Explorations in Elementary School Science

Practice and Theory, K–8

ERMINIA PEDRETTI

Ontario Institute for Studies in Education,
University of Toronto

KATHERINE BELLOMO

Ontario Institute for Studies in Education,
University of Toronto

SUSAN JAGGER

Ontario Institute for Studies in Education,
University of Toronto

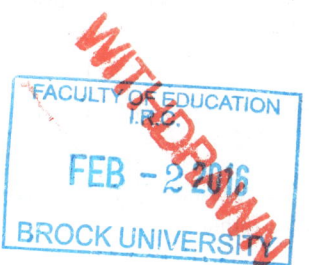
PEARSON

Toronto

Editor-in-Chief: Michelle Sartor
Acquisitions Editor: Carolin Sweig
Marketing Manager: Loula March
Program Manager: John Polanszky
Project Manager: Susan Johnson
Developmental Editor: Johanna Schlaepfer
Media Editor: Marisa D'Andrea
Media Producer: Tiffany Palmer
Production Services: Cenveo® Publisher Services
Permissions Project Manager: Marnie Lamb
Photo Permissions Research: Jamey O'Quinn, PreMediaGlobal
Text Permissions Research: Anna Waluk, Electronic Publshing Services
Art Director: Zena Denchik
Cover Designer: Alex Li
Interior Designer: Jerilyn Bockorick, Cenveo Publisher Services
Cover Image: ©abstract/Shutterstock

10 9 8 7 6 5 4 3 2 1 WC

Library and Archives Canada Cataloguing in Publication

Pedretti, Erminia, 1964-, author
    Explorations in elementary school science : practice and theory, K–8 / Erminia Pedretti, Ontario Institute for Studies in Education, University of Toronto, Katherine Bellomo, Ontario Institute for Studies in Education, University of Toronto, Susan Jagger, Ontario Institute for Studies in Education, University of Toronto.

Includes bibliographical references and indexes.
ISBN 978-0-13-335543-7 (pbk.)

    1. Science—Study and teaching (Elementary).   I. Bellomo, Katherine, author II. Jagger, Susan, author   III. Title.

LB1585.P43 2014   372.35'044   C2013–908283–2

ISBN 978-0-13-335543-7

To the children in our lives:

Joshua

Olivia

Madelyne

Lilianna

Tyler

Dante

Roman

Luca

Maia

Breanna

Kaitlyn

who inspire us with their sense of wonder and delight in, and with, the world.

A PERSONAL MESSAGE

We hope this book serves you well on your journey to becoming an elementary teacher of science, and that it nurtures your passion and enthusiasm for a subject that is exciting and relevant. Our intent is to provide support as you refine, redefine, and expand your practice and your theoretical perspectives. We invite you to imagine a science education that is student-centred, inclusive, joyous, inspiring, and filled with possibilities for transformative teaching and learning.

Brief Contents

PART 1   A VISION FOR SCIENCE EDUCATION

Chapter 1   Teaching Science: Beginning the Journey 1

Chapter 2   Nature of Science 21

Chapter 3   Environmental Education 39

Chapter 4   Equity, Diversity, and Social Justice in Science Education 59

PART 2   CURRICULUM DESIGN

Chapter 5   Curriculum that Meets the Needs of Students 79

Chapter 6   Curriculum Planning and Implementation 99

Chapter 7   Curriculum Fundamentals 127

PART 3   SCIENTIFIC INQUIRY

Chapter 8   Scientific Inquiry and Investigations 149

Chapter 9   Planning for Scientific Inquiry and Investigations 175

PART 4   SCIENCE, TECHNOLOGY, SOCIETY, AND THE ENVIRONMENT (STSE)

Chapter 10   Exploring Science, Technology, Society, and Environment (STSE) 199

Chapter 11   STSE Education: Planning and Pedagogy 223

PART 5   KNOWLEDGE

Chapter 12   Knowledge and Learning 247

Chapter 13   Teaching Content Knowledge: Pedagogy and Principles 267

APPENDICES

Appendix A   Strategies and Graphic Organizers 285

Appendix B   Preparing for Your Practicum 309

Appendix C   Making a Successful Beginning to the School Year 315

Appendix D   Favourite Assignments 321

Appendix E   Suggested Children's Literature for Elementary Science 333

Appendix F   Planning for Field Trips 339

References 343

Name Index 355

Subject Index 359

Contents

Preface xi
Acknowledgements xvi

PART 1
A VISION FOR SCIENCE EDUCATION

1 Teaching Science: Beginning the Journey 1

Learning Objectives 1
Introduction 2
What Makes a Good Teacher? 2
  Getting to Know your Students 3
Developing a Philosophy of Teaching and Learning 5
  Transmissive, Transactive, and Transformative Approaches to Education 7
  Domains of Teacher Knowledge 8
What is Science Education for? 9
  Arguments: What is Science Education for? 9
Scientific Literacy 10
  Toward a Comprehensive Vision of Scientific Literacy 11
  Scientific Literacy in Curriculum Documents and Policies 12
Literacy and Numeracy 14
The Role of Technology in Teaching Science 15
  Exploring the Relationship Between Science and Technology 15
  Information and Communication Technologies (ICT) and Teaching Science 16
  Science, Technology, and the Curriculum 16
Science Beyond the Classroom 17
Science Education Research 18
Contemporary Issues in Science Education 18
  Standardized Testing 18
  Conflicting Visions of Science Education 19
  Science Specialists in Elementary Schools 19

Concluding Thoughts 19
Bringing it all Together: Final Questions 20

APPENDIX 1.A Find a classmate who… 20

2 Nature of Science 21

Learning Objectives 21
Introduction 22
What is the Nature of Science? 22
  Tenets of the Nature of Science 24
  What is the Scientific Method? 25
Laws and Theories 26
Teaching Through, With, and for the Nature of Science 27
  Arguments for the Inclusion of Nature of Science 28

Nature of Science: Tensions and Challenges 30
  Incorporating NOS in the Classroom 32
Teacher Beliefs and Practices about NOS 33
Connecting Practice and Theory 34
Science Beyond the Classroom 35

Concluding Thoughts 36
Bringing it all Together: Final Questions 37

APPENDIX 2.A Modified Card Exchange Statements for Elementary Students 37

3 Environmental Education 39

Learning Objectives 39
Introduction 40
What is Environment? 40
  Why Environmental Education? 41
  Environmental Education: A Brief History of Policy and Practice 41
Environmental Education in Canada 44
  Aboriginal Perspectives and Environmental Education 46
Conceptualizing Environmental Education 48
  Education About-In-For the Environment 48
  Environmental Education Orientations 49
Toward a More Critical Approach to Environmental Education 50
Science Beyond the Classroom 51
  Place-Based Education 51
  Outdoor Education 52
Environmental Education Resources for Planning 53
Contemporary Issues and Ongoing Debates 55

Concluding Thoughts 56
Bringing it all Together: Final Questions 56

APPENDIX 3.A Ecological Footprint Calculator Activity 57

APPENDIX 3.B Environmental Education Curriculum and Instruction Resources 58

4 Equity, Diversity, and Social Justice in Science Education 59

Learning Objectives 59
Introduction 60
A Framework for Equity, Diversity, and Social Justice in Science 60
  Social Justice in the Digital Age 62
Marginalized Students and Issues of Identity 62
  Student Identity and Diversity 63
  Teacher Identity 64
Exploring Aboriginal Science Education as a Social Justice Issue 65
Fixed Borders/Fuzzy Borders: Border Crossings 68

Foundations for Social Justice in Science Education 69
Classroom Teaching 70
Culturally Relevant Pedagogy 71
Science Curriculum Guidelines and Social Justice 72
Science Curriculum for Social Justice: Some Program Suggestions 75
Suggestion 1: Inquiry and the Nature of Science 75
Suggestion 2: STSE, Problem Solving, and Community 75
Suggestion 3: The History of Science from Non-western Traditions 75
Suggestion 4: European Inventors and Inventors from Non-western Perspectives 76

Concluding Thoughts 76
Bringing it all Together: Final Questions 77

APPENDIX 4.A *Curriculum Resources for Social Justice 77*
APPENDIX 4.B *Grades 4–6 Outcomes and Expectations from Provincial and Territorial Guidelines 78*

PART 2
CURRICULUM DESIGN

5 Curriculum that Meets the Needs of Students 79
Learning Objectives 79
Introduction 80
Curricular Design and Creating a Supportive and Inclusive Learning Environment 80
Culturally Relevant Teaching 80
Differentiated Instruction (DI) 82
Knowing Students and Meeting Their Learning Needs 83
Theories of Learning 83
The Role of Affect 83
Multiple Intelligences 84
Planning for Unique Learning Needs 85
Science, Language, and Mathematics 86
Science and Language 87
Reading and Cueing Systems in Science Programs 87
Textbooks in Science 88
Science and Mathematics 89
Assessment and Evaluation 92
Types of Assessment 93
Assessment Strategies and Tools 93
Self-Assessment 96
Peer Assessment 96

Concluding Thoughts 96
Bringing it all Together: Final Questions 97

6 Curriculum Planning and Implementation 99
Learning Objectives 99
Introduction 100
Lesson and Unit Planning: An Overview 100
Unit Planning 101
Ensuring a Balanced Approach 102
Pre-planning Considerations and Decisions 103
Drafting the Unit Plan: Start with the End in Mind 106
Post-implementation Reflections 109
Lesson Planning 109
Planning Lessons: Student Considerations 109
What is a Lesson Plan? 110
Instructional Strategies 111
Lesson Design 112
Three-Part Lesson 112
Lesson Plan Components 113
The Art of Questioning 115
Bloom's Taxonomy 116
Strategies to Extend Student Thinking 117
Classroom Management: Creating a Positive Classroom Climate 117
Program Planning 118
Awareness of Student Needs 118
Techniques and Strategies 118
Styles of Classroom Management 120
Science Beyond the Classroom: Planning Field Trips 121

Concluding Thoughts 121
Bringing it all Together: Final Questions 122

APPENDIX 6.A *Year Overview Example 122*
APPENDIX 6.B *Lesson Plan Templates 123*

7 Curriculum Fundamentals 127
Learning Objectives 127
Introduction 128
Curriculum Theory and Theorists 128
Curriculum Theorists 129
Fundamentals of Curriculum Development 132
The What, Why, and How of Curriculum 133
Students' Needs Revisited 133
Constructing Curriculum: Practical Considerations 134
What Do the Ministry Curriculum Documents Say? 134
How to Construct a Student Task 134
Curriculum Validations for Science Education 137
Re-visiting Activity 7.6 138
Issues and Influences Shaping Curriculum 138
Subject Matter Content Knowledge (CK) and Pedagogical Content Knowledge (PCK) 140

Exploring Elementary Science in Creative Ways: Human Body Systems 140

Concluding Thoughts 142
Bringing it all Together: Final Questions 142

APPENDIX 7.A Technological Challenge 143
APPENDIX 7.B Research Project with Presentation and Poster 143
APPENDIX 7.C Science Investigation and Science Notebook Activity 146

PART 3
SCIENTIFIC INQUIRY

8 Scientific Inquiry and Investigations 149
Learning Objectives 149
Introduction 150
Why do we do Science Investigations? 150
Scientific Inquiry and Types of Science Investigations 152
Verification (Confirmation) 153
Problem Solving (Structured and Guided Inquiry) 153
Experiments (Open Inquiry) 153
Other Types of Science Activities 158
Skills Development 158
Developing Process Skills with Elementary School Students: Classification 160
Demonstrations in the Science Classroom 161
Using Computer Technologies in Science Investigations 162
Data Collection and Management 163
Communication of Findings 163
Problem-Solving Investigations through Design Technology 167
Science Beyond the Classroom 169
Exploring Elementary Science in Creative Ways: Magnets and Magnetism 170

Concluding Thoughts 172
Bringing it all Together: Final Questions 173

APPENDIX 8.A Template for Activity 8.4: Exploring paper helicopters 174
APPENDIX 8.B Sample Student Worksheet 174

9 Planning for Scientific Inquiry and Investigations 175
Learning Objectives 175
Introduction 176
Planning for Investigations 176
Pre-Investigation Planning 176
Doing the Science Investigation 181
Post-Investigation Planning 181

Linking Investigations to Planning 187
Scaffolding for Open-Ended Experiments 187
Planning with Safety in Mind 187
Planning for Safe Science Investigations 188
Planning with Assessment in Mind 191
Science Beyond the Classroom 193
Contemporary Issues and Ongoing Debates in Science Investigations 194
Exploring Elementary Science in Creative Ways: Animal Life Cycles 194

Concluding Thoughts 196
Bringing it all Together: Final Questions 197

APPENDIX 9.A Smarter Science 197
APPENDIX 9.B Safety Symbols Found on Products in the Home 198

PART 4
SCIENCE, TECHNOLOGY, SOCIETY, AND THE ENVIRONMENT (STSE)

10 Exploring Science, Technology, Society, and Environment (STSE) 199
Learning Objectives 199
Introduction 200
STSE: A Brief History 200
Benefits of STSE Education 201
Characteristics of STSE Education 203
Analyzing the Characteristics of STSE Education 205
Stewardship 205
Decision-Making 207
Values 209
Action 210
Nature of Science 213
STSE Challenges and Tensions 215
Values and Student Identity 215
Teacher Positioning 216
The Politicization of the Curriculum 217
A Research Perspective 217
Exploring Elementary Science in Creative Ways: The Rock Cycle 218

Concluding Thoughts 220
Bringing it all Together: Final Questions 221

11 STSE Education: Planning and Pedagogy 223
Learning Objectives 223
Introduction 224
Revisiting the Characteristics of STSE 224
STSE Emphases and Approaches to Planning 225
Issues-Based Approach 225
Historical Approach 228

Pedagogical Strategies for STSE Education 229
  Role Play and Drama 229
  Six Thinking Hats 230
  Values Continuum 230
  Consequence Mapping 230
  Debate 230
  Town Hall 230
Action-Based Community Project 233
Assessment and STSE Education 234
Planning with an STSE Focus 237
Navigating Controversy in the Science Classroom 239
  Planning for Controversy in the Curriculum 240
Science Beyond the Classroom 241
Exploring Elementary Science in Creative Ways: The Water Cycle 242

Concluding Thoughts 243
Bringing it all Together: Final Questions 244

APPENDIX 11.A Data Collection Sheet for Using Skateboarding to Debate Speeding (Activity 11.3) 245

PART 5
KNOWLEDGE

12 Knowledge and Learning 247
Learning Objectives 247
Introduction 248
Ways of Knowing 248
  Science as a Way of Knowing 248
Categories of Knowledge 251
Theories of Knowledge and Theories of Learning 252
  Theories of Knowledge 252
  Theories of Learning 254
  Summary of Theories of Learning 257
Alternative Frameworks, Misconceptions, and Conceptual Change 258
  Examples of Alternative Frameworks or Misconceptions 259
  Conceptual Change Theory 260
Exploring Elementary Science in Creative Ways: Seasonal Change 262

Concluding Thoughts 264
Bringing it all Together: Final Questions 265

13 Teaching Content Knowledge: Pedagogy and Principles 267
Learning Objectives 267
Introduction 268
Students, Content Knowledge, and Meaningful Understanding 268
  Exploring Scale 269
Teaching with Analogies and Models 272
  Strategies for using Analogies and Models 272
Teaching with Games 273
  Strategies for using Games 274
Using Questions to Promote Learning 274
  Types of Questions 275
  Bloom's Taxonomy 275
Teaching Content Knowledge with and through Technology 276
  Developing a Critical Lens when Using Technology 278
Teachers' Work and Professional Development 279
  A Case Study: Teaching about Light and Sound 279
  Professional Learning Communities 281
Continuing the Journey 281

Concluding Thoughts 282
Bringing it all Together: Final Questions 282

Appendix A   Strategies and Graphic Organizers 285
Appendix B   Preparing for Your Practicum 309
Appendix C   Making a Successful Beginning to the School Year 315
Appendix D   Favourite Assignments 321
Appendix E   Suggested Children's Literature for Elementary Science 333
Appendix F   Planning for Field Trips 339

References 343
Name Index 355
Subject Index 359

Preface

INTRODUCTION

Elementary school science is a place where wonder, experience, and imagination come together. It is a place where children can play, investigate, and learn about the natural world they inhabit. Children's natural curiosity contributes to the magic of the elementary classroom. As a teacher of science, we hope you will nurture children's multiple perspectives, while challenging them to learn new and relevant material.

Each of you has a unique school science experience. Some of you may have fond memories of hands-on explorations, field trips, or demonstrations, while others may recall a science program dominated by reading of textbooks and answering end-of-chapter questions. Furthermore, you have different academic backgrounds in science. For some, science may have been a major in university; and for others, Grade 11 may have been the last time you thought about beakers and Bunsen burners, Newton's laws, or the Kreb's cycle. As you begin this professional journey, you have a wonderful opportunity to revisit the subject of science, develop pedagogical skills, and work collaboratively to explore the type of science program you want to create.

An elementary school teacher has the dual challenge of being both a generalist and a specialist in many areas—a feat that can be overwhelming. This textbook will support you as you become a teacher of elementary school science. We intentionally designed a book that merged practice and theory in synergistic ways. Some books on methods of teaching elementary science are collections of practical ideas and tips presented in the absence of theoretical underpinnings; others are too theoretical in nature and lack practical insights. Our aim is to strike a balance and to challenge your assumptions about what science is and how it can be taught. We hope this book will help you to feel confident and inspired as you begin your career in this important profession.

OUR VISION

We envision this book as a guide for elementary school teacher candidates. Our goals are two-fold: to provide teacher candidates with knowledge, pedagogy, and skills to be successful in a contemporary classroom, and to equip them with strategies to critique, re-imagine, and transform the elementary science experience for their students. Additionally, in-service teachers and graduate students who are looking to refine and improve their praxis may well benefit from the book.

We have deliberately incorporated a broad range of education research perspectives and activities to support teacher candidates as they explore their beliefs, improve pedagogical knowledge, and develop judgment and decision-making skills. Furthermore, we hope that a modest immersion into the science education research literature will inspire teacher candidates in the present and inform their practice in the future.

Throughout the book we have merged practice and theory with what we consider fundamental to school science in the twenty-first century. These fundamentals include an understanding of scientific literacy as a broad concept; an appreciation of the beauty and limits of science; an understanding of the nature of science (NOS) both as a process and as a product; the integration of environmental education; and a commitment to equity, social justice, and inclusive science education that meets the needs of a diverse student population.

UNIQUE APPROACH OF THE TEXTBOOK

In determining the specific features of this book, we drew upon our experiences as elementary, middle, and secondary teachers of science; science consultants; researchers; teacher education instructors; and graduate-level instructors. Our collective teaching experience spans Western, Central, and Atlantic Canada. Over the years we have surveyed preservice students across the country to gauge what they felt was important to include in a science methods textbook. Their thoughtful comments helped shape the direction and substance of this work.

Unique Features We believe this book is unique in the way that it:

- includes activities that support literacy and numeracy
- addresses science subject matter content knowledge
- provides activities for elementary students
- highlights cross-curricular connections
- raises thoughtful questions for discussion
- provides appendices containing practical guidance and support for elementary teachers
- infuses information and communications technologies
- merges educational practice, theory, and research
- features a range of practical teacher development activities

Canadian Perspectives The book is distinctly Canadian in its perspective and focus as it:

- aligns with Canadian values such as multiculturalism and inclusiveness
- draws on critical research by renowned Canadian, as well as international, science educators
- refers to Canadian provincial and territorial curriculum frameworks
- includes environmental education practice and theory
- supports equity, diversity, and social justice teaching
- incorporates Indigenous and Aboriginal ways of knowing

21st Century Learning The Canadian education system is undergoing significant change in support of the twenty-first-century classroom. The focus has shifted from *what* students learn to *how* students learn, and includes skills and competencies that can be transferred and applied in new situations. Every province has its own vocabulary to describe this body of knowledge. We have chosen to focus on seven **21st Century Skills and Competencies** to respond to the challenges of the evolving classroom across the country:

❶ **Communication**

❷ **Critical thinking**

❸ **Collaboration**

❹ **Creativity**

❺ **Literacy and numeracy**

❻ **Media literacy**

❼ **Technological literacy**

Each of the activities throughout the book indicates which of these 21st Century Skills and Competencies are called on. The list is featured near the beginning of each chapter for easy reference. We believe that focusing on these seven skills and competencies in the classroom will create innovative learning opportunities that will prepare both students and teachers for the complex environments of the twenty-first century.

Activities

A variety of **Activities** are placed throughout each chapter to help teacher candidates explore content in context. Activities are followed by **Discussion Questions** that ask students to reflect on their experience and provide further learning. These activities and discussion questions should prompt conversations and sharing of ideas to develop rich and comprehensive views of teaching and learning science. We have provided more activities than most courses have time for, in order to give the user freedom to choose according to needs and context. Some activities are organized around the following themes:

- *Exploring Prior Knowledge and Experience*: Intended for teacher candidates to access their prior knowledge related to the focus of the chapter.
- *Working with Resources*: Designed to familiarize teacher candidates with curriculum documents, policies, and frameworks relevant to their province or territory, as well as other resources and materials.
- *Read and Reflect*: Designed to encourage teacher candidates to read and reflect on the findings of research in science education.
- *Connecting Practice and Theory*: Designed to help teacher candidates bring practice and theory together in coherent and beneficial ways.

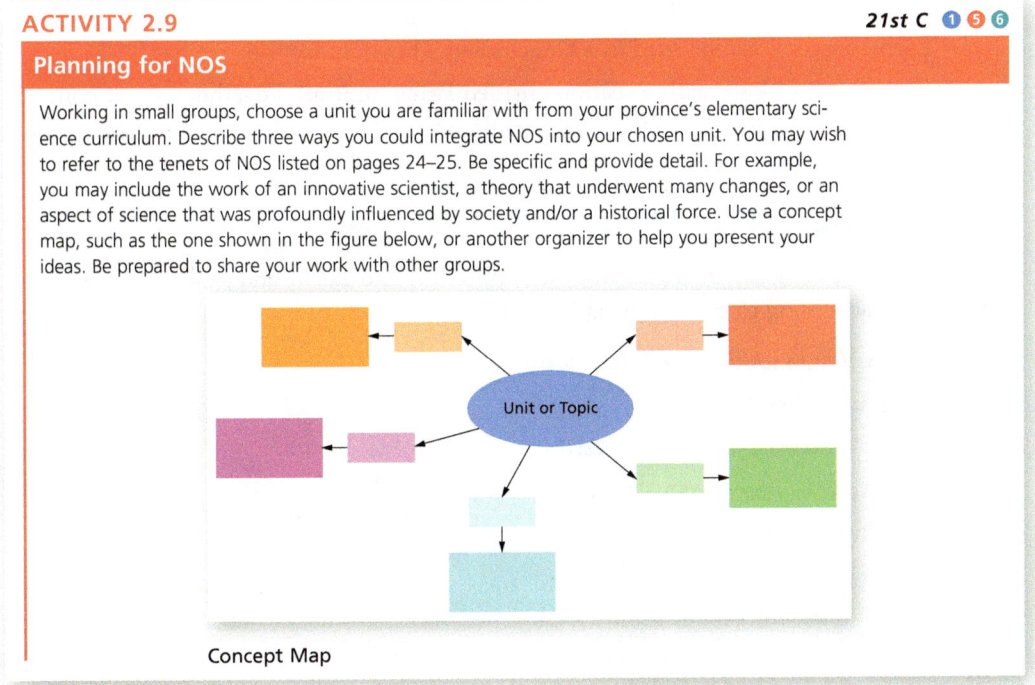

ACTIVITY 2.9   *21st C* ❶ ❺ ❻

Planning for NOS

Working in small groups, choose a unit you are familiar with from your province's elementary science curriculum. Describe three ways you could integrate NOS into your chosen unit. You may wish to refer to the tenets of NOS listed on pages 24–25. Be specific and provide detail. For example, you may include the work of an innovative scientist, a theory that underwent many changes, or an aspect of science that was profoundly influenced by society and/or a historical force. Use a concept map, such as the one shown in the figure below, or another organizer to help you present your ideas. Be prepared to share your work with other groups.

Unit or Topic

Concept Map

Appendices The book concludes with a series of appendices that may be helpful as you prepare for your practicum and plan for teaching and learning in your future classroom. For example, you will find appendices on Strategies and Graphic Organizers, Preparing for Your Practicum, Making a Successful Beginning to the School Year, Suggested Children's Literature for Elementary Science (with over 70 annotated titles), and Planning for Field Trips.

Other Features

CONCLUDING THOUGHTS

Teaching NOS can enhance the student learning experience. NOS tenets reflect a comprehensive and authentic view of science and complement the teaching of science as a body of knowledge. Determine your own knowledge base and comfort level with respect to NOS perspectives, and consider how NOS will impact your pedagogy. What follows is a summary of the key ideas related to the learning objectives provided at the beginning of the chapter.

Tenets of the nature of science (NOS)
Teachers bring to the classroom various philosophies of science, as illustrated in "The Nature of Science Card Exchange" (page 22). It is important to recognize a wide variety of perspectives, and appreciate how this human element can bring science to life for many students. McComas et al. (1998) summarize 14 tenets of NOS.

Arguments for including NOS in elementary science
Understanding NOS can enhance student learning, increase interest in science, improve science instruction, promote equity and diversity, foster students' appreciation of cultural aspects of science, and support understanding of knowledge construction.

Tensions and challenges of teaching NOS
Some teachers feel ill equipped to address NOS perspectives due to their own perceived lack of knowledge. Assessment and evaluation, time constraints, and a lack of resources can also make teaching NOS challenging, as can students' positivist views of science. Still, when teachers include NOS in their teaching and assessment practices, and use diverse resources, it can make science worthwhile and meaningful for students.

The relationship between beliefs about NOS and teacher practice
Teachers' own beliefs about NOS, and their science content knowledge, are often reflected in their explicit and implicit curricula and instruction. Teachers' content knowledge is a key factor in classroom practice, and beliefs about science influence both implicit and explicit lessons about NOS.

Science curriculum that includes NOS
NOS can be included in science curricula and instruction in many ways. While not every tenet of NOS can be included in each lesson or each unit, try to incorporate them across units and over the course of the year. Build your confidence in NOS and expand your pedagogical repertoire to acquire expertise in this area.

NOS as a lens to explore science practices and institutions
It is important to create opportunities in which a lens of NOS can be used to assess issues relevant to students' lives. Students who have opportunities to explore NOS in their classrooms will have a better appreciation of the practice of science and of the institutions that support science in the community.

Educational research related to NOS
NOS is a rich, growing field. Researchers we have drawn upon include Fouad Abd-El-Khalick, Larry Bencze, William Cobern, Derek Hodson, Norm Lederman, Cathleen Loving, and William McComas.

BRINGING IT ALL TOGETHER: FINAL QUESTIONS

1. Reflect on how your understanding of NOS has changed from reading this chapter. In a paragraph or two, describe your current understanding of NOS and critique the place of NOS in elementary and middle school science education.

2. Work in pairs or groups of three to discuss what you predict will be the biggest challenges to implementing NOS perspectives in science curriculum planning and classroom practice. How might you overcome these challenges?

- Each chapter opens with a series of thought-provoking **quotations** from students, preservice teachers, in-service teachers, and notable individuals.

- A set of **Learning Objectives** is listed at the beginning of each chapter to enable the reader to see exactly where the chapter is going and guide them to a higher-level understanding of the content.

- The *Safety* **icon** alerts preservice teachers to safety issues related to the activity or investigation in question.

- Each chapter is summarized in a **Concluding Thoughts** section.

- Each chapter closes with a section entitled **Bringing it all Together**, which contains two or three synthesis questions to stimulate class discussion or assign as homework.

ORGANIZATION OF THE BOOK

The book draws upon examples from life, physical, and Earth and space science and is organized according to the following five themes:

1. A Vision for Science Education
2. Curriculum Design
3. Scientific Inquiry and Investigations
4. Science, Technology, Society, and the Environment (STSE)
5. Knowledge

Parts 1 and 2 provide grounding in areas such as scientific literacy, the nature of science, environmental education, social justice, meeting student needs, curriculum planning and assessment, and curriculum theory. These themes reappear throughout the book. Parts 3, 4, and 5 reflect the organization of most science curriculum documents in many provinces and territories across the country, as well as the *Common Framework of Science Learning Outcomes K-12: Pan-Canadian Protocol for Collaboration on School Curriculum.* (CMEC, 1997).

Admittedly, we struggled with the order of topics; indeed, the table of contents went through a number of iterations. For example, some reviewers suggested that STSE should be at the beginning of the book, while others wanted to start with Scientific Inquiry. Some argued that Knowledge, which is foundational to science, should appear earlier in the text. In the end, we chose an organization that reflects our way of conceptualizing a science education program, with the understanding that the chapters can be used in any order.

Each of the five parts comprises chapters that, while different in purpose and content, have commonalities. In general, each chapter attends to practice and theory, encourages the development of teacher judgment with respect to pedagogy, provides opportunities to connect literacy and numeracy to teaching science, and reflects teacher realities related to curriculum planning and implementation. Additionally, we have infused technology, assessment, and evaluation throughout. We recognize that information and communications technologies (ICT) can be powerful tools for accessing information, analyzing scientific processes, conducting scientific investigations, and supporting connections among students as they learn. We encourage teacher candidates to expand their own knowledge about the range of technologies available and to cultivate and apply a critical lens while developing sound pedagogical practices. Similarly, assessment and evaluation are interwoven throughout the book, so that teacher candidates can consider them in the context of inquiry, STSE, and knowledge, and as central to curriculum planning. In several chapters we highlight Aboriginal worldviews and learning science beyond the classroom. We also incorporate ready-to-use activities that teacher candidates may use with their own students in elementary and middle schools.

TECHNOLOGY RESOURCES

MyEducationLab®

The moment you know. Educators know it. Students know it. It's that inspired moment when something that was difficult to understand suddenly makes perfect sense. Our MyLab products have been designed and refined with a single purpose in mind—to help educators create that moment of understanding with their students.

MyEducationLab® delivers **proven results** in helping individual students succeed. It provides **engaging experiences** that personalize, stimulate, and measure learning for each student. And, it comes from a **trusted partner** with educational expertise and an eye on the future.

MyEducationLab® can be used by itself or linked to any learning management system. To learn more about how MyEducationLab combines proven learning applications with powerful assessment, visit **www.MyEducationLab.com**.

MyEducationLab®—the moment you know.

Pearson eText Pearson eText gives students access to the text whenever and wherever they have access to the Internet. eText pages look exactly like the printed text, offering powerful new functionality for students and instructors. Users can create notes, highlight text in different colours, create bookmarks, zoom, click hyperlinked words and phrases to view definitions, and view in single-page or two-page view. Pearson eText allows for quick navigation to key parts of the eText using a table of contents, and provides full-text search.

CourseSmart for Instructors CourseSmart goes beyond traditional expectations—providing instant, online access to the textbooks and course materials you need at a lower cost for students. And even as students save money, you can save time and hassle with a digital eTextbook that allows you to search for the most relevant content at the very moment you need it. Whether it's evaluating textbooks or creating lecture notes to help students with difficult concepts, CourseSmart can make life a little easier. See how when you visit www.coursesmart.com/instructors.

CourseSmart for Students CourseSmart goes beyond traditional expectations—providing instant, online access to the textbooks and course materials you need at an average savings of 60 percent. With instant access from any computer and the ability to search your text, you'll find the content you need quickly, no matter where you are. And with online tools like highlighting and note-taking, you can save time and study efficiently. See all the benefits at www.coursesmart.com/students.

Pearson Custom Library For enrolments of at least 25 students, you can create your own textbook by choosing the chapters that best suit your own course needs. To begin building your custom text, visit www.pearsoncustomlibrary.com. You may also work with a dedicated Pearson Custom editor to create your ideal text—publishing your own original content or mixing and matching Pearson content. Contact your local Pearson Representative to get started.

Technology Specialists Pearson's Technology Specialists work with faculty and campus course designers to ensure that Pearson technology products, assessment tools, and online course materials are tailored to meet your specific needs. This highly qualified team is dedicated to helping schools take full advantage of a wide range of educational resources, by assisting in the integration of a variety of instructional materials and media formats. Your local Pearson sales representative can provide you with more details on this service program.

SUPPLEMENTS

The following instructor supplements are available for downloading from a password-protected section of Pearson Canada's online catalogue (catalogue.pearsoned.ca). Navigate to this book's catalogue page to view a list of those supplements that are available. See your local sales representative for details and access.

- **Instructor's Manual:** This useful teaching aid provides an overview of the material within each chapter, as well as features such as Activities-at-a-Glance charts, modifiable line masters, and references.
- **PowerPoint™ Slides:** PowerPoint presentations combine graphics and text to provide premade lecture slides.

ACKNOWLEDGEMENTS

We are grateful to our students, both in elementary and middle schools and in teacher education programs, who have taught us to be better teachers of science. Their enthusiastic participation in our classrooms and their openness to new ideas, strategies, and approaches to teaching science have inspired us to write this book.

We are appreciative of the support and collaboration from the many talented and dedicated science educators we have worked with over the years—in particular Elgin Wolfe, Don Galbraith, Judith Burt, Denis Cooke, and Robbie Olivero. They have inspired and challenged us, and generously shared their wisdom and craft.

We acknowledge the immense influence of our teachers and mentors, in particular, the impact that Derek Hodson, Larry Yore, and John Wallace have had on our thinking, practice, theoretical work, and research.

Our sincere thanks to Joanne Nazir, our personal Science Education Consultant, who contributed professional opinions, research, and editorial assistance—always with a smile and good sense. A special thank you to Michelle Dubek for contributing her expertise in both science teacher education and elementary education in the supplementary materials to this book. Thank you as well to Olivia, Michelle, Nenad, Amy, James, Peter, Erin, Barb, and Limin for patiently listening and offering supportive advice.

We thank the folks at Pearson, specifically Reid McAlpine, Carolin Sweig, and Johanna Schlaepfer, for conversations that helped shape and inform this book, for their continued support (especially during pregnancies and broken arms), and for their wise counsel.

During the development of this book, we obtained many helpful and invaluable suggestions and comments from colleagues from across the country. We are indebted to the following reviewers whose insights helped improve our final manuscript:

Ron Ballentine, New Street Education Centre

Jennifer Brokofsky, Saskatoon Public Schools

H. Bruce Burton, Memorial University

L.J. Dowell-Hantelmann, Regina Public Schools

Paul Elliott, Trent University

Jane Forbes, OISE University of Toronto

Edwin Gibb, Western University

Douglas D. Karrow, Brock University

Giuliano Reis, University of Ottawa

Hyacinth Schaeffer, University of Calgary

Azza Sharkawy, Queen's University

Aamer Shujah, University of Windsor

Jim Wiese, University of the Fraser Valley

To family and friends who graciously accepted our absences and cancellations—thank you for your understanding! Finally, a special thank you to John, Renata, Roxane, Sally, and Heather, whose unwavering support, love, and patience made this all possible.

Chapter 1

Teaching Science: Beginning the Journey

Stock Connection Blue / Alamy

[The teacher] if he is indeed wise does not bid you to enter the house of his wisdom but rather leads you to the threshold of your mind.

—Khalil Gibran

I had an amazing teacher. He was inspiring regarding his hands-on-minds-on science approaches. We built a pond, used magnets, set up simple circuits.

—Madelyne, elementary school teacher

I do not recall learning anything about how to teach science…not one thing…I can remember literacy and math and general instructional methods and theory…but in terms of curriculum, nothing on science.

—Gallaway, elementary school teacher

LEARNING OBJECTIVES

- Describe what constitutes good or effective teaching.

- Develop a personal philosophy of teaching and learning.

- Explain the domains of teacher knowledge.

- Outline three arguments to explain the purpose of science education.

- Develop a comprehensive understanding of scientific literacy, and discuss how it is enacted in the science curriculum in your province or territory.

- Explore the relationship between science and technology, and describe the role of information and communication technologies in science education.

- Explain how informal environments can be used to teach science.

- Discuss the role of education research in teacher development.

INTRODUCTION

Welcome to the world of teaching and learning! You have chosen to embark on a wonderful profession. No two days are alike, and your journey will be rewarding, exciting, and challenging. You will be teaching and learning in various contexts; working with a range of students; collaborating with other teachers, school staff, and parents; developing curricula; and using an array of materials and resources in creative and interesting ways. Most importantly, you can make a difference in your students' lives as you help prepare them for the future. Your interactions with students can inspire and motivate them, and instill in them a lifelong love of learning. We are inspired by Lisa Delpit's (1995) sentiment: As teachers we have the incredible responsibility of caring for children who are not our own.

As a teacher of science you will be able to share your curiosity and sense of wonder in the natural world. The landscape of science education is varied and rich, and includes exploring new ideas, participating in science investigations, learning science content, and critically engaging with issues that cut across science and society. You will no doubt have many questions: Do I know enough science to teach it? What topics do I teach? How will I run investigations smoothly and safely? How can I use technology in my teaching practice? Will I be able to manage 30 students? These concerns are natural, and are part of your professional growth. Although there are no simple answers, this book will provide some guidance, as well as activities that will help you realize your strengths and potential for growth. We'll also help you build a repertoire of effective strategies, tools, and pedagogical practices.

This book serves as an introduction to becoming a teacher, and in particular to teaching science. Learning to teach is a lifelong process. Throughout this chapter, we invite you to examine your ideas about science education, scientific literacy, and what it means to be a teacher. You will have the opportunity to think critically about teaching and learning and to develop skills of reflective practice. Donald Schon (1983) describes the *reflective practitioner* as one who is able to reflect upon and analyze his or her own teaching practice. Schon defines reflection *in* action as what happens *during* teaching (in other words, thinking on your feet and in the moment), and reflection *on* action as what happens when you think back on events. The reflective practitioner looks to experience, practice, and theory in building new understandings that inform the skill of teaching. It is our hope that as you begin this journey, you will become thoughtful, judicious educators who care about students and are enthusiastic about teaching science.

Finally, we offer a vision of science education that may challenge some of your assumptions about science and how it should be taught. We hope this book will inspire you to re-imagine a science education that is transformative, relevant, and reflective of a diverse student population.

WHAT MAKES A GOOD TEACHER?

ACTIVITY 1.1   *21st C* ❶ ❸

Prior Knowledge and Experience

Think back to when you were an elementary or secondary school student. Recall a "good" teacher you had and explain why he or she was effective. Next, think about a "good" teacher of science you had (either a specialized teacher of science or a classroom teacher whose science lessons you enjoyed) and consider why he or she was effective. Compare your recollections with a peer.

As a class, make two lists: 1) characteristics of good teachers and 2) characteristics of good teachers of science. You might display the similarities and differences in a Venn diagram.

The lists you generated in Activity 1.1 probably include the following characteristics of a good teacher:

- is prepared and organized
- plans lessons thoughtfully
- uses different instructional techniques
- is enthusiastic
- has good classroom management skills
- uses students' ideas
- cares about students
- includes all students
- assesses fairly and in different ways
- sets clear goals

Of course, this is not an exhaustive list, and there are certainly many more traits that constitute effective teaching. You may be beginning to think about which of these traits you possess, which ones you'd like to develop, and some of the challenges you might encounter along the way.

While effective teaching is a critical component of students' learning experiences, it is not easily defined. Rather, it is informed by a range of assumptions and therefore holds multiple definitions. Kennedy (2008) discusses teacher effectiveness and the importance of recognizing the qualities that support it. She proposes three broad categories of characteristics: 1) personal resources; 2) performance; and 3) effectiveness. A teacher's *personal resources* are those qualities that she or he naturally brings to the profession. These include beliefs, attitudes, and values; personality traits; knowledge, skills, and expertise; and credentials. *Performance* comprises the work done by a teacher on a day-to-day basis, including practices within the classroom (e.g., sharing clear expectations with students), student learning activities (e.g., complex problem-solving tasks), and practices outside the classroom (e.g., interaction with parents and colleagues). Finally, teacher *effectiveness* typically relates to how well a teacher raises student achievement. Such practices might include fostering student learning, motivating students, and encouraging personal and social responsibility. Good teaching is informed by all of these qualities working together.

Getting to Know Your Students

Effective teachers are cognizant of the importance of interpersonal relations. Broadly speaking, this means treating all students with integrity. Being positive and setting high expectations is key. Get to know your students; understand their diverse (and sometimes challenging) contexts and try to help them grow. Students will come to class with their own experiences that shape their beliefs about science and about what a teacher of science should do. Often students view science as a body of facts to memorize and a pursuit that yields definite answers from specific methods. Sometimes students may need to examine biases about science and teaching science before they can be intellectually available for a science education that is empowering and authentic.

Knowing your students is an important part of teaching, and much more will be said about meeting student needs in Chapter 5. For now, we make the point that creating a safe and trusting environment requires, in part, knowing your students, and your students knowing one another. Activity 1.2 is a simple community-building activity that encourages movement, discussion, and sharing of experiences about lives and science. Our version, for you as teacher candidates, appears below and an adaptation you can use with your elementary school students is provided in Appendix 1.A on page 20. Throughout the book, we will provide such paired activities that are ready for use in elementary science teaching.

ACTIVITY 1.2   *21st C*

Find Someone Who...

Distribute a copy of the table below to each person in the class. For each box, find two people in your class who match the description and record their names. Try to include as many different people as possible. Be prepared to introduce to the class two people from your list.

Find someone who...

Enjoys reading popular science books	Studied science in university	Enjoys the outdoors	Watches nature programs
Name: Name:	Name: Name:	Name: Name:	Name: Name:
Enjoys bird watching	Has a food garden	Plays an instrument	Speaks three languages
Name: Name:	Name: Name:	Name: Name:	Name: Name:
Has a food allergy	Has participated in a local cleanup project	Has a composter	Enjoys cooking
Name: Name:	Name: Name:	Name: Name:	Name: Name:

DISCUSSION QUESTIONS

1. What descriptions might you change? What descriptions might you add?
2. What are some of the benefits of an activity like this?

USING THIS ACTIVITY WITH ELEMENTARY SCHOOL STUDENTS

This activity is best used at the start of the school year. It can help you learn about your students and their experiences in science, and it encourages students get to know each other. Adapt the descriptions as needed to best suit the grade of your students. Be mindful of any students who are new to the school, and support their first few interactions as they make the transition into a new peer group.

1. Have students sit together on the carpet or gathering space in your classroom. Describe the activity and explain that by participating in the activity they will get to know each other and you.

2. Distribute a copy of "Find a classmate who…" You might wish to clarify some descriptions with personal examples, such as "My pet is a dog named Brandy" or "I watch the science program *Bill Nye the Science Guy.*" Additionally, you can modify the descriptions with local examples (e.g., the Royal British Columbia Museum, the Ontario Science Centre, the Halifax Discovery Centre, the Montreal Botanical Gardens, or the Yukon Northern Lights Space and Science Centre). For younger students, you may want to include pictures with the text. You might consider going through the descriptions together with students, perhaps using an interactive whiteboard, before they begin the activity to ensure that everyone understands the descriptions.

3. Allow 10 to 15 minutes for students to find at least two classmates who match each description. Encourage them to get as many different names as possible rather than using one student's name multiple times. Also, ask students to write their own names on their peers' sheets. Be sure to participate with your own recording sheet.

4. When students have found peers who match all (or nearly all) descriptions, bring the class together again. Ask students to share one thing they found out about a peer. You might challenge your students (and yourself) by creating a game that combines this activity with learning everyone's name.

DEVELOPING A PHILOSOPHY OF TEACHING AND LEARNING

In this section we explore your ideas about teaching and learning, and help you identify a personal philosophy. It is important to understand, and sometimes to challenge, the values and beliefs that inform teaching practice. It is equally important to articulate a philosophy that underpins our actions. As mentioned, this is only the beginning of your journey. Your teaching philosophy will evolve over time and change with each new experience.

You and your fellow students likely hold a variety of expectations about teaching. Understanding the similarities and differences in these goals is important to your professional growth. In Activity 1.3, you will examine your ideas about teaching and learning through metaphors. Metaphors can provide a powerful way to think about particular concepts, and they convey meaning and advance understanding (Mulholland & Wallace, 2008). They often generate interesting discussion about how we view, for example, teaching, learning, and knowledge. As you work through Activity 1.3, you may find that there is more than one metaphor that illustrates your views. Different metaphors can suit different contexts, and these can, in turn, carry implications for practice.

ACTIVITY 1.3   *21st C* ①②③④

Conceptions of Teaching and Learning[1]

Part A
Individually, consider the three visual metaphors on the next page. For each, decide who or what represents the learner and the teacher, and what each is doing. Choose one that you feel best captures your views about how teaching and learning in science should occur.

Part B
Form groups of four and compare your individual responses. In your group, rank the metaphors from 1 to 3, with 1 being the metaphor that is best representative of your group's view of teaching and learning and 3 being the least representative. Be prepared to share your group rankings with the class.

[1] Thank you to Elgin Wolfe and Don Galbraith for introducing us to this activity.

continued on next page

Teaching and learning metaphors a. Tending a garden b. Withdrawing money from the bank c. Creating a vase

DISCUSSION QUESTIONS

1. What are the strengths and weaknesses of each metaphor?
2. What does the metaphor the group chose convey about the relationship between teacher and learner?
3. How difficult was it for the group to come to consensus about ranking the metaphors? Explain your answer.
4. What are some of your concerns as a beginning teacher of science?

👁—**Watch**

The Learning Cycle
Explanation
Expansion
Evaluation

In completing Activity 1.3, it becomes clear that there are many metaphors that describe teaching and learning. For example, the teacher can be viewed as a guide, a facilitator, or a sage on the stage. At different times in your career you will take on different roles as appropriate to the context and lesson you have planned. Students also have complex roles, with varying degrees of autonomy and participation. Throughout this book, we encourage developing good judgment as you navigate the principles of effective teaching.

Transmissive, Transactive, and Transformative Approaches to Education

Depending on how you interpreted the metaphors in Activity 1.3, you may have alluded to different educational orientations. Miller (2007) suggests the following three educational orientations: 1) transmission; 2) transaction; and 3) transformation. In the *transmission* model, the teacher presents knowledge and skills that are *absorbed* or *accepted* by the student. This reflects Paulo Freire's (1970) banking model of education, in which students receive, file, and store knowledge deposits. Knowledge is viewed as a fixed entity, and is broken down into steps to be mastered by students, typically through imitation and repetition. In Activity 1.3, which metaphor(s) reflect a transmission model? The transmissive relationship between the curriculum and the student is shown in Figure 1.1.

The *transaction* orientation involves more interaction, and emphasizes dialogue, between student and teacher, which includes curricula. Often, students solve a problem or undertake some kind of inquiry-based learning activity. Unlike transmission, where knowledge is seen as fixed, the transaction model views knowledge as dynamic. While dialogue is emphasized, this model focuses on cognitive interactions that highlight analysis rather than on synthesizing or feeling (Miller, 2007). In Activity 1.3, which metaphor(s) reflect a transaction position? Figure 1.2 depicts the relationship between the teacher and the curriculum, and the student.

Finally, the *transformation* approach views the teacher, curriculum, and student as connected rather than separate entities. This position focuses on the development of the whole person rather than just on a set of learning competencies or skills. Pedagogical strategies include creative problem solving, cooperative learning, and artistic approaches that make learning both personally and socially meaningful for students (Miller, 2007). In Activity 1.3, which metaphor(s) might reflect a transformation position? Figure 1.3 illustrates the relationship between curriculum, teacher, and learner in this approach.

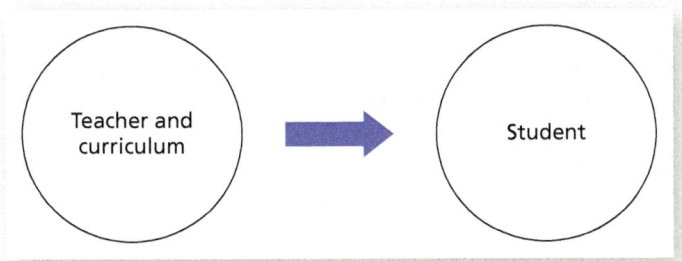

Figure 1.1 The transmission orientation

Source: Adapted from Miller, J. P. (2007). *The holistic curriculum* (2nd ed.). Toronto, ON: University of Toronto Press. Reprinted with permission of the publisher.

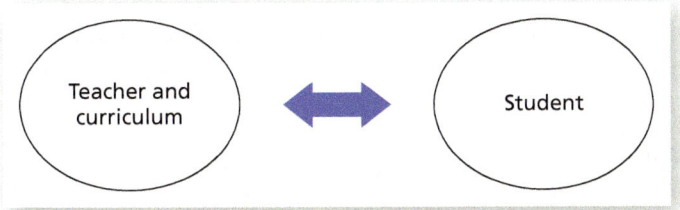

Figure 1.2 The transaction orientation

Source: Adapted from Miller, J. P. (2007). *The holistic curriculum* (2nd ed.). Toronto, ON: University of Toronto Press. Reprinted with permission of the publisher.

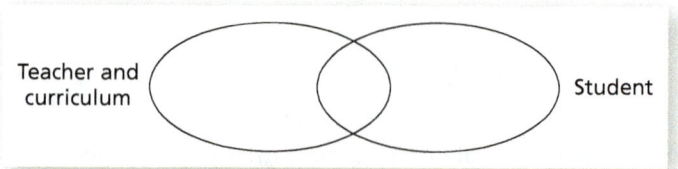

Figure 1.3 The transformation orientation

Source: Adapted from Miller, J. P. (2007). *The holistic curriculum* (2nd ed.). Toronto, ON: University of Toronto Press. Reprinted with permission of the publisher.

Domains of Teacher Knowledge

Teaching science is a demanding job with many responsibilities. It is replete with choices (e.g., about content, pedagogy, and representation); teachers are constantly making decisions, building up their repertoire of practices, and developing their craft (Wallace & Louden, 2000; 2002; 2003). Wallace and Louden (2000) remind us that knowledge about teaching develops from a gradual expanding of horizons over time and through experience, rather than through sudden leaps of insight or quick-fix answers. In this section we explore teacher knowledge in an effort to understand practice.

Many theories have been proposed about the art of teaching. One particularly useful theory comes from Lee Shulman. Published in the 1980s, Shulman's work (1986, 1987) remains relevant to thinking about what it means to be a teacher and, in particular, a teacher of science. His theory of the complex knowledge base required for teaching identifies three domains of teacher knowledge: 1) *content knowledge*, which is knowledge of the concepts and principles of a discipline; 2) *curriculum knowledge*, which includes understanding curriculum documents, school policies, available resources, and educational structures; and 3) *pedagogical content knowledge* (PCK), which is knowledge of how to teach particular content—in other words, it blends content and pedagogy.

Imagine you are teaching the movement of objects in the solar system to a Grade 3 class. The content knowledge includes reviewing objects in the solar system and related vocabulary and concepts. Curriculum knowledge might be achieved by examining Ministry curriculum documents; print, media, and community resources; and other educational materials. Now, how do you teach this topic? What pedagogical tools should you use in order to effectively teach it? One way would be to simply lecture, or, alternatively, you could have students physically act it out using Styrofoam models and other props, or you could make use of computer simulation. Good teachers are able to draw on pedagogical content knowledge to create contextually appropriate learning experiences.

Building on Shulman's work, Barnett and Hodson (2001) coined the term *pedagogical context knowledge* to refer to knowledge of teaching that is situated in the details of everyday classroom life. The source of this knowledge is both internal and external. It arises from teaching experiences and from interactions with parents, students, other teachers, government regulations, and policies. Barnett and Hodson argue that pedagogical context knowledge can lead to a cultural awareness that involves the following:

   a. understanding the social location of beliefs and practices
   b. acknowledging the context-dependence of what we do
   c. recognizing the existence of distinctive socio-cultural aspects of teaching

Pedagogical context knowledge enables teachers to engage in reflection, look outward for other sources of knowledge, and critique perceptions, while considering the socio-cultural landscapes that influence personal frameworks and understandings.

WHAT IS SCIENCE EDUCATION FOR?

This seemingly simple question has long been the subject of debate, often creating tension in the development of curricula and policy. Many have attempted to shed light on the complexities of this central question (see for example, Aikenhead, 2006; Hodson, 1998; Roth & Calabrese Barton, 2004). Part of the complexity stems from the understanding that science education serves many purposes. For example, it aims to teach subject matter, to prepare students to enter science and technology careers, to foster economic growth, and to develop responsible, informed citizens. Sometimes these purposes are at odds with one another; one purpose may be privileged over another, depending on the context, curricula expectations, and goals for a particular lesson. It soon becomes clear, however, that a variety of goals in science education are required, partly to make science interesting and accessible to diverse student populations, and also to facilitate excellence and equity in science education (Pedretti & Little, 2008). As we plan curricula, we need to be aware of the multiple purposes of science education and able to respond to a question that students inevitably ask: *Why are we doing this?*

Arguments: What Is Science Education for?

Wellington (2001) provides three succinct justifications in response to the question of what science education is for: intrinsic value, citizenship, and utilitarianism.

Intrinsic Value Science is recognized as a major cultural activity, and all young people should be able to understand and celebrate its achievements. This argument seeks to demystify science while making sense of the natural world. It supports the notion of science for the sake of science, and suggests that science education is intrinsically interesting and exciting.

Citizenship Science This justification argues that an understanding of science is necessary for individuals and key decision makers in a democracy in order to participate in debate and make decisions about issues that span the realms of science and society (e.g., waste disposal, climate change, genetically modified foods, and health). Citizenship science includes understanding scientific knowledge, the nature of scientists' work, scientific evidence, and the scientific enterprise (see Chapter 2).

Utilitarianism The utilitarianism justification for science education suggests that science can be useful. Some parts of this argument relate to individuals, others to the economy. A utilitarian argument includes developing process skills that may be of value to all (e.g., measuring, estimating, evaluating); developing attitudes such as curiosity, skepticism, and a critical disposition; preparing students for careers that include science and technology; and preparing students to become scientists.

Wellington's justifications are compelling and they can help us understand why particular science topics are in the curriculum. In Activity 1.4, you will examine topics in the science curriculum in the context of Wellington's justifications.

ACTIVITY 1.4   *21st C* ① ② ③ ④

What Should Be in the Science Curriculum, and Why?

(adapted from Wellington, 2001)

Imagine you are a member of a Ministry of Education committee tasked with the job of determining which topics in a science curriculum should remain and which could be removed.

1. On your own, using the table on the next page, categorize each science topic and provide the reasoning for your selection. (Some topics may have more than one justification.) These topics have been drawn from the Manitoba K-4 science curriculum, but you might alternatively choose topics from your province or territory.

continued on next page

2. Using Wellington's justifications, determine which of the following categories each topic should be placed in:

U—utilitarian justification
C—citizenship science justification
I—intrinsic value justification
X—it is not necessary that everyone know this; it need not be included in the science curriculum

3. In groups of four, share your responses, and try to come to consensus for each topic. Be prepared to share your results with the class.

Analyzing Curriculum Topics

	Science Topic	Your Categorization	Your Reasoning
1	Sources of drinking water		
2	Basic parts of a tree		
3	The effect of forces on structures		
4	Properties of light		
5	The importance of senses in various activities, hobbies, and jobs		
6	Uses of inclined planes		
7	Magnets and magnetism		
8	Fossil formation		
9	Characteristics of soils		
10	Seasonal changes		

DISCUSSION QUESTIONS

1. How difficult or easy was it to categorize each topic? Explain your answer.
2. Did any topics fall into more than one category? Which ones?
3. How difficult or easy was it to determine whether something should be removed from the curriculum?
4. What role do values play in determining what is "worthwhile" knowledge?
5. Imagine that, in light of teacher complaints about an overcrowded curriculum, two of the science topics had to be removed. Which two would you remove? Why?

SCIENTIFIC LITERACY

Scientific literacy is often described as a way to conceptualize the purpose of science education. Scientific literacy has become increasingly significant to discussions about the purposes of science education, national and international education policy, and the development of science curricula. It captures the most admirable aspirations for students in the context of science education; in other words, we hope our students become scientifically literate through science education. Although a highly desirable goal, the phrase *scientific literacy* has become so commonplace that, for some, its meaning has become lost or vague. In Activity 1.5, we ask you to consider what scientific literacy means to you.

ACTIVITY 1.5
21st C

Exploring Scientific Literacy

Using the mind map on the next page and in groups of three, brainstorm what scientific literacy means to you. Be prepared to share your results with the class in order to generate a comprehensive mind map. You might consider using an online mapping tool (e.g., https://bubbl.us). Analyze your mind map and try to cluster similar ideas together. (See Appendix A for more information about mind mapping.)

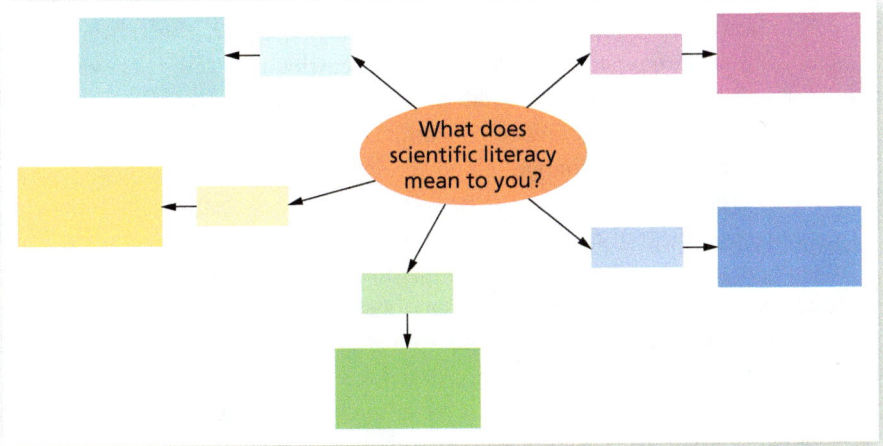

Mind Map for Scientific Literacy

DISCUSSION QUESTIONS

1. Describe how you clustered your ideas.
2. What were the predominant themes that emerged?
3. What surprised you, if anything, as a possible component of scientific literacy?

It is likely that the mind maps generated will include understanding scientific principles as one of the main outcomes of scientific literacy. Indeed this is central to any understanding of scientific literacy. For example, many countries have attempted to measure scientific literacy and the quality of their science education programs by measuring students' understanding of scientific content (e.g., laws, theories, principles) through standardized testing. Such an approach is problematic for a number of reasons. Generalizations about scientific literacy levels based on comparison of test scores do not take into account the broader goals of science education, the highly contextualized nature of teaching and learning, variation in science curricula across jurisdictions, or the myriad social, cultural, political, and economic factors that affect the teaching and learning process (Pedretti & Little, 2008). We would like you to consider a scientific literacy that is more comprehensive and includes understanding key concepts in science, participating in the procedures of science, and preparing for active citizenship. Scientifically literate people are able to navigate the complexities of a world where science is infused in all aspects of life. These ideas are discussed in more detail below.

Concept Mapping

Toward a Comprehensive Vision of Scientific Literacy

More recent calls for scientific literacy offer frameworks that are comprehensive and inclusive. (See, for example, Fensham, 2002; Hodson, 1998, 2008; Jenkins, 1990; Roth & Désautels, 2002.)

Hodson's (1998, p. 5) framework for conceptualizing scientific literacy captures three important aspects of science education:

1. Learning science: developing conceptual and theoretical knowledge
2. Doing science: engaging in, performing, and developing expertise in scientific inquiry and problem solving

3. Learning about science: developing an understanding of the nature and methods of science, an appreciation of its history and development, and an awareness of the complex interactions among science, technology, society, and environment

Hodson (2008) embeds these three elements within the notion of *critical scientific literacy*, which argues for a more politicized curriculum, one that will equip students to engage in responsible decision making, particularly in matters of scientific, environmental, and social consequence. Science education must have a transformative agenda—one that embodies principles of change, empowerment, and action. Furthermore, Hodson argues that educators and researchers must pay attention to obstacles experienced by students, many of them related to socio-economic status, ethnicity, and gender. In response, it is incumbent upon science educators to address inherent biases in science, and to provide authentic and culturally sensitive images of scientific practices. We need to create a learning environment that allows students to feel a sense of belonging; in other words a *science for all* approach, not science for a privileged few. And so we are challenged with the task of creating a more authentic and inclusive environment that is inviting to all students, while encouraging them to *learn*, *do*, and *learn about* science.

Others (e.g., Aikenhead 2006; Bencze & Carter, 2011; Norris & Phillips, 2002; Roth & Calabrese Barton, 2004) concur with a vision of scientific literacy that is outward and transformative. In *Rethinking Scientific Literacy*, Roth and Calabrese Barton (2004) argue that school science today fosters social reproduction, remains virtually unchanged, and privileges few. Little has been done to engage diverse and marginalized audiences. Students continue to opt out of science in large numbers; the discipline has become a mechanism to control and sort, rather than to empower and include. Roth and Calabrese Barton argue for what some would call a radical vision of scientific literacy that advocates for expanded agency, social justice, and social reconstruction to improve lives and build positive science identities. In summary, at the heart of our vision is a commitment to scientific literacy—in its broadest sense—as a guiding principle for science education.

Scientific Literacy in Curriculum Documents and Policies

Scientific literacy is part of curriculum documents and policy, and it has helped define science education worldwide for decades. For example, in *Science for all Americans* (American Association for the Advancement of Science, 1989), a scientifically literate person is described as

> one who is aware that science, mathematics, and technology are interdependent human enterprises with strengths and limitations; understands key concepts and principles of science; is familiar with the natural world and recognizes both its diversity and unity; and uses scientific knowledge and scientific ways of thinking for individual and social purposes. (p. 4)

In Canada, the Council of Ministers of Education (1997) developed what has come to be known as the *Pan Canadian Framework*. Its purpose was to set out a common vision and foundation statements for scientific literacy in Canada and to clearly articulate that all Canadian students, "regardless of gender or cultural background" (p. 4), have an opportunity to develop scientific literacy. Furthermore, it provided general and specific learning outcomes, along with examples to illustrate these outcomes. The *Pan Canadian Framework* served as a guide to assist provinces and territories in developing and reforming their science curricula.

The vision for scientific literacy in the *Pan Canadian Framework* (Council of Ministers of Education, 1997, p. 6) is based on four foundation statements, each delineating an important aspect of students' scientific literacy. These statements, although presented separately, are overlapping and mutually supportive, and reflect the interconnectedness of learning.

Foundation 1: Science, technology, society, and the environment (STSE)
Students will develop an understanding of the nature of science and technology, of the relationships between science and technology, and of the social and environmental contexts of science and technology.

Foundation 2: Skills
Students will develop the skills required for scientific and technological inquiry, for solving problems, for communicating scientific ideas and results, for working collaboratively, and for making informed decisions.

Foundation 3: Knowledge
Students will construct knowledge and understandings of concepts in life science, physical science, and Earth and space science, and apply these understandings to interpret, integrate, and extend their knowledge.

Foundation 4: Attitudes
Students will be encouraged to develop attitudes that support the responsible acquisition and application of scientific and technological knowledge to the mutual benefit of self, society, and the environment.

Source: Council of Ministers of Education, Canada. (1997). *Common framework of science learning outcomes, Pan-Canadian protocol for collaboration on school curriculum.* Printed with permission.

Although the document is from 1997, it is considered critical to science education and to science education reform in Canada. Milford, Jagger, Yore, and Anderson (2010) examined the influence of the framework on the development of provincial science curricula. In general, provincial science curriculum documents followed the framework through either specific reference or by using similar design principles; namely, outlining the four foundations of STSE, skills, knowledge, and attitudes.

Provinces and territories have taken up the call for scientific literacy in varied ways. What differs is the relative emphasis that each curriculum places on these foundation statements. In Activity 1.6, you will have an opportunity to explore how scientific literacy is conceptualized in your province or territory.

ACTIVITY 1.6

21st C ❷❸❺

Working with Curriculum Documents

Part A: Analyzing the Front Matter or Introduction to Curriculum Documents

Read the front matter (the introductory materials that precede actual curriculum units and outcomes or expectations) of a science curriculum document in your jurisdiction. Describe the vision of science education and scientific literacy in the document.

DISCUSSION QUESTIONS

1. How does the curriculum document describe scientific literacy?
2. What theoretical assumptions do you think underpin the view of science education and scientific literacy in your document?
3. Is there evidence of a commitment to critical scientific literacy as a goal? Explain, providing examples if possible.

continued on next page

Part B: Analyzing a topic or unit in the curriculum document

Choose a topic or unit from a science curriculum document in your jurisdiction. Read what you are expected to teach. Analyze how the terms of the foundational statements (STSE, skills, knowledge, attitudes) are represented. For example, in Ontario, skills are referred to under the heading "Developing Skills of Investigation and Communication"; in Alberta, STSE is combined with knowledge outcomes; and in some provinces the statements remain unchanged.

DISCUSSION QUESTIONS

1. How do your documents describe the foundation statements?
2. Are some foundations emphasized more than others? Speculate as to why this might be the case.

LITERACY AND NUMERACY

Science education inherently includes literacy and numeracy (Lemke, 1990; Yore et al., 2004). Students, for example, need to solve problems; describe their findings from science investigations in prose, numerically, or graphically; explain phenomena orally or in writing; and produce and interpret graphs. Indeed, science is a wonderful way to address literacy and numeracy skills that are promoted in policy documents.

Fundamental to scientific literacy is *literacy* itself. Norris and Phillips (2002) identify two distinct yet related understandings of literacy: A *fundamental sense of literacy* refers to reading and writing, and a *derived sense of literacy* refers to being knowledgeable and educated in a discipline such as science. Typically, when we speak of scientific literacy, we refer to this derived sense. However, as argued by Norris and Phillips, a derived sense of scientific literacy is dependent on possession of fundamental literacy—in this case, being able to read and write science. Noted by Yore, Bisanz, and Hand (2003), language is a critical component of science and scientific literacy, for it is

> a means to doing science and to constructing science understandings [and] also an end in that it is used to communicate about inquiries, procedures, and science understandings to other people so that they can make informed decisions and take informed action. (p. 691)

As a teacher, particularly of elementary school students, recognizing and supporting the development of both fundamental and derived senses of literacy is key. Curriculum and instruction that support reading and writing permeate all subject areas.

The importance of language in science is also evident in mathematics. Numeracy is critical in informed citizenry and is similarly important in science education. Many mathematical skills, such as basic computations, measurement, spatial sense, patterning, graphing, and data management, are foundational to science topics (see Bowen & Roth, 2005; Frykolm & Glasson, 2005; Roth & Bowen, 2001a). For example, it is difficult to be successful in many topics of physical science without the ability to perform basic number operations, measure mass, and calculate area and volume. Specific math skills may need to be explicitly taught or reviewed in the context of your science program.

Throughout this book, we recognize the importance of literacy and numeracy across the elementary curriculum and specifically highlight activities that support them. We suggest activities that cross disciplinary boundaries and provide opportunities to meaningfully bring other components of education into your science teaching. We revisit literacy and numeracy in more detail in Chapter 5, with a focus on the language and mathematics of science and the challenges they can present to learners. Take time to investigate children's literature online and in your local library or school board.

ACTIVITY 1.7

21st C

Teaching Science, Literacy, and Numeracy Through Children's Literature

Imagine you are teaching a Grade 1 or 2 class. Locate Graeme Bases's book *The Waterhole*, a wonderful story that weaves together reading and counting with ecology. With a partner, read the book and brainstorm how you might use it in a cross-curricular lesson that launches a unit on ecology. Include in your lesson both a literacy component and a numeracy component. Consider the different types of literacy you could include as well as a range of numeracy applications. In a chart, table, or other graphic format, outline what your goals are for the activity, what your students would be doing, and how literacy and numeracy are integrated into the lesson. Locate other examples of children's literature to support your theme. Share your ideas on your class wiki or another online learning environment.

THE ROLE OF TECHNOLOGY IN TEACHING SCIENCE

In the following section we consider the relationship between science and technology and the role of information and communication technologies (ICT) in the teaching and learning of science. (These topics are revisited and analyzed throughout the text.) The relationship between science and technology is complex and fluid, and the boundaries between the two have become increasingly blurred.

A Dinosaur WebQuest

Exploring the Relationship Between Science and Technology

Conventionally, science is thought to be about the pursuit of knowledge that is often abstract and decontextualized, while technology is viewed as the application of knowledge in more contextualized ways. We are reminded of Ursula Franklin's (1999, p. viii) whimsical definition of technology as "practice—as the way things are done around here."

Technology and Science Learning (Part 2)

Many view science as the attempt to understand natural phenomenon and to organize these understandings into ordered systems; technology involves applying ideas to design tools that affect quality of life. Bencze (2001) describes their respective goals. The scientific intent, he states, has traditionally been to document, explain, and predict natural phenomena (e.g., species growth and propagation), while the technological intent is to change objects and events in ways considered desirable (e.g., "stopping" invasive species). The argument that there are differences between science and technology with respect to contextualization is also helpful. At one extreme, some science can be conducted in an idealized context (e.g., studying the Higgs Boson or God particle), while technology is often more contextualized and takes into account a number of variables (e.g., designing hybrid cars). Innovation and design are hallmarks of technological pursuits; in elementary science, this is often referred to as design and technology (further explored in Chapter 8).

While science and technology can be viewed as separate enterprises, they are often practised together and are deeply interconnected. Each discipline informs the other, propelling it forward. As Bencze (2001) explains, both are theory-driven (that is, both make use of conceptual structures and knowledge); both make use of similar processes; both rely on some form of rigorous debate; and both inform one another. Indeed, science and technology have become so intertwined that numerous hybrid fields have emerged, such as biotechnology, genetic engineering, and robotics. Science and technology impact human relationships, work, community, citizenship, and the notion of collective social responsibility (Franklin, 1999). As future teachers of science, we encourage you to adopt a critical stance about the purposes of science and technology.

Information and Communication Technologies (ICT) and Teaching Science

Information and communications technology (ICT) provides a range of tools that can enrich teachers' instructional strategies and support students' learning in science (Shanahan, 2011). Hewitt (2005) describes three compelling reasons for using ICT: a) concretizing abstract concepts; b) providing students with tools for conducting and analyzing scientific processes; and c) supporting connections between people as they learn. To this list we add using technology to enhance lesson delivery and assessment practices and to provide tools that can support student needs.

The use of ICT to concretize abstract concepts is particularly important to help science students visualize abstract ideas. Imagine you are teaching about forces in natural hazards, the properties of air, or tidal patterns. These concepts can be difficult to visualize or even observe firsthand. Tools to assist student learning might include simulations (e.g., Starry Night to investigate astronomical principles), virtual manipulatives (e.g., Gizmos), application software, CD-ROMS, and DVDs. Other technologies play a more significant role in conducting inquiry and research. For example, probes and sensors are helpful for data collection, storage, and analyses. Through online and CD-ROM technology, students can access primary sources held in libraries and other public institutions for research purposes.

ICT can be used in creative ways to connect students and provide access to the global community—for example, through virtual learning environments such as Moodle and Blackboard, and through social media technologies like wikis, Facebook, and Twitter. There is also a range of web-based collaborative tools that allow students to participate in online discussion forums, peer reviews, and debates. In this way, students can learn from one another and engage in scientific inquiry (Shanahan, 2010; Slotta & Linn, 2009). While powerful, virtual learning environments and social media technologies provide a level of anonymity that can be problematic. We urge you to adopt a critical stance with regard to their appropriateness and to consider carefully how to prepare students for their use in order to avoid exclusion, alienation, or bullying.

Teaching and learning can be further supported by presentation software (e.g., PowerPoint, Keynote) and technologies such as interactive whiteboards (e.g., SMART Boards), which operate on the principle of touch detection and allow for dynamic, collaborative lessons. Many schools are equipped with interactive whiteboards. Another interactive technology is the clicker, a personal response device that resembles a remote control and can be registered to a specific student in order that he or she can participate in class discussions. In response to questions set by the teacher, each student registers her or his opinion or answer anonymously. Class responses are tabulated immediately and can be seen by the whole class via a projector or monitor. This technology can provide formative and summative assessment and provide direction for further discussion.

Technology is ubiquitous in our homes, places of work, and schools. Advocates of technology-rich classrooms argue that ICT has the potential to transform teaching and learning. We agree that technology can be a powerful learning tool; however, as Hewitt suggests, we need to move beyond broad generalizations and "move towards developing a deeper sense of the kinds of situations in which technology is best used" (2005, p. 161). In other words, the teacher needs to consider if, how, when, and why technology is appropriate for the particular goals he or she has set. Context is important, as is the premise that ICT is best used alongside classroom practices that effectively support learning.

Science, Technology, and the Curriculum

How then, do science and technology play out in curricula? Most provinces and territories have dedicated science courses and dedicated technology courses at the secondary level. In British Columbia, students can study industrial design and electronics, for example, in addition to the usual selection of science courses. Similarly, Quebec offers science education in the traditional domains as well as in manual and technical courses. However, provincial elementary curricula tell a different story. Ontario explicitly combines science and technology at the K–3 and 4–6 levels in the *Grades 1-8 Science and Technology Curriculum* (Ministry of Education, 2007). Elementary science is similarly combined with technology in Quebec. Unlike in Ontario and Quebec, though, the British Columbia elementary curriculum focuses on science alone; it is not explicitly combined with technology. This is also the case in other western provinces and in Atlantic Canada. That said, all curricula make use of ICT.

The boundaries between science and technology are not distinct; rather, they are interconnected and impact one other. It is important to understand how science and technologies are addressed in your province or territory. We invite you to consider the relationship of technology, in all its manifestations, to teaching and learning science today, and how you can help prepare students to understand and critique the role of technology in the new millennium.

ACTIVITY 1.8   *21st C* ❶ ❸ ❹ ❼

Using Technology to Support Learning

As a class, create a virtual learning environment to post responses to discussion questions and to share resources throughout the year. For example, you might collaborate on a class wiki or blog.

SCIENCE BEYOND THE CLASSROOM

Whether through school trips to science centres and museums, media, or engagement in recreational activities (e.g., hiking and camping), we are always learning. It is widely recognized that science learning occurs in both school and non-school settings and throughout our lives.

◉—Watch

Physics at an Amusement Park

The learning that occurs beyond schools is often referred to as *informal learning*, and can occur in museums, science centres, aquaria, botanical gardens, and zoos (Davidson, Passmore, & Anderson, 2009; Falk & Dierking, 2001; Jagger, Dubek, & Pedretti, 2012; Pedretti, 2012; Stocklmayer, Rennie, & Gilbert, 2010). These are typical destinations for school field trips, which are organized on the premise that they complement the curriculum and support learning in meaningful ways. Furthermore, such sites can create a holistic, inclusive approach to curricula and provide experiences that students may otherwise never have. Millions of other visitors also flock to these places, for both entertainment and education purposes. As you consider informal learning venues, be sensitive to the beliefs, values, and emotions of your students and their families. Some venues may be viewed as controversial and can be potentially upsetting (e.g., zoos, issues-based exhibitions). Be sure to maintain open conversation with parents and guardians when considering these types of learning experiences.

Media provide another source of science learning beyond the classroom (e.g., television, popular science books, and magazines). Television programs increasingly portray a variety of scientists and forensic specialists at work. Virtual worlds are increasingly available and accessible through information and communication technologies (Braund & Reiss, 2006). Community organizations, after-school programs, and local areas such as parks and ravines can provide yet another place to explore science beyond the classroom.

Research suggests that informal learning can enhance attitudes toward science and foster interest and enthusiasm (Falk & Dierking, 2001; Hodson, 1998). Learning opportunities outside the classroom can be a powerful experience for students, teachers, and the community. For example, Mayer-Smith, Bartosh, and Peterat's (2007) *Intergenerational Landed Learning Project* brought together students, elders, and teachers on an urban farm to explore how farming practices can be integrated with curricula to promote environmental knowing, and an ethic of care and responsibility. Calabrese Barton (2003) describes the positive effects of after-school programs for marginalized youth. There are many other examples. We urge you to consider the role of informal learning as you plan your curriculum, and to make use of the rich resources available beyond the walls of the classroom.

SCIENCE EDUCATION RESEARCH

A vast research literature base exists to provide science educators with empirical and theoretical perspectives to inform practice. We encourage you to delve into the science education research literature. Well known academic journals include *Science Education; Journal of Research in Science Teaching; Canadian Journal of Science, Mathematics, and Technology Education; School Science Review; Science and Education; International Journal of Science Education; Cultural Studies in Science Education;* and *School Science and Mathematics.* Activity 1.9 asks you to read some peer-reviewed articles. Another resource is professional organizations, which produce journals such as *Science and Children, Science Scope, the Science Teacher, the American Biology Teacher,* and *Interactions.* One of our goals throughout the book is to engage you in the research literature in an effort to connect practice and theory. Reading journals and publications will become an important part of your professional learning journey.

ACTIVITY 1.9   *21st C* ❶ ❷ ❻

Read and Reflect: Learning About Science Education Research

Choose one of the three articles listed below from your university library or Google Scholar. Read the article, and answer the questions that follow. Be prepared to share your responses in small groups of your peers who have read the same article.

1. Does this article help you become a better teacher? If so, how?
2. What are the implications for students? For the classroom?
3. What ideas in the paper challenged you? Surprised you?

Hodson, D. (2003). Time for action: Science education for an alternative future. *International Journal of Science Education, 25*(6), 645–670.

Lemke, J.L. (2001). Articulating communities: Sociocultural perspectives on science education. *Journal of Research in Science Teaching, 38*(3), 296–316.

Hurd, P. D. (1998). Scientific literacy: New minds for a changing world. *Science Education, 82*(3), 407–416.

CONTEMPORARY ISSUES IN SCIENCE EDUCATION

Periodically throughout the book we will raise issues pertaining to science education, such as constructivism as a theory of learning, the use of computer simulations in place of hands-on work, and the role of informal learning in science curricula. There is no end to the issues faced by contemporary science educators. In this chapter, we present a few concerns related to science literacy and to conflicting views of the aims of science education. In the spirit of critical thinking, get together with your classmates and discuss the following issues.

Standardized Testing

Watch

Standardized Tests

In groups of four, research the structure and use of standardized tests such as the Trends in Mathematics and Science Studies (TIMSS) and the Programme for International Student

Assessment (PISA). Find the most recent published reports for either TIMSS or PISA. How does Canada perform in relation to other countries?

1. What is your position on standardized testing (consider cost, purpose, etc.)?
2. What are the implications of standardized testing for teaching at the elementary level?
3. What are the implications of standardized testing with respect to scientific literacy?
4. What are the implications of standardized testing for students?

Conflicting Visions of Science Education

In groups of four, share your vision of an *ideal* science program. Now imagine you are part of a staff that has a different vision for the science program.

1. How do you work with others who have different views?
2. Is there a view of science education that is *better* for students? Explain.

Science Specialists in Elementary Schools

Many elementary schools have music and language specialists. Should elementary schools also have science specialists? In groups of four, discuss the pros and cons of having science specialists in elementary schools.

1. What are the benefits of having specialist teachers of science in elementary schools?
2. What are the drawbacks?
3. What are the implications of science specialists at the elementary level for teacher education programs?

CONCLUDING THOUGHTS

Teaching is a complex enterprise. No two students are alike; no two teachers or communities are alike. While teaching occurs within a rich myriad of variables that challenge us and require constant sensitivities, it is also the diverse nature of students and communities from which we draw strength and inspiration. What follows is a summary of the key ideas related to the learning objectives provided at the beginning of the chapter.

Good or effective teaching
Although no two teaching situations are alike, there is consistency in what constitutes good or effective teaching. A good teacher is someone who is prepared, plans lessons thoughtfully, uses different instructional techniques, is enthusiastic, has good classroom management skills, uses students' ideas, cares about students, assesses students regularly and in different ways, knows his or her science, and sets clear goals. The reflective practitioner looks to experience, theory, and practice in an attempt to build new understandings of teaching and to inform and improve their pedagogy.

Philosophy of teaching and learning
It is important to develop a philosophy of teaching and learning that can be articulated and can guide practice.

Particular views—for example, about the roles of teacher and student—carry implications for curriculum planning, implementation, and assessment.

Domains of teacher knowledge
Shulman's (1986, 1987) theory of the complex knowledge base that is required for teaching identified domains of teacher knowledge as content knowledge, pedagogical content knowledge (PCK), and curriculum knowledge. Barnett and Hodson (2001) introduced the idea of pedagogical context knowledge.

Arguments to explain the purpose of science education
The question, "What is science education for?" has been the subject of debate for decades. Wellington (2001) provides three justifications in response to this question: He describes science education as having intrinsic value, promoting citizenship science, and having utilitarian functions.

Scientific literacy
Scientific literacy has become increasingly significant to discussions about the purposes of school science education, guiding national and international education policy

and the development of science curricula. We advocate a framework for scientific literacy that is comprehensive and inclusive, and includes learning science and doing science (Hodson, 1998). Central to this formulation are the guiding principles of transformation and social justice.

Science and technology, and the role of information and communication technologies in science education

Science is thought to be about the pursuit of knowledge that is often abstract and decontextualized, while technology is viewed as the application of knowledge in more contextualized ways. However, they are often practised together and are deeply interconnected. Information and communications technology (ICT) provides tools that can enrich teachers' instructional strategies and support students' learning through concretizing abstract concepts, providing students with tools for conducting and analyzing scientific processes, and supporting connections among people as they learn. It is important to adopt a critical stance with regard to appropriateness of ICT.

The role of informal environments to teach science

Science learning occurs in both school and non-school settings and throughout our lives. The learning that occurs beyond schools is often referred to as *informal learning*, and can take place in museums, science centres, aquaria, botanical gardens, and zoos. Other informal learning environments include media, the internet, community organizations, after-school programs, and local parks. Research suggests that informal learning can enhance attitudes toward science and foster enthusiasm.

Education research

The field of education has a large research literature that can provide educators with empirical and theoretical perspectives to inform practice. It is important to be familiar with the academic and professional journals in the field.

BRINGING IT ALL TOGETHER: FINAL QUESTIONS

1. Describe your personal philosophy of teaching and learning.
2. What makes a teacher different from a caring and knowledgeable adult?

MyEducationLab®   Visit MyEducationLab® to access an electronic version of the text, as well as a variety of topics that enhance the text material. The topics include the following to support your learning in the course:

- Assessments, including interactive case studies, activities, and video assignments
- Discussion board questions
- Videos, simulations, a lesson plan builder, and other useful course resources

---

APPENDIX 1.A   Find a Classmate Who...

Likes to read books about science	Has a pet	Likes to explore the outdoors	Likes to watch programs about science
Name: Name:	Name: Name:	Name: Name:	Name: Name:
Likes bird watching	Likes cooking	Can play a musical instrument	Can speak more than two languages
Name: Name:	Name: Name:	Name: Name:	Name: Name:
Has an allergy	Recycles at home and in the community	Has a brother or sister	Has been to a museum or science centre
Name: Name:	Name: Name:	Name: Name:	Name: Name:

Chapter 2
Nature of Science

Pavel Svoboda/Fotolia

LEARNING OBJECTIVES

- Examine tenets of the nature of science (NOS).

- Outline arguments for including NOS in elementary science.

- Investigate tensions and challenges of teaching NOS.

- Explore the relationship between beliefs about NOS and teacher practice.

- Design curriculum that includes NOS.

- Use a NOS lens to explore science practices and institutions.

- Explore educational research related to NOS.

Scientists make potions and study dinosaurs.

—Roland, Grade 3 student

Scientists live alone and have funny hair.

—Luca, Grade 2 student

I think it's important to de-mystify science for my students.

—James, elementary school teacher

21st CENTURY LEARNING SKILLS & COMPETENCIES

1 Communication

2 Critical thinking

3 Collaboration

4 Creativity

5 Literacy and numeracy

6 Media literacy

7 Technological literacy

INTRODUCTION

The nature of science (NOS) has gained prominence in educational practice and theory in the past two decades. Still, many science textbooks begin with science defined as a search for truth and understanding of natural phenomena in the physical world. There is usually mention of the predictive power of science, its ability to explain, the importance of inquiry, and a perceived universal *scientific method*. While this captures some of the features of science, school science is often overwhelmingly concerned with facts, information, and end products of science and less about knowledge construction and processes. Little attention is paid to how scientists decide what they believe is *true* and how people—both practising scientists and the general public—use scientific knowledge and skills in their personal lives and in society.

Effective teachers of elementary science use a variety of resources and experiences that portray a comprehensive and diverse view of science. For example, how astronomers conduct research and engage in scientific practice differs from that of geneticists, biochemists, string theorists, and ecologists. Embracing NOS attends to the diversity of science processes methods, as well as aspects of the discipline's history and philosophy.

In this chapter, you will explore your own understanding of NOS, current thinking about NOS in the science education community, and how to include NOS in your teaching practice.

WHAT IS THE NATURE OF SCIENCE?

Activity 2.1 will help you to explore and articulate your current perspectives about NOS.

ACTIVITY 2.1

21st C **1** **3**

Prior Knowledge and Experience

Your instructor will provide a set of six cards related to NOS that have been created from statements from Cobern and Loving (1998). Alternatively, your instructor may create his or her own set of cards. For example, one card might read "Science is always objective," while another might be "Science is never objective since it is culturally determined."

Read over the cards and decide which statements you agree with and which you do not. Order the cards from the ones you strongly agree with (and would like to keep) to the ones you strongly disagree with (and want to get rid of). Find another student to exchange cards with. You may exchange one or more, but you must always have six cards. Repeat the exchange as many times as you need in order to get rid of cards you do not agree with and to accept cards that are close to your own views. In the end you should have six cards you agree with.

DISCUSSION QUESTIONS

1. Which statements surprised you?
2. Which statements were difficult to make a decision about and why?
3. Which cards did you have difficulty getting rid of? Why do you think this was the case?
4. Did some of the statements that others agreed or disagreed with surprise you?
5. On your own, using the cards you've kept and information from class, write a paragraph that describes your view of NOS.

USING THIS ACTIVITY WITH ELEMENTARY SCHOOL STUDENTS

As presented here, Activity 2.1 is geared toward preservice teachers. However, some statements can be easily modified and used as prompts for classroom discussion with upper elementary school students. (See Appendix 2.A for modified statements.) For example, students might debate the statement *Science has made possible some of the best things in life and some of the worst*. This is also a good opportunity to integrate science with other areas, such as social studies and language arts. You might, for example, consider traditional ecological knowledge and wisdom (TEKW) and science when studying Aboriginal cultures in social studies.

You can also explore NOS with all elementary school students through the following mystery box activity (adapted from Cavallo, 2007). The activity presents several aspects of NOS: science as tentative, subjective, creative, and evidence-based. Allow plenty of time for exploration and discussion.

1. Using small boxes (jewellery or small gift boxes work well), create mystery boxes of known objects. For example, one box might contain three pennies, another might have a paper clip, and a third might have two marbles. Be sure to have at least one mystery box for each group of three to four students. Number and seal each box.
2. In groups, students make and record observations about what is in each box. This can be done in science notebooks, journals, tables, or other organizers. (See Appendix A.)
3. Based on their observations, the groups will draw a conclusion about what they believe is in the box.
4. Have the groups exchange boxes, and repeat steps 2 and 3. Each group should examine at least two mystery boxes.
5. Groups should present their observations and conclusions to the class. Students from other groups are encouraged to ask questions, and you can model questioning that encourages thinking (e.g., "How do you know that the object is a penny and not a quarter?" or "What makes you think there are three objects in the box?"
6. Pose the following question to the class: "How can we be more sure of our conclusions without opening the boxes?" Have each group work on determining how more data can be gathered. Groups can record their method of exploration and additional observations and revisit their initial conclusions.
7. Groups should present their methods, observations, and refined conclusions to the class.
8. Ask questions related to NOS: How were their observations and conclusions similar and different? Did their conclusions change with additional data collection? How did they change? How did methods vary between groups? Which conclusions were groups most sure of, and why? Your questions should illuminate the tentative, subjective, creative, and evidence-based NOS, as well as the role of observation and inference.
9. Have groups open the boxes.
10. *Assessment*: Your assessment will depend in part on how students record their findings. You might use individual or group rubrics, checklists, anecdotal comments, or journal entries to determine students' understanding. This activity can be used as formative assessment of what your students know of NOS early in the school year, and can be used in planning your science curriculum.

👁 **Watch**

Concept Application

School science is often represented as an orderly, objective, abstract pursuit that employs a reliable algorithmic method to find factual knowledge about the universe. The human element, the idiosyncratic nature of doing science, and the real life messiness and creativity of research are often overlooked. School science can seem void of context or connections to students' lives; it is often presented as taking place in a laboratory and done only by trained scientists. Such a depersonalized view can alienate students, leading to a characterization of science as boring, difficult, and abstract (Hodson, 1998; 2008).

A more realistic image of science includes an understanding of NOS—of how scientific knowledge is generated and validated, an appreciation of what scientists do, and how the scientific enterprise operates (see, for example, Aikenhead, 2006; Hodson, 1998). As McComas, Clough, and Almazroa (1998) state,

> NOS . . . blends aspects of various social studies of science including the history, sociology and philosophy of science combined with research from the cognitive sciences . . . into a rich description of what science is, how it works, and how scientists operate as a social group and how society itself both directs and reacts to scientific endeavours. (p. 4)

Tenets of the Nature of Science

McComas et al. (1998) reviewed eight international science education documents and generated a consensus view of 14 NOS objectives. These objectives and descriptions can be useful to science educators as they develop curricula:

Concept Invention

1. *Scientific knowledge, while durable, has a tentative character.* When new evidence is found or old evidence is viewed in a different way, new patterns can be developed and scientific knowledge and ideas can change (Crowther, Lederman, & Lederman, 2005).

2. *Scientific knowledge relies heavily, but not entirely, on observation, experimental evidence, rational arguments, and scepticism.* Ideas and understandings in science are informed through multiple methods, including observation, exploration, analysis, speculation, review of existing literature, and experimentation (McComas, 1996).

3. *There is no one way to do science; therefore, there is no universal step-by-step scientific method.* Doing science does not just follow the linear sequence of defining a problem, gathering background information, developing a hypothesis, making observations, and stating conclusions. Instead, science investigations can follow any number of different and often complex pathways and include imagination, creativity, and prior knowledge (McComas, 1996).

4. *Science is an attempt to explain natural phenomena.* Through scientific knowledge and processes, we can better understand the patterns and phenomena existing in nature.

5. *Laws and theories are related but serve different roles in science; therefore, students should note that theories do not become laws, even with additional evidence.* Scientific laws and theories are supported by evidence and observation. A common misconception is that laws are simply mature theories and are of more value than theories. This is not the case. Laws are generalizations observed in the natural world under specific conditions, whereas theories explain laws and provide frameworks for additional research. For example, Charles's law states that when heated, gases tend to expand. On the other hand, kinetic theory asserts that atoms and molecules within gases are constantly moving, and that increases in temperature increase particle movement (Clough, 2000; McComas, 2004).

6. *People from all cultures contribute to science.* This can be expanded to include people of all ethnicities, regardless of race, class, gender, or sexual orientation. Everyone can participate in science, including you and your students!

7. *New knowledge must be reported clearly and openly.* Scientists have a responsibility to share their findings in a way that is readily available and accessible to others.

8. *Scientists require accurate record keeping, peer review, and replicability.* In order for scientific findings to be valid, the scientist must keep careful records and be open to review by others. Experiments must be able to be reproduced by others.

9. *Observations are theory laden.* Scientists hold prior knowledge and biases about how the world works, and these ideas influence their ability to make and interpret observations.

10. *Scientists are creative.* Imagination and creativity are important in developing research questions, designing experiments, analyzing data, and explaining findings. These qualities are not exclusive to the arts!

11. *The history of science reveals both an evolutionary and a revolutionary character.* Looking back at the history of science, it is clear that scientific knowledge and processes are ever changing and can greatly inform thinking across disciplines.

12. *Science is part of social and cultural traditions.* Science does not occur in isolation, but rather is embedded within social and cultural contexts.

13. *Science and technology impact each other.* Recall from Chapter 1 that science and technology influence each other, but they are not synonymous. Science seeks to explain the nature of reality; it is "knowledge for knowledge's sake." Technology is developed to meet a particular need; it is the application of scientific knowledge. For example, the nature of a particular bacterium might be studied (science) and a medication could be developed to treat it (technology).

14. *Scientific ideas are affected by their social and historical milieu.* Scientific research is greatly influenced by historical, cultural, and social contexts. For example, stem cell research is highly controversial for a number of reasons beyond science. These influences can both encourage and impede scientific explorations.

We acknowledge that much of the discourse about NOS has a western bias. Other cultural groups, including Indigenous peoples worldwide, also contribute to science. School science warrants a comprehensive and pluralistic view of how the discipline operates and how knowledge is generated. Multiple perspectives encourage all students to see themselves as potential contributors to science in their future.

What Is the Scientific Method?

Understanding NOS includes examining the *scientific method*. What does this phrase mean to teachers of elementary science? How do we understand *observation*, *purpose*, *hypothesis*, or *theory*? Activity 2.2 will help you consider the common practices of scientists and whether there is one method used by all.

ACTIVITY 2.2   *21st C* ❶❷❸❹

Doing Science

Working in small groups, organize the words and phrases below (using a flow chart, a web, or a mind map) to represent the processes and products of science. Once you have reached group consensus, glue your arrangement onto chart paper and post it in the classroom or on an interactive whiteboard. Explore the charts posted by your fellow classmates, looking for similarities and differences in the arrangement of the words and phrases, and add comments using sticky notes.

- Collection of data
- Hypothesis
- Interpretation of data
- Procedure
- Data
- Prediction
- Control of variables
- Consulting with others
- Law

- Communicating with others
- Theory
- Analysis of data
- Conclusion
- Observation(s)
- Inference(s)
- Experiment
- Question
- Equipment and materials

DISCUSSION QUESTIONS

1. List any words or phrases you felt unsure about.

2. List any words or phrases that were difficult to incorporate into your arrangement.

continued on next page

3. What does this activity tell you about NOS with respect to methods and processes?

4. What are the implications for your future students?

5. In a few sentences, describe how science knowledge is generated according to your arrangement.

6. How is the work of an astronomer different from that of a geneticist? What are the implications for science methods?

USING THIS ACTIVITY WITH ELEMENTARY SCHOOL STUDENTS

1. Choose a few key terms or phrases from the list above that your students are familiar with (e.g., observation, question, prediction, conclusion). These will depend on what science vocabulary and skills you have already taught. Have students work in small groups to create a concept map, flow chart, web, or other organizer showing the connections between the terms.

2. Have groups complete a science investigation; for example, an exploration of floating and sinking. Groups can test a variety of materials (wooden block, pen, ice cube, etc.) to determine whether they sink or float in water. Have students use the key terms in their work.

3. Groups should revisit the concept maps they created in step 1, making any additions in another colour. You and your students should easily see their pre- and post-investigation ideas.

4. Groups can present their maps to the class. Encourage students to discuss their decisions for arranging the words, using specific examples from their exploration.

5. *Assessment*: This activity and its list of terms can be revisited with each science exploration. Have students think about the processes of science and how they fit into a particular exploration and, more broadly, into how science is done.

⊙─Watch

Water Wheels Part 1

Your class no doubt created a variety of arrangements of words that describe the scientific method. Often in science resource books, the scientific method is presented in steps: State your purpose, make a hypothesis, describe your method, make observations, and draw conclusions. Science students are often asked to describe investigations in this way. This might be helpful as a reporting tool, but it does not reflect what many scientists actually do. Sometimes scientists begin with observations of the natural world, which lead them to a question; for example, an astronomer might make observations of the night sky and later pose research questions related to those observations. Sometimes scientists use data that has been collected by others to make a model of a phenomenon. For example, scientists studying climate change use data collected over a long period of time to create a computer simulation and predict future patterns. Scientists also identify and control variables to investigate relationships. A botanist might want to investigate the effects of water on plant growth and set up an experiment with several plants. Each plant would receive a different amount of water (the variable under study), while keeping all other conditions the same (these variables are controlled—such as amount of sunlight, soil, and air). We want to emphasize the point that science as a process is not a simple algorithm.

LAWS AND THEORIES

Learning the language of science is part of learning science, and we encourage the correct use of science terminology with students. Words such as *hypothesis* and *prediction* are at times used to mean an educated guess, and *observations* and *inferences* are often confused.

In this section we turn our attention to scientific laws and scientific theories, which are often used interchangeably. For example, why do we say the *law* of universal gravitation but the *theory* of evolution, or the *law* of independent assortment but gene *theory*? Activity 2.3 explores this concept further.

ACTIVITY 2.3

21st C

Laws and Theories

In groups, brainstorm three laws and three theories in science (e.g., theory of relativity, particle theory of matter, law of universal gravitation). Consult websites, textbooks, and curriculum documents for ideas, and be sure to include the disciplines of life science, physical science, and Earth and space science.

1. What is your understanding of the difference between scientific law and scientific theory?
2. How is a scientific theory different from saying *I have a theory about why my friend is late all the time*?
3. Explain each of the laws or theories you named.
4. Why do we say *law* of universal gravitation but the *theory* of evolution?
5. What differentiates a law from a theory in science? Are there consistent definitions? Do we use them in teaching and learning science?

Question 5 is difficult to answer, and indeed, literature is often conflicting or simplistic about the respective meanings of theory and law. McComas, Almazroa, and Clough (1998) write about the myth that with increased evidence, theories become laws. Although theories and laws are related, they are different, and they do not have a hierarchical relationship. McComas et al. (1998) describe laws as generalizations, principles, or patterns in nature, while theories are the explanations of those laws. Refer to Kugler (2002) for a more detailed examination of laws and theories.

Although the context of Kugler's article is biology, the issues raised and research described have implications for all branches of science and all teachers of science. Kugler explores the use of *law* and *theory* by examining a number of textbooks. He found a lack of consistent definitions for these terms, which are used daily by teachers and found in science resources.

TEACHING THROUGH, WITH, AND FOR THE NATURE OF SCIENCE

A large body of literature and policy documents recommend that school science include NOS perspectives. (See, for example, Abd-El-Khalick & Lederman, 2000; Bencze, Bowen, & Alsop, 2006; Bencze et al., 2003; Brickhouse, 1990; Clough, 2000; Council of Ministers of Education, 1997; Crowther et al., 2005; Hodson, 1998; Khishfe & Lederman 2006; Lederman & Lederman, 2005; McComas, 1996, 2004; McComas et al., 1998; Olson, 2003.) Many contemporary science educators argue that understanding NOS—its goals, assumptions, presuppositions, and limitations—should be central to teaching science (McComas et al., 1998). The arguments for incorporating NOS are compelling; in this section, we discuss why teaching NOS matters.

ACTIVITY 2.4

21st C

Working with Resources

Examine the *front matter* (introductory materials that precede actual curriculum units and expectations) of science curriculum documents in your jurisdiction and any other sections that describe NOS.

DISCUSSION QUESTIONS

1. Analyze what aspects of NOS are reflected in the document. Make a list of these features.
2. Using the outcomes or expectations for particular units of study, identify different aspects of NOS that are explicitly addressed.

continued on next page

3. If an elementary science textbook is used in your school district, comment on how it could be used to support the teaching of NOS. Provide two examples.

4. Why is the inclusion of NOS perspectives in teaching and learning science important for students?

Arguments for the Inclusion of Nature of Science

Enhancing Teaching and Learning Science Studies indicate that understanding NOS, and specifically how science operates, enhances students' understanding about the behaviour of the natural world (McComas et al., 1998; Peters & Kitsantas, 2010; Pocovi, 2007). For example, having a view of science as dynamic and changing rather than static and constant suggests that knowledge is tentative, builds on prior work, is fallible, and is constantly revised by a community of scientists. Students who hold a more dynamic view of how science operates are less likely to believe that learning science means rote memorization. As such, these students often build more integrated understandings of the topics they are studying in science class. Understanding terms such as models, laws, and theories, or the relationship between evidence and explanation, can help students better appreciate what scientific ideas mean and how they are generated. Consider, for example, the controversy surrounding evolution and how NOS might help alleviate some of the tensions between science and religion.

Anchoring a lesson in NOS can increase student interest and motivation, and students can begin to make connections between science and the broader contexts of their lives. An understanding of how science works makes the field more accessible to a diverse student population. NOS perspectives situate science and technology within historical, philosophical, economic, sociological, political, and cultural contexts.

It is also argued that exposure to NOS enhances instructional delivery (McComas et al., 1998). For example, in science explorations, the idea that there is a "single approach" or a "right answer" can be disheartening for students, particularly if they cannot see connections that seem obvious to others. NOS can diminish these feelings if students understand, for example, that theories are tentative and offer *possible* explanations that are subject to change. NOS also provides space for the teacher to allow for multiple outcomes and to avoid the trap of *telling* students the *correct* answer.

Humanizing Science One of the strengths of including NOS perspectives is the promotion of equity and diversity by demystifying science (Hodson, 2008). NOS gives science a human face; we begin to see that scientists are human beings and, as such, are subject to the visions and vagaries of the human spirit. (The historical dimensions of NOS are particularly helpful here.) Students begin to see at a personal level that they, too, can participate in science—for example, by understanding issues around science, technology, society, and environment; participating in decision making; managing technological objects and processes; or pursuing a career in science.

NOS teaches that it matters who *does* science, because different scientists ask different questions, and different research projects are given priority and funding. Therefore, it is important that all students see themselves as participants in science.

Exploring Contemporary Cultural Aspects of Science Understanding NOS helps students see science as a significant part of contemporary culture. NOS illustrates the powerful, elegant structures that have been developed in our attempt to understand natural phenomena (Driver, Leach, Miller, & Scott, 1997). This invariably requires discussion about epistemological issues (i.e., questions about how knowledge is created), and the social, cultural, and political milieu from which scientific ideas emerge.

NOS also provides insight into the institution of science as a subculture. In other words, NOS incorporates the realities of the scientific community, including the politics and funding aspects. Also, it provides students with insight into the subculture of science, as well as the tools to allow them to access this subculture.

Understanding Knowledge Construction in Science Understanding knowledge generation, or epistemology, and its relationship to knowledge construction is an integral part of NOS. Why does this matter? Consider the popular view that science is *correct*, *reliable*, and *authoritative*. How will students interpret scientific claims? How might conflicting positions be viewed as a way in which science progresses? How will the messiness of real-world situations and the application of fundamental models be interpreted? These questions are particularly important when making decisions around socio-scientific issues, such as reproductive technologies, genetically modified foods, and the proposed Northern Gateway pipeline. Understanding how knowledge, within the scientific context, is constructed, negotiated, and tested emphasizes science as *expertise* about the natural world, rather than *certainty* about knowledge (Driver et al., 1997).

ACTIVITY 2.5   *21st C* ② ⑤ ⑥

Science in the Media

Find a current newspaper or magazine article, or a trending article in online news feeds, that reports on recent science research or developments. For example, there are often headlines about chemicals in the environment, bacterial or viral disease transmission, caffeine, or the discoveries of planets that can support life. Read the article and the scientific claims that are made.

DISCUSSION QUESTIONS

1. Who conducted the research?
2. Who asked the original question under consideration?
3. Where does the funding for the research originate? Who owns the research results?
4. How was the research conducted? For example, was the research conducted using an experimental design, a correlational study, or a survey?
5. Describe how social, cultural, religious, political, or economic factors might impinge on the priorities of this research.
6. Are the scientific claims made in the article backed by evidence? How was the evidence gathered?
7. Are alternative interpretations and conclusions possible?
8. Does the article direct you to the original publication or full report of the research?

USING THIS ACTIVITY WITH ELEMENTARY SCHOOL STUDENTS

Activity 2.5 can be adapted for elementary school students by ensuring that the material is at a suitable reading or viewing level. Consider news sources specifically written for young readers (e.g., *Teaching Kids News*). Language arts and media literacy are inherent in this activity.

1. If reading an article, distribute copies to students or share it on an interactive whiteboard. If viewing, show the video clip.
2. In small groups, have students discuss content and NOS-related questions, such as who conducted the research, how the research was done, who the research affects, and how it affects them. Remind students to consider not only the written text but also the visual text (e.g., pictures, graphs, figures). The questions you choose will depend on the level of your students and their understanding of NOS.
3. Groups can share their findings as a class.
4. *Assessment*: Make anecdotal comments as students are working in groups. Be sure to circulate among groups and ask additional questions to extend students' critique.

NATURE OF SCIENCE: TENSIONS AND CHALLENGES

In spite of international endorsement, local policy, and research about NOS, there is still some resistance to its inclusion in teaching and learning science, as well as some very real challenges for teachers. For example, to what extent should NOS be included in teaching science? Is NOS infused in an indirect and *implicit* way in the science curriculum? Or is it purposefully and *explicitly* addressed? We believe it can be both. It is not enough, for example, to hope that students will figure out how science proceeds, or see its broader social, political, historical, or cultural context without explicit or purposeful dialogue. Context is important, and the curriculum topic you are covering will help guide your decisions.

Many teachers feel ill equipped to address NOS perspectives, believing they lack sufficient knowledge in the philosophy, history, or sociology of science; this is understandable. The goal is not to teach the philosophy of science or the history of science as a discipline, but rather to help students understand how science operates and how scientific knowledge is generated. Other ongoing challenges include the assessment of students' understandings of NOS, and locating resources that support NOS teaching. Collaborating to develop curricula with colleagues, participating in professional development opportunities that focus on NOS, and generating NOS resources[1] are a few ways to address teacher concerns.

Lastly, many students hold rather conventional, positivist views of science (i.e., science is an objective and unbiased field of study), and therefore may wonder why history, economics, philosophy, politics, and cultural issues are included in their "science" class. For some, the certainty of science is what attracts them to the field, so disrupting their ideas through NOS may cause unease or resistance (Bellomo, 2003). Often such students are more interested in the body of scientific knowledge, and less so in scientific practice or epistemological issues. Alternatively, students who dislike science and view it as memorization might find NOS perspectives inspiring.

ACTIVITY 2.6

21st C  ❶ ❷ ❸ ❹ ❻

Images of Scientists

Part A: Draw a Scientist

This activity is appropriate for any age group from kindergarten to adult, and draws from the works of Chambers (1983), Barman (1997), and Huber and Burton (1995).

In this activity, the student is given a blank sheet of paper and asked to draw a scientist at work. The resulting drawings are examined for commonalities, and students can describe what the scientist is doing. A common response is a white male, with wild hair like Albert Einstein, in a white lab coat and using test tubes or beakers to pour a smoky potion.

USING THIS ACTIVITY WITH ELEMENTARY SCHOOL STUDENTS

1. Distribute a blank sheet of paper to each student.
2. Ask students to draw a scientist at work and to describe what the scientist is doing. Be mindful of giving too much direction; you want to see how your students perceive scientists and their work.
3. Share drawings and discuss similarities and differences.
4. *Assessment*: The drawings can be used to discuss student preconceptions and misconceptions about who can be a scientist and how science is done. You might repeat this activity throughout the school year to follow changes in student perceptions.

Part B: Examine Images of Scientists from Popular Media and the Internet

In this activity, students are presented with a variety of cartoons or images of scientists and are asked, "What can we deduce about the sort of person a scientist is?"

---

[1]We highly recommend McComas's (1998) book *The nature of science in science education: Rationales and strategies*. Also, the National Science Teacher Association's *Science and Children and Science Scope* are great resources for NOS-related elementary and middle school lesson and unit plans.

Stereotypical Images of Scientists

You can try this activity using the images from above and the discussion questions that follow.

DISCUSSION QUESTIONS

1. Describe the personality traits, physical traits, social group, and personal life conveyed by each image.

2. What other traits do scientists have that are not represented in the images?

3. Consider the image of a scientist from television, film, and popular culture—for example *The Big Bang Theory, CSI, Outbreak, GATTACA,* or *Bill Nye the Science Guy.* Using specific examples, discuss how scientists are portrayed. Are they fairly portrayed, or are they caricatures? Where do such images originate, and what are the messages they convey?

4. What are the implications of these portrayals for elementary school students? Do they inspire or alienate?

USING THIS ACTIVITY WITH ELEMENTARY SCHOOL STUDENTS

1. In small groups, students can examine a variety of images of scientists from the media and popular culture. These might be from the internet, television, and film.

continued on next page

2. In groups, have students discuss and record the personality traits, physical traits, social group, and personal life conveyed by each image.
3. Pose the following questions to your groups: What traits of scientists are missing from these images? Is each image a fair portrayal of a scientist? Why or why not? Where do these images come from, and what do they say about scientists?
4. *Assessment*: As with the "Draw a Scientist" activity, this activity can be revisited throughout the year to follow changes in students' perceptions.

Incorporating NOS in the Classroom

How can we incorporate NOS into teaching and planning science lessons? Below is a list of ideas to consider when planning your lessons.

- Visit a laboratory to see scientists at work or invite scientists to visit your class.
- Follow a Twitter feed or blog (e.g., Chris Hadfield's live tweets from space) related to active research.
- Organize science fairs (see Chapter 8).
- Use historical material or case studies.
- Conduct "The Nature of Science Card Exchange" (Activity 2.1) to inspire discussion and debate.
- Explore mystery boxes (page 23).
- Read and discuss biographies of scientists (Activity 2.7).
- Use the "Draw a Scientist" activity (Activity 2.6) for Grade 4–6 students.
- Use media images of scientists to examine stereotypes (Activity 2.6).
- Examine how media and advertising use the power of science to persuade.
- Analyze the impact of social media on scientists' work.

Rich and meaningful connections can be made across the curriculum through the integration of NOS with language arts, social studies, mathematics, or fine arts. Activity 2.7 brings together NOS and language arts. Visit the website of the Cooperative Children's Book Center, School of Education, University of Wisconsin-Madison for other useful resources (www.education.wisc.edu/ccbc/books/detailList-Books.asp?idBookLists=76).

ACTIVITY 2.7   *21st C*

Science Biographies to Support Literacy

Biographies of scientists often examine the historical, social, and cultural aspects of NOS. Search your school or local library, or online, for biographies of scientists written for children. Choose a working scientist and describe what she does, his contributions to the field, and how she or he communicates their work to the public. Be mindful of how science and scientists are represented in your source and how these representations align, or do not align, with the characteristics of NOS. For further insights into the portrayal of scientists in biographies for children, see Dagher and Ford (2005). As a starting point, we provide a few biographies of scientists written for children.

Atkins, Jeannine. *Girls Who Looked Under Rocks: The Lives of Six Pioneering Naturalists*. Illustrated by Paula Conner. Dawn Publications, 2000. 63 pages. Ages 8–11.

Ehrlich, Amy. Rachel: *The Story of Rachel Carson*. Illustrated by Wendell Minor. Harcourt, 2003. 32 pages. Ages 5–9.

McGinty, Alice B. *Darwin*. Illustrated by Mary Azarian. Houghton Mifflin / Houghton Mifflin Harcourt, 2009. 48 pages. Ages 8–12.

Dendy, Leslie, and Mel Boring. *Guinea Pig Scientists: Bold Self-Experimenters in Science and Medicine*. Illustrated by C.B. Mordan. Henry Holt, 2005. 213 pages. Ages 10–15.

Other scientists you might consider researching include the following:

Roberta Bondar (neuroscience and astronomy)
Ursula Franklin (metallurgy)
John Percy (astronomy)
Jane Goodall (primatology)
Marie Curie (chemistry and physics)
Alexander Graham Bell (engineering)
Albert Einstein (physics)
Galileo Galilei (astronomy)
Gregor Mendel (genetics)

USING THIS ACTIVITY WITH ELEMENTARY SCHOOL STUDENTS

1. Read aloud a biography of a scientist with the class or, if enough copies are available, have groups read together. Select a biography written at a suitable level for your students—there are many to choose from for elementary readers. If you have classroom volunteers, they can support each group's reading, writing, and discussion.

2. In groups, have students discuss the scientist's work, both in general (e.g., What does the scientist study?) and in relation to NOS (e.g., Does the scientist work with others?). You may choose some guiding questions specific to the biography. Students can record their findings, and supporting details from the text, in a web or other graphic organizer.

3. Discuss the groups' findings.

4. Give each group a second biography to read together and similarly discuss.

5. Have groups come together and present their findings to the class.

6. Record the groups' analysis of each biography on a chart or interactive whiteboard.

7. Questions for discussion might include: What characteristics of NOS do you see in this scientist's work? How do you know?

8. *Assessment*: You might use a checklist or rubric to assess each group's discussion, as well as anecdotal comments.

TEACHER BELIEFS AND PRACTICES ABOUT NOS

Many science education researchers have written about NOS and its relationship to teaching. Nancy Brickhouse (1990) interviewed three teachers and observed their classes to explore the effects of their beliefs about NOS on their classroom practice. The teachers differed in their views on the nature of scientific theories, scientific processes, and the progression of scientific knowledge. For example, one teacher thought of scientific theories as tools that could be used to solve problems, and that, in having students test theories, they would become better scientists and better understand how a theory develops. A second teacher saw theories as absolute truths that were derived from numerous experiments and testing. A third relied heavily on the information in the textbook, presenting the textbook material as fact and teaching the scientific method as a linear process. Brickhouse also explored scientific knowledge with respect to the nature of scientific theories, scientific processes, and scientific progress, and addressed the role of content knowledge and the influence of prior knowledge. She concluded that teachers' content knowledge is a key factor in their classroom practice, and that teachers' beliefs about science influenced both explicit lessons concerning NOS and implicit curricula about the nature of scientific knowledge.

ACTIVITY 2.8   *21st C*

Read and Reflect: Teacher Beliefs and Practices

Read Brickhouse, N. W. (1990). Teachers' beliefs about the nature of science and their relationship to classroom practice. *Journal of Teacher Education, 41*(3), 53-62 and consider the following questions.

DISCUSSION QUESTIONS

1. How do the beliefs of the teachers in the article manifest in, and inform, practice?
2. How does the view of science (as a process) projected by the teacher affect student learning?
3. Which of the teachers in the article are you most like? Explain.
4. What is the importance of content knowledge in teaching science?
5. What is the relationship between content knowledge and NOS?
6. What are the consequences of assessment practices that depend primarily on the acquisition of knowledge?

CONNECTING PRACTICE AND THEORY

How might you include NOS perspectives in your own curriculum planning? Activity 2.9 asks you to consider the theoretical perspectives and practical considerations raised in this chapter in the context of teaching specific content.

ACTIVITY 2.9   *21st C*

Planning for NOS

Working in small groups, choose a unit you are familiar with from your province's elementary science curriculum. Describe three ways you could integrate NOS into your chosen unit. You may wish to refer to the tenets of NOS listed on pages 24–25. Be specific and provide detail. For example, you may include the work of an innovative scientist, a theory that underwent many changes, or an aspect of science that was profoundly influenced by society and/or a historical force. Use a concept map, such as the one shown in the figure below, or another organizer to help you present your ideas. Be prepared to share your work with other groups.

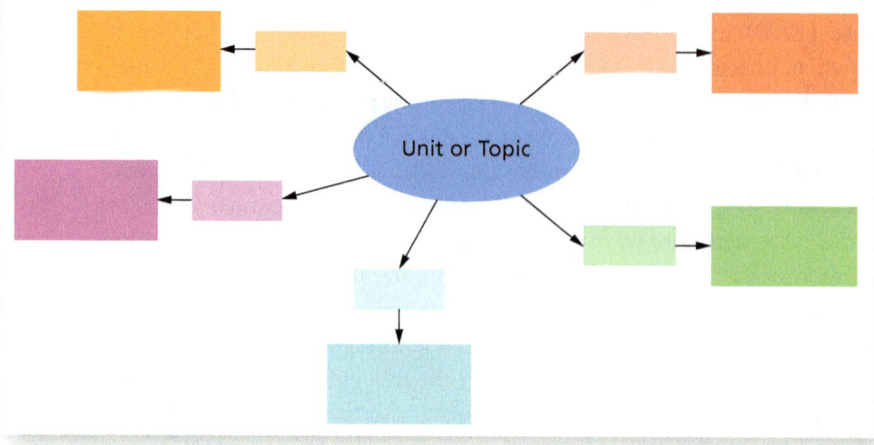

Concept Map

DISCUSSION QUESTIONS

1. How easy or difficult was this task? Explain.
2. Would you be explicit or implicit with respect to teaching about NOS in the future? Explain.
3. Comment on your own comfort and commitment to teaching NOS.

SCIENCE BEYOND THE CLASSROOM

Ideally, students who understand NOS perspectives will see its implications beyond the classroom. There are ample opportunities in which a NOS lens can be used to critique or assess issues relevant to students' lives. For example, decisions about future educational options and careers are informed by understanding what scientists do. The overwhelming amount of scientific information easily accessible on the internet requires a healthy dose of scepticism and the ability to critically assess content and claims. A clear understanding of NOS can help all students become better informed citizens as they interact in their communities at the municipal, provincial, and federal levels. Students who have an opportunity to explore NOS in the classroom have a better appreciation for the practice of science and for the institutions that support science in the community.

ACTIVITY 2.10   *21st C*

Visiting a Science Centre or Museum

Visit a local science centre or museum. Choose an exhibition—your instructor may direct you to an appropriate one. Briefly describe the exhibition and note NOS perspectives and how scientists are portrayed.

DISCUSSION QUESTIONS

1. How is science represented in the exhibition? For example, is the emphasis on concepts or the process?
2. Are there stereotypical portrayals of scientists in the exhibition?
3. What NOS perspectives, if any, are represented (e.g., Is the science situated in an historical perspective)?
4. What images of science and scientists are supported by the exhibit?
5. Is it important to include NOS perspectives at science centres and museums? Explain.

USING THIS ACTIVITY WITH ELEMENTARY SCHOOL STUDENTS

Science centres and museums can present unique opportunities for teaching and learning science. Prior to a field trip, it is important to carefully plan your visit. Often, these venues have special days or evenings where teachers can visit for free or at a reduced rate. Your visit will help you to plan for practical matters (e.g., mapping out potential meeting places, lunch room and locker locations). Venue websites also provide information to guide your planning. It is best not to take on too much on a field trip—do not try to see everything! Instead, focus on one exhibit, perhaps including a workshop or guided session, and allow free time for students to explore. Be sure to have several adults help with supervision so that students can explore in small groups. Most importantly, incorporate the exhibition into lessons at school before the trip, and follow up once the class is back at school. Field trips should not be stand-alone experiences. Appendix F includes additional suggestions for planning and leading field trips and out–of-school learning experiences.

1. Choose an exhibition that relates to a topic you are teaching in class.
2. Prepare a guiding activity for your students' visit to the exhibition; for example, a worksheet, graphic organizer, or draw-and-tell sheet.

continued on next page

3. Give each group a NOS-related question or statement from the modified card exchange activity (Appendix 2.A) to keep in mind as they explore the exhibit. Be sure that these elements of NOS are familiar to your students, as they will be applying what they have learned to their field-trip experience. You might give all groups the same question, or you could give each group a different one. Students can record their findings on the guiding activity sheet.
4. When the class comes together at the end of the trip, discuss the questions or statements. Do the students' experiences support NOS? What are specific examples from the exhibit that show, or do not show, NOS?
5. *Assessment*: Anecdotal comments can be recorded on groups' application of NOS understandings to their field-trip experience.

CONCLUDING THOUGHTS

Teaching NOS can enhance the student learning experience. NOS tenets reflect a comprehensive and authentic view of science and complement the teaching of science as a body of knowledge. Determine your own knowledge base and comfort level with respect to NOS perspectives, and consider how NOS will impact your pedagogy. What follows is a summary of the key ideas related to the learning objectives provided at the beginning of the chapter.

Tenets of the nature of science (NOS)
Teachers bring to the classroom various philosophies of science, as illustrated in "The Nature of Science Card Exchange" (page 22). It is important to recognize a wide variety of perspectives, and appreciate how this human element can bring science to life for many students. McComas et al. (1998) summarize 14 tenets of NOS.

Arguments for including NOS in elementary science
Understanding NOS can enhance student learning, increase interest in science, improve science instruction, promote equity and diversity, foster students' appreciation of cultural aspects of science, and support understanding of knowledge construction.

Tensions and challenges of teaching NOS
Some teachers feel ill equipped to address NOS perspectives due to their own perceived lack of knowledge. Assessment and evaluation, time constraints, and a lack of resources can also make teaching NOS challenging, as can students' positivist views of science. Still, when teachers include NOS in their teaching and assessment practices, and use diverse resources, it can make science worthwhile and meaningful for students.

The relationship between beliefs about NOS and teacher practice
Teachers' own beliefs about NOS, and their science content knowledge, are often reflected in their explicit and implicit curricula and instruction. Teachers' content knowledge is a key factor in classroom practice, and beliefs about science influence both implicit and explicit lessons about NOS.

Science curriculum that includes NOS
NOS can be included in science curricula and instruction in many ways. While not every tenet of NOS can be included in each lesson or each unit, try to incorporate them across units and over the course of the year. Build your confidence in NOS and expand your pedagogical repertoire to acquire expertise in this area.

NOS as a lens to explore science practices and institutions
It is important to create opportunities in which a lens of NOS can be used to assess issues relevant to students' lives. Students who have opportunities to explore NOS in their classrooms will have a better appreciation of the practice of science and of the institutions that support science in the community.

Educational research related to NOS
NOS is a rich, growing field. Researchers we have drawn upon include Fouad Abd-El-Khalick, Larry Bencze, William Cobern, Derek Hodson, Norm Lederman, Cathleen Loving, and William McComas.

BRINGING IT ALL TOGETHER: FINAL QUESTIONS

1. Reflect on how your understanding of NOS has changed from reading this chapter. In a paragraph or two, describe your current understanding of NOS, and critique the place of NOS in elementary and middle school science education.

2. Work in pairs or groups of three to discuss what you predict will be the biggest challenges to implementing NOS perspectives in science curriculum planning and classroom practice. How might you overcome these challenges?

MyEducationLab® Visit MyEducationLab® to access an electronic version of the text, as well as a variety of topics that enhance the text material. The topics include the following to support your learning in the course:

- Assessments, including interactive case studies, activities, and video assignments
- Discussion board questions
- Videos, simulations, a lesson plan builder, and other useful course resources

---

APPENDIX 2.A   ## Modified Card Exchange Statements for Elementary School Students

1. A scientific theory is made up of facts that explain the world we live in.

2. Science gives us definite answers—facts that cannot be questioned.

3. Observations are important in science. If you can't see it, you can't believe it.

4. Science can cause harm to people and the world. Scientists need to take responsibility for any harm caused by their work.

5. Because science changes, we cannot depend on it.

6. Money spent on science would be better spent on helping people in need.

7. Science is done in specific and organized steps; it follows a kind of recipe.

8. The way we live is possible because of science and scientists' work.

9. Science and scientists are always right.

10. Science is done when people work together, not alone.

11. Some people are left out of science.

12. Science helps us understand the world, but cannot answer all our questions.

These statements were inspired by Cobern and Loving (1998). Please refer to their paper for their complete list: The card exchange: Introducing the philosophy of science. In W. McComas (Ed.), *The nature of science in science education: Rationales and strategies* (pp. 73–82). London, UK: Kluwer Academic Publishers.

Chapter 3
Environmental Education

Eugene Mio

LEARNING OBJECTIVES

- Describe the characteristics and rationale for environmental education.

- Appreciate the history of environmental education policy and understand its current status in your province or territory.

- Explore the role of Aboriginal knowledge and perspectives in curricula.

- Discuss different conceptualizations of environmental education.

- Describe a critical approach to environmental education.

- Understand place-based and outdoor education in relation to environmental education.

- Explore resources related to environmental education and planning.

- Identify and discuss issues and research related to environmental education.

INTRODUCTION

It is becoming increasingly clear that the environment is in crisis: Climate change, acid rain, ozone depletion, deforestation, and pollution are among the factors leading to loss of biodiversity and threatening Earth's ability to sustain all forms of life, including human. Many argue that our connection to the land and environment is in jeopardy, even absent altogether, and requires our immediate attention. Calls for environmental education (EE) globally are plentiful (Council of Ministers of Education Canada, 2010; UNESCO, 2005; North American Association of Environmental Education, 2010). Indeed, the period between 2005 and 2014 has been declared the United Nations Decade of Education for Sustainable Development.

Environmental educators advocate working together to identify and address socio-ecological problems through positive, proactive change. EE is a direct response to concerns for the environment and includes appreciating the interconnectedness of all life, making wise and responsible decisions about the environment and its resources, and acting in ways that protect Earth and all its inhabitants. One of the ultimate aims of EE is to foster in citizens a responsible attitude toward the planet, an appreciation of its biodiversity and beauty, an environmental ethic, and the will to act justly and responsibly in navigating the tensions between economic prosperity and environmental sustainability. EE is a movement with many interests. Nature studies, field work, outdoor education, place-based education, conservation education, and sustainable development are a few examples of different historical and recent conceptualizations of what we understand as EE. For our purposes, *environmental education* is an umbrella term that includes these many orientations.

In this chapter we explore teaching and learning about EE through science education. Central to this is a commitment to a continuum that includes the use of school buildings and grounds, the local and broader community, and outdoor education centres. These sites can help teachers and students explore EE. While in this text we focus on EE within science curricula, it can be approached, and is often best realized, across multiple disciplines including arts, humanities, and social sciences. This is particularly relevant in the elementary classroom.

WHAT IS ENVIRONMENT?

Before delving into EE practice and theory, it is important to consider what we mean when we speak of the *environment*. Just as our understandings of science influence our science curricula and instruction, so do our perceptions of the environment and its elements. The term *environment* holds multiple definitions—so many that it is impossible to pin down. Some view the environment as solely a physical space: It includes living things and the land they live on, and may or may not include humans. Some understand environment to be a holistic series of ecological relationships. Still others extend environment further to include the physical world as well as social, political, cultural, economic, and philosophical domains. Your understanding of *environment* will likely influence how you choose to include EE in your curriculum—as a stand-alone unit in one discipline, infused throughout your entire curricula, or something in between. Activity 3.1 calls to your identification of environment and how it influences your view of EE in the curriculum.

ACTIVITY 3.1   *21st C* ❶ ❷

Exploring Prior Knowledge and Experience

Think back to your experiences as a student (from elementary to post-secondary). Describe a memorable incident, unrelated to school, that involved the environment. Next, identify an example of where a teacher incorporated some features of EE into a class, either in science or another subject area. Describe the environmental topic that was introduced and how it was taught. How did the teacher present it (e.g., lecture, discussion, current events, YouTube clip)? What did you as a student do?

◉─Watch
Experiential Learning

DISCUSSION QUESTIONS

1. Looking back on your experience, what made it memorable? Was this a significant event for you? Describe any lasting influence it has had.
2. Comment on the EE you experienced as a student. Was it included in one subject area or across disciplines? Did you see it as relevant? Inspiring? Uncomfortable? Explain.
3. What role do you think EE should play in schools?

Why Environmental Education?

To paraphrase Suzuki (2010), we *are* the environment, and any sense of separation from the environment is simply an illusion. While there is a wide range of material published about EE, there are similarities across the literature that speak to its importance and to the commitment of educators to include it in school curricula. All of these features are inherent in the understanding that humans are members of the environment; that our relationships with all other members of the environment should be acknowledged; and that our actions within the environment should reflect a respect of these relations. Characteristics common to EE, and embedded throughout this chapter, include stewardship, decision making, values education, taking action, and nature of science (NOS) perspectives.

Your responses in Activity 3.1 likely share similarities with the following aspects of EE:

- concern for the environment and the need to protect and care for it
- the need to come up with creative, just, and feasible solutions to environmental issues (e.g., climate change, waste)
- the acquisition of knowledge about the environment (i.e., ecosystems, biomes) and humankind's relationship to it
- awareness that science and technology are not without negative consequences
- understanding resource management
- the need to curb consumption and what some call our addiction to *stuff*
- understanding political pressures that advocate and support environmental education
- reconnecting to nature—loss of this connection has been coined *nature deficit disorder* (see Richard Louv's 2008 *Last Child in the Woods*)
- belief in promoting responsible action for eco and social justice

Environmental Education: A Brief History of Policy and Practice

The history of EE is complex and diverse. It is generally agreed upon that UNESCO/UNEP produced the first inter-governmental statement on EE at Belgrade in 1975. The brief but comprehensive objectives are summarized below:

- to foster clear awareness of and concern about economic, social, political, and ecological interdependence in urban and rural areas
- to provide every person with opportunities to acquire the knowledge, values, attitudes, commitment, and skills needed to protect and improve the environment
- to create new patterns of behaviour toward the environment in individuals, groups, and society (UNESCO, 1975)

The Belgrade Charter was ratified in 1977 as the Tbilisi Declaration (UNESCO/UNEP, 1978), and laid the foundation for subsequent work in EE. In 1987 a report titled *Our Common Future*, more commonly known as the *Brundtland Report*, was published by the World Commission on Environment and Development (WCED, 1987). The idea of sustainable development was introduced and defined as "development that meets the needs of the present without compromising the ability of future generations to meet their own needs" (p. 54). The Earth Summit, held in Rio de Janeiro in 1992, resulted in Agenda 21, which served as an action program for nations to achieve sustainable development. And, as mentioned, the United Nations declared the years from 2005 to 2014 the Decade of Education for Sustainable Development. These reports reflect a collective desire to respect human rights. They also reflect a commitment to a) social and economic justice for all; b) intergenerational responsibility, protection, and restoration of life in all its diversity; and c) building a culture of tolerance and peace. Accordingly, many programs and policies have emerged globally in an effort to develop and implement EE.

The history of EE reaches further back, however, predating the publication of preeminent international policy documents like the Tbilisi Declaration. Jean-Jacques Rousseau, 18th-century philosopher, asserted the value of interactions with the environment in learning in *Émile: Or, On Education* (1911/1966). John Dewey, foundational curriculum and pedagogy theorist, outlined the importance of experiences in the natural world in children's construction of knowledge (Dewey, 1925/1997; 1938/1997). Localized nature study formed a considerable component of science curricula of the early 1900s and was broadly supported by the community. School gardening projects were common, and were viewed as sites not only of pedagogical innovation but also as models of learning (Gaylie, 2011). Following World War I, the Great Depression, and World War II, the focus of EE practice shifted to conservation education and became motivated by scientific advancement. Rachel Carson's pivotal *Silent Spring* (1962) and the social and political activist movements of the late 1960s and early 1970s revitalized a movement in EE that focused on the health and well-being of the whole environment, inclusive of humans. While historic and current policy and prescribed curriculum documents do not always encourage, or even support, EE, quality grassroots and school and community curricula and pedagogy have quietly persisted over time.

ACTIVITY 3.2   *21st C* ❷❹❼

Calculating Your Ecological Footprint

In 1975, sustainability advocates Mathis Wackernagel and William Rees (1998) coined the phrase *ecological footprint*. Our ecological footprint reflects the demands we make on Earth's resources to produce food, material goods, and energy, and to absorb waste. Calculating your ecological footprint provides a powerful way to demonstrate personal impact on Earth's resources and systems, and allows us to assess the sustainability of our lifestyle. We highly recommend reading Wackernagel and Rees's work to learn more about the concept of ecological footprints.

In this activity, you will calculate your personal ecological footprint using the Ecological Footprint Calculator Activity. (Please see Appendix 3.A.) Compare your results with your peers. Note: To complete the activity, you will need to visit one of the many online ecological footprint calculators (e.g., www.islandwood.org/forkids/footprint) to score your footprint. There are also many other versions available online and in print.

DISCUSSION QUESTIONS

1. As North Americans, what are the issues that arise from our large footprints?

2. Choose another part of the world, and speculate how and why the ecological footprint might be different.

3. What are some of the challenges you might encounter in using an activity such as the one above?

4. Describe how you would wrap up the activity.

5. Describe an extension to this activity.

USING THIS ACTIVITY WITH ELEMENTARY SCHOOL STUDENTS

As you prepare for this activity, consider the other versions available online and in print. Be sure to check the suitability of any site and test any footprint calculators yourself before having your students work with them. We have selected a version that would be appropriate for a group of elementary school students with respect to language, length, and level of detail. Please see Appendix 3.A for the activity. Also think about how this activity can support particular curriculum topics such as water use and energy.

Conduct a general discussion with your students about how our choices impact Earth and its resources. Also, discuss how the print made by an actual foot is different from an ecological footprint, which gives a measure of how much land is needed to support our current lifestyle. With older students you might choose to discuss the concepts of producers, consumers, and decomposers; abiotic and biotic needs; and energy flow and matter recycling. The following questions might be helpful to introduce the idea of ecological footprints and consumption of resources. As each question is addressed (perhaps via a student poll), discuss the implications.

- How do you travel: by foot, car, bicycle, or bus?
- How much water do you use for bathing, showering, or brushing teeth?
- What are your clothes made of—for example, cotton, rayon, or wood cellulose?
- How much does your house need in terms of heat in winter and air conditioning in summer?
- Where do you play or do sports—parks, arenas, gyms, and so on?
- Where does your food come from? How far does it travel from where it is grown to your plate? Does it need to travel long distances to get to your community? Do you and your family grow your own food or eat produce grown close to home?
- Do you recycle at home? At school? What do you recycle?

It is important to provide context for this activity. Having done so, ask your students to complete the ecological footprint calculator activity. We offer the following procedure:

1. Complete the ecological footprint calculator activity as a teacher-led discussion. If possible, project the calculator onto a screen or interactive whiteboard and walk through the questions as a class.
2. Depending on the age of your students, they could also complete it individually, or at home with their families.
3. Ask some students to share their scores. Were students surprised?
4. Using a bar graph, display the scores of each student and discuss the class results.
5. Ask students to find a partner and brainstorm ways to lower their ecological footprints at school and at home, using a Venn diagram to organize their ideas. (If need be, review how to use Venn diagrams; see Appendix A for details.) Students can label one side of their diagram "school" and the other "home." Those changes that are relevant to both school and home can be placed in the overlap of the circles.
6. Bring the class together with their Venn diagrams. Have students sit in a circle with their papers in the centre; this will allow other groups to easily view their peers' diagrams. On an interactive whiteboard, create a class Venn diagram of positive changes for school and home.

continued on next page

7. As a class, decide on a change that can be enacted at school and create a way to monitor the outcomes over the next month.
8. Now ask students to choose how they can make a change at home. Students can keep a journal (e.g., one entry a week, for four weeks) recording and reflecting on the progress they are making.
9. *Assessment*: You might assess students' ecological footprints, Venn diagrams, participation in the class discussion, or journal reflections by using a marking scheme or anecdotal comments.

ENVIRONMENTAL EDUCATION IN CANADA

While EE in one form or another has been present since the early 1900s, formalized EE in Canada emerged in the 1960s and consists of a range of narratives (Russell, Bell, & Fawcett, 2000) that are simultaneously a strength and a challenge. There are a few federal reports that speak to EE across the country (see, for example, CMEC, 2010; Government of Canada, 2007) and inform different views and practices. In sum, these reports state that education must be reoriented to motivate people to become responsible citizens of the planet, capable of making informed and responsible decisions and acting with respect to the environment, economy, and society. Goals include the acquisition of interdisciplinary knowledge and the development of critical-thinking skills in order to address environmental challenges. EE is meant to be authentic, action-oriented, and linked to values and ethics. *The Framework for Environmental Learning* (Government of Canada, 2007, pp. 14–15) offers the following principles:

- Environmental learning should be participatory, transformative, and a life-long process;
- Environmental learning should promote big picture thinking with local and personal applications;
- Environmental learning must inspire a sense of wonder and awe about nature;
- Children need to be surrounded by caring, knowledgeable and committed educators;
- Recovering, restoring, honouring, and using the traditional knowledge and wisdom of aboriginal peoples will provide a sound basis for environmental learning and sustainability;
- Environmental learning should value local knowledge, and call on many modes of knowing;
- A sense of place, beginning with one's own home and community, is one of the many ways in which citizens can learn environmentally;
- Learning should be intergenerational, interdisciplinary, taking place at all levels of education, and occur in and beyond school classrooms; and
- Environmental education must acknowledge the global nature of environmental and sustainability issues.

Depending on your province or territory, formalized EE may take many forms and purposes. Sometimes it exists as a stand-alone course; other times it is embedded within science education or infused across all subjects (e.g., mathematics, geography, history, art, and physical education). For example, in Ontario, secondary school environmental science courses were introduced in 1973 as stand-alone courses. In the 1990s, these separate environmental studies courses were eliminated. In the Ontario elementary curriculum, there has never been a separate environmental studies subject; it has always been included within other subject areas (e.g., science, social studies). Over time, this approach, along with the changing political climate, led to the release of a report titled *Shaping Our Schools,*

Shaping our Future: Environmental Education in Ontario Schools (Ontario Working Group on Environmental Education, Ontario, 2007). The authors argue the following:

> Over the past decade, changes in the Earth's environment and its natural systems have emerged as a matter of increasingly urgent concern around the world. While the issues are complex and diverse, there is a shared and universal recognition that solutions will arise only through committed action on a global, national, regional, local, and individual scale. Schools have a vital role to play in preparing our young people to take their place as informed, engaged, and empowered citizens who will be pivotal in shaping the future of our communities, our province, our country, and our global environment. (p. 1)

This report led to EE being infused across subject areas, as well as to the development of Environmental Science as a stand-alone course in secondary education. The *Standards for Environmental Education in the Curriculum* (Ontario Ministry of Education, 2008) recommends that the themes of community, knowledge, and action guide curriculum and instruction.

The British Columbia Ministry of Education built upon its first environmental education framework, *Environmental Concepts in the Classroom: A Guide for Teachers* (1995), with *Environmental Learning and Experience: An Interdisciplinary Guide for Teachers* (British Columbia Ministry of Education, 2007). This updated guide offers teachers a conceptual interdisciplinary framework for guiding environmental learning across all subjects and grades, based on the principles of complexity, aesthetics, responsibility, and ethics (CARE). *The Western and Northern Canadian Protocol* (Alberta et al., 2011), developed by the governments of Alberta, Manitoba, Saskatchewan, the Northwest Territories, Nunavut, and the Yukon, outlines principles of sustainability built upon understanding knowledge, including Indigenous knowledge that explicitly links nature to the healthy functioning of democratic, diverse, multicultural First Nations, Métis, and Inuit societies. As revisions to provincial and territorial curricula are made, most jurisdictions include a strong EE component.

We encourage you to read some of the work of environmental educators in Canada, including Glen Aikenhead, Veronica Gaylie, David Greenwood, Paul Hart, Bob Jickling, Rick Kool, Jolie Mayer-Smith, Milton McClaren, Connie Russell, Lucie Sauvé, Gloria Snively, Astrid Steele, David Zandvliet, and others. Their insights span broadly across EE and present a range of theoretical discourses. Within the limited scope of this chapter, we have referred to these scholars and practitioners as much as possible.

ACTIVITY 3.3   *21st C* 2 6

Working with Resources: Environmental Education Curriculum and Policy

In this activity you will examine how EE is positioned in your province or territory. For example, is it presented as an integrated model across subject areas, or as a distinct vision? Begin by scanning appropriate provincial policy documents to determine how and where EE is addressed. Briefly summarize the status of EE in your jurisdiction. Next, choose an environmental studies curriculum document (if there is one in your jurisdiction) or a science education curriculum document. Focus on those sections that speak to the environment. Choose a topic or unit, analyze the outcomes or expectations, and comment, for example, on the language used, suggested activities, and accompanying strategies. Use specific examples to support your analyses.

 **Watch**

Investigating Goldfish
(Part 4)

continued on next page

DISCUSSION QUESTIONS

1. What is your view on how EE is positioned in your province or territory?
2. a) If there is a specific EE curriculum in your province or territory, briefly describe its goals and intent. Do you find them satisfactory?
b) If there is not a separate EE curriculum, briefly describe the goals and intent presented in the science curriculum document. Are they satisfactory? How would you characterize the relative emphasis of EE in the curriculum you analyzed? In other words, how important does it seem? Explain.
3. Describe and critique the role of Aboriginal perspectives in the documents you analyzed.
4. What are students expected to know, do, and value with respect to environmental objectives?
5. In the documents and units you analyzed, what, if anything, surprised you? What did you find lacking? What did you find exciting about these documents?

EXTENSION

We suggest reading Paul Hart's work: Hart, P. (2002). Environment in the science curriculum: The politics of change in the Pan-Canadian science curriculum development process. *International Journal of Science Education, 24*(11), 1239–1254. Hart problematizes the issue of incorporating EE into the science curriculum through an examination of the Pan-Canadian science curriculum process. He argues for closing the gap between curriculum policy development and professional development, as well as reimagining science education.

Aboriginal Perspectives and Environmental Education

There is much to be learned from Aboriginal peoples and their relationships to the environment. Although traditional knowledge and ways of being vary across the First Nations, there is a set of shared commonalities that speak to ways of living in nature. Their inherent relationship with nature is recognized and honoured by First Nations peoples through respectful interactions with the environment. It is place-based, holistic, relational, mysterious, dynamic, systematically empirical, based on cyclical time, and highly spiritual (Aikenhead & Michell, 2011). The words of F. Henry Lickers, biologist and member of the Turtle Clan of the Seneca Nation, eloquently capture First Nations peoples' view about the interconnectedness of the earth and humankind:

> The First Nations people view themselves not as custodians, stewards or having dominion over the Earth, but as an integrated part in the family of the Earth. The Earth is my mother and the animals, plants and minerals are my brothers and sisters. (Cited in Canadian Council of Learning, 2007, p. 2)

Similarly, and succinctly, the Nuu-Chah-Nulth of Vancouver Island echo this relationship in their phrase *Hishukishts'awalk*, "everything is one" (Turner, 2005).

Over time, around the globe, we have witnessed the unjust exclusion of Indigenous peoples from the decision-making process regarding, for example, resource management, and seen the devastating effects of this exclusion on communities. However, more recently, the unique understandings afforded by traditional practices are being acknowledged by the scientific community and have helped to deepen and enrich our approach to environmental biology, ecology, and science. As Aikenhead and Michell (2011) suggest, the environmental crisis cannot be solved with Eurocentric science and technology alone, but, rather, must call upon Aboriginal knowledge that has at its very heart a reverence for all life. Indigenous knowledge and practices learned from Elders have led to an emerging field called Traditional Ecological Knowledge and Wisdom (TEKW). TEKW comprises elements that are foundational to many EE programs: the principles of ecology, use of ecological indicators, adaptive strategies for sustainably harvesting resources, effective systems of learning and communicating ecological knowledge, respectful and interactive philosophies, close connections to traditional lands, and beliefs that highlight nature's power and spirituality (Turner, Ignace, & Ignace, 2000). TEKW is time-tested, with sustainability and environmental integrity at its very core. (For a more detailed discussion of TEKW, see, for example Aikenhead & Michell, 2011; Alsop & Fawcett, 2010; Reis & Ng-A-Fook, 2010; Snively & Corsiglia, 2001; Turner, Ignace, & Ignace, 2000; van Eijck & Roth, 2007.)

Provinces and territories have incorporated Aboriginal perspectives into their respective curricula in different ways. In some jurisdictions, Aboriginal knowledge deeply informs curriculum development and implementation, while in other places, TEKW is embedded, where appropriate, into different units or topics. For example, in *Pinasuaqtavut 2004–2009: Our Commitment to Building Nunavut's Future* (Government of Nunavut, 2004), the knowledge and wisdom of Elders is established, along with the concept of Inuit *Qaujimajatuqangit*—that is, the Inuit way of life, which includes

- respecting others, valuing relationships, and caring for people
- fostering good spirit by being open, welcoming, and inclusive
- serving and providing for family and community
- decision making through discussion and consensus
- developing skills through practice, effort, and action
- working together for a common cause
- being innovative and resourceful
- respecting and caring for land, animals, and the environment

Accordingly, the Nunavut Department of Education, working closely with Elders and educators from across the territory, has produced foundation documents such as the 2012–2013 *Nunavut Approved Curriculum and Teaching Resources* to support curriculum development. The proposed program of studies for Nunavut schools consists of interdisciplinary curricular strands derived from Inuit *Qaujimajatuqangit*. Strands replace the subjects of the traditional school curriculum. In some other provinces, Aboriginal perspectives are integrated into curriculum expectations and outcomes in a less explicit way.

ACTIVITY 3.4

21st C

First Nations Communities and Water

(Source: Adapted from Boulton, J., Brockman, A., Johanson, T., Wallace, M., & View, T. (2010). *Saskatchewan Science 8*, Pearson)

For Aboriginal peoples, water is sacred—it is the lifeblood. Albert Scott of Nakawe (Saulteaux) Nation in Saskatchewan describes water in the following way:

> Our people believe that water never remains still. It is always moving whether as rain or as snow or as a river. [Water] was told by the Creator to come down as rain, hail, or snow; it was made to cleanse and to give.... I remember drinking water right from the river but now we cannot do that. The natural system is being interrupted now the drinking water that our reserve uses is bottled. Our old men [Elders] told us long ago we would have to pay for water. Back then, I did not understand what they meant. I see it now. (Boulton et al., 2000, p. 274)

continued on next page

Imagine you are teaching a unit on water to your elementary school students. You have decided to use an *issues-based approach*—that is, you are going to organize your curriculum planning around an issue that is important to people, is often controversial, and cuts across science, society, technology, environment, economics, and so on. (Chapter 11 looks more closely at issues-based planning.)

In groups of four, brainstorm issues related to water in First Nations communities (e.g., the disruption of natural drinking water, protection of fresh water resources). If possible, invite members of local First Nations to participate in the planning and teaching of the unit. Choose one issue from your list, identify the specific problem, and investigate how it affects people, the environment, health, economics, government, etc. Keep in mind voices from multiple perspectives, the process of decision making, and possibilities for taking action. Record your ideas in a concept map (see Appendix A), and propose possible solutions to the issue you have identified.

DISCUSSION QUESTIONS

1. Examine the solutions you proposed. How do TEKW and Eurocentric scientific knowledge work together to address the issue?
2. Discuss three strengths and three challenges to incorporating Aboriginal perspectives.
3. What aspects of NOS are reflected in this activity? Refer to Chapter 2 if necessary.
4. Discuss how you might do this activity with elementary school students in your community.

CONCEPTUALIZING ENVIRONMENTAL EDUCATION

It is important to recognize the many different conceptualizations of EE. Much of what you do will be guided by the curriculum documents you are working from, and as you plan your EE lessons, we encourage you to include a range of approaches. Keep in mind that there is no right way to do EE, and that you have an incredible amount of flexibility in how you bring EE goals to life for students.

Over time, the nature of EE and the language used to describe its purposes have evolved. EE can take many forms, both in practice and theory. For example, are you interested in developing in your students stewardship and an ethic of care? Is it important that your students be able to recognize and name local flora and fauna? Are they going to engage in a stream study, or perhaps organize a cleanup of a local watershed? These examples reflect different emphases. As mentioned, earlier versions of EE focused on localized nature studies and field work—learning about plants, animals, and the physical systems that support them. More recent characterizations from the 1990s and 2000s emphasize EE for sustainability, and include creative and critical approaches to socio-ecological issues, long-term thinking, innovation, empowerment, and the interconnectedness of environment, economy, society, and cultural diversity. More will be said about this later in the chapter.

For a more detailed discussion of the history of EE orientations, explore the works of Arthur Lucas (1979), Joy Palmer (1998), and Lucie Sauvé (2005). The following sections highlight some of their work.

Education *About-In-For* the Environment

The *about-in-for* conceptualization of EE is often credited to Lucas (1979) and is found in many EE programs today (see, for example, Working Group on Environmental Education, Ontario, 2007). Interestingly, it parallels the structure of many curriculum documents (i.e., knowledge, inquiry and investigation, connections to science and society). Education *about-in-for* the environment can be useful to keep in mind as you plan your curriculum. Palmer (1998, p. 44) describes Lucas's work as follows:

- education about the environment—basic knowledge and understanding of the environment including scientific theories, concepts, laws etc. (e.g., knowing the roles of different plants and animals in an ecosystem)

- education in the environment—using the environment as a resource with an emphasis both on planned inquiry and on investigations providing students with the opportunity to engage in first-hand personal experiences (e.g., exploring food chains in a local wetland ecosystem)

- education for the environment—concerned with values, attitudes, and positive actions reflecting an ethical framework (e.g., participating in a campaign to preserve a local wetland ecosystem)

ACTIVITY 3.5

21st C

Education *about-in-for* the Environment

In pairs, choose one non-fiction and one fiction resource related to EE. Non-fiction examples include websites or periodicals such as *The Green Teacher.* Fiction examples include Shel Silverstein's *The Giving Tree*, which tells the story of a tree, a little boy, and the gift of giving, or Jeannie Baker's *Window*, a picture book that speaks to urban sprawl. (See Appendix E for an annotated bibliography of children's literature titles.)

Science and Literacy
(Part 1)

Consider how these resources reflect education *about-in-for* the environment. For each, identify whether it could be used for students in K–3, 4–8, or both. Post your resources on the class wiki or blackboard.

DISCUSSION QUESTIONS

1. Discuss how these resources can be used for each of:

- education *about* the environment
- education *in* the environment
- education *for* the environment

2. How might the non-fiction resource be used to supplement or support the use of fiction?
3. What science themes are reflected in each resource?

Environmental Education Orientations

Lucie Sauvé (2005) uses the metaphor of currents to describe 15 different forms of EE. These currents, or orientations, are not mutually exclusive; instead they often work together. Sauvé's intention was to highlight and celebrate the richness of EE and its accompanying pedagogies and to encourage discourse around EE initiatives among educators. For our purposes, we have brought together the work of Palmer (1998), who traces key trends in environmental education over time, and Sauvé into six orientations, summarized in Table 3.1.

ACTIVITY 3.6

21st C

Analyzing Environmental Education Orientations

In pairs, discuss the advantages and challenges of adopting each of the EE orientations presented in Table 3.1. Then, go back to the resources you selected in Activity 3.5 and analyze each according to the orientations in the table.

DISCUSSION QUESTIONS

1. Which orientation(s) would you feel most comfortable using? Why?
2. Which would you find challenging to include in your teaching? Explain.
3. Discuss which orientations are reflected in your resources.

Table 3.1	Environmental Education Orientations
Environmental education orientations	**Characteristics**
Nature Study	Learning about plants, animals, and the physical systems that support them; reconstructing a link with nature (e.g., identifying trees, plants, flowers)
Outdoor Education	Increasing the use of the natural environment for firsthand experiences (e.g., visiting outdoor education centres)
Conservation Education and Stewardship	Teaching about conservation issues, adopting behaviours compatible with conservation (e.g., protecting and caring for parks and zoos, learning about endangered species, creating butterfly gardens)
Development Education	Developing a more political dimension to EE (e.g., building wells in Africa, participating in international aid organizations)
Sustainable Development	Promoting economic development that takes care of social equity and ecological sustainability and focuses on economic theory rather than changing lifestyles (e.g., paying a carbon tax, automobile industry producing hybrid or electric cars)
Advocacy and Eco-justice	Promoting social justice, change, action, and activism. It is less about the economy and more about living in harmony with nature. This orientation is characterized by critical thinking and changes in values, and is less anthropocentric in its view of nature (e.g., reclaiming land, buying local produce, growing your own food)

Source: Adapted from Palmer (1998) and Sauvé (2005).

TOWARD A MORE CRITICAL APPROACH TO ENVIRONMENTAL EDUCATION

Many argue that it is not enough to learn about the environment and to raise awareness of local and global issues. In addition, we need to empower students with the tools to critique issues related to EE and equip them to be active, informed, and engaged citizens, not just for the future but also in the present. Empowerment, politicization, ethical reasoning, decision making, and agency are additional important goals of EE. Your students' actions can be powerful, particularly within their families and communities.

The eco-justice orientation reflects a critical approach, recognizing that social inequalities are central to environmental issues. Eco-justice advocates go beyond, for example, celebrating wilderness through ecotourism or engaging in green consumerism (Bowers, 2002; Furman & Gruenewald, 2004). Connections between social and ecological conflicts are made transparent (Bowers, 2002). Consider, for example, the placement of power plants and waste management sites in areas of lower socio-economic status, the cleanup of industrial waste, and access to clean water and healthy food. These topics can be very difficult to discuss and may evoke strongly emotional responses in your students; be sure to frame your teaching within a space of hope, and allow your students opportunities to make positive change.

What does a critical approach to EE look like? Among other things, it includes an awareness of relationships of power, privilege, and socio-economic status. The following list is meant to help teachers conceptualize and plan for a more critical approach to EE:

- analyze the issue—*why is this happening?*
- be critical—*look beneath the surface*

- recognize the relations of power that always underpin decisions—*in whose best interest is this decision?*
- re-imagine the future—*what kind of future do we want?*
- look for creative solutions—*think outside the box*
- engage in action—*what can I do to make a difference?*

ACTIVITY 3.7

21st C

Power, Place, and the Environment

TED (Technology, Entertainment, and Design) talks are an impressive compilation of videos from TED Conferences around the world. Under the banner of *Ideas Worth Spreading*, TED talks provide easy access to some of the world's most inspiring people. They are 18 minutes in length and can be an excellent teaching resource. For this activity, view one of our favourite TED talks (recorded in 2006) that focuses on issues of power, place, and environmental advocacy: Majora Carter's *Greening the Ghetto* (www.ted.com/index.php/talks/majora_carter_s_tale_of_urban_renewal .html).

   After you have watched the clip, form small groups, summarize what you viewed, and answer the questions below.

DISCUSSION QUESTIONS

1. Discuss how this TED talk reflects a critical approach to EE.
2. Discuss the role of power, politics, race, and poverty in *Greening of the Ghetto*.
3. How did Majora Carter make a difference?
4. How, if at all, might you use the TED talk with students?
5. What are some of the challenges for educators to adopting a more critical approach to teaching?

SCIENCE BEYOND THE CLASSROOM

Place-Based Education

Place-based education has become popular among environmental educators over the past few years, but it is certainly not a new concept. Situating curriculum and instruction in the local community predates our current standardized system of schooling. Curriculum theorists of the early 20th century, most famously John Dewey, asserted the value of learning through firsthand experience and the importance of knowing place. As discussed earlier in the chapter, *place* is an integral part of Aboriginal ways of knowing and being. Place-based education seeks to develop in young people a connection to the place they live, enhancing their "familiarity with what is beautiful and worth preserving in the territory they call home" (Smith, 2007, p. 192). Broadly, place-based education grounds students in their local communities, connecting them to nature and building a sense of ownership and ultimately empowerment (Foster & Linney 2007; Gruenewald, 2008). It involves tapping into local communities, learning about ecological systems, understanding the relationship between humans and their environment, and making a commitment to being active and engaged citizens. Gruenewald (2008) argues that in order for children to flourish, we need to provide them with time to love the earth before asking them to evaluate and save it. Sites for place-based learning are plentiful, and include school grounds, local parks, ravines, streams, and outdoor education centres.

 **Watch**

Investigating Moon Phases (Part 3)

David Sobel (1996) emphasizes the importance of children learning in places close to home. He identifies three cumulative stages of children's bonding with the natural world: 1) empathy; 2) exploration; and 3) social action. These stages align with clear patterns he found on neighbourhood maps made by children in early childhood, elementary years, and early adolescence. Children aged three to seven focused their maps on their homes and the natural world within sight and earshot of home. At this stage, children tend to feel empathy toward animals and feel protective of those familiar to them such as, the squirrels and birds that visit their yards. They might also move like animals—hopping like rabbits, slithering like snakes, and leaping like deer. From eight to eleven years, children's maps expanded to include the wider neighbourhood. At this stage, children might build forts, follow trails and pathways, tend to gardens, and create maps. Experiencing the natural world through the five senses is key. Finally, children eleven years and older mapped the broader community, including downtown areas. This stage is marked by social action, where adolescents consider and take action on real issues in their communities, such as initiating recycling and waste reduction campaigns.

Sobel's three stages of bonding with the natural world are not mutually exclusive but rather build upon each other, resulting in cognitive, affective, and physical understandings of place. These deep connections were highlighted in Jagger's (2013) study of the influence of community mapping on students' environmental worldviews. A Grade 4 class in British Columbia participated in a three-month place-based mapping project of a local provincial park. Students showed an increased and lasting understanding of the natural history of the park and of humans' influence on its ecosystems, less anthropocentric views of the natural world, identification of the park as a peaceful place of refuge, and rich and personal connections to the park.

Outdoor Education

In many ways, outdoor education can be considered a type of place-based education. It is a field with a long, well-documented history, often linked to adventure education and experiential education. Outdoor education can include such activities as nature walks, field studies, camping, hiking, school-ground greening projects, ropes courses, and other recreational activities. It can take place in local, remote, urban, and wilderness settings. The diverse goals of outdoor education are captured in Foster and Linney's (2007) work, *Reconnecting children through outdoor education: A research summary*. In this document, they summarize the goals of outdoor education as:

- environmental education
- education for character development
- education to support curriculum or in-school learning of traditional subjects
- education for physical, emotional, and spiritual well-being

The resurgence of interest in outdoor education coincides with Richard Louv's (2008) popular book *Last Child in the Woods*. In it he coins the phrase *nature deficit disorder* to refer to society's growing disconnect to the natural world. He argues that young people are increasingly more connected to technology and to the indoors at the expense of connections to nature and the outdoors. In his view, this increasing alienation can cause many kinds of distress—social, emotional, spiritual, and physical. We agree, and contend that outdoor education can be a powerful tool for learning about the environment while attending to social, emotional, spiritual, and physical well-being.

In a study conducted by Pedretti, Nazir, Tan, Bellomo, and Ayyavoo (2012), 377 Ontario teachers responded to a survey about environmental and outdoor education.

Educators tended to view the goals of outdoor education as helping students connect to the natural environment, understand the role of nature in their lives, and make choices about socio-political action. Respondents also indicated that they recognized the importance of field trips and activities outside the classroom. Despite this, many of the respondents did not include the outdoors in their teaching. This gap between practice and theory is not new; it speaks to the many pedagogical, systemic, and administrative challenges inherent in extending your classroom to the outdoors. Do not let this deter you! Through careful and deliberate planning, administrative and parental support, and a commitment to outdoor education as an important part of environmental learning, you can begin to plan powerful and inspiring experiences for your students. The many factors that must be considered when planning a field trip or outdoor education are explored in Appendix F.

Outdoor education centres are an important component of outdoor education, and have significant intersections with EE. Most of the outdoor education centres in North America were established in the 1960s and '70s as places that promote physical fitness, build character, and develop outdoor skills. They are permanent sites with outdoor specialist staff committed to providing programs that increasingly link directly to school curricula. Some operate as day centres, while others are residential and offer programs for students and teachers that last anywhere from a couple of days to a week. Be mindful when using outdoor education centres that you do not minimize the value of natural spaces in your students' own community, particularly those in urban environments.

ACTIVITY 3.8   *21st* C ② ④ ⑤

Read and Reflect: Environmental Poetry

Read Gaylie, V. (2008). The poetry garden: Ecoliteracy in an urban school. *Language and Literacy, 10*(2). Retrieved from http://ejournals.library.ualberta.ca/index.php/langandlit/article/view/9778/7692. This interdisciplinary narrative explores elementary students' ecoliteracy as expressed through environmental poetry. Answer the questions below, and be prepared to share your answers with the class.

DISCUSSION QUESTIONS

1. Many components of EE discussed in this chapter are reflected in Gaylie's article. Describe these features and how they are incorporated into the students' learning.
2. How are students' understandings of place and environment reflected in their poems?
3. Which EE orientations do you see reflected in this article? Explain.
4. Gaylie describes how poetry about a school garden was used as a means of expressing ecoliteracy. How could you integrate mathematics, social studies, and art into a garden-based environmental study?
5. Gaylie's inquiry focused on Grade 6 and 7 students. How might you use a similar approach with Grade 2 and 3 students?

ENVIRONMENTAL EDUCATION RESOURCES FOR PLANNING

One of the challenges of teaching is locating resources, assessing their value, and deciding how to incorporate them into lessons. There are many EE resources available in print, media, and online to help you create an inspiring, exciting EE curriculum. At times, however, the sheer volume of materials related to EE can make the task of planning overwhelming.

Some of our favourite children's literature, curriculum and pedagogy resources, films, websites, and periodicals are listed in Appendix 3.B. While not all of these resources can be used in the elementary classroom, they can help you build your background knowledge on environmental issues, provide you with ideas for EE instruction, and motivate you with positive and proactive environmental stories. You will need to critique their value and suitability for your classroom.

We strongly encourage you to seek out the resources from your province or territory and school board that will assist in planning for effective EE. *Environmental learning and experience: An interdisciplinary guide for teachers* (British Columbia Ministry of Education, 2007, p. 10) provides nine suggestions for practice when designing environmental learning experiences for your students:

- encourage the integration of subjects/interdisciplinary approaches
- encourage critical reflection on a range of perspectives
- examine issues for their currency and authenticity
- acknowledge Aboriginal perspectives
- acknowledge other perspectives
- consider the place of action
- consider issues from both local and global perspectives
- occur with a context of hope
- encourage humility

Note the context of hope; all too often we present environmental issues as doom-and-gloom scenarios, and students can be left feeling helpless and fearful. Also, be mindful of the content you present to your students. Environmental issues can be overwhelming, particularly for young learners. Begin with local issues that students can directly relate to (e.g., planting a community garden or classroom recycling) and that allow for noticeable positive impacts.

ACTIVITY 3.9

21st C

Connecting Practice and Theory: Resources for Planning

Working in pairs, choose an environmental issue from the list below and decide if it will be taught to K–3, 4–6, or middle-school students. Locate an example for each type of resource (see the table on next page) to support the issue you have chosen. For each, provide a full citation and brief description, an idea for incorporating the resource into a lesson, and possible cross-curricular connections to other subjects such as mathematics, language arts, social studies, or visual arts. Be sure to upload your findings to the class wiki or other virtual learning environment.

Environmental Issues:

- water and air pollution
- wildlife conservation
- climate change
- disposal of computers

- intensive farming
- logging of old growth forest
- strip mining
- waste management

Environmental Education Resources

Type of resource	Full citation and brief description	Ideas for incorporating the resource into a lesson	Cross-curricular connections
Popular books			
Children's literature			
Curriculum and pedagogy books			
Films			
Websites			
Community groups and organizations			
Periodicals			
Databases and reports			
Other			

CONTEMPORARY ISSUES AND ONGOING DEBATES

While few would deny the merits of EE, there remain several challenges. We encourage you to examine these issues and consider their practical and theoretical complexities as you develop your understanding of EE. What follows is a brief overview of some issues inherent in EE that you may want to explore.

- The term *sustainable development* is considered by some (e.g., Jickling, 1992; Jickling & Wals, 2008) to be an oxymoron, or at the very least a conceptual muddle. They argue that a logical inconsistency arises when the term *sustainability* is juxtaposed with *development*. What is your understanding of sustainable development, and what impact does it have on EE?

- Often, we hear about "presenting both sides of an issue," when in reality, there may be multiple sides. How do we know what the other perspectives are?

- EE draws upon different disciplines. What is the role of interdisciplinary knowledge? Is there a place for interdisciplinary courses?

- Teaching science (and curriculum and instruction in most other disciplines) typically focuses on content knowledge, whereas EE places a high importance on affect and action in its learning goals. What does this mean for EE? What does this mean for science education?

- EE provides a foundational understanding of the environment as a network of relationships, and its curriculum reflects these inherent interactions. However, the school system is divided into separate disciplines and, often, curricula are geared toward development of the individual citizen. How does EE fit into this system?

- There is considerable disagreement on what magnitude of action is needed to make a difference to our current environmental crises. Can small steps make a difference? What about the inaction of others? Is it worth making changes when others do not? How will you address these concerns in EE teaching?

- Ecology and economy share the same root—*oikos*, or home—and yet they are usually seen as separate. Often ecological health is overlooked in favour of strengthening the economy. Can both ecology and economy be strong in our current social and political world? How will your teaching address this perceived divide?

● Action is a major part of EE. We want students to be self-motivated rather than told to take action. How will your EE curriculum encourage and motivate students to take positive action?

CONCLUDING THOUGHTS

Environmental education is a complex and value-laden field; it brings together aesthetic, spiritual, social, political, and economic aspects with scientific knowledge. We hope you and your students will appreciate the magic of the natural world, develop ecological thinking and an environmental ethic, and exercise responsible and informed decision making. What follows is a summary of the key ideas related to the learning objectives provided at the beginning of the chapter.

Characteristics and rationale for environmental education

EE seeks to prepare students to be environmentally minded, responsible citizens. It includes understanding the interconnectedness of all life, making wise and responsible decisions about the environment and its resources, and acting in ways that respect Earth and all of its inhabitants. There are many compelling reasons for including EE in the curriculum.

History and status of environmental education

EE has a long history and multiple strands, interests, and goals. Depending on your province or territory, it can take many forms. For example, EE might be a stand-alone subject, embedded in science education, or taught across subject areas. Understand the EE policy in your province and familiarize yourself with the programs available in your area.

Aboriginal knowledge and perspectives in curricula

Although traditional knowledge and ways of knowing vary across Aboriginal groups, a shared set of features speaks to ways of living in nature. These commonalities describe a relationship with nature that is place-based, holistic, relational, dynamic, cyclical, and spiritual. Understand the role of Traditional Ecological Knowledge and Wisdom (TEKW) and how it is incorporated into your curriculum and policy documents.

Conceptualizations of environmental education

Education *about-in-for* the environment is a useful conceptualization for planning EE that includes a basic knowledge of the environment, opportunities to be in the environment, and environmental advocacy. Another conceptualization is based on the metaphor of currents and includes nature studies, outdoor education, conservation, development education, sustainable development, and advocacy and ecojustice.

A critical approach to environmental education

It is not enough to learn about the environment and raise local and global issues; we must provide students with the means to critique issues and be active, engaged citizens. A critical approach to EE includes analyzing issues, recognizing inherent power structures, re-imagining the future, looking for creative solutions, and engaging in action.

Place-based and outdoor education

Place-based education seeks to develop in young people an affiliation with the places they live, grounding students in their local communities and connecting them to nature. Outdoor education can be a powerful tool for learning about the environment and attending to social, emotional, spiritual, and physical well-being.

Resources related to environmental education planning

Seek out the resources available in your province or territory and through your school board that will assist you in planning for effective EE. There is a broad range of resources you can draw upon that can be used for cross-curricular purposes.

Research related to environmental education

While few would argue about the merits of teaching EE, it still carries with it various challenges and concerns. Examine these issues as you develop your understanding of EE. We drew upon a few researchers in the field, including Glen Aikenhead, Veronica Gaylie, David Greenwood, Bob Jickling, Connie Russell, Lucie Sauvé, Gloria Snively, and Veronica Gaylie. We encourage you to explore the work of these researchers as well as the many others who have contributed to this field over the past few decades.

BRINGING IT ALL TOGETHER: FINAL QUESTIONS

1. Environmental education is often marginalized in the school system (in spite of supporting policies and curricula). Why? What can you, as a beginning teacher, do to address this situation?

2. How do we reconcile the contradictions between what we teach and what we do with respect to EE?

APPENDIX 3.A   Ecological Footprint Calculator Activity

Transportation

How did I travel today? Think about each time you went somewhere...

> I drove in a car.
> I took a bus.
> I rode my bike.
> I walked.

Water Use

How much water did I use?

> I did not shower.
> I had a shower for 1-2 minutes.
> I had a shower for 3-6 minutes.
> I had a shower for 7-10 minutes.
> I bathed in a full tub.
> I bathed in a half-full tub.

When I brushed my teeth.

> I let the water run the whole time.
> I turned off the tap.

When I use the toilet,

> I flush every time.
> I use a low-flow toilet or put a one-litre plastic container full of water or rocks to displace water in the toilet, so each flush uses less water.
> I sometimes let the "yellow mellow," especially if other people will be using the toilet soon (i.e., first thing in the morning and before bed).

Clothing

I am wearing

> Only brand new clothes.
> Some secondhand or hand-me-down clothing.
> Almost all secondhand or hand-me-down clothing.

Play

In the sports and games I like to play, the equipment I need is

> A lot (full jersey and pads, computers, etc.)
> Not so much (balls, hoops, game boards, etc.)
> None or very little

This much land was made into a field, arena, pools, ski slopes, and parking lots for the sports and games I like to play:

> Lots (more than the area of a football field)
> Some (about the area of a football field)
> None or very little

In general, I spend this much money a day on recreational activities:

> $20 or more
> $10
> $5

Food

When I eat a meal there is this much left on my plate:

> Half the food there was to begin with
> A bit of the food
> I clean my plate

In a typical day, I eat meat

> At every meal
> At one or two meals
> Never

In my lunch, this much food is wrapped in paper or plastic that I throw away

> All of it
> Some of it
> None of it

School

When my class leaves the classroom for recess or another activity we turn off the lights

> Never
> Sometimes
> Always

My classroom recycles

> Nothing
> Some paper
> All of our paper, cans, and drink boxes

Source: www.islandwood.org/forkids/footprint.

| APPENDIX 3.B | Environmental Education Curriculum and Instruction Resources |

Popular books	• *The Legacy* (Suzuki, 2010) • *Last Child in the Woods* (Louv, 2005) • *Silent Spring* (Carson, 1962) • *The Big Picture* (Suzuki, 2009) • *Keeping Our Cool* (Weaver, 2008) • *The Sense of Wonder* (Carson, 1956/1998) • *The Sacred Balance* (Suzuki, 2002) • *The Earth's Blanket* (Turner, 2005)
Children's literature	• *Winston of Churchill, One Bear's Battle Against Global Warming* (Okimoto, 2007) • *The Lorax* (Dr. Seuss, 1971) • *The Elders are Watching* (Bouchard & Vickers, 2004) • *Jessie's Island* (McFarlane, 1992) • *Waiting for Whales* (McFarlane, 1991)
Curriculum and pedagogy books	• *Natural Curiosity* (The Laboratory School, 2011) • *Beyond Ecophobia: Reclaiming the Heart in Nature Education* (Sobel, 1996) • *Keepers of the Animals: Native American Stories and Wildlife Activities for Children* (Caduto & Bruchac, 1997) • *Earth in Mind* (Orr, 2004) • *Ecological Literacy: Education and the Transition to a Postmodern World* (Orr, 1992) • *Roots and Research in Urban School Gardens* (Gaylie, 2011) • *The Learning Garden: Ecology, Teaching, and Transformation* (Gaylie, 2009) • *Learning Gardens and Sustainability Education* (Williams & Brown, 2012) • *Ecological Literacy: Educating our Children for a Sustainable World* (Stone & Barlow, 2005)
Films	• *An Inconvenient Truth* (Al Gore) • *The Sacred Balance* (David Suzuki) • *Planet Earth* (BBC) • *The Blue Planet* (BBC)
Websites	• The Story of Stuff Project (www.storyofstuff.com)
Community groups and organizations	• Wildlife Federation • Green Leaf • Green Thumbs Growing Kids • Evergreen • Canadian Network for Environmental Education and Communication (EECOM) • Ontario Society for Environmental Education (OSEE) • Environmental Educators Provincial Specialists Association (British Columbia)
Periodicals	• *The Green Teacher* • *Clearing* (www.clearingmagazine.org) • *Canadian Journal of Environmental Education* • *Journal of Environmental Education* • *Environmental Education Research*
Databases and reports	• Statistics Canada (www.statcan.gc.ca/start-debut-eng.html) • Environment Canada (www.ec.gc.ca/default.asp?lang=en) • World Health Organization (www.who.int/en)

Chapter 4
Equity, Diversity, and Social Justice in Science Education

Eugene Mio

What does science have to do with social justice?

—Kim, preservice teacher candidate

I don't think science and social justice are compatible—science deals with facts and social justice is about feelings and emotions.

—Zu-Zhang, preservice teacher candidate

In science we learn about communities.

—Lilly, Grade 1 student

LEARNING OBJECTIVES

- Construct a framework for equity, diversity, and social justice.

- Explore how marginalization and identity affect teaching and learning science.

- Explore Aboriginal world views in the context of science education.

- Identify and describe border crossings for students.

- Summarize the foundations of social justice in science education, including culturally relevant pedagogy and teaching.

- Explore social justice issues and resources for science curricula.

*21st CENTURY
LEARNING SKILLS &
COMPETENCIES*

❶ **Communication**

❷ **Critical thinking**

❸ **Collaboration**

❹ **Creativity**

❺ **Literacy and numeracy**

❻ **Media literacy**

❼ **Technological literacy**

INTRODUCTION

Teaching for social justice is an educational choice that has implications for students and for curricular resources. What is the place of social justice in science education? There is controversy about what to include in contemporary science programs. Conventional teaching of science most often includes, according to Hodson (2003), "dealing with established and secure knowledge, while contested knowledge, multiple solutions, controversy, and ethics have been excluded" (p. 664). Science teaching that is grounded in social justice takes into account multiple perspectives, treats all knowledge as potentially problematic, and addresses issues of power.

Social justice includes values, ideologies, and practices that can be applied to individuals, groups, communities, or institutions such as schools as well as to society in the broader sense. Social justice is referred to as *the elimination of behavioural and institutional barriers*, including prejudice and discrimination, that preclude equality of opportunity, freedom, and choice (Sen, 2009). "It is about the right treatment of others and the fair distribution of resources or opportunities" (Reiss, 2003, p. 160).

There are aspects of school science that propagate *science* as elitist and powerful without problematizing how it can be used to reproduce the status quo in our society. Social justice science education questions structural barriers in society that prevent some students from succeeding in school (Gitari, 2003). It is not, and does not try to be, neutral, as decisions in education are never neutral, but rather are laden with the hopes, fears, beliefs, and culture of those who create the curriculum. Social justice science education is instead a more holistic representation of science, going beyond the *facts* of science to an understanding of the influences, power structures, and privileges that contribute to knowledge construction. Social justice science pedagogy helps students to understand the power and influence of science in our world, and to explore social justice and social responsibility issues related to science.

In this chapter we explore how to confront and change exclusionary practices when teaching science. Social justice issues can make science education richer, more equitable, and accessible to all. We will revisit some ideas from Chapter 2 about NOS and how it can encourage all students to *see* themselves as part of science. The chapter also explores pedagogy, identity, urban education, marginalization, Aboriginal education, and the development of an equity lens.

A FRAMEWORK FOR EQUITY, DIVERSITY, AND SOCIAL JUSTICE IN SCIENCE

Have you ever wondered why some children love science and others do not? Some of you may have enjoyed science in school. What were your reasons? What was engaging about it? You might have liked learning about how it impacts many aspects of life, from health to energy production and how chemicals in our environment affect us at work and home. Was your teacher welcoming and respectful? Did you enjoy conducting investigations? Were they relevant to your interests? What can teachers of science do to develop programs that invite students to participate in science in the classroom and outside of school?

Using a framework of equity, diversity, and social justice for planning science curricula can be helpful. At the heart of such a framework are the needs and aspirations of all students, including those who are marginalized. It incorporates NOS, acknowledges the bias within the discipline of science, and addresses issues of power and control. Such a framework prompts us to be more attentive to multiple perspectives in content choices we make and to include examples that present science as sometimes beneficial and sometimes implicated in injustice (Gill & Levidow, 1987). The framework shown in Figure 4.1 (inspired by Hodson, 1993) is organized into three parts that inform teaching: 1) interactions with students; 2) curriculum choices and examples; and 3) bias.

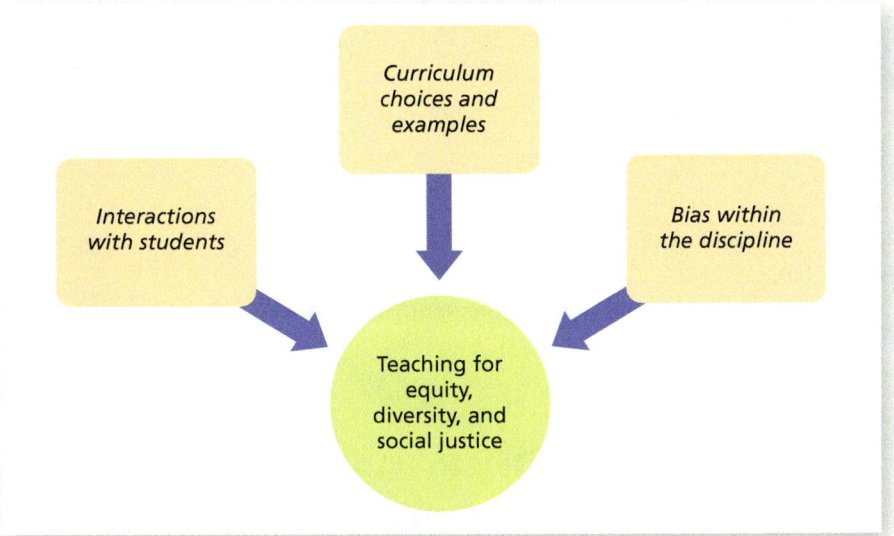

Figure 4.1 Framework for equity, diversity, and social justice in science

1. *Interactions with Students* In their daily interactions with students, teachers aim to create a positive classroom climate. This includes being respectful of students and providing an ethic of care; acknowledging diverse needs and accommodating student learning styles; recognizing cultural differences and Aboriginal status, race, class, gender, sexual orientation, and ability; and giving students opportunities for choice and control. (Please see Chapter 6 for a more comprehensive discussion of creating a positive classroom climate.)

2. *Curriculum Choices and Examples* As teachers plan their lessons around specific topics, they are faced with myriad decisions. These include choosing resources, selecting examples, identifying how our choices include or exclude students, demystifying the knowledge construction process, promoting content that will help students enter the subculture of science, and making modifications to the curriculum depending on student needs and interests. (See Chapters 6 and 7 for a more comprehensive discussion of curriculum design.)

3. *Bias Within the Discipline* Every academic discipline has inherent biases. Knowledge construction is never neutral; it is always context driven. All knowledge construction happens within the contexts of society, culture, time, and place, and, as James Banks (1996) notes, "students should be given opportunities to investigate and determine how cultural assumption, frames of reference, perspectives, and the biases within a discipline, influence the ways knowledge is constructed" (p. 169). It is important for teachers of science to understand these biases, recognize that science knowledge is created within a social context, and explore how science knowledge does or does not become part of school curricula.

ACTIVITY 4.1   *21st C* ❶❷❸❻

Using the Framework for Equity, Diversity, and Social Justice

It may be difficult to envision the equity framework in action without seeing students in the classroom setting. For this activity, your instructor will make available a video recording of a science lesson. Watch the video and, in groups, critique it with respect to the equity, diversity, and social

continued on next page

justice framework (Figure 4.1). Consider the interactions between the teacher and students, list the curriculum choices made and examples used by the teacher, and identify any instances where bias occurred.

Note that the framework can be adapted to other subjects, including social studies, language arts, and visual arts.

DISCUSSION QUESTIONS

1. What aspects of the framework were evident in the video?
2. Describe examples of inclusive teaching.
3. In your teaching experience, recall and describe an instance where your teaching reflected one or more aspects of the framework.

Social Justice in the Digital Age

In 2007, the General Assembly of the United Nations proclaimed February 20 a *World Day of Social Justice*. The UN stated that "observance of World Day of Social Justice should support efforts of the international community in poverty eradication, the promotion of full employment and decent work, gender equity and access to social well-being and justice for all" (United Nations, n.d.). The World Day of Social Justice encourages us to work toward removing all forms of exclusion. In our rapidly changing world, access to technology allows the inclusion of more people, more often, in more ways, However, it is important to note that digital exclusion and marginalization can be barriers to achieving social justice. (See www.infoxchange.net.au/news/social-justice-digital-age.)

Although print materials continue to be used in schools, as we move into the 21st century technologies are becoming more widely used in many aspects of teaching science. (See also Chapters 1 and 8.) Within the context of this chapter, think about how technology can be related to justice issues. For example, we should question practices such as pairing students who have smartphones with those who do not in order to complete a science task, or assigning work that must be done at home on the assumption that all students have access to a computer or the internet. Schools that are committed to social justice must equip classrooms and teachers of science with appropriate technology so that all students can participate and succeed.

MARGINALIZED STUDENTS AND ISSUES OF IDENTITY

Terms such as *urban*, *inner city*, or *at-risk* are used in different ways. Sometimes, when used to describe students, they imply low socio-economic status and racialization. Lack of access to resources, living in poverty, and low academic performance can lead to reduced achievement. Students, regardless of whether they live in the inner city, in suburban areas, or in rural areas, can face marginalization in science classrooms and run the risk of failing or dropping out. Often, such students are labelled as *at-risk* and are at the centre of a deficit discourse in education.

Teachers often view science as special and requiring unique qualities from students in order for them to succeed (Prime & Miranda, 2006). James (2012b) examines, for example, how stereotypes operate in the social construction of African Canadian males as at-risk students, while Emdin (2011) writes about the state of urban science education and African-American males' experience within it. After exploring underachievement, low participation, and, for some, dropping out, Emdin says,

> Teachers in urban science classrooms enact pedagogical practices that they believe are best for their African-American male students despite the fact that these practices are subversive to larger societal goals surrounding effective science education. These practices are triggers for the academic disinterest of African-American male students in school and science, and issues seemingly separate from science education, such as culture, rituals, identity, and stereotypes, may ultimately trigger changes to the exclusionary nature of the discipline. (p. 76)

As educators navigate issues of underachievement, it is important to be aware of how they are constructing student identity based on generalities and stereotypes. It is equally important to remember that a particular student may not represent the group with which the student is identified.

Student Identity and Diversity

Science has historical and contemporary connections to issues of identity such as race, gender, and sexual orientation (Willinsky, 1998). When we say *a diverse group of students*, what do we mean? Teachers must consider the impact of racism, classism, sexism, homophobia, and ableism on their students' lives. Educators would do well to reflect upon how they understand diversity, and whether they see it as something that needs to be changed, ignored, or recognized as a strength (Cochran-Smith, 2003; 2004). Teachers of science have the unique opportunity to address issues of diversity within the context of the curriculum, while exploring how humans interact with the natural world.

McLaren (1998) contends that teachers and researchers must understand the complexity of diversity and its relationship to curriculum construction. Diversity is understood to be individuals having, among other factors, identifications related to Aboriginal heritage, language, race, ethnicity, class, gender, and sexuality. Diversity must be understood in terms of its implications for individuals and for society. A re-envisioned science curriculum has the potential to allow students to *see* themselves in their lived realities. Students can be inspired and motivated to engage in science, and to study science beyond compulsory requirements.

A body of research explores student identity formation in the science classroom (Brickhouse & Potter, 2001; Carlone & Johnson, 2007). For example, Costa (1995) gathered qualitative data on 43 high school students enrolled in chemistry or earth science in two schools with diverse student populations. She concluded that, despite a range of descriptions of student worlds and science, there were distinct patterns of relations between students' worlds of family and friends and their successes in school science. Costa describes these patterns and creates five categories: potential scientists; other smart kids; "I don't know" students; outsiders; and inside outsiders (see Table 4.1). Although the context of Costa's study was a high school, her findings have implications for all students.

Aikenhead (1996) used Costa's categories to help clarify the curricular implications of a cultural perspective for science education. These consequences for teaching are also summarized in Table 4.1.

Table 4.1	Student Identities in Science	
Category	**Description**	**Consequences for teaching**
Potential Scientists	Worlds of family and friends are congruent with worlds of school and science.	These students enjoy the challenges of the academic subject matter.
Other Smart Kids	Worlds of family and friends are congruent with world of school but inconsistent with world of science.	These students prefer to engage in creative activities that require self-expression and human interactions.
"I Don't Know" Students	Worlds of family and friends are inconsistent with worlds of school and science.	These students see science classes as no different than other classes at school. They may have learned to play the school game of passing a course without understanding the content. They do not care to replace their commonsense conceptions with self-constructed scientific knowledge or to engage in scientific inquiry other than going through the motions of getting the right answer.

continued on next page

Table 4.1 Student Identities in Science *(Continued)*		
Category	**Description**	**Consequences for teaching**
Outsiders	Worlds of family and friends are discordant with worlds of school and science.	Outsiders view scientists as experts who are always right, drab, and boring. Even when science content makes sense to them, they may not care enough to hand in homework or pass examinations.
Inside Outsiders	Worlds of family and friends are irreconcilable with world of school, but are potentially compatible with world of science.	These students possess an intense curiosity about the physical world but developed mistrust for the schools' teachers and administrators, which is an obstacle to engaging in science.

Source: Adapted from Costa, 1995 (p. 316), and Aikenhead, 1996 (pp. 15–18).

ACTIVITY 4.2   *21st C* ❷

Using Student Identities in Science

In pairs, consider each of Costa's five student identities in science. For each, describe what inclusive teaching might look like and how it could affect students in that category.

Investigating Moon Phases
(Part 1)

DISCUSSION QUESTION

1. How might you begin to understand what categories your students fall into?
2. How would you describe your own identity (as a K–12 or university student) using Costa's categories? Explain.
3. What use can you make of these categories in your teaching?
4. What are their limitations?

Teacher Identity

In order to fully understand teaching practices and decisions that are made with respect to curriculum development and implementation, teachers can begin by interrogating their own identity and factors that influence their identity formation (Grant & Zeichner, 1995). How we teach is a result of who we are. There is a robust body of literature that examines how teacher beliefs influence what science they teach and how they teach it; this literature is explored at various points throughout this book (see, for example, Brickhouse, 1990, and Mulholland & Wallace, 2001).

Identity is a relationship of characteristics that make you who you are. (See Figure 4.2.) These factors are often dynamic in meaning and emphases, and they interact with each other. In order to explore your identity in relation to specific categories and other personal factors, such as volunteer service, use Activity 4.3 to create an identity wheel (Figure 4.2; adapted from Lee, 1985; see James, 2010, for a more contextualized identity wheel).

ACTIVITY 4.3   *21st C* ❶❷❹

Create an Identity Wheel

Create an identity wheel like the one in Figure 4.2 and display as many factors as you wish to include about yourself. Share your wheel with a peer and describe your factors. Choose two factors and speculate as to how they might influence your work both as a general elementary school teacher and as a teacher of science.

DISCUSSION QUESTIONS

1. What aspects of your identity do you think will most influence your teaching practice? Explain.
2. What aspects do you think will least influence your practice? Explain.
3. Describe how you relate to people who are not like you.
4. How might different teacher identities within your school influence curriculum and collegial planning?

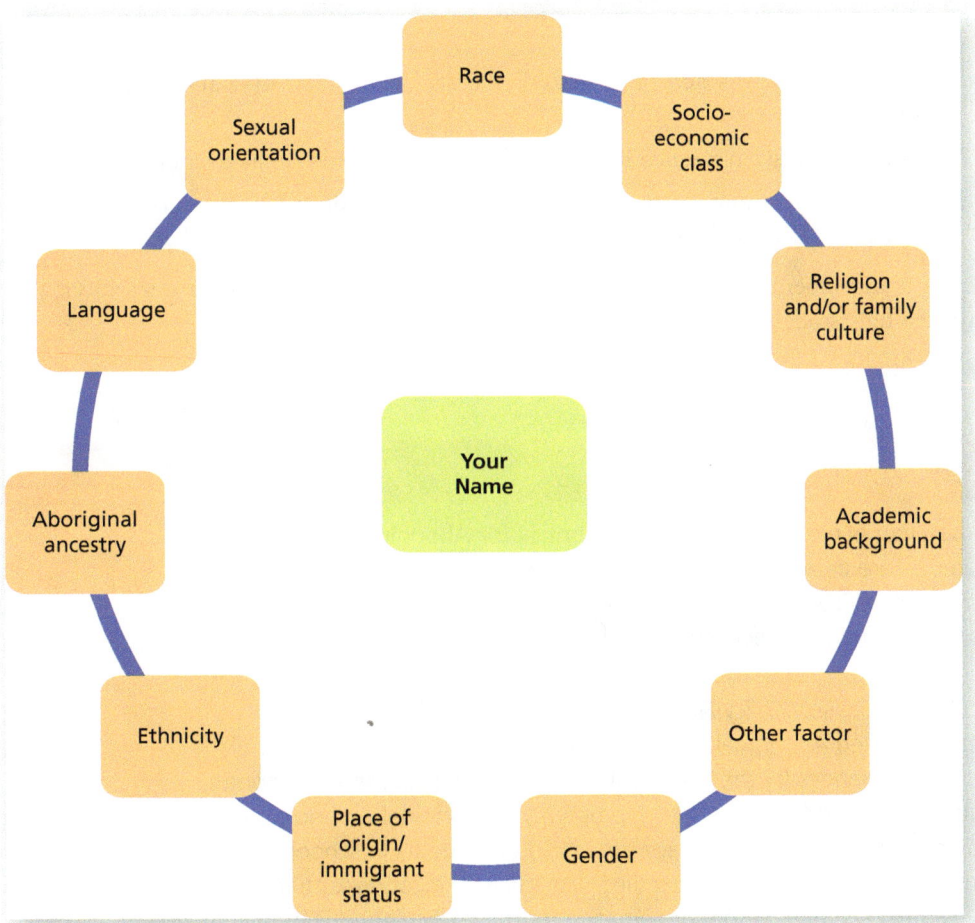

Figure 4.2 Identity wheel

EXPLORING ABORIGINAL SCIENCE EDUCATION AS A SOCIAL JUSTICE ISSUE

Issues of power and access are interwoven with the needs, identities, aspirations, and achievement of Aboriginal students. The underrepresentation of Indigenous students in senior high school science and in science-related careers is complex, with many factors (for example, generations of colonization) undermining support for students' education (Aikenhead & Michell, 2011). Teachers of science can positively influence this underrepresentation by creating a science classroom experience that respects cultural identities and infuses Indigenous knowledge within the curriculum.

Western science can conflict with the cultural beliefs of Aboriginal students, who might view science instruction as an attempt to assimilate them into the dominant culture (Aikenhead & Michell, 2011). When Aboriginal students feel excluded or experience "a cultural mismatch, between the values and philosophy of western science (particularly as these are typically exemplified in the classroom) and the values and philosophy held by many Aboriginal people and communities" (Canadian Council on Learning, 2007, p. 2), they can become marginalized from science curriculum and instruction. For example, Aboriginal peoples may view nature as a spiritual whole that is sacred and connected to all other things, whereas western science often reduces nature to a system of component parts that can be manipulated. (Aboriginal world views about nature are explored in more detail in Chapter 3.) The implications of conflicting world views in the classroom include the following:

1. Aboriginal students accept a western science world view and abandon Aboriginal values.

2. They learn western science in a superficial way to avoid threats to their identity.

3. They avoid learning science at all and often fail or drop out of science. (Canadian Council on Learning, 2007)

It is incumbent on educators to be respectful and inclusive of diverse world views in order to help students navigate multiple perspectives.

ACTIVITY 4.4

21st C

Aboriginal Science Education: Provincial Perspectives

Some jurisdictions have specific statements regarding goals and priorities for Aboriginal education and Aboriginal science. Four examples are detailed below. Some aspects of these policy statements intersect with the framework for social justice education described on page 61. Read each and answer the discussion questions at the end of the activity.

Ontario First Nations, Métis, and Inuit Education Policy Framework
  The Ministry of Education has identified Aboriginal education as one of its key priorities, with a focus on meeting two primary challenges by the year 2016—to improve achievement among First Nation, Métis, and Inuit students and to close the gap between Aboriginal and non-Aboriginal students in the areas of literacy and numeracy, retention of students in school, graduation rates, and advancement to postsecondary studies. The ministry recognizes that, to achieve these goals, effective strategies must be developed to meet the particular educational needs of First Nation, Métis, and Inuit students. (Ontario Ministry of Education, 2007a, p. 5)

Science 5
  The aim of K–12 science education is to enable all Saskatchewan students to develop scientific literacy. Scientific literacy today embraces Euro-Canadian and Indigenous heritages, both of which have developed an empirical and rational knowledge of nature. A Euro-Canadian way of knowing about the natural and constructed world is called science, while First Nations and Métis ways of knowing nature are found within the broader category of Indigenous knowledge. (Saskatchewan Ministry of Education, 2011, p. 6)

Science K–7 Integrated Resource Package
  The incorporating of Aboriginal science with western science can provide a meaningful context for Aboriginal students and enhance the learning experience for all students. The inclusion of Aboriginal examples of science and technologies can make the subject more authentic, exciting, relevant, and interesting for all students. (British Columbia Ministry

of Education. (2005). *Science K–7 integrated resource package.* Victoria, BC: Author. Copyright © Province of British Columbia. All rights reserved. Reproduced with permission of the Province of British Columbia. www.ipp.gov.bc.ca)

Aboriginal Education in Quebec

While lively debates take place about how best to improve Aboriginal education, there is little disagreement on its priority as a goal... In contrast to the scarring policies of the past, the goal of education reform is not to eliminate Aboriginal cultures. On the other hand, primary/secondary education is about more than cultural transmission—its goal is to impart core competencies in reading, writing, mathematics and science, necessary knowledge if Aboriginal students are to enjoy a realistic choice as adults between participation in Canada's urban industrial society or a rural, more collective style of life. *(Aboriginal Education in Quebec: C.D. Howe Institute Commentary—The Education Papers* (2011, p. i)).

DISCUSSION QUESTIONS

1. How can the spirit and substance of these statements be realized within elementary science?
2. What specific topics or examples can be incorporated into science curricula in order to meet the goals of Aboriginal students?
3. Describe your understanding of an Aboriginal world view.
4. What are some effective strategies for meeting educational needs of First Nations, Métis, and Inuit students?

Finding resources to broaden knowledge and enhance teaching can be a challenge. Refer to your provincial policy documents as well as resources such as *The Cultural Divide in Science Education for Aboriginal Learners* from the Canadian Council on Learning (2007), available online at www.ccl-cca.ca/CCL/Home.html, to help you develop an inclusive science education for Aboriginal students.

Consider the following two scenarios and reflect upon

- the topics usually included and excluded from science class

- the consequences for Aboriginal students of experiencing an exclusively western science education

- how a student's world view may be at odds or may be interwoven with the world view of western science

Beaver

Cree hunters and their organizations have held management authority over beaver in northern Quebec since 1975. The Cree hunters have been able to combine their own traditional approach to monitoring beaver populations with a complementary Western science approach in order to generate accurate beaver population measures covering enormous geographic areas. The Cree hunters are skilled at determining the proportion of beaver lodges in a given area that are occupied. On their own, though, they have no way of generalizing this information over the full expanse of their vast territory. Conversely, the provincial resource managers can provide aerial survey data giving an accurate count of the number of beaver lodges over a large area, but these data provide no information concerning the number of lodges actually occupied. Combining these two approaches to population monitoring yields precise counts over large areas. (Canadian Council on Learning, 2007, p. 7)

Titi Chicks

In New Zealand, rakiura Maori harvest titi chicks every fall. Through years of observation, rakiura Maori titi harvesters have noticed that chicks tend to be fat during years of high abundance and thin during years of low abundance because chick size and abundance both depend on the adult birds' ability to feed their chicks. Recently, however, titi harvesters noticed surprising occurrences in which there were small numbers of fat chicks. When the harvesters drew attention to this event, Western scientists began using state-of-the-art technology to track adult titi over their trans-equatorial migrations in order to identify the causes of the event. Combining aboriginal knowledge of normal titi patterns with Western technology for studying aberrations in these patterns allowed scientists and titi harvesters to discover that titi were suffering from the effects of global climate perturbations. (Canadian Council on Learning, 2007, p. 7)

How might teachers of science help students to navigate diverse world views while maintaining their own cultural identities?

FIXED BORDERS/FUZZY BORDERS: BORDER CROSSINGS

The metaphor of border crossings (Giroux, 2005) can be useful in understanding what some students experience during a science class—it can feel as though they have crossed a border into a foreign place. Some students feel as though they do not belong, cannot speak the language, and do not understand the customs. For example, students who identify as something other than male or female may find their identities excluded in science curriculum materials (Bazzul & Sykes, 2011), or students who have had a refugee experience or have been displaced for other reasons may feel alienated from school (Bash & Zezlina-Phillips, 2006). Aikenhead (1996) categorizes the process of "border crossing into the subculture of science" as smooth, managed, hazardous, or impossible (see Table 4.2).

Many students dislike science, never opt in, opt in half-heartedly and may not develop deep understandings, or opt out as soon as their compulsory requirements are met. Opting out of science education can limit students' future possibilities. Additionally, society misses out on the wider range of perspectives held by these students that may inform future science practice. To help students navigate the different worlds they inhabit, Calabrese Barton (1998) suggests blurring the fixed borders between cultures:

> If the borders of science are expanded or made fuzzy, then there will be more room to fit children's experiences that cannot be neatly labeled as science. Valuing these experiences shifts the dynamics of what counts as science and who can do science because children would not have to silence certain experiences or feelings traditionally labeled outside of science. (p. 386)

An expanded view of science education is essential to the challenge of empowering students to successfully cross borders. Table 4.2 revisits the student categories described in Table 4.1, focusing on the relationship of student profiles to border crossings. As you study the table, ask yourself what strategies might make science less foreign and border crossings smoother and easier to navigate.

ACTIVITY 4.5

21st C

Read and Reflect: Border Crossings

This chapter highlights some of the ideas from Glen Aikenhead's (1996) paper on border crossings as a way to think about how students participate in science and the implications for social justice issues. We encourage you to read the entire paper: Aikenhead, G. S. (1996). Science education: Border crossings into the subculture of science. *Studies in Science Education*. 27(1), 1–52. We also refer to this paper in Chapter 12. As you read the paper, think about the ways that students experience border crossing in science and how we can help them navigate difficulties.

Table 4.2 Revisiting Student Border Crossings: Smooth, Managed, Hazardous, or Impossible Consequences

Category of students	Consequences for border crossing
Potential Scientists	Border crossing into school science is so smooth and natural that borders appear invisible.
Other Smart Kids	Students find the subculture of science to be personally unimportant and inconsistent with the subcultures of their school, peers, and family. However, border crossing into school science is managed so well that few students express any sense of science being a foreign subculture.
"I Don't Know" Students	Students do not know much about the subculture of science and when asked they simply submit to the wisdom of the media and treat scientists as experts. Border crossing into school science poses real hazards, but these students generally navigate successfully around those hazards.
Outsiders	Subcultures of science are highly discordant with the subcultures of peers and family. Students do not know or care about the subculture of science. School and science are indeed foreign subcultures for most outsider students and border crossing into school science is virtually impossible.
Inside Outsiders	Because of their unconventional lives, these students find border crossing into the subculture of school to be almost impossible, preventing participation in school science.

Source: Adapted from Aikenhead, 1996.

FOUNDATIONS FOR SOCIAL JUSTICE IN SCIENCE EDUCATION

Social justice is important in science for two separate but overlapping reasons: a) the power of science and its relationship to access and inclusion for students of all cultural backgrounds and b) the selection of science topics and examples of a social justice nature that affect individuals, communities, and society.

Social Justice and Issues of Power, Access, and Inclusion Social justice in this context relates to how science can be used to reproduce social stratification and addresses issues such as inequality, oppression, and the unequal distribution of wealth. Teaching science for social justice should include presenting the discipline as dynamic and socially constructed in order to allow students to see themselves as participants in science. When students understand NOS perspectives, including the impact of funding for research and socio-political pressures, they understand science in a more authentic way. You might explore questions such as why and how groups of individuals are represented or underrepresented in science.

Science holds social power in schools and in society (Sleeter, 2000, 2009; Young, 1987). It is often associated with success in schools and affects access to higher education. Furthermore, material taught in science classrooms can be seen as more valuable than other forms of knowledge. Science content is constructed knowledge (Aikenhead, 1994; Harding, 1998; Kuhn, 1996), and exploring NOS perspectives can help students understand the limitations of the enduring power of science in our society. Teachers must be willing to ask questions of themselves and of their teaching, such as the following:

- How can we help all students to see themselves as "having potential to participate in society's power structures and to generate knowledge" (Aikenhead, 1996, p. 15)?

- How can we demystify science and make it more accessible to students (Hodson, 2003)?

- Why and how do schools reproduce oppressive structures seen in society (Cummins, 1996)?

Social Justice and Science Curriculum Topics Many science curriculum topics lend themselves to a social justice approach to instruction. For example, we might explore who pollutes and who lives near polluted land, where our food comes from and how it is distributed, what the impact of mining is on Aboriginal communities and farmers, and how classroom waste affects the school community.

Teachers want to create a more inclusive curriculum, but often feel discouraged and frustrated in their attempts to do so. Teachers face challenges and barriers, including insufficient background knowledge, time restraints, school expectations, or anxiety about being controversial in the classroom. Another source of tension is resistance from students who have varying ideas about what science is and what should be taught in a science class (Bellomo, 2003).

Science, technology, society, and the environment (STSE) can be an entry point for teachers to consider curricula in terms of social justice. For example, issues such as poverty overlap with health and disease, economy with energy resources and production. Conducting inquiry and exploring the tenets of NOS also serve as appropriate entry points for science lessons.

Moje (2007) acknowledges that while all teachers want to be socially just and provide equal opportunities for all, this is different from a *social justice pedagogy* that provides opportunities for transformation and the reconstruction of knowledge. This is a particular challenge in science, which many identify as a neutral discipline that involves understanding or memorizing without questioning (Hodson, 2003, 2011). Calabrese Barton (2003) shares stories from students as they explore meaningful science experiences that help them construct science knowledge. She promotes a vision of teaching science that is responsive to student needs. According to Calabrese Barton and Upadhyay, 2010, p.5:

> The history of social justice research in science education is still in its infancy—[but]—it is clear that science education for social justice is premised on three broad assumptions:
>
> - Having the opportunity to learn science as content knowledge, discourse, and practice is a civil right.
> - Teaching and learning science involves critical activism and citizenship.
> - The goals of science literacy involve personal, social, and economic empowerment.

Classroom Teaching

Teaching is at the intersection of the two foundations: power and inclusion, and social justice curriculum topics and examples. (See Figure 4.3.) Science pedagogy should acknowledge each. A science program for social justice, equity, and diversity, then, is not an added on, extra notion, but central to the curriculum development process and embedded into the daily experiences of students.

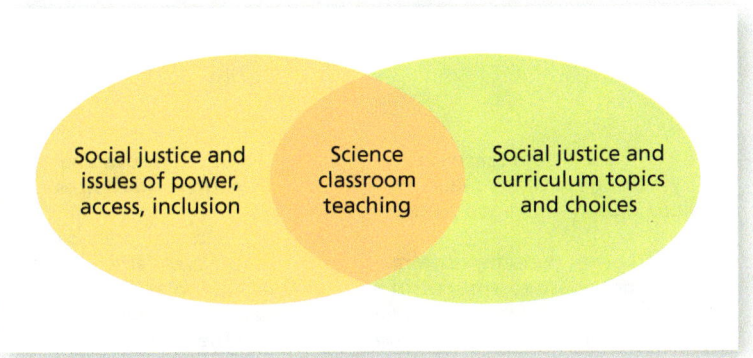

Figure 4.3 Science classroom teaching in relation to social justice

Culturally Relevant Pedagogy

Socially just teaching overlaps with what Ladson-Billings (1995a) describes as *culturally relevant pedagogy*: "a pedagogy of opposition not unlike critical pedagogy but specifically committed to collective, not merely individual empowerment" (p. 160). Culturally relevant pedagogy focuses on helping students experience academic success and develop a critical consciousness through which they are enabled to challenge the status quo. James (2012a) uses the term *community-informed pedagogy*, since the communities to which our students belong, or from which they have come, shape them and should inform teachers' practice.

Understanding that there is cultural multiplicity within a community, the following list expands on the notion of culturally relevant and community-informed pedagogy. All teachers can

a) explore privilege, power, and economics, and the unequal distribution of these elements in our society

b) question school and institutional practices that are coercive or oppressive

c) recognize the value of the knowledge and experience that all students bring to classrooms

d) ensure that students see themselves in curricula

e) address marginalization in society and how it can be reproduced in schools

f) question the notion of meritocracy

g) recognize how knowledge construction practices operate in science

h) understand the power structures that underpin and fund scientific research

i) recognize science as a process of inquiry and encourage students to see themselves as able to participate in that process

j) understand how social justice issues can influence the content of science

k) examine bias in interpersonal relationships, curricular choices, and the discipline of science

l) incorporate the contributions of a diverse body of scientists, including historical, non-western, Aboriginal, Indigenous, neo-Indigenous, and western traditions

The Venn diagram in Figure 4.4 illustrates how culturally relevant pedagogy can be incorporated into curricula.

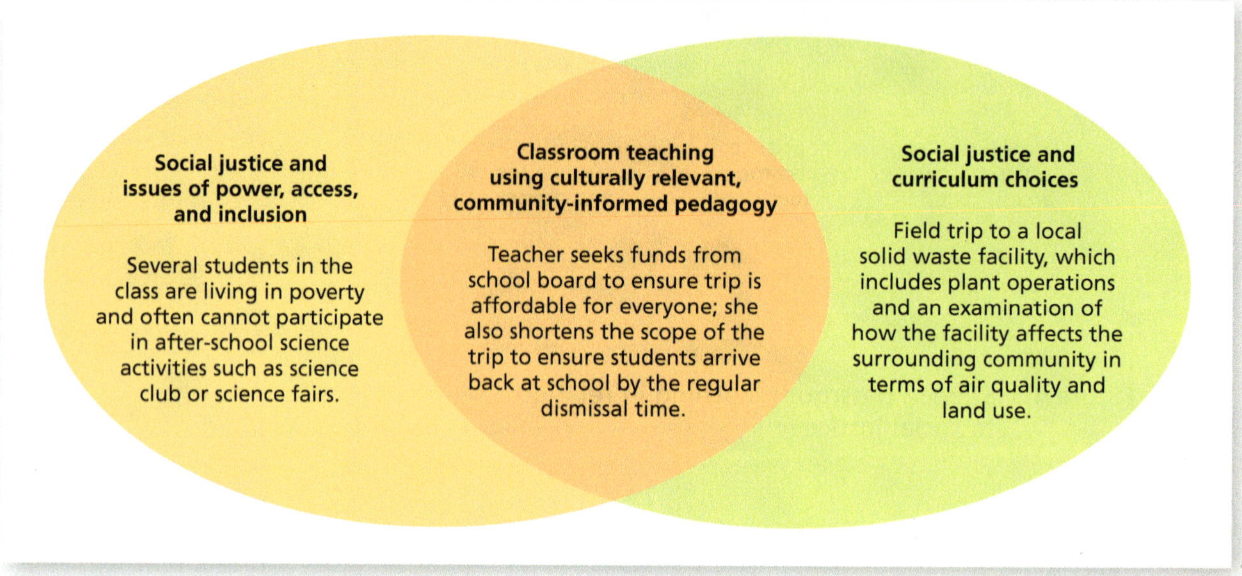

Figure 4.4 Teaching for social justice in science education

Science Curriculum Guidelines and Social Justice

Social justice issues can be woven through many topics. In this section we explore *food*—a common theme in most curriculum guidelines. We might begin, for example, by asking students (a) what they already know about food and (b) what they would like to learn more about. Their ideas might include the following:

- types of plants used for food
- types of foods eaten around the world
- foods children like to eat
- organic food
- food for good nutrition and health
- soil nutrients needed for food crops
- reasons some people do not have enough to eat and are hungry
- feeding the world population
- ways to cultivate more of the available land on the planet
- clearing land for cultivation and the resulting loss of forests

Provincial guidelines incorporate many expectations related to food; below are a few from K–3. As you read through the list, think of how ideas from earlier in this chapter might influence the way you would teach these outcomes, keeping in mind:

a) the equity framework

b) foundations for social justice in science education

c) culturally relevant, community-informed pedagogy

Sample Outcomes from Various Provincial and Territorial Curriculum Guidelines

Grade 1:

- Students can try to guess the identity of types of food by closing their eyes and smelling, touching it, or if possible tasting it. (Nova Scotia Department of Education, 2005, p. 22)

- Students might explore how their sense of smell can help them identify when food has gone bad. For example, students could discuss previous experiences with food that has gone bad—mouldy bread, sour milk . . .). (Nova Scotia Department of Education, 2005, p. 22)

Grade 2:

- We shouldn't waste water, for the same reasons that we shouldn't waste food—for example, because others don't have enough and it costs money. (Ontario Ministry of Education, 2007b, p. 67)
- Recognize that food is a form of energy and that healthy eating is essential for growth and development. (Manitoba Education and Training, 1999, p. 3.28)
- Investigate food groups and plan a menu for one day based on the four food groups outlined in *Canada's Food Guide to Healthy Eating*. (Manitoba Education and Training, 1999, p. 3.28)

Grade 3:

- Recognize that plants use the sun's energy to make their own food. (Manitoba Education and Training, 1999, p. 38)
- Identify how humans from various cultures use plant parts for food and medicine. (Manitoba Education and Training, 1999, p. 3.39)
- Describe various local and domestic plants used in food preparation (e.g., vegetables, fruits, spices, herbs) and identify places where they can be grown. (Northwest Territories, Education, Culture and Employment, 2004, p. 27)
- Identify some functions of different local plants (for example, trees for shade or to break wind or bind soil; trees also provide building materials). (Northwest Territories Education, Culture and Employment, 2004, p. 27)

Activity 4.6 explores how justice issues can be incorporated into science through the theme of food.

ACTIVITY 4.6   *21st C* ① ② ③ ④

Exploring Social Justice Teaching Through the Topic of Food

Part A

The table below lists specific outcomes or expectations from the K–3 provincial guidelines discussed above along with some ideas about how to teach them through a social justice lens. Complete the table using two other expectations from the K–3 guidelines. Brainstorm teaching strategies, activities, ideas, or issues that children could explore.

Social Justice and Food	
Outcome or expectation	**Using a social justice lens**
Investigate food groups and plan a menu for one day based on the four food groups outlined in *Canada's Food Guide to Healthy Eating*.	Explore what healthy eating means in other parts of the world. Plan a healthy menu for one day based on food that is grown in other parts of the world.

continued on next page

cience Inves

Social Justice and Food (Continued)

Outcome or expectation	Using a social justice lens
Recognize that plants use the sun's energy to make their own food.	Explore the idea that plants need water, soil, and the sun to grow. If land is degraded or polluted, it may not be suitable for plant growth, perhaps resulting in food shortages for humans and other animals. Climate change may also affect rainfall or droughts and so affect food supply.
We shouldn't waste water for the same reasons that we shouldn't waste food—for example, because others don't have enough and it costs money.	Research parts of the world experiencing food shortages. Organize a food drive for a local food bank.
Your choice	
Your choice	

Part B

Repeat this activity for Grades 4 to 6 using one of the following:

a) a theme such as water or energy
b) a theme of your choice (perhaps a topic you will be teaching during your practicum)
c) continue the theme of food using the outcomes and expectations found in Appendix 4.B

As you may have noted, it can be challenging to view a topic through a social justice perspective while adhering to curriculum guidelines. While food lends itself to many aspects of social justice, not all science topics are so rich in possibilities. Still, always be mindful of issues of power, access, and inclusion, and the curriculum choices we make. As Angela Calabrese Barton (2003, p. 18) argues, "Until an approach to science and science education in our (urban) classrooms focuses on what it might mean to create a more just world, then we will fall short of our goal of truly building a *science education for all*."

ACTIVITY 4.7

21st C

Read and Reflect: Exploring Research

The journal *Equity & Excellence in Education* published a special issue titled Teaching and Learning Science for Social Justice (Volume 43, 2010). Read one of these articles, from this issue, and reflect on how it fits within the framework outlined in Figure 4.1.

Buxton, C. A. (2010). Social problem solving through science: An approach to critical, place-based, science teaching and learning. *Equity & Excellence in Education*, *43*(1), 120–135.

O'Neill, T. B. (2010). Fostering spaces of student ownership in middle school science. *Equity & Excellence in Education*, *43*(1), 6–20.

DISCUSSION QUESTIONS

1. How does the article you read address the following three components of Figure 4.1:
   a. social justice and issues of power, access, inclusion, and NOS
   b. social justice and *curriculum* choices
   c. science classroom *teaching*
2. How is inquiry (doing science) related to social justice?
3. How is urban education defined? How is it described in the context of science classrooms with respect to challenges and solutions?
4. How is specific subject matter knowledge, such as health or the environment, addressed in social justice classrooms?

SCIENCE CURRICULUM FOR SOCIAL JUSTICE: SOME PROGRAM SUGGESTIONS

Teaching science for social justice can be rewarding for teachers and students as they engage in a more holistic approach to societal inequities. Some aspects of the issues raised in this chapter may be viewed by some teachers as controversial. We argue that all decisions are value laden, and so ignoring or omitting controversial social justice issues is inherently just as contentious as confronting them. Below are four program suggestions for how to include social justice in your teaching of science. These suggestions raise questions about where teachers and students can find appropriate resources—this issue is addressed in the last section of the chapter.

Suggestion 1: Inquiry and the Nature of Science

Science instruction should reflect what science is and how it is done. An inclusive science curriculum includes access to resources and ideas that give students experiences with the nature of science. This can be achieved by engaging students in scientific inquiry and asking them to do, and assess, science as a practice (Thadani, Cook, Griffis, Wise, & Blakey, 2010). As students view science as a process of knowledge construction and not just content, they begin to see themselves as able to actively participate in the process. Authentic experiences involving open-ended inquiry, experimental design, data collection, and the interpretation of data can contribute to an understanding of NOS and can "position students as knowledge-constructors and critics (rather than passive recipients) [and] can help promote social justice in science education" (Thadani et al., 2010, p. 22).

Nature of Science: Scientific Method

Suggestion 2: STSE, Problem Solving, and Community

Community problem solving and content that is anchored in the lives of students can further social justice education. When school science has a focus on community issues, then society and community can intersect with education in an authentic way. Sometimes this is related to an STSE approach, which is detailed in Chapters 10 and 11 (see, for example, Buxton, 2010; Pedretti & Little, 2008).

Suggestion 3: The History of Science from Non-western Traditions

The history of science from non-western traditions can contribute to an understanding of historical and global perspectives. The inclusion of non-western traditions provides avenues to explore social justice, and to address marginalized or forgotten science. Refer to provincial documents that suggest how to incorporate history. (See, for example, Quebec (1998, p. 26), which states, "The history of science will be a major focus of the science program. This will contribute to a proper appreciation of the contributions of different cultures to the development of the sciences.")

The following are suggestions for how to incorporate history into science topics:

- astronomy from Chinese perspectives
- metallurgy and jewellery engraving in West Coast Aboriginal cultures
- chemistry and alchemy in Islam and the Arab world
- crop breeding in Africa or Asia
- medicine and healing in non-western cultures

Recognizing science from non-western perspectives can also be explored in terms of what knowledge is valued and whose knowledge has influence and power. Additionally teachers can address what knowledge is included in the science curriculum and what knowledge is marginalized and why.

Suggestion 4: European Inventors and Inventors from Non-western Perspectives

In addition to teaching about European contributions to science, incorporate the inventions of Aboriginal, Indigenous, African, Asian, and other populations. Recognize and include the experiences of diverse groups, the lives of the inventors, and the social, cultural, and political contexts from which their work emerged. You might consider teaching about the following inventors:

- Ibn Sina (Avicenna), a polymath renowned for his philosophy and medical expertise
- Gurtej Sandhu, who produced thin film processes and materials, very large-scale integration, and semiconductor device fabrication
- Jan Ernst Matzeliger, inventor of a shoemaking machine that increased shoemaking speed by 900 percent
- Otis Boykin, who invented 28 different electronic devices, including control devices for guided missiles, IBM computers, and the pacemaker

◉▸ Watch

A Web-based Music Project

Begin to build your own library of print, media, and web-based resources that you can use to help plan for topics with specific outcomes or expectations. Appendix 4.A includes a few suggestions. You may want to simultaneously refer to curriculum outcomes to determine if and how your teaching can be enhanced with these resources.

CONCLUDING THOUGHTS

Teaching for social justice is an educational choice that has implications for how we include all students and for the curricular resources and examples we use. Social justice science education is an inclusive representation of what science is that goes beyond *facts* of science to an understanding of influences, power structures, and privileges that contribute to knowledge construction. Social justice science pedagogy supports students in understanding the power, influence, and authority of science in our world, and exploring social justice issues related to the discipline. Below we summarize key ideas related to the learning objectives provided at the beginning of the chapter.

Framework for equity, diversity, and social justice

Using an equity, diversity, and social justice framework for planning science curricula means including multiple perspectives in content choices and examples that present science as sometimes beneficial and sometimes implicated in injustice. The framework we suggest is organized into three parts: interactions with students; curriculum choices and examples; and bias within the discipline of science as knowledge construction occurs.

Marginalization and identity

Regardless of whether students live in the inner city, in suburban areas, or in rural communities, they can face marginalization in science classrooms and can run the risk of not being successful. Often, such students are described as at-risk. Effective teachers consider the impact of Aboriginal heritage, language, ethnicity, class, gender, and sexuality on students' lives.

Aboriginal world views in the context of science education

Issues of power, access, inclusion, and social justice in the curriculum are interwoven with the needs, aspirations, and achievements of Aboriginal students. Western science at times conflicts with the culture of Aboriginal students, who may view science instruction as an attempt to assimilate them into western culture.

Border crossings for students

The idea of border crossings is a metaphor for what some students face when they enter a science class. Often they feel as though they do not belong; they cannot speak the language; and they want to leave. The process of border crossing into the subculture of science can be smooth, managed, hazardous, or impossible.

Foundations of social justice in science education, including culturally relevant pedagogy and teaching

Social justice in science is foundational in building an inclusive and just science education. The first foundation is the power of science and its relationship to access for students of all cultural backgrounds. The second founda-

tion relates to science issues of a social justice nature that affect individuals, communities, and society. Some of these issues are implicated in injustice. A social justice science education questions structural barriers in society that prevent some students from succeeding in school. Just pedagogy and teaching overlap with culturally relevant curricula.

Social justice issues and resources for science curricula

Four program suggestions are presented as examples of how to include social justice in science education. Explore inquiry and NOS; STSE; problem solving and community; the history of science from non-western traditions; and European and non-western inventors.

BRINGING IT ALL TOGETHER: FINAL QUESTIONS

1. Describe your understanding of the foundations of social justice within a science classroom from reading this chapter.

2. What are obstacles to including social justice in the science classroom?

3. Work in pairs or groups of three and discuss (a) ways to make your class more socially just (by addressing issues of power, access, and inclusion) and (b) ways to include social justice issues that are connected to science content.

MyEducationLab®

Visit MyEducationLab® to access an electronic version of the text, as well as a variety of topics that enhance the text material. The topics include the following to support your learning in the course:

- Assessments, including interactive case studies, activities, and video assignments
- Discussion board questions
- Videos, simulations, a lesson plan builder, and other useful course resources

APPENDIX 4.A   Curriculum Resources for Social Justice

Curriculum Services Canada (CSC)

www.curriculum.org/content/home
CSC works with government agencies, NGOs, and private organizations from across Canada to develop and evaluate print, multimedia, and web-based resources that support learning. It provides educational services that promote professional growth. Its services include, for example, webcasts (such as "Creating the conditions for learning mathematics") and sites with a specific theme (Black Canadians

Portal for Educators—a portal listing resources to support teachers and students in learning about the contributions of African Canadians).

Canadian International Development Agency (CIDA)

www.acdi-cida.gc.ca/acdi-cida/acdi-cida.nsf/eng/home
CIDA is Canada's lead agency for development assistance. Its mission is to lead Canada's international effort

to help people living in poverty, and its mandate is to manage the nation's resources effectively and accountably to achieve meaningful, sustainable results. The organization engages in policy development in Canada and internationally, enabling Canada's effort to realize its development objectives.

Canadian Council On Learning (CCL)

www.ccl-cca.ca/CCL/Home.html
CCL is an independent, non-profit corporation that promotes and supports research to improve all aspects of learning across the country and across all walks of life. In 2012 the organization was dissolved. However, CCL has taken measures to ensure that the work they have done is still accessible to all Canadians. Sample CCL publications include:

- Lessons in Learning
  www.ccl-cca.ca/CCL/Reports/LessonsInLearning.html#2007
- Aboriginal Learning
  www.ccl-cca.ca/CCL/AboutCCL/KnowledgeCentres/AboriginalLearning/index.html
- Gender Differences In Career Choices: Why Girls Don't Like Science
  www.ccl-cca.ca/CCL/Reports/LessonsInLearning/LinL20071101_Gender_differences_in_science.html

---

APPENDIX 4.B

Grades 4–6 Outcomes and Expectations from Provincial and Territorial Guidelines

Grade 4

- Classify organisms and draw diagrams to illustrate their role in the food chain. (Nova Scotia Department of Education, 2006, p. 13)
- Demonstrate an understanding of the food chain as a system in which energy from the sun is transferred eventually to animals. (Northwest Territories, Education, Culture and Employment, 2004, p. 28)
- Humans depend on natural habitats and communities for many things, including food, building materials, clothing, and medicine. (Ontario Ministry of Education, 2007b, p. 85)
- When scarce farmland is used for development, we lose family farms and a way of life, as well as local sources of fresh food and important open spaces. To lessen such impacts, we need to think of alternative ways of meeting our needs. (Ontario Ministry of Education, 2007b, p. 85)

Grade 5

- Students could discuss the following questions: Why do we need to eat? How does food give us energy? What do my lungs do, and how do they work? What happens to food after I eat it? (New Brunswick Department of Education, 2002, p. 20)
- Describe how the digestive and excretory systems work together to make certain the body uses the food you eat and the waste is processed properly. (New Brunswick Department of Education, 2002, p. 29)

- Research one of the following topics to find out how it affects the growth and development of the body: tobacco, alcohol, steroids, marijuana, tanning salons, junk food. (New Brunswick Department of Education, 2002, p. 31)
- The use of chemical preservatives makes foods last longer, but the preservatives may have an impact on human health. (Ontario Ministry of Education, 2007b, p. 105)

Grade 6

- Analyze the roles of organisms as part of interconnected food webs, populations, communities, and ecosystems. (British Columbia Ministry of Education, 2005, p. 39)
- Explain and provide several examples of how energy is transferred through food webs and food chains within an ecosystem. (British Columbia Ministry of Education, 2005, p. 117)
- Assess the benefits that human societies derive from biodiversity (e.g., thousands of products such as food, clothing, medicine, and building materials come from plants and animals) and the problems that occur when biodiversity is diminished (e.g., monocultures are more vulnerable to pests and diseases). (Ontario Ministry of Education, 2007b, p. 113)
- Explore the transformation of energy in living things: food chains and ecological pyramids. (Quebec Education Program, Preschool and Elementary Education, 2001, p. 176)

Chapter 5

Curriculum That Meets the Needs of Students

Morgan Lane Photography/Shutterstock

LEARNING OBJECTIVES

- Outline factors contributing to the creation of an inclusive learning environment.

- Summarize strategies for knowing students and meeting their learning needs.

- Outline the impact of language and mathematics in teaching science.

- Describe assessment and evaluation strategies and tools for science classrooms.

I find I can engage [my students] better when I really get to know them.

—Sunita, preservice teacher candidate

Treat people as if they were what they might be, and you will help them become capable of being.

—Goethe

When I make the effort to meet the needs of all of my students, they experience success!

—Jake, elementary school teacher

**21st CENTURY
LEARNING SKILLS &
COMPETENCIES**

1 Communication

2 Critical thinking

3 Collaboration

4 Creativity

5 Literacy and numeracy

6 Media literacy

7 Technological literacy

INTRODUCTION

We know that education serves many purposes. Tyler (1949) described education as a process of developing student behaviours inclusive of actions, thoughts, and emotions. Course outcomes and expectations are related to those changes we wish to support in our students and calls for curriculum that centralizes students within the educational process (Tyler, 1949). Today, the prevailing ethos for many teachers is the need to teach the whole child, and, in doing so, identify each student's unique learning needs. Designing a curriculum that meets the needs of all students can be a significant challenge. All teachers at one time or another voice concerns about student engagement and motivation. Yet often these concerns are framed in terms of student deficiency (e.g., how can students be disinterested when science is so fascinating?) rather than student strengths (e.g., my students bring a variety of rich life experiences and come from many cultures—how can I understand what they know already and use it in my planning and implementation of curriculum?).

Our students represent our multicultural society, with a wide range of ethnic, linguistic, cultural, spiritual, and socio-economic backgrounds. We might ask ourselves:

- What assumptions am I making about my students?
- Does my curriculum and instruction exclude some students?
- How will I create a positive classroom climate that supports learning?
- How will I design curriculum that meets the individual needs of my students while affirming their personal identity?
- How will I use assessment both to help students learn and to help me plan?

Teachers can plan individualized approaches rather than apply a *one-size-fits-all* approach to curriculum development (Lynch, 2000). One starting point is to consider the understandings that students bring to class, and then to plan curriculum that honours those ways of knowing and learning (Hollins, 1993). As Corson (1998) suggests, different curricula and different practices are needed for all students, particularly those who have been marginalized. An inclusive curriculum takes into account, among other things, students' language, race, ethnicity, class, beliefs, gender, sexual orientation, and ability. It is helpful to remember that we teach children, not subjects!

Easily, an entire book could be written—and many have been (for example, Schwartz & Pollishuke, 2013)—about strategies that support student needs. This chapter serves as a starting point to the following broad areas: curricular design that creates an inclusive classroom; support for students and their learning needs; considerations for creating a positive classroom climate; issues of literacy and numeracy; and matters related to assessment and evaluation.

CURRICULAR DESIGN AND CREATING A SUPPORTIVE AND INCLUSIVE LEARNING ENVIRONMENT

Culturally Relevant Teaching

In this section, we briefly revisit the idea of culturally responsive pedagogy and curricula. (See Chapter 4.) Ladson-Billings (1994) describes culturally relevant teaching as instruction relevant to and inclusive of students' cultural backgrounds, and in which students experience success and develop a critical consciousness. It includes, among other strategies, relationships with parents, student-centred instruction, teaching from multiple perspectives, and reshaping curricula (Hollins, 1996; Ladson-Billings, 1994; Nieto, 1996). Some strategies for culturally responsive teaching are using varied resources, incorporating cooperative learning strategies, and developing integrated units (see, for example, Hollins, 1996; Ladson-Billings, 1994; Nieto, 1996). Scholars have written about the challenges of planning culturally relevant and community-informed lessons for diverse students. (See, for example, Eslinger, 2012; James, 2012a.)

Below is a list of additional strategies that support culturally relevant teaching and culturally responsive curriculum:

- planning with your students' cultural perspectives and identity (e.g., Indigenous and neo-Indigenous) in mind
- choosing resources that are appropriate to the age, ability, and interests of students
- choosing resources that present science content from both western and non-western traditions
- being aware of how students may be included or excluded
- using a variety of student groupings (e.g., individual, paired, or small-group activities, or whole-class instruction)
- varying teaching strategies (e.g., give students the option of reading about a topic on their own versus listening to the teacher explain it, use stations around the room that cover the same material but in different ways)
- reviewing previous years' material for those who need it (e.g., if some students have covered a topic but others have not, split the class and go over prerequisite material with those who missed it)
- encouraging students to teach each other as needed and appropriate
- using different and varied assessment strategies
- offering students choice whenever possible (e.g., choice of topic, task, assignment, or assessment
- being flexible with timelines and deadlines
- having regular times for students to seek help from the teacher (e.g., lunch club, after-school extra-help sessions)
- making sure that all students understand the goals for a particular unit

ACTIVITY 5.1   *21st C* ❶

Exploring Prior Knowledge and Experience

Recall two experiences from your K–12 schooling or university; one should be a lesson or assignment in which you felt included and honoured, the second should be one in which you felt excluded. Then consider the discussion questions below.

Hint: You might choose a lesson or assignment on a topic that resonated for you; perhaps you were given the choice to pursue your own interests, or perhaps you felt that science came alive and was relevant to your life. It would be the opposite of a lesson where you felt like an outsider or marginalized, or felt that you were forced to learn random abstract ideas that you can hardly remember.

DISCUSSION QUESTIONS

1. Describe how each lesson made you feel.
2. In each case, what was it about the lesson or assignment that made you feel included or excluded? Consider your answer in terms of the course content or the teaching methods and teacher pedagogy.

Differentiated Instruction (DI)

Watch

Learning Centers

Differentiated instruction (DI) is effective instruction that is responsive to the learning preferences, interests, and readiness of individual learners. DI is best thought of as an organizing framework for thinking about teaching and learning (Ontario Ministry of Education, 2010a).

DI is adapting instruction to meet the needs of individual students. Teachers can modify their content, the process, or the product (Tomlinson, 1999). *Content* is the subject matter or concepts that students are expected to learn, whereas *process* describes the activities that students engage with in order to make sense of content. *Product*, as the name suggests, is the work students produce. For example, some students need help identifying gaps in their background knowledge and may require direct instruction. The products they are asked to create may call for structured, concrete direction with prescribed pacing. Other students may be able to skip previously learned material and work at a brisker pace. A basic premise of DI is to help students identify their needs and strengths and to determine how we can use student strengths for engagement.

A key idea that underpins DI is understanding how students learn best (and this might not be the way you learn best). This process involves ensuring that students are ready for learning and providing them with a variety of experiences that address their needs. For example, what approach might you take if you expect a student to write about a science investigation if you know the student has strong speaking skills but has difficulty with writing? You might ask the student to speak about her or his findings in a conference. In this way the student can demonstrate understanding of the activity and build confidence. Next, you might ask the student to write about the activity in order to develop written skills. Since you know that writing is a challenge for him or her, create an opportunity for the student to submit a draft that can be revised after some feedback, or use peer editors. Alternatively, make use of different writing genres such as stories, poems, or scripts (DeCoito, 2009) to support how students learn best.

DI involves more than providing variety—it is the process of matching instructional strategies to different needs. Challenges for teachers include knowing what instruction is best for a particular student and for a specific piece of content and being prepared to facilitate multiple processes in the classroom at one time. In some classes, it may be more practical for the whole class to participate in the same activity (such as an investigation).

The activities that follow explore ways of achieving DI in a science class.

ACTIVITY 5.2

21st C ❶ ❹

Differentiated Instruction in a Lesson on Structures

Imagine you are teaching a lesson on strong and stable structures and you want students to understand the similarities and differences between *strength* (capacity to withstand forces that tend to break an object or change its shape) and *stability* (capacity to maintain balance and stay fixed in one position). Plan two activities that cover the same material, but use different instructional methods to meet the needs of the following four student profiles:

a. Joshua is studious, consistently works hard, and welcomes challenges.

b. Jason is capable, but is easily distracted and enjoys wandering to his friends' desks to talk.

c. Mimi is engaged and wants to do well but is reading below grade level and struggles with new science content.

d. Francois is often disinterested in science class but tends to be more engaged when he is making something with his hands.

DISCUSSION QUESTION

1. How do your activities differentiate instruction with respect to content, process, or product?

KNOWING STUDENTS AND MEETING THEIR LEARNING NEEDS

Theories of Learning

Learning involves the whole person, not just the mind, but also emotions, affect, and context. Think about your own learning for a moment. What is your learning style?

- Do you learn best by reading material several times? Or do you prefer to write things out?
- Do you like to work individually or in groups?
- Do you prefer to use diagrams (e.g., flow charts, concept maps) that map out connections across ideas and concepts?
- Do you learn best by talking with a partner about ideas?

Over the years, much research has been dedicated to understanding how people, particularly children, learn. It is often difficult to fully understand how students learn best. However, we can begin by observing students carefully, paying attention to their needs, and providing them with opportunities to show us, in different ways, what they have learned. These understandings are further informed by theories of learning, which are discussed in more detail in Chapter 12.

The Role of Affect

What is affect, and what role does it play in the science classroom? Affect can include emotions, mood, feelings, and attitudes (Reiss, 2005). Alsop and Watts (2003) note that it is important to acknowledge how the emotional aspects of students' lives impact teaching and learning science, and Reiss (2005) makes a case for challenging the notion that science and emotions operate in different worlds. Lemke (2001) suggests that being motivated to learn science is not simply a neutral process that requires students to exhibit logical thought and application of content. Culture and class (and we would add all aspects of a student's identity) are other significant factors in students' attitudes toward science. These matters of affect, when included in the curriculum design process, create an inclusive curriculum that truly meets student needs and interests.

Osborne, Simon, and Collins (2003) provide some helpful suggestions for enhancing student attitudes, such as setting clear goals and encouraging student input, reviewing content of lessons, and embedding lessons in students' experiences. They also suggest an approach that supports differentiated instruction, including respecting individual needs and making appropriate modifications.

If affect is important to teaching and learning, then how can teachers understand what students are feeling? Carefully and respectfully listen, watch, ask, and respond to what you learn about your students. Ask them about their class experience as they leave, using "one-minute reflection" or "ticket out the door" technique. Students take a minute to complete the reflection before they leave the room. Ask one or two questions such as the following:

- What did you learn in class today? How did you feel about what you learned?
- How did you feel about what was happening in class?
- What were the best and worst things that happened in class today?

The first time you use this strategy, students might give brief answers like "everything was okay" or "the person next to me was bugging me" or "you went too fast." If you summarize the responses anonymously and report common themes to the class, students may provide more detailed and thoughtful responses in subsequent one-minute reflections. This information can be useful in involving students and acknowledging and honouring their aspirations and concerns.

Multiple Intelligences

◉ **Watch**

Water Wheels Part 3

We know that people have different strengths, talents, and learning preferences. For example, you might prefer to learn by writing things down rather than just listening, while your friend may prefer a more hands-on approach. Howard Gardner's (1985) work can inform how you address student strengths and areas for growth. He defines eight intelligences, as summarized in Table 5.1, and suggests that teachers use these multiple intelligences in different contexts. The implication is that teachers need to be cognizant of students' diverse strengths and preferences, and plan with those differences in mind. Gardner's categories offer us a way to think about different learning styles.

It is important to remember that the lines between the different intelligences can be blurred. Students are unlikely to exhibit only one type of intelligence, but instead express strengths across intelligences. Learning is context dependent, and students may draw on different intelligences for different purposes. The challenge for teachers is to recognize

Table 5.1 Summary of Gardner's Multiple Intelligences		
Intelligence	**Description**	**A student who**
Verbal-Linguistic Intelligence	Ability to understand and be comfortable with the different functions of language and the sounds, rhythms, and meanings of words	Likes to read Enjoys writing Likes crosswords and word games
Bodily-Kinesthetic Intelligence	Ability to control physical movements with comfort and to handle objects skillfully; a preference for learning kinesthetically	Prefers to learn by doing rather than watching or listening Tends to gesture while explaining things Likes to move while thinking
Musical-Rhythmic Intelligence	Ability to produce and appreciate pitch, timbre, rhythm, and different forms of musical expression	Remembers melodies Likes listening to and performing music Has a good sense of rhythm
Logical-Mathematical Intelligence	Ability to distinguish logical and numerical patterns and to manage complex reasoning	Approaches problems logically Enjoys math Likes number and strategy games
Visual-Spatial Intelligence	Ability to perceive the visual-spatial world accurately and understand graphic displays Ability to make transformations from perceptions	Uses pictures and maps to help remember Likes to sketch or doodle; has a good sense of direction
Naturalist Intelligence	Ability to feel comfortable with the natural world and to relate to information about the environment	Likes being outdoors with plants and animals Knows details about nature Easily recognizes the sounds of nature
Interpersonal Intelligence	Capacity to discern and respond appropriately to the moods, temperaments, motivations, and desires of others	Prefers working in groups rather than alone Can tell how people are feeling Talks to people in order to learn
Intrapersonal Intelligence	Perceptiveness about one's own emotional state and knowledge of one's strengths and weaknesses	Knows self well Likes to learn or sort out ideas by thinking about them Thinks about and plans next steps

Source: Based on Gardner, 1993.

which intelligences students have and which can be further developed. When planning curriculum and specific classroom activities, teachers must decide whether to focus on student strengths or areas for growth. For example, if a student exhibits strong verbal-linguistic intelligence, and the potential for growth in visual-spatial intelligence, should she or he be encouraged to submit a poem for assessment? Or should that student be challenged to create a visual representation to demonstrate what she or he has learned? Alternatively, you might plan an activity that involves both intelligences (e.g., an arts-based project that combines drawing with creative writing).

Planning for Unique Learning Needs

English Language Learners English language learners are students for whom English is not their first language and (usually) not the language they speak at home. Such students come from diverse backgrounds; some are born in Canada, some are recent immigrants, and some may be refugees with no formal schooling. Students usually acquire *conversational language* within one to two years of exposure to English. However, to acquire *academic language proficiency*, students typically need at least five years (Cummins, 2011). Academic language in science can be specific, difficult, and technical. Furthermore, new words are not used often in conversational English (e.g., herbivore, diffusion, kinetic), or may be used in other contexts (e.g., energy, work, lift, respiration). We will explore this concept further later in the chapter.

Cummins (2011) suggests the following strategies to enhance language proficiency:

- Support literacy by reading and providing opportunities to discuss the meanings of the readings.
- Scaffold instruction through graphic organizers, visuals, and demonstrations.
- Connect to students' lives through prior experience and build background knowledge.
- Affirm students' identities through the validation of their culture.

These strategies, while supporting English language learners, also support good teaching, DI, and a culturally relevant pedagogy. Furthermore, some English language learners new to the country may need support as they learn new classroom practices (Jao, 2012).

Special Needs There may be students in your class who have been assessed as having special learning needs and who require specific accommodations, such as more time to complete tests or assignments. Some students have visual or auditory challenges or require assistive devices such as wheelchairs. The physical constraints of many classrooms can present a challenge. Students with special needs may require either modifications to the goals of lessons or accommodations with respect to process or product. Teacher sensitivity to these students' needs will benefit everyone in the classroom. Effective teaching requires that teachers examine their own beliefs about the nature of student ability and knowledge (see Jordan, Schwartz, & McGhie-Richmond, 2009). Be sure to read related policy documents and resources in your province or territory.

Using Technology for Special Circumstances Accommodations through technology (e.g., assistive technology) can help both English language learners and students with special needs. Technology can allow students access to a subject or course without altering the knowledge and skills they are expected to demonstrate (Ontario Ministry of Education, 2011). Teachers can make use of computer-assisted technology or computer-assisted language labs to help students with special needs. The software program *Read and Write Gold* is one example of assistive technology that provides support for reading and writing text. Using this type of technology, students can develop literacy skills—and do so with greater independence. Speech recognition software that converts the spoken word to written text can also be useful. Find out what resources are available through your school.

◉─|Watch

Lesson on Birds

ACTIVITY 5.3

21st C **2** **3** **4**

Watch

Active Learning

Affect, Multiple Intelligences, Unique Learning Needs and Teaching Science

In this activity you will combine your general understanding of affect, multiple intelligences, and special needs to think about the particulars of science education. In pairs, complete the table by suggesting pedagogical actions that attend to affect, multiple intelligences, and unique learning needs in the context of teaching and learning strategies for science lessons. Some examples are provided.

Attending to Affect, Multiple Intelligences and Unique Learning Needs when Teaching Science

Teaching and learning strategy (some examples)	Attending to affect	Attending to multiple intelligences	Attending to unique learning needs
Teacher demonstration			
Cooperative small group learning	Ensure shy student feels comfortable in the group		
Guest speaker or other community resource			
Class discussion			
Independent study		Give choice of written, oral, or visual presentation of work	
Investigation			
Field trip			
Game			Have students work in pairs
Question and answer			

SCIENCE, LANGUAGE, AND MATHEMATICS

Science education inherently includes literacy and numeracy (Lemke, 1990; Yore et al., 2004). Students need to solve problems; describe their findings from investigations in prose, numerically, or graphically; explain phenomena orally or in writing; and produce and interpret graphs. Indeed, science is a wonderful way to address the literacy and numeracy skills that are promoted in policy documents. In the sections that follow, we explore the role of language and mathematics in science education and the implications for teachers, and offer some strategies to help support students in these areas.

Science and Language

Literacy skills are developed as students read, write, listen, and speak in science classes. Regardless of the subject, students are expected to read many forms of print—in books and electronically—they need to be able to interpret what they read. Reading for meaning is different from decoding text. Good teaching strategies support learning to read while reading to learn in science (Ontario Ministry of Education, 2007). When students lack grapho-phonic, syntactic, or semantic cues, they face a barrier to reading for meaning.

Grapho-phonic cues refer to the relationship between symbols (letters) and sounds that helps us break words into letters, sounds, and syllables and allows us to *read* a word, even if it is gibberish. However, in order to make meaning from reading, we need both syntactic and semantic cues. *Syntactic cues* involve knowledge about language systems and how words are sequenced for meaning. These include experiences with written language that enable us to predict what might come next in a sentence. *Semantic cues* refer to prior knowledge of a topic, as well as experience with the reading process. When we read, we add meaning. As such, semantic cues in science can pose difficulties for students who have no prior knowledge to bring to the context. Many words have both colloquial and scientific meanings, such as *force, energy, power, work, fitness, gas, cell,* and *weight.* Meaning depends on the context, adding additional complexity for students.

Table 5.2 summarizes cueing systems and provides some instructional strategies for helping students read for meaning.

Reading and Cueing Systems in Science Programs

As students become independent readers, teachers expect them to make meaning of what they read. While many students, regardless of their reading level, can read and make

👁—Watch

Memory

Table 5.2   Cueing Systems and Instructional Strategies

Grapho-phonic (visual)	Syntactic (structure)	Semantic (meaning)
Teachers can help students to understand the relationships between symbols and sounds, and to decode text.	Teachers can model complex sentence structures and sentence reconstruction with familiar stories.	Teachers can help students understand the purpose of reading: Does the word fit and make sense? What information do the illustrations provide? What has happened so far and what might happen next?
• word sorts • word analogies • sounds and symbols • directionality • beginnings and endings • word families • root words • syllables • prefixes and suffixes	• organizing words and phrases into sentences • re-reading • reading ahead • capitalization • punctuation	• oral predicting • prior knowledge • pictures • connections • graphic organizers (webs, KWL) • context clues, pictures, text • a cloze activity (determine the covered word)

Source: Adapted from Hastings and Prince Edward District School Board, 2007.

meaning of fiction books, they may have more difficulty with non-fiction texts. Science texts in particular, which can include a great deal of new and specialized vocabulary, can be very challenging to read.

Consider, for example, introducing the properties of liquids and solids. With K–3 students, you might begin with a children's book such as *Bartholomew and the Oobleck* by Dr. Seuss. This is a story of a boy, Bartholomew, who must contend with a sticky substance (Oobleck[1]) that is falling from the sky. Bartholomew helps his king to rid the kingdom of this strange, sticky substance.

On the other hand, older students might read a science text for information about how solids and liquids differ. For example,

> Properties of solids and liquids: Both solids and liquids have mass and occupy space. While a liquid will take the shape of a container, a solid does not. Solids are rigid and not easily compressed. They have a fixed shape and a definite volume. Liquids, on the other hand, have a fixed volume but not a fixed shape and, as stated above, take the shape of their container. Liquids have a melting point below room temperature and that is why they appear as liquids—although at colder temperatures they may solidify. Water, for example, is a liquid at room temperature but will solidify into ice if cooled to a temperature below its freezing point. Both water (a liquid) and ice (a solid) are made up of the same type of particles but the motion of the particles is different. In liquid water the particles move about easily past one another, whereas in solid water (ice) the particles do not move easily past one another.

This passage highlights the issue of reading for meaning and the importance of cueing systems. A student might be able to read this passage (decode the text), but the key ideas might be unclear. While he or she can read the words *melting point* and *temperature*, can he or she make meaning from them? Learning science can, in many ways, be like learning a new language (Wellington & Osborne, 2001). Strategies to help students become comfortable with the often highly specialized language of science include word walls, word games, crossword puzzles, creating a class glossary or dictionary of science terms for a specific unit, and using pictures, diagrams, and illustrations rather than relying solely on oral and written language.

ACTIVITY 5.4   *21st C* 3 4 5

Making Sense of Cueing Systems in Science Programs

Form groups of two and choose a topic from your provincial or territorial science curriculum document that is rich in science vocabulary. Identify the grade level and choose two resources (one fiction and one non-fiction) that would support students' learning about this topic through reading. Brainstorm how you might use the two resources to help students develop strategies for reading unfamiliar science material. Outline one strategy you would use to support each of the graphophonic, syntactic, and semantic cues.

Textbooks in Science

Science textbooks can be used to support science curriculum and instruction in elementary schools. Reading textbooks requires a different skill set than reading fiction. Students may be asked, for example, to read passages and answer questions, to use the textbook for investigations, or to refer to the glossary. Textbooks can be challenging to navigate for

---

[1]An Oobleck-like substance can be made by combining 1 part water with 2 parts cornstarch. The resulting mixture has properties of both liquids and solids.

ACTIVITY 5.5   *21st C*

Textbook Scavenger Hunt

A scavenger hunt can be a fun way to familiarize students with the textbook they will be using, while also developing language skills. As students search for answers, they may be encouraged to flip through the book more and more.

Select a textbook you might use in your first year of teaching. Create a scavenger hunt that asks one question about each of the following:

- table of contents (e.g., Use the table of contents to find out how many sections or chapters are in the book.)
- index (e.g., On what pages are there references to topic "x"?)
- glossary (e.g., Use the glossary to find the meaning of these words.)
- structure of each section or chapter (e.g., Explore the introduction, margin notes, section headings, or review questions at the end of each chapter or section.)
- organization of the activities and investigations in the book
- visuals (e.g., Compare the images on pages x and y and explain which one is more informative.)

EXTENSION

If you are using a virtual textbook or an ebook, how would you adapt these questions? How would you help students navigate the virtual environment?

children unfamiliar with their structure. It is important that teachers scaffold the use of the textbook. Be mindful of its organization, its use of language, and its readability.

Science and Mathematics

Many mathematical skills are foundational to science topics (Frykolm & Glasson, 2005). Learning some aspects of science content can be difficult if students do not have basic math skills. In addition to basic computational skills, students need to be able to use fractions, decimals, and percentages; to produce or interpret graphs; and to have strategies for problem solving. Difficulties in these areas can be a barrier to learning science. Specific math skills may need to be explicitly taught or reviewed in order for students to successfully approach new science content material. In the following sections, we highlight two aspects of numeracy: graphing and problem-solving.

Graphing The importance of using graphs is well established in science. (See Roth & Bowen, 2001b.) Students use graphs to summarize and present data that they have collected during lab work. They are often asked to *read* graphs in order to extract data and understand scientific principles, such as the difference between arithmetic and exponential growth in organisms, for example, or what information can be derived from a distance-time graph. Graphing skills such as constructing a graph or analyzing one to interpret meaning are generally taught in mathematics classes. However, graph interpretation can be difficult for students who may not be able to easily transfer their mathematic graphing skills to a science context. Additionally, graphing may be used for a different purpose in science. Creating graphs to display data and *reading* graphs for a specific purpose, such as to persuade an audience, may be new concepts for students. Activity 5.6 allows you to explore how graphing can be included in science teaching.

ACTIVITY 5.6

21st C **3** **5**

Using Graphs to Present Data

(adapted from Bosak, 2000)

Working with a partner and using a tape measure, make the following measurements:

- distance from tip of longest finger to longest finger with arms outstretched (arm span)
- height
- length of your head (chin to top of head)
- distance around closed fist
- distance between elbow and wrist
- distance between elbow and shoulder
- length of your foot

Record the measurements in the table below.

Measuring Body Dimensions

What to measure?	Measurement (in cm)
Arm span	
Height	
Chin to top of head	
Around closed fist	
Elbow to wrist	
Elbow to shoulder	
Length of foot	

Make a bar graph of the results, either by hand or computer, and compare the measurements. Are any similar? Which ones? Compare these similarities to those of another student.

Creating ratios is another way to compare the measurements. Complete the table below using the data you generated above. (We have completed one for you.) Compare your ratios with your peers and your teacher.

Comparing Measurements Using Ratios

What to compare?	Raw measurements	Ratio	Ratio (in the form of X:1)
Height to length of head	Height = 167 cm Length of head = 22 cm	167 : 22	7.5 : 1
Height to arm span			
Around closed fist to Length of foot			
Other			

DISCUSSION QUESTIONS

1. The lengths of arm span and height are approximately the same, as are the distances around a closed fist, from elbow to wrist, from elbow to shoulder, and the length of a foot. How do your own measurements compare? Did you have similar findings?

2. How did your length of head to height ratio compare to someone else in the class?

3. Height is between 6 and 7.5 times the length of your head. How did your ratio compare to this?

4. You displayed your measurements in a table, in a bar graph, and as ratios. Which display allowed for easier comparison of measurements?

USING THIS ACTIVITY WITH ELEMENTARY SCHOOL STUDENTS

The measurements of many parts of the human body are related, either as approximately the same measure or as a ratio. Artists use these measurements to maintain proportions in drawings, paintings, and sculpture. In the following activity, students will explore these unique measures and use ratios to make comparisons.

With a partner, use a measuring tape to find the distances listed below. Make a table in your science notebook to record your findings.

Measuring Body Dimensions	
What to measure?	**Measurement (in cm)**
Arm span. Stretching your arms out to either side, measure the distance from tip to tip of your longest fingers.	
Height	
Length of your head from chin to top of head	
Distance around closed fist	
Elbow to wrist	
Elbow to shoulder	
Length of foot	

Make a bar graph of the measurements, either by hand or computer. Compare the bars. Are any similar? Which ones? Compare your bar graph with another student's graph.

Another way to compare the measurements involves ratios. Complete the table below using the data you generated above. (We have completed one for you.) Compare your ratios with your peers and your teacher.

Comparing Measurements Using Ratios			
What to compare?	**Raw measurements**	**Ratio**	**Ratio (in the form of X:1)**
Height to length of head	Height = 145cm Length of head = 22 cm	145 : 22	6.6 : 1
Height to arm span			
Distance around closed fist to length of foot			
Distance around closed fist to distance from elbow to shoulder			
Other			

Assessment: You can use students' science notebooks and a rubric to evaluate students' understandings and skills.

Problem Solving Being able to analyze and solve a problem using multiple strategies is important in science education. According to Van de Walle and Lovin (2006), a problem is defined as a task or activity for which students have no prescribed or memorized rules or methods. Problems must begin where the students are at and must be engaging. George Polya (1957) proposed a four-phase problem-solving model for open-ended problems or those that might have more than one solution. Table 5.3 summarizes Polya's framework.

Table 5.3   A Problem-Solving Model
Understand the Problem (the exploratory stage)
• Reread and restate the problem.
• Identify the information given and the information that needs to be determined.
Communication: talk about the problem to understand it better
Make a Plan
• Relate the problem to similar problems solved in the past.
• Consider possible strategies*.
• Select a strategy or a combination of strategies.
Communication: discuss ideas with others to clarify which strategy or strategies would work best
Carry Out the Plan
• Execute the chosen strategy.
• Do the necessary calculations.
• Monitor success.
• Revise or apply different strategies as necessary.
Communication: draw pictures, use manipulatives to represent interim results, use words and symbols to represent the steps in carrying out the plan or doing the calculations, share results of computer or calculator operations
Look Back at the Solution
• Check the reasonableness of the answer.
• Review the method used: Did it make sense? Is there a better way to approach the problem?
• Consider extensions or variations.
Communication: describe how the solution was reached, using the most suitable format, and explain the solution

Source: Ontario Ministry of Education, *Mathematics, Grades 1–8*, 2005, p.13 © Queen's Printer for Ontario, 2005. Reproduced with permission.

*Strategies can take the form of looking for patterns, using a model, using a formula, solving an equation, or working from a similar but simpler problem. Students usually need guidance with choosing an appropriate strategy.

Regardless of the type of problem that students are to solve in science, they may need to be taught these steps and practise them in many different contexts before becoming proficient. Teaching the steps can demystify the process of problem solving, which is sometimes seen by students as guesswork or lacking structure. Even so, it is important to recognize and allow students to solve problems in different ways. Students should be encouraged to be creative and to seek alternative ways of arriving at a solution.

ASSESSMENT AND EVALUATION

As a teacher candidate, you will likely take a separate course that deals with assessment and evaluation in detail. This section, meant to complement your other courses, examines assessment and evaluation in elementary science.

According to *Equity and Inclusive Education for Ontario Schools* (Ontario Ministry of Education, 2009, p. 22), assessment and evaluation practices need to identify any discriminatory biases that prevent students from fulfilling their learning potential. In order to support valid and reliable assessment and evaluation, teachers must use strategies that:

- address both what students learn and how well they learn
- are based on the categories of knowledge and on achievement

- match descriptions given in the achievement chart that appears in the curriculum policy document
- are varied in nature, administered over a period of time, and designed to provide opportunities for students to demonstrate the full range of their learning
- are appropriate for the learning activities used, the purposes of instruction, and the needs and experiences of the students
- are fair to all students
- accommodate students with special education needs, consistent with the strategies outlined in their Individual Education Plans
- accommodate the needs of English language learners
- ensure that each student is given clear directions for improvement
- promote students' ability to assess their own learning and to set specific goals
- include the use of samples of students' work that provide evidence of their achievement
- are communicated clearly to students and parents at the beginning of the course and at other appropriate points

"Assessment and Evaluation" from page 22 of *Equity and inclusive education for Ontario schools: Guidelines for policy development and implementation* (2009), http://www.edu.gov.on.ca/eng/policyfunding/inclusiveguide.pdf © Queen's Printer for Ontaio, 2009. Reproduced with permission.

Assessment refers to the ongoing collection of data using a variety of methods. It is the process of gathering information, from a variety of sources, that accurately reflects how well a student is achieving the curriculum expectations in a subject or course (Ontario Ministry of Education, 2010b).

Evaluation is making a judgment based on evidence. It is the determination of the level of understanding, the level of retention, and the ability to apply what the student has learned, and involves judging the quality of student learning on the basis of established criteria and assigning a value to represent that quality. Evaluation is based on assessments of learning that provide data on student achievement at strategic times, typically at the end of a period of learning (Ontario Ministry of Education, 2010b).

Types of Assessment

While provinces and territories are not consistent with how assessment and evaluation are to be addressed, one shared framework is assessment *for* learning, *as* learning, and *of* learning. Tables 5.4 and 5.5 present interpretations of these terms by British Columbia and Ontario, respectively. A distinction is made between formative and summative assessment and criterion, norm, and student-referenced (also called self-referenced) criteria.

Assessment Strategies and Tools

The term *assessment strategies* refers to the tasks we are asking students to engage in or the product we are asking them to create. Teachers use recording devices or assessment tools to examine and assess student work. For example, if you asked students to give a presentation to the class, you might assess the presentation using a rubric. If you asked students to conduct a science investigation, you might use a checklist of expected behaviours as the recording device.

Table 5.6 summarizes a selection of assessment strategies and recording devices or assessment tools. Teachers can choose from a range of assessment strategies that are appropriate to their expectations. Some topics—for example, pollution—lend themselves to oral presentations, while others are more suited to drawings (e.g., classifying leaves) or journal entries (e.g., making observations of the night sky). It is important to use different assessment strategies within and between units.

For each of the assessment strategies in Table 5.6, identify the most appropriate recording device or assessment tool; for example, drawings may be assessed with a rubric. Some assessments in science are particular to the discipline, while others, such as tests, are common across disciplines. Activity 5.8 provides an opportunity to explore some common assessment strategies used in science.

Watch

Assessment

Table 5.4	British Columbia Assessment *for* Learning, *as* Learning, and *of* Learning	
Assessment *for* learning	**Assessment *as* learning**	**Assessment *of* learning**
Formative assessment *ongoing in the classroom*	Formative assessment *ongoing in the classroom*	Summative assessment *occurs at end of year or at key stages*
• teacher assessment, student self-assessment, and/or student peer assessment • criterion-referenced—criteria based on prescribed learning outcomes identified in the provincial curriculum, reflecting performance in relation to a specific learning task • involves both teacher and student in a process of continual reflection and review about progress • teachers adjust their plans and engage in corrective teaching in response to formative assessment	• self-assessment • provides students with information on their own achievement and prompts them to consider how they can continue to improve their learning • student-determined criteria based on previous learning and personal learning goals • students use assessment information to make adaptations to their learning process and to develop new understandings	• teacher assessment • may be either criterion-referenced (based on prescribed learning outcomes) or norm-referenced (comparing student achievement to that of others) • information on student performance can be shared with parents/guardians, school and district staff, and other education professionals (e.g., for the purposes of curriculum development) • used to make judgments about students' performance in relation to provincial standards

Source: British Columbia Ministry of Education. (2006). *Science grade: Integrated resource package 2006*. Victoria, BC: Author. Copyright © Province of British Columbia. All rights reserved. Reproduced with permission of the Province of British Columbia. www.ipp.gov.bc.ca

 **Watch**

Forms of Assessment

ACTIVITY 5.7

21st C

Purpose of Assessment

In groups of three of four, brainstorm the purpose that assessment serves for you, for students, and for parents. Discuss the benefits and challenges of using formative assessments and the strengths and problems inherent in each of norm-referenced, criterion-referenced, and student-referenced assessments. (See Tables 5.4 and 5.5 for definitions.)

Table 5.5	Ontario Assessment *for* Learning, *as* Learning, and *of* Learning	
Assessment *for* learning	**Assessment *as* learning**	**Assessment *of* learning**
"Assessment for learning is the process of seeking and interpreting evidence for use by learners and their teachers to decide where the learners are in their learning, where they need to go, and how best to get there."[1]	"Assessment as learning focuses on the explicit fostering of students' capacity over time to be their own best assessors, but teachers need to start by presenting and modeling external, structured opportunities for students to assess themselves."[2]	"Assessment of learning is the assessment that becomes public and results in statements or symbols about how well students are learning. It often contributes to pivotal decisions that will affect students' futures."[3]

Source: *Growing success: Assessment, evaluation, and reporting in Ontario schools,* First Edition, Covering Grades 1 to 12, page 31. Ministry of Education's website, at http://www.edu.gov.on.ca. © Queen's Printeer for Ontario, 2010. Reproduced with permission.

[1]Assessment Reform Group. (2002). Assessment for learning: 10 principles. p. 2. Available at www.assessment-reform-group.org.

[2]Western and Northern Canadian Protocol for Collaboration in Education. (2006). Rethinking classroom assessment with purpose in mind. Winnipeg: Manitoba Education, Citizenship and Youth. p. 42. Available at www.wncp.ca.

[3]Western and Northern Canadian Protocol, p. 55.

Table 5.6   Assessment Strategies and Recording Devices or Assessment Tools

Assessment strategy	Recording device (or assessment tool)
Culminating task	Anecdotal record
Drawings	Checklist
Interview or conference	Rating scale
Journal or learning log	Rubric
Science notebook	Marking scheme
Presentation	
Portfolio or e-portfolio	
Poster	
Project	
Question and answer	
Test or quiz	
Science investigation (practical)	
Science investigation (report)	
Scrapbook	

ACTIVITY 5.8

21st C ❶ ❹

Matching Assessment Strategies and Recording Devices in Teaching Science

Part A. Complete the table and compare your answers with a peer. Discuss which of the assessment strategies you have seen used successfully, and which you see yourself using and why.

Describing Assessment Strategies

Assessment strategy	Description and purpose	How the strategy might be used	Appropriate recording device
Culminating task			
Quiz			
Science investigation report			
Data table from a science investigation			
Project			
Notebook			
Science investigation performance			
Tests (could include short answer, multiple choice, or long answer questions)			

continued on next page

Observing Children in
Authentic Contexts

Part B. Creating assessment tools
1. Create a checklist for a set of science investigation skills (such as the use of the microscope) or a journal or learning log.
2. Create a rubric for a presentation on the pros and cons of nuclear power.

Self-Assessment

Student self-assessment can be a powerful meta-cognitive device that encourages students to reflect upon, regulate, and monitor how they learn, in order to reach their potential. Self-assessment can offer teachers valuable insight into the reasons for student success or lack of achievement. Strategies for self-assessment include checklists or written answers related to the process and product being assessed, and can be assessments *for* or *as* learning.

Peer Assessment

Peer assessment is often employed as part of the assessment process during cooperative group work. Students can give each other and the teacher valuable feedback. Most often, students are honest and fair; however, some might be uncomfortable with peer evaluation. Teachers who use peer assessment should carefully review student comments before sharing with the class, and should establish clear expectations about constructive and respectful feedback.

CONCLUDING THOUGHTS

Today, the prevailing ethos for many teachers is to teach the whole child and address individual needs. Designing curriculum that meets the needs of students can be a significant challenge for teachers of science. Teachers can modify practices according to the knowledge students bring to class rather than forcing student learning into existing structures and practices. Varied curriculum and practices are needed, particularly for students who are marginalized. Inclusive curricula take into account students' language, unique learning needs, ethnicity, class, gender, and sexual orientation. What follows is a summary of key ideas related to the learning objectives provided at the beginning of the chapter.

Curricular design that creates an inclusive learning environment
Culturally relevant teaching recognizes the importance of including students' cultural backgrounds. Differentiated instruction adapts instruction to meet the needs of individual students. Teachers can customize their program by modifying the content, the process, or the product.

Strategies for understanding students and meeting their learning needs
It is important to acknowledge how the emotional aspects of students' lives impact teaching and learning in science. Howard Gardner (1985) identifies eight intelligences that can inform how teachers address student strengths and areas for growth. He suggests that these multiple intelligences be applied in different contexts. Students with special circumstances and needs may require support as well as modifications and accommodations.

Impact of language and mathematics on learning science
Science education inherently includes literacy and numeracy. Literacy skills are developed as students read, write, listen, and speak in science classrooms. Cueing systems, reading for meaning, and scientific definitions of everyday words should all be explored. Mathematics can pose a barrier for students who do not have basic operational skills, graphing skills, or problem-solving strategies—all of which may need to be explicitly taught.

Assessment and evaluation in teaching science

Assessment refers to the ongoing collection of data using a variety of methods, while *evaluation* refers to making a judgment based on evidence. *Assessment strategies* are the tasks that teachers ask students to engage in or the products they are asked to create. Teachers use recording devices or assessment tools to examine to assess students' work. A collection of assessments can lead to an evaluation or formal grade. Assessment and evaluation practices need to address any discriminatory biases that prevent students from fulfilling their learning potential. Teachers need to address assessment *for* learning, *as* learning, and *of* learning.

BRINGING IT ALL TOGETHER: FINAL QUESTIONS

1. Discuss ways that you can provide a supportive learning environment.
2. Describe specific assessment strategies that are effective in science classrooms.

MyEducationLab®

Visit MyEducationLab® to access an electronic version of the text, as well as a variety of topics that enhance the text material. The topics include the following to support your learning in the course:

- Assessments, including interactive case studies, activities, and video assignments
- Discussion board questions
- Videos, simulations, a lesson plan builder, and other useful course resources

Chapter 6
Curriculum Planning and Implementation

Image Source/Getty Images

LEARNING OBJECTIVES

- Describe the elements of unit planning for teaching science.

- Construct a unit plan, including an evaluation plan and a sequence of topics.

- Explain the factors and considerations inherent in good lesson planning.

- Explore instructional strategies for teaching science.

- Describe and apply the components of lesson plans.

- Explore how to use questioning to extend student thinking.

- Describe how to create a positive classroom climate.

I want to integrate my science with language arts and math.

—Steve, pre-service teacher candidate

How do I do my long-term planning, like three months or the whole year?

—Jen, pre-service teacher candidate

I love that I get to plan everything around themes.

—Ellen, pre-service teacher candidate

21st CENTURY LEARNING SKILLS & COMPETENCIES

❶ Communication

❷ Critical thinking

❸ Collaboration

❹ Creativity

❺ Literacy and numeracy

❻ Media literacy

❼ Technological literacy

INTRODUCTION

This chapter explores the process of curriculum planning, implementation, and assessment, as well as the art of questioning. We will also consider the basic tenets of classroom management as they relate to creating a positive and productive classroom climate and to thoughtful program planning.

Unit planning is examined with student learning in mind. For our purposes, a unit of study takes several weeks to implement, and elementary science curriculum is typically organized into four or five units over the course of the school year. Lesson planning refers to the daily planning of curriculum and instruction, where each lesson takes about one class period to implement.

We are assuming that unit plans are more abstract and may be developed without a particular group of students in mind, whereas lessons are designed for your own students. You may plan a unit that requires additional enrichment activities for gifted students. Similarly you may prepare a unit with a considerable reading and writing component that needs to be adapted for students with varying abilities in literacy. Alternatively, you may plan a unit with several group activities, such as debates or role-plays, but your lessons may require adaptation for students who find collaborative work challenging.

Curricular planning must attend to diverse learners, and it takes into account differentiated instruction, culturally relevant pedagogy, and assessment issues. Remember the importance of an equity framework when planning. Ask yourself how you interact with students; how you make choices in the examples, materials, and resources you use to build curriculum; and what bias exists within the discipline. Refer to Chapter 4 for a full explanation of the framework.

LESSON AND UNIT PLANNING: AN OVERVIEW

👁‍🗨 Watch

Planning for Instruction

In general, unit plans provide an overall road map of how the unit will unfold, what topics will be covered, and activities and strategies that will be utilized. A unit plan follows a basic route, while lesson plans provide the detailed itinerary of the day. Table 6.1 compares lesson and unit plans.

Table 6.1 Comparison of Lesson and Unit Plans

	Lesson plan	Unit plan
When to prepare	Daily/weekly. Try to plan a few lessons in advance and then adapt as needed. This will help you stay organized.	Prior to a new unit. Ideally planning should take place before the school year, or well before the start of the unit.
Student issues	Plan with specific students in mind; meets specific student needs.	Plan with a generic student profile based on what you know about students from past experiences.
Level of specificity	Detailed; includes outcomes or expectations, teaching and assessment strategies, materials required, time allotment, questions to ask, homework to assign, and so on.	General; broad strokes that provide a guide for pre-planning—such as field trip bookings, materials to order, resources to gather, community or parent involvement.
Assessment	Depends on context; might be diagnostic, formative, or summative.	Plan includes indicators of what students are expected to do and know by the end of the unit, what will be evaluated, and how a grade will be derived.
Metaphor of a road trip	This is the detailed plan for one day out of a trip. It might be: Get up early, go to a market in the morning, a museum in afternoon, and a restaurant for dinner. Another day might be: Sleep in, eat brunch, hike in the afternoon, and have a picnic dinner.	This is the itinerary that indicates where you will be on any given day and the general route you will follow, including the attractions along the way.

UNIT PLANNING

For our purposes, *unit of study* refers to the entire teaching and learning sequence, from the introduction of the unit to the final evaluation. A unit of study typically takes 25–30 hours to complete; however, it is important to be flexible with scheduling. Once you put your unit plan into practice, it will inevitably change. Student questions, ideas, and interests may present meaningful new directions of study. It is a good idea to leave time at the end of each unit to allow for this flexibility.

Elementary school teachers would be wise to consider even longer-term planning by creating a year overview or year-at-a-glance plan that maps out all the topics that will be taught across the curriculum. This overview will allow you to make meaningful cross-curricular connections between science and other subject areas, to plan across the curriculum according to themes (e.g., harvest, weather patterns), and to time your teaching to align with seasonal activities (e.g., connecting a unit on forces with the annual school skating trip) and unique occurrences (e.g., timing an astronomy unit to coincide with a solar eclipse). You will also be able to coordinate your plan with other teachers to allow for collaborative teaching opportunities and to ensure access to shared learning resources and science equipment. An example of a year overview is provided in Appendix 6.A.

The language of curriculum documents varies across provinces and territories. For example some jurisdictions use the terms *objectives*, *outcomes*, *expectations*, or *standards* to refer to what students are expected to learn. Curriculum documents also use organizational language such as *strand*, *module*, *topic*, or *unit*. Activity 6.1 provides an opportunity to examine the language of the curriculum documents in your region.

ACTIVITY 6.1   *21st C* ② ⑤ ⑥

Working with Resources: How Are Science Curriculum Documents Organized?

For this activity, you will need access to your provincial or territorial elementary science curriculum documents, which are usually available on your ministry or department of education website. Each province has a unique organizational structure, and as such this activity might have to be adjusted to fit your requirements. For our purposes here, *unit* and *topic* are synonymous.

1. Read the introductory pages, sometimes referred to as the *front matter*, of your elementary science curriculum document. What key ideas are described in the document with respect to the following? (Your provincial document may not explicitly include all of these topics.)

   - the goals of science programs
   - the nature of science (NOS)
   - fundamental concepts, big ideas, or enduring understandings
   - curriculum outcomes, expectations, or objectives
   - skills of scientific investigation
   - literacy and numeracy
   - cross-curricular integration
   - Aboriginal content
   - environmental education
   - the role of information and communications technology in science
   - involvement of parents and guardians

2. Identify the organizing labels of the document, such as *physical science* or *Earth and space science*.
3. Describe how specific outcomes or expectations are organized within each strand (for example, knowledge, skills, values, STSE, inquiry).
4. List the units for a curriculum you might teach during your practicum (there is usually one unit per strand).

continued on next page

DISCUSSION QUESTIONS

1. Look through the outcomes for each of the Grade 3 and Grade 7 units. Which are you most comfortable with? Least comfortable with?
2. What does the curriculum document say (if anything) about assessment and evaluation? For example, is there an achievement chart to guide your planning?
3. Comment on the clarity of the teaching outcomes and expectations.

When planning a unit of study, many perspectives will come into play. Some of them are obvious, some are subtle, and many are teacher-specific. Teachers are constantly making practical and philosophical decisions. For example, you might ask yourself what resources will you use; what will you ask students to do; what teaching and assessment strategies will you employ; how will you motivate uninterested and marginalized youth; how will you challenge gifted students; how will you organize the classroom; what skills of inquiry will you highlight; what emphasis will you choose; how will you include NOS, social justice, and STSE perspectives; and what teaching philosophy will underpin your work? The remainder of the chapter can serve as a planning guide. Adapt it as needed to meet the needs of the diverse learners in your classroom.

> Choose a unit that you are likely to teach during your practicum to anchor the activities in the remainder of this chapter (e.g., Grade 1: Needs of Living Things or Grade 5: Forces and Simple Machines). If possible, discuss with your sponsor practicum teacher what science topics you will be teaching.

ACTIVITY 6.2   21st C ② ⑤ ⑥

Planning with Equity in Mind

For your unit of choice, examine the outcomes or expectations you will be teaching. Summarize, in a few sentences, the main ideas in the unit. Locate two resources, such as books, videos, websites, magazines, or articles, that will help you plan your unit. Critique these resources with respect to the equity framework discussed in Chapter 4: a) interactions with students; b) curriculum choices; and c) bias within the discipline of science.

DISCUSSION QUESTIONS

1. Give one aspect of each of the resources that supports the framework.
2. Detail any bias inherent in the resources you chose.
3. Would you recommend your resources to a colleague? Explain.
4. In what ways is the framework helpful in planning inclusive curricula?

Ensuring a Balanced Approach

Every unit in science is distinct and lends itself to a unique approach. Teachers need to determine a balance between teaching the concepts, observing phenomena, designing and doing science investigations and developing skills of inquiry, and connecting science, technology, society, and environment (STSE). For example, a unit on astronomy may involve a field trip to a planetarium, but it is unlikely to involve an open-ended experiment. A unit that explores the properties of matter will likely have several investigations, and a unit on climate change may involve a research project. As you plan units, choose appropriate instructional strategies that support a balanced approach and ensure students have a meaningful learning experience.

Learning outcomes and expectations and selected instructional strategies need to be directly aligned with assessment strategies and tools. The tools you choose for assessing content and skills learning will necessarily be different. Be sure to select a range of assessment strategies that fit with the student expectations, activities, and tasks. Assessment is discussed further throughout the chapter.

Additionally as you plan units of study, consider the degree to which you will include student-centred and teacher-centred experiences to address knowledge, inquiry, and STSE components.

Activity 6.3 explores how a unit can be planned with a balanced approach. You may need to refer to Chapter 8 for more details on science investigations.

ACTIVITY 6.3   *21st C* ❸ ❹

Exploring a Balanced Approach

Work individually, in pairs, or in small groups. For your unit of choice, brainstorm one or two possible activities and assessment strategies you might use in your classroom for each of the suggested student experiences in the table. Refer to your curriculum documents.

Next, repeat the exercise for a different unit from a different grade. If you have already brainstormed activities for K–3, choose a unit from Grades 4–8, and vice versa.

Exploring a Balanced Approach

Student experiences	Outcomes or expectations addressed	Description of activity or task	Assessment strategies and tools
Independent reading about science content			
Science investigation to confirm a science concept			
Open-ended science investigation			
Research project with a presentation			
STSE-focused activity			
Field trip			
Other			

DISCUSSION QUESTIONS

1. Which components of the table were easiest to complete? Why?
2. Which components of the table were most difficult to complete? Why?
3. Are there some student experiences that are more difficult to create tasks for? Which ones? Why do you think this is the case?

Team Work

Pre-planning Considerations and Decisions

There are many considerations to be addressed even *before* creating a unit plan. Begin by reading through your curriculum document's outcomes or expectations and familiarize yourself with what is mandated in the unit. The following are some pre-planning considerations.

1. Identifying Themes

Identify general themes from the outcomes or expectations in the curriculum document and from local contexts that can act as a focal point for the unit. Themes help link ideas in a relevant and meaningful way for students and can make planning easier when we link science topics to other subject areas. For example, a Grade 4 class in Northern Ontario might use the theme of mining to study rocks and minerals. This theme could also connect to the geography of the region and the influence of mining on the local economy, environment, and culture.

2. Fundamental Concepts, Big Ideas, and Enduring Understandings

Establishing curriculum priorities is one of the first steps of long-term or unit planning. You will need to decide what you consider to be an essential understanding (*must* know), what you consider to be important (*should* know), and what you think is worth being familiar with (*good* to know). In a perfect world without time restrictions, you would be able to teach all of the material in the unit in depth; in reality it is important to ensure that you focus on the big ideas. We are not suggesting that there are curriculum outcomes or expectations that you ignore or dismiss, but rather that you prioritize what you see as central. It is important to be mindful of these fundamental concepts while making decisions about resources, materials, student abilities, and skills and concepts that will be built upon in further science learning.

3. Assessing the Unit

As you plan the unit, keep in mind the three major types of assessment: assessment *for* learning, assessment *as* learning, and assessment *of* learning. Assessment for learning helps students know what they need to learn in order to be successful. Assessment as learning is student-driven formative assessment that allows the student to trace their learning and decide how to best improve their achievement. While assessment as learning consists primarily of student self-assessment, teachers can act as facilitators by providing time for student reflection and supporting students' critical analyses. Assessment of learning is typically a summative assessment at the end of a unit of study that is used to communicate student performance to parents and guardians. How will you assess students' understanding of fundamental concepts? How will you know that your students have learned the fundamental concepts of the lesson? What strategies will you use that will allow students to show what they know and can do? Which assessment tools will you use? Assessment strategies should align with the knowledge and skills to be learned. Consider assessment throughout the unit planning process, as it will inform both your long-term planning and day-to-day practice.

4. Launching the Unit

A launch introduces students to a new topic. It may be a modest introduction, such as an explanation of what they may expect during the unit, or a brainstorming session to assess what they know and want to know about the topic. It could also involve a guest speaker, a field trip, or another special event. Think about resources within your school and community that might be used to make the launch of a unit memorable and inspiring. Launches provide an opportunity to motivate students, to assess prior knowledge, and to create a need to know.

5. Bringing Closure to the Unit

Closure can take many forms, including a celebration of work produced, a culminating task, a summative test, or an event that provides consolidation of the key concepts from the unit. It could also take the form of a presentation of work to an audience of peers, parents, or community members.

6. Designing a Major Project

Some units are planned to include a major project that can address several unit outcomes and expectations. A major project may involve research in the library and on the web, and a subsequent presentation to the class. The project may also include a culminating activity. Alternately, it may include an open-ended scientific investigation or a technology design project. Project-based work can include both written and oral components and can support the development of independent study skills. When planning for major projects, identify what students will do and what they will produce. If appropriate, include your students in the process of setting project requirements and goals. Be mindful of and realistic about the time required to complete the project. Will the work be done at school? Will work also be done at home?

7. Identifying Resources

Resources can help engage students in a unit of study. Make a list of learning resources such as books, course profiles, media, visual aids (e.g., posters and charts), audio-visual materials, computer simulations, computer-assisted activities, and relevant websites. Preview as many of these resources as possible and flag ideas that might help in planning. During the process, be mindful of bias and how science is represented. Be aware of spending too much time gathering resources without scheduling sufficient time to preview them carefully and effectively. Confer with colleagues about resources they found useful, and speak with your school librarian about science-related literature and trade books that might support your teaching.

8. Mastering the Subject Matter Content Knowledge

Teachers have different strengths with respect to knowledge of science content. For example, you may feel comfortable teaching physical science units but unsure about some topics in Earth and space science. Refer to a textbook or other reference books to refresh and fill any gaps in your science content knowledge (CK); websites can also help answer specific questions. Some pedagogical content knowledge (PCK), such as co-operative learning strategies, may also need to be reviewed in preparation for specific student activities.

9. Selecting Appropriate Instructional Strategies and Activities

Throughout any unit, there will be opportunities for students to learn through listening, speaking, reading, and writing. Students may appreciate opportunities to make choices about what they will do. Choosing the appropriate strategy depends on several factors, such as the purpose and content of the lesson, and how it will support learning goals. Are the strategies new to your students? What is required for students to be able to successfully participate in any of these strategies? Some strategies can be combined. For example, you might assign a research project or laboratory exercise that includes an oral presentation. Below is a list of instructional strategies you might incorporate into a unit (for more information, refer to Appendix A).

- science investigations (guided, structured, or open-ended)
- design challenge
- teacher demonstration
- problem-solving exercise
- reading exercise
- cooperative small group activity (e.g., jigsaw)
- simulation
- computer-assisted activity
- research project
- case study
- role-play
- oral presentation

- debate
- question and answer
- short lecture
- class discussion of an issue or problem
- guest speaker or other community resource
- video
- field trip
- meta-cognition exercises
- research projects

10. Choosing Equipment and Supplies

It is necessary to identify and order any materials that are not available in the school, and to ensure that all needed equipment is in good working order. If purchasing equipment or supplies, be sure to find out if your school has designated funds for science equipment. You may be required to pre-book equipment at the school or within the school district.

11. Nurturing Positive Parent and Guardian Involvement

In elementary school, it is important to actively include parents and guardians in their children's learning. You might have parents visit your class as guest speakers with special expertise, or they could help provide supervision during field trips. Parents and guardians can be invited to be part of an audience for the presentation of a culminating task, a final exhibit of student work, or student presentations. Discussing upcoming topics can encourage open communication with parents and guardians and foster a positive and supportive relationship.

12. Meeting Student Needs

Part of good planning is considering diversity and situating all students at the centre of your plan. Be mindful of the different ways that students learn, including special needs, and of how your plan will support their learning. Pay attention to culturally relevant and community-informed practices.

Drafting the Unit Plan: Start with the End in Mind

We suggest that you begin a unit plan draft by becoming familiar with the outcomes or expectations for which you are responsible. Determine the unit's fundamental concepts, make an evaluation plan, create a logical sequence of content and activities, and establish a timeline. It can be helpful to draft your plan as a flow chart, concept map, or learning hierarchy. For elementary school teachers, it can be particularly useful to plan using a mind map or concept map, which will allow you to easily make connections between activities. As you make your plan, consider assessment strategies and determine what students will be required to do in order to show what they have learned.

Assessment planning is often left to the end of unit planning, however as assessment must align directly with learning objectives, it should always be planned simultaneously. This process is often referred to as backward design, or planning with the end in mind (McTighe & Thomas, 2005; Wiggins & McTighe, 1998).

Pacing of unit activities is an ongoing challenge for many teachers. Carefully plan timelines, including deadlines, so that the content of the entire unit is addressed and no important part of learning is missed or rushed. Planning a timeline also helps with booking library visits, field trips, and guest speakers. Activity 6.4 will guide you through a unit drafting process.

ACTIVITY 6.4

21st C

Unit Planning: Making a Draft

Part A. Determine Enduring Understandings

Use your unit of choice from the previous activities and the curriculum documents. Summarize what students will know, understand, and be able to do by the end of this unit. Identify enduring understandings with an asterisk.

Enduring Understandings

What students will know, understand, and be able to do:

Part B. Assessment and Evaluation

When you draft an evaluation plan, make the distinction between the assessment strategy (how students will demonstrate what they know and can do), and the assessment tool or recording device (what you will use to evaluate student work). The table below outlines a few examples of assessment strategies and tools.

Assessment Strategies and Tools

Some sample assessment strategies	Assessment tools
Culminating task	Anecdotal record
Interview	Checklist
Journal or learning log	Marking scheme
Oral presentation	Rating scale
Portfolio/ePortfolio	Rubric
Project	
Question and answer	
Science investigation performance	
Science notebook	
Test or quiz	

Using your unit of choice, complete the next table to create an evaluation plan. You may need to return to this table and make adjustments as you complete your unit plan. We provide two examples for a unit on simple machines.

continued on next page

Making an Evaluation Plan

Outcomes or expectations	Assessment strategy	Assessment tool
Design a toy that incorporates two simple machines.	Project	Rubric
Investigate the structure and function of simple machines.	Science investigation performance	Checklist

Part C. Planning the Sequence of Lessons

Briefly outline what each lesson will include, assuming 25–30 hours per unit. This is only a guide, though, and you will likely need to adjust the schedule as you progress. Your lessons might range in length from 20 to 90 minutes depending on your schedule, the grade level and age of your students, and the specific activities you intend to include. Find a flow of lessons that works for you and your students that is also flexible in sequence to allow for teachable moments and changes of direction. Remember to include a range of instructional strategies and activities.

You might use the computer to cluster your curriculum outcomes or expectations, or you could cluster them manually using strips of paper. Match the expectations to the lesson titles, identify how you will assess them, and briefly draft what you and your students will do for each lesson. Complete the table below and extend as needed.

Draft Unit Plan: Sequence of Lessons

Lesson title or topic	Outcomes or expectations	Assessment or evaluation	What will the teacher do?	What will the students do?
1				
2				
3				
4				
5				
6				
7				
8				
9				
10				

REFLECTING ON THE UNIT PLAN DRAFT

Once you have drafted your unit overview, look at the unit as a whole. Consider the following:

- Is each intended outcome or expectation supported by a suitable teaching or learning strategy?

- Is a valid assessment strategy included for each enduring understanding?
- Will students have opportunities to be involved in sensory, experiential learning with concrete materials?
- Will students have opportunities to sufficiently develop their inquiry and communication skills, regardless of their initial skill level?

Post-Implementation Reflections

At the end of every unit, it is a good idea to reflect on the experience and the efficacy of the plan. Record any changes you would make if you used this unit plan again. Keep a folder with the unit plan and any handouts marked with the needed revisions.

As you consider the efficacy of your unit, think about your evaluation plan. Did you follow it? Did you assess too much or too little? Did you vary your assessment strategies? What were your students' experiences of the unit? How well did you promote student learning? What could you change about the unit so that more students are successful? What might be modified to reflect greater student inclusion?

Reflect as well on your planned and actual curriculum. What did you intend to teach? What did you actually teach? What did you opt to omit and why? What did you choose to teach explicitly and what did you choose to teach implicitly?

LESSON PLANNING

As you gain experience, you will develop your own planning and organizational style. We believe that teachers should develop a lesson planning method that suits their own preferences. Lesson planning is complex and non-linear; it does not involve following a simple algorithm. Instead, it details what learning will occur, teaching notes, student materials, teaching and learning strategies, and how learning will be assessed.

Central to lesson planning is meeting the individual needs of diverse student groups. When the unique experiences and understandings that students bring to the classroom are embraced, you can begin to meet the needs of all students. Your planning will evolve to include differentiated instruction and fair practices for assessment. Consider how each of your teacher education courses helps you to analyze your assumptions about teaching and learning, about yourself, and about what science education is for. Teaching to a diverse student population and meeting needs of individuals is a life-long learning journey.

Daily lesson planning takes into account all aspects of pedagogical content (Shulman, 1986; see also Gess-Newsome, 2002) and context knowledge (Barnett & Hodson, 2001). We explore lesson planning as pedagogy refinement, planning as the development of judgment, and lesson plans as manifestations of theory into practice.

Planning Lessons: Student Considerations

1. Assessing Prior Knowledge and Identifying Misconceptions

David Ausubel (1968) is known for stressing that the most important issue for teachers as they plan how to teach new material is to consider what students already know. Always assess the prior knowledge of your students before beginning to implement your plan, and consider how to proceed if students' background knowledge is disparate. It is essential to fill in any knowledge or skill gaps students might have and yet not become bogged down with too much review. Determine any misconceptions (Chapter 12 will explore misconceptions in more detail) that students may hold; these will inform what you teach and how you teach it. Also think about what you might do if there is a wide range of understandings in your students.

Watch

Student Ideas about What Is Moving in Plants [positive]

2. Motivating Students

Students will be more engaged in learning if they are interested in, and motivated by, the material being taught. It is helpful to incorporate students' interests in curriculum planning whenever possible. For example, a group of students might be interested in robots; you could incorporate this interest in a design project for a unit on simple machines. Find out about students' interests, what they would like to learn, and how you might actively include them in the planning process.

3. Knowing Your Students and Fostering Inclusion

It is important to plan lessons that recognize the cultural traditions of students and respect students' privacy, personal beliefs, and unique personalities. When teachers *know* their students, they can work to create a safe and inclusive learning environment where all students feel they can take risks, contribute, and share in the decision-making processes of the class community. When planning lessons, ensure that all students feel included regardless of ethnicity, language differences, cultural traditions, religion, socio-economic class, gender, sexual orientation, learning style, and ability.

ACTIVITY 6.5

21st C **2 3 4**

Factors That Influence Planning

Read the two scenarios that follow, and list all of the factors that would inform your planning. In pairs, answer the discussion questions.

Scenario 1

You are teaching in an urban elementary school and most of your students live in surrounding high-rise apartments. There are few parks nearby, and your students' opportunities to spend time in natural spaces are limited. Much of their free time is spent playing with friends in the apartment courtyards and alone playing video games. As part of your life science unit, you decide to take the class on a field trip to a natural wooded area with a marsh and stream.

Scenario 2

You are teaching at a rural elementary school. Your school's catchment area is large, covering a small town and an agricultural community, and most students are bused in to school. Most of them live in town or on farms. There are also several First Nations students in the class. As part of your unit on environmental science, you plan to take your students on a field trip to a beaver dam near the school.

DISCUSSION QUESTIONS

1. With your partner, compare your list of factors to be considered in each scenario.
2. How would you structure a field trip for each group?
3. What would you expect students to do and how would you assess what they already know?

What Is a Lesson Plan?

Lesson plans—the daily plans and materials used with students—fulfill many purposes and are used differently by every teacher. Good lessons have clear learning outcomes or expectations and goals. Ask the following: Do your students know what to do? Are students doing what is expected? How can you assess whether they have learned what was intended? Lesson plans are a guide to help ensure that these three things happen.

For our purposes, a lesson is a teaching and learning episode that lasts for one class period. However, every elementary school timetable is different, and your science lessons might range from 20 minutes to 90 minutes, depending on your schedule, the age of your students, and the activities you have planned. For these reasons, many teachers view lessons differently; some see each period in the timetable as one lesson, while others see a sequence of periods as a lesson even though it may extend over several days.

Good lessons include a variety of instructional strategies, some degree of individualization for students to pursue interests, a range of assessment strategies, probing questions, and a balance of teacher talk and student talk. Good lessons also take into consideration how to motivate students, make the science lesson relevant, and address the unique strengths and needs of diverse learners.

Lesson plans are highly personal, and highlight teacher beliefs about behaviour and classroom management. For example, some teachers follow a routine: They may begin each lesson with a review of the last class or with a problem to solve. While each teacher might have the same purpose—to focus students—each will do so in a different way. Your lessons provide insight into your students' needs and what you believe is important about science. Teachers are constantly negotiating between being in control and being controlling. They must decide whether to be a facilitator, manager, guide, or coach as different needs arise. In implementing lesson plans, teachers regularly have to react in the moment and make impromptu revisions. Be flexible, but do not abandon your underlying purpose, and maintain high expectations for both your students and yourself.

Instructional Strategies

Effective lessons include a variety of instructional strategies; Table 6.2 provides examples of strategies used in elementary science classrooms. The strategies are grouped into six categories for the purposes of the activity that follows. For additional instructional strategies used in teaching elementary science, see Appendix A.

Table 6.2   Instructional Strategies

Teacher-Directed Activities	*Student-Centred and Small-Group Activities*
• Teacher demonstrations • Short lectures • Questions and answers • Field trips	• Computer-assisted activities • Simulations • Cooperative small group activities • Case studies
Independent Study	*Whole-Class Activities*
• Problem-solving exercises • Research projects • Reading exercises • Meta-cognition exercises	• Class discussions • Role-plays • Debates
Science Investigations	*Whole-Class Focus*
• Guided or structured problem-solving investigations • Experiments or open-ended investigations • Design challenges	• Oral presentations • Guest speakers • Videos

ACTIVITY 6.6   *21st C* ❷

Instructional Strategies: Opportunities for Inclusive Teaching and Learning

Choose two of the categories in Table 6.2. For each, answer the following questions:

1. What is the role of the teacher?

2. What are the learning goals for students?

continued on next page

3. What kind of information can be collected to assess achievement?
4. What opportunities will students have to learn through listening, speaking, reading, and writing?
5. Are students given the chance to work independently, in pairs, or in groups?
6. Explain how the strategy might be active or passive.
7. How does your your choice of teaching strategy support or hinder an inclusive classroom environment. Are some strategies more inclusive than others? Provide examples.

LESSON DESIGN

There are many models of lesson design that inform lesson planning. (See, for example, Maynes, 2010, and Schwartz & Pollishuke, 2013.) In this section, we share models commonly used by elementary school teachers and describe the components that are typically included in elementary science lesson plans.

Three-Part Lesson

(Adapted from Ontario College of Teachers, 2010; Schwartz & Pollishuke, 2013)

The three-part lesson consists of three parts that, depending on the resource (e.g., Ontario College of Teachers, 2010; Schwartz & Pollishuke, 2013), are named differently. Typically, the lesson includes the following three components:

1. introduction
2. body
3. closing

The introduction (also referred to as the *opening, mental set, hook,* or *getting started*) prepares students by briefly reviewing previous lessons and prerequisite knowledge; capturing and engaging student attention with a motivating story, question, problem, demonstration, or visual; and sharing the purpose, expectations, and assessment of the lesson. The opening is typically teacher-focused and takes about 10 to 15 minutes.

The body of the lesson (also called *work session,* or *working on it*) is the activity component of the lesson—the *doing* part. Here, students will be actively involved in learning through group work, partner activities, and independent practice. The body of a lesson should be student-focused; the teacher provides input to students on their work, demonstrates and models activities, poses questions to extend thinking, and checks for student understanding. This part of the lesson can take 30 to 45 minutes, depending on the age of your students and the length of your class periods.

The closing of the lesson (also called *conclusion, closure,* or *consolidation and practice*) brings together the big ideas learned in the lesson; ideas are summarized and connected to prior knowledge, and new understandings are reflected upon. During this component, work might be shared in whole class discussions, or students might provide a ticket out the door or apply what they have learned to their own lives. All too often, the closing of a lesson is minimized or left out because of time constraints. However, it is an important component; if time is running short, reduce the time spent on the body of the lesson to allow for a proper closure. Closing typically takes 10 to 15 minutes.

Lesson Plan Components

Some teachers write out their teaching notes, outlining in detail what they will say and what questions they will pose. Others simply jot rough notes of the lesson outcomes, assessments, and activities. However, as a beginning teacher, it is advantageous to be thorough in your planning. As you become more experienced, you will determine what works best for you. The lesson components listed below, and the sample lesson plan templates in Appendix 6.B, can help you to organize your planning. Sample 4 in Appendix 6.B draws on Targeted Implementation and Planning Supports (TIPS), a three-part lesson plan developed by the Ontario Ministry of Education for implementation of mathematics curricula.

Prescribed Outcomes or Expectations and Learning Goals The ministry or department of education sets out prescribed learning outcomes or expectations. In this part of the lesson plan, you will identify specific prescribed outcomes or expectations and determine how they will be addressed in your lesson. Be realistic about what a lesson can cover; it is best to focus on teaching one or two outcomes well rather than attempting to get through several. You might find it helpful to make a list of learning goals (i.e., what you tell students is the purpose of the lesson) in simple, student-friendly language.

Assessment You will need to determine whether your students are meeting the learning goals of the lesson. Your assessment strategy will differ from lesson to lesson, and may be formative, summative, or both. As in unit planning, assessment is often left to the end of the lesson plan, but given its importance in informing curriculum and instruction, make direct connections between assessment strategies and lesson objectives early in the planning process. Refer to the evaluation plan discussed in Activity 6.4—such a plan can help you to outline assessments that support your overall strategy.

Adaptations and Modifications Make note of any adaptations or modifications to your plan that are necessary to meet the needs of students with individualized education plans (IEPs) and unique learning needs. These might include changes to the outcomes or expectations of the lesson, to the activities, or to the assessment strategies.

Introduction The introduction describes what will be used to engage and motivate students in the first few minutes of the lesson. It should help to establish a positive classroom climate. An introduction may take the form of, for example, a focus question, a review of previous material, a brainstorming activity, or a demonstration.

Materials, Equipment, and Safety Considerations List the materials, equipment, and technology you will use in your lesson. Also note any safety considerations that need to be taught to or reviewed with students.

Instructional Strategies, Sequence, and Timing Map out the sequence of the lesson and how to move students forward in knowledge, skills, and values. The body of the lesson plan details what you and the students will be doing, what instructional strategies are used, and what support materials are needed. Your instructional strategies support students in learning the specific science concepts or skills. When planning the strategies, sequence, and timing of your lesson, ask yourself the following: Do your students have opportunities to discuss, construct, and communicate new knowledge? How will you differentiate instruction? How will your students use higher-order thinking skills to develop concepts? Are your students working individually, in pairs, or in small groups? What will your students be doing (listening, speaking, reading, writing), and what materials will they be using (paper, pencil, technology, science supplies)? How will your choice of strategies determine the way you will interact with students?

Closure Your plan should include a way to end the lesson that pulls together the big ideas of the lesson and consolidates the concepts and skills learned. It might include a check for conceptual understanding, and should prepare students for the follow-up activity or lesson. Often this involves a whole-class discussion.

Notes and Post-Lesson Reflections Make notes during or at the end of the lesson. These reflections allow you to compare what you had hoped to achieve in the lesson with what was achieved. Jot down reminders for the next day or revisions to the lesson for future use.

ACTIVITY 6.7   *21st C*

So Many Ideas—But What's the Plan?

In pairs, examine the various teaching suggestions outlined below for teaching a Grade 1 unit on daily and seasonal changes. Decide which ones you would use, and order them in a coherent sequence. If you decide not to use any of the ideas, replace them with your own, and add additional strategies as you see fit. You may want to consult a textbook or a curriculum document to assist you.

A) Question and answer with pictures
With students at the carpet, go through pictures of plants and animals in different seasons (e.g., tree with leaves changing colours in autumn, flowering plants in spring, migrating birds in spring and autumn, a hibernating bear in winter). Ask students in what seasons they think the pictures were taken and how they know. Also ask what else students might see in that season.

B) Weather chart and graph
Each day, during the morning routine or calendar time, observe the weather and make note of the temperature, wind, clouds, and precipitation. Record on a class chart, and also have students keep track in their science notebooks in drawings and words. Have students discuss and compare the weather patterns across weeks and months.

C) Clothes-sorting activity
Seat students in a circle and place a bag of clothing in the centre. Ask students to help you sort through the clothes and organize the articles according to season. Four volunteers can hold boxes for each of the seasons. Go through the clothes piece by piece, asking students what season the clothing would be worn in and why, and then place in the corresponding box. Be sure to include some challenging pieces that could fit into more than one season.

D) Computer simulation
Using an interactive whiteboard, show your students a computer simulation that illustrates the movement of Earth on its axis and in its orbit around the Sun.

E) Flip book of the Sun's position in the sky
Give students photocopied drawings that show the Sun's position in the sky from sunrise to sunset. Have students order them from sunrise to sunset. You might wish to have the drawings precut on card stock. Students can check their order with two partners, and then come to you to staple the cards together. As you staple each student's book, have the student briefly describe the daily movement of the Sun across the sky.

F) Seasonal schoolyard drawings

Give each student a piece of paper that is divided into four sections labelled spring, summer, autumn, and winter. As an example brainstorm with your students what they might see in the schoolyard in the spring, and list these on the board or on chart paper. Have students draw their own schoolyard ideas for each season. When complete, students can share their drawings with the class, describing what they have drawn and why.

G) Tracing shadows activity

Before the lesson, draw a chalk line several metres long on a sunny, paved area of the schoolyard. Mark points about one metre apart along the line. Students will be working in pairs; make one point per pair. At different time intervals (e.g., 9:00 a.m., 10:00 a.m., 11:00 a.m., noon, and so on) throughout the day, have students go outside with their partners and, standing on their point on the line, trace their shadows with chalk. After the last tracing of the day, have students talk with their partners about the changes in their shadow (size, direction, etc.). Photograph each of the pairs' tracings to use in later lessons.

H) Matching memory game

Create two sets of cards—one labelled spring, summer, autumn, and winter, and the other showing pictures characteristic of each of the seasons (e.g., sports, activities). With a partner, students turn all cards facedown and take turns turning over two cards and trying to make a match between the season and picture. This game could also be played between the teacher and class, using a projector.

I) Children's literature

Share a story that involves daily or seasonal changes. As you read, ask students about the changes that are occurring, why they are occurring, and how they know. Some books you might share include Eve Bunting's *Sunflower House*, Julie Fogliano's *And then it's Spring*, and Sheryl MacFarlane's *Waiting for Whales*.

DISCUSSION QUESTIONS

1. Share and compare your lesson sequence with another group.
2. Which suggestions did you like, reject, or modify? What did you add? Why?
3. What prior knowledge is assumed for these activities?
4. Which lessons would you use to assess your students' understanding? How?
5. What is the logical next step or follow-up to these lessons?

THE ART OF QUESTIONING

Questions are at the heart of good teaching and learning. Sometimes teachers carefully plan a series of questions in advance to help develop specific skills, knowledge, or attitudes, or to meet specific learning outcomes or expectations. Teachers also use questions "in the moment" to help students clarify their learning and to assess understanding.

Teachers ask question in all learning contexts to support student learning. When you enter an elementary classroom you might see, for example, the teacher:

- circulating and asking probing questions as students work in groups
- asking students to apply what they have learned from an activity in a learning centre
- asking questions to check student understanding during a science investigation
- posing questions to focus the class while performing a demonstration
- asking students to clarify their explanations of a science phenomenon
- wrapping up a unit of study with review questions to consolidate student learning

Watch

Investigating Goldfish
(Part 1)

Questions are a significant aspect of designing and implementing curricula that meets students' needs. They can help establish relationships, involve students, and draw on students' experiences.

On the surface, asking questions seems straightforward; we do it all the time in our daily interactions. However, from a pedagogical perspective, asking questions—good questions—requires careful planning on the part of the teacher. As Kestner (2012) said, "If kids can Google the answers, maybe we are asking them the wrong questions."

Bloom's Taxonomy

In 1956 Benjamin Bloom published a taxonomy that captured an array of cognitive thinking skills, ranging from lower-order thinking skills (LOTS; e.g., recalling a piece of information) to higher-order thinking skills (HOTS; e.g., critiquing a piece of work). His taxonomy has been used to help teachers think about the kinds of goals they set for their students. Bloom's original taxonomy includes knowledge, comprehension, application, analysis, synthesis, and evaluation. More recently, his taxonomy has been modified slightly (see, for example, Anderson & Krathwohl, 2001) to replace synthesis with creating, and knowledge with recall or remembering. Table 6.3 provides a summary of the taxonomy (from Bloom, 1956; Anderson & Krathwohl, 2001), sample questions or tasks, and key words to help you form questions that move students from lower- to higher-order thinking skills. As students develop higher-order thinking skills they will be able to pose higher-order questions.

Table 6.3 Bloom's Taxonomy			
Category	**Definition**	**Sample questions or tasks**	**Sample verbs**
Remembering (LOTS)	Recall of previously learned material	Which planet is about the same size as Earth? Define force, tension, compression, and load.	Choose, copy, name, recall, state, match, find, define, tell, list, describe, relate, locate, write
Understanding (LOTS)	Ability to grasp and explain meaning	How are living and nonliving things different? Summarize and describe forces resulting from natural phenomena (e.g. wind, tornadoes) that can have consequences for structures.	Calculate, change, compare, match, relate, show, explain, interpret, outline, discuss, distinguish, predict, restate, describe, summarize
Applying (LOTS)	Use of knowledge in a new situation, to consider elements, relationships, organizational structures	Classify rocks as igneous, sedimentary, or metamorphic. Apply knowledge of force to explain how sports equipment (e.g. helmets) protects the body	Produce, perform, modify, experiment, interpret, construct, solve, show, use, illustrate, complete, examine, classify, apply
Analyzing (HOTS)	Break information into component parts and determine how the parts relate to one another	Compare and contrast different types of mechanical systems (e.g., pulley, lever, gear).	Research, illustrate, investigate, classify, compare, contrast, analyze, distinguish, categorize, identify, explain, separate
Evaluating (HOTS)	The ability to make judgments about information, validate of ideas, or develop opinions	Decide if you support the creation of a neighbourhood playground and defend your decision. Evaluate the impact of the environment on structures or mechanisms (e.g., building on frozen ground).	Appraise, assess, critique, defend, justify, support, judge, select, choose, decide, debate, verify, argue, recommend, determine
Creating (HOTS)	Compile and synthesize information in new ways to create something new, or propose new solutions.	Construct a glider made of balsa wood that will travel 10 metres.	Compose, construct, create design, hypothesize, plan, produce, revise, invent predict, imagine, propose, devise, formulate

Source: Adapted from Bloom, (1956); Anderson & Krathwohl (2001).

Strategies to Extend Student Thinking

- *Remember to use wait time.* Allow at least ten seconds for students to think about your question and formulate their response. Do not be afraid to wait even longer; beginning teachers often worry about not having enough time in their lessons, or feeling uncomfortable with the silence. But it is worth being generous with wait time. Along with allowing students enough time to form answers, you demonstrate that you will not answer your own question and will wait to hear their responses.

- *Use think–pair–share.* It is often beneficial to ask a question and have students turn to a partner to discuss their ideas, which can then be shared with the class. In doing this, students can clarify their ideas before sharing with a larger audience. For those who are not sure of the question or concept, discussion with a peer can help clarify what is being asked.

- *Ask follow-up questions.* Follow-up questions are particularly important if the response is not clear or needs elaboration. Follow-up questions can also segue into new topics.

- *Provide a safe and comfortable environment for all students.* Welcome all contributions in order that students feel that they can venture an answer, even if it may be incorrect. Remind students to respect all ideas and contributions from peers.

- *Distribute your questions.* Be sure to call on as many students as possible so that everyone is included, and be aware of how you respond to the boys and girls in your class.

- *Encourage students to explain their thinking.* Ask students to elaborate and unpack their thinking, and allow them to modify or correct their responses.

- *Call on all students.* This is sometimes a point of contention among educators. What should you do if a student never raises her or his hand to answer questions? It is okay to call upon those students; however, it must be done in a careful and sensitive way. Some students are shy, some prefer to listen, and some are afraid of giving the wrong answer. Cultural norms might affect how students participate in class. If a student is unsure of how to answer a question, you might let her or him know that you will come back to them after a few more students have shared their ideas. This will give them ample time to prepare an answer. No matter what you do, you need to know your students and develop a good rapport with them so they feel comfortable being called upon.

Provide positive reinforcement and, if responses are not what you expected, be mindful of how you react. There are many ways of responding without being judgmental or suggesting that students are wrong. For example, you might say, "Tell me how you got to your answer," or ask, "Can you explain your answer?" Think carefully about how your questions are worded, and avoid confusing students with several questions rolled into one. Avoid questions that have double negatives—it may be unclear what you are actually asking. Incomplete questions (such as fill-in-the-blank queries), or over-involved questions (questions that have too many ideas and are therefore complex) can elicit few responses. Be sure to use a range of questions, from lower-order to higher-order thinking questions.

A Final Word about Questioning . . .
We discourage you from using questions to control the class. You have likely seen or experienced a situation in which a teacher asks a question as a classroom management tool or to control behaviour. A positive classroom climate can be achieved in more effective ways.

CLASSROOM MANAGEMENT: CREATING A POSITIVE CLASSROOM CLIMATE

Creating a positive classroom climate requires a conscious effort and careful planning. In this section, we explore strategies for creating a safe environment where learning can take place, where all students feel safe, and where deep understanding can be achieved. It is essential to establish and maintain a positive classroom climate at all times, and in

Watch
Science, Technology and Society

Watch
Feedback

particular during science investigations, where safety can quickly be compromised. Please note that this chapter does not address more acute issues that might arise; make yourself aware of your school's supports and processes for addressing serious behaviour concerns.

Many classroom management issues can be examined in terms of three factors:

a. program planning, pedagogy, and curriculum decisions
b. awareness of student needs
c. techniques and strategies for dealing with disruptive behaviour

Program Planning

At the core of a productive and positive classroom is a curriculum that is well planned and effectively implemented. In many ways, this entire book supports curriculum design and development. As with all subjects, if a science program is poorly planned and students are not engaged in class activities, behavioural issues can arise. For our purposes here, let us emphasize that effective teaching employs a variety of teaching and assessment strategies that are well-suited to students and have clear expectations for student participation. When students are disruptive, it may signal that they are unable to engage in the activity or that they are either bored or lost.

Awareness of Student Needs

Every student has unique needs with respect to all aspects of their learning, from noise tolerance and concentration levels to diverse interests. Some students are easily distracted, others find it hard to follow oral directions, and others feel they are not good at science and may tune out. Understanding your students will help engage them in their learning. For example, a teacher who is aware that her or his students need repetition of instructions might provide instructions orally, ask a class member to summarize them for the class, and write the instructions on the board. This chapter attests to the importance of placing students at the centre of planning.

Techniques and Strategies

There are numerous books available that promote tools for effective classroom management. (See, for example, Bennett & Rolheiser, 2008; Wong, Wong, & Seroyer, 2005.) They include specific strategies such as learning student names as quickly as possible (preferably within the first day or two of school), and noting and dealing with misbehaviour when it happens rather than ignoring it in the hope that it will disappear. Other strategies include beginning each class with a hook or a student challenge in order to engage students in a positive way, and having clear expectations for the lesson. Explicit instructions for student behaviour can help motivate and ensure that students are focused during lessons, on task during activities, safe and productive during investigations, and prepared for assessment and evaluation. Moving around the room, standing near a disruptive student, or quietly and casually asking a student to focus can also be affective. However, no technique can take the place of a well-planned, prepared, and organized lesson that is engaging and at a suitable level for all students.

The following activities will allow you to consider how you might address specific classroom-management issues in the classroom.

ACTIVITY 6.8   *21st C* ② ④

Causes, Actions, and Proactive Strategies for Disruptive Behaviours

The table lays out some possible classroom scenarios. For each, think about the cause, possible courses of action, and proactive strategies. Use the table headings to guide your decision about what you might do in each case.

Unpacking Classroom Scenarios

Scenario	Causes: What are possible causes of the behaviour?	Actions: What might you do at the time and what action might be appropriate later?	Proactive strategies: What strategies might be used to prevent this in future?
A student continues to talk with classmates—even when asked to focus.			
A portion of the class has not done their science homework, and you were counting on it being complete to further your lesson.			
During a science investigation, students are using materials inappropriately or throwing them around the room.			
Students are arguing about who does what during a design and technology challenge.			
On a field trip at the science centre one group of students, is running through the galleries and not staying with the parent chaperone.			

DISCUSSION QUESTIONS

1. Have you experienced any of these scenarios during your practicum or other teaching experience? How was the situation dealt with?
2. Discuss other scenarios you have experienced involving disruptive behaviour and how they were handled.

ACTIVITY 6.9   21st C ❷ ❹

Program Planning to Avoid Classroom Management Problems

Many classroom management problems can be avoided with careful planning. For this activity, complete the table below, understanding that in a classroom not every strategy would require something to be collected. The first row has been completed as an example.

Avoiding Classroom Management Issues

Teaching and learning strategy	What will the students actually do?	What could be collected?
Demonstration	Make notes: On a teacher-prepared worksheet, students record their observations and what it means	Completed worksheet
Cooperative small group learning		
Guest speaker or other community resource		
Class discussion		
Independent study		
Science investigation		
Field trip		
Game		
Question and answer		

continued on next page

DISCUSSION QUESTIONS

1. For which strategy was it the most difficult to describe a student action? Why do you think this is so?
2. For which strategy was it the most difficult to determine what will be assessed? Why do you think this is so?
3. In which strategy do you think there is greatest potential for classroom management issues? Explain.
4. In groups, brainstorm routines or ways to prepare students for each of the strategies in the table in order to lessen the likelihood of classroom management problems.

Styles of Classroom Management

Different styles of classroom management have been identified in educational literature. (See for example Hand, 1996.) The following are different roles that classroom teachers might assume:

- Manager: Teachers focus on maintaining firm classroom control with teacher-centred lessons.
- Facilitator: Teachers engage in fewer teacher-controlled activities and collaborate with students to be problem solvers.
- Empowerer: Teachers encourage students to identify and solve problems.

Classroom management can also be framed with respect to power relations (Cummins, 1996). Although Cummins's discussion refers to society as a whole, it inherently has implications for the classroom. He makes the distinction between coercive and collaborative control. *Coercive control* implies that the teacher defines the rules and controls students' learning opportunities. *Collaborative control*, on the other hand, seeks to empower students by creating shared learning opportunities in order to develop their motivation to succeed.

ACTIVITY 6.10   *21st C*

What Are My Beliefs with Respect to Classroom Management?

Examine the list of statements below. Indicate whether you would *never*, *sometimes*, or *always* do the following:

I would:

- use a list of rules that I have developed for the classroom and posted so that I can point to it to remind students
- use rules that have been established in collaboration with students
- give after-school detentions for misbehaviour
- ask students to leave the classroom for disruptive behaviour
- treat all students equally
- vary my reaction to the particular student profile
- give rewards when students are cooperative and productive in class
- engage the entire class in a group discussion to solve any problems that arise—even if only a few students are involved
- speak with a misbehaving student privately to resolve any conflict
- call parents to report student misbehaviour
- attempt to involve parents whenever possible
- seek help for my classroom problems from the principal—at the end of the day

- revisit an incident the next day to discuss it
- seek help and advice from the guidance counsellors
- ask a colleague to observe my class to offer suggestions regarding classroom management

DISCUSSION QUESTIONS

1. For each statement, explain to a peer your reasons for making the decision you made.

2. Describe your classroom management style.

3. What classroom management issues are unique to teaching science?

SCIENCE BEYOND THE CLASSROOM: PLANNING FIELD TRIPS

When planning a unit of study, you may wish to include a field trip that will supplement your classroom teaching. This might be as modest as a 30-minute visit to a local grocery store or as ambitious as a three-day camping trip to an outdoor education centre. Field trips can enhance learning, foster the development of social and interpersonal skills, and allow students to experience places and settings that they might otherwise not visit. Organizing field trips includes planning what your students will do and linking activities to the curriculum; arranging for transportation and lunches; attending to permission forms and supervision, including possible parent volunteers; and considering how to debrief the field trip back at school. Appendix F outlines in detail how to plan for field trips.

CONCLUDING THOUGHTS

Planning is an important part of teaching. Carefully designed lesson and unit plans can support student learning and create productive and positive classrooms. What follows is a summary of the key ideas related to the learning objectives provided at the beginning of the chapter.

Elements of unit planning for science programs

As part of the pre-planning process, identify themes and fundamental concepts; choose how to assess student understanding; and decide how to introduce and bring closure to the unit. Teachers learn or review the content of the unit, select instructional strategies, and review resources that support student learning. Teachers can actively include parents and guardians in their science curriculum and instruction.

Constructing a unit plan (including an evaluation plan and a sequence of topics)

When drafting a unit plan overview, teachers can begin by summarizing ministry outcomes or expectations and what students should understand and be able to do by the end of the unit. In this process, they identify the fundamental concepts for students to learn and can determine the most appropriate assessment strategies and tools. In planning a sequence of lessons, teachers can choose instructional strategies that best support their students' learning.

Factors and considerations inherent in good lesson planning

Central to lesson planning is meeting the individual needs of a diverse student population. Daily lesson planning takes into account all aspects of pedagogical content and context knowledge. Lesson planning depends upon students' backgrounds, their strengths and areas for growth, the course content, and contextual factors. Lesson plans also take into account students' prior knowledge and motivation.

Instructional strategies for teaching science

When planning individual lessons, teachers can choose from a variety of instructional strategies. Some are teacher-directed and some student-centred; some involve science investigations or whole class participation. Some are independent in nature, while others involve students working in groups. The chosen strategies should be clearly explained to students and take into account unique student needs and strengths, as well as other issues of student identity.

The components of lesson plans

Several components are typically considered in the creation of lesson plans. These include: outcomes or expectations and learning goals; how the learning of these outcomes will be assessed; students' prior knowledge; a clear introduction to engage and motivate students; instructional strategies, sequence, and timing of the lesson; materials, equipment, and safety considerations; how the teacher will bring closure to the lesson; and reflections and notes for future lessons.

Effective questioning and Bloom's taxonomy

Teachers ask questions in all sorts of contexts and for a variety of purposes that support student learning. Teachers might ask questions to check student understanding or to consolidate student learning, for example. The type and purpose of questions are a significant aspect of designing and implementing curriculum that meets students' needs.

Bloom's taxonomy can help teachers formulate effective questions and develop higher-order thinking skills.

Creating a positive classroom climate

Classroom management issues can be examined in terms of three factors: program planning, pedagogy, and curriculum decisions; awareness of student needs; and strategies for dealing with disruptive behaviour. Examining causes, actions, and prevention of disruptive behaviours, as well as strategies to avoid problems, can result in a positive classroom climate. It is useful to consider your style of classroom management as manager, facilitator, or empowerer.

BRINGING IT ALL TOGETHER: FINAL QUESTIONS

1. Individually reflect upon what you consider will be your biggest challenge in the unit planning process.

2. In pairs or small groups, discuss the types and structure of lessons you have observed and experienced. Share some memorable lessons with the group. What ideas from this chapter were reflected in or missing from the lessons you recall?

MyEducationLab®

Visit MyEducationLab® to access an electronic version of the text, as well as a variety of topics that enhance the text material. The topics include the following to support your learning in the course:

- Assessments, including interactive case studies, activities, and video assignments
- Discussion board questions
- Videos, simulations, a lesson plan builder, and other useful course resources

APPENDIX 6.A   Year Overview Example

Subject	September–October	November–December	January–February	March–April	May–June
Language Arts	Poetry	Novel study	Information texts, persuasive writing	Novel study	Myths and legends, Shakespeare
Mathematics	Numbers				
	Patterns data analysis	Chance and uncertainty	Measurement	3D objects and 2D shapes	Transformations
Social Studies	Skills and Processes of Social Studies				
	Identity, society, and culture	Identity, society, and culture	Governance	Economy and technology	
				Human and physical environment	

Science	Processes and Skills of Science				
	Human body	Human body	Forces and simple machines	Renewable resources	Non-renewable resources
Music and Drama	Prep Time				
Art	Life drawing	Sculpture	Printmaking	Group of Seven, painting	Emily Carr, painting, year-end art exhibition
Health and Career Education	Goals and decision making	Health	Health	Career development	Career development
Physical Education	Active Living; Safety, Fair Play, & Leadership				
	Movement dance	Movement dance	Movement gymnastics	Movement games	Movement games
Activities, Breaks, etc.	Curriculum night	Public health nurse visit	Skating	Ski trip: March Spring break	Field trip: First Nations village

Note: This example uses the British Columbia Grade 5 curriculum.

APPENDIX 6.B   Lesson Plan Templates

Sample 1

Unit: Lesson:	Date: Time:
Learning Outcomes:	**Assessment:**
Prior Knowledge:	**Adaptations and Modifications:**
Materials:	

Introduction (timing)	
Body of Lesson (timing)	
Closure (timing)	

Next Steps:
Reflection and Notes:

Sample 2

Unit:	Lesson:

Differentiated Instruction Details

Knowledge of Students

Differentiation based on
☐ Readiness _____
☐ Interests _____
☐ Style/Intelligence _____
☐ Other _____

Differentiated Instruction Response:
☐ Topic (content) _____
☐ Ways of learning (process) _____
☐ Learning environment _____
☐ Ways of demonstrating learning (product)

Backward Design Question 1: *What will students learn?*

Curriculum Expectations: *List overall and specific expectations that you will address and assess.*

Learning Goals: *State learning goals in direct, explicit, and student-friendly language.*
We are learning to

Guiding Questions: *List two or three questions that will frame students' learning in the lesson.*

Instructional Components and Context

Readiness: List the prior knowledge and skills that students need before beginning new learning.

Terminology: List key terms that are used in the lesson as either a conceptual learning focus or a functional, shared vocabulary.

Materials: List all materials required by the teacher and the student for the lesson.

Backward Design Question 2: *How will I know students are learning? Assessment for, as, and of learning.*

Assessment Strategies	Assessment Tools

Backward Design Question 3: *How will assessment and instruction be organized for teaching and learning?*

Minds On: Activating Prior Knowledge

Action: *Introducing new learning or extending/reinforcing prior learning, providing opportunities for practice and application*
Consolidation
Self Reflection

Sample 3

Unit:
Topic:

Academic Expectations

Learning Skills and Work Habits		
☐ Responsibility	☐ Independent Work	☐ Initiative
☐ Organization	☐ Collaboration	☐ Self-Regulation

Instructional Strategies		
☐ Carousel	☐ Learning Centres	☐ Six Thinking Hats
☐ Concept Map	☐ Literature Circles	☐ Think Pair Share
☐ Consequence Mapping	☐ KWL	☐ Town Hall Meeting
☐ Debate	☐ Mind Map	☐ Values Continuum
☐ Flow Chart	☐ Role Play and Drama	☐ Venn Diagram
☐ Jigsaw	☐ Science Notebook	☐ Other
Assessment Strategies and Tools		
☐ Assignment	☐ Observation	☐ Quiz
☐ Checklist	☐ Peer Assessment	☐ Rubric
☐ Conference	☐ Performance Task	☐ Self-Assessment
☐ Homework	☐ Portfolio	☐ Unit Test
☐ Journal	☐ Presentation	☐ Other

Resources	Lesson Sequence	Time
Homework & Reminders		

Reflections and Improvements
☐ Needs work _____
☐ Satisfactory _____
☐ Good _____
☐ Amazing _____

Sample 4

Lesson title: _____

Ministry outcomes or expectations:

Learning goals:

Expected prior knowledge:

Technology needs:

Time	Teaching/Learning Strategies and Reasons for Choices	Materials, Laboratory Equipment, and Safety Considerations
	MINDS ON	
	ACTION(S)	
	CONSOLIDATION	
	DEBRIEF	

Source: Ontario Ministry of Education. *Targeted implementation & planning supports (TIPS): Grade 7, 8, and 9 applied mathematics.* Toronto, ON: Queen's Printer for Ontario, 2003. Retrieved from http://www.edu.gov.on.ca/eng/studentsuccess/lms/tips4rm.html. Reproduced with permission.

Chapter 7
Curriculum Fundamentals

Monkey Business Images/Shutterstock

I thought curriculum was just the lesson plan.

—Emily, preservice teacher candidate

Curriculum means expectations in curriculum documents, right?

—Amal, preservice teacher candidate

INTRODUCTION

Curriculum is an often-used term in education and yet has many definitions. For our purposes, we understand curriculum to be inclusive of ministry or department of education policy documents that outline the guidelines for science courses as well as the *program* (including units of study and specific lessons) that teachers create and implement. When teachers refer to the curriculum for their students, they may be referring to everything the student experiences, including daily tasks and activities, major projects, extended investigation and research opportunities, field trips, and homework. Curriculum, then, is a complex notion dealing with the content, purpose, and strategies of teaching and learning plans. In many instances, teacher choices regarding content ideas and examples are inextricable from other considerations of pedagogy. Curriculum, according to Pinar, Reynolds, Slattery, and Taubman (1995), is a very complicated conversation that includes among other factors the historical, political, racial, gendered, autobiographical, and aesthetic. Indeed, all teacher choices are affected by the purpose of curricula, what we believe is important for our students, and the philosophical underpinnings of our discipline. Curriculum planning, construction, and implementation are at the heart of all teaching. What teachers understand to be possible in a particular educational context affects what they choose to do and how they do it. In this chapter, we explore curriculum fundamentals in an effort to help you consider the *what*, *why*, and *how* of curriculum creation.

CURRICULUM THEORY AND THEORISTS

The idea of curriculum conjures many meanings and perspectives. In this section we highlight some curriculum theorists and researchers to help you navigate its complexities. What we present is by no means a definitive list. However, before we examine the theorists, consider your own understanding of *curriculum*.

You will likely have come to the conclusion that curriculum is a complex term, one Ted Aoki (1993) refers to as a "weasel word," and one that defies definition. Curriculum is both the lesson and the unit plan, and it includes the outcomes or expectations teachers are trying to meet. Curriculum is also the teachable moment; it is the newspaper article read aloud from the morning paper; it is the unexpected student question and how and when a teacher chooses to answer it, dismiss it, or save it for a future lesson. Curriculum development must take into account how teachers follow up on a topic and how they choose resources. Curriculum reflects the vision of what students should learn. Quite simply, it is everything teachers do—and do not do: what they teach (and do not teach), what they assess (and do not assess), and what is implied by their choices.

ACTIVITY 7.1   *21st C* ❷❸

Examining Your Prior Knowledge: What Does Curriculum Mean to You?

Describe the term *curriculum* and record your ideas. Next, form groups of four and compare your responses. Compile a description, in a PowerPoint presentation or on chart paper, that captures all of the ideas from your group. Use a Venn diagram, as shown on the next page, to organize your group's responses into three categories: what is curriculum, what is not curriculum, and those elements that are not clearly categorized. Share your description with the class and consider the responses shared by other groups.

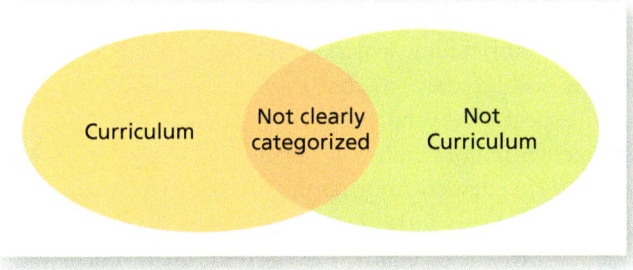

What is curriculum? What is not curriculum?

DISCUSSION QUESTIONS

1. How would you describe curriculum?

2. Discuss the range of descriptions of curriculum offered by your peers. How easy or difficult was it to come to consensus, if at all, on a description?

Curriculum Theorists

Like curriculum itself, curriculum theory is tricky to summarize; it is like "nailing Jell-O to the wall" (Wright, 2000, p. 4). Wright asserts that curriculum theorizing is always political and evolving; its body is composed of multiple discourses that both complement and contrast with each other but inherently inform the direction of curriculum. In this section we highlight some key curriculum theorists and their contributions.

Schwab (1973) describes four *commonplaces* that should be part of any curriculum work: the subject, the learner, the teacher, and the milieu. He suggests that each is central to any curriculum deliberation and that all need to be considered in a balanced and cogent way. Figure 7.1 summarizes Schwab's ideas.

Elliot Eisner (1979), a student of Schwab, makes the distinction between the *explicit curriculum* (the academic goals of a school), the *implicit curriculum* (the organizational structure and pedagogical rules of a school), and the *null curriculum* (what is not taught).

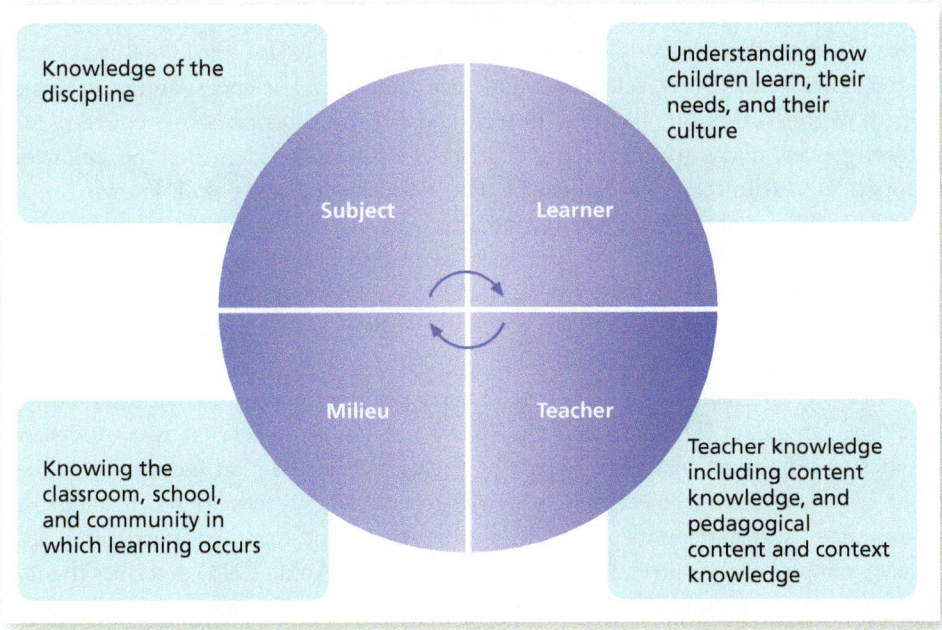

Figure 7.1 Schwab's four commonplaces

Jackson (1968) and Apple (2004) refer to a *hidden curriculum*—an idea that overlaps with Eisner's implicit curriculum, which Apple describes as "the tacit teaching to students of norms, values, and dispositions that goes on simply by their living and coping with the institutional expectations and routines of the schools" (2004, p. 13). It is important for teachers to recognize how each of these curricula are at work within their teaching.

Cuban (1995) suggests another and different four curricula. First, *official* curriculum is what provinces or territories would refer to as curriculum documents, set forth by the ministry or department of education. Second, *taught* curriculum is the lessons that take into account teacher planning, teacher preference, teacher comfort with different topics, and the adjustments that are made for specific groups of students. Third, *learned* curriculum includes the taught curriculum as well as all the other things that students might learn, such as classroom behaviours and attitudes that comply with teacher goals. For example, students may learn to respect others, ask questions, consider multiple perspectives, or memorize without questioning. *Tested* curriculum is comprised of parts from the other three. Cuban argues for teacher construction of tests, contending that standardized assessments are poor measures of student learning.

Connelly and Clandinin (1988) suggest that within schools and from the perspective of many teachers, curriculum is usually thought of as the plan or government document that outlines what to teach. However, they contend that teachers are the curriculum makers and planners, and bring their own experiences, beliefs, and situational contexts to their planning. Young (1998) makes the distinction between curriculum as practice and curriculum as fact:

> From this view teachers' practices are crucial in both sustaining and challenging prevailing views of knowledge and curriculum. The curriculum thus ceases to be separate from the activities through which teachers devise assignments, produce marks and grades and differentiate between subjects and identify pupil achievements. The implication of such a view is that if teachers subject the assumptions underlying their practices to critical examination, they will understand how to change curriculum. (p. 27)

Schubert (1996) recognizes curriculum as dealing with what is worth knowing and, in turn, what is worth experiencing, doing, and being. He points out that examinations of curriculum bring to the surface questions about the lives of individuals and about issues of social justice. He suggests four positions on curriculum thinking, noting that educators and researchers tend to embody a blend of these positions. The *intellectual traditionalist* values the classics in the arts, sciences, humanities, and social sciences, and positions the great ideas of truth, beauty, goodness, liberty, equality, and justice above concerns such as culture, gender, class, and ethnicity. The *social behaviourist* identifies the behaviours that support success in today's social world. The *experientialist* views skill, knowledge, and value as "a seamless fabric" and asserts that the learning that comes from interests and real concerns is best. The *critical reconstructionist* critiques schools as sites of reproduction of inequity, where, depending on context, students are afforded different opportunities to learn. Schubert (1996) reminds us of the need to continuously ask what is worth knowing, and to do so through a variety of lenses.

Aoki (1993) embraces the multiplicity of curricula as framed by the *curriculum-as-plan* and the *lived curriculum*. The curriculum-as-plan embodies the interests, assumptions, and approaches of curriculum planners. Typically, the curriculum-as-plan includes statements of intent (e.g., goals, aims, objectives), activities to be done by students and teachers, suggested resources, and statements of evaluation. Provincial and territorial curriculum documents are examples of the curriculum-as-plan. Alternately, Aoki (1993) describes the lived curriculum as "not the curriculum as laid out in a plan, but a plan more or less lived out" (p. 257). The lived curriculum includes daily contextual elements and the uniqueness of all members of the learning community.

Curriculum theory is increasingly informed by social and cultural theory and "post-discourses." Social cultural theory recognizes that socio-political forces and culture influence curriculum theorizing, pedagogy, and education. (See, for example, education research from Carl James, Gloria Ladson-Billings, and Wolff-Michael Roth.) The works of French philosophers Michel Foucault and Jacques Derrida are helpful in understanding post-discourses, including postmodernism and poststructuralism. (For an accessible overview of Foucault's and Derrida's contributions to the theory and practice of education, please see Cherryholmes, 1988.)

Wright (2000) highlights the complexity of contemporary and traditional discourses and their influence on the unfolding landscape of curriculum and curriculum theory. He emphasizes the importance of flexibility and open-mindedness in engaging with the complex and multiple conceptualizations of curriculum. Teachers face many challenges in the curriculum development process, such as having a deep understanding of the content, planning for and conducting meaningful investigations, and integrating science and technology with society and the environment. Concerns around meeting the demands set out by curriculum documents need to be contextualized within the curriculum teachers develop. Teachers must acknowledge their responsibility in developing a curriculum that will improve science education for all. (Chapter 5 further explores student needs as a core of the curriculum development process.) Creating, implementing, and reflecting on curriculum can help teachers review the decisions they make in the curriculum writing process. These decisions are value laden, never neutral, and reflect teachers' personal perspectives of what is important in science. Table 7.1 below summarizes curriculum theorists and theories.

Table 7.1	Selected Curriculum Theorists and Theories
Curriculum Theorist	**Features**
Schwab	Four commonplaces inform curriculum work: subject, learner, teacher, and milieu.
Eisner	Distinctions are made between explicit curriculum, implicit curriculum, and null curriculum.
Cuban	Four curricula are taught in schools: official curriculum, taught curriculum, learned curriculum, and tested curriculum.
Connelly & Clandinin	Curriculum is viewed as government documents, yet teachers are the curriculum makers and planners, and are influenced by the personal.
Schubert	Four positions on curriculum theorizing include intellectual traditionalist, social behaviourist, experientialist, and critical reconstructionist.
Aoki	Curriculum is a multiplicity of human endeavours, including curriculum-as-planned and curriculum-as-lived.

ACTIVITY 7.2   *21st C* ① ② ⑤

Continuing the Curriculum Conversation through Quotations

The source for each quotation in this activity is provided; however, we have adapted them for our purposes.

Part A.
Read the following quotations. Beside each, indicate if you agree or disagree with it. Choose one quotation that resonates for you, and write a short paragraph to explain why. In

continued on next page

groups of four, share your paragraphs and list similarities and differences in your reactions.

1. Curriculum is a cultural construction, not a concept—it is a way of shaping educational practices. (Grundy, 1987)
2. Curriculum is the study of all things educational. (Egan, 1978)
3. Curriculum is more meaningful when we understand ourselves, and can express the reasons for what we are doing and why we are doing it. (Connelly & Clandinin, 1988)
4. Curriculum debates are about different views of society and the future. (Young, 1998)
5. Curriculum is a product of choice. The choice we make, from different possibilities, is a political act. (Hood, 1998)
6. Curriculum is institutional text and practice reinforcing and perpetuating normative descriptions of racial categories, class, gender, and (hetero) sexuality that exist in society. (Chambers, 1999)

Part B.

Your personal philosophy of teaching informs how you develop curriculum. In your groups, articulate your developing philosophy of teaching and your beliefs about what is most important in a science curriculum. Keep in mind that your teaching philosophy will change over time, particularly during the first few years of your career. Focus on those big ideas about teaching and learning that are important to you. Now, look ahead and speculate as to how your philosophy will affect your curriculum development in the future.

FUNDAMENTALS OF CURRICULUM DEVELOPMENT

Curriculum theorists have proposed many ways of organizing curriculum. Franklin Bobbitt's (1918/2004) work and later the Tyler Rationale (Tyler, 1949/2004) closely align with common assumptions about schooling and curriculum planning. Their work presents four questions to be addressed by curriculum: What are the educational objectives to be attained? What experiences are to be provided? How are those experiences organized? How will the attainment of the objectives be assessed?

In Chapter 6, we discussed lesson and unit planning. It is always worthwhile to step back and consider the broader questions about curriculum design and its purposes, both for individual lessons and for an entire year plan. Eisner and Vallance (1974) and Petrina (1998, 1993) argue that all curriculum design is a bricolage of various orientations. For example, is the curriculum oriented toward knowledge acquisition? Does it stress individuality and personal expression? Does it emphasize social conditions or social justice? Are many orientations reflected? It is from questions such as these that the notions of transmissive (teacher telling students), transactive (teacher and students working together), and transformative (curriculum for change) curriculum evolved (Miller, 2007), as well as the notion that neutral orientations for curriculum design do not exist (Petrina, 1998). With respect to the latter, all curriculum design is and should be contextually driven, and is stamped by the multiple biases and ideologies that a teacher holds, as well as the needs, aspirations, and world views of students. Furthermore, curriculum design and change is not about following a correct technique, but rather is a complex journey (Blades, 1997).

William E. Doll, Jr. (1993/2004) presents an alternative to the Tyler Rationale, the four Rs that can be used to evaluate a postmodern curriculum: *richness*, *recursion*, *relations*, and *rigour*. Richness refers to the depth of the curriculum and its multiplicity of interpretations. Recursion relates to the circularity of the curriculum; it has no fixed beginning or ending. Relations are of importance in pedagogical and cultural ways that complement each other. Rigour in the postmodern sense draws upon indeterminacy and interpretation; teachers must continually explore new combinations and be cognizant of assumptions and how they inform interpretations.

Regardless of the lens through which curriculum development is viewed, organized, and evaluated, teachers need to ask what is to be taught, how it will be taught, and why it is to be taught. In the next sections we consider these questions, as well as other factors related to student learning that impact the curriculum writing process.

Watch

Emergent Curriculum Built on Children's Interests

The What, Why, and How of Curriculum

As just mentioned, the curriculum development process depends on what is to be taught, why or for what purpose it is taught, and how it will be taught. Table 7.2 outlines these aspects of the curriculum design process.

Table 7.2 The What, Why, and How of Curriculum	
	Considerations and questions for curriculum design
What is taught refers to what is included in the official documents and what teachers and students bring to the curriculum.	Ministry documents provide lists of expectations or outcomes as well as other guiding principles related to the discipline. Teachers bring their preferences, expertise, and personal philosophy to the curriculum. Consider what your students bring to the curriculum—their interests, prior knowledge and skills, and personal backgrounds.
Why, or the purpose of a curriculum, may be multi-faceted. It may refer to students, groups, or society.	Curriculum encompasses what teachers do every day. What purpose does a teacher's vision have in terms of student needs and aspirations (e.g., a kindergarten science lesson will be quite different from a Grade 8 science class)? What purpose does the vision have in terms of societal needs and political pressures? What purpose does it serve in terms of the discipline and knowledge acquisition? Does your curriculum help students learn? Does it help them become critical thinkers and decision makers?
How curriculum is taught refers to the myriad strategies and approaches that teachers use and that students experience (pedagogy in action).	From question-and-answer sessions, to cooperative small group work, to independent study and long-term projects, teachers choose strategies that support the teaching and learning process. Student needs and strengths also influence how the curriculum is developed. Teachers need to take time to assess what students know in order to create a curriculum that moves them forward. This challenge is compounded by large classes of students, whose knowledge base can be varied and learning needs different.

Students' Needs Revisited

We address teaching that meets the needs of students in Chapter 5. In this section, we revisit three salient points that relate to creating any curriculum.

What Do Students Already Know? David Ausubel (1968) is famous for saying that the most important thing teachers need to consider before they plan what to teach is what students already know. Teachers must ascertain what students understand about a topic before finalizing a curriculum plan. Once students' prior knowledge is determined, pedagogical support and foundational knowledge can be embedded within the curriculum. Then, students can build on what they already know to expand their understandings.

How Does Curriculum Support Student Literacy and Numeracy? It is important to ask how curriculum will foster the development of literacy and numeracy skills. Language is fundamental to teaching and learning. Curriculum develops language skills such as reading, writing, listening, and speaking, and the curriculum implementation process *depends* on such skills. Just as language is important to learning science, so, too, is mathematics. For example, learning in science requires basic operational and problem-solving skills.

It is essential to carefully consider students' competencies with literacy and numeracy and to weigh what they need to learn in order to engage in the curriculum. For further discussion about language, literacy, and mathematics in teaching and learning science, and for teaching strategies, see, for example, DeCoito (2009), Frykholm and Glasson (2005), and Yore et al. (2004).

What Is the Role of Affect? Affect includes emotions, mood, feelings, and attitudes (Reiss, 2005). Teachers need to acknowledge how the emotional aspects of students' lives impact teaching and learning in science (Alsop & Watts, 2003). Furthermore, affect does not operate in isolation from other classroom factors, but rather works in concert with cultural, sociological, and psychological aspects.

CONSTRUCTING CURRICULUM: PRACTICAL CONSIDERATIONS

What Do the Ministry Curriculum Documents Say?

Typically, Canadian teachers use provincial and territorial curriculum documents as a starting point when designing science curriculum. These documents present a context for science education in the introduction, usually providing an overview of the prescribed curriculum, organizers, and suggestions for instructional time frames. Often, when educators speak of "the curriculum," they are referring to these documents. Activity 7.3 provides an opportunity to examine your provincial or territorial curriculum documents.

ACTIVITY 7.3   *21st C*

Working with Documents to Plan Curriculum

You will need the elementary science curriculum documents for your province or territory. These are usually available on the ministry or department of education website. Each province and territory has unique organizational structures for curriculum documents, this activity will likely have to be adjusted to fit your region's document. Work in groups of four, ideally with peers who will be teaching the same grade.

1. Choose a grade from Kindergarten to Grade 8 and examine the science curriculum. (If you know what grade you will be teaching on your practicum, use this grade.) Familiarize yourself with the topics and the curriculum outcomes or expectations.
2. Describe the main themes or topics covered.
3. Choose one of these topics and, with your group, brainstorm activities, investigations, resources, and assessment tools that could support your teaching and your students' learning of the topic. How do these teaching strategies and resources support student learning?

How to Construct a Student Task

There are many factors to consider in the curriculum design process, such as the purpose for the assignment; what you would like students to learn; student interest, ability, level, and needs; teacher content and pedagogical knowledge; context; and the site of learning. When planning, ask yourself the following questions:

- Will the curriculum be relevant to students?
- How can I create conditions for maximum success for all students?
- What skills will students develop?

When teachers plan curriculum, they often design a specific assignment or activity that supports their purpose. What follows are some samples of such assignments that range from a day to a few weeks in duration and could be part of a larger unit of study.

Activity 7.4 involves a technological challenge (building a mousetrap), a research project (learning about planets), and a science investigation (exploring plant growth). Design-technology challenges ask students to solve a problem by creating or constructing a device or product, and students often work in groups to develop their problem solving and cooperative group skills. A research project, with a poster and presentation like this one, can take many forms, but usually involves a theme, research conducted at the library or online, organization of information, and presentation of findings to the class or to a larger audience. A science investigation, and a science notebook activity like the one that follows, involve active exploration of a scientific phenomena that is documented through drawings, written text, and graphic displays that involve questions, predictions, observations, and reflections. The use of science notebooks in teaching is further outlined in Appendix A at the end of the book.

Watch

Science Fair Projects

ACTIVITY 7.4

21st C 5 7

Analyzing Curriculum: Sample Assignments

Central to this activity are the ideas that curriculum development involves more than covering outcomes or expectations and that good curriculum is inextricable from good pedagogy. This activity explores a particular aspect of curriculum design—student assignments.

Three sample assignments are included at the end of this chapter: a technological challenge (Appendix 7.A), a research project with poster presentation (Appendix 7.B), and a science investigation and notebook activity (Appendix 7.C). Your instructor may provide additional samples of assignments used in schools in your area. Examine each one and complete the following table.

Analyzing Curriculum Examples			
	Type of assignment		
Criteria related to curriculum development	**Technological challenge**	**Research project with presentation and poster**	**Science investigation with science notebook**
List the main features of this assignment.			
What is the purpose of this type of assignment?			
What do students need to know in order to be successful in this assignment?			
How are literacy and numeracy supported?			
List features that would appeal to elementary school students.			
Describe how students are assessed.			

continued on next page

DISCUSSION QUESTIONS

1. How is each activity relevant to students?
2. How does each activity support maximum success for all students?
3. What skills will students develop?
4. What other forms of assessment could be used in each case?
5. How does each assignment support your own beliefs about good curriculum?
6. How could you use information and communication technologies such as podcasts, presentation software, wikis, blogs, and websites to support or enhance each assignment?

Many provinces and territories include in their curriculum documents learning skills or work habits, such as collaboration, responsibility, and organization. Each of the samples in Activity 7.4 support the development of these skills; we recommend that they not be taught independently but rather be embedded within comprehensive tasks. School-wide expectations or goals also often include these work habits. Furthermore, learning skills may be included as part of the evaluation and reporting process, as a complement to a grade for achievement, or as additional information for parents.

ACTIVITY 7.5   *21st C* ❹

What Work Habits Do Teachers Promote and Support?

Re-examine Appendices 7.A, 7.B, and 7.C from Activity 7.4. Consider the list of work habits in the table below, and indicate how each of these assignments might foster the development of these skills.

Exploring Work Habits

	Type of assignment		
Learning skill or work	**Technological challenge**	**Research project with presentation and poster**	**Science investigation with science notebook**
Collaboration			
Independence			
Organization			
Responsibility			
Initiative			
Self-regulation			

DISCUSSION QUESTIONS

1. How might each activity be modified to enhance particular work habits?
2. What other skills might be developed through each of the assignments?
3. How might the 21st-century skills listed on page 128 be supported by each of the curriculum assignments in Appendices 7.A, 7.B, and 7.C?

 **Watch**

Exploration

ACTIVITY 7.6   *21st C* ① ③ ④ ⑤ ⑥

Connecting Theory and Practice: Designing an Assignment

Below is a list of elementary science topics. In groups of three, choose one and find the related unit (as best you can!) in your ministry or territory's curriculum document. Read the outcomes or expectations and chose two or three that might form the basis of a project. Make a draft plan of a project that includes

   a) the purpose of the project
   b) outcomes or expectations addressed
   c) what students will be expected to do (be sure to consider Aboriginal and non-western perspectives) and
   d) how student achievement will be assessed

Topics

   - classifying living and non-living things
   - food chains
   - properties of solids, liquids, and gases
   - electricity
   - weather
   - the formation of rocks

DISCUSSION QUESTIONS

   1. How is the assignment you drafted relevant to students?
   2. Will all students feel connected to the material? Explain.
   3. What will you do to support your students' success?
   4. What skills will students develop?
   5. What science will they learn from this project?
   6. Discuss how your assessment, both formative and summative, relates to your project learning outcomes and to the student activities.
   7. How will literacy and numeracy be supported?
   8. How does the project address a range of student abilities, levels, and needs?
   9. In what ways can projects meet the needs of a diverse student population?

CURRICULUM VALIDATIONS FOR SCIENCE EDUCATION

Curriculum validations are fundamental to constructing curriculum. Doug Roberts (1982) suggests using curricular emphases that broadly organize the teaching of science teaching, and can form the basis of curriculum and instruction. For example, he writes about skill development and foundational knowledge, decision making, and science for everyday use as organizers for curriculum design. His emphases can be used in isolation or in unison in the design of science curriculum (please refer to Roberts and Ostman [1998] for a detailed description of Roberts's emphases). Table 7.3 builds upon a long history of curriculum theorists who suggest that teachers be explicit about purpose during the curriculum design process.

Table 7.3 presents four validations, or purposes, to help guide teachers as they develop curriculum that meets students' interests, needs, and aspirations. What teachers consider relevant may not be meaningful to their students. However, if students find a topic to be useful and interesting, or if it appeals to their sense of social responsibility or their understanding of science principles, then they will likely find relevance in it. Depending on the student, science content may fall into different or multiple categories.

Table 7.3 Curriculum Validations

Validation	What a student might say	Explanation	Example
Usefulness (worthwhile)	I can use this information. I'm going to tell my family about this.	The curriculum is designed to help students learn material and ideas they can use in their lives.	Know the parts of the human body and their functions; identify the four food groups and examples from each; identify hazardous materials based on symbols
Interest (excitement)	Wow—this is so interesting. I never knew that. That's cool!	The curriculum is designed to help students appreciate the wonder of science in terms of both the mystery of the natural world and the rich history of scientific thought.	Explore electricity using a variety of materials; know what causes volcanic eruptions; using simple machines, lift a heavy object with your finger
Social responsibility (being a good citizen; caring about others, our communities, and the environment)	This will help me take care of the environment. This is good for me, my family, and my neighbourhood.	The curriculum is designed to help students explore issues and ideas of societal, political, cultural, and economic importance to themselves and their community.	Demonstrate ways to reduce, reuse, and recycle at school; know alternate sources of energy; clean up a local watershed
Science expertise (learning content, skills, knowledge)	I want to be an astronaut, a scientist, a vet. Now I get it.	The curriculum is designed to help students learn theories, principles, laws, and the "current dogma" of science.	Measure forces; understand planetary motion; describe the properties of light

Re-Visiting Activity 7.6

Go back to Activity 7.6 and reassess your draft project in the context of Table 7.3 by answering the following questions. Describe which validation(s) are present in your project.

1. Do you favour one or more of these validations? Why do you think this is the case?

2. As a group, discuss which of these validations you feel positive about using as a basis for curriculum focus; which ones you like but perhaps feel unsure about incorporating; and which, if any, you reject. Explain your answers.

ACTIVITY 7.7

21st C ➋ ➍

Analyzing Commercially Produced Curricular Resources

Find a commercially produced curriculum unit or resource, either in print or on the internet, on a specific science topic. Examine it to determine what purpose or validation underpins the resource and what views about curriculum are revealed. How might you use it, and what modifications would be needed for students in your community?

ISSUES AND INFLUENCES SHAPING CURRICULUM

Teachers need to develop curriculum that helps students construct meaning. It should meet students' needs and help them navigate science as both a body of knowledge and a process for creating knowledge. Curriculum construction does not follow a set series of steps;

instead it is complex, contextually driven, and never neutral in its focus or implementation. It is influenced by, among other factors, history, politics, ethnicity, gender, class, and personal forces. As teachers strive to develop student-centred science curricula we encourage consideration of the following categories and questions:

The nature of science

- What science knowledge is worth learning in a science classroom?
- How do scientists and the science community create and direct science knowledge?
- How is science connected to the economy, to economic forces, and to institutional funding?

Environmental education

- How is science implicated in environmental issues in both positive and negative ways?
- How is environmental education integrated into the curriculum in meaningful ways?

Social justice

- How can we explicitly create curriculum that is reflective of a diverse student population?
- How are issues of power, access, and inclusion reflected in the science curriculum?
- How is social justice reflected in curriculum topics and choices?

The curriculum development process

- What do you hope students will know from your curriculum five years from now?
- How have historical, social, and cultural influences been realized in curriculum documents?
- How does your definition of a good teacher of science affect the curriculum development process?
- How does your content knowledge affect the curriculum design process?

ACTIVITY 7.8   *21st C*

Read and Reflect: Curriculum Theory and Development

Curriculum theory literature is vast and varied. We encourage you to explore the works of Eisner, Pinar, Tyler, Aoki, and Doll Jr., and direct you in particular to Petrina (2004) and Aoki (1993), who highlight interesting perspectives about the curriculum development process:

Petrina, S. (2004). The politics of curriculum and instructional design/theory/form: Critical problems, projects, units, and modules. *Interchange, 35*(1), 81–126; Aoki, T. T. (1993). Legitimating lived curriculum: Towards a curricular landscape of multiplicity. *Journal of Curriculum and Supervision, 8*(3), 255–268.

Petrina (2004) focuses on the role of teachers in developing curriculum, while Aoki (1993) explores curriculum-as-plan and the lived curriculum through the narratives of teachers and students. For each article, summarize and reflect on the following questions:

DISCUSSION QUESTIONS

1. How do the articles help you to
   a) plan curriculum
   b) meet student needs
   c) address your questions about curriculum
   d) develop expertise

SUBJECT MATTER CONTENT KNOWLEDGE (CK) AND PEDAGOGICAL CONTENT KNOWLEDGE (PCK)

An important part of curriculum planning is subject matter content knowledge (CK), and representing content in forms that students understand—in other words, blending content and pedagogy (PCK). The concept of CK and PCK are inextricably linked and affect all aspects of the practice of teaching science (Appleton, 2006; Mulholland & Wallace, 2005). Elementary school teachers have the added challenge of having to learn across different science disciplines—life science, physical science, and Earth and space science. No one expects you to know all of these fields thoroughly, but some basics are helpful. You will learn alongside your students as you plan lessons on material that is new or less familiar to you. Research suggests that preservice teachers of science often have unformed or unstable understanding of subject matter, and what they do know is remembered from high school and university courses (Lederman, Gess-Newsome, & Latz, 1994).

Elementary school teachers' science content knowledge may not always align with currently held conventions (Kallery & Psillos, 2001). Understanding science CK can impact confidence, teaching, and students' learning (Harlen & Holroyd, 1997; Murphy, Neil, & Beggs, 2007); thus it is important that you determine what you know and any gaps that exist in your knowledge base. While some would argue for the inclusion of specific science content courses in teacher education programs (Usak, Ozden, & Eilks, 2011), this is not usually the case. Indeed, there is a dearth of research on elementary school teachers' science CK gained from teacher education or other programs. The task to broaden your science CK will likely fall to you and your own initiative!

From our experience working with preservice teachers, we can report a range of content knowledge among students and a range of reactions to the gaps that become unveiled. Every preservice teacher approaches the issue of learning science CK differently. Still, we have identified some common challenges for all teachers of science—at all levels:

- learning the CK well enough to be able to teach it
- staying current with new research and developments in science
- developing a science curriculum that promotes active engagement for all students

The activities and examples in the next section and throughout later chapters reflect elementary science CK that you may need to learn or review for teaching science for kindergarten through Grade 8. It is beyond the scope of this book to include all content topics in life, physical, and Earth and space science; however, we hope these examples serve as a beginning. The purpose is twofold: to build your own CK while also developing pedagogical content knowledge (PCK). Each topic is organized around the following components: reviewing content, making literacy and numeracy connections, and exploring activities for elementary school students.

EXPLORING ELEMENTARY SCIENCE IN CREATIVE WAYS: HUMAN BODY SYSTEMS

In order to teach any topic confidently and effectively, it is helpful to have a broad knowledge base. In this section, we present some ideas to help develop your CK and PCK for a specific topic. The topic is introduced with a visual that might appear in a print or media resource. We encourage you to search for other resources, as well. As you learn or review the content, keep in mind other issues such as terminology, abstract processes, integration with mathematics and language arts, and activities to support student learning. Additionally, consider the meta-cognitive aspect of the activity, such as understanding how you learn, what you know, and what you need to know.

ACTIVITY 7.9

21st C ⑤

Human Body Systems

The human body is a common topic across many grades. From senses in Grade 1 or 2 to food and nutrition or studies of body systems in Grade 5, students learn about the body in units across the elementary science curriculum. In the British Columbia Grade 5 science curriculum, the following learning outcomes are outlined: Describe the basic structure and functions of the human respiratory, digestive, circulatory, skeletal, muscular, and nervous systems; and explain how the different body systems are interconnected. The Atlantic provinces include a unit on the healthy body. Similarly, in Saskatchewan, Grade 5 students investigate the structure and function of the major organs of human body systems and how they work together to allow us to move, grow, and respond to stimuli. For this activity, we will focus on the digestive system.

Reviewing the Content

1. Learn or review the content associated with the digestive system. For example, what is the liver and what is its function? What are two functions of saliva? Use the visual below to guide your exploration.
2. Make a list and write definitions for important or unfamiliar vocabulary and processes associated with this topic.
3. When you feel comfortable with the content, use the figure below to explain to a peer what happens to a piece of bread as it passes through the digestive system.

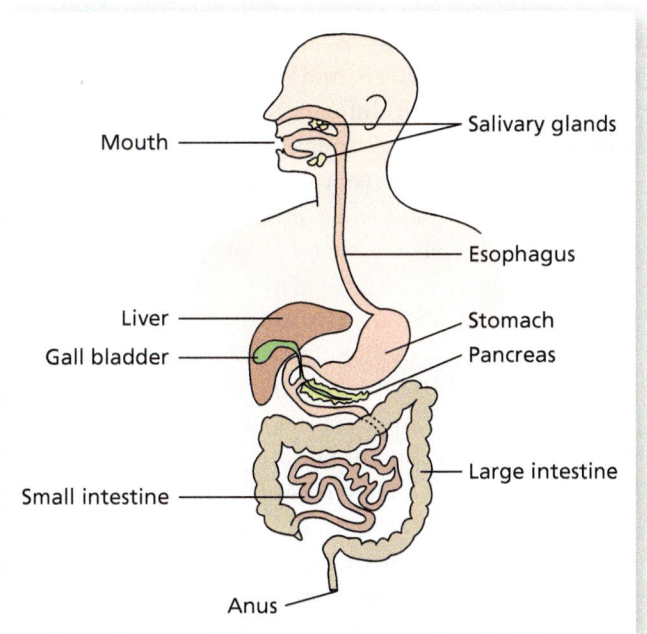

The human digestive system

Literacy and Numeracy Connections

1. *Moira's Birthday* by Robert Munsch is a fun story to include in a study of the digestive system. Moira invites all the students at her school to her birthday party and tries unsuccessfully to have enough pizza and cake for all of her guests. Students could trace the path followed by the birthday treats through the digestive system.
2. Also using *Moira's Birthday*, mathematics can be integrated into life science through problem solving, fractions, and data management activities related to the central question of the story: Does Moira have enough pizza and cake to divide among all of her guests?

continued on next page

Activities for Elementary school Students

1. With a partner, students can trace the outline of their bodies and draw in the organs of the digestive system.
2. Students can keep track of the foods they eat for one or two weeks and then analyze what they ate, using Canada's Food Guide.
3. Using different found materials (e.g., tubing, plastic jugs, plastic bottles), students can create a model of the human digestive system.

CONCLUDING THOUGHTS

Curriculum is a complex notion dealing with the content, purpose, and strategies of teaching and learning plans. Choices teachers make regarding content ideas and examples inextricably link to other pedagogical considerations. Curriculum development is at the heart of all teaching. What teachers understand to be possible in a particular educational context affects what they choose to do and how they do it. What follows is a summary of the key ideas related to the learning objectives provided at the beginning of the chapter.

Curriculum

Curriculum is inclusive of all educational experiences; it is everything teachers do—and do not do. Pragmatically, it is includes provincial and territorial curriculum documents as well as teachers' own planned and lived curricula.

Curriculum theory and theorists

There is a rich history of curriculum theory, and its evolution can be traced through the works of major curriculum theorists. It is important to recognize the many ways teachers can theorize about curriculum, and that their philosophical underpinnings influence how they develop curriculum.

Fundamentals of curriculum development

The curriculum development process depends on what is to be taught, how it will be taught, and why it is to be taught. What students already know, literacy and numeracy, and the role of affect should inform curriculum design.

Practical considerations in the curriculum construction process

The choice of strategies, support materials, and resources, together with other pedagogical considerations, make up curriculum. Beginning with ministry documents, teachers determine the best way to teach topics and plan accordingly.

Validations or purposes for curriculum

We provide four validations, or purposes, meant to guide teachers as they develop curriculum that meets students' interests, needs, and aspirations: usefulness, interest, social responsibility, and science expertise.

Issues and influences shaping curriculum

Curriculum construction is complex, contextually driven, and never neutral in its focus or implementation. It is influenced by many factors, including history, politics, ethnicity, gender, class, and personal forces. As you plan your science curriculum, be sure to consider nature of science, environmental education, and social justice issues.

Science content knowledge and pedagogy

An important part of curriculum planning for all teachers is subject matter content knowledge and blending content and pedagogy. Understanding science subject matter content knowledge can impact confidence, teaching, and children's learning. Common challenges for teachers of science at all levels include learning the subject matter content well enough to be able to teach it, staying current, and developing a science program that promotes active engagement for all students.

BRINGING IT ALL TOGETHER: FINAL QUESTIONS

1. Looking back and looking forward, how would you describe curriculum?

2. With your school community in mind, what do you anticipate will be the biggest challenges to developing meaningful, student-centred, and inclusive curriculum?

MyEducationLab® Visit MyEducationLab® to access an electronic version of the text, as well as a variety of topics that enhance the text material. The topics include the following to support your learning in the course:

- Assessments, including interactive case studies, activities, and video assignments
- Discussion board questions
- Videos, simulations, a lesson plan builder, and other useful course resources

APPENDIX 7.A   Technological Challenge

Grade 7 Science Design Technology Challenge: Make a Mousetrap

Assignment

You will be working in groups of three or four. Your challenge is to build a device to capture a mouse. It must have the following features:

a. Once a mouse enters it cannot leave.
b. You must not have to touch the mouse to release it.
c. The mouse must not be harmed.
d. It must work without human action (i.e., a human does not need to do anything for it to work).

Materials provided

Paper
Wood
Bits of food
Tape
Glue
Dowelling, popsicle sticks, or twigs
Any other materials that can be easily be found around the house or outdoors.

You are encouraged to bring in materials from home (e.g., a pie plate, a shoe box) with parents' permission.

Details

You will have two class periods of 40 minutes to complete this challenge. Your mousetrap will be tested with a mechanical wind-up toy mouse that will enter the trap.

Evaluation criteria

You are expected to design, build, test, and refine the mousetrap until it successfully captures a mouse according to the features outlined above. All students will eventually get full marks or a level 4.

APPENDIX 7.B   Research Project with Presentation and Poster

Grade 3 Science Research Project: Planets

Assignment Details:

You will be working in a group of three or four on a research project on planets. Together with your group, you will find information on the internet and in books to learn about a planet, and then you and your group members will teach the class about that planet. Your project will include a presentation, a poster, research notes, and group work.

1. Presentation

- Create a five- to seven-minute presentation to teach the class about your planet.

- Include all of the required content, such as a drawing of the planet, its diameter, its number of moons, etc. (See the Research notes that follow.)
- Present visual images using PowerPoint.
- Each group member needs to participate in the presentation.

2. Poster

- Create a Bristol board poster (or Prezi) to use in your presentation, and display it in a gallery walk that helps to teach the class about your planet.
- Include all of the required content. (See the Research notes that follow.)

- Present material in a clear, creative, and visually appealing way.
- Each group member needs to participate in creating the poster.

3. Research notes

- Each group member needs to complete a research notes sheet.
- Include all required content.

4. Group work

- All group members need to participate equally.
- Group members will cooperate and share responsibility.
- Group members need to organize themselves.

Steps:

1. Form a group of three or four.
2. With your group members, decide on a planet to research and present.
3. During library and computer time, investigate your planet and complete a Research Notes sheet.

(See sample below.) You might wish to divide the characteristics found on the sheet and then share with each other when finished. You might also choose to do additional research at home.

4. Work with your group members to plan out your teaching presentation. Be sure that each member is included in the planning and presentation.
5. Create PowerPoint slides to show during your presentation.
6. Create a poster that displays your presentation visually. Be sure to include all of the characteristics you found about your planet and a hand-drawn picture of the planet.
7. As a group, present your planet and poster to the class, and display your poster in a gallery walk.

Planets to choose from:

- Mercury
- Venus
- Mars
- Jupiter

- Saturn
- Uranus
- Neptune

Student names:

RESEARCH NOTES

DRAWING OF PLANET (don't forget to add colour!)

Diameter of planet (distance across)	Number of moons
(Diameter of Earth is 12 576 km.)	(Earth has one moon.)
Maximum distance from the Sun _____ planet is _____ kilometres from the Sun (Earth is 152.1 million kilometres from the Sun.)	Average surface temperature (The average temperature of Earth is 22° C.)
Length of day Length of year (Earth's day is 24 hours, or 1 Earth day long; Earth's year is 365 days.)	Unique features (Earth is the only planet where there is life.)
Myths, legends, or stories	

Evaluation

You will be evaluated on your presentation, poster, research notes, and group work according to the following rating scale:

Criteria for presentation	Level			
Presentation is well organized, with a beginning, middle, and end	1	2	3	4
All planetary characteristics are thoroughly covered.	1	2	3	4
Voice is loud and clear, and pacing is good.	1	2	3	4
All presenters are prepared and organized.	1	2	3	4
All presenters are enthusiastic and knowledgeable.	1	2	3	4
Presentation Total	/20			

Criteria for poster	Level			
All characteristics are presented.	1	2	3	4
All characteristics are thoroughly covered.	1	2	3	4
Poster is visually appealing.	1	2	3	4
Poster complements the presentation.	1	2	3	4
Poster Total	/16			

Criteria for research notes	Level			
Detailed notes were taken.	1	2	3	4
You used your own words.	1	2	3	4
Notes were taken for all characteristics.	1	2	3	4
Research Notes Total	/12			

Criteria for group work	Level			
All contributed to completing research.	1	2	3	4
All participated in presentation.	1	2	3	4
All contributed to creating poster.	1	2	3	4
Group Work Total	/12			

APPENDIX 7.C   Science Investigation and Science Notebook Activity

Science notebooks are useful in teaching science and learning as they bring together language, data, and experience and can help students gain a better understanding of the products, processes, and big picture of science (Klentschy, 2005). Science notebooks can be openly structured but often include six components: questions, problems, or purposes; predictions; planning; observations or data; conclusions; and next steps and new questions. For more information on using science notebooks in your teaching, read Michael Klentschy's (2005) *Science Notebook Essentials*. Depending on your students' prior experience with science notebooks, you will want to adjust the amount of scaffolding you provide students. In the following activity, we have included a structured notebook page as an example. Feel free to allow your students to organize their books as they, and you, see fit, and adjust your assessment accordingly.

Grade 1 Science: What are the basic needs of plants?

In this investigation, you and a partner will explore how having and not having these basic needs affect plant growth. You will use drawings and writing in your science notebook for planning, predicting, and making observations and conclusions.

Class Discussion:

What have you learned so far about the basic needs of plants? Create a list as a class.

Partner Work:

Find a partner and choose one plant need (e.g., soil, sunlight, air, water) to explore. Complete the following steps, using the sheets in your science notebook. Show your teacher each step before going on to the next one.

1. State your question. (e.g., What happens if my plant gets too much water?)
2. Make a prediction about will happen to your plant.
3. Make a plan and try it out (using the materials provided—see list below).
4. Make observations.
5. What did you find? (This is your conclusion.)
6. Think about the activity and explain what you learned, how you felt, and what you would like to do now. (These are your reflections.)

You can use any of the following materials:

- Plastic yogurt pots
- Bean seeds
- Soil
- Gravel

- Paper towel
- Compost
- Water
- Aluminum foil

- Labels
- Rulers

Sample notebook organization sheet

My name: My partner's name:	
My question	**My prediction about what I expect will happen to my plant**
My plan **Step 1** **Step 2** **Step 3** **Step 4** **Step 5** **etc.**	
My observations **(drawings, photos, words)** **Day 1** **Day 2** **Day 3** **etc.**	
What I found (my conclusion) **(drawings, photos, words)**	**What I learned and how I felt (my reflections)** **(drawings, photos, words)**

**What I would like to do next
(drawings, photos, words)**

Rubric for evaluation of science investigation and science notebook

Components	Level 1	Level 2	Level 3	Level 4
Questions	Question posed shows little or no development from what has been taught in the unit	Question posed shows some development from what has been taught in the unit	Question posed shows considerable development from what has been taught in the unit	Question posed shows strong development from what has been taught in the unit
Predictions	Predictions show little or no connection to what has been taught in the unit	Predictions show some connection to what has been taught in the unit	Predictions show considerable connection to what has been taught in the unit	Predictions show strong connection to what has been taught in the unit
Procedure (Plan)	Steps of investigation not outlined	Some steps of investigation outlined	Most steps of investigation outlined	All steps of investigation outlined
Observations	Regular and detailed observations and measurements not made	Some regular and detailed observations and measurements made	Regular and detailed observations and measurements consistently made	Regular and highly detailed observations and measurements made
Conclusions	Little or no application of findings to support conclusion	Some use of application to support conclusion	Substantial application of findings to support conclusion	Exemplary application of findings to support conclusion
Science Notebook Organization	Shows little or no use of drawings, writing, and organization	Shows some use of drawings, writing, and organization	Shows substantial use of drawings, writing, and organization	Shows exemplary use of drawings, writing, and organization
Work Habits	Shows little or no collaboration and cooperation in partner work	Shows some collaboration and cooperation in partner work	Shows considerable collaboration and cooperation in partner work	Shows exemplary collaboration and cooperation in partner work

Chapter 8
Scientific Inquiry and Investigations

Heather Ashdown

Kids really like hands-on science, but aren't too interested in textbook learning.

—Ms. R., elementary school teacher

Once we created a cheese substance—we mixed vinegar and milk. There was a piece of solid in the test tube, but we didn't eat it!

—Angelica, Grade 5 student

We went for a walk to see electricity stuff around the school. We found posts to hold electricity and lights on streets.

—Roman, Grade 1 student

LEARNING OBJECTIVES

- Discuss reasons for doing science investigations.

- Describe types of inquiry and science investigations.

- Investigate skills of inquiry and describe the range of skills students use during science investigations.

- Summarize the role of demonstrations in science programs.

- Describe, use, and critique various computer-based technologies for science investigations.

- Explore the role of design and technology in elementary science.

- Outline the use of science fairs in elementary science.

- Identify and describe educational research related to inquiry.

**21st CENTURY
LEARNING SKILLS &
COMPETENCIES**

1 Communication

2 Critical thinking

3 Collaboration

4 Creativity

5 Literacy and numeracy

6 Media literacy

7 Technological literacy

INTRODUCTION

If you visit any elementary science classroom in Canada, you will likely find students engaged in all sorts of class activities that teachers collectively call *science investigations*.[1] For example, students might be following step-by-step instructions to explore properties of matter, using a spring scale to measure forces required to lift a load, or designing an experiment to determine the amount of water and sunlight needed to maximize plant growth. These tasks reflect different categories of science investigations. Throughout the chapter, work by prominent researchers in science education will be used to build a foundation for understanding inquiry.

Curriculum policy documents for science education worldwide emphasize the centrality of scientific inquiry. According to the U.S. National Research Council (1996), *scientific inquiry* refers to

> the diverse ways with which scientists study the natural world and propose explanations based on the evidence derived from their work. Inquiry also refers to the activities of students in which they develop knowledge and understanding of scientific ideas as well as an understanding of how scientists study the natural world. (p. 23)

Science investigations reflect many aspects of scientific inquiry and emphasize the "doing science" aspect of Hodson's (1998) framework. When doing science students, are "engaging in and developing expertise in scientific inquiry and problem-solving" (Hodson, 1998, p. 5). In this chapter, we explore the place of investigations in elementary school science, and examine practice and theory that underpins inquiry.

WHY DO WE DO SCIENCE INVESTIGATIONS?

As we consider the relevance of investigations in science classrooms, a number of questions emerge. Why are investigations important? What kinds of investigations do teachers do, and why do they do them? What do teachers hope students learn from investigations? Ask teachers of science anywhere in the world why they conduct science investigations, and common themes emerge. (Science education researchers echo similar perspectives.) Activity 8.1 allows you to explore some of these questions.

ACTIVITY 8.1   *21st C*

Exploring Prior Knowledge and Experience

Think back to your experiences as a student in elementary, secondary, or university science, and also think forward to your future as a teacher of elementary school science.

Part A.
Describe an investigation you did as a student. What do you think its purpose was, and what did you learn from it?

Part B.
Examine the three investigations described in the table that follows. Complete the table by suggesting the purpose of each investigation and what students might learn from each experience.

---

[1]A number of synonymous terms have been used in provincial and territorial curricular and policy documents, including laboratory and field work, experiments, science activities, science inquiries, and school laboratory investigations. We use *science investigation* or just *investigation* to indicate activities where elementary school students are "doing science." Later in the chapter, we suggest a framework for bringing meaning and scope to these varied terms.

Example Science Investigations and their Purposes

Examples of science investigations	Purpose	What might students learn beyond the stated purpose?
Students set up apparatus to show how simple machines help us move objects.	To explore levers, pulleys, inclined planes, wedges, screws, and wheels	Students learn to manipulate equipment and materials, follow instructions, and work cooperatively with others.
Students use a magnet to separate mixed materials (e.g., mixture of salt and iron filings).		
Students explore the needs of plants by growing them in various locations in the schoolyard.		
Your choice		

DISCUSSION QUESTIONS

1. Create a list of possible reasons that teachers of science do investigations with their students.

2. Comment on the range of knowledge and skills students learn (generated from the table above).

3. Why do you think some teachers might be reluctant to do science investigations with students?

The list you generated with your students likely contains many of the reasons cited in the research literature for conducting investigations. (See for example, Hodson, 2008; Johnstone & Al-Shuaili, 2001; Reid & Shah, 2007; Wellington, 1998.):

- motivating students
- increasing interest and enjoyment
- teaching science inquiry skills
- developing manipulative and fine motor skills
- strengthening theoretical knowledge
- teaching how scientific knowledge may be used in daily life
- increasing creative thinking skills
- nurturing scientific working methods and higher-order thinking skills
- developing communication skills

Wellington (1998) conducted research with preservice teachers to investigate the purposes of practical investigations. Based on their responses, three arguments emerged. The *cognitive* argument asserts that practical work promotes students' conceptual understanding of science by allowing them to visualize the laws and theories of science. For example, students might better understand properties of matter after actively exploring the effects of heating and cooling water. The *affective* argument suggests that practical work is motivating and exciting, thus generating student interest and enthusiasm; while the *skills* argument suggests that manipulative and higher-level skills such as observation, measurement, data analysis, and prediction are developed. Wellington also gives counterviews for each of these arguments. For example, not all students enjoy practical work, and they can become stressed and confused during science investigations. There is also potential for investigations to go wrong; students don't see the point of what they are doing; and most skills are context dependent and therefore not easily transferable to other inquiry situations. In Chapter 9 we will discuss how teachers can help students overcome some of the difficulties of investigations with careful planning and organization, and by being clear about the intended purpose.

The U.S. National Research Council (2000, p. 29) outlines five essential features of classroom inquiry: "1) engaging a scientifically oriented question; 2) gathering and evaluating evidence; 3) formulating evidence-based explanations to answer a scientific question, 4) demonstrating scientific understanding by evaluating explanations in light of alternatives; and 5) communicating and justifying proposed explanation(s)." These features are common across many science curriculum documents and policies. For example, in Ontario, curriculum documents state that science classrooms should "develop the skills, strategies, and habits of mind required for scientific inquiry and technological problem solving" (Ministry of Education, 2007, p. 4), while in the Atlantic Canada Science Curriculum, scientific inquiry "involves the posing of questions and the search for explanations of phenomena" (n.d., p. 8). In British Columbia, science education includes providing students with opportunities to "develop the skills required for scientific and technological inquiry, for solving problems, for communicating scientific ideas and results, for working collaboratively, and for making informed decisions" (British Columbia Ministry of Education, 2005, p. 11).

ACTIVITY 8.2   *21st C* ⑤

Working with Resources

Using the ministry or department of education science curriculum document in your province or territory, summarize how the curriculum guidelines explain or describe scientific inquiry. For example, is language such as *investigation*, *problem solving*, or *experiment* used? List the skills of inquiry students are expected to develop.

DISCUSSION QUESTIONS

1. What do the curriculum guidelines state with respect to scientific inquiry?
2. How is scientific inquiry positioned within the guidelines (e.g., as a separate section, infused into each unit)?

SCIENTIFIC INQUIRY AND TYPES OF SCIENCE INVESTIGATIONS

According to Bell, Smetana, and Binns (2005) scientific inquiry involves student learning through questioning, data analysis, and critical thinking. Similarly, Llewellyn (2005) describes inquiry as active exploration involving critical, logical, and creative thinking skills to pursue questions of interest. A review of science education literature and resources reveals a rich landscape of science investigations. For example, students might be observing the properties of matter, investigating weather patterns, designing and constructing a simple machine, exploring the properties of light, or demonstrating the effects of magnets. All of these activities capture different aspects of scientific inquiry.

Many frameworks have been put forward that describe various models of science investigations. (See, for example, Llewellyn, 2005; Rezba, Auldridge, & Rhea, 1999; Windschitl, 2002.) The framework here, which draws from many existing frameworks, reflects a balance between teacher practice and research in the field and consists of three categories: *verification, problem solving,* and *experiments.* Intended to help teachers plan for a variety of science investigations, the framework is based on our experiences navigating the field of inquiry, attending to different needs of students, meeting the demands of the curriculum, and reading the research.

Verification (Confirmation)

Verification investigations are predictable and reliable. Students follow specified proce-dures in order to confirm previously learned principles or content (Hodson, 1998). These investigations are sometimes referred to as confirmation, cookbook, or recipe investiga-tions. Examples include confirming the melting and boiling points of water, demonstrating that warm air rises and cool air sinks, and verifying that similarly charged magnetic poles repel each other and oppositely charged poles attract each other. Students follow a step-by-step procedure and work toward one answer that is known by the teacher. Verification investigations have distinct beginnings, middles, and ends, and can be useful for engaging students, developing skills and background knowledge, affording common experiences to address questions, demonstrating understandings for assessment, and stimulating questions for further exploration. Overuse of these prepackaged types of investigations is described as *activitymania* (Moscovici & Holmlund Nelson, 1998). A science program consisting only of these verification activities in the absence of other more open-ended forms of inquiry does not reflect the scope of scientific inquiry.

Problem Solving (Structured and Guided Inquiry)

In problem-solving investigations, students explore questions posed by the teacher. The procedural elements of the task, such as materials needed and time allotted, are usually suggested by the teacher, but may be directed by the student.

The teacher may outline a specific procedure to be used. This is sometimes referred to as structured inquiry (Bell et al., 2005; Rezba et al., 1999). For example, the teacher might ask, "Which paper towel is best?" and students could investigate absorbency of two brands of paper towel, following a procedure provided by the teacher. The teacher might instruct students to determine the amount of water that can be held by a paper towel measuring 10 cm^2. Step-by-step instructions, and often a table to record data, are provided. Other examples of structured problem solving are exploring the interactions that occur from mix-ing different solids and liquids, or investigating the characteristics of water.

If the student designs and plans the procedure, it becomes less a structured investiga-tion and more a guided inquiry (Bell et al., 2005; Rezba et al., 1999). Using the example above, when the teacher asks, "Which paper towel product is best?" students are expected to design a procedure to investigate the problem. The degree of autonomy in student planning and implementation will depend on the question posed, the students' level of experience, and safety concerns. Guided or student-planned procedures are appropriate when students are asked, for example, to construct an apparatus to measure air pressure or to examine the effect of light on plant growth.

Problem-solving investigations can be messier and less predictable than verification investigations, and your students will likely approach problem solving in unique ways. Whether teachers or students design the procedure, critical thinking skills are developed, with many opportunities to discuss results. Messiness and lack of predictability are both strengths and challenges of this approach.

Experiments (Open Inquiry)

In experimental investigations, students design an experiment to collect data and draw conclusions about a question they have posed. Although the term *experiment* is commonly used by teachers and students to refer to all sorts of science investigations, we identify experiments as a particular kind of investigation—one in which students plan and design the procedure, control variables, collect and analyze data, and report their findings. Some of the literature refers to this as open inquiry (Bell et al., 2005; Rezba et al., 1999). Examples include investigating which brand of bubble gum allows the biggest bubbles, or determining factors that affect plant growth (such as water, light, and soil type). Not surprisingly, an analysis of textbooks reveals few experiments as we have described them for students to do in class. The spirit of experimental investigations is often at the core of science fairs. This sort of science investigation can motivate and engage students, allowing them to explore areas of interest to them and providing insights into the processes of scientific inquiry.

In summary, it is important to note that the categories we present here have different functions. At times they can be thought of as a continuum, and at other times they are mutually exclusive. (See Banchi & Bell, 2008; Lott, 2011.) For example, after the relative acidity of a cola is determined (using pH paper), students could engage in a problem-solving investigation to determine the effects of cola on teeth. This is a teacher-posed question that could be investigated by students in a structured or guided way. Students might then be inspired to ask their own questions about effects of other soft drinks or other foods on teeth and to design an experiment to investigate their question. At other times, the categories are exclusive. For example, verifying the melting point of water through an investigation does not lend itself to promoting student experiments or open inquiry.

We encourage teachers to embrace the idea of providing students with opportunities to ask their own questions and to design experiments. Such open inquiry provides rich opportunities for students to exercise creativity, critical thinking skills, and strengths that may not always emerge in rigid, one-size-fits-all investigations. In Table 8.1, we demonstrate how a topic may be developed using different types of investigations.

Table 8.1 Types of Investigation Using Magnets

Comparison criteria	Type of investigation		
	Verification (confirmation)	**Problem solving (structured and guided inquiry)**	**Experiment (open inquiry)**
The question to be explored	Posed by teacher	Posed by teacher	Posed by student
The procedure	Supplied by teacher	Students plan a way to investigate the question (often with suggestions and guidance from the teacher); they collect data and make a conclusion based on their findings.	Designed by students (but with some teacher input and feedback along the way depending on other factors). Students collect data and make a conclusion based on their findings.
The solution, answer, or findings	There is an expected solution.	May or may not know the answer, depending on the question posed and the procedure.	May or may not know the answer, depending on the question posed and the procedure.
What do students do?	Follow directions to answer a question posed by the teacher in order to verify a science concept.	Carry out their plan to collect data, answer their question, and support their answer with evidence.	Design an experiment to investigate a question they have posed. Students collect and analyze data, and draw conclusions (which may or may not be what the teacher expected).
Example using magnets	Students verify that north and south poles of a bar magnet will attract while like poles will repel.	Students investigate questions such as: What sorts of materials will magnets attract and not attract? Will a magnet exert a force and attract another magnet through a piece of wood or through Styrofoam?	Students pose a question. (Often the question arises from other investigations.) Students may ask: How is a bar magnet different from a fridge magnet? Which magnets are strongest?

ACTIVITY 8.3

21st C ❷ ❹ ❺

Read and Reflect: Exploring Inquiry

Read the following article and answer the questions below.
Lott, K. (2011). Fire up the inquiry. Science and Children. 48(7), 29–33.

DISCUSSION QUESTIONS

1. Which type of investigation do you think would be easiest to plan for? Speculate as to why this might be the case.
2. Which type of investigation do you think is most challenging for students? Why?
3. How would you scaffold student learning for each type of investigation? (For example, for verification investigations, students must be able to read and follow directions. What might you do to support emergent readers?)
4. What criteria might you use to decide which kind of investigation is most appropriate?

ACTIVITY 8.4

21st C ❸ ❹ ❺

Exploring Paper Helicopters

In this activity, you will examine a simple investigation called Exploring Paper Helicopters (found in many textbooks) and think about how that investigation can be tweaked to reflect the different types of investigation identified in the framework. We have chosen this investigation because it is easy to set up, requires very few materials, is fun to do, and draws on a number of scientific ideas and principles. Furthermore, this activity can be carried out in different ways, depending on the needs of your students, the degree of freedom you choose to provide, and your learning goals for the investigation.

Divide the class into two groups. Group one performs investigation Version A, while group two performs investigation Version B. See Appendix 8.A for templates for making helicopters. Cut along the solid lines and fold along the dotted lines. Use the figure below as a guide.

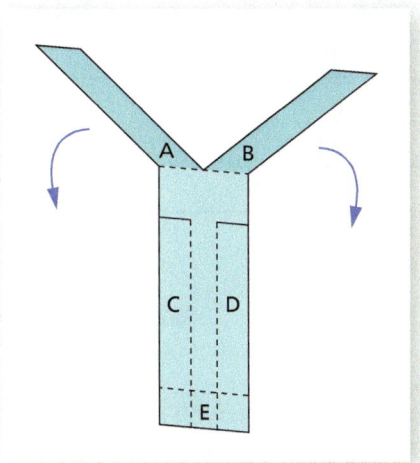

**Making a Paper Helicopter
from a Template**

continued on next page

Helicopter Investigation—Version A

- Make a paper helicopter using a template in Appendix 8.A.
- Observe the way the helicopter falls. What factors affect its rate of descent? Can you make it fall faster or slower?
- Make one or more modifications to your helicopter and see how it falls. You may use scissors to change the helicopter or use paper clips to change its mass.
- How did your modification(s) affect the helicopter's descent?

EXTEND YOUR UNDERSTANDING

1. Describe the modifications you made and why.
2. What variables were you testing?
3. Did you make the helicopter fall faster or slower? How?
4. Write a short paragraph (three or four sentences) that summarizes at least two things you learned about paper helicopters.

When you have completed your version of the investigation and answered the "Extend your understanding" questions, find a partner who performed the other investigation—version B below. Compare the two approaches by answering the discussion questions at the end of the activity.

Helicopter Investigation—Version B

- Make a paper helicopter using a template in Appendix 8.A. Be sure to use the same size template for each trial.
- Drop the helicopter from a height of two metres, and time the fall.
- Add a paper clip to the bottom of the helicopter. Predict what will happen. Let it fall and record the time.
- Repeat to get a second reading.
- Add a second paper clip. Again predict and time the helicopter's fall and repeat to get a second reading.
- Use the table below to record your results.

Data Table for Helicopter Investigation B			
Trial	Number of paper clips	Predicted time to fall two metres	Measured time to fall two metres
A	0		
B	1		
C	1		
D	2		
E	2		

EXTEND YOUR UNDERSTANDING

1. Explain your findings from trials A (no paper clips), B and C (one paper clip), and D and E (two paper clips) in terms of air pressure, gravity, mass, and acceleration.
2. Which of these variables are you testing?
3. What do you think would happen in a vacuum?
4. Is timing the descent the best way to measure the fall? Is there a better way? Explain.
5. Were you surprised by the results? Be specific.
6. Analyze experimental design. How would you modify it to get "better" results?

When you have completed your version of the investigation and answered the "Extend your understanding" questions, find a partner who performed the other investigation—version A above. Compare the two approaches by answering the discussion questions below.

DISCUSSION QUESTIONS

1. What is the purpose of each investigation?
2. Categorize the two approaches in terms of the types of science investigation described in the framework from pages 152–154.
3. How are the two approaches different in terms of student autonomy, the degree of free exploration allowed, and the role of the teacher?
4. What are advantages and disadvantages of each approach?
5. What skills are learned with each set of instructions?
6. How engaging was each investigation and why?
7. Compile a list of what you learned in each investigation. Are the lists the same? Do they overlap and if so, what is shared?

USING THIS ACTIVITY WITH ELEMENTARY SCHOOL STUDENTS

This activity brings together elements of versions A and B from above. We suggest beginning with free explorations and letting students play with the paper helicopters. Once they have had a chance to freely explore, they will likely have generated several ideas about what they would like to investigate. These ideas can help them formulate a list of variables that might be explored further. Depending on the grade level and prior knowledge of your students, you might include discussions of forces and flight, or you might choose to focus on science inquiry skills.

1. Model for students how to fold the helicopter template. Also demonstrate dropping the helicopter and timing its fall.
2. Distribute a copied helicopter template to each pair of students. Have them cut out and make the helicopter. For younger students, you might use precut templates and go through the folding step by step, pausing after each step to check that students are folding correctly.
3. Allow some time for free exploration and ask students to generate a list of questions that arise from their play. These questions can lead to potential helicopter modifications.
4. Provide each pair of students with a stopwatch and several paper clips. Ask students to explore the way the helicopter falls, both unaltered and with a modification of their choosing (for example, by adding a paper clip to the bottom or by cutting the blades in half). For K–3 students, you can explore the rate of falling qualitatively—i.e., using words such as slower, faster, fastest—or by dropping two helicopters simultaneously from the same height to compare. You might ask two volunteers to help you model dropping the paper helicopter and timing its fall.
5. After giving students a chance to play, ask them to describe what they observed and to consider a possible reason for it, and to think of a way to test their idea.
6. Introduce the idea of a fair test. For example, if you drop two helicopters from different heights, is it fair to compare them? Since it is not, introduce the idea of changing only one variable at a time and controlling all other variables.
7. Ask students to record their modifications and the steps of their investigations in writing or pictures in their science notebooks, journals, or logs, or on a data sheet.
8. As a class, discuss findings. What modifications were made? How did these modifications change the helicopter and its fall?
9. Follow up this investigation by exploring a) forces acting on the helicopter; b) principles of flight such as lift, gravity, drag, and thrust; and c) how to construct a paper airplane that flies (glides) the farthest.
10. *Assessment*: Use a rubric or anecdotal notes to assess student performance and inquiry skills, or a checklist to assess student science notebooks and data sheets.

Child as Scientist

If you introduce Activity 8.4, you will likely note that giving students time for free exploration increases motivation and curiosity and enhances the quality of questions asked. Students are better prepared to focus on subsequent related tasks. Play-based science investigation can enhance young students' developing understandings of science concepts. Much related literature builds upon Vygotsky's (1987) work on concept formation, and asserts the importance of familiarity and context in conceptual change stemming from play-based science investigations. For further discussion of play and science investigation, see, for example, Fleer (1996, 2009), Jordan (1992), and Martins and Veiga (2001).

Other Types of Science Activities

Sometimes students are engaged in activities that do not fit into the framework we presented earlier in the chapter; for example, building a solar system model. Such activities usually support content learning and are designed to be fun and to use non-traditional materials that are easily found in the classroom or home. For example, creating a model of how muscles and bones work together can help students understand how the actions of muscle contraction and relaxation move bones, and how muscles and bones work together to give us support and help us move. As valuable as these activities are, they should not be confused with scientific inquiry—question posing, data collection and analysis, and critical thinking are at the heart of inquiry.

SKILLS DEVELOPMENT

In this section, we explore the role of skills development in the context of investigations. An analysis of science policy documents from across Canada confirms that skills of inquiry are an important part of scientific literacy. The *Pan Canadian Framework* (Council of Ministers of Education Canada, 1997) states,

> Students use a variety of skills in the process of answering questions, solving problems, and making decisions. While these skills are not unique to science, they play an important role in the development of scientific understandings and in the application of science and technology to new situations. The listing of the skills is not intended to imply a linear sequence or to identify a single set of skills required in each science investigation. Every investigation and application of science has unique features that determine the particular mix and sequence of skills involved. (p. 6)

The *Pan Canadian Framework* outlines four broad categories of skills that students should develop: a) initiating and planning, b) performing and recording, c) analyzing and interpreting, and d) communication and teamwork. These skills are incorporated into the provincial and territorial science curricula in various forms. For example, British Columbia outlines a continuum of processes and skills that are built upon in each grade, starting with observing and communicating in Kindergarten and adding two more skills (e.g., classifying, interpreting observations, making inferences, questioning, interpreting data, and developing models) in each subsequent grade (British Columbia Ministry of Education, 2005). Similarly, the Foundation for the Atlantic Canada Science Curriculum (n.d., p. 3) notes that skills such as questioning, designing experiments, collecting data, and interpreting data are fundamental to engaging in science.

Many such lists have been generated to describe the range of skills students need for science in general and inquiry in particular. For example, Padilla (1990) outlines basic and integrated process skills:

Watch

Keeping Observation Records

Basic science process skills:

- *observing* (using the senses to gather information)
- *inferring* (making an educated guess based on previously known information)
- *measuring* (using standard and nonstandard measures and estimating to describe an object or event)
- *communicating* (using written or oral language or graphic symbols to describe an object or event)
- *classifying* (sorting or grouping objects or events based on properties or criteria)
- *predicting* (stating a future outcome based on patterns of evidence)

Integrated science process skills:

- *controlling variables* (identifying variables in an investigation and changing only the independent variable)
- *defining operationally* (stating how and in what units a variable is measured)
- *formulating hypotheses* (stating the anticipated outcome of an investigation)
- *interpreting data* (organizing and drawing conclusions from data)
- *experimenting* (conducting all steps of an experiment—posing a question; stating a hypothesis; identifying, controlling, and operationally defining variables; designing a fair test; and conducting and interpreting the results)
- *formulating models* (creating physical or mental models of an object or event)

Process skills are applicable to all areas of science. The *basic* process skills act as a foundation for *integrated* process skills. All these skills cannot be taught in one investigation, but rather must be developed over time and with appropriate tasks. All skills have varying levels of difficulty depending on the context. Making observations can be simple and rudimentary (e.g., observing colour changes) or complex and more nuanced (e.g., observing animal behaviour). Likewise, manipulating equipment can be simple (e.g., using an electronic scale with a digital display) or more complex (e.g., designing and building a device that incorporates multiple simple machines to perform a task). It is important to recognize that skills need to be taught explicitly (and often separately from the investigation itself) and that students need opportunities to practise the same skill in different situations.

ACTIVITY 8.5   *21st C* ❶ ❷

Exploring Skill Development

In this activity, you will consider investigations commonly found in elementary science textbooks or resources—i.e., exploring properties of light and the helicopter activity. If you know what you will be teaching in an upcoming practicum, you may choose to use the textbook used in your practicum school. Using the table below, describe the skills your students may develop while performing these two investigations and one of your choosing. We have used the basic science process skills, but the activity can easily be extended to include additional skills. An investigation of the basic properties of light is provided as an example. Light and sound are topics usually found in the Grade 4 science curriculum. Typical student investigations show that light travels in a straight path, is reflected from shiny surfaces, refracts or bends when travelling from one medium to another, and is made up of many colours.

continued on next page

Developing Process Skills

Investigation skill	Investigating the properties of light	Helicopter activity	Choose your own
Observing	Yes (e.g., students observe that light travels in straight lines)		
Inferring	Yes (e.g., students make inferences about the spectrum of visible light with rainbows in mind)		
Measuring	Yes (e.g., students measure angles of refraction)		
Communicating	No		
Classifying	No		
Predicting	Yes (e.g., students make predictions about how light will travel through different mediums)		

👁 **Watch**

Science (teacher introducing snails to young class)

DISCUSSION QUESTIONS

1. Which skills seem overemphasized and which are overlooked? Why do you think this is so?
2. Which skills do you predict you will overemphasize, and which skills do you predict you might overlook in your classroom? Why?
3. List other skills, not included here, you would highlight.

Developing Process Skills with Elementary School Students: Classification

👁 **Watch**

Animal Classification

Be mindful of including too many skills and too much content within a single investigation. This can result in student frustration and withdrawal. Instead, include one or two skills into each investigation, knowing that you will be able to bring additional skills that build upon them into your science curriculum over the course of the year. Consider the process skill of *classifying*. One way to approach a classifying activity is to gather a collection of objects—for example, fruit, pictures of animals or plants, classroom objects, or fossil samples—for examination. Ask students to sort the objects (for example, five different fruits) and to create rules for sorting (for example, by colour, shape, or texture).

Another example might be to create learning centres around the theme of classification. Organize four centres, with different objects at each. Examples are vegetables, fossils, photos of animals, or pencils. At each table, students can create their own rules to sort the objects into groups. Depending on your students' experience with classification, you might have them simply create two groups based on one characteristic, or sort into more complex classifications. Students can record the classification criteria they used on chart paper or in their science notebooks using words or pictures. As students rotate through the centres, they will develop the skill of classifying in different ways. Groups can share their classification systems at the end of the activity. Please see Appendix A for more information on creating learning centres.

Extension: Choose a basic or integrated process skill. Create four learning centres to help students develop the skill. Describe how you could explicitly incorporate numeracy and literacy into the centres.

DEMONSTRATIONS IN THE SCIENCE CLASSROOM

A particularly valuable science activity is the demonstration, which can be an important and exciting part of science class. It might be an attention getter to start a topic, an activity that addresses a misconception, or something fun and interesting that is worth sharing with the class. Demonstrations usually take about 10 minutes to perform and include questions that promote critical thinking and participation. There are many interesting and important aspects of science that are best observed rather than performed by students due to safety issues.

Despite the popularity of demonstrations, they have also been criticized as being just entertaining, without enabling valuable learning. (See Crouch, Fagen, Callan, & Mazur, 2004.) Crouch et al. (2004) suggest that students who simply observe a demonstration do not necessarily understand the science concept presented any better than students who have not seen the demonstration at all. We suggest that demonstrations should be coupled with a student observation activity that incorporates making a prediction about what will happen, if appropriate, recording observations from the demo, or trying to explain what was seen. This is commonly called a Predict, Observe, Explain (POE) exercise. (See Appendix 8.B for a sample student worksheet.) The POE sequence elicits student ideas and encourages discussion (White & Gunstone, 1992). It can be used not only with demonstrations but also as an organizational tool for science investigations.

Choosing a Demonstration Be mindful of where you source demonstration ideas. YouTube has a multitude of demonstrations, but several are dangerous and give no information about amounts of materials, procedures, or safety. Should you choose to use an online resource, it *must* be carefully tested for safety, accuracy, and appropriateness prior to use in the classroom. We strongly recommend consulting an established, reputable source, or using a procedure that has been tested by an experienced teacher. Some resources that might be useful are listed below:

- Bilash, B., & Shields, M. (2001). *A demo a day: A year of biological demonstrations.* Botavia, IL: FLINN Scientific Ltd.
- Bosak S. V. (1991). *Science is…* Markham, ON: Scholastic.
- Gross, G.R., Koob, J., & Bilash, B. (1995). *A demo a day: A year of chemical demonstrations.* Botavia, IL: FLINN Scientific Ltd.
- Liem, T. L. (1987). *Invitations to science inquiry* (2nd ed.). Lexington, MA: Ginn Press.

Preparation and Practice In order for a demonstration to be successful, always practise it well in advance of performing it for others.

Student Participation and Engagement Consider carefully how your students will participate in the demonstration experience. At times you will want them to gather at the carpet to observe if safety is not a concern. At other times, students may use their science notebooks or a worksheet to record their observations. The science notebook would allow students to make a prediction, record their observations of the demonstration, and give an explanation of what was seen.

When using demonstrations in teaching science, explore ways to provide a genuine learning experience by incorporating science process skills, such as observing, predicting, and hypothesizing. As you consider including a demonstration, ask yourself the following questions:

1. Would this activity be best done as a demonstration for the whole class or as a science investigation done by students?
2. Besides observing, what process skills will I ask students to engage in during the demonstration?

3. When do students need to manipulate equipment and materials and feel both the elation and frustration associated with data collection, and when is it better for them to watch a teacher demonstration?

Teachers feel more comfortable giving demos when they have observed or practised them. Activity 8.6 provides an opportunity for each teacher candidate to peruse demonstration resources and to choose, practise, and present a demonstration. As a class, you may choose to create a repertoire of demonstrations in a shared wiki. We hope teachers will be both inspired and more comfortable doing demonstrations they have seen or tried.

ACTIVITY 8.6

21st C ① ⑦

Do a Demonstration for the Class

Working in pairs or individually, prepare and present a 10-minute demonstration to your peers. Your instructor can provide guidance about your choice. Be sure to check your sources, particularly if you found them online. Gather your materials and practise your demonstration before presenting it.

Prepare a summary of the demonstration so that other teachers may easily do it in their classrooms. Be sure to upload your demonstration resource to the class wiki or another online platform. The summary should include the following:

Watch
Demonstrating a Method of Teaching

- Notes for teachers (one or two pages) that include safety considerations, materials needed, a description or diagram of the setup, a description of what to do, questions to ask during the demo, and an explanation of the theory or science underpinning the demonstration
- A student worksheet that could be used by students for recording purposes. (See Appendix 8.B.)

USING COMPUTER TECHNOLOGIES IN SCIENCE INVESTIGATIONS

Students' abilities to collect, analyze, interpret, and present data are central to scientific inquiry. Computer technologies play an important role in helping to facilitate these goals. A range of technologies such as software packages, probeware, computer simulations, and application software for smartphones and tablets are available to educators (Hewitt, 2005; Linn & Slotta, 2000; Slotta & Linn, 2009). Data management technologies can be helpful for storing and analyzing data. Inclusion of data management and statistics in your science curriculum and instruction also allows for meaningful connection to your mathematics teaching. Furthermore, there is a range of communications technologies that support sharing, analysis, and presentation of data. Be sure to inquire about what technologies are available at your school and within your school district.

As technologies become ubiquitous in schools, it is important for teachers to learn how to use them appropriately. In general, technologies, if used effectively, can facilitate student learning, provide interactions with phenomena that in real time or space would be difficult or impossible to do, render invisible interactions visible, and provide three-dimensional models. They allow students to focus on particular learning outcomes in an interactive and engaging way, and contribute to students' developing technological literacy. It should be emphasized, however, that these technologies are not meant to replace the teacher or other instructional strategies, but rather complement instruction and enhance student learning (Hewitt, 2005). They are yet another potentially powerful teaching tool to add to your growing repertoire of strategies. Accordingly, you will need to exercise judgment and critique the technology you are planning to use with your students. For example, consider if the technology is appropriate for the learning goals you have in mind, if it enhances student learning, or if it emphasizes particular scientific concepts clearly. Is the purpose of the investigation to collect data? Or to learn to graph? Or to interpret data? For internet use, is parent or guardian consent needed, and if so, has it been obtained? Depending on your answers, you might choose to use a particular technology in a particular way for a particular purpose. Many teachers say they must be willing to initially invest time and energy to learn to use a technology, but after mastering it, the technology's use becomes easy, fast, and fruitful for developing richer science investigations for students.

Data Collection and Management

Software Various software packages are commonly on networked systems in schools. Software that can support your students in learning science processes and concepts include tutorials and games, multimedia, spreadsheets, databases, word processing, and PowerPoint presentations.

Computer simulations Computer simulations are readily available and can be easily accessed via the internet or with the use of various computer software programs. Computer simulations are essentially models of systems, real-world events, or scientific phenomena. Topics that can be taught using simulations include, for example, climate change, rock formation, and structures and functions of body systems. We suggest building a library of computer simulations that you might use to complement your science investigations.

Probeware Probeware are electronic systems or sensors that can be used to collect, analyze, and interpret data. They can be connected to computers, calculators, or handheld devices; examples include probes that collect data about motion and temperature. Probeware allow students to easily manipulate variables and to collect data accurately and over specific amounts of time—particularly data collection that happens very quickly. Initially quite expensive, the price of probeware has dropped, and some elementary schools are equipped with various probeware tools.

Application software for smartphones and tablets Application software (apps), smartphones, and tablets are other tools that are becoming increasingly common in many science classrooms for data collection purposes. They are small, easy to use, and often unique in what they are able to accomplish. For example, there are stethoscope, sphygmomanometer, electroencephalograph, and oscilloscope apps. Other apps can measure angles, distance, and light intensity.

While some students today own a smartphone or tablet, teachers should not assume that all do. You will need to ensure that if they are used in your classroom, all students have their own access to the tools necessary to do the work.

Communication of Findings

Technology can also be useful for helping students share, store, and communicate their findings. Wikis, blogs, and online learning platforms such as Moodle and Blackboard are powerful tools for sharing class data and accompanying discussions. Spreadsheets allow for organization and analysis of other forms of data, and presentation tools such as PowerPoint, Prezi, and Keynote can be used by students to share findings with their peers.

Activities 8.7 and 8.8 provide an opportunity to use and critique some of the computer technologies available to teachers.

ACTIVITY 8.7

Using Data Management in Science Investigations: Monitoring Heart Rate

In this activity, you will collect data regarding heart rate in two different ways. This is a typical investigation found in many elementary science textbooks across the country. Its purpose is to investigate how heart rate changes with different activities, and to graph and interpret data.

BACKGROUND INFORMATION

- Most adults have a heart rate of 60–80 beats per minute. In children the heart rate is typically higher. The heartbeat (or heart sound) is sometimes called lub-dub. Each time the heart beats, the muscles of the atria and ventricles contract, but the atria and ventricles contract slightly out of sync, causing the lub-dub sound.
- Heart rate is recorded in heartbeats per minute. Each heartbeat causes a pulse. In this activity we will use pulse rate as a measure of heart rate.
- The pulse is a measure of the bulge in an artery as the blood is pumped. There are several pulse points on the human body. The most commonly used ones are the wrist and neck. We suggest you use the wrist pulse.
- To feel the wrist pulse, find the artery in the wrist. Place the tips of the first two fingers of one hand on the inside of the wrist closest to the thumb. You may need to press firmly in order to feel the pulse of blood that each heartbeat sends through the artery. Do not use your thumb to feel the pulse, as it has a pulse of its own.

MATERIALS

- Computer
- Graph paper or a graphing program
- Heart rate monitor (i.e. a handheld heart-rate monitor, a chest pressure belt, or a pulse rate finger-clip,)
- Stopwatch or clock

PROCEDURE

1. Work in pairs. One partner will act as time-keeper and recorder while the other has his or her heart rate monitored. Partners then switch roles.
2. To measure pulse rate, count the number of pulses in 15 seconds. Multiply that number by four to get heartbeats per minute. This is the resting state.
3. Measure and record pulse rate for each of the resting or activity situations in the table below. It is important to record the time of each manual data collection point in order to compare data later.
4. If you are using a heart-rate monitor, attach it to the first exerciser.
5. You will collect data from the manual recording of pulse rates and from the heart rate monitor. Be sure the monitor data is stored. Compile both sets of data in the table below.
6. Using a graphing program or graph paper, plot the data from the table on a heart rate/pulse rate versus time graph. Show both graphs on the same axis.

Data Table for Heart Rate/Pulse Rate

Time	Activity for the subject	Instructions for measuring heart rate/pulse rate	Beats in 15 seconds	x 4 =	Heart rate/ pulse rate (beats/ min)	Heart rate monitor reading
	The subject is at rest (resting state)	Take the pulse at rest.		x 4 =		
	Walking on the spot for two minutes	Take pulse after the subject has walked on the spot for two minutes.		x 4 =		

Running on the spot for two minutes	Take pulse after the subject has run on the spot for two minutes.	x 4 =
Doing jumping jacks for two minutes	Take pulse after the subject has done jumping jacks for two minutes.	x 4 =

DISCUSSION QUESTIONS

1. What can you conclude about the relationship between heart rate and exercise? How do you know?

2. If using a heart-rate monitor, compare the two graphs. Do you arrive at the same conclusion from each graph?

3. What are the advantages of collecting the data manually? Of using a heart-rate monitor?

4. What are the disadvantages of each data collection method?

5. Imagine you were to perform this heart-rate investigation with elementary school students. Which data collection method would you prefer? Why?

6. What factors might affect your choice of using technology (e.g., a temperature probe, a simulation) as you plan investigations for your students?

USING THIS ACTIVITY WITH ELEMENTARY SCHOOL STUDENTS

In this investigation, students explore how their pulse rate changes with different types of exercise. It includes connections to numeracy (students apply their multiplication and data management skills) and physical education (measurement of pulse rates can become part of a post-gym class routine). If heart rate monitors are available at your school, do include them in data collection. The investigation works well set up as centres that students rotate through; this is how it is outlined below. It can be helpful to create instruction cards at each centre so that students can quickly check the procedures to follow. You may wish to have all students go through each of the measurements together. Be sure that all students start by measuring their resting heart rate. This is an ideal time to review your expectations for their participation.

MATERIALS

- Stopwatch
- Graph paper or computer with spreadsheet program

1. Have students rest for two minutes or begin investigation after quiet seat work (e.g., reading).

2. Distribute data tables or have students create their own in their science notebooks.

3. Demonstrate for students how to find their pulse, and practise by finding their own. You might have students find their pulse on their neck first—the neck pulse can be easier to find, especially if this is new to your students. When they recognize the rhythm of the pulse, have them find their wrist pulse. Ensure that students are not using their thumbs to check!

4. Have students count the number of beats in 15 seconds, and then record in their data tables. Multiply this number by four to get the number of beats per minute. Alternatively students could count the number of beats in one minute, in 30 seconds and multiply by two, or in 20 seconds and multiply by three.

continued on next page

5. Ask students to rotate through the following centres with a partner:
   - Walking: One student walks on the spot for two minutes; partner measures the walker's pulse for 15 seconds and records it. Partners switch roles and repeat.
   - Running: One student runs on the spot for two minutes; partner measures the runner's pulse for 15 seconds and records it. Partners switch roles and repeat.
   - Jumping jacks: One student does jumping jacks for two minutes; partner measures the jumper's pulse for 15 seconds and records it. Partners switch roles and repeat.

6. Distribute graph paper and have students record their pulse rate/heart rate data on a bar graph—see the figure below for an example. You might give them specific directions on how to set up their graph using an appropriate scale, or you may have students set up a bar graph as they see fit. Students could also input their data into a spreadsheet program and create a graph this way.

7. Have student describe, orally or in writing, how their pulse rate/heart rate changed after each activity. Why do they think this was the case?

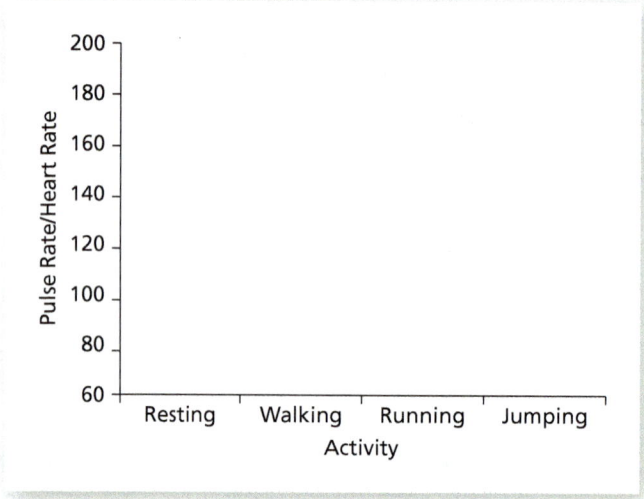

Activity-Pulse Rate/Heart Rate Bar Graph

Source: ArtPlus

ACTIVITY 8.8

21st C

Using Simulations in Science Investigations

Find a simulation that shows the result of exercise on heart rate, and compare with your results from Activity 8.7. Locate two other simulations on the Internet. Try to find ones from different disciplines of science—life science, physical science, or Earth and space science. Record the website and try the simulation. As you engage with the simulation, answer the questions below.

POSSIBLE SOURCES
- www.explorelearning.com
- http://phet.colorado.edu/en/simulations/category/physics
- http://smartr.edc.org

DISCUSSION QUESTIONS

1. Discuss two strengths and two weaknesses of each simulation.
2. Would you use this simulation in your classroom? Why or why not?

3. Brainstorm three places in the science curriculum where a simulation would be ideal for showing a scientific phenomenon or principle (e.g., climate change, functioning of organ systems, a tour of the cell).

USING THIS ACTIVITY WITH ELEMENTARY SCHOOL STUDENTS

This activity incorporates literacy, as students tell or write a story about what happens to their bodies as they exercise. Depending on the resources at your school, have students work with their heart-rate investigation partners in the computer lab, or show a heart rate simulation to the class on an interactive whiteboard.

1. Discuss the heart rate investigation, reviewing the students' findings and explanations of how exercise changes heart rate. Let students know that they will be viewing a computer simulation of the heart during exercise and that, with their partners, they will be writing the story of an exercising heart.
2. In pairs, students view the heart rate simulation and relate what they are seeing to their own investigation (when they are doing light exercise, vigorous exercise, resting). Be sure to give ample time for students to view it several times! Circulating and talking with students about the changes in heart rate will allow you to assess their understanding of the concept.
3. With their partners, have students create a story of what happens to the heart during exercise. Encourage them to include text and images—their stories might take the form of a graphic novel or a comic.
4. Have students share their stories with the class.
5. *Extension:* Have students investigate through simulations other factors that can affect heart rate, such as drinking cola. Older students could incorporate these factors into a more complex story.
6. *Assessment:* This activity can be assessed with anecdotal comments, a checklist, or a rubric.

> ⊙ **Watch**
>
> Investigating Moon Phases (Part 5)

PROBLEM-SOLVING INVESTIGATIONS THROUGH DESIGN TECHNOLOGY

As mentioned, problem-solving investigations allow students to explore questions or problems posed by the teacher. Often the equipment and materials are suggested by the teacher but may involve student input. A specific type of problem solving involves designing and constructing a device or product that will perform a task or address a specific need. This is often referred to as *design technology*. For example, students may be asked to create a solar cooker. Design technology tasks are an important aspect of the science investigation experience, and can foster creativity, collaboration, and critical thinking. Furthermore, they are fun! A common approach to help students through the design process is called *identify-design-make-appraise*. This approach can be helpful in scaffolding student learning. Students:

- identify the problem to be solved
- design a plan, which may include drawings or diagrams
- make or construct the device, object, or product based on the plan
- appraise or evaluate the results

Some argue that the design process does not actually work in this way—neither in workplaces nor in the classroom (Mawson, 2003). Rather, students (and designers, innovators, inventors) go through a process that is far from linear as they proceed toward completing the task. The process is usually cyclical in nature, often involving trial and error and multiple iterations and deliberations.

Design technology challenges are one way of addressing the design component of science and technology curricula. In a typical science challenge, students work in teams to construct devices that have a particular function. (See Chapter 6 for an example of a design technology assignment and assessment.) Some examples of design challenges appear below. As you will see, some are prescriptive, and others less so.

- Design and construct a package that will protect a raw egg from breaking when dropped from the greatest height.
- Design and construct a device that will make a sound (such as a ringing bell) after 10 seconds, using whatever materials are available.
- Design and build, using a piece of aluminum foil 15 cm x 15 cm, and 35 cm of tape, a boat that will float under a load of the greatest number of coins.
- Construct, using eight straws and two pieces of standard 8 ½ by 11-inch paper, the tallest free-standing structure that you can.

ACTIVITY 8.9

21st C

Design Technology Challenges

In groups of four, design and build a boat that will float under a load of the greatest number of coins. Use a 15 cm x 15 cm piece of aluminum foil and 35 cm of tape. Once you have built your boat, determine how many coins it can hold and still stay afloat.

DISCUSSION QUESTIONS

1. What design factors enhance the effectiveness of your boat?
2. Compare your results with the results of other teams. Which boat construction held the most coins and why?
3. What scientific principles did you learn through this challenge?
4. What skills were developed through this activity?
5. When might you use a design technology activity with your students?
6. What are some of the benefits of using design technology activities?

USING THIS ACTIVITY WITH ELEMENTARY SCHOOL STUDENTS

For this activity, pre-cut 15 cm x 15 cm squares of aluminum foil, allowing one for each group plus a few extra squares. Numeracy can be incorporated into the activity by having students measure and cut squares of foil—be sure to factor the time for students to do this into your planning. Use large storage tubs filled with water for testing the boats and remember to cover the surrounding floor with newspaper or do this challenge outside.

1. Discuss with your class the concepts of sinking and floating—what objects sink, what objects float, etc. Read aloud Pamela Allen's *Who Sank the Boat?*, a book that chronicles a number of large animals getting into a small boat. As each animal climbs into the boat, it sinks lower into the water, but it does not sink until a tiny mouse climbs aboard!
2. Challenge students to design and build a boat, using limited supplies, that will carry a maximum number of coins without sinking.
3. Working together in groups of two to four, students brainstorm ideas for how they might design their boat using only a 15 cm x 15 cm piece of aluminum foil and 35 cm of tape.

Students can make sketches and notes in their science notebooks or on large sheets of paper.

4. Each group predicts how many coins their boat will carry and records this number in their notebook or on their planning sheet.

5. As groups complete their planning, have them share with you what their design is and how they will build their boat. After checking the group's plan, distribute the foil square, tape, and several coins. Give groups ample time to construct their boats.

6. In the tubs of water, have groups test how many coins their boat can carry, and record the number of coins the boat held before it sank. Groups might also measure the mass of the maximum load of coins to bring additional measurement into the investigation. As in *Who Sank the Boat?*, the constructed boat will finally sink, in this case under the load of one additional coin.

7. As a class, share and discuss your results. How many coins did each boat carry before sinking? What were the designs of the boats? Which design could hold the largest load? Why do you think this was the case?

8. If time permits, students can revisit their design and, in light of their discussion, make changes and test a second boat design. Does the second boat hold more coins before sinking? Why do you think this is the case?

9. *Assessment:* A checklist or rubric could be used for this investigation. You might want to assess students' ability to work collaboratively, their boat design, or their understanding of floating and sinking.

SCIENCE BEYOND THE CLASSROOM

Science fairs have been a part of Canadian science education since 1959, when Winnipeg, Edmonton, Hamilton, Toronto, Montreal, and Vancouver all hosted their first fairs.

Canada's National Science Fair program falls under the umbrella of Youth Science Canada, which has chapters in every province and territory, and plays a "vital role in nurturing the scientific impulse amongst our youth—encouraging them to get their hands dirty and develop scientific and technological knowledge and skills through project-based science" (www.youthscience.ca). Regional science fairs (for example, Sci-Tech in Ontario, Central Alberta Regional Science Fair, Prince Edward Island Science Fair, Sahtu Northwest Territories Regional Science Fair) provide opportunities for students to investigate a scientific question, topic, or phenomenon of their own choosing, encouraging participation, excellence, and innovation in science and technology. Students may work individually or with a partner to design and perform an experiment, or perhaps to create and design an artefact or innovation. Students' work is then presented, usually on a display board that includes materials and a written report. The exhibits are often set up in a central location where other students, parents, teachers, and the public can view the work and talk with the young researchers. Traditionally, but not always, science fairs are judged by experts. Winners of local fairs move forward to regional competitions, and, if successful, advance to the Canada Wide Science Fair. The Canada Wide Science Fair takes place every year in May in a different Canadian city.

While science fairs have the potential to motivate and encourage students' participation in scientific inquiry, they must be approached critically. Science fairs are competitive and can thus present a number of ethical, equity, and social justice issues. They can be exclusive, privileging some students and ideas over others. Research on

Canadian science fairs (Bencze & Bowen, 2009; Bowen & Bencze, 2009) has indicated that those participants who reach the national level tend to have access to resources not available to all students (e.g., expensive technologies, costly displays, and university or private laboratories). Many projects have significant commercial application, and the fairs themselves can prominently display corporate logos and branding. Sometimes science achievements are commodified through monetary prizes and scholarships. When considering your students' participation in science fairs, keep these concerns at the forefront of your planning. Speak with other teachers at your school about the purpose of the school science fair and how it should be framed (e.g., a competition, a celebration, an exhibition). Encourage your students to explore topics that are of interest to them and that they can investigate on their own. Send a letter to parents and guardians expressing that the goal of the science fair is to participate in student-driven scientific inquiry. Remind your students that you want to see the science they do, not that others do for them.

EXPLORING ELEMENTARY SCIENCE IN CREATIVE WAYS: MAGNETS AND MAGNETISM

In order to teach any topic confidently and effectively, it is helpful to have a broad knowledge base. In this section, we present some ideas to help develop your subject matter content knowledge (CK) and pedagogical content knowledge (PCK) on the topic of magnets. The topic is presented with a visual that might appear in a print or media resource. We encourage you to consider other resources as well. As you learn or review the content, keep in mind issues such as terminology, abstract processes, integration with mathematics and language arts, and activities that support student learning. Additionally, consider the metacognitive aspect of the activity, such as understanding how you learn, what you know, and what you need to know.

ACTIVITY 8.10

21st C ❶ ❸ ❺

Magnets and Magnetism

Magnets and magnetism are included in elementary science curricula in several grades. Most provinces and territories introduce magnets in the early elementary grades and revisit them in later units on electricity. In Manitoba, related learning outcomes are included in the Grade 3 science curriculum within the Forces That Attract or Repel cluster. In Ontario, magnets and magnetism are also included in the Grade 3 curriculum, this time under the unit Forces Causing Movement, while the British Columbia science curriculum includes magnets and magnetism in the Grade 1 science unit Forces and Motion. The Alberta science curriculum includes expectations on the topic in its Grade 5 unit on Electricity and Magnetism. All of the curricular outcomes anticipate that students will be able to identify materials that are attracted by magnets and those that can be magnetized, to determine the orientation of a magnet's poles, and to show that opposite poles attract while like poles repel.

Reviewing the Content

1. Learn or review the content associated with magnets and magnetism. For example, what is a magnet and what causes magnetism? Use the visual that follows to guide your exploration.
2. Write a list of definitions of important or unfamiliar vocabulary and processes associated with this topic.
3. When you feel comfortable with the content, use the figure that follows to explain magnets and magnetism to a peer.

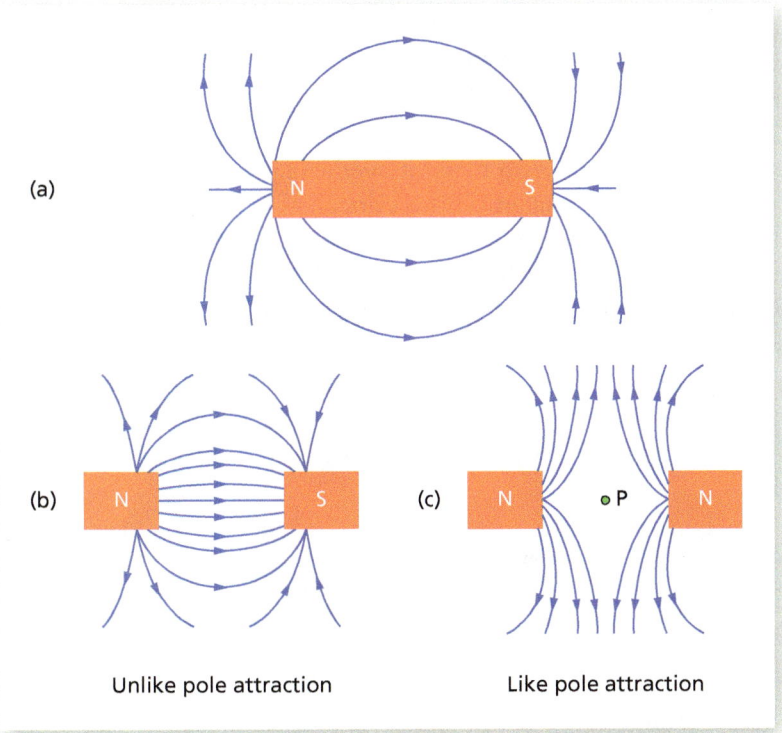

Magnetic Fields

Literacy and Numeracy Connections

1. Share the story *The Wiener Dog Magnet* by Hayes Roberts (www.magickeys.com/books/wienerdog/index.html) with your students. In the story, the wiener dogs are able to use their magnetism to make a bridge to rescue a pair of stranded alligators. Brainstorm similar creative and fun ways that the properties of magnets can be used to do things, and write a story about it.

2. Graph the results of a class investigation of materials that can be picked up by a magnet.
   - Step 1: From the following list (iron nail, paper clip, glass, pencil, copper wire, rock, screw, aluminum can, feather, and paper) predict which objects will be attracted by a magnet.
   - Step 2: Record the prediction using a bar graph.
   - Step 3: Test each object with a magnet, and record the result.
   - Step 4: Create a new bar graph with your results.

EXPLANATIONS USING SCIENTIFIC KNOWLEDGE

- Compare your two graphs. Were any predictions incorrect? What predictions were you surprised to find were wrong. Why?
- What type of objects or materials will magnets attract?
- Do magnets attract all metals? Explain.

Activities for Elementary School Students

1. *Pick Up* (adapted from Bosak, 1991)—Explore which objects and through which media magnets are able to exert their attraction. Use a magnet to sort through a group of metallic and nonmetallic objects and to find paper clips hidden in a box of sand. Try to pick up paper clips

continued on next page

in a glass of water using a magnet. With a strong magnet in the palm of your hand, can you lift another strong bar magnet at the back of your hand by simply raising your hand? Predict and test how many paper clips a magnet will pick up. Will a magnet pick up paper clips through a piece of paper? How many pieces of paper?

2. *Magnetic patterns*—This investigation works well using an Elmo or overhead projector. Place an acetate sheet or piece of glass over a strong bar magnet. This is critical, as you will not be able to remove the filings from the bare magnets. Sprinkle iron filings over the magnet and observe the patterns created. Arrange bar magnets with like (i.e., N and N) and unlike (i.e., N and S) poles together, sprinkle iron filings over the acetate, and observe the patterns created. What do the patterns of filings show?

3. *Make a magnet*—Using a strong permanent magnet, stroke the length of an iron nail in one direction with one pole of the magnet. Will the nail pick up a paper clip? Repeat the first step until the nail is magnetized and then continue to strengthen its magnetic power. How many paper clips can you get the nail to pick up?

CONCLUDING THOUGHTS

Science investigations are the hallmark of science classes. For many students, investigations are what they look forward to most in science. Investigations are an opportunity to "do science," to engage with materials and ideas, and to ask questions and pursue answers. They can be an exciting part of the science curriculum. Planning and implementing meaningful science investigations can be challenging but rewarding. It is clear that teachers need to make careful and informed decisions about the "what and why" of investigations. What follows is a summary of the key ideas related to the learning objectives provided at the beginning of this chapter.

Reasons for doing science investigations

Science investigations support students' learning in a multitude of ways. Investigations can motivate students, teach science inquiry skills, foster development of manipulative and communication skills, strengthen theoretical knowledge, encourage critical thinking, and teach the daily applications of scientific knowledge. Practical experiences in the science classroom can support students' cognitive, affective, and skills development.

Types of science investigations

There are a number of frameworks that classify science investigations. One such framework balances teacher practice and research as it organizes investigations into three categories: 1) verifications—investigations that follow a specific procedure toward a predetermined endpoint,

2) problem solving—investigations (structured or guided inquiries) in which students freely explore questions posed by the teacher; and 3) experiments—investigations in which students plan and conduct investigations related to their own questions. These investigations differ in terms of the role of the teacher, the outcomes of the investigation, and the degree of student autonomy.

Skills of inquiry

In science investigations, students learn and apply a range of skills that allow them to answer questions, solve problems, and make decisions. The *Pan Canadian Framework* outlines four broad categories of skills: initiating and planning, performing and recording, analyzing and interpreting, and communication and teamwork. Skills need to be taught explicitly, and students need opportunities to practise the same skill in different situations.

Using demonstrations in the science classroom

Demonstrations are a way to explore concepts, reactions, equipment, and phenomena with students. They generate curiosity, and can pique students' interest in particular topics or concepts. Sometimes demonstrations are used to introduce a topic and provide a hook; at other times they complete a unit and bring a number of concepts or principles together. Demonstrations should be coupled with an activity that incorporates making predictions, recording observations, and an explanation of the science concepts introduced in the demonstration.

Information and communication technologies in science investigations

Computer technologies play an important role in helping to facilitate and achieve student learning in the lab. A range of technologies such as software packages, probeware, computer simulations, and application software for smartphones and tablets are available to educators. Furthermore, there is a range of communication technologies to support sharing, analysis, and presentation of data. Exercise judgment as you determine the appropriate computer technology to enhance and augment the student experience in the lab.

Problem-solving investigations through design technology

A specific type of problem solving involves designing and constructing, often referred to as *design technology*. Students may be asked to create a device or product that will perform a task or to address a specific need. A common framework that can scaffold student learning is identify-design-make-appraise. These tasks are important aspects of science investigations and can foster creativity, collaboration, and critical thinking.

Science fairs

Geared toward promoting participation, excellence, and innovation in science and technology, science fairs provide an opportunity for students to explore a topic and research a question of their own choice. Science fairs provide a unique venue for students, parents, teachers, and experts to come together and celebrate young people's science explorations. However, science fairs and participation in them should be critically considered prior to including them in your students' science learning experience.

Educational research related to inquiry

Research focusing on science investigations and inquiry is vast (and often overwhelming)! We have drawn upon a few researchers in the field, including Randy Bell, Larry Bencze, Michael Bowen, Derek Hodson, Roger Lock, Jerry Wellington, and Mark Windschitl. We encourage you to read the work of these researchers as well as the many others who have contributed to this field over the past few decades.

BRINGING IT ALL TOGETHER: FINAL QUESTIONS

1. Choose two ideas about science investigations from this chapter that resonate with you. Explain why you have chosen them.

2. Work in pairs or groups of three and discuss why some teachers might resist conducting science investigations with their students. How might these barriers be overcome?

Visit MyEducationLab® to access an electronic version of the text, as well as a variety of topics that enhance the text material. The topics include the following to support your learning in the course:

- Assessments, including interactive case studies, activities, and video assignments
- Discussion board questions
- Videos, simulations, a lesson plan builder, and other useful course resources

APPENDIX 8.A   **Template for Activity 8.4: Exploring Paper Helicopters**

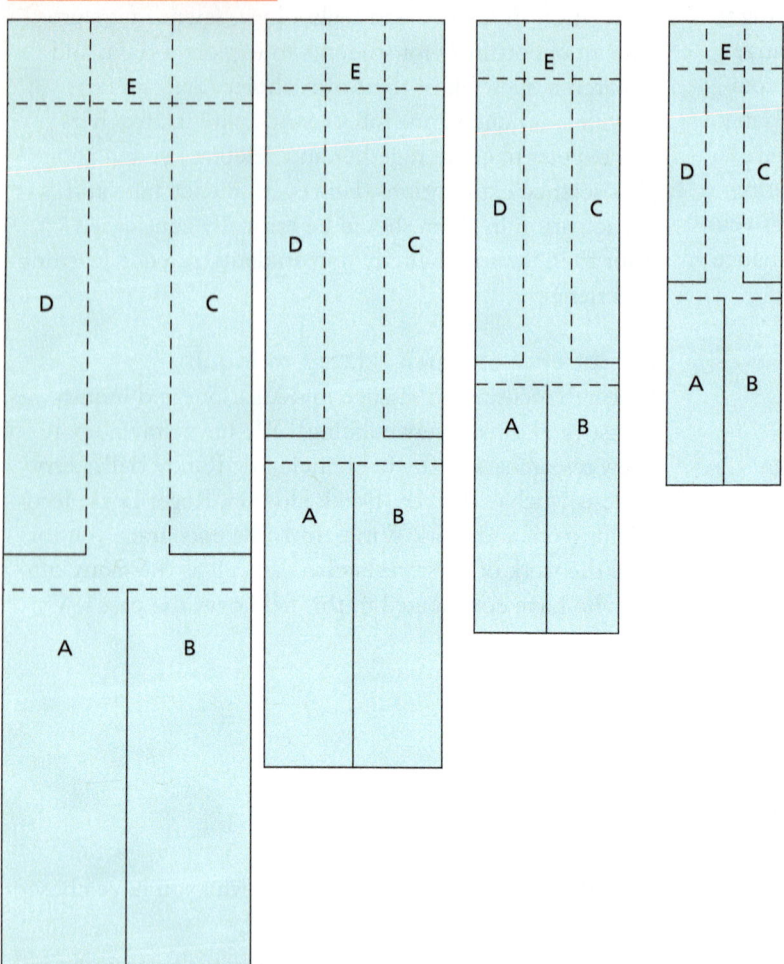

APPENDIX 8.B   **Sample Student Worksheet**

Demonstration title:	
Draw a labelled diagram of the demonstration setup.	**P**redict Make a prediction of what you think will happen.
	Observe Record your observations.
	Explain Give an explanation for what you saw in this demonstration.

Chapter 9
Planning for Scientific Inquiry and Investigations

Blend Images / Alamy

I love the idea of doing investigations—but I'm not sure where to start.

—Alex, preservice teacher candidate

I am afraid of letting my Grade 2s do investigations. It'll be a mess!

—Sania, elementary school teacher

We tested baking powder, cornstarch, and sugar and we tested it with water and Iodine and vinegar.

—Angelica, Grade 5 student

21st CENTURY LEARNING SKILLS & COMPETENCIES

1 **Communication**

2 **Critical thinking**

3 **Collaboration**

4 **Creativity**

5 **Literacy and numeracy**

6 **Media literacy**

7 **Technological literacy**

INTRODUCTION

Part of teaching science is planning for investigations. There is no simple, straightforward way to decide which types of investigations to do, when to do them, or how to approach them. Planning for science investigations can be simultaneously systematic and idiosyncratic, collaborative and isolating. Initially, planning and conducting investigations can seem overwhelming; however, with experience and collaboration with other teachers, your confidence will grow and you will develop a repertoire of enriching and effective investigations. When planning for investigations, ask yourself questions about all aspects of teaching and learning. Careful preparation ensures that investigations run smoothly and are a meaningful and fun experience for you and your students. Science investigations provide rich opportunities for integration with literacy and numeracy, and to make cross-curricular connections with other subjects.

In this chapter, we explore a number of considerations related to *preparing* for investigations, *conducting* investigations with your students, and *following up* the investigation with appropriate activities. We explore a number of ideas and planning tools that may serve as a guide as you plan for science investigations. We have tried to be both general in terms of a variety of planning considerations and also specific in advice and strategies.

PLANNING FOR INVESTIGATIONS

ACTIVITY 9.1

21st C 1 2

Prior Knowledge and Experience: Recollections from the Past

Recall two investigations or laboratory activities that you did in elementary or secondary school or university. Describe one that was enjoyable and motivating, and one that was overwhelming or stressful. Briefly describe the experiences and provide contextual information such as course content and level.

DISCUSSION QUESTIONS

1. Identify what you think made the first experience enjoyable and motivating.
2. For the second experience, identify what you think were the main sources of your anxiety (e.g., unfamiliarity with equipment, poor instructions, or concern over grades).
3. What might have helped to lessen your anxiety?

The first step in planning for science investigations is to establish your purpose. When your purpose is clear (for example, to verify previously learned material or to introduce new content), and the investigation matches your purpose, you can move on to the contextual considerations of planning. To ensure success, planning begins in advance of investigation day. Every investigation, classroom space, and group of students are different and you will need to decide what is required in a specific context. Let's begin by considering the teacher, the students, and the classroom setting.

Pre-Investigation Planning

When we use the term *investigation*, we refer to any of the verification (confirmation), problem solving (structured and guided inquiry), and experimental (open inquiry) investigations. Regardless of the type of investigation you choose, there are common planning considerations. Later we will explore specific aspects of planning for verification, problem solving, and open-ended investigations.

Teacher Considerations Investigations can be enjoyable for teachers. It can be rewarding to work with students and to see new skills and strengths emerge. However, they can also be a source of anxiety for teachers who feel pressed for preparation and instructional time. In this section, we present four aspects of pre-planning that will help reduce anxiety and make science investigations more valuable for all.

1. **Finding Appropriate Science Investigations.** The first planning consideration is finding age-appropriate, relevant, and safe science investigations for your students. For example, will you use an investigation from a textbook? If so, will you use it as is, or will you modify it to make it clearer, shorter, or more challenging? If a textbook does not approach an investigation in a way that best suits you and your students, where might you search for other ideas? Textbooks are edited and reviewed resources, and are likely to contain investigations that are appropriate; other sources may be untested. We raise this point due to the explosion of investigation ideas on the internet: Proceed carefully in choosing appropriate and safe investigations! There are many reputable books (e.g., *Science Is...* by Susan Bosak) and journals for teachers of science (e.g., *Science and Children* and *Science Scope*) full of ideas for science investigations available for your consideration. Provincial science specialist associations (e.g., Science Teachers' Association of Ontario, Alberta Teachers Association Science Council) and collaborations between educators and scientists (e.g., British Columbia's Scientist in Residence program) can be another source of ideas. Also check out Smarter Science (www.smarterscience.ca; Appendix 9.A).

2. **Testing the Investigation.** Once you have chosen an investigation, begin your pre-planning by performing the investigation as a student would. (Yes! Wear those goggles that students complain about!) This is always a good idea, particularly when you are unfamiliar with the procedure or equipment. Check the quantity of materials needed, the working order of equipment, the steps in the procedure, and the time required to do the investigation. By performing the investigation yourself, you will be able to identify any skills that need to be taught or reviewed prior to the investigation. You can also determine gaps in your own background knowledge and potential gaps your students may have. By using the same instructions that students will use, you can identify any instructions that are unclear or safety precautions that need to be emphasized. If a teacher's guide is available, do refer to it. After working through the investigation, you may need to rewrite the instructions. It is always helpful to perform the investigation with others and share ideas and tasks—this can easily be done with grade partners or teachers covering similar topics. Not only will you be able to identify the practical considerations of the investigation, but you will also be able to determine whether the investigation fits with your curricular goals. Will it be an activity or guided inquiry, or will students have the flexibility to explore more freely?

3. **Making Connections.** Ensure that the content of a particular investigation is meaningfully connected to the course and the topics you are covering. Students should clearly understand the purpose of the investigation, and you should be clear as to what learning outcomes or expectations the investigation supports. You may need to explicitly teach new material and address the connections to related course content. Later, as the year progresses, you might decide to refer back to the investigation, or even do the investigation again.

> *REMINDER CHECKLIST*
> ☐ Do I have a procedure that is appropriate for my needs?
> ☐ Have I examined resources carefully for a suitable investigation?
> ☐ Have I searched other sources, including colleagues, for an investigation?
> ☐ What skills and knowledge do students need in order to successfully do an investigation?
> ☐ Are the instructions clear?
> ☐ Where is the best placement of a particular investigation within a specific unit?
> ☐ How will I assess student understanding?

Student Considerations Science investigations can be used to motivate students; however, this is unlikely to happen if they are feeling confused, frustrated, or bored. Good planning keeps student needs central. Below are six aspects of planning that impact the student experience.

1. **Equipment Use and the Acquisition of Skills.** You may need to teach or review specific skills before students do the science investigation. For example, can the students operate a microscope with care and accuracy? Can they make reliable measurements with a ruler or thermometer? Do students understand the distinction between the independent variable (the variable being manipulated or changed), the dependent variable (the variable being observed or measured), and controlled variables (those that are kept the same)? Addressing skills prior to an investigation can increase your students' confidence and decrease frustration.

2. **Knowledge Scaffolding.** It may be necessary, after some initial formative assessment, to provide students with specific science content knowledge that is required for the investigation. For example, a science investigation designed to examine changes of states of matter due to absorption or release of heat assumes prior knowledge of properties of solids, liquids, and gases. If prior knowledge is assessed, and required knowledge is taught, the resultant scaffolding will enhance students' learning.

3. **Pre-investigation Student Tasks.** You may choose to incorporate a pre-investigation discussion or activity to ensure that students are prepared. These might include asking students to design a flow chart that represents the procedure, to define terms that are unfamiliar, or to review safety procedures. These tasks should not be too time-consuming. Teaching time for science may be limited in the elementary classroom, and you want to ensure plenty of time for the hands-on aspects of the investigation.

4. **Inclusivity.** It is your responsibility to make certain that all students feel included. Consider student diversity, as well as ability, language skills, and social skills and how they intersect within the science investigation. For example, you might include visual instructions in your investigation to allow those students learning English to participate fully, or you might infuse Aboriginal science with western science in order to recognize multiple ways of knowing. Planning with student diversity and differences in mind allows for all students to be supported in their learning.

5. **Student Grouping.** Working in groups has many benefits for students. Students can improve social skills as they work together to set up materials and equipment, refine communication skills as they discuss procedures and data, and develop knowledge and understanding of scientific content through group discussions. However, in larger groups, a number of challenges can emerge. There are fewer opportunities for students to participate in all aspects of the investigation. It is important to determine the best group size for a particular investigation. For example, microscope work lends itself to partner work but not groups of four. Each investigation is different, and group size will depend on materials available, the class profile, and student needs. Generally, students

Watch

Cooperative Learning

in groups of four or fewer stay more engaged and on task, as there are meaningful ways for each member to participate. You will also need to consider the composition of groups. For example, which students work well together? When you know your students well, you can best determine the size and composition of student groupings.

6. **Student Duties.** During science investigations some students show their enthusiasm by rushing to do everything or handling and setting up all equipment. Others may be hesitant and are only willing to participate minimally. One way to address these issues is to establish a set of science investigation jobs and ensure that each student rotates through all jobs. Assuming that setup and cleanup can be done by all group members, and that the group composition is stable over several investigations, you can create a duty roster based on your own student profile like that shown in Figure 9.1.

Duties Name	Equipment manager	Time manager	Safety monitor	Recorder
Jean-Marc	Sept. 10	Sept. 17	Sept. 23	Oct. 4
Maia	Oct. 4	Sept. 10	Sept. 17	Sept. 23
Aziz	Sept. 23	Oct. 4	Sept. 10	Sept. 17
Joshua	Sept. 17	Sept. 23	Oct. 4	Sept. 10

Equipment manager: Ensures all equipment is collected and returned in good order and reports any problems to teacher.

Time manager: Keeps an eye on the clock to ensure all work gets done in the allotted time.

Safety monitor: Ensures that safety considerations are addressed, such as wearing goggles or any other issue specific to the lab.

Recorder: Records data collected during the investigation.

Figure 9.1 Student duties

REMINDER CHECKLIST

☐ How will I meet the diverse needs and interests of my students?

☐ How will I determine if students have the necessary knowledge to do an investigation?

☐ How will I determine if the students have learned the expected material?

☐ Will I collect part of the investigation, such as a data table, or will I collect a formal write-up?

☐ What pre-investigation task will I ask students to prepare?

Classroom Considerations The physical setting of the classroom is an important consideration. Planning with safety in mind is discussed later in the chapter; here, we consider planning related to equipment and materials. Students typically conduct investigations at their desks or at a designated science learning centre. A challenge is that some elementary classrooms do not have running water or a sink.

1. **Equipment and Materials.** Equipment and materials need to be gathered and checked well in advance of your science investigation. For example, check that thermometers have a continuous column of liquid and that the range is appropriate for your needs, or that microscopes have working bulbs. Ensure that you have more than enough of each material for your investigation. You may need to place an order for specific materials. Contact your school board science consultant, who can provide you with a list of companies (e.g., Boreal Science, Sargent Welch) that supply schools with materials and other consumables. Some

school boards have contracts with approved suppliers. Also contact the science department at the local secondary school—you may be able to borrow supplies from them.

2. **Organizing and Dispensing Materials.** Once you have gathered sufficient quantities of materials and equipment, decide where they will be positioned and how they will be distributed in the classroom. Your organization of materials will depend on the investigation requirements and the layout of your classroom. Are your students' desks or tables arranged in groups, in rows, or individually? Will desks and chairs need to be moved? Is there a separate science room at your school? Also consider where your sink is (if you have one in your classroom) and where you will place waste containers. Generally one of two methods is used to distribute equipment and materials: 1) they are located centrally and students gather what is needed for the investigation; or 2) they are organized into bins and each student group is given one bin containing all of the materials needed for the investigation. Some schools create kits that contain all or most of what is need for a particular investigation in labelled containers or plastic zip bags. Use the method that works best for you, your students, and the particular investigation you will be doing.

REMINDER CHECKLIST

☐ How does the classroom layout affect the investigation?

☐ How will I organize and position the equipment and materials?

☐ Where is the safety equipment in the classroom, and is it in good working order?

☐ Have I checked for the needed equipment and materials? What is my plan if there are insufficient quantities?

☐ Does my school or school board have a published list of banned or restricted materials that will guide my planning?

ACTIVITY 9.2

21st C ① ② ④

Working with Resources: Textbook Analysis and Pre-planning

Choose two investigations from an elementary science textbook or other resource, and imagine you are planning to conduct them with students, perhaps during a practicum. Analyze each investigation in terms of the teacher, student, and classroom pre-planning considerations presented in the table below. An investigation of properties of light is included as an example.

Pre-planning for Science Investigations

Considerations	Name of investigation: properties of light	Name of investigation: (choose any investigation of interest)	Name of investigation: (choose any investigation of interest)
Describe your reasons for choosing the investigation.	To explore properties of light		
List all *safety* precautions that students need to take.	Never directly look at the sun or the sun's reflection in a mirror; do not direct light into eyes; and keep water away from electrical equipment		

What *equipment* is needed, and are you familiar with it?	Mirrors, prisms, flashlights or ray boxes, container of water, pencil, paper, ruler
Identify any *background knowledge* students need to review prior to doing the investigation.	Reflection, refraction, visible light spectrum, concave, convex
Assess the *quality* of the instructions.	Clear explanation of how to set up equipment; anticipated outcomes
Are there aspects of the investigation that might *exclude* some students?	Fine motor skills required to adjust placement of equipment
Design a *pre-investigation student task* appropriate to this investigation.	Name properties of light; practise using a ray box

Doing the Science Investigation

On the day of the investigation, pre-planning should be complete. Before students conduct the investigation, however, the teacher might:

- review with students the reason the investigation and the instructions
- review key concepts if applicable
- model the equipment set-up to review any difficult steps
- review and stress all safety precautions
- instruct students as to how the materials will be distributed and retrieved (orally and in writing on the board)
- remind students what you will collect for assessment purposes (for example, a data table at the end of the period or a formal investigation report later)
- remind students of the expectations for cleaning up

You might also select students to review for the class the investigation's procedure, important safety precautions, or special instructions for cleanup.

During the investigation, circulate, watching for potential problems, and redirect students' focus as needed. Try to avoid unnecessary interruptions that stop the whole class, and carefully monitor overall timing issues, including instructing the students when to begin cleaning up and returning equipment. Students will need to be reminded of where to safely dispose of materials and to inform you immediately of any broken or damaged equipment. While the end of the investigation period can be very busy, students should have a clear idea of what they need to prepare for any post-investigation discussion.

Post-Investigation Planning

The post-investigation lesson can take many forms. After doing an investigation, students should have opportunities to communicate their findings. Communication technologies might be helpful. A whole-class or small-group discussion about the significance of data can be a valuable and worthwhile part of a science investigation. Post-investigation activities enable students to bring their collective judgments to bear on a problem by comparing data and qualifying conclusions. Although students may find discrepancies in their data, different results can give rise to productive discussions and are part of the nature of science. It is through the discussion of results that students begin to see how data are analyzed and evaluated by scientists.

Your post-investigation lesson will depend on the purpose and approach you used, and as such you will need to determine the most appropriate follow-up. For example, are you verifying data, or is the investigation a way to explore data analysis? Do you wish to reinforce content previously learned, or does the investigation help you to intlroduce a new concept or establish a generalization? You may choose to explore any or all of the following:

- the purpose of the investigation
- observations and results
- class sets of data and trends or generalizations from the data
- discrepancies in results and sources of these differences
- connections with course content

The post-investigation lesson nurtures higher-order thinking skills, creative thinking, and communication skills. It also helps students to synthesize class results and to move from a specific observation to a broader generalization, and serves as an introduction to the next topic. Any post-investigation lesson will be guided by what you intend to assess.

ACTIVITY 9.3
21st C

Experiencing the Science Investigation

In this activity you will be conducting two investigations: The Kitchen Detective and Blast Off. Our purpose for you is two-fold:

  a. to experience what elementary school students might be asked to do

  b. to evaluate the procedures from a teacher perspective

Both investigations could be adapted to suit different grades and abilities. If doing these investigations with children, they may need to be modified due to heath and safety concerns (for example, replacing talc with another powder).

INVESTIGATION ONE: The Kitchen Detective

Imagine you are helping bake cookies. You need cornstarch, baking soda, and baking powder for the recipe, but the labels have worn off the containers. Which is which? Appearances can be deceiving. Scientists work like detectives to determine the identity of unknown materials using physical and chemical properties of matter. This investigation uses materials commonly found in the kitchen to reveal the identity of five "mystery" powders.

Safety Precautions

Wear safety equipment at all times.
Follow your teacher's instructions to dispose of materials.
Immediately inform your teacher about any spills.
Wash your hands after completing the investigation.
Do not taste or eat anything in the investigation.
If you have allergies be sure to inform your teacher.

MATERIALS

- Plastic egg cartons
- Teaspoons
- Hand lens
- Iodine solution (Lugol's solution)
- Vinegar
- 2 small beakers

- 2 eye droppers
- Salt
- Corn starch
- Baking soda
- Baking powder
- Cream of tartar (talc-based, not cornstarch-based)

NOTE TO TEACHER

- Before the investigation, label five beakers as A, B, C, D, and E, and fill each with a "mystery" powder (salt, corn starch, baking soda, baking powder, cream of tartar).

• To reduce the amount of time spent retrieving materials, the investigation can be organized into five investigation centres, one for each unknown. Have small groups of students rotate through the centres, spending five to ten minutes at each. Adult helpers at each centre can help younger students. Be sure to remind students to clean up each centre for the next group.

PROCEDURE

1. Create a data table like the one below to record your observations and results of each test.

Mystery Powder Data Table	A	B	C	D	E
Appearance					
Texture					
Drawing					
Reaction with vinegar					
Reaction with iodine solution					
Identity of mystery powder					

2. Wearing safety equipment, work with a partner to label the cups of an egg carton as A, B, C, D, and E along the top row and repeat along the bottom row. (See the figure below.) Collect mystery powders from the materials table. Do not mix up the spoons for each! Place one teaspoon of mystery powder A in each of the two cups labelled A. Repeat for B, C, D, and E. Ten cups will be filled.

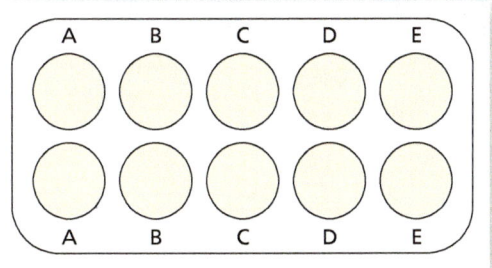

Labelled Egg Carton

3. In the data table, record your observations about the appearance of each powder.
4. Rub a small amount of each powder between your thumb and index finger to determine its texture. Using a hand lens, observe the particles. Are they powder or crystal? Record your observations in the data table. Be sure to wash and dry your hands thoroughly after handling each powder.
5. You will now test the mystery powders with vinegar and iodine solution.
   a. Vinegar is an acid that reacts with some substances (such as bicarbonate) to produce carbon dioxide. Place a small amount of vinegar into a beaker. Using an eyedropper, add two drops of vinegar to powder A in the top row. Record your observations. Repeat for powders B, C, D, and E along the top row.
   b. Iodine acts as an indicator of starch. If starch is present, it will turn black; if starch is not present, there will be no colour change. Add two drops of iodine to powder A in the bottom row. Record your observations. Repeat for powders B, C, D, and E along the bottom row.
6. Use the flow chart shown below to identify the mystery powders.
7. Dispose of the samples as directed. Clean the egg carton, spoons, and beakers, and dry them thoroughly.

continued on next page

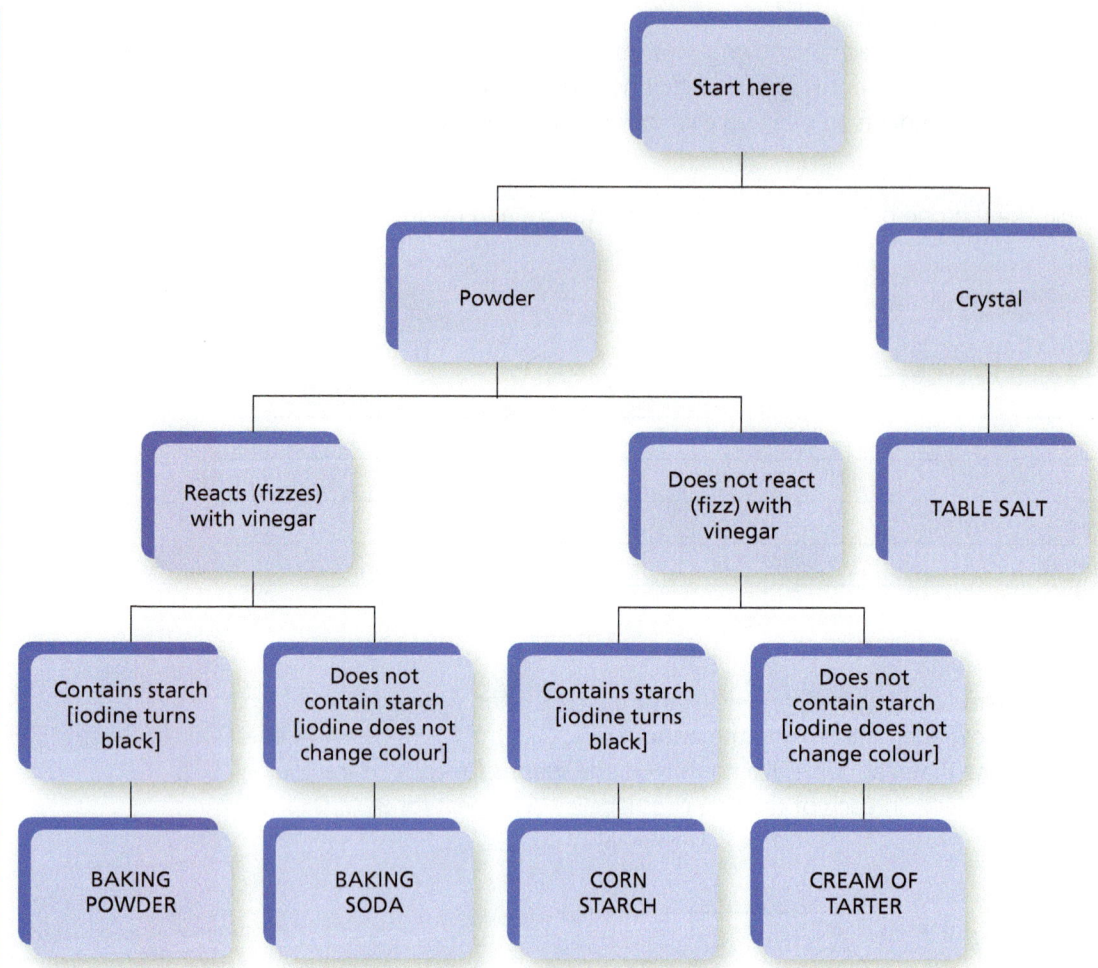

Mystery Powder Identification Flow Chart

EXTEND YOUR UNDERSTANDING

1. What did the powders have in common?
2. Why was it important to use multiple tests to identify the mystery powders?
3. Design another investigation that follows a different series of steps to identify salt, sugar, flour, and starch. Create a flow chart.

INVESTIGATION TWO: Blast Off!

A chemical reaction is defined as a change in matter in which at least one new substance with new properties is formed. Evidence of a chemical reaction includes one or more of the following: colour change, production of gas, temperature change, light or sound emission, or the formation of a precipitate. Some chemical reactions occur slowly and others very quickly. There are many ways to accelerate reactions (e.g., adding heat, shaking, increasing concentration), several of which are explored in this investigation of the reaction between an acid (vinegar) and a base (baking soda).

As this investigation can be messy and requires a lot of space, it is ideally done outside. It can be done indoors, but be sure to put down a lot of newspaper to soak up spills. Alternately, the procedure could be conducted in a plastic zip bag, in which case students would observe gas produced rather than distance travelled by a canister filled with baking soda and vinegar. You might opt to use antacid tablets (1/4 or 1/2 tablet for each trial) in place of baking soda; both are basic and react with the acidic vinegar. For younger students, consider doing this investigation as a demonstration or at a centre with an adult helper.

QUESTION

How far can you make a canister travel?

DESIGN

You will design an experiment that maximizes the distance travelled by a canister filled with baking soda and vinegar.

Working in a group, discuss the variables that might affect the reaction between vinegar and baking soda. Record your ideas.

Plan a series of trials to investigate the effects of several variables on the reaction and distance travelled by the canister.

Set up an observation table to record variables and times.

Have your experimental design approved by your teacher.

Safety Precautions

The canister and lid can come apart quickly and suddenly. Wear safety goggles at all times. Everyone should stand well back from the canister as it pops.

MATERIALS

- Apron
- Safety goggles
- Baking soda
- Clear plastic film canister and lid

- Vinegar
- Aluminum foil, cut into 5 cm squares
- Measuring spoons
- Graduated cylinder

NOTE TO TEACHER

Given the popularity of digital cameras, it might be difficult to source plastic film canisters. Contact film developers and camera equipment stores in your community to see if they have empty canisters and lids. Also, check with other teachers at your school—this is a common exploration activity and your colleagues may have canisters and lids you can borrow. Wash and dry the canisters after the investigation for reuse the next time you do the investigation.

PROCEDURE

1. Your teacher will demonstrate the general procedure: Make a small foil cup, add vinegar to film canister, put baking soda in the foil cup, float the cup in the canister of vinegar, put the lid on the canister and place the canister on its side and observe how far it travels.

2. Put on your apron and safety goggles, and collect your materials. You may not have more than five foil squares, so you should plan accordingly. Be sure to save one square for your final "blast off"!

continued on next page

3. Carry out your planned trials. Record your results.
4. Analyze your results and decide on a procedure for the final blast off.
5. Join the other groups for the blast off.
6. Each group will carry out their plan, and the teacher will record the distance travelled by each canister. The winning team is the one whose canister travels the farthest.
7. Dispose of the mixtures in the sink with plenty of water, and put away your materials as instructed by your teacher.
8. Clean up your workstation and wash your hands.

EXTEND YOUR UNDERSTANDING

1. What evidence was there that a chemical reaction occurred?
2. What variables affected distance travelled by the canisters?
3. Which variables had the greatest effect? Explain. Which variables had little or no effect?
4. Hold a class discussion comparing the various experimental designs used. Which was most successful in the blast off? Why?
5. How might you have improved your experimental design if you had been given more time and more materials?

DISCUSSION QUESTIONS

1. What is the purpose of each investigation?
2. What skills do students need for each investigation?
3. Comment on the clarity of the procedures for elementary school students.
4. What safety considerations would need to be addressed prior to performing these investigations?
5. What modifications would need to be made for English language learners (ELL)?
6. What modifications would need to be made for students with special learning needs, or who have an IEP?
7. How would you assess each investigation? Provide a sample assessment strategy for each.
8. How would you modify the follow-up questions? Can they be used "as is"?
9. Compare and contrast the level of engagement for each investigation.
10. Compare and contrast the type of data collected in each investigation.
11. What is the strength of each investigation with respect to approach, and what does it convey to students about the nature of science?
12. What might you do in a pre-investigation lesson to support each investigation?

ACTIVITY 9.4   *21st C* ④ ⑤ ⑦

Following Up

Create a brief post-investigation lesson outline for either the Kitchen Detective or Blast Off investigation. Include the following in point form:
- key terms and concepts to be discussed
- data, observations, and results to be discussed
- model answers to the investigation discussion questions
- teacher notes and materials—perhaps a diagram, graph, or chart—that could be helpful in clarifying the content of the investigation
- possible connections to numeracy and literacy
- potential cross-curricular connections to other subjects
- possible uses of technology
- other points you deem relevant

LINKING INVESTIGATIONS TO PLANNING

While all investigations benefit from the considerations outlined in this chapter, some issues are specific to the approach and type of investigation you choose. For example, in verification investigations, you *want* students to verify an existing principle, and as such you want the investigation to work as expected. In open-ended investigations, you might need additional equipment and resources for students to choose from.

Scaffolding for Open-Ended Experiments

Recall from earlier sections that in an open-ended investigation, students design an experiment in order to collect data and draw conclusions to a specific question. The results are open-ended, and students have control of their work while the teacher acts as a guide. When doing an open-ended investigation, like Blast Off from Activity 9.3, some steps in the planning process will change. You may choose to have a planning session where students tell you what they will need. If applicable, you might need to plan for students to be able to store their experiments in progress. For example, if the experiment involves plant growth, the plants need to be stored and watered, which requires a secure space. In addition, for open-ended investigations and some structured or guided inquiries (see Chapter 8), pre-investigation sessions may involve far more brainstorming of ideas. The post-investigation activity may include the presentation of results to the class, as each group may have used a different procedure and obtained different results.

Ideally students pose a question of interest, although the teacher will need to consider safety, materials needed, space for storage, time required, and connections to the curriculum. Developing process skills such as posing questions; forming hypotheses; identifying variables; collecting, analyzing, and interpreting data; and drawing conclusions based on evidence is central to this approach. There is no simple algorithm for conducting open-ended experiments; it is a dialogue between students and teachers that calls for flexibility in planning.

PLANNING WITH SAFETY IN MIND

Safety is more than a set of rules or a checklist. It includes classroom organization, what students are asked to do, movement of individuals during a science investigation, materials, and disposal of waste. It is as important for the teacher as for the students.

All teachers want their students to be safe, to take all safety precautions very seriously, and to feel comfortable while doing investigations. Sometimes, however, teachers can feel so overloaded with safety concerns that they are anxious about doing any investigations at all. In this instance, discussion with colleagues and local school board curriculum coordinators can be invaluable. Connect with teachers of science at the local secondary school, if possible. Not only will they be able to advise you on safe practices with specific materials and procedures, but they can also help source materials and might even provide science experts (i.e., secondary science students) to buddy with your students. More broadly, provincial and territorial science curriculum documents also provide guidelines for safety in the elementary science classroom, and some ministries and departments of education publish science safety resource manuals.

You can create a safe classroom environment by making sure you address all safety precautions and support materials while not overwhelming your students or yourself. Ongoing and consistent safety expectations and attention to student preparation will serve you well. By developing a safety ethos in your work, as you plan each new lesson, you and your students can feel safe and responsible with each new situation.

Planning for Safe Science Investigations

Instruction on safety equipment, symbols, and safe practice is a good way to begin your teaching of science. Do not assume that students remember all this information when it is needed later in the year. It is important to review and be clear about the safety precautions specific to a particular investigation, as well as general practices relevant to all science investigations. Activities 9.5, 9.6, and 9.7 allow you to explore characteristics of safe and unsafe science classrooms, to learn safety symbols and procedures, and to create a safety contract. Each of these activities can be taken into your elementary classroom.

ACTIVITY 9.5   *21st C* ❶ ❷ ❻

Examining Safety in the Elementary Classroom

Examine the following cartoon and identify as many unsafe practices as you can. Describe those practices and how they should be addressed with students. Share your list with classmates.

👁 **Watch**

Safety Goggles

Heating Use of Alcohol Burner

Use of a Wool Fire Blanket

Use of an Eye Wash

Use of a Fire Extinguisher

Electrical Safety Outlets and Covers

Use of a Hot Plate

What's Not Safe?

USING THIS ACTIVITY WITH ELEMENTARY SCHOOL STUDENTS

In this activity, you will ask students to identify the unsafe practices in the figure above (or another that you would like to use). You can extend your students' thinking by having them apply their knowledge of safety in science investigations to a safe science classroom cartoon of their own and ask them to label the safety features. This adds an artistic element into the science curriculum, and it also allows you to easily assess your students' knowledge of safety practices specific to your classroom. As always, adapt the activity to suit the age and level of your students, providing more or less instruction as appropriate.

1. Show the cartoon of the unsafe science classroom to students on the whiteboard. For one or two minutes, have students individually look for unsafe practices in the cartoon, noting as many as they can. Alternatively, each student can be given a copy of the cartoon to review.
2. Ask students to turn to a partner and share the unsafe practices they spotted.
3. Generate a class list of the unsafe practices in the cartoon.
4. Ask students how these practices could be changed to make them safe and, in a different colour, add their suggestions to the class list.
5. Have students think of their own classroom and the safety features in it. Here, take one minute to allow students to quietly look around the room. Brainstorm the safety features present in the room (e.g., fire extinguisher, fire blanket, first-aid kit, goggles cabinet, etc.).
6. Ask students to draw a safe science classroom cartoon. Distribute large sheets of paper (11" x 14") and be sure to remind students to clearly label their cartoons.
7. *Assessment:* You can assess the cartoons using the brainstormed list of classroom safety features. You might also have students complete self- and peer-evaluation rubrics.

ACTIVITY 9.6   *21st C*

Safety Symbols and Procedures

Check around your home for consumer product safety symbols (see the figure below) on household products. Record the name of the product and the symbol on the label.

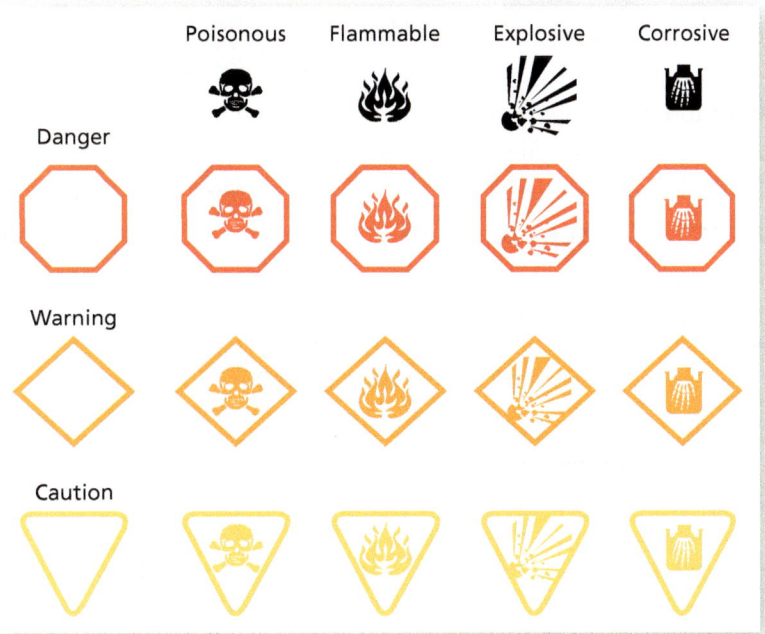

Consumer Product Safety Symbols

DISCUSSION QUESTIONS

1. Do any of the product warnings surprise you? Which ones, and why?
2. Discuss and research safer alternatives to the products you found (e.g., vinegar to clean windows, baking soda for scrubbing surfaces).

USING THIS ACTIVITY WITH ELEMENTARY SCHOOL STUDENTS

This activity brings parents and guardians into science learning as students explore safety symbols in their homes. It also encourages discussion of science topics between students and their parents

continued on next page

or guardians. Ideally this will be an activity that has both at-home and at-school components, but it can be adapted into a school activity in which you bring in a variety of products for students to examine. Should you choose this route, please be sure that the containers are emptied and cleaned thoroughly and that students are only looking at the labels.

1. After teaching or reviewing the safety symbols from the figure above, ask students to conduct a search, together with a parent or guardian, for these symbols on products at home. Go through the data sheet included in Appendix 9.B, and check that all students are clear on the instructions.
2. Distribute data sheets for students to record their findings.
3. In the next class, ask students to share their findings and create a class list of found household products, the warnings on those products, and the warning levels.
4. Ask students about their findings: Were there any surprises? Were your parents surprised by any warnings? In what rooms did you find the products?
5. Discuss safer alternatives for some of the products. Ask for examples from home (e.g., parent uses newspaper and vinegar to clean the windows).
6. *Assessment:* You can assess the students' data sheets using a marking scheme.

ACTIVITY 9.7

21st C ❸ ❹ ❺

Creating a Safety Contract

Compile a class list of all the unsafe practices that were identified in Activity 9.5. As a class, brainstorm rules that the class should follow in order to create and maintain a safe environment for science investigations (e.g., no running, no food or drinks, hair tied back, wear goggles). Create a safety contract for students to potentially sign at the beginning of the school year.

USING THIS ACTIVITY WITH ELEMENTARY SCHOOL STUDENTS

It is a great idea to create a safety contract at the beginning of the school year before any science investigations are done. This can be even more effective if its creation is a collaborative effort between students and the teacher. Encourage student discussion and try to step back and take on the role of facilitator and recorder. This activity nicely follows Activities 9.5 and 9.6, drawing on and applying what was learned in each.

1. Have students sit together in a circle at the carpet.
2. Review what was learned in the safe classroom cartoon and safety symbols activities using examples of student work and referring to class lists.
3. Tell students that the class will be creating a safety contract of expectations for behaviour during science investigations and that you want the list to be generated by the class rather than by you.
4. As a class, brainstorm safe behaviours that could be included on the contract (e.g., no running, wear goggles) and write these on the board.
5. Have students discuss which behaviours are important to include in the contract, and create a list. Try to limit the list to a maximum of 10 points that cover all safety concerns.
6. Create a contract on a piece of chart paper, using student words and contributions. Have all students sign the contract and post it in a visible place in the room so that it can be referred to during science investigations throughout the year.
7. *Assessment:* You can use a rubric to assess student participation and contribution to class discussion.

PLANNING WITH ASSESSMENT IN MIND

An important aspect of planning for science investigations is determining what type of assessment will be used. Both you and your students should be clear as to how investigations will be assessed, and whether those assessments will be formal or informal. The following two activities are a way for you to explore formal assessment strategies for science investigations. Additionally, you will need to consider whether you will assess students individually or in groups, as well as the challenges associated with each method. You may need to refer to your school guidelines regarding assessment of group assignments.

ACTIVITY 9.8   *21st C* ❶ ❸ ❹

Pairing Assessment Strategies and Tools with Investigations

With a partner, brainstorm and record all of the aspects of science investigations that might be assessed. Beside each, identify an appropriate strategy and tool for assessment. As a class, compile a list of possible aspects of investigations and an appropriate assessment strategy and tool for each. In practice, it is not feasible, or even possible, to assess every aspect of every investigation for each of your students. Instead, focus on one or two aspects that complement the science content and process learning objectives of the investigation.

Assessment Strategies and Tools for Science Investigations

Aspect of investigation	Appropriate assessment strategy	Appropriate assessment tool
e.g., pre-investigation questions about set-up of the materials and procedure	e.g., pre-investigation quiz	e.g., marking scheme
e.g., measure the mass of objects using a scale	e.g., observation of student conducting investigation	e.g., anecdotal record

DISCUSSION QUESTIONS

1. Was there agreement in the class as to what strategies and tools best assessed the investigations?
2. Classify the aspects of an investigation to be assessed in terms of skills and knowledge.
3. Using the list of assessment strategies and tools generated in this activity, consider when each type of assessment would be most appropriate. Explain.

As discussed in Chapter 8, the *Pan Canadian Framework* (CMEC, 1997, p. 12) outlines four broad categories of skills that students should develop:

- *Initiating and planning:* skills of questioning, identifying problems, and developing preliminary ideas and plans
- *Performing and recording:* skills of carrying out a plan of action, gathering evidence by observation, and manipulating materials and equipment

- *Analyzing and interpreting:* skills of examining information and evidence, processing and presenting data so that it can be interpreted, and interpreting, evaluating, and applying results
- *Communication and teamwork:* skills that support the development and application of science ideas as a collaborative process with ideas being developed, tested, interpreted, debated, and agreed upon

Activity 9.9 provides an opportunity to examine the inquiry skills that are highlighted in your jurisdiction and possible assessment of those skills.

ACTIVITY 9.9

21st C

Working with Resources: Assessing Skills of Scientific Inquiry

1. Examine science curriculum documents from your ministry or department of education and make a list of the skills for which there is an expectation that achievement will be measured.
2. Describe science investigations that would support each of the categories of skills described.
3. Create a rubric for one of the investigations you described in Question 2 and the category of skill described. You might choose to build upon the rubric framework in the table below. We have filled in an example using the Kitchen Detective investigation from earlier in the chapter.

Rubric for Assessing Skills of Scientific Inquiry

Criteria	Level 1: Not yet within expectations	Level 2: Approaching expectations	Level 3: Meets expectations	Level 4: Exceeds expectations
Performing and recording	Makes observations of either colour, colour changes, texture, and particle shape by drawing a picture or writing notes	Makes observations that include two of the following: colour, colour changes, texture, and particle shape by drawing pictures of observations and writing notes	Makes observations that include three or four of the following: colour, colour changes, texture, and particle shape by drawing labelled pictures of observations and writing notes	Makes detailed observations of all of colour, colour changes, texture, and particle shape by drawing detailed and labelled pictures of observations and writing descriptive notes
Initiating and planning				
Analyzing and interpreting				
Communication and teamwork				

DISCUSSION QUESTIONS

1. For the science investigations you chose, describe how you would assess each of these skills.
2. Re-examine the science investigations presented in this chapter and determine which of the four broad categories of skills—initiating and planning, performing and recording, analyzing and interpreting, or communication and teamwork—are supported. Describe how you would assess the categories included.

SCIENCE BEYOND THE CLASSROOM

For the most part, this chapter has dealt with investigations conducted within the classroom. Of course, scientific inquiry in its many forms can also be done outside the school. For example, using fieldwork is common for many life science units. As a teacher, you might consider the following: When would it be best to plan an investigation outside the classroom? Is this unit best taught by going out into the field? Why? Can you make use of the schoolyard or neighbourhood to support an aspect of your teaching? Activity 9.10 explores planning for an investigation in the field.

ACTIVITY 9.10   *21st C* 1 2 4

Planning for an Investigation in the Field

Choose a unit that you may be teaching or would like to teach. Plan an appropriate field trip using the headings in the table below, and be prepared to share with the class. Remember that some of the best field trips are close to home—a walk around the neighbourhood or an exploration of the school grounds, for example. Appendix F outlines practical considerations to keep in mind for field trip planning.

Planning for an Investigation in the Field

Considerations	Planning
Unit and grade	
Topic of inquiry to be conducted in the field	
Field trip location Provide details regarding location for the field trip, why the location is suitable, and what students will investigate while on site.	
Prepare permission forms Gather necessary permission forms used in your school board. These include permission from the principal, school board, and parents. Often schools have general permission forms that cover neighbourhood visits; be sure to check if your school does, and collect signed forms early in the school year.	
Connection to curriculum Describe how the substance of the field trip supports the curriculum.	
Student materials Create all the needed students materials. This might include lists of what students should bring on the field trip, the equipment you will provide, what students will be asked to do, and what they will submit. Also consider alternate plans for students who do not have permission to participate in the field trip.	
Assessment What will you assess, and how?	
Accommodation for students with special needs Are there students who require wheelchair access, for example, or have food restrictions or allergies?	

CONTEMPORARY ISSUES AND ONGOING DEBATES IN SCIENCE INVESTIGATIONS

👁•⎡Watch

Moral Dimensions

Many issues pertaining to science investigations are explored in this chapter. Debates arise, for example, from educational research on constructivism (Hofstein & Lunetta, 2003; Jenkins, 2000); the nature of science (Abd-El-Khalick & Lederman, 2000; Hodson, 2008; Lederman, 1999); the role of technology in classrooms (Hewitt, 2005; Slotta & Linn, 2009); and moral and ethical concerns (Blades, 2006; Reiss, 2008; Zeidler & Keefer, 2003). Much can be learned from spirited conversation in these matters. You may choose to do some outside reading, beginning with the sources provided above. Below are some questions for you to reflect upon and discuss with colleagues.

1. What are the implications of constructivist theories of learning for investigations?
2. How important is it that your investigations reflect nature of science (NOS) principles? Explain.
3. What will you do if some students raise moral, ethical, and environmental concerns related to investigations and refuse to participate in them?
4. What is your experience (if any) with dissection simulations?
5. What is your stance on replacing hands-on investigations with computer simulations?
6. What role will technology play in your classroom?
7. What are some challenges related to using technology in science investigations?
8. What are the challenges of planning for elementary science investigations, and how might these be addressed?

EXPLORING ELEMENTARY SCIENCE IN CREATIVE WAYS: ANIMAL LIFE CYCLES

In order to teach any topic effectively, it is helpful to have a deep and broad knowledge base. In this section we present some ideas to help develop your subject matter content knowledge (CK) and pedagogical content knowledge (PCK) for a specific topic—in this case the butterfly life cycle. The topic is introduced with a visual that might appear in a print or media resource. We encourage you to search for other resources as well. As you learn or relearn the content, keep in mind issues such as terminology, abstract processes, integration with mathematics and language arts, and activities to support student learning. Additionally, consider the meta-cognitive aspect of the activity, such as understanding how you learn, what you know, and what you need to know.

ACTIVITY 9.11   *21st C*

Animal Life Cycles

A science topic such as animal life cycles can form the anchor to a rich, cross-curricular unit that incorporates science with other areas. For example, the life cycle of the butterfly, characteristics of insects, migratory patterns, the ecological niche of butterflies, reading fiction and non-fiction, and art activities related to butterflies' beauty and form can be brought together meaningfully in a study of animal life cycles.

Animal life cycles are covered in the Grade 2 or 3 science curriculum in most provinces and territories. In Saskatchewan, students are expected to analyze the growth and development of familiar animals. Specifically, students should be able to describe the characteristics common to each stage of the life cycle, create representations (physical, visual, or dramatic) of growth and development through the life cycle, and recognize the cyclic nature of Mother Earth in the Medicine Wheel. The Manitoba Grade 2 science curriculum includes animal life cycles within Cluster 1: Growth and

👁•⎡Watch

A Scientific
Investigation
in Preschool:
From Tadpole
to Frog

Changes in Animals. In Alberta's Grade 3 science curriculum, students are expected to describe the appearances and life cycles of some common animals and to identify how they have adapted to their environments. In this activity, we examine the life cycle of the butterfly. Advanced planning for this activity (e.g., ordering materials, careful storage) is crucial for its success.

Reviewing the Content

1. Review or learn the content associated with animal life cycles. For example, what is a larva? What is a pupa? Use the visual below to guide your exploration.
2. Make a list of definitions for important or unfamiliar vocabulary and processes associated with this topic.
3. When you feel comfortable with the content, use the figure below to explain the life cycle of a butterfly to a peer.

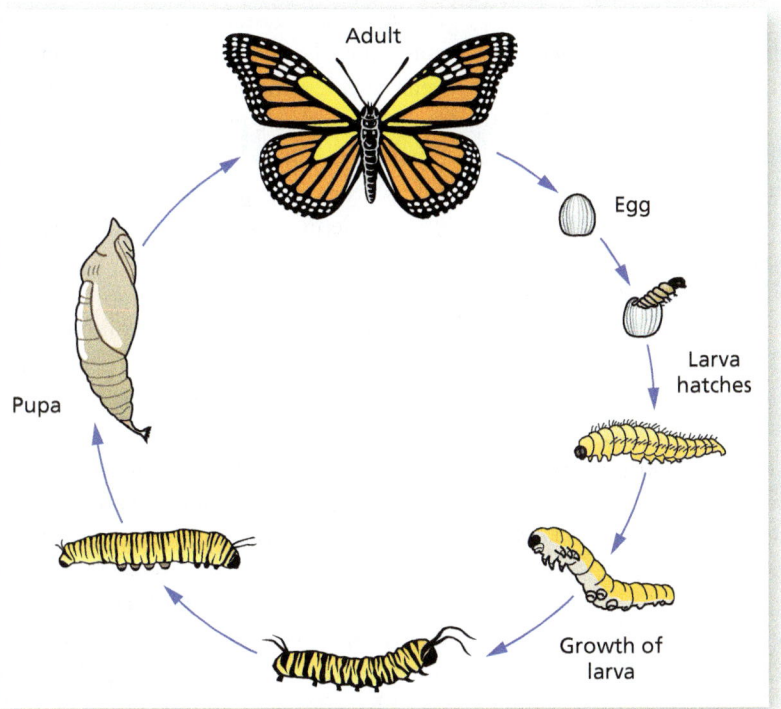

Life Cycle of a Butterfly

Literacy and Numeracy Connections

1. Many children's books involve stories about the butterfly life cycle. *Eggs, Legs, Wings: A Butterfly Life Cycle* by Shannon Knudsen is a graphic novel that nicely illustrates the details involved in the stages of the butterfly life cycle. You might use this book as an introduction or to review the study of butterfly life cycles
2. There are several opportunities to include measurement in a study of the butterfly life cycle. Students can measure the time in days for each stage and the length of the larva, pupa, and butterfly. Students can create tables, graphs, or diagrams to show their observations.

Activities for Elementary School Students

1. Students observe caterpillars over time (butterfly-rearing kits can be ordered from many biological supply companies). Ask students to keep a daily log with written and drawn observations of changes.
2. In small groups, have students use drama and physical actions to illustrate the stages of the butterfly life cycle to the class.
3. Create flip-books that illustrate the stages of the life cycle.
4. View *Flight of the Butterflies*, an IMAX movie that depicts the work of Canadian scientist Fred Urquhart, who tracked the migration patterns of the monarch butterfly.

CONCLUDING THOUGHTS

Science investigations can be fun and exciting; they can also be enriching, motivating, and relevant when they are embedded contextually within both the curriculum and the students' lived experience. Furthermore, science investigations are important for developing particular aspects of scientific literacy. Careful planning will help to alleviate the anxiety that you and your students might experience in doing investigations. In your journey to becoming a teacher, nothing can take the place of deliberate, comprehensive, and judicious planning. What follows is a summary of the key ideas related to the learning objectives provided at the beginning of the chapter.

Pre-investigation planning considerations

Teacher considerations include finding suitable investigations for your students, testing investigations, ensuring that the investigation clearly supports the unit and curriculum, and determining appropriate assessment. Student considerations include teaching or reviewing relevant science content or skills related to the investigation, creating appropriate tasks that will prepare students, ensuring an inclusive learning environment, and determining group and duty arrangements. Finally, classroom setting considerations such as equipment distribution, retrieval and storage, and safety need to be addressed. Safety must be a priority—be sure to remind students of safety procedures before each investigation.

Science investigations from the perspective of both student and teacher

It is helpful for teachers to evaluate an investigation from the perspective of the student experience. When analyzing an investigation, consider its purpose, the skills needed by students, the clarity of the procedure, important safety precautions, modifications for students with IEPs and unique learning needs, assessment strategies and tools, and the NOS perspectives conveyed.

Appropriate post-investigation lesson

Post-investigation lessons can take many forms, ranging from informal discussion of results to full lessons that support and enhance the experience of the investigation. You may decide to review key terms and concepts from the investigation; to discuss data collection, observations, and results (including unexpected data); to take up answers to the discussion questions; or to include any other teaching episodes that could be helpful in clarifying the content or inquiry skills explored.

Investigations with safety in mind

Planning for safety includes consideration of classroom organization, what students are asked to do, movement of students during an investigation, the materials used, and the disposal of waste. It is good practice to start the school year with lessons and instruction on safety equipment, symbols, and safe practice during science investigations. There is much to be mindful of, but when you develop a safety ethos in your curriculum and instruction, you and your students can safely deal with each new situation.

Investigations with assessment in mind

An important aspect of planning for investigations is planning for assessment. Different aspects of an investigation should be matched to the appropriate strategy and tool. It is also important to consider all the skills of inquiry that students develop, and how initiating, planning, and performing an investigation; recording, analyzing, and, interpreting data; and communicating results will be evaluated.

Inquiry outside the classroom

Many aspects of scientific inquiry can be conducted outside the classroom. By using the school grounds, the neighbourhood, or an informal science learning venue as an extension of your science classroom, you can add rich, meaningful connections to your students' lives as well as increase student interest.

Issues and debates related to science investigations

There are many ongoing debates related to doing science investigation, including topics of constructivism, the nature of science, the role of technology in classrooms, and moral and ethical concerns. Each of these issues requires teachers to consider their own class profiles and to determine the best approach to meet student needs and to expose students to a variety of procedures.

BRINGING IT ALL TOGETHER: FINAL QUESTIONS

1. Reflect upon which skills of inquiry are best supported by each of the investigation ideas presented in this chapter.

2. Which aspects of planning discussed in the chapter are you most worried about and why? What strategies might help you overcome your fears?

3. Work in pairs to develop an investigation for a topic from a curriculum guideline that you intend to use. Make a list of all pre- and post-planning considerations. Create three brief lesson plan outlines for the pre-investigation, investigation, and post-investigation periods.

MyEducationLab®

Visit MyEducationLab® to access an electronic version of the text, as well as a variety of topics that enhance the text material. The topics include the following to support your learning in the course:

- Assessments, including interactive case studies, activities, and video assignments
- Discussion board questions
- Videos, simulations, a lesson plan builder, and other useful course resources

---

APPENDIX 9.A   **Smarter Science**

Smarter Science (see **www.smarterscience.ca**) provides a framework for teaching and learning science in Grades 1–12 and for developing skills of inquiry, creativity, and innovation in a meaningful and engaging manner. The open-source website also shares resources for teachers. Originally developed in the Thames Valley District School Board, Ontario, Smarter Science is now part of Youth Science Canada's program for engaging youth in science and providing a curricular connection to project-based science and science fairs. Students engaged in Smarter Science–based activities are actively investigating and problem solving, and become increasingly independent and self-confident learners. A key feature of Smarter Science is its open-source nature. All resources developed by cooperating school boards and contributing teachers can be accessed online, at no cost, through http://smarterscience.ca, and resources may be freely reproduced and distributed.

APPENDIX 9.B	**Safety Symbols Found on Products in the Home**

For this activity, work with your parent or guardian and look for products at home that have one or more of the safety symbols shown below on their labels. Some labels carry written warnings instead—include these as well. Be sure to let your parent or guardian handle the products and do not open the containers.

Use the table below to record your findings. An example has been done for you. Use the back of the page if needed.

Safety Symbols

Source: Health Canada. "Hazard Symbols." http://www.hc-sc.gc.ca/cps-spc/legislation/acts-lois/hazard-symbol-danger-eng.php

Table 9B   Recording Safety Symbols Found in the Home

Product	Room where it was found	Safety warning and level
e.g. Static Guard	Kitchen	Flammable: danger
		Explosive: caution

Talk with your parent or guardian about safer alternatives. What might be substituted?

_____

_____

_____

Chapter 10

Exploring Science, Technology, Society, and Environment (STSE)

Bob Daemmrich/Alamy

LEARNING OBJECTIVES

- Describe the history and context of STSE education.

- Summarize the benefits of STSE education in science curriculum and instruction.

- Outline five characteristics of STSE education.

- Describe practical and ideological challenges in adopting an STSE perspective, and ways of overcoming these challenges.

- Identify and discuss education research related to STSE education.

STSE? What do those letters stand for, anyway?

—Heather, elementary school teacher

I'd like to teach about issues but am not sure how to include activism in my teaching.

—Abdul, preservice teacher candidate

Imagine if you went with your grandpa to the pond where you always go fishing and the fish were dead and floating.

—Tyler, Kindergarten student

21st CENTURY LEARNING SKILLS & COMPETENCIES

❶ Communication

❷ Critical thinking

❸ Collaboration

❹ Creativity

❺ Literacy and numeracy

❻ Media literacy

❼ Technological literacy

INTRODUCTION

We live in a time of rapid scientific and technological change. Issues and controversy abound within the scientific community and the public at large. For example, how do we understand and make decisions about genetically modified foods or drinking bottled water? Should the Northern Gateway pipeline be built through northern Alberta and British Columbia, and crude oil transported through B.C. fjords and open waterways? What can we do about depleting forests? How do teachers and students understand such complex issues—many of which have moral and ethical implications? How are informed, responsible decisions made? What is the relationship between science and social responsibility? Science, technology, society, and environment (STSE)[1] education provides an avenue to explore some of these questions within the science curriculum.

STSE education is multidisciplinary and includes moral and ethical perspectives as well as political, philosophical, historical, and economic considerations. These perspectives explore and critique the connections among science, technology, society, and the environment. Simply put, STSE positions science within larger social, cultural, and political contexts and equips students to understand socio-scientific subject matter, to make informed and responsible decisions, and to take action. In our view, STSE education offers hope and a way of re-imagining the world, our relationship with nature, and solutions to problems.

The intentions of this chapter are to introduce you to STSE education and to explore some of the theoretical and practical issues it entails. We explored the "E" in STSE in Chapter 3, Environmental Education. Given the interdisciplinary and complex nature of STSE education, you will find that STSE-informed teaching of science naturally draws from multiple subjects, including social studies, language arts, and media literacy.

STSE: A BRIEF HISTORY

There are many reasons for the evolution and growth of STSE education. Increased attention toward science and social responsibility, the prevalence of issues that cut across science and society, a desire to humanize science, decreased enrolment in physical sciences, and a renewed concern for the environment have provided a fertile ground from which STSE education has developed. One of the earliest mentions of STSE appeared in a 1971 *Science Education* article written by Jim Gallagher. He wrote, "For future citizens in a democratic society, understanding the interrelationships of science, technology and society may be as important as understanding the concepts and processes of science" (p. 337). This statement marked the beginning of a new way of conceptualizing science education.

A range of significant texts published between 1970 and 1990 marked an ongoing commitment to STSE education and a collective desire for fundamental change in school science. (See, for example, Hurd, 1986; Pedretti, 1996; Solomon, 1993; Solomon & Aikenhead, 1994; Yager, 1996; Ziman, 1980.) In 1994, well-known researchers and educators Joan Solomon and Glen Aikenhead edited the landmark book *STS Education: International Perspectives on Reform*. This publication did much to bring STSE to the fore. Solomon and Aikenhead describe STSE education as being "relevant, challenging, realistic, and rigorous. STS[E] science teaching aims to prepare future scientists, engineers, and citizens alike to participate in a society increasingly shaped by research and development involving science and technology" (Solomon & Aikenhead, 1994, p. 59).

These and other publications challenged the status quo, calling for a science education that was both accessible and relevant to everyone—a *science for all* philosophy. Recall from Chapter 1 that *science for all* recognizes the need for science education for everyone (not

---

[1]Note that the STSE movement has its origins in STS education. For the purposes of our work, we will refer to STSE, understanding that its roots are in STS education.

just scientists!), so that we have the knowledge and skills to think critically, communicate effectively, make informed decisions, and act on matters related to science and technology. This era marked the beginning of citizenship science.

At the same time, STSE policy and curriculum projects and themes were developed in many countries around the world. For example, governments in Canada, the United States, the United Kingdom, Australia, and Israel developed documents that consistently called for science education to be more than simply the acquisition of scientific concepts.

The Science Council of Canada published *Science Education in Canadian Schools, Volume 1* (Orpwood & Souque, 1984), which described a science curriculum that included emphasis on science and society. The Council of Ministers of Education, Canada (1997) publication entitled *Common Framework of Science Learning Outcomes: Pan-Canadian Protocol for Collaboration on School Curriculum* provided a vision for scientific literacy that emphasized and prioritized STSE education. The document boldly asserts that scientific literacy would be best achieved through STSE education:

> The vision of scientific literacy included in this document sets out the need for students to acquire science-related skills, knowledge, and attitudes, and emphasized that this is best done through the study and analyses of the interrelationships among science, technology, society and the environment. (STSE) (CMEC, 1997, p. ii)

ACTIVITY 10.1   *21st C* ❶

Exploring Prior Knowledge and Experience: Science and Society

Think about your own experiences as a student, both in K–12 and in university. Identify an example of when your teacher of science raised issues of science or technology and its effect on society. Your teacher might have presented a controversial topic or explored an historical example of science and society. Describe the issue or event, and discuss what methods your teacher used (e.g., lecture, discussion, current events presentation, video clip). What activities did students do?

DISCUSSION QUESTIONS
1. What was your response to this approach?
2. Did you see it as relevant? Inspiring? Uncomfortable? Explain.
3. Make a list of the reasons why you as a teacher might include issues related to how science, technology, and the environment are affected by society, and vice versa.

Benefits of STSE Education

Over the past 40 years, much has been written about why educators and policy-makers should prioritize STSE education. (See, for example, Hodson, 2011; Pedretti & Little, 2008; Solomon & Aikenhead, 1994.) Recall from Chapter 1 that calls for science education include goals of scientific literacy, citizenship education, public understanding of science, and science and social responsibility. These goals are also consistently articulated by STSE advocates and programs worldwide. In summary, STSE education:

- fosters student engagement and raises student interest in science
- empowers learners
- requires collaboration among students and teachers
- raises awareness of current issues

- includes global and local perspectives
- promotes active, global citizenship for social good
- enhances student learning
- nurtures intellectual independence
- develops critical thinking skills
- advocates for social justice
- contextualizes science
- provides a more balanced view of science and scientists
- reflects a humanistic approach
- encompasses a broad vision of scientific literacy
- is interdisciplinary
- seeks to prepare young people to meet the challenges of the present and future

One of the criticisms levelled against STSE education is that science content is watered down or not attended to at all. Indeed this is not the case; science content is taught, but situated in the *context* of STSE. In other words, the teaching of scientific concepts and processes occurs within a rich science and society context. Researchers (such as Aikenhead, 2006; and Bennett, Lubben, & Hogarth, 2007) concluded that an STSE approach to teaching results in improvement of student attitudes toward science while maintaining their understanding of scientific ideas. For example, imagine your students are learning about energy sources—solar, wind, coal, hydroelectric, and tidal, to name a few. Each of these sources could be taught in a conventional lecture where sources are identified and discussed, with little consideration for the complex context in which they operate. Alternatively, a teacher may decide to engage in the political, social, and, economic complexity that each energy source brings to the table—an STSE approach. In both cases, students are learning about sources of energy but in very different ways.

Historically, proponents of STSE education have argued for a vision of science education that is inclusive, relevant, and reflective of the interconnectedness of science and society. Today, this desire for change in science education continues. In provinces and territories across Canada, STSE education has become an important part of the student science experience. However, STSE education is taken up differently by each province and territory. In Ontario, for example, STSE education has a central position, in the Curriculum Consortium of Canada's four Atlantic Provinces, the STSE approach is viewed as a means of achieving balance and integration in the science curriculum and is combined with NOS. In Alberta, STSE education and knowledge learning outcomes are combined, followed by skills and attitude outcomes. The extent to which STSE is prioritized carries important implications for policy and practice across the country. Activity 10.2 presents an opportunity to examine STSE policy and curriculum in your own province or territory.

ACTIVITY 10.2

21st C

Working with Resources: STSE Curriculum and Policy

Read, individually and then in pairs, the general section (usually located in the front matter) that pertains to STSE education in your province or territory's elementary science curriculum document. Briefly summarize what is said about STSE education. Then choose a K–3 topic or unit and read the outcomes or expectations for STSE education and comment, for example, on the language used, suggested activities, and accompanying strategies. Use specific examples to support your analysis. Repeat this exercise for a Grade 4–7 topic or unit.

DISCUSSION QUESTIONS

1. In general, how would you characterize the relative emphasis of STSE in the science curriculum? In other words, how important does it seem?
2. What are students expected to know, do, and value with respect to STSE outcomes and expectations?
3. Is there a difference in how STSE education is presented in the K–3 and Grades 4–7 expectations or outcomes? Explain and support with examples.

CHARACTERISTICS OF STSE EDUCATION

STSE education is multidisciplinary, drawing from, for example, history, economics, environmental studies, politics, sociology, and ethics. It would be a mistake to assume that STSE education is a single, well-articulated approach to science education. Rather, it is a movement with a number of different strands, each with a distinct history, and not without tensions. What is clear is that there is no single, widely accepted view of STSE education. By its very nature, it defies definition, which is both a strength and a weakness. As Ziman (1994) writes:

> The movement for STS[E] education springs from so many different sources, and flows in so many different channels that it does not have a shape that can be grasped mentally and described as a whole. That is not necessarily a defect. The same would apply to other great movements of our times, such as those for peace and for the environment. Such movements are kept alive by countless personal and collective commitments that cannot be captured in a few thousand words of didactic prose. (p. 21)

Solomon (1993, p. 18) used the following list to describe the general characteristics of STSE education:

1. an understanding of the environmental threats, including global ones, to the quality of life
2. the economic and industrial aspects of technology
3. some understudying of the fallible nature of science
4. discussion of personal opinion and values, as well as democratic action
5. a multi-cultural dimension

Table 10.1 summarizes the characteristics that typify STSE education. The list is the result of an analysis of national and international STSE research, curriculum, and policy documents. The following characteristics of STSE education consistently emerged: stewardship, decision making, values, action, and nature of science.

It is important to note that these characteristics often overlap; they are not mutually exclusive, and no single characteristic is more important than another. Many work in tandem, and different characteristics are used at different points in the curriculum for different purposes. Not all of the characteristics can be included in each lesson or unit—nor should they be. However, try to include all of the characteristics within your year of teaching science. It is up to you as the teacher to be judicious about STSE planning.

Technology and Science Learning (Part 1)

Table 10.1	Characteristics of STSE Education
Characteristic	**Description**
Stewardship	Caring for the environment, studying the utilization of resources, and considering long-term human needs in an effort to maintain a life-giving and life-sustaining environment.
Decision Making	Understanding how decisions are made at local, provincial, and national levels of government and within the private and industrial sectors; helping people make informed, responsible decisions.
Values	Coupling of science and values education, which departs from the traditional presentation of science as a value-free, objective, linear enterprise.
Action	Empowering citizens to become responsible agents of change at personal and social levels; promoting responsible participation in society; developing the potential to act and the disposition to do so. Exercising intellectual and ethical skills in determining the benefits and costs of any scientific or technological development, recognizing that underlying political and social forces drive the development and distribution of scientific and technological knowledge and artefacts; honouring principles of social justice.
Nature of Science	Recognizing that scientific knowledge is tentative (subject to change); empirical (based on or derived from observations of the natural world); subjective (theory laden); the product of human inference, imagination, and creativity; and socially and culturally embedded.

Source: Based on Pedretti & Little (2008).

ACTIVITY 10.3   21st C ② ④ ⑤

Read and Reflect: A Case Study of STSE in Practice

For this activity, read the following article:

Amirshokoohi, A., & Kazempour, M. (2010). The biodiversity community action project: An STS investigation. *The American Biology Teacher*, *72*(5), 288–293.

The article is an account of an STSE investigation that allowed students to gain an in-depth understanding of the interactions between organisms and their environment, as well as to connect science to society and their lives. Briefly describe what this project was about and answer the questions below. Be prepared to share your answers with the class.

DISCUSSION QUESTIONS

1. What motivated the class to embark on this project?
2. What characteristics of STSE education are reflected in this project? Describe the inclusion of each of these characteristics with examples from the project.
3. What is the relationship between content (understanding relevant science concepts) and STSE education?
4. Assessment can be a challenge in a project like this. Discuss how assessment was handled and what students were assessed on (content, collaboration, communication, etc.).
5. What is your response to a project of this magnitude?
6. This article describes a project done with Grade 9 and 10 students. How might you undertake a similar project with elementary school students?

ANALYZING THE CHARACTERISTICS OF STSE EDUCATION

In the sections below, we discuss in more detail the characteristics of STSE education outlined in Table 10.1. We include an activity and series of questions as entry points for personal reflection and dialogue with your peers as you begin to think about developing and implementing curricula with an STSE orientation.

Stewardship

Our environment is in crisis: climate change, acid rain, ozone depletion, species extinction, deforestation, and pollution are but a few examples. It seems that our relationships with and within the environment are precarious and require our immediate attention. Many issues arise when we consider, for example, what we preserve and how, over what timeline, and who should make these decisions. Some argue that the standard of living in North America and our related ecological footprint far exceed the limits of our environment and are predicated upon bountiful supplies of inexpensive fuel and other commodities, often at the expense of underdeveloped countries and those who are economically disadvantaged.

Over the years, there has been a resurgence of interest in environmental education at all levels. For example, the years 2005–2014 were declared the United Nations Decade of Education for Sustainable Development. A review of the literature (for example, Bateson, 2000; Hart & Nolan, 1999; Palmer, 1998; Suzuki & Hanington, 2012) describes education for stewardship as the following:

- heightening appreciation for all forms of life and for Earth as the only life-sustaining environment we know
- enabling people to understand the interdependence of all life on Earth
- making explicit the natural structures and processes that sustain life
- critiquing the way humans alter the integrity of ecosystems
- engaging students in a process through which they come to recognize personal and societal practices, attitudes, and forces (i.e., economic, political, social, cultural, technological, philosophical, ideological) that foster or impede sustainability
- challenging the imagination to envision alternative practices and life-enhancing roles for humans in the web of ecosphere relationships
- providing students with the skills, knowledge, and values they need to live responsibly as global citizens

It has been argued that stewardship and sustainability can (and should) be infused across the curriculum. However, STSE (with an emphasis on the E) education provides a natural starting point to teach and learn about stewardship in the context of science education. (See Chapter 3.) Stewardship includes caring, protecting, and preserving the natural world for future generations. Environmental stewardship entails conserving and preserving healthy ecosystems and restoring damaged and endangered ones. It requires governments, organizations, and communities to work together to accomplish these goals. As you continue reading, think about how you might weave environmental education and stewardship toward Earth into your teaching of science. What role do science and technology play in stewardship? How might different value perspectives affect stewardship? For example, Aboriginal people in Canada recognize that the land and its people are inextricably linked:

> Embedded within the Aboriginal world view is the concept of collective responsibility for tending the land and using only that which is needed for sustenance. Important, as well, is the interconnectedness and interdependence of all life forms—humankind, flora and fauna, and all that exists on the Earth. (Manitoba Education and Training, 2000, p. 49)

ACTIVITY 10.4

Studying the Locavore Movement

Locavores are people interested in eating foods that are locally produced, rather than foods that are grown elsewhere and often shipped long distances to reach their destination. Every attempt is made to eat foods grown within 100 miles of its point of cultivation. The local food movement benefited greatly from the popularity of Vancouver couple Alisa Smith and J. B. MacKinnon's book *The 100 Mile Diet: A Year of Local Eating*. In groups of four, research the locavore movement with the following questions in mind.

- Explain what motivated the locavore movement.
- Describe three benefits of eating locally produced foods.
- What are some of the criticisms levelled against locavores? Do you agree? Why or why not?
- Do you already choose to eat locally grown food? If not, would you consider changing your diet to consume more locally grown food? Why or why not? If so, what changes would you need to make?
- Now imagine it is autumn in your community and you are planning a dinner party. Plan a three-course meal according to locavore practices. (Be sure to describe the specific foods used.)

DISCUSSION QUESTIONS

1. Would you use an activity like this with your students? Why or why not?
2. What science content do your students need to understand in order to complete this activity?
3. What might be some of the challenges for you and your students in using this activity?

USING THIS ACTIVITY WITH ELEMENTARY SCHOOL STUDENTS

This activity takes you and your class on a field trip to a neighbourhood grocery store to explore where fruits and vegetables come from. Back at school, students will map out the path that each food takes from its origin (where it is grown) to their dinner plates. As with all field trips, be sure that you plan logistics (time, transport, etc.) well in advance and that you have enough adult supervisory support (Refer to Appendix F: Planning for Field Trips). If a visit to a grocery store or market is not feasible, you can also use grocery store flyers and a selection of produce for the activity. Alternatively, you might ask a local farmer or the grocery store produce manager to be a guest speaker in your classroom; if this is the case, you will need to adapt the activity below accordingly. The activity easily connects to social studies, mathematics, language arts, and fine arts curricula. The activity as presented here has many steps—adapt it to suit your students. For additional ideas for mapping with students, see, for example, Jagger (2009) and Sobel (1998).

1. Before the field trip, organize student groups and data collection supplies (e.g., pencils, science notebooks, digital cameras). Also, contact the store manager or supervisor to check that classes are able to make store visits, and arrange a time for the visit.
2. As a class, discuss where food comes from. You might ask what students ate for breakfast or for dinner the day before and where those foods came from. Don't be surprised if some students think that vegetables come from the store or the fridge, not the ground!
3. Arrange students into groups and distribute their data collection supplies. Be sure to remind them of the expectations for field trips (e.g., stay with group, listen carefully, and follow instructions).
4. At the grocery store or market, ask students to choose 5 or 10 fruits and vegetables that they eat or like and record in as much detail as possible where they are from. For example, an apple could be described as from the Okanagan Valley in British Columbia rather than just as an apple from Canada. Encourage groups to talk to employees in the produce section about how fruits and vegetables get to the store. Data might be recorded in drawings, notes, and digital photographs.
5. Back at school, create a class list on chart paper of fruits and vegetables and their origins. Are there any patterns? Consider the time of year. Which fruits and vegetables are local? From within the province? Within Canada? Somewhere else in the world?
6. On large maps—one each of your region, your province, Canada, and world—have groups locate and mark the origins of the listed fruits and vegetables. For younger students, you might do this step together.

7. Discuss steps it takes to get food from the field to the table. (These are known as *foodways*.) This is a good place to use role-play with students as farmers, produce pickers, truck drivers, and so on. Talk about the impact of foodways that have multiple steps and cross long distances. What can we do to reduce the amount of energy expended?

8. Using fruits and vegetables that are grown close to home (ideally locally), have groups create a recipe for a salad or a smoothie. Put together a local-food cookbook of the recipes to keep in the class library and share with families. If possible, have groups prepare their salad or smoothie as a morning or afternoon snack for the class.

9. *Assessment:* This activity has many components, and it is important to determine what you plan to assess. For example, will you assess the recording sheet from Step 4, the explanation of the foodway of one item, or the recipe students create as a group? Possible assessment tools include a checklist, a rubric, or anecdotal comments. Students could also complete a self-assessment rubric.

Decision Making

Science and technology play a vital role in the lives of individuals and societies. At the individual level, we often make decisions based on scientific evidence. For example, we choose to consume certain foods and reject others, or we might use particular cleaners over others in our homes. STSE education can enhance students' risk literacy—their understanding and application of probability—through the examination of authentic problems (Radakovic & McDougall, 2012). For example, students might explore the statistics related to nuclear power, and decide whether it is an acceptable risk to live next to a nuclear power plant. Almost all of these decisions are guided by scientific authorities in whom the public often places implicit trust: "Science and technology are essential social enterprises, but alone they can only indicate what can happen, not what should happen. [What should happen] involves human decisions about the use of knowledge" (National Research Council, 1996, p. 199). STSE education is rooted in understanding and participating in the decision-making process. Students are encouraged to gain a clear understanding of how decisions are made at the local, provincial, and national government levels, and within the private and industrial sectors, while developing skills to make informed personal decisions.

Decision making is a complex process encumbered by multiple values and agendas. To navigate this complexity, decision makers rely on understanding the underlying value positions of stakeholders as well as the criteria and cost-benefit analyses for the various alternatives. Experts can be found to support a number of different perspectives stemming from a single issue, often making it difficult to form firm conclusions. However, this should not preclude science educators from attempting to teach decision making. Rather, it highlights the need to teach students the critical thinking skills that will assist them in evaluating alternative solutions while participating as citizens in a democratic society.

The Foundation for the Atlantic Canada Science Curriculum (n.d., p. 3), for example, outlines the following steps involved in the decision-making process:

- identifying the problem or situation
- generating possible solutions or courses of action
- evaluating alternatives
- making a thoughtful decision based on the information available

In the Saskatchewan Science 5 curriculum (Adapted from Saskatchewan Ministry of Education. (2011). *Saskatchewan Curriculum Science 5*. Retrieved from https://www.edonline.sk.ca/bbcswebdav/library/curricula/English/Science/Science_5_2011.pdf. Adapted and used with permission of Saskatchewan Ministry of Education.), a framework for engaging students in STSE education includes:

- clarifying an issue
- evaluating available research and different viewpoints on the issue
- generating possible courses of action or solutions

- evaluating the pros and cons for each action or solution
- identifying a fundamental value associated with each action or solution
- making a thoughtful decision
- examining the impact of the decision
- reflecting back on the process of decision making

As you continue reading, think about the following questions. What should inform decision making? What is the role of science and technology in contemporary (social) decision making? How might teachers encourage informed decision making in students?

ACTIVITY 10.5

21st C

Do We Need Plastic Shopping Bags?

Adapted from Sandner, L., Ellis, C., Lacy, D., Little, C., & Mace, H. (2009). *Investigating Science 9*. Pearson Canada, Inc., p. 133. Reprinted with permission by Pearson Canada Inc.

When we are finished using a plastic bag, we are faced with the dilemma of its disposal. Recycling is one option, but it uses energy and resources, possibly more than making the plastic bag in the first place. Plastic bags and other polyethylene products often end up in landfill—or as litter—and may not break down for decades. Consider whether we need plastic shopping bags as you complete the following.

In groups of four, perform the following steps:

- Identify and research two advantages and disadvantages of using plastic bags.
- Identify two alternatives to using plastic bags and both the pros and cons of those alternatives.
- Create a table to record your results.
- Decide your position on the issue and defend your stance.

DISCUSSION QUESTIONS

1. Would you use an activity like this with your students? Why or why not?
2. What science content do your students need to understand in order to complete this activity?
3. What are some of the challenges or barriers that you foresee in implementing decision-making activities?

USING THIS ACTIVITY WITH ELEMENTARY SCHOOL STUDENTS

The following activity as written is suited for older students but can be used with younger students in a whole-class or group discussion.

1. Arrange students in groups of three or four. Give each group a large piece of chart paper and markers, or a tablet, and have them set up a table like the one below:

Advantages, Disadvantages, and Alternatives to Using Plastic Shopping Bags	
Advantages of Using Plastic Bags	**Disadvantages of Using Plastic Bags**
Alternative #1 to Using Plastic Bags	**Alternative #2 to Using Plastic Bags**

2. Groups brainstorm and record in one colour the advantages and disadvantages of using plastic shopping bags.

3. Discuss ideas as a class and from the discussion, groups can add additional advantages and disadvantages in different colours.

4. Groups then identify two possible alternatives and list pros and cons for each.

5. Together, group members discuss which option—plastic shopping bags, alternative 1, or alternative 2—they support and present their position to the class.

6. As a class, discuss whether groups agreed or disagreed. Compare and contrast the groups' positions. Is there a consensus? How do decisions differ?

7. *Assessment*: You might use the groups' brainstorming tables and a rubric for assessment. This is a good opportunity to have students complete a self- and a group-assessment rubric that covers both content and group work goals.

Values

As mentioned, STSE education seeks to bring together science and values education, departing from a traditional representation of science as value-free and objective. The underlying assumption is that science cannot be separated from its moral and ethical responsibilities to society, nor can society abdicate responsibility to science (Venville & Dawson, 2012). However, deeply embedded within these issues is the question of values—specifically, which values, and who decides. For our purposes, we use Aspin's (2002, p. 15) definition of *values* as those "ideas, conventions, principles, rules, objects, products, activities, practices, procedures or judgments that people accept, agree to, treasure, cherish, prefer, incline toward, see as important and indeed act upon." This can present some challenges for educators in science, as they strive to take into account alternative cultural perceptions, values, and customs.

STSE education should to be sensitive to a range of values and ideologies, especially in Canada's rich multicultural society. Conceptual ideologies about progress, sustainability, democracy, and educational purposes differ. STSE educators, particularly when dealing with controversial subject matter, face the challenge of recognizing pluralism, biases, and indoctrination, while simultaneously taking account of alternative values. For example, students might study different cultural beliefs about food choices or the multiple value positions regarding the building of a quarry on farmland. As you continue reading, consider the following: How should teachers accommodate diverse views, cultural contexts, and ways of thinking about the world? Whose values are advocated? Whose are ignored? Are there topics that you might use with your students that show how values or biases are implicated in scientific research?

ACTIVITY 10.6   *21st C*

Not in My Backyard!

Adapted from Ellis, L., Hounjet, C., Johanson, T., Walter, C., O'Soup, D., Racette, C., & View, T. (2012). *Saskatchewan Science 5*, Toronto: Pearson Canada Inc., p. 101.

Manufacturers create products from raw materials, and there are often drawbacks to this process, particularly if goods are manufactured in neighbourhoods and communities. For example, a manufacturing plant might create loud noise or unpleasant smells. Think about the natural resources in your region and how they are extracted and processed to make products. Examples include logging, mining, fisheries, and agriculture. As a class, choose an industry in your region.

1. Divide the class equally into the following roles (or stakeholders): consumer, individual/corporation or federal agency that owns the raw materials, individual who extracts, harvests, and/or processes the raw materials (e.g., logger, miner, farm labourer), government official, environmentalist, manufacturer, salesperson, scientist, and role of your choice.

continued on next page

2. Conduct research to answer the following questions from the perspective of your role (or stakeholder position).
   - What are the benefits of the product?
   - What are the benefits of manufacturing the product in your region?
   - What are the drawbacks of the product?
   - What are the drawbacks of manufacturing the product in your region?
3. Conduct a town hall meeting to present your view on whether the industry should be located in your community. (Refer to Appendix A for details on how to conduct a town hall meeting.)
4. Try to reach consensus regarding the industry's presence in your community.

DISCUSSION QUESTIONS

1. Compare and contrast the views of the different stakeholders. How are they similar? How are they different?

2. As a teacher, would you share your personal views? Explain.

3. Describe three challenges or barriers that you foresee when including values in your teaching of science

USING THIS ACTIVITY WITH ELEMENTARY SCHOOL STUDENTS

In this activity, your students will be participating in a town hall meeting to decide if the benefits of the industry outweigh the drawbacks. As above, think about natural resources and manufacturing that occurs in your community or region. For example, in British Columbia you might choose logging; in Saskatchewan you might look at agriculture; and in Nova Scotia you might use fishing. Be mindful of connections that your students may have to those industries (e.g., parents employed by a mill, uncle is a farmer) and remind students of expectations of respectful and inclusive discussions. This activity fits well within a unit on resources and can also complement social studies and language arts.

1. In small groups, brainstorm and record the benefits of the product and having the industry in your community or region. Then brainstorm and record the drawbacks of the product and having it in your community or region. A T-chart can be a good way to organize ideas.
2. As a class, discuss the benefits and drawbacks. Tell students they will role-play a town hall meeting about whether the industry should be in the community. Assign students to the following roles: consumer; individual, corporation, or federal agency that owns the raw materials; individual who extracts, harvests, or processes the raw materials (e.g., logger, miner, farm labourer); government official; environmentalist; manufacturer; salesperson; scientist; and role of your choice. There should be three to five students per role.
3. Students will work in their role groups to discuss their viewpoints and establish an argument on whether the industry should be in their town.
4. Groups will present their arguments in a town hall meeting. (Refer to Appendix A for details on how to conduct a town hall meeting.)
5. As a class, discuss all of the viewpoints and try to come to a decision that will benefit the whole community.
6. *Assessment*: A rubric and anecdotal comments can be used to assess students' argument and position, their presentation to the group, or overall participation in the activity.

Action

If education is to enable young citizens to look critically at society, analyze the values underpinning that society, and ask what can be done to create a more socially just society, then science education must also contribute to this active citizenry (Bencze & Carter, 2011; Hodson, 2011; Pedretti, 2003; Roth & Désautels 2002; Sperling & Bencze, 2010). An STSE orientation is one way for science curricula to explore the goals of social reconstruction and social justice. For example, how can we ensure that people have access to safe drinking water? Or that local green spaces are protected? It is not enough to simply develop awareness or make decisions about what might be done. Science educators must also provide, when appropriate, opportunities for students to take action. For example, students might engage in an activity to clean up a local ravine or write letters to a local politician concerning a community issue.

Hodson (2003) describes four levels that help students prepare to take action. The first level helps students explore and appreciate that science and technology impact society. Level two is about understanding how power, wealth, and special interests affect decisions about science and technology. In level three, teachers help students develop personal positions and value perspectives, and level four encourages students to take action. Educators often attend to levels one, two, and three, and for many it comes easily and intuitively. However, level four is the real challenge. This final level—action—can take many forms—for example, organizing petitions, engaging in "greening" the community, conducting surveys, lobbying local governments, boycotting environmentally unsafe products, publishing newsletters, or monitoring the school's energy consumption. The key to translating knowledge into action is ownership and empowerment. Students need to have a personal understanding of the issue, a feeling of investment in addressing and solving the problem, and the opportunity to practise action.

In *Teaching Science for Social Justice*, Angela Calabrese Barton (2003) describes her work with inner city youth living in poverty. Her book includes stories of marginalized youth engaged in community-based science projects and transforming their spaces, essentially empowering them to build a socially just world. She argues that science, schooling, and society must intersect to help build a more socially just, critically informed, and sustainable society. Closer to home, Larry Bencze (in, for example, Bencze & Sperling, 2012; Bencze & Carter, 2011) developed STEPWISE (Science and Technology Education Promoting Well-being for Individuals, Society and Environment), a framework to assist teachers and students in taking informed and responsible actions to address STSE issues.

In summary, engaging in action necessitates a shift from transmission learning (that is, the passive transfer of knowledge from teacher to student) to a transformation position (the development of the whole person in connection with their community and society at large) (Miller, 2008). A transformative lens supports a pedagogy that promotes critical thinking, problem-solving, analysis, synthesis, and evaluation is more action oriented and politically motivated. This shift inevitably raises questions about the purpose of schooling, the form we wish society to take, and what constitutes science curriculum and science education. As you continue reading, think about the following questions: Should teachers advocate social reconstruction within science classrooms? Why or why not? Do you think that it is appropriate for teachers to politicize the science curriculum? What kinds of action, if any, should teachers encourage students to take? What role might science and technology play in social reconstruction?

ACTIVITY 10.7

21st C

Taking Action

Imagine you live in a community that is about to build a shopping centre on prized parkland. Many families use the park, and there is an abundance of flora and fauna that is native to the region. After extensive research and engaging in a cost/benefit analyses, you have come to the decision to oppose construction of the shopping centre. In groups of four, choose one of the methods below to get your message across to the public.

    a.   Design a pamphlet for distribution to community members and local politicians.

    b.   Create a three-minute commercial for television or radio.

    c.   Write a short article (250 words) for a community newsletter.

continued on next page

DISCUSSION QUESTIONS

1. What is your response to the inclusion of action in your science classroom?
2. What kinds of action, if any, should teachers encourage students to take?
3. Do you think social justice should be part of the mandate of science education? Why or why not?
4. Do you think it is appropriate for teachers to politicize the science curriculum? Why or why not?
5. Describe three challenges or barriers that you foresee in promoting action in your science classroom.

USING THIS ACTIVITY WITH ELEMENTARY SCHOOL STUDENTS

Consider your local school community. What are some of the real-life concerns of the community? For example, are there few or poorly maintained playgrounds? Is overdevelopment a concern? Are there any green spaces? In this activity, your students will take a neighbourhood walk, pinpoint a community issue, and plan and take action to address their concerns. The example of a poorly maintained playground is outlined in the activity description below. Adapt as necessary to fit with your community issue. Depending on your students' interest and the flexibility of your curriculum and schedule, you might choose to extend this activity into a much larger community research and action project. It can be easily integrated with social studies, language arts, and fine arts curricula, and can also incorporate technology. This activity could also be a great buddy activity for younger and older elementary classes.

1. Preparation: Before the activity, gather data collection materials—sketch books, pencils, clipboards, digital cameras, copies of neighbourhood maps, etc. Depending on the age of your students, you might pre-sort the supplies and store them in plastic zip bags. Be sure that you have enough adult supervisory support. Check with your school what the required ratio of adults to students is, and try to have an extra adult or two present.
2. Launch: Talk to students about the local playground. Is it used? What actions could be taken to improve it? Who would take action? Tell students that they will be taking a neighbourhood walk to the playground to collect data about the site. Arrange students in groups and distribute materials.
3. Visiting the site and data collection: On the walk and at the playground, ask students to take digital photographs, make sketches, and take field notes in order to answer questions such as
   - What equipment is present?
   - Is it in good working order?
   - What equipment could be added?
   - Is the playground safe?
   - Is there grass covering?
   - Is there a water feature (e.g., pond, paddling pool)?
4. Data analysis: Back at school, create a class list of observations from the playground and complete the following table:

Community Site Exploration Data Table

What do I see? Include positive and negative features	Evidence to support observations (field notes, sketches, photos)	My reaction and thoughts about what I see
e.g., broken swing	photo	I cannot use it; it might hurt someone; who can fix it?
e.g., lots of trees	field note	pretty, provides shade

5. Making a plan: As a class, discuss what can be done to improve the playground. Create an action plan, using the following questions as a guide.
   - What changes would make the playground better?
   - What do you know about the playground with respect to who is responsible for its maintenance and who uses it?
   - What do you need to find out?

   Working with a partners, students can use the internet to research these questions. This step can be skipped if your students are in the early elementary years. You might also provide questions that students can pose to their parents.

6. Preparing for action: Remind students that an important step of an action project is getting the message across to the public. Students will choose one of three options to work on with a partner: Design a pamphlet to distribute to community members and local politicians; plan a short commercial for the morning announcements; or create a poster to go in the school hallways and newsletter. Students can use a computer to make pamphlets and posters.

7. Taking action: Students communicate their findings to the community with pamphlets, announcements, and posters.

8. *Assessment*: You will need to determine what you plan to assess. For example, you might interview students with respect to what they learned and how they participated, or collect students' field notes and/or the improvement plans, or assess the product of the action project. Assessment tools include a checklist for the interview or field notes and a rubric for the improvement plan or action project. For any project work, student self-assessments can be valuable.

Nature of Science

It is often communicated to students that science is objective—only concerned with facts. Some argue that throughout the history of western science, human emotions and biases have influenced developments in science and technology. Nature of science (NOS) is an important part of STSE education because it can help students understand how scientific knowledge is constructed, how claims are made and used to support arguments, and how science is practised. Typically in schools, little attention is paid to how scientific knowledge is generated (epistemology), how scientists decide what they believe to be *true*, or how science is practised. Consequently, many school curricula misrepresent science as an orderly, abstract pursuit employing a set and reliable method to find factual information about the universe. However, NOS is a field of research that provides a realistic image of science and scientific practice. (Please refer to Chapter 2 for a more thorough overview of NOS.) As you continue reading, keep the following questions in mind: How do scientists create knowledge? Is it important to teach students about how science works? Why or why not?

ACTIVITY 10.8   *21st C* 6

Media Literacy and NOS

Almost every day, in local or national newspapers, there are articles written that have connections to STSE. Examples might be articles that question the value of eating organic food or that promote flu vaccinations. Locate a newspaper or magazine article (either in print or online) or a video news clip that has a science and society focus. Briefly describe the story and answer the following questions.

continued on next page

DISCUSSION QUESTIONS

1. What techniques, if any, are used to persuade the reader or viewer to take a particular position?
2. What claim(s) does the news story make?
3. What evidence is used to support the claims? Is this valid use of data?
4. Is the argument compelling? Trustworthy? Why or why not?
5. What are the challenges of using media resources in your teaching of science?

ACTIVITY 10.9

21st C

Connecting Practice and Theory: STSE Education

In small groups, choose one of the three topics in the table below and complete the chart. Be prepared to share your results with the class. Working with your particular science topic, brainstorm how the different characteristics of STSE education can be included in your planning. Locate two online resources, as well as textbooks, to assist you. An example using *conservation of energy and resources* is completed for you.

Exploring STSE Education Through Science Topics

STSE characteristics	Topic: Conservation of energy and resources	Topic: Habitats and communities	Topic: Air and water in the environment	Topic: Properties of liquids and solids
Stewardship	Protecting energy resources. How can we move to using more renewable resources for energy generation?			
Decision making	Brown-outs can happen when the energy demand exceeds the supply. To avoid these, should more energy be made available, or should consumers be encouraged to reduce their energy usage?			
Values	Many living near wind turbines and wind farms oppose their use due to issues such as increased headaches, noise pollution, and interference with birds and other animals. Others espouse their benefits. Should we use wind turbines as an alternative source of energy?			
Action	You have concluded that you want to reduce energy consumption in your home or school. Create an action plan.			
Nature of Science (NOS)	A trans-provincial pipeline project has been proposed to transport crude oil from Alberta to coastal British Columbia. What research has been done to explore the viability of this option? Who is doing the research, and how is it funded?			

1. Having shared your results, compare how easy or difficult it was to complete the table for each of the life science, Earth and space science, and physical science topics.
2. Which of the characteristics of STSE education resonated for you and why?
3. Which ones, if any, are problematic for you, and why?
4. What aspects of STSE education seem to be favoured in science? What is absent? Speculate as to why this might be the case.
5. Discuss the strengths and limitations for teaching science that includes STSE characteristics. Be prepared to share your ideas with the class.
6. Discuss the strengths and limitations of the two websites you used. Would you use these sites to help you in your planning? In your science instruction? Why or why not?

STSE CHALLENGES AND TENSIONS

An emphasis on STSE education can present both practical and ideological challenges for educators. As you worked through some of the activities in this chapter, you may have come to a similar conclusion. In spite of the challenges, support for STSE education continues to grow. STSE education can engage and increase students' interest in science; make science accessible, meaningful, and relevant; connect science to social, cultural, and political contexts; and convey a humanistic view of the institution and practice of science. In this section, we explore the practical and ideological challenges of STSE education for teachers and students. We also examine ways to address these tensions.

A number of challenges relate to STSE pedagogy and teaching. For example, some teachers may believe they lack content expertise required to engage in STSE education in rich and complex ways. The interdisciplinary nature of STSE education further complicates this issue and prompts teachers to ask: How do I integrate politics, economics, and history into my science lessons? The challenge of translating outcomes and expectations into teaching practices (i.e., pedagogical content knowledge) that support STSE characteristics can be another tension. Finally, assessment presents a particular challenge—the pedagogy of STSE education often includes teaching strategies (e.g., debates, town hall meetings) that can be difficult to assess. Chapter 11 explores planning and pedagogy in the context of STSE education.

Values and Student Identity

How do teachers reconcile the coupling of science and values in their teaching? How do teachers address personal values in the classroom and accommodate diverse views, cultural contexts, and ways of thinking? Students who feel marginalized may have difficulty participating in discussions, particularly if the issues are controversial. Students may feel vulnerable for many reasons, including:

- being an English language learner
- lacking previous academic success and confidence
- being shy
- not being a member of the dominant culture
- being with more outspoken peers

There may be a social hierarchy in your classroom that you are not aware of. Ideas should be judged based on their merit rather than on who voiced them. As the teacher, it is critical that you ensure a safe and trusting environment in which all of your students belong, and in which diversity is respected and celebrated. The following list offers some suggestions regarding how to accomplish this:

- Start building relationships among students early in the year, even in the first few days of school in September. Create opportunities for small-group discussion and ensure that students work with different people in the class.
- Discuss expectations for discussion at the outset, repeating them when necessary. It is a great idea to generate a list of expectations for discussion so that it is reflective of students' expectations, not just your own.
- Actively ensure that all students have a chance to speak during class discussions. Be mindful of student identity.
- For whole class discussions, have students sit together in a circle so that everyone is facing each other and no backs are turned. It seems simple but physical openness and inclusivity can really bring a group together.
- Form small groups for discussion to allow more chances for each individual to contribute.
- Within small groups, use techniques that allow everyone equal time (e.g., give students four playing cards each—every time they speak, they throw a card into the circle. Once all of their cards are gone, they cannot have them back until everyone else has used up their four cards). You might use similar strategies for whole class discussions (e.g., talking sticks or beanbags).
- Intervene in the discussion when students express disrespectful views. These comments serve to silence those students who identify with the group or the individual who is being denounced. You may not even know which students are being affected. It is essential that you deal with such comments as they happen.

Discussion of ethics and science can easily deteriorate into a values clarification discussion, where students believe that anything goes if they can justify it. The other extreme is indoctrination, where students are *told* what to believe, support, or choose (usually by the teacher). It is a slippery slope between relativism and indoctrination, and a road that teachers must tread carefully.

Teacher Positioning

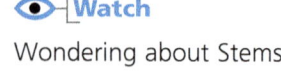

Watch

Wondering about Stems

As you consider the place of STSE education in science classes, consider the role of the teacher, particularly with respect to controversial issues. Our experience—as teachers in the K–12 school system—has consistently shown that students want to know where you stand on specific issues and why. Unfortunately, there is no definitive rule or governing orthodoxy about the role of a teacher. It is not surprising that different educators and researchers have differing views. Regardless of the choice you make, remember that you have an enormous influence not only on what views are expressed in class, but also on what views students adopt. Below are three positions a teacher might assume: neutrality, commitment, and balance (Van Rooy, 2012).

Neutrality In this position, the teacher either supports all viewpoints or withholds support for any viewpoint. If you decide not to disclose your opinion and remain neutral, it is helpful to explain to your students why you have decided to keep your opinion to yourself (i.e., to avoid influencing the discussion and to allow students to explore possibilities). In reality, remaining neutral is difficult to do, if not impossible. You might believe you are being neutral, but facial expressions and other cues can convey bias. Students know that you have a view, and often want to know what it is. Further, it can be argued that neutrality can stifle communication.

Watch

Investigating Goldfish
(Part 2)

Commitment In this case, the teacher makes his or her view clear by disclosing her or his personal position at an appropriate time in the unit. The teacher's endorsement of a particular position could imply to students that it is the best position, so teachers must be mindful when making their position known. There are situations in which you may feel that you cannot keep your opinion to yourself. If you choose this route, it is crucial that you have established a safe and accepting classroom atmosphere where students feel comfortable in knowing that you will assess their arguments and not expect them to hold the same view as you do.

Balance   In this position, the teacher ensures that all viewpoints are represented equally. Viewpoints are presented either through student statements or published sources. The teacher organizes and facilitates student contributions by observing procedural rules, yet refrains from stating personal positions. This may allow for freer discussion among students and avoids the issue of indoctrination. At times, the teacher might play the role of devil's advocate by carefully but deliberately adopting provocative and oppositional stances, irrespective of personal viewpoint.

ACTIVITY 10.10   *21st C* ❷

Exploring Teacher Roles

Discuss the pros and cons of each of the three positions described above. Provide concrete examples to explain your reasoning, and describe circumstances in which you might adopt a neutral position, a committed position, or a balanced position.

The Politicization of the Curriculum

Sometimes action is political in nature—for example, writing a letter to a local Member of Parliament regarding a development in the community that may have detrimental effects on the environment, or becoming involved in a project to provide clean drinking water to a community in need. Action and the politicization of science present yet another set of tensions. The notion of a socio-political science curriculum that promotes social justice and transformation provides a very different vision of teaching science and science education that can be disconcerting for some. There are a number of considerations to keep in mind:

- How might you involve parents?
- What student actions, if any, are appropriate to promote (for example, letter writing, cleaning up a local ravine, planting a school garden, picketing)?
- What is the school ethos?
- What are the school norms?
- To what extent is action supported in your curriculum, policy documents, and school board?
- How comfortable do you feel in promoting action with your students?

Some would argue that it is not a teacher's job to promote action or to be political in the classroom. Others feel that it is vital to teach students that there are different perspectives to issues. Still others assert that choosing *not* to politicize issues is a political decision in itself. We argue that students need opportunities to develop skills for asserting their political positions and for taking action. However, as a teacher, you need to consider, in light of your particular school context, the needs of your students and the curriculum, and act accordingly.

A Research Perspective

Many have written about the challenges inherent to adopting an STSE approach. In a study conducted with preservice students, Pedretti, Bencze, Hewitt, Romkey, and Jivraj (2008) were interested in determining teacher candidates' inclinations toward teaching with an

STSE orientation and how the identity of "science teacher" intersected with the adoption of STSE education. These preservice teachers watched a video case study of a teacher and her students working through a unit on climate change. Central to the unit was a town hall debate on the Kyoto Protocol. The research found that these preservice teachers supported STSE education, even expressed confidence and motivation to teach it, but were unlikely to engage in it in their early years of teaching. Their comments included the following:

> My first consideration when implementing STSE would be about my expertise. I have to take an inventory of my own expertise, identify my limitations and my strengths. (p. 952)
>
> There's so much to cover in the curriculum, STSE would take a lot of time away from that. (p. 952)
>
> Other teachers are probably using a standard teaching approach and a teacher using STSE would be concerned about whether the students are going to retain the same amount of information. (p. 952)
>
> I was impressed with the project overall...spending all that time looking at the politics of Kyoto and she mentioned having her students read *The Globe and Mail*, *The Post*, and *The Star*...but should a science class spend that much time on politics? (p. 953).

In trying to understand this paradox, five problems of practice consistently emerged, including issues related to control and autonomy, support and belonging, expertise and negotiating the curriculum, politicization and action, and ideological perspectives. Activity 10.11 explores this research in more detail.

ACTIVITY 10.11
21st C ❷ ❺

Read and Reflect: Identity and Ideology

For this activity read the following article:

Pedretti, E., Bencze, L., Hewitt, J., Romkey, L., & Jivraj, A. (2008). Promoting issues-based STSE perspectives in science teacher education: Problems of identity and ideology. *Science and Education, 17*(8/9), 941–960.

Answer the following questions and be prepared to share your responses.

DISCUSSION QUESTIONS

1. Explain the concept of teacher of science identity and its relationship to STSE education.
2. Describe each problem of practice and your response to it.
3. Which, if any, of these tensions are you most worried about and why?
4. What might you do to alleviate these possible problems of practice?

EXPLORING ELEMENTARY SCIENCE IN CREATIVE WAYS: THE ROCK CYCLE

In order to teach any topic effectively, it is helpful to have a deep and broad knowledge base. This is particularly true in the context of STSE education, where content can be minimized in the context of larger social issues. In this section, we present some ideas to help develop your subject matter content knowledge (CK) and pedagogical content knowledge (PCK) for a specific topic. The topic, the rock cycle, is introduced with a visual that might appear in a print or media resource. We encourage you to search for other resources, as well. As you learn or review the content, keep in mind other issues such as terminology, abstract processes, integration with mathematics and language arts, and activities that support student learning. Additionally, consider the meta-cognitive aspect of the activity, such as understanding how you learn, what you know, and what you need to know.

ACTIVITY 10.12

21st C ⑤

The Rock Cycle

Rock and minerals are found in the curriculum documents of most elementary science programs. The rock cycle is related to STSE perspectives in terms of how, for example, extracting and refining rocks and minerals for human use can impact on society and the environment. In Ontario, the Grade 4 Rocks and Minerals unit has the following expectation: Describe how igneous, sedimentary, and metamorphic rocks are formed. Grade 3 students in Alberta learn about the rock cycle within their Rocks and Minerals unit; the provincial science curriculum includes the expectation that students will demonstrate knowledge of the materials that make up Earth's crust and be able to classify those materials. Saskatchewan includes rocks and minerals in the Grade 4 science curriculum, in which students investigate the properties of rocks and minerals, paying special attention to those in the local environment. Similarly, Nova Scotia has a Grade 4 unit called Rocks, Minerals, and Erosion.

Reviewing the Content

1. Review or learn the content associated with the formation of rocks. For example, what is igneous rock? How is it formed? Use the visual below to guide your exploration.
2. Make a list of definitions for important or unfamiliar vocabulary and processes associated with this topic.
3. When you feel comfortable with the content, use the figure below to explain the rock cycle to a peer.

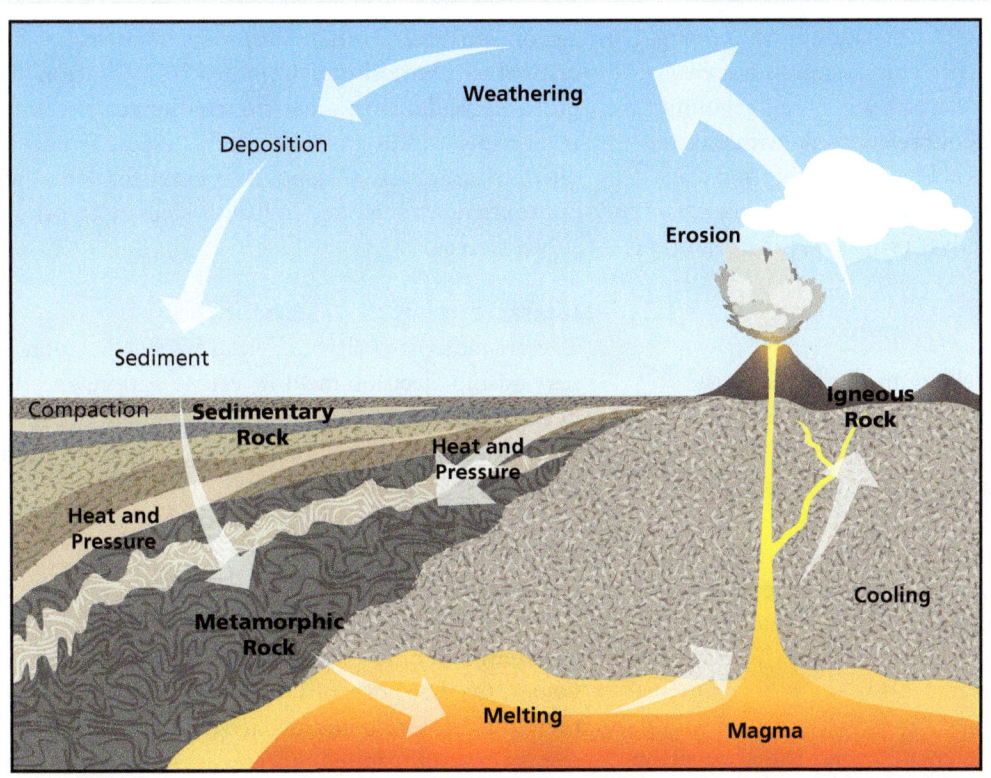

The Rock Cycle

continued on next page

Literacy and Numeracy Connections

1. Locate the book *Everybody Needs a Rock* by Byrd Baylor (1985), a lyrical and beautifully illustrated guide to finding a special rock.
2. You will notice that the author provides 10 simple rules for finding a special rock. Consider how you might use the book in the rocks and minerals unit to bring a personal element to this topic. For example, your students could begin their own rock collection.

Activities for Elementary School Students

1. Provide students with a collection of rocks (or ask students to bring in their rock collections). Ask students to sort the rocks according to their own criteria (e.g., size, colour, texture), and then sort them according to criteria provided by the teacher (igneous, metamorphic, sedimentary).
2. Use the game *I Spy* to identify objects that are made from, or contain, rock.
3. Make your own rock. Using granite as a model, combine and glue shredded coloured paper to create a granite rock. The coloured paper represents the minerals in granite. For example, feldspar is pink, quartz is yellow, and mica is brown. Alternatively, you could use clay or plasticine and dried beans and legumes to create smaller granite rocks.

CONCLUDING THOUGHTS

What is science education for? If science education is about transformation and agency, as well as understanding the discipline of science, then STSE education holds a prominent place in the school science curriculum. In our view, STSE education offers an optimistic way of re-imagining our world, a revitalization of our relationship with nature, and alternative solutions to problems in society and the environment. What follows is a summary of the key ideas related to the learning objectives provided at the beginning of the chapter.

STSE education

STSE education is an umbrella term that explores the interplay between science and society. STSE education positions science within larger social, cultural, and political contexts, equipping students with the skills to understand socio-scientific subject matter, to make informed and responsible decisions, and to take action. There is no single, widely accepted approach to STSE education. Rather, it draws from number of different strands.

The benefits of STSE education in science education

STSE education teaches science beyond the acquisition of facts or content. Studies have shown that students engaged in STSE education are motivated, empowered, and interested in what they are learning. STSE education nurtures intellectual independence, develops critical thinking skills, promotes collaboration, and prepares students to meet the challenges of the future. It also raises awareness of current issues, promotes citizenship for social good, advocates for social justice, contextualizes science, and links science to other subject areas.

Characteristics of STSE education

The characteristics that underpin STSE education include stewardship, decision making, values, action, and nature of science (NOS). These characteristics are not mutually exclusive and often complement one another and the goals of the curriculum.

STSE challenges and tensions

An emphasis on STSE education presents challenges for educators—both practical and ideological. Challenges include the coupling of science and values, teacher positions, the place of action, and issues related to teaching and pedagogy, such as lack of time, resources, and teacher confidence, and assessment concerns.

Educational research related to STSE education

There is no shortage of research in the area of STSE education. We have drawn upon a few researchers in the field, including Glen Aikenhead, Larry Bencze, Derek Hodson, Erminia Pedretti, and Wolff-Michael Roth. We encourage you to read the work of these researchers as well as the many others who have contributed to the field over the past few decades.

BRINGING IT ALL TOGETHER: FINAL QUESTIONS

1. What is the relationship between learning and understanding science content and STSE education?
2. How does STSE education contribute to scientific literacy?

MyEducationLab®

Visit MyEducationLab® to access an electronic version of the text, as well as a variety of topics that enhance the text material. The topics include the following to support your learning in the course:

- Assessments, including interactive case studies, activities, and video assignments
- Discussion board questions
- Videos, simulations, a lesson plan builder, and other useful course resources

Chapter 11
STSE Education: Planning and Pedagogy

Iain Smith/Getty Images

I found that the [STSE] part of the unit had a significant impact on the students. They were better able to express themselves in relation to their experience.... Expectations were covered in a lesson that was fun and interesting. This is the way that STSE was meant to be.

—Hamza, elementary school teacher

The sun picks up the water and turns it into mist and it moves up and gets colder and colder and it forms inside the cloud and when there is too much water it pushes out by little drops and it rains.

—Evan, Grade 1 student

LEARNING OBJECTIVES

- Review the characteristics and general principles of science, technology, society, and environment (STSE) education.

- Discuss two approaches to STSE education: issues-based and historical.

- Develop a repertoire of strategies for teaching and assessing with an STSE orientation.

- Engage in curriculum planning and assessment with an STSE focus.

- Discuss the complexities of introducing controversial issues when teaching science.

- Identify and describe education research related to STSE education.

INTRODUCTION

Science, technology, society, and environment (STSE) education can be highly motivating and engaging for students. An STSE focus can help students make personal connections and bring meaning to what they are learning. It is an opportunity to integrate community-informed pedagogy into your classroom. The extent to which you emphasize STSE education in your planning will depend on many factors, including your goals for your students, their needs, the context in which you are teaching, your comfort level with the material, and the curriculum.

Teaching with an STSE orientation generates a number of pedagogical questions and challenges. For example, how might you present various viewpoints fairly and equitably? How will you scaffold the student learning experience? Which viewpoints will you include? Which will you exclude? What strategies and resources are available? What role does controversy play in the classroom? What is the best way to plan a debate in the science classroom? How can you teach informed and responsible decision making? How will you assess students' work? In this chapter, we consider these questions and issues as we explore planning for STSE education.

REVISITING THE CHARACTERISTICS OF STSE

Recall from Chapter 10 the five characteristics that define STSE education: stewardship, coupling of science and values, decision making, the nature of science, and action. In Activity 11.1, we explore these characteristics alongside some of the other general principles of STSE education.

ACTIVITY 11.1

21st C ❷❸❹

Exploring STSE Education

In groups of four, create a concept map that illustrates the relationships among the characteristics and principles associated with STSE education. You might use chart paper or a tablet to create your map. Be prepared to share your concept map with the class. The figure on the next page, of a blank concept map template, provides a starting point. (See Appendix A for a more detailed description of how to create concept maps). You do not need to use the exact format provided below; adapt as you see fit. Please use the words in the following list in your map and provide links between the ideas:

- science
- action
- politicization
- stewardship
- social justice
- sustainability
- decision making
- technology
- society
- environment
- values
- nature of science

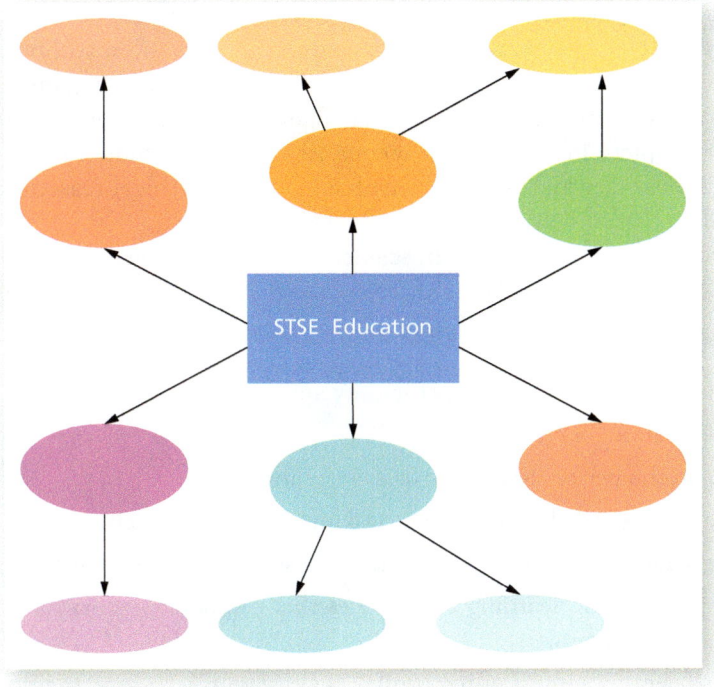

STSE Concept Map

STSE EMPHASES AND APPROACHES TO PLANNING

Depending on the content or unit, STSE curriculum and planning can take many forms. Sometimes the STSE aspect of your curriculum might be a single exercise or activity in the classroom infused at the appropriate time in a unit. For example, imagine you are teaching a life science unit on the basic needs of local plants and animals. You might choose to address some STSE outcomes or expectations (e.g., local biodiversity and habitat loss) at the end of the unit. At other times, STSE education becomes a more substantial integrated theme from which the rest of the unit develops. For example, an Earth and space science unit on the dynamics of tectonic plate movement and land-mass formation might begin with the reading of historical case studies highlighting the impact of earthquakes along the British Columbia coast. Your choice will be dependent upon a myriad of factors. Furthermore, STSE emphases provide for natural integration with other subjects, such as language arts, mathematics, social studies, and health and physical education. (See Rennie, Venville, and Wallace (2012), for case study examples of integrating science with other subjects.)

In this section, we offer two broad approaches for bringing STSE education to life in the classroom: an issues-based approach and the use of historical case studies. Each approach has its own rationale, thematic virtue, and pedagogical advantage. The approach you choose will depend on the curriculum, learners, and the learning goals you set for your students.

Issues-Based Approach

Many advocate for STSE education through the exploration of issues (for example, Pedretti, 2005; Roth & Désautels, 2002). Some educators refer to societal issues as socio-scientific issues (SSI; Zeidler, Sadler, Simmons, & Howe, 2005)—in other words, subject matter that cuts across science and society. We use the terms *issues* and *socio-scientific issues* interchangeably here. Socio-scientific subject matter embeds science in social, cultural, and political contexts, recognizing the inherent messiness of science and, perhaps most importantly, connecting science to students' lives. Socio-scientific issues describe societal dilemmas with conceptual, procedural, or technological links to science (Sadler, Barab, & Scott, 2007). Such issues involve forming opinions and making choices at a personal and societal level. They are frequently reported in the media, deal with incomplete information or incomplete scientific evidence, require an understanding of probability and risk, and involve values and ethical reasoning (Ratcliffe & Grace, 2003).

The advantages of using issues in science classrooms are well documented (Alsop & Pedretti, 2001; Hodson, 1998; Pedretti, 2005; Van Rooy, 2012; Venville & Dawson, 2012) and include the following:

- providing students with a sense of inquiry and investigation
- addressing nature of science
- assisting in the personalization of understanding
- fostering skills needed to make informed and responsible decisions
- building knowledge about the biological, physical, and technological world
- providing authentic learning experiences that promote personal, intellectual, emotional, and social growth
- raising student awareness of responsibilities toward themselves, their future children, others in the community, and the global environment
- providing opportunities to challenge beliefs, values, and fears
- engaging in action
- providing opportunities to pursue students' own questions of interest

According to Ramsey (1994, p. 241), an STSE issue, when "utilized as a context for instruction, offers the greatest potential for capturing the dynamic interplay of science, technology and society." Many issues extend across the strands of science as well as across discipinary boundaries. Examples that might be included in any science curriculum are:

- life science: food production and justice, animal research, intensive agriculture, loss of biodiversity, environmental degradation and habitat loss, endangered species, health and wellbeing, pesticide use
- physical science: energy production and conservation, nuclear power, light pollution, industrial use of chemicals, acid rain, water pollution
- earth and space science: management of resources, resource extraction, impact of mining, space exploration, climate change

In issues-based learning, societal concerns are potential organizers for science curriculum and instruction. These issues emanate from the interplay of science, technology, society, and environment, and are often controversial in nature; that is, they involve various individuals and stakeholders supporting conflicting courses of action. You can imagine students learning about an issue from multiple perspectives, conducting research, engaging in inquiry, and moving toward a reasoned and informed decision. Ultimately, and if appropriate, students may have the opportunity to engage in action (e.g., greening their school, using energy-saving strategies at home or in the community, writing letters). Figure 11.1 depicts a model for using issues as central organizers or as a culminating activity in a unit:

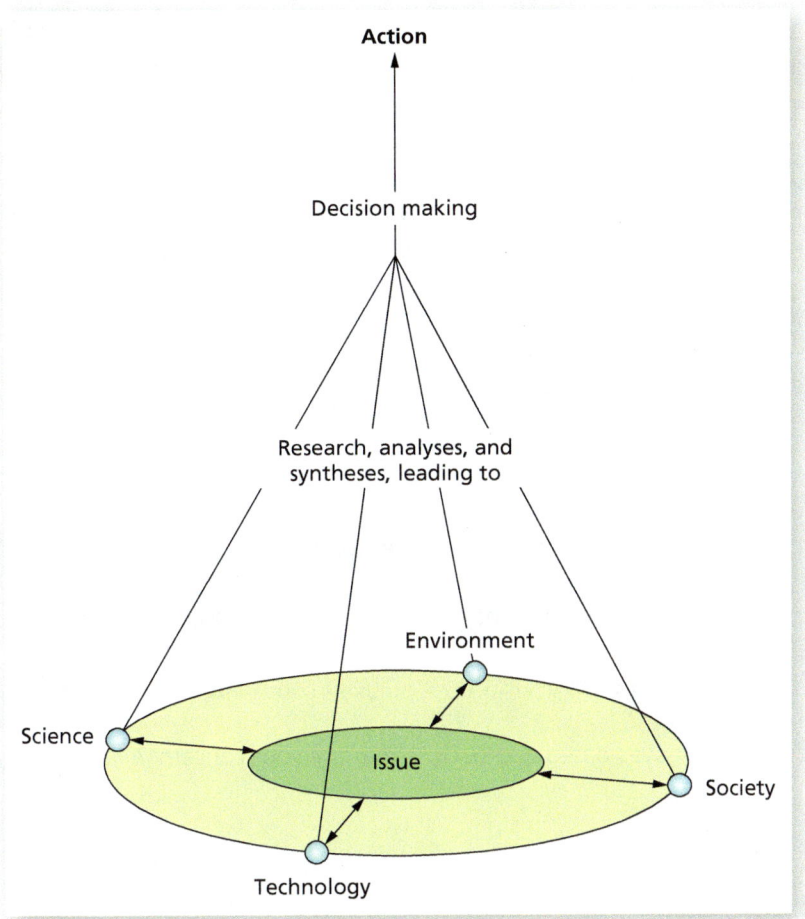

Figure 11.1 A model for issues-based planning

Source: Pedretti (1996), Pedretti & Little (2008).

The model provides a conceptual tool for planning STSE education. For example, for a study of weather or water systems, a teacher might decide to explore an issue such as the flooding of the Red River in Manitoba. Students could examine the many factors that can lead to flooding, as well as explore human interventions that have been used to help prevent damage from flooding. Students might also consider the sociological and economic implications of flooding and preventative technologies (e.g., measures to protect Winnipeg at the expense of small rural towns and villages), and engage in decision making and action for communities affected by flooding.

Notice that STSE issues—both local and global—can become central to the curriculum and encourage explorations that are socially relevant, personally compelling, and community informed. It is important to consider issues and events that are of relevance and interest to students to ensure that learning takes account of their knowledge, values, attitudes, aspirations, and personal experiences, thus presenting science and technology as person-oriented (Hodson, 1998). In this spirit, we suggest you provide students with opportunities to brainstorm issues they would like to study in depth. You will likely be surprised at what they come up with! Moreover, encouraging students to choose issues nurtures a sense of empowerment and increases motivation.

ACTIVITY 11.2

Read and Reflect: Issues-Based Case Studies

For this activity read the following case studies:

Cooper, S., Motley, T., & Thomas, J. (2011). No duck left behind: Fourth grade students' data analysis supports scientists' theory of declining duck populations. *Science & Children, 48*(5), 45–49.

Nelson, C., & Ponder, J. (2010). Turtle girls: A visit to a sea turtle hospital inspires civic involvement. *Science & Children, 47*(6), 27–31.

These two case studies illustrate issues-based approaches to STSE education in elementary classes. Briefly describe what was done in each class, using Figure 11.1 where appropriate. As you read through the cases, answer the questions below. Be prepared to share your thoughts with the class.

DISCUSSION QUESTIONS

1. What motivated the teachers in these cases to adopt an STSE perspective? What personal characteristics and social factors would you suggest allowed them to feel comfortable in choosing their respective routes?
2. Describe three strategies the teachers used to facilitate different aspects of an issues-based approach. Why were they effective?
3. What are some of the challenges for teachers and students as they engage in issues-based STSE education?
4. How comfortable do *you* feel in adopting an issues-based approach? What are your concerns?

Historical Approach

Exploring the history of science (for example, the development of vaccines, Darwin's voyage on the *Beagle*, Galileo's trial) is widely recognized as an important dimension of teaching and learning science (Pedretti & Nazir, 2011; Ziman, 1994). Understanding the historical and socio-cultural contexts of scientific ideas and the work of scientists helps us appreciate more fully the richness of the scientific process.

The history of science is one of the most natural mediums for humanizing the discipline—challenging traditional images of science as cold, linear, and separate from social relations. According to Ziman (1994, p. 26),

> [The history of science] is an indispensable dimension for any understanding of the nature of science itself. STS[E] education must encompass this dimension. It must show that science and technology grow and change in association with the societies in which they are embedded. It must show the increasingly influential role of science and technology in society, and the increasing demands of society on science and technology. This historical approach, by showing how things got the way they are, is one of the most compelling ways of explaining this present state and also laying out the ground for a discussion of how it might change.

The potential benefits to students of using an historical approach include the following (Alsop & Pedretti, 2001):

- developing a better understanding of the process of science (i.e., NOS)
- understanding that science is conducted by people who hold particular views, attitudes, passions, and biases
- exploring the role and impact of context, politics, and belief systems on the institution and practice of science
- understanding the underlying scientific concepts, theories, and principles

• recognizing the contributions of women and men from diverse groups, thereby moving beyond the western male bias that is present in much of the science taught in schools

We describe three ways of utilizing history or narratives in teaching science. In the first instance, students might explore the work of famous scientists such as Frederick Banting and Charles Best, Sandford Fleming, Elijah McCoy, Albert Einstein, Vandana Shiva, or Jane Goodall, to name a few. Their stories hold the potential to capture the imagination and interest of students and help bring the diverse activities of science to life. Historical case studies touch upon such underlying themes as ethics, environmental protection, gender and equity, politics, and the human spirit. Furthermore, this approach provides opportunities for students to explore the scientific contributions of Indigenous peoples and civilizations (e.g., Egyptians, Persians, Indians, Chinese) from ancient to contemporary times.

The second approach focuses on a scientific concept and explores its development over time. For example, students might study the evolution of geocentric models of the solar system to heliocentric models, or the history of nuclear power as a way of understanding how an idea progresses within a social, cultural, and political milieu.

Finally, historical case studies may be incorporated into science curriculum and instruction to examine socio-scientific topics that emerge from the interplay of science, technology, society, and environment, including the resolution of the issues and their long-term outcomes. Examples include the collapse of the Newfoundland cod fisheries, the zebra mussel controversy of the Great Lakes, and the *Exxon Valdez* oil spill in Prince William Sound.

By now you will have developed a good understanding of STSE education. You may have read a few case studies of teachers and students engaged in STSE work and various related activities. Now it is your turn to begin some initial planning of STSE curriculum, making use of an issues-based or an historical approach.

PEDAGOGICAL STRATEGIES FOR STSE EDUCATION

In the section that follows, we focus on helping you develop pedagogical content knowledge (PCK) within the context of STSE teaching. We encourage you to make use of an issues-based or historical approach and to incorporate the characteristics of STSE mentioned on page 224. We begin by exploring some useful strategies for transforming STSE curriculum outcomes and expectations into engaging and thoughtful practice.

STSE education requires developing a range of teaching strategies, and knowing when and how to use them effectively. Some strategies include jigsaw, concept maps, and role play. Additionally, teachers can involve the community, make use of non-school settings, and draw on media and technology resources to enrich their planning and teaching of STSE education. The following strategies are particularly well suited to exploring socio-scientific issues. (These and other strategies are outlined in more detail in Appendix A.)

• role play and drama
• six thinking hats
• values continuum
• consequence mapping
• debate
• town hall

Role Play and Drama

Role play and drama can encourage students to use their artistic talents to engage with issues in a creative and engaging way. When using role play and drama, students typically take on particular roles and actions of different interest groups with the objective of understanding the positions of various stakeholders and the mechanics of decision making. For example, students might explore the construction of a major road through a greenspace using roles such as scientist, builder, mayor, local shop owner, environmentalist, hiker, or bird watcher.

Six Thinking Hats

The six thinking hats strategy (adapted from de Bono, 1985) is often used to help students understand the decision-making process, particularly around tricky ethical questions. Each student adopts a certain "thinking approach," which is symbolized by a coloured hat (real or imaginary). Students are often organized into groups, and each student picks a coloured hat out and then assumes that role. The roles focus on information and questions, benefits, judgment and consequences, creative possibilities, affective considerations, and next steps.

Values Continuum

In this strategy, students are asked to respond to a thought-provoking statement by physically standing on a line that represents a continuum of positions. At one end of the line is the position *really agree*; at the other end is *really disagree*. Students position themselves according to the degree to which they agree or disagree with the statement. This method allows the teacher to quickly determine where students stand on an issue, and allows students to give their opinion nonverbally. Sometimes this is preferable—particularly if the issue is sensitive. The results of the activity can then be used to initiate discussion.

Consequence Mapping

In consequence mapping, students have the opportunity to illustrate with a diagram or web the many kinds of effects related to a real or imagined event, issue, trend, or developing technology. It encourages students to think about the future and involves creating a flow diagram stemming from a central "what if" question. "What if" questions might include: What if we ran out of oil? What if a wind turbine farm were planned in your community? What if we had more robots in society? Scientific, social, ethical, legal, economic, environmental, and personal consequences are considered.

Debate

Students have the opportunity to debate an issue, which engages learners in a combination of activities such as research, active listening, public speaking, decision making, and critical thinking. Debate enables students to interact with controversial topics arising from the science curriculum. Formal debate is bound by rules that vary by location and participants. The process can be adjudicated and a winner declared based on the quality of their arguments. Depending on the level of your students, you will need to adapt the format accordingly by modifying and omitting steps as you see fit. Do not shy away from having K–3 students participate in modified debates—they often have very strong opinions and are eager to voice them!

Town Hall

The town hall meeting strategy can be an authentic introduction to democracy; it can be used to conduct research and bring personal meaning to topics in the science curriculum. Generally speaking, a town hall meeting gives members of a community the opportunity to come together to discuss community concerns. At the meeting's end, people might be asked to make a decision, or a summary of the main points of discussion could be shared. As with debating, town hall meetings are part of the democratic process in modern societies.

ACTIVITY 11.3

Read and Reflect: Using Skateboarding to Debate Speeding

Read and critique the student activity below titled Using Skateboarding to Debate Speeding (adapted from Dolan and Zeidler, 2009). Working in pairs, reflect on how this activity supports the emphases and approaches of STSE education, and how strategies such as role play and debate can be used with elementary school students. Before beginning this activity, you may want to review your understanding of speed (a scalar quantity) and velocity (a vector quantity), mass, friction, and momentum.

Using Skateboarding to Debate Speeding

In this activity, students explore the science involved in skateboarding and then apply their understanding in a debate about speed limits. Students learn about the relationships between forces, momentum, mass, and velocity. Geared toward older elementary school students, it can be included in physical science units on forces and motion and also brings mathematics and language arts into the science curriculum. Parts A and B each take one class to complete, and Part C can take two or three classes.

Part A—Skateboarding Data Collection

1. Prior to the activity, gather equipment (long skateboard, adjustable helmet, knee pads, elbow pads, stopwatch, tape measure, masking tape) and ask all students to wear running shoes or sneakers. In a long hallway or the gymnasium, mark a starting line with masking tape, and then mark a finish line 10 metres away. Do not do this activity on a paved surface, as you want to minimize friction.
2. Discuss friction, speed, velocity, momentum, and mass with your students. This might be a review or presentation of new material.
3. Distribute data sheets (Appendix 11.A) and have students work in partners. One partner sits on the skateboard with his or her feet on the front of the board, holding onto the sides. The other partner pushes at a controlled velocity from the start to finish lines. Remind students about safety and ask that they do not push too quickly. Have a student volunteer act as a timer. Partners record their time on their data sheet and then switch. Each student will have one trial.
4. To maintain privacy, after each partner has finished the trial, measure the student's mass (in kg) individually, and record on the data sheet.
5. Collect students' data sheets.

Part B—Calculations

1. Review friction, velocity, momentum, and mass as needed.
2. Model calculations of velocity and momentum for trial 1 (the recorded time). For trial 2, add two seconds to the recorded time. For trial 3, subtract two seconds from the recorded time. Trial 2 will be the "slow" trial and trial 3 will be the "fast" trial.
3. Distribute calculators and data sheets.
4. Have students work with their partners to complete the calculations on their data sheets to determine their velocity and momentum for the three trials. Remind students to add two seconds to their times for trial 2, and to subtract two seconds for trial 3.
5. Have students use think-pair-share to think about and discuss friction, velocity, momentum, and mass in light of their calculations. Be sure that students understand that two things—mass and velocity—affect momentum.
6. Ask students to draw some conclusions from their data about the relationship between mass, velocity, and momentum.

continued on next page

Part C—Planning and Debating

INTRODUCTION

Share the following paragraph on a whiteboard:

Recently, there has been an increase in injuries to children involved in vehicle accidents. Concerned parents have demanded that the local government come up with a solution to the problem. After considerable debate, a law has been proposed to reduce speed limits by half to prevent more accidents involving children. A meeting has been called to debate the proposed law.

1. Individually, have students write how they feel about the proposed law. Do they agree or disagree with the proposed changes? Ask them to provide support for their decision.
2. With their partners, students read a pros and cons article on vehicular speed and its effects. You can ask students to locate articles on the internet, or you can provide them with direct links. Have students discuss what might be the societal implications of lower speed limits.
3. Explain to students that they will be participating in a town hall debate involving four role-play groups: local business leaders, parents, police officers, and taxi drivers. "Parents" and "police officers" will support the law; "local business leaders" and "taxi drivers" will oppose it. Divide students into these four groups, and have them form a persuasive argument on the proposed law with support from their reading and their exploration of friction, mass, velocity, and momentum.
4. Allow students additional time to gather more information that supports their argument.
5. Establish some general rules for the town hall debate. Have students make suggestions for rules and then negotiate as a class which ones should be adhered to. Be sure to include respect of all contributions and opinions in the rules. Describe the teacher role of selecting speakers and recording notes from the debate. You might also want to be the final arbitrator of the town hall debate.
6. Each group selects one member to present an opening argument. When all groups have presented, open the floor to anyone wishing to speak, either in support of their position, in refute of another group's argument, or to question another group's information. Ensure the students understand the debate rules as needed.
7. Ask students to vote on whether or not to pass the proposal into law. Students can use a secret ballot or a show of hands. Tally the votes and declare the outcome.
8. When the debate has finished, discuss as a class how the debate went. What went well, and what could have been done differently?
9. *Assessment*: Assess students' completed data sheets and their participation in the debate process. A rubric or anecdotal comments can be used.

DISCUSSION QUESTIONS

1. How does this activity reflect the STSE education emphases and approaches discussed earlier in the chapter?
2. You will note that this activity integrates STSE education and scientific knowledge. Comment on the effectiveness of teaching knowledge (in this case, velocity and momentum) through this role-play and debate activity.
3. Redesign part C of the activity using six thinking hats and values continuum strategies.
4. Formulate four questions to ask students as they conduct this activity (e.g., how does the velocity change as the time taken increases?).

ACTIVITY 11.4

21st C ❸ ❹ ❺ ❼

Connecting Practice and Theory: Your Turn

Form groups of four. Each group chooses from a hat two of the strategies discussed above—role play and drama, six thinking hats, values continuum, consequence mapping, debate, and town hall meeting—and develops an activity for each. Embed the activity in one of the topics in the science curriculum. Identify the grade, unit, and topic. Develop the activity in ready-to-use form as part of a lesson plan or overview of a series of activities. Be sure to include an assessment tool that could be used for each strategy. Each group will present their work and share in a common format (e.g., upload to class Moodle site or wiki).

DISCUSSION QUESTIONS

1. Why would you use each activity with your students?
2. What are some of the strengths of the two strategies you chose?
3. What were some of the challenges in developing the activities?
4. Describe what could be assessed (e.g., content, communication skills, work habits such as collaboration or initiative, making connections to STSE).

ACTION-BASED COMMUNITY PROJECT

We have argued for incorporating socio-scientific issues into the curriculum and for providing students with opportunities to engage in action. Alsop and Bencze (2012) describe *activist pedagogy* that is predicated upon students gathering information and research through inquiry in order to take informed and appropriate action. STSE education and inquiry can be integrated through a community-based project where students identify an issue, gather and analyze data, and propose and take action. Younger children may need guidance in identifying an issue that is appropriate for investigation. It is important to be sensitive to the dynamics and relationships of the community in action-based projects. A framework for engaging in action-based projects is outlined below.

1. Identify an issue that is community based and authentic to students. Community members may help define the issue and set the context—reflect on community-informed pedagogy (James, 2012a; see Chapter 4).
2. Gather information about the issue in a number of ways, such as through inquiry (and designing experiments), by using existing databases, using technology to pool student-gathered data from different sites, or conducting surveys with community members.
3. Analyze and interpret data, and identify themes and patterns.
4. Propose action. Students can suggest possible courses of action to address the issue.
5. Take action. Students choose, for example, to write a letter to the local newspaper, set up a blog, create a podcast, plant a school garden, or create a pamphlet for distribution.

Table 11.1 uses the framework to demonstrate how an action-based community project (in this case, the problem of cars idling in front of the school) can be developed.

Table 11.1   Idling Cars: An Action-Based Inquiry Project

Process	Example
Identify the issue.	Cars idling in front of the school
Gather information.	Students gather information about why cars are idling (for example, parents drive students to school because there is no public transit and students live too far to walk, or because their children sleep in and are driven to school to avoid being late).
	Students investigate the effects of car exhaust on the environment.
	Students research media sources to investigate how the issue has been reported locally or nationally.
Analyze and interpret data.	Students look for common themes and patterns to explain the large number of cars idling in front of school and the subsequent effects.
Propose action.	Students encourage car-pooling, walking groups, or public transit use, and/or create a designated drop-off space that is away from pedestrian traffic.
Take action.	Students create a flyer to distribute to the community about the benefits of walking and why idling in front of schools is a problem. Organize walking groups so that children can walk to school with an older student.

ACTIVITY 11.5

21st C ❶ ❹ ❺ ❻

Planning an Action-Based Community Project

Think about where your practicum school is located and brainstorm potential issues within that community (e.g., littering, traffic congestion). If possible, discuss this with your host teacher to ensure that you are being aware of, and responsive to, the community's needs, interests, and expectations. You might use a mind map to help organize your ideas, with the school community at the centre of the map and issues radiating out. Choose one issue and a grade grouping (K–3 or 4–7) and, using the framework above, draft a plan for a student action-based community project. Include each of the five components from Table 11.1. Share your project plans with your peers.

DISCUSSION QUESTIONS

1. Which components of the framework were easy to plan? Which were challenging? Why?
2. What are the benefits for students of this type of action-based community project?
3. If you planned for K–3, how might your planning be adapted for Grades 4–7? Alternately, if you planned for Grades 4–7, how would your plans be adapted for K–3?
4. If you were to implement your plan at your practicum school, what measures would you take to ensure that community relationships are respected and all voices are heard?
5. Identify ways to assess students' work at each stage of the framework.

ASSESSMENT AND STSE EDUCATION

Teachers have identified assessment as one of the challenges related to STSE education. Many feel ill-equipped to assess students' work related to, for example, debates, position papers, action-oriented activities, and decision-making exercises. Clarity is key with respect to what is being assessed and for what purpose. Sometimes teachers assess content; sometimes product, and sometimes process. Some assessments contribute to formal student evaluation, and some are for feedback purposes only. Below are examples of *what* can be assessed (strategies) and *how* they can be assessed (tools). We provide examples of assessment strategies that can be particularly useful and appropriate in STSE education. These lists are not exhaustive but provide a good starting point. Throughout the remainder of the chapter, you will have an opportunity to practise creating and applying some of these tools.

Examples of what to assess include the following:

- research projects
- performance pieces (drama, poetry, etc.)
- portfolios
- essays
- debates
- town hall meetings
- concept maps
- art projects
- community maps

Teachers (for formative and summative assessment) and students (for self-and peer assessment) might use the following assessment tools:

- anecdotal record (e.g., Two Stars and a Wish)
- rubric
- checklist
- tracking sheet
- marking scheme
- rating scale

Scenario 1:

Grade 5 students Breanna and Kaitlyn created and performed a commercial for the class as part of a science assignment to convince local government to stop the building of a road through a large, undisturbed greenspace near to the school. Students were asked to include research to back up their position, and their commercial had to be two minutes long and make use of supporting materials and props. The teacher used a rubric, as shown in Figure 11.2, (which students were given in advance) to assess their performance.

	Level 1	Level 2	Level 3	Level 4	Notes
Organization and flow	Information and viewpoints were presented with little or no organization and flow	Information and viewpoints were presented with some organization and flow	Information and viewpoints were presented with good organization and flow	Information and viewpoints were presented with professionalism, excellent organization, and flow	
Research	Information and arguments were presented with little or no support from research or evidence	Information and arguments were supported with some research or evidence	Information and arguments were supported by good research and evidence	Information and arguments were supported by excellent research and abundant evidence	
Supporting materials	Visual aid(s) were not used or had little or no connection to the presentation	Visual aid(s) were somewhat appropriate and used to support the presentation	Visual aid(s) were good and well used to support and enhance the presentation	Visual aid(s) were excellent and used to greatly support and enhance the presentation	
Presenters:					
Comments/Notes:					

Figure 11.2 Rubric for presentation

Scenario 2:

Working in groups of four, Grade 8 students Michelle, Nenad, Amy, and Clint worked to research the issue of whether plastic shopping bags should be used in their community and created a poster displaying their findings. Among other assessments, the teacher wanted students to reflect upon how well they worked together. She decided to use peer- and self-evaluation tools as shown in Figure 11.3.

STUDENT SELF ASSESSMENT

Name: _____
Date: _____

Rating: 0 = disagree   1 = mostly agree   2 = strongly agree

CRITERIA	Rating
I made a significant contribution to my group (e.g., I came up with interesting ideas, I encouraged and helped others).	
I made a significant contribution to our research (e.g., I found books and websites, I made notes).	
I made a significant contribution to our final product (e.g., I created charts and drew diagrams, I wrote sentences and paragraphs about the topic).	
I worked cooperatively with all of the group members and we all worked well as a group.	
I am proud of the way I contributed to this group project.	
Comments:	Total: /10 marks

STUDENT PEER ASSESSMENT

Name of the student I am evaluating: _____
Date: _____

Rating: 0 = disagree   1 = mostly agree   2 = strongly agree

CRITERIA	Rating
Made a significant contribution to our group (e.g., Came up with interesting ideas, encouraged and helped others).	
Made a significant contribution to our research.	
Made a significant contribution to our final product.	
Worked cooperatively with me and other group members.	
I would like to work with this person again.	
Comments:	Total: /10 marks
My name: _____	

Figure 11.3 Student peer and self-assessment samples

Scenario 3:

Grade 3 students Dante and Roman made a presentation to the class regarding the planting of a school garden. They brought in seeds and explained what they wanted to grow and why. The teacher used Two Stars and a Wish, an assessment tool that can be used by teachers and in peer and self-assessment (Figure 11.4). The student or teacher anecdotally describes two elements of the activity, assignment, or project that they liked or were particularly strong and identifies one thing they would have liked to experience. Two Stars and a Wish is a good substitute for simply listing strengths and weaknesses, as it removes

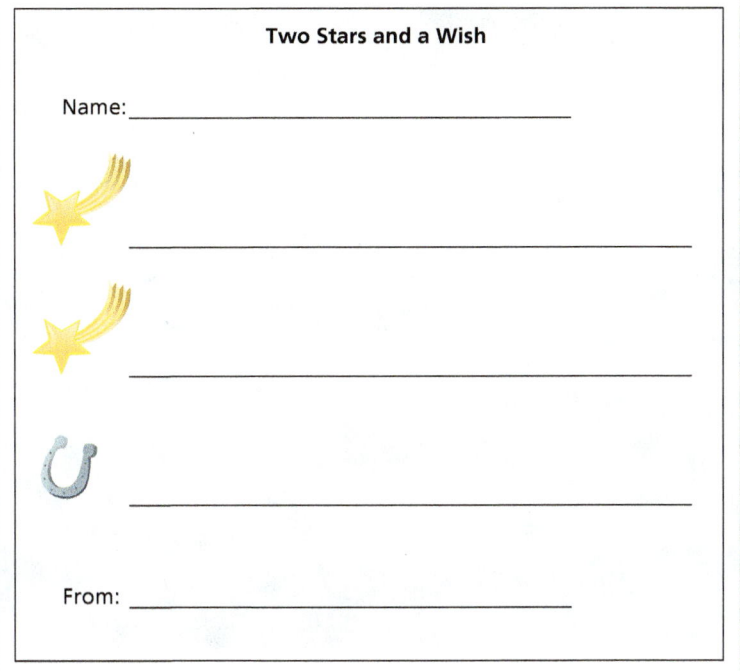

Figure 11.4 Two stars and a wish

the binary of positive and negative and instead highlights what was enjoyed or important and notes a suggestion for improvement.

PLANNING WITH AN STSE FOCUS

Planning for STSE education can be rewarding and challenging. Our experiences over the years have confirmed that working with colleagues, sharing resources, and engaging in dialogue can lead to the creation of co-constructed curriculum that is exciting and innovative. Working together in a sustained way, and over time, is a particularly powerful model for professional learning and development. Professional learning communities (PLCs) are one such way to do this. (More will be said about PLCs in Chapter 13.)

In 2006, we were fortunate to be able to form STSE-focused PLCs with elementary school teachers and outdoor educators from a large urban school district. These teachers volunteered to be part of the PLC because they wanted to learn more about STSE education and work with other teachers to develop curriculum. Twenty-four teachers participated in this five-month project, coming together regularly to investigate STSE theory and practice and to discuss, plan, and implement a unit of study (Pedretti & Bellomo, in press). At the end of the five months, teachers were interviewed and asked to submit written feedback about their experiences. Two examples of their comments include: "Based on the unit we did, I feel more confident in using the STSE approach and using Big Ideas to produce more thought-provoking questions" (Roger, post-study interview), and "Social justice is a possible way to approach STSE education" (Amanda, feedback form).

Working in small groups, often with colleagues from other schools, teachers developed and field-tested STSE units of study. Examples included building school gardens, doing revitalization projects, cleaning up a local ravine, and growing food. Other action projects reflected a design orientation and included building a solar oven and designing insulated clothing. Figure 11.5 depicts two examples that capture work generated by students during the curriculum implementation phase: One reflects a revitalization project and the other an energy consumption project.

Watch

Water Wheels Part 5

Watch

Investigating Goldfish
(Part 3)

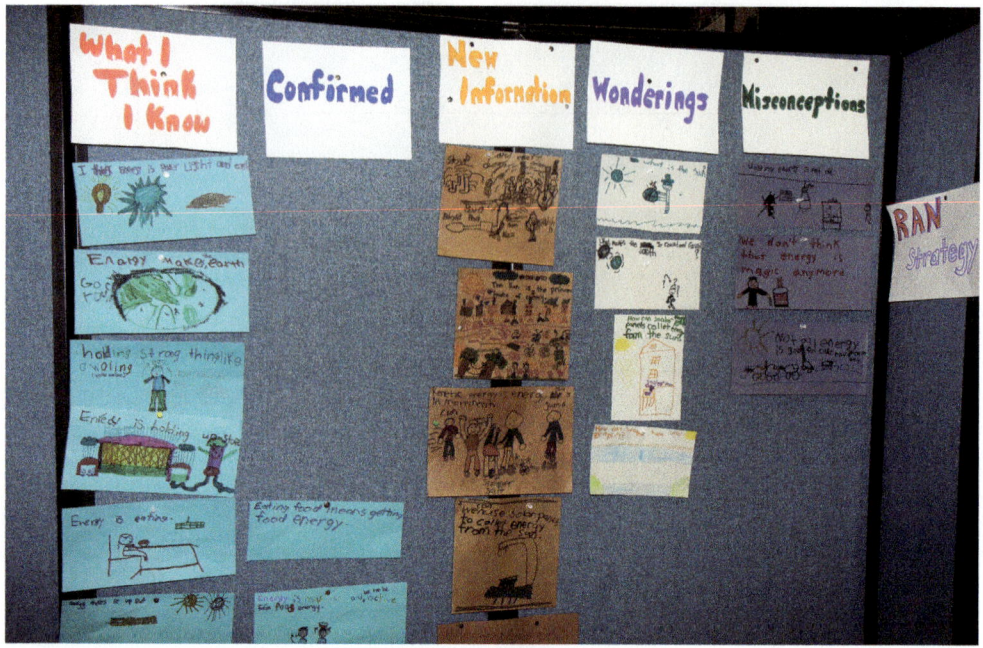

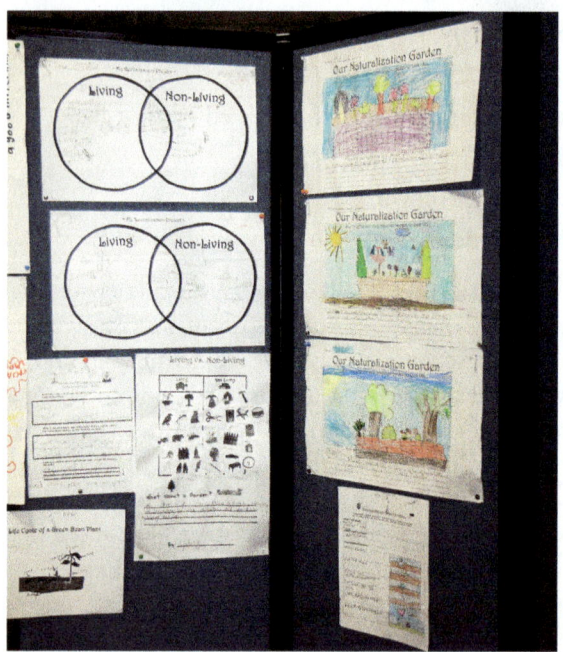

Figure 11.5 STSE and student work

ACTIVITY 11.6

21st C ❸ ❹ ❺

Connecting Practice and Theory: Planning for STSE Education

Imagine you are about to plan lessons for one of the units listed below. In groups of four, choose one of the units and read all of the ministry outcomes or expectations for that unit, paying particular attention to those related to STSE education. Brainstorm how the unit might be approached with an STSE focus, and create three lessons to support your students' learning. Use the table to guide your planning. Your lessons should include the following:

- some integration with at least one other subject area
- evidence of students' decision making and choices
- a taking-action component
- assessment (one assessment strategy and the corresponding assessment tool)
- one book of children's literature connected to the topic (See Appendix E for an annotated bibliography of science-related children's literature.)

Units to consider:

- Life Science: Plant Growth and Change (K–3) or Ecosystems (4–6)
- Physical Science: Properties of Objects and Materials (K–3) or Sound and Light (4–6)
- Earth and Space Science: Air, Water, and Soil (K–3) or Exploration of Extreme Environments (4–6)

Planning with an STSE Focus

General Information

Names of group members:

Grade and unit:

What is the focus of the lessons (e.g., a project, an historical or contemporary issue, a debate, a field trip)? Provide a brief description of each lesson.

Write a rationale for adopting a particular approach for this topic.

State the outcomes or expectations addressed (include STSE, knowledge, inquiry, and attitudes as applicable).

DISCUSSION QUESTIONS

1. How did your group decide on the approach and focus of the lessons?
2. What are the advantages of the approach you chose?
3. Discuss some of the challenges you foresee in planning for this unit. How might you overcome them?
4. How will your lessons engage students? How does your curriculum planning reflect one or more of the validations? (See Chapter 7 for a review of the validations.)

NAVIGATING CONTROVERSY IN THE SCIENCE CLASSROOM

By now it is likely clear that many of the issues in science education are controversial. Often, socio-scientific issues cut across other disciplines and challenge our beliefs, values, and fears. What is a controversial issue? According to Stenhouse (1970, p. 8), a controversial issue involves "a problem about which different individual and groups urge conflicting courses of action." Controversial issues can spark intense and passionate responses from people and involve problems in which different individuals and groups support conflicting courses of action. Consider, for example, genetic engineering, wind farms, fad diets and related health concerns, or space research.

Such issues are typically contentious, open-ended, and subject to multiple perspectives. Individuals may interpret the same information differently, and reasoning based on science alone may not be enough to resolve the conflict. In other words, different views may be based on value judgments rather than on empirical evidence (Van Rooy, 2012).

When addressing controversial issues in a science class, teachers must be judicious in their planning, thinking, and organizing. (Be sure to contact the school board in your area and ask for any documents or policies concerning teaching controversial issues in the classroom.) There are several reasons for using controversial issues in science lessons. They can be stimulating, motivating, and relevant to students; they often address topics of interest to students; and they often involve *real life* science. In other words, it is not just science in the abstract. Another important reason relates to citizen science. Today's students will be tomorrow's decision makers, and they need opportunities to think critically about complex socio-scientific subject matter. The growing expectation in society that schools should teach values and ethics makes the coupling of science and values important. Finally, the classroom provides a safe environment where students can engage with multiple perspectives and practise making decisions.

Planning for Controversy in the Curriculum

Engaging in STSE education can be challenging for teachers and students alike. Adding a controversial component can create even more complexity, both practically (e.g., resources, time, crowded curriculum, assessment issues) and ideologically (e.g., coupling of science and values, the role of action and politicization in science). In this section, we provide some curriculum planning recommendations. We begin with general guiding principles followed by teacher and student considerations (adapted from Dawson, 2001).

General Guiding Principles
In general it is important that:

- clear objectives or outcomes are set (what can students do?)
- science content underlying the issue is introduced
- lessons are student centred (students are active rather than passive)
- sharing of ideas is encouraged (using different discussion strategies)
- a decision-making process, if appropriate, is explicitly taught
- the examination of an issue is taught in the context of learning, not as a "rainy day" activity
- controversial issues should not be an add-on
- one topic in depth is better than one issue a lesson
- assessment tools are determined in conjunction with your unit and lesson planning

Role of the Teacher
As the teacher, you need to:

- take on multiple roles (information provider, facilitator of discussion)
- decide how you will position yourself
- create a safe learning environment where students feel comfortable talking
- establish ground rules for guiding discussions
- avoid indoctrinating or imposing your view

- model appropriate behaviour
- assume a facilitative role, rather than the "sage on the stage"
- have a plan for dealing with extreme or opposing student views

Student Considerations

Teachers need to consider carefully who their students are as well as their needs and contexts. Keep the following in mind:

- Students will show considerable variation in ethical maturity and moral development.
- Students bring strongly held values and viewpoints to the classroom.
- Students may feel threatened if asked to discuss personal views.
- Young learners can focus predominantly on short-term consequences and not necessarily the long-term implications of their choices.
- Students may make naive and idealistic decisions, with an overemphasis on the rights of individuals, often at the expense of justice, avoiding harm, and promoting good.
- Young learners tend to have entrenched expectations or views of their role and the teacher's role—which may need to be expanded upon explicitly.

SCIENCE BEYOND THE CLASSROOM

The STSE aspects of the curriculum are rife with opportunities for your students to experience science beyond the classroom. Hodson (2003, p. 664) states that "it is well documented that informal learning experiences can sometimes be more effective than formal schooling in bringing about awareness of issues, attitudinal shifts and willingness to engage in sociopolitical action." There are many ways to do this, including the following:

- Bring your students to the experts (e.g., visit a science research laboratory, industrial labs, community experts).
- Organize field trips and excursions (e.g., to conservation areas, zoos, museums, and science centres).
- Become involved in local projects (e.g., cleaning up ravines, reclaiming abandoned school grounds).
- Make use of community organizations to support the curriculum (e.g., food banks, conservation authorities, Habitat for Humanity).

With respect to visiting science centres, be sure to look for exhibitions that are issues based. Traditionally, science centres create exhibitions that are phenomenon based—that is, visitors learn scientific concepts (such as about light, dinosaurs, animal behaviour, chemical processes) through hands-on activities and galleries. More recently, science centres are also turning their attention to issues-based exhibitions, many of which are controversial. (See, for example, Jagger, Dubek, & Pedretti, 2012; Pedretti, 2004, 2012.) Examples include exhibitions that explore genetic engineering, oil spills, and energy resources. These contemporary and controversial explorations locate science and technology within the social and political contexts in which they operate. Should you consider visiting, for example, a zoo or game farm, keep in mind that the site and its practices can be controversial, and discussion of a potential visit could be a science activity itself.

EXPLORING ELEMENTARY SCIENCE IN CREATIVE WAYS: THE WATER CYCLE

In order to teach any topic confidently and effectively, it is helpful to have a deep and broad knowledge base. In this section we present some ideas to help develop your subject matter content knowledge (CK) and pedagogical content knowledge (PCK) for the water cycle. The topic is introduced below with a visual that might appear in a print or media resource. We encourage you to search for other resources to aid you as well. As you learn or re-learn the content, keep in mind other issues such as terminology, abstract processes, integration with mathematics and language arts, and activities that support student learning. Additionally, consider the meta-cognitive aspect of the activity, such as understanding how you learn, what you know, and what you need to know.

ACTIVITY 11.7   21st C

The Water Cycle

The water cycle is an important element of the global ecosystem that all children experience in their daily lives as they see, for example, rain or snow falling, clouds moving across the sky, or puddles of rainwater disappearing on a hot day. Some aspects of the water cycle are more difficult for students to perceive (such as transpiration of water from trees), but they do experience the ensuing humidity. A good understanding of the water cycle will allow you to contextualize societal problems related to consumption, recycling, and water management.

Watch

Interviewing Sam about Condensation

The stages of the water cycle are typically covered in the Grade 2 science curriculum. In Ontario, Grade 2 students investigate the stages of the water cycle, examine water in the natural environment (e.g., observe and measure precipitation), and use appropriate vocabulary (e.g., solid, liquid, vapour, evaporation, condensation, precipitation). Similarly, the Saskatchewan Grade 2 science curriculum includes outcomes in which students are expected to investigate the physical changes in water during each change of state (i.e., freezing, melting, evaporation, condensation, sublimation, and deposition) and also to investigate ways of increasing or decreasing the rate at which water changes state. The water cycle is revisited in later grades in most provinces and territories in units on

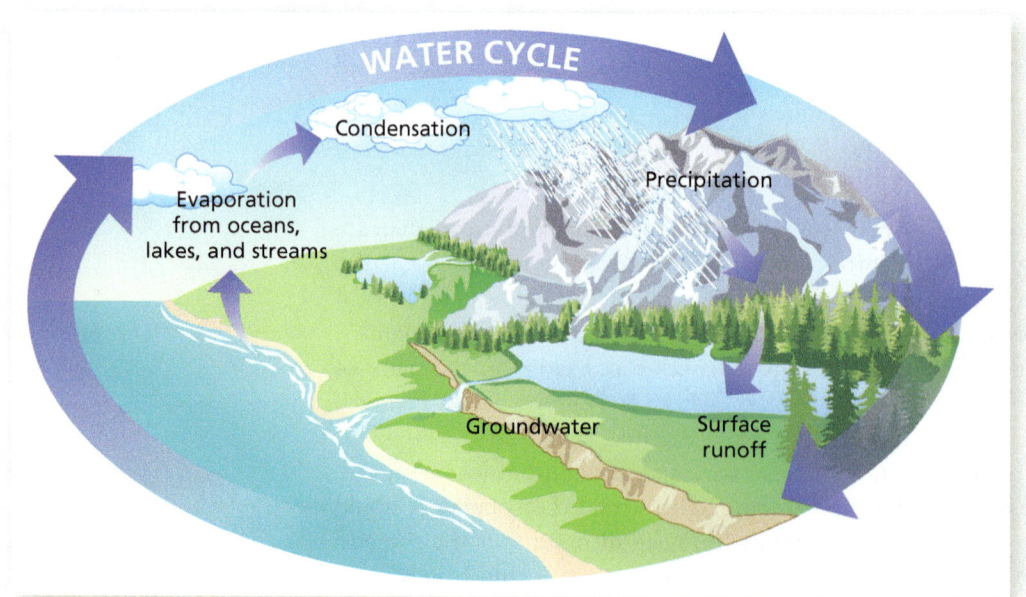

The Water Cycle

weather, resources, and ecosystems. Depending on your region, the depth at which you will cover the water cycle will vary, but by having strong foundational content knowledge, you will be able to confidently allow your students opportunities for extension and enrichment.

Reviewing the Content

1. Review or learn the content associated with the water cycle. For example, what is condensation? How is it related to precipitation? Use the visual to guide your exploration.
2. Make a list of definitions for important or unfamiliar vocabulary and processes associated with this topic.
3. When you feel comfortable with the content, use the visual to explain the water cycle to a peer.

Literacy and Numeracy Connections

1. Students can extend and apply their knowledge of the water cycle by sharing *One Well: The Story of Water on Earth* by Rochelle Strauss (2007). This book integrates social justice, environmental education, and STSE into teaching science. Discuss the importance of water, and brainstorm ways to conserve it.
2. Set up clean, recycled plastic drums to collect rainwater over a one-month period. Students can paint and install these rain barrels around the schoolyard or in a school garden. Monitor the amount (the depth in mm) of rain captured on a daily basis, and record results on a graph. Discuss the advantages of collecting rainwater and its possible uses.

Activities for Elementary School Students

1. Water cycle demonstration (adapted from Bosak, 1991): For safety reasons, this demonstration should be done by an adult. Pour cold water and ice cubes into a saucepan and set aside. Heat water in a kettle. When the water comes to a boil, hold the saucepan just above the steam. Oven mitts should be worn for protection. Place a baking tray below the saucepan. Observe what occurs and relate each component of the model to the water cycle.
2. Create a word wall of vocabulary related to the water cycle. Use the vocabulary to build concept maps connecting terms to show the interconnectedness of states and processes occurring in the water cycle. Be sure to identify if heat is lost or gained for any of the changes of state.
3. Research places in Canada that have experienced a boil water advisory within the past year. Describe where the advisory occurred, possible reasons for the advisory, and if and how the problem was resolved with municipal, provincial, territorial, or federal involvement.

CONCLUDING THOUGHTS

STSE education is an important part of the curriculum. The tenets of STSE education are central to scientific literacy and citizenship science—and students overwhelmingly respond positively to STSE components of the curriculum. What follows is a summary of the key ideas related to the learning objectives provided at the beginning of the chapter.

Characteristics of STSE education

STSE education includes the following principles: stewardship, the coupling of science and values, decision making,

action, and nature of science. Often these characteristics work in tandem.

Issues-based and historical approaches

Two common approaches to implementing STSE education include an issues-based approach and the historical case study approach. In the first approach, a socio-scientific issue (such as local biodiversity and habitat loss) frames the unit. An historical approach includes researching the work of scientists and recognizing the socio-cultural context in which scientists lived, exploring the historical development of a concept (for example, the history of the atom), or studying historical socio-scientific issues (for example, the *Exxon Valdez* oil spill).

Some useful strategies for STSE education

There are many useful strategies available for designing and implementing STSE aspects of the curriculum. Strategies that are particularly suited to STSE education include simulations and role play, six thinking hats, values continuum, consequence mapping, debate, and town hall meeting.

Planning and assessment for STSE education

Assessment is often identified as a challenge in STSE education. Teachers can feel ill-equipped to evaluate debates, position papers, action-oriented activities, and decision-making exercises. Assessment can be a concern, particularly when students' work includes a range of products such as position papers, research projects, performance pieces, portfolios, essays, or participation in debates and town hall meetings. Useful assessment include peer evaluation, self-evaluation, rubrics, checklists, and tracking sheets. Planning for STSE education, while rewarding, can be similarly challenging. Collaboration with other teachers and community members, perhaps in a PLC, can help to enhance your STSE education planning and teaching as well as your students' learning.

Navigating controversial issues in the science classroom

Many of the issues in science education are controversial and multidisciplinary. Using such issues can be motivating, stimulating, and relevant to students, while providing opportunities to develop citizenship skills such as informed and responsible decision making, taking action, and thinking critically. Controversy in the classroom can be a challenge for teachers and students, and teachers need to be judicious and sensitive in their planning and pedagogy.

Education research related to STSE education

There is no shortage of research in the area of STSE education or related concepts. We have drawn upon a few researchers in the field, including Glen Aikenhead, Steve Alsop, Larry Bencze, Jacques Désautel, Derek Hodson, Wolff-Michael Roth, Erminia Pedretti, Troy Sadler, and Dana Zeidler. We encourage you to read the work of these researchers as well as the many others who have contributed to this field over the past few decades.

BRINGING IT ALL TOGETHER: FINAL QUESTIONS

1. Some educators and researchers propose that STSE courses should be stand-alone programs. Discuss the benefits and limitations of this proposal. Where do you stand on this proposition and why?

2. In spite of its growing prominence in curriculum policy and development, STSE education is often marginalized. Why do you think this is the case? What is your response?

Visit MyEducationLab® to access an electronic version of the text, as well as a variety of topics that enhance the text material. The topics include the following to support your learning in the course:

- Assessments, including interactive case studies, activities, and video assignments
- Discussion board questions
- Videos, simulations, a lesson plan builder, and other useful course resources

APPENDIX 11.A	Data Collection Sheet for Using Skateboarding to Debate Speeding (Activity 11.3)

Name: _____

Mass: _____ kg

Velocity Calculations

Trial	Displacement (in m)	÷	Time (in sec)	=	Velocity (in m/sec)
Example	10 m	÷	12 sec	=	0.83 m/sec
1	10 m	÷		=	
2	10 m	÷		=	
3	10 m	÷		=	

Momentum Calculations

Trial	Mass (in kg)	×	Velocity (in m/sec)	=	Momentum (in kg m/sec)
Example	45 kg	×	0.83 m/sec	=	37.35 kg m/sec
1		×		=	
2		×		=	
3		×		=	

Chapter 12
Knowledge and Learning

Gunter Marx / Alamy

There's so much to know—it makes me nervous.

—Ben, teacher candidate

My biggest fear is not knowing the material.

—Ting, teacher candidate, first day of class

In science we learned about Arctic animals. The polar bear has white fur but the skin is black—but the fur makes it white. The black skin absorbs the sun. He eats fish and seals.

—Evan, Grade 1 student

LEARNING OBJECTIVES

- Describe what is meant by *science as a way of knowing*, and discuss the implications of this with respect to Indigenous and neo-Indigenous ways of knowing.

- Describe different categories of knowledge.

- Compare and contrast major theories of knowledge.

- Outline the major theories of learning.

- Explain misconceptions (or alternative frameworks) and conceptual change theory, and the implications for teaching.

- Identify and discuss education research related to knowledge and learning in science education.

21st CENTURY LEARNING SKILLS & COMPETENCIES

1 Communication

2 Critical thinking

3 Collaboration

4 Creativity

5 Literacy and numeracy

6 Media literacy

7 Technological literacy

INTRODUCTION

Knowledge is central to what teachers do, and to student learning. It forms the foundation of practices in schools and classrooms, and is an important part of all curriculum documents. Knowledge is a complex construct and warrants examination—philosophically and practically. Although teachers understand that science, for example, has a corpus of knowledge that makes up the discipline, they may be less familiar with the epistemological perspectives underpinning the generation of that knowledge. (Recall our discussion of NOS in Chapter 2.) By *epistemology*, we are referring to how we know what we know. How is knowledge generated? What are the different types of knowledge, and how does knowledge become part of the broader community?

As Plato asked in *The Republic,* What knowledge is of most worth? Today this question is still relevant. In this chapter, we invite you to explore the intersections of knowledge, learning, teaching, and pedagogy, and, in particular, the role these play in the context of science education. Our focus is philosophical and theoretical; practice and pedagogy will be taken up in more detail in Chapter 13.

WAYS OF KNOWING

We know all kinds of things—for example, when we are feeling happy or sad, the temperature outside, how to cook food to our liking, how to tend to a garden, and how to calculate tax on a purchase. However, we rarely stop to ask *how* we know, or how our knowledge is shaped and changed over time. Figure 12.1 depicts contributing factors to what we accept as knowledge.

◉▸Watch

Investigating Particles: Part 1

Science as a Way of Knowing

Science is *a* way of knowing (rather than *the* way of knowing); it represents only one of many ways of knowing the physical world. Consider, for example, knowledge and knowing

Figure 12.1 Factors related to knowledge

ACTIVITY 12.1

21st C ❷❸❹

Exploring Prior Knowledge and Experience

Choose three of the factors shown in Figure 12.1 that contribute to knowledge, and state a specific example that illustrates each. For example, we know from experience and evidence that the sun rises in the east. In groups of four, compare your examples and answer the questions below.

DISCUSSION QUESTIONS

1. Which examples of knowledge were easiest to generate? Which were more difficult? Explain.

2. When is something *science* knowledge?

3. How is science knowledge created?

that comes from perception, spirituality, emotion, or aesthetics (Aikenhead & Michell, 2011; Gitari, 2008; Harding, 1991; Hodson, 2011), and how they contribute to different world views. *World view* refers to a set of assumptions and beliefs that people hold about the world around them. Cobern (1996) describes world views as providing people "with pre-suppositions about what the world is really like and what constitutes valid and important knowledge about the world" (p. 27).

Different world views and ways of knowing are often marginalized (particularly in schools) and experienced by some students as incompatible with school science. For some, it is not easy to relate to a *scientific way of knowing* or a *scientific world view*, and consequently individuals may regard school science as a foreign culture (Aikenhead & Michell, 2011). For example, Gitari (2008) discusses the fragmentation and disconnect experienced by African students between their school science knowledge and the knowledge they use in their day-to-day interactions within their local community or family. Sutherland (2005), working with Cree students in Northern Manitoba, found that some students held two sources of knowledge to explain some science concepts and adopted learning strategies where they held two often conflicting schema.

Aikenhead and Michell (2011), in their book *Bridging Cultures: Indigenous and Scientific Ways of Knowing Nature*, describe how Indigenous students can feel alienated and frustrated by their school science experiences. These researchers sought to explore fundamental commonalities and differences between Eurocentric sciences and Indigenous knowledge, and to provide insights and strategies for teachers of science to build bridges across the scientific and other ways of knowing. They argue that multiple ways of knowing can enrich our understanding of science and nature; these knowledges are complementary and can co-exist.

Although Indigenous knowledge is addressed throughout the text, keep in mind that there are other ancestries that are neither European nor Indigenous. Aikenhead and Michell (2011) describe Eurocentric and western ways of knowing, Indigenous ways of knowing, and neo-Indigenous ways of knowing that are significant to the journey of becoming a teacher of science: Eurocentric science uses a Euro-American culture-based perspective; Indigenous science is based on Indigenous knowledge, Maori science, Yupiaq science, African science, and West Indian science; and neo-Indigenous ways of knowing include Islamic science, Chinese science, and Japanese ways of knowing nature (Aikenhead & Michell, 2011). These perspectives can help inform your pedagogy for a diverse student population in both urban and rural settings and encompass a shared understanding of science as a rational, culturally based, empirically sound way of knowing nature that yields, in part, descriptions and explanations of nature (Aikenhead & Michell, 2011; Ogawa, 1995). If teachers recognize science as encompassing several ways of knowing nature, then they can have a more equitable perspective on ways of knowing the world and can foster culturally responsive teaching. Many ministries and departments of education in Canada are responding to this call and producing curriculum and policy that honour Indigenous knowledge. (See, for example, Aboriginal Education Office, Ontario Ministry of Education, 2007a; Government of Nunavut, 2007; Manitoba Education and Youth, 2003.)

Historically, Eurocentric science has been the predominant view of science in most curriculum documents and textbooks. Recently, however, textbooks are incorporating non-western ways of knowing. The *Saskatchewan Science* textbook series integrates Indigenous knowledge in deep and meaningful ways, and includes for example: interviews with Elders; a chapter entitled "Cultural Explanations" that explores different explanations for the creation of the universe; examples of traditional uses of land; First Nations understandings of lightening, medicine and healing traditions, and much more. We encourage you to be sensitive to different ways of knowing, in order to attend to your diverse student populations. In Activity 12.2, you will have an opportunity to explore how—if at all—different ways of knowing are addressed in science textbooks in your region.

Science as a Culture and Border Crossing It can be helpful to think of science as a culture, with its own language, norms, practices, conventions, beliefs, and history. Be aware that many students experience school science as a foreign culture (Aikenhead, 2001; Aikenhead, Allen & Jegede, 1999). Aikenhead's (1996) notion of *border crossing* provides a useful construct for understanding how students negotiate these different cultures. Border crossings are not always difficult, but in some cases can be problematic; transitions can be smooth, managed, hazardous, or, for some students, virtually impossible. The ease with which students are able to cross these cultural borders (i.e., between their life-world and the world of school science) with the assistance of teachers who are sensitive and competent affects their educational outcomes and aspirations. (See Aikenhead Chapter 4 for a more detailed discussion of border crossing.) The challenge is that some students are able to move easily between cultures, while others struggle, resist, or experience failure. How can teachers move students toward understanding accepted scientific knowledge while honouring multiple ways of knowing? Teachers need to recognize the different ways students experience border crossing and work toward helping those students navigate difficulties.

ACTIVITY 12.2

21st C **2** **3** **4**

Working with Resources: Analyzing Science Resources for Indigenous and Neo-Indigenous Content

Choose a science resource (e.g., textbook, resource kit) used in your school district or board. Describe the content and context of the resource (i.e., the topic, unit, grade). Working in pairs, look for examples of Indigenous knowledge and neo-Indigenous knowledge. Be prepared to discuss your examples with the class.

DISCUSSION QUESTIONS

1. Describe the examples of Indigenous knowledge in the science resource.
2. Describe the examples of neo-Indigenous knowledge in the science resource.
3. Critique how these examples are presented (e.g., as peripheral to the main content of the chapter, as a token message, or as deeply integrated).
4. Discuss how you might further integrate Indigenous and neo-Indigenous content into your curriculum.

CATEGORIES OF KNOWLEDGE

When we think of knowledge in the context of teaching science, what often comes to mind is the acquisition of subject matter content knowledge—for example, knowing the stages of the rock cycle; understanding the influence of different forces on objects; or knowing the behaviours of solids, liquids, and gases. While this emphasis is prevalent, there are many other categories of knowledge. In this section we explore some of those different categories of knowledge in an effort to understand their referents and purposes.

There are many different schemas for categorizing knowledge. The categorization of knowledge presented in Table 12.1 draws from Anderson and Krathwohl (2001), de Jong and Ferguson-Hessler (1996), and Wallace, Venville, and Rennie (2010), and serves as a way to think about different kinds of knowledge. This list is not definitive, and the categories are not mutually exclusive—there are times when they overlap and work in synergy.

Consider, for example, a Grade 6 class studying biodiversity, which is important to environmental health and supports the resilience of species. In planning for this topic, the

Table 12.1   Categories of Knowledge

Category	Description	Example
Propositional or Factual Knowledge	Refers to knowledge of specific details and terminology, knowledge of facts	Knowing that plastic comes from petroleum; knowing that the heart has four chambers
Conceptual Knowledge	Refers to knowledge of classifications and categories, principles and generalizations, theories, models, and structures	Understanding the effect of gravity; being able to classify living things as producers, consumers, or decomposers
Procedural Knowledge	Refers to knowledge related to specific skills and algorithms, techniques, and methods; knowing when to use appropriate procedures; knowledge of how to do something	Knowing how to measure temperature using a thermometer; knowing how to follow appropriate safety procedures
Meta-Cognitive Knowledge	Refers to self-knowledge, knowledge about cognitive tasks, knowing about knowing, understanding your cognitive processes, self-monitoring, self-regulation	Knowing when to use a particular strategy, recognizing that you are having trouble solving a problem, and double checking your thinking about the process
Personal Knowledge	Refers to knowledge by acquaintance or experience first-hand knowledge, familiarity with something, tacit knowledge	Knowing that in autumn deciduous tree leaves change colour; knowing that soap feels slippery
Critical or Emancipatory Knowledge	Refers to knowledge related to questioning practices and taken-for-granted assumptions, and how practices may be changed. Such knowledge balances personal, community, and generational needs	Choosing to walk to school instead of being driven; writing a letter to the editor of a local newspaper
Strategic Knowledge	Refers to knowledge of how to investigate a question, organize problem-solving, and apply knowledge	Knowing how to design a mechanism that includes at least one simple machine; knowing how to design an investigation to determine which paper towel is most absorbent

teacher integrates different categories of knowledge. Students need propositional knowledge (e.g., insects have three basic body parts), conceptual knowledge (e.g., birds and bees spread pollen between plants), procedural knowledge (e.g., using a microscope to observe microorganisms), and critical knowledge (e.g., discussing loss of biodiversity and its causes while planning a butterfly garden at school). Teachers and students might also make use of personal knowledge, based on experience and familiarity with the topic.

ACTIVITY 12.3   *21st C* ② ③ ④

Working with Resources: Analyzing Curricula

Analyze the outcomes or expectations in a science curriculum in your province or territory in light of the categories of knowledge discussed in Table 12.1. Locate curriculum expectations that support each category, if possible.

DISCUSSION QUESTIONS

1. What categories of knowledge are predominant in the document? Why do you think this is the case?
2. What categories of knowledge seem least prevalent? Speculate as to why.

ACTIVITY 12.4   *21st C* ② ③ ④

Connecting Practice and Theory: Categories of Knowledge

Imagine you are teaching plant growth and change to Grade 3 students. (See, for example, Aspen-Baxter, Brockman, Molnar, & Shields (2013)). As a culminating activity, you would like your students to design a vegetable garden and a poster that shares the design. In groups of four, brainstorm the types of knowledge that are needed to complete this task. Identify the category of knowledge needed and provide specific examples of what students need to accomplish the assignment.

DISCUSSION QUESTIONS

1. What kinds of knowledge are needed? Which were absent?
2. What are the implications of privileging certain categories of knowledge?
3. Provide two examples of how you might assess student work.

THEORIES OF KNOWLEDGE AND THEORIES OF LEARNING

In this section, we consider the intersections between the theories of knowledge and learning and their implications for education and teaching. A detailed discussion of these domains is beyond the scope of this chapter. We hope, however, that this serves as an introduction to the landscape of knowledge and learning, one that you can pursue in more detail throughout your educational journey. We encourage you to read more of the rich research literature available in this area.

Theories of Knowledge

For centuries, philosophers have grappled with the question of what we know and how we come to know it. These ideas are equally important for educators. For example, the question *where does knowledge reside*, although philosophical in nature, is inherent in developing an educational theory that encompasses knowledge, teaching, and pedagogy. As we will demonstrate later in this section, the answer has implications for practice.

Traditionally, there have been two opposing philosophical positions to whether knowledge exists external to the knower or within our minds. It can be argued that knowledge exists independently of individuals—external to the knower. The real world exists, independent of our ideas. Epistemological theorists often refer to this position as *realism*. The opposite position is *idealism*, the idea that knowledge exists only in the minds of individuals (so, for example, there can be no "laws of nature except in the minds of people who invent and hold these views" (Hein, 1998, p. 17)). These polarized positions are problematic. If, for example, knowledge is indeed external, then how do we come to know it? If it resides within us, how do we share it (Hein, 1998)? Many other positions have been developed in response. For example, Osborne (1996) writes about the *modest realist position*, which acknowledges the existence of knowledge as corresponding to the behaviour of real objects in the world, as well as humanly constructed constructs and theories. Von Glaserfeld (1989) argues that, although he does not deny the existence of an absolute reality, we have no way of knowing it, and therefore we define the meaning of *to exist* only within the realm of our experiential world.

In contrast to idealism's and realism's emphasis on disciplines, subject matter, and content, *pragmatism* and *existentialism* emerged at the turn of the twentieth century. Pragmatism asserts that knowledge is a dynamic process in which reality is in constant change. Learning occurs through problem solving and is transferable to a variety of contexts, and knowing is identified as an exchange between the learner and the environment. The principles of pragmatism were developed by Charles Pierce and William James, mathematician and psychologist, respectively, and reject assertions of preconceived truths, instead promoting the testing and verification of ideas. Truth (knowledge) is not absolute or universal; it is proven in relation to facts, experience, and behaviour. John Dewey, a pragmatist, applied these principles as he emphasized the importance of experience in learning. Existentialism asserts that people are faced with situations in which they make choices, both major and minor, and that the decisions made lead to self-definition and the creation of one's own essence. Essentially, we choose what we are, and, as such, what we are differs across individuals. To the existentialist, the most important knowledge relates to the human condition and the choices made by the individual. Social, political, and religious norms, authority, and orders are rejected and eternal truths are not recognized; this is at odds with idealism and realism (Ornstein & Hunkins, 1993). Table 12.2 summarizes these four philosophies.

Teachers' approaches to teaching, and to teaching science, are informed by these philosophies. For example, a teacher who identifies with realist philosophy might view his or her role as an authority or expert, and that teacher's curriculum may emphasize acquisition of subject matter content knowledge. On the other hand, a pragmatist teacher might

Table 12.2	Four Major Philosophies Informing Education	
Philosophy	**Reality**	**Knowledge**
Idealism	Unchanging; spiritual, moral, or mental	Based on latent ideas
Realism	Objective and universal; based on natural laws	Based on sensation and abstraction
Pragmatism	Changing; interaction of individuals with environment	Based on experience; scientific methods
Existentialism	Subjective	Based on personal choice and self-definition

Source: Orstein, Allan C., Hunkis, Francis P., *Curriculum: Foundations, principles, and issues,* 6th Ed., © 2012, p.33. Adapted and electronically reproduced by permission of Pearson Education, Inc. Upper Saddle River, New Jersey.

see her or himself as a facilitator encouraging critical thinking, and might develop a curriculum that includes a focus on problem-solving across disciplines. Philosophical beliefs are inherent in teachers' actions as curriculum workers.

Theories of Learning

Theories of learning are intricately connected to theories of knowledge. Both impact theories of teaching. Learning is a complex process that involves accessing, understanding, processing, internalizing, and expressing information. Learning involves the whole person, including cognition, emotion, affect, and context. Over the years, much research has been done in an attempt to understand how people, particularly children, learn.

Think about your own learning for a moment:

- What is your learning style?
- Do you learn best by reading material several times, or do you prefer to write things out?
- Do you like to work in groups?
- Do you use diagrams (flow charts, webs) to map out connections across concepts?

It is clear that there are different ways of learning; each individual has personal preferences and uses different approaches in different contexts. In this section, we provide a brief overview of theories of learning that have been influential in education over the past few decades. As you read through this section, you will notice how successive theories of learning have built upon past work, and how theories of learning are connected to theories of knowledge. We draw on psychological and educational research to help explain various theories. Think about how these theories underpin what teachers do and how they plan curricula.

Davis, Sumara, and Luce-Kapler (2008) identify two types of learning theories: *correspondence theories* and *coherence theories*. Correspondence theories are grounded in the assumptions that learning occurs in a mechanistic, predictable, and easily manipulated way, and takes place in the individual (*learner* and *individual* are viewed as synonymous). Behaviourism and mentalism are two correspondence theories in which learning is identified as the alignment of subjective, internal models with objective, external realities (Davis, Sumara, & Luce-Kapler, 2008).

Correspondence Theories

1. *Behaviourism* is a theory of learning based on the idea that learning occurs through conditioning (Skinner, 1953). In behaviourism, the emphasis is on external manifestations of learning or observable behaviours, rather than internal physiological events or constructs such as thoughts and beliefs. Learning is essentially the acquisition of new behaviours based on contextual conditions. Adhering to a behaviourist view of learning often translates to the teacher holding a dominant role and controlling learning and evaluation. The learner (or student) typically has little opportunity to evaluate or reflect on her or his own learning processes. Essentially, it is stimulus-response learning. Behaviourism has been criticized on many fronts. Mainly, it does not take into account the activities and processes occurring in the mind, and it does not explain how individuals adapt reinforced patterns to new information. It also fails to explain the many ways that people opt to learn, and reduces learning to an extrinsic and superficial process. That said, there are traces of behaviourism at work in many educational settings, such as the use of external rewards or reinforcements (e.g., watching a movie as a reward for completing a unit of study on time) to encourage particular behaviours.

2. *Mentalism*, a second correspondence theory, holds that learning involves assembling an internal mental model that corresponds with the external world (Davis, Sumara, & Luce-Kapler, 2008). Essentially, mentalism asserts that the mind has a map or image that aligns with the real world. Traditionally these maps have been viewed in terms of sculpting, filming, and photographing, to name a few, but now many metaphoric representations of mentalism use computers and digital encoding to illustrate the processes of learning, such as internalizing information and storing and processing knowledge. One example of mentalism is in the construct of multiple learner styles. These types, including auditory, visual, and kinesthetic learning, rest on the assumption that knowledge is filtered from the real world into an internal model. Mentalism has been criticized for focusing on internal representations rather than on mechanisms of learning; learning is much more complex than an organization of parts into a sensible whole (Davis, Sumara, & Luce-Kapler, 2008).

Coherence Theories In response to criticisms of correspondence theories, a number of coherence theories of learning have been put forward. Coherence theories reject a number of fundamental assumptions of correspondence theories. Mind and body, self and other, individual and collective, knower and knowledge, and human and non-human are not viewed as being in opposition, but as depending on the interests of the theorist and recognized as agents within larger systems. Four prominent coherence theories of learning are outlined below.

1. *Constructivism* is a theory of learning (not teaching!) that postulates that people, especially children, learn by constructing and building new ideas in their minds. Learning is about building and constructing knowledge, and depends greatly on what the learner already knows. People create meaning of the world through individual constructs (Driver, Guesne, & Tiberghien, 1985; von Glaserfeld, 1989) and through experiencing an environment first-hand. Here there are echoes of Dewey's (1938/1997) philosophy that education should be experiential and child-centred. Earlier forms of constructivism focused on the individual as the unit of analysis, while latter work introduced the idea of *social constructivism*, where social interactions, discourse, and cultural mediation are central. Learning is influenced by a person's background, culture, and embedded world view. Constructivism is supported by many school boards across the country, leading to what many call *constructivist-informed pedagogy*.

   Constructivism is rooted in the work of Jean Piaget, one of the leading 20th-century figures in child development and learning. Piaget's cognitive development theory (1926, 1929) postulates that people move through a series of stages from infancy to adulthood, as summarized in Table 12.3.

Watch

Conservation of Matter

Table 12.3   Piaget's Stages of Development

Age (in years)	Stage	Features
0–2	Sensorimotor	The child learns to differentiate between "me "and "not me" through interactions with objects in its environment.
2–7	Pre-operational	The child learns to classify objects in general ways, using important and obvious characteristics. The child is egocentric.
7–12	Concrete operational	The child begins to use logical operations such as reversal, deliberate classifications, and serialization. Thinking becomes less egocentric, and there is increased awareness of external events.
12 and up	Formal operational	The child begins to think in more abstract ways and use symbols related to abstract concepts. Hypothetico-deductive reasoning emerges.

Source: Adapted from Cook & Cook (2005).

Watch

Conservation of
Matter, Volume

Piaget's work has many implications for education. First, instruction should be consistent with the developmental level of the learner. Second, the teacher is viewed as a facilitator of learning, providing a range of experiences and scaffolding for the learner. Some describe this as *discovery* learning, where students explore their environment to gain new understandings. Piaget's theory also implies that educators should use concrete props, visual aids, and models, beginning with the familiar and moving to the abstract.

Constructivism is not without its critics. Some argue that it denies a body of knowledge that exists in the world outside the learner or that, ironically, it only works if you have a strong knowledge base (Lui & Matthews, 2005). In other words, discovery learning, through investigations or experiences with little or no assistance or prior knowledge, is a misnomer. For many, guided discovery is a more accurate description of what is really happening to and with students. So, for example, if you were teaching the periodic table, students would not be able to reconstruct it from first principles— or *discover* the periodic table. That took hundreds of years of research, organization, reorganization, and additions. However, students can come to understand how it is organized into families and periods through an exploration of patterns (e.g., atomic size, reactivity).

Constructivism has become highly influential in teacher training programs and educational research. In our view, the constructivist theory of learning can be useful in that it reminds us of the centrality of the learner; that she or he comes with ideas about the world and how it works and that we need to provide students with a range of experiences to help them build their knowledge. If learning is constructed, then the foundation provided by the teacher becomes key. Learning is viewed as an active process, often constructed in a social context but ultimately taken up by individuals. It is a process that involves interaction between what is already known and the current learning experience. For learning to be lasting and meaningful, it must connect with prior knowledge, prior conceptions, and prior experience—otherwise, it becomes rote learning. Bonnie Shapiro (1994), in *What Children Bring to Light: A Constructivist Perspective on Children's Learning in Science*, explores the importance of the personal experience of the learner. While acknowledging that learning is a cognitive process, she extends what it means to learn to include emotional, personal, social, and cultural contexts. Her theoretical work is illustrated through six case studies of a Grade 5 class exploring the topic of light.

2. *Constructionism* departs from constructivism as, rather than focusing on the individual learner, it views the individual as a learning system within a larger system of learning. Cognition is inherently collective, embedded within and directed by language, history, tradition, interests, and assumptions. The mind is the product of complex social and physical relations. Constructionism—also known as social constructivism—is deeply informed by the works of Lev Vygotsky (for example, Vygotsky, 1962, 1978; Wertsch, 1985), who believed that a child's cultural background and social interactions affect learning, and that learning does not necessarily occur in a hierarchy of succession as proposed by Piaget. Cultural mediation and interpersonal communication are introduced as important to child development. Consequently, Vygotsky (1978) developed the concept of *zone of proximal development*, which refers to a range of tasks children can complete independently and with the assistance of a capable instructor. The *zone of proximal development* explains the relationship between children's learning and cognitive development. It represents the space that allows for challenge, but not so much so that the learner is frustrated and gives up. Here, the notion of scaffolding learning becomes

important as the knowing educator provides tasks that may be initially beyond the learner's capacity but within the range of his or her competence. Situated learning is an example of constructionism that uses the metaphor of apprenticeship to describe how children learn and reproduce social norms (Davis, Sumara, & Luce-Kapler, 2008).

3. *Cultural and critical theories* reflect a movement from seeing how the individual shapes the world to how the social and cultural world shapes the individual. Educational theorists have traditionally drawn from psychology and sociology (e.g., Piaget, Dewey, Vygotsky), but in the 1960s and 1970s, theories of learning were increasingly informed by anthropology and philosophy, thereby acknowledging *cultural and social contexts* and their implications for education. Cultural and critical theories of learning consider ethics and morality and identify the interpretations and associations that produce (and reproduce) social norms. These theories of learning highlight the privilege afforded to some disciplines in contemporary academia, such as science and mathematics. Prominent among these theories is the work of Paulo Freire, which recognized the interactions of the individual with social organizations and the cultural world (Davis, Sumara, & Luce-Kapler, 2008).

4. *Ecological theories* of learning extend thinking beyond individual, social, and cultural contexts to include the more-than-human world and dynamic relationships among species. These theories view humans as but one species inextricably linked to others within a web of relations, and as such identify cognition as an evolving interaction between agents to create new understandings. Learning is at once about memory and knowing, activities within agents, and actions interacting with other agents. Ecological theories are similar to other coherence theories in that they apply the same metaphors and logic but assert that knowledge aligns and evolves with the natural world as well as with the individual, social, and cultural worlds (Davis, Sumara, & Luce-Kapler, 2008).

Complexity Theory Complexity theory brings together all of these coherence theories of learning and recognizes that they inherently inform and are informed by each other. Complexity theory, as a unifying theory, departs from linear cause-and-effect models or analytically fragmented approaches to understanding phenomena, and replaces them with holistic approaches that honour relationships and interconnectedness (Morrison, 2006). As Morrison (2006) states, the teacher informed by complexity theory strives to heighten connectivity and interactivity between her or himself and students. In other words, various levels of learning—individual, social group, and species and ecosystem—interact and thus should be considered in educational practice and theory (Davis, Sumara, & Luce-Kapler, 2008).

Summary of Theories of Learning

We can think about these various theories of learning using a continuum with two distinct positions (adapted from Hein, 1998, p. 21). At one end is a theory of learning as transmission; students learn by absorbing material that the teacher transmits to them. Learning happens incrementally, bit by bit, step by step; the image of students as an empty vessel to be filled is often used to describe this position. It is inclusive of correspondence theories of learning. The other extreme represents a network of learning theories that include the works of Piaget, Dewey, Vygotsky, von Glaserfeld, and Freire. This end of the continuum suggests that the learner actively constructs knowledge, and that learning is not the simple addition of pieces of information but rather

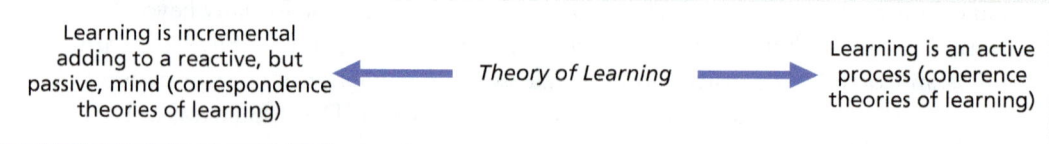

Figure 12.2 Theory of learning continuum

Source: Based on Hein, G. (1998). *Learning in the museum.* New York: Routledge.

a transformation of schemas in the learner's mind. The learner plays an active role in making sense of a range of experiences and phenomena. This position aligns with coherence theories of learning.

This *theory of learning* continuum (based on Hein, 1998) provides a useful way to represent these different positions. Think about where you might position yourself on this continuum, as shown in Figure 12.2, and why.

ACTIVITY 12.5   *21st C* ② ③ ④

Read and Reflect: Theories of Learning

In this activity you will have an opportunity to choose an article that focuses on some aspect of learning. Locate one of the following three articles, and briefly summarize it and answer the questions below. Form groups of three, making sure that each person in your group has read a different paper. Be prepared to share your answers.

Colburn, A. (2000). Constructivism: Science education's "grand unifying theory." *The Clearing House, 7*(41), 9–12.

Davis, B., & Sumara, D. J. (1997). Cognition, complexity, and teacher education. *Harvard Educational Review, 67*(1), 105–125.

Quay, J. (2003). Experience and participation: Relating theories of learning. *Journal of Experiential Education, 26*(2), 105–116.

DISCUSSION QUESTIONS

1. How does the author describe the learning theory? What are its core ideas?
2. What are some of the challenges of the theory of learning?
3. What are the implications of this theory for a beginning teacher of science?
4. Describe three teaching strategies that are underpinned by the learning theory. Explain the connection to that theory.

ALTERNATIVE FRAMEWORKS, MISCONCEPTIONS, AND CONCEPTUAL CHANGE

There is much agreement among education researchers today that students are active learners who are continually building knowledge. This belief is captured in coherence theories of learning, which suggest that children come with a wealth of experiences that lead them to develop common-sense ideas about the social and natural environment in which they live (Driver, 1989; Read, 2004). These ideas evolve from their direct experiences in the world, media, interactions with others, and past education. However, students' informal understandings can be misaligned with formal scientific knowledge of how the world works (Thompson & Logue, 2006).

In the educational literature, these erroneous views are often called *alternative frameworks* or *misconceptions* because they do not necessarily align with the accepted scientific view. These terms are often used interchangeably. Alternative frameworks often serve as an effective starting point when a teacher begins a new topic or lesson. What do students already know about this topic? What are their current understandings? Where do their ideas come from? How will the teacher begin to challenge the students' ideas? It is important to recognize that students bring with them a range of experiences and understandings that inevitably influence what they do and how they learn in your classroom. Always let this guide your science curriculum and instruction. In doing so, you will not only align your curriculum with students' understandings, but you will also be able to realize rich pedagogical opportunities (e.g., inquiry-based learning). For further reading on students' misconceptions in elementary science, please see Allen (2010).

◉─[Watch

Interviewing Jessie about Water Cycle Concepts

Examples of Alternative Frameworks or Misconceptions

The research literature is replete with examples of alternative frameworks held by children and older students. Even teachers often unknowingly hold alternative frameworks. Some common examples of elementary school students' science misconceptions appear in Table 12.4.

Table 12.4   Elementary School Students' Science Misconceptions

Topic	Misconception	Scientific Explanation or Accepted Theory
Seasons	Seasons are caused by the changing distances of Earth from the Sun on its elliptical orbit.	Seasonal change is caused by the tilting of Earth relative to the Sun's rays.
Gravity	Heavier objects fall faster than lighter objects.	Objects fall at the same rate.
Buoyancy and Density	Things float if they are light and sink if they are heavy.	Whether something sinks or floats is dependent upon buoyancy, density, and effect on surface tension.
Properties of Matter	Any crystal that can scratch glass is diamond.	Diamond is a hard crystal but is not the only one that will scratch glass.
Planetary Motion	The Sun orbits Earth.	Earth orbits the Sun.
Properties of Matter	Mass and weight are the same and always equal.	Mass is the amount of matter and weight is the force of gravity on a mass.
Energy	Heat and temperature are the same thing.	Heat is energy and temperature is a measure of the average kinetic energy of particles.

ACTIVITY 12.6

Read and Reflect: Common Student Misconceptions

For this activity, read Thompson, F. & Logue, S. (2006). An exploration of common student misconceptions in science. *International Education Journal, 7*(4), 553–559.

    This article describes an assignment that was undertaken by a group of teacher candidates enrolled in a science methods course. The objective was to identify three scientific concepts and misconceptions that students commonly hold. Six students between the ages of 6 and 15 were interviewed to probe their understandings (and misconceptions, if any) on a particular topic, and determine where their ideas came from.

    After reading the article, answer the following questions and be prepared to share your responses.

👁 Watch

Interviewing Amber about Water Cycle Concepts

DISCUSSION QUESTIONS

1. What three misconceptions were identified by the teacher candidates?
2. Choose one of the misconceptions and describe the students' beliefs about the concept. Speculate as to where their ideas came from.
3. Why is it important to probe students' ideas about scientific concepts or phenomena?
4. What might challenge a teacher who adheres to a constructivist theory of learning?

Conceptual Change Theory

Student misconceptions can be problematic for a number of reasons. First, research suggests that students hold on to their ideas tightly, even when presented with contradictory evidence. Second, misconceptions can seriously influence learning as students resist new ideas or schemas. For example, if students are conducting an investigation and come across unexpected data, they might ignore, reject, exclude, or reinterpret the data in order to protect their pre-instructional ideas (Read, 2004). Third, students may appear to have learned a concept yet have simply memorized an equation and have a weak understanding of the underlying scientific principles. For example, students might be able to solve problems using algorithms but perform poorly on tasks involving conceptual understanding. Finally, in attempting to please the teacher or do well on a test, students might provide scientifically accepted explanations but may revert to their naive explanations later on.

    How do learners change their views? How do they adapt, modify, or replace old schemas? Posner, Strike, Hewson, and Gertzog (1982) posited the *conceptual change model*, in which conceptual change begins when the learner experiences dissatisfaction with an existing conception because it fails, for example, to resolve a new problem or explain an anomaly. The researchers suggested that there are three conditions that must be met in order for conceptual change to occur. A new concept must be:

1. *intelligible* or meaningful to the learner (i.e., Does the learner know what it means? Do the words make sense? Can it be described in his or her own words?)

2. *plausible* (i.e., There must be a possibility of resolving the problem, and it must be compatible with existing knowledge about the concept.)

3. *fruitful* (i.e., It can actually solve the problem that the old idea could not. Does it suggest new directions or possibilities? Is it useful?)

    Hodson (1998, 2011) highlights a further condition: Students must feel comfortable with a new idea or concept in that it meets their emotional needs and is culturally safe. Feelings can be influenced by class members, by personal world view and culture, and by socialized values. If students view an idea as personally or socially relevant, they are more likely to accept it.

Coherence theories of learning can help teachers recognize that students have previously constructed misconceptions about the natural world. If you subscribe to this view of learning, then, within the context of teaching science, your pedagogy will likely acknowledge the following:

- Learners come to the classroom with ideas and experience, and these ideas can contradict western science and the scientific community. The corollary is that learners' minds are not blank slates or empty vessels ready to be *filled* with knowledge. Instead students must be provided with experiences that will help them build understandings, challenge existing ideas, and create new knowledge.

- Learners need others to help them learn. Learning does not happen in a vacuum, and learners need opportunities to engage in dialogue with peers, teachers, and other experts. The social aspect of learning is critical to building knowledge.

- Learners have different learning styles and needs, and curricula must reflect the many unique ways that learners construct knowledge.

- Responsibility for learning should reside with the learner.

- Teachers need to portray scientific and technological knowledge as constructed.

- The teacher is a facilitator; that is, the learner and teacher are equally involved in learning, and the process is dynamic and interactive.

- Context is important. Educators should consider the classroom milieu, the lives of students, and the influence of popular culture and media.

Finally, it is important to note that it is the learner, and not the teacher, who decides if the conditions have been met for conceptual change. However, the teacher is responsible for creating curricular experiences for students that challenge their ideas and move them toward current scientific concepts, principles, and procedures. Consequently, the teacher needs to consider what educational research says about students' misconceptions as a first step in designing appropriate instructional activities; to develop methods for diagnosing students' misconceptions before and after instruction; and to review their own understandings of difficult concepts (Cakir, 2008).

ACTIVITY 12.7   *21st C* ❷❸❹

Examining Misconceptions and Teaching for Conceptual Change

In groups of four, choose one of the science topics below and explore what the educational research literature indicates are common student misconceptions about the topic. Create three specific activities that a teacher could use to address these misconceptions and challenge students' ideas. One of the activities must be independent work, one must involve cooperative group learning, and one must involve technology. Be prepared to share your ideas with the other groups in the class.

TOPICS
- electricity
- properties of matter
- forces and fluids
- daily and seasonal changes
- human body
- astronomy
- Earth's crust

EXPLORING ELEMENTARY SCIENCE IN CREATIVE WAYS: SEASONAL CHANGE

In order to teach any topic confidently and effectively, it is helpful to have a deep and broad knowledge base. In this section we present some ideas to help develop your subject matter content knowledge (CK) and pedagogical content knowledge (PCK) for a specific topic—seasonal change. The topic is introduced with a visual that might appear in a print or media resource. We encourage you to search for other resources to help you. As you learn or re-learn the content, keep in mind other issues, such as terminology, abstract processes, integration with mathematics and language arts, and activities to support student learning. Additionally, consider the meta-cognitive aspect of the activity such as understanding how you learn, what you know, and what you need to know.

Students (and adults) have many misconceptions related to the seasons and to seasonal changes (see Table 12.4). Seasonal changes, while experienced by all students living in Canadian climates, are difficult to explain as they require understandings of abstract ideas such as planetary motion and the tilt of Earth. Mental models and simulations can be helpful in teaching about seasonal change.

ACTIVITY 12.8

21st C ② ③ ④

Seasonal Change

The topic of seasonal change is found in the Grade 1 science curriculum in many provinces and territories. The British Columbia Grade 1 curriculum expects that all students will be able to describe the changes that occur in seasonal cycles and their effects on living things. Similarly, the Manitoba Grade 1 curriculum includes learning outcomes related to characteristics of the seasons, preparations of living things for seasonal changes, and safety considerations for each season, while the Ontario Grade 1 science curriculum expects that students will investigate seasonal changes and assess their impact on living things, including humans. The Atlantic provinces also include the topic of seasonal change in the Grade 1 science curriculum.

Reviewing the Content

1. Review or learn the content associated with seasonal change. For example, how does Earth's axis influence seasons? Use the figure below to guide your exploration of the topic.
2. Make a list of definitions for important or unfamiliar vocabulary and processes associated with this topic.
3. When you feel comfortable with the content, use the figure below to explain the topic of seasonal change to a peer.

Literacy and Numeracy Connections

1. Read *And then it's spring* by Julie Fogliano (2012), a lovely story of a young boy and his dog who plant a garden after a long winter and wait patiently for the seeds to grow. Students might plant seeds and write similar stories about their own gardens.
2. A study of seasons could include a parallel exploration of fractions and equivalent fractions. Students could look at fourths (four seasons per year) and twelfths (three months/twelve months per season), and show those fractions in a variety of ways (pie graph, calendar, etc.).

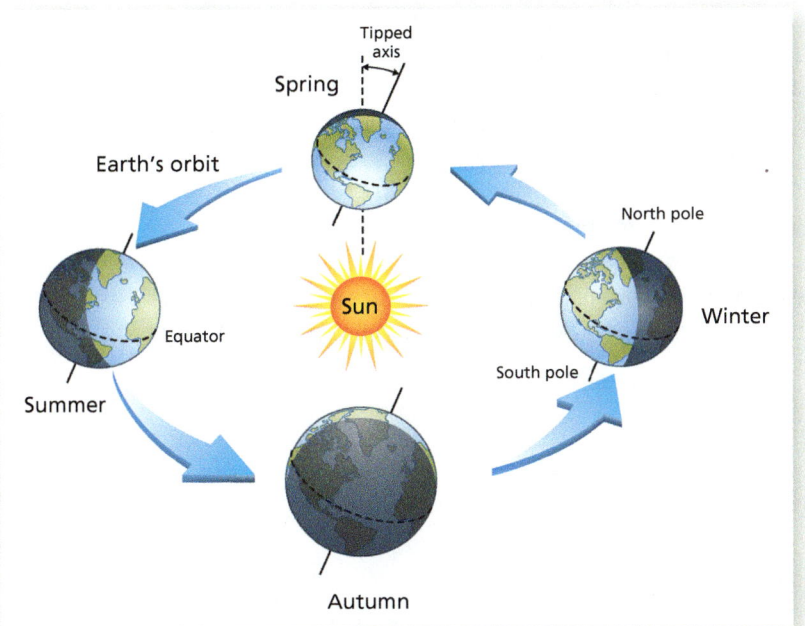

The Seasons

Watch

Investigating Moon
Phases (Part 4)

Activities for Elementary School Students

1. Modelling the Seasons. (Adapted from Bosak, S. (1991). Science is…: *A Source book of fascinating facts, projects and activities*. TCP Press.) Place a table lamp with its shade removed at the centre of a floor space. Identify and label NORTH in the room. On a globe that rotates on a tilted axis, tape a small nail, head down, where you live. Place the globe about 1.5 metres away from and level with the lamp and opposite NORTH, with the axis tilted toward NORTH. This is summer in the northern hemisphere. Moving counterclockwise, move through autumn, winter, spring, and back to summer, keeping the axis directed toward NORTH. (See the figure below.) Make observations about the areas of the globe illuminated and the length of the nail's shadow in each season. In which season is the shadow longest? Shortest?

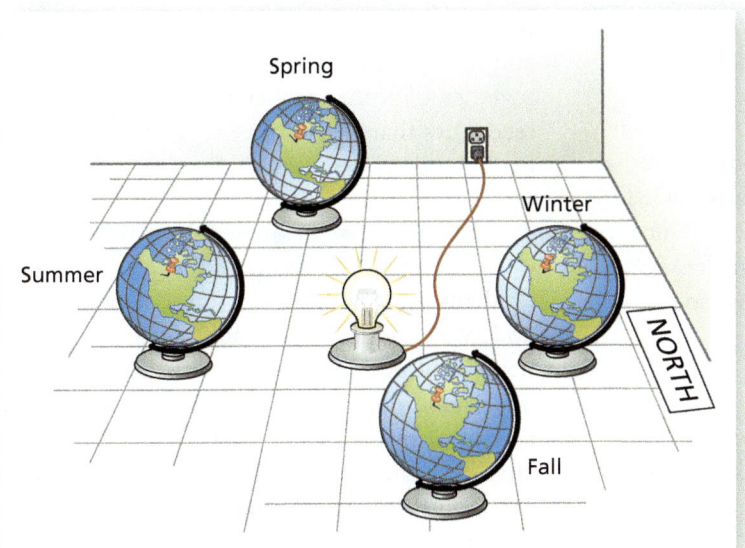

Seasons Demonstration

continued on next page

2. Observing Seasonal Changes. Visit a local park or green space every three to four weeks, and in a log book or science notebook make field notes and drawings of the surroundings. Also, take photographs to add to a digital log. Be sure to include the date of the observations. You might focus on a particular tree or small ecosystem. Note any changes in the plants and animals. What changes do you see from autumn to winter? Winter to spring? Spring to summer?

3. Picture Sort. Have students categorize pictures from spring, summer, autumn, and winter into their respective seasons. Include images of changes in plants (e.g., leaves falling from trees, flowers blooming), animals (e.g., hare with white fur, duck with ducklings), and human activities (e.g., playing Frisbee on the beach, wearing a winter coat). Which pictures are easy to classify and why? Which are difficult and why?

CONCLUDING THOUGHTS

The intention of this chapter was to engage you with some of the philosophical and historical ideas related to knowledge and learning, and to explore students' ideas in science. What follows is a summary of key ideas related to the learning objectives provided at the beginning of the chapter.

Science as a way of knowing

Science represents one way of knowing the physical world. In schools, Eurocentric science is dominant. For some students, this view is alienating, fragmented, and incompatible with their world views, which may include Indigenous and neo-Indigenous perspectives. Honouring multiple ways of knowing can enrich teachers' understanding of science and nature, as these knowledges are complementary and can co-exist in a science curriculum.

Categories of knowledge

There are many different schemas and categories for conceptualizing knowledge, including propositional or factual knowledge, conceptual knowledge, procedural knowledge, meta-cognitive knowledge, personal knowledge, critical or emancipatory knowledge, and strategic knowledge. School science tends to emphasize factual, conceptual, and procedural knowledge.

Theories of knowledge

Traditionally, two opposing philosophies informed education. The realist position argues that knowledge exists independently of individuals, external to the knower. The other extreme is idealism, the idea that knowledge exists only in the minds of individuals, by virtue of being within the realm of our experiential world. Two contemporary positions that inform education are pragmatism and existentialism. Pragmatism asserts that knowledge is dynamic, and its production occurs through interactions between the learner and the environment. Existentialism relates knowledge to decisions made by individuals and the creation of one's own essence. All of these positions carry implications for teaching and learning.

Theories of learning

Correspondence theories of learning are grounded in the assumption that learning occurs in a mechanistic and predictable way. Behaviourism and mentalism are examples of correspondence theories. A number of coherence theories of learning have been put forward in response to criticisms of correspondence theories. Constructivism, constructionism, cultural and critical theories, and ecological theories reflect the connectedness of individual, social, cultural, and ecological worlds. Complexity thinking brings together all of these coherence theories of learning and recognizes that they inherently inform and are informed by each other.

Misconceptions (or alternative frameworks) and conceptual change theory

Students bring with them a range of experiences and understandings that inevitably affect what they do and how they learn in your classroom. Erroneous views or understandings about science are often called *misconceptions* or *alternative frameworks* because they don't necessarily align with the accepted scientific view. The *conceptual change model* describes how new schemas replace old ones. In it, three conditions must be met: The new concept must be *intelligible*, *plausible*, and *fruitful*. The teacher has the responsibility of creating experiences for students that challenge their ideas and move them toward accepting current scientific knowledge.

Educational research related to knowledge and learning in science education

There is no shortage of research in the area of epistemology and learning. We have drawn upon a few researchers in the field, including Glen Aikenhead, David Ausubel, Brent Davis, Rosalind Driver, Wanja Gitari, Rebecca Luce-Kapler, Herman Michell, Jean Piaget, and Dennis Sumara. We encourage you to read the work of these researchers as well as the many others who have contributed to this field over the past few decades.

BRINGING IT ALL TOGETHER: FINAL QUESTIONS

1. How will you attend to different ways of knowing in your science class?
2. What are the strengths and limitations of adopting a correspondence theory of learning? Of adopting a coherence theory of learning?

MyEducationLab®

Visit MyEducationLab® to access an electronic version of the text, as well as a variety of topics that enhance the text material. The topics include the following to support your learning in the course:

- Assessments, including interactive case studies, activities, and video assignments
- Discussion board questions
- Videos, simulations, a lesson plan builder, and other useful course resources

Chapter 13

Teaching Content Knowledge: Pedagogy and Principles

Tetra Images/Alamy

I can name six simple machines. Do you know what kind of machine a boat is? I do.

—Olivia, Grade 2 student

We are talking about habitats, and seeing how animals adapt, and I did a report on the bald eagle. Here's an interesting fact about the bald eagle: If a feather from one wing falls off, in the same place on the other wing, it will also fall off to keep balance.

—Dante, Grade 4 student

I've wanted to be an elementary school teacher all my life!

—Sandeep, preservice teacher candidate

LEARNING OBJECTIVES

- Discuss the role of, and relationship between, content knowledge in the science curriculum and pedagogical content knowledge.

- Describe three levels of scientific concepts that students are expected to navigate and link together.

- Explain how a teacher can use questioning to enhance student learning of content.

- Summarize Bloom's taxonomy and its relevance to pedagogy.

- Explain how a teacher can use analogies, models, and games to enhance student learning of content.

- Describe how technology can enhance student learning of content.

- Discuss the role of education research in teacher development.

21st CENTURY LEARNING SKILLS & COMPETENCIES

❶ Communication

❷ Critical thinking

❸ Collaboration

❹ Creativity

❺ Literacy and numeracy

❻ Media literacy

❼ Technological literacy

INTRODUCTION

We begin this chapter by perhaps stating the obvious: Schooling seems to be largely about understanding and acquiring knowledge of subject matter. By now you are well aware that curricula across the country include knowledge outcomes and expectations in every subject area—be it science, history, English, or physical education. Each discipline has its own body of knowledge that helps define it and that is evolving and dynamic. Science is one such dynamic body of knowledge. The content of science, however, is not simply an archive of facts, but rather is a complex set of interconnected concepts, theories, and laws. "Science is a highly conceptual business, and learning science is about building—and developing—interconnecting frameworks of scientific concepts" (Taber, 2005, p. 127).

Shulman's (1987) theory of teachers' complex knowledge base requires that they have content knowledge (CK) and pedagogical content knowledge (PCK). This chapter focuses primarily on PCK, or the interaction of subject matter and pedagogy, and how teachers transform content into meaningful learning experiences for students. We focus on pedagogy and principles as they relate to knowledge outcomes, particularly knowledge that is categorized as *propositional (factual)*, or *conceptual* in the science curriculum.

There are two core principles underpinning this chapter. The first is the centrality of the learner; the second is the need to attend to diverse learners, keeping in mind that each student brings unique strengths and challenges to your class. Multiple intelligences (see, for example, Gardner, 2006) and differentiated instruction (see, for example, Tomlinson & McTighe, 2006) are other ideas to keep in mind as you develop your PCK.

STUDENTS, CONTENT KNOWLEDGE, AND MEANINGFUL UNDERSTANDING

In Chapter 12, we explored the idea that students may hold misconceptions or alternative frameworks about science concepts and the way the natural world works. These ideas come from a variety of places—media, family, prior school experiences, and students' interactions with the world. However, there is another important reason that students' ideas and understandings can be erroneous or incomplete: Science concepts and content are often complex, abstract, and difficult to grasp.

Lawson, Alkhoury, Benford, Clark, and Falconcer (2000) describe different levels of scientific concepts that students are expected to navigate and link together in science classes; *descriptive, theoretical,* and *hypothetical* concepts. *Descriptive concepts* are those that order and describe experiences. This includes knowing, for example, that fish have gills, and that a rainbow is made up of red, orange, yellow, green, blue, indigo, and violet light. These concepts are usually easiest to grasp and often provide the starting place for learning. *Theoretical concepts* are those concepts that are not directly visible, but are understood and accepted based on empirical evidence, other theories, or models. Examples of theoretical concepts include the concept of gravity and the properties of sound. Finally, *hypothetical concepts* are those that are difficult to observe or describe because of the length of time in which they occur. Hypothetical knowledge can be approached like descriptive knowledge if you were able to observe the phenomenon for a long time. For example, the rock cycle is descriptive in nature but can be observed only over a long period of time—much longer than the human lifespan. Another example is climate change.

ACTIVITY 13.1

21st C **2** **3** **4**

Working with Resources: Descriptive, Theoretical, and Hypothetical Concepts, and the Science Curriculum

In pairs, revisit your knowledge of human body systems, magnets and magnetism, the animal life cycle, the water cycle, the rock cycle, and seasonal changes. Locate a science resource or textbook to support the topics. For each, identify examples of descriptive, theoretical, and hypothetical concepts (if applicable), and complete the table below. We have provided two examples.

Examples of Descriptive, Theoretical, and Hypothetical Concepts

Topic	Descriptive Concepts	Theoretical Concepts	Hypothetical Concepts (if applicable)
Example 1: Human Body Systems			
Example 2: Magnets and Magnetism			
Example 3: Animal Life Cycle			
Example 4: Rock Cycle	Rocks are naturally occurring, solid aggregates of one or more minerals. We can see rocks and describe their appearance.	The composition of rocks represents different combinations of atoms.	If we could wait and watch, we would see rocks being pushed by tectonic forces and eroded by wind and rain.
Example 5: Water Cycle	When it rains, water falls from the clouds. Snow is made up of water. When water is heated (for example, in a kettle), steam is released.	As water particles move faster and faster due to absorption of heat, they change states from a liquid to a gas (one aspect of the particle theory of matter).	If we could wait and watch, we would see aspects of the water cycle (such as rain), but we cannot see the entire cycle as it is happening over time.
Example 6: Seasonal Changes			

As a teacher it is important to (1) understand that there are different types of content; (2) recognize that CK can be difficult for students to learn; and (3) develop PCK that will help students link different knowledge in meaningful ways.

Exploring Scale

A difficult idea for students is the concept of scale, particularly with respect to very large distances or periods of time and very small distances or periods of time. For example, it is difficult for students to understand how small a bacterium or an atom is, or how large the solar system is. Similarly, it is difficult to comprehend what a thousand years means, or how a chemical reaction can take place in a fraction of a second. John Percy, renowned astronomer and winner of the 2013 American Astronomical Society Education Prize, has discussed issues of scale in the teaching of astronomy (2002). He notes that poor understanding of time and distance scales can be a barrier to deep understandings. Activities 13.2 and 13.3 explore scale further.

ACTIVITY 13.2

21st C

Exploring Scale: Deep Time

Time and deep time (very long periods of time) can be challenging for students. Examining a geologic time scale can be helpful, but often students get lost in memorizing names and the order of eras or epochs, such as Cenozoic, Cretaceous, or Miocene. For this activity, you will work in pairs to create a calendar and determine where in time particular events or episodes occurred. A geological time calendar provides a visual of long periods of time. To make a geologic time calendar, find a blank calendar with pages for January to December; January 1 represents the Big Bang, and December 31 is the present. Alternatively, you might create a linear scroll for your calendar that spans several walls. A calendar year of 365 days will represent about 4.5 billion years (or the approximate age of Earth); each day of the calendar is _____ years (round your answer to simplify).

In the calendar, mark the following events on the correct day:

- First single-celled life appears
- First multi-cellular life
- Cambrian "explosion" and trilobites
- First flowering plants
- Pangaea forms
- First fish
- First mammals
- Dinosaurs appear
- Dinosaurs become extinct

- First humans
- Invention of the wheel
- Invention of the printing press
- Pyramids are built
- War of 1812
- First telephone
- First TV
- First cell phone

Try to include at least one milestone event in each month of the calendar. You have now produced a geologic time scale that can be referred to as needed or can be posted in a classroom as a permanent visual aid. Continue to add to the calendar throughout the year as you learn about other significant historical scientific events.

ACTIVITY 13.3

21st C

Exploring Scale: Length and Distance

Adapted from Bosak, S. (1991). Science is…: *A Source book of fascinating facts, projects and activities*. TCP Press.

Diagrams can add to the challenge of understanding conceptual knowledge embedded in scale. For example, long distances between celestial bodies in space and small dimensions of microorganisms can pose conceptual challenges for students. Diagrams, such as the one on the next page that shows the order of planets as evenly spaced, confound the issue and can perpetuate misconceptions. What is the relative distance between the planets and from Earth to the moon, the sun, or other planets?

First, as a class, create a one-page information sheet for each planet, for the asteroid belt, and for the Kuiper belt, noting for each the distance from the sun. Along the school hallway, ask students to represent the sun, each planet, the asteroid belt, and the Kuiper belt by accurately spacing

The Solar System

themselves according to a predetermined scale. Place the sun at one end of the hall. Unravel a roll of paper towel along the floor, and ask students to tape their information sheets to the paper in the correct place.

USING THIS ACTIVITY WITH ELEMENTARY SCHOOL STUDENTS

The following activity has students physically creating a scale model of the solar system using a huge balloon, marbles, tennis balls, a ping pong ball, a basketball, a soccer ball, and baseballs to represent the sun and planets. Alternatively, you could make papier-mâché planets scaled to size. You will need a lot of room; this activity is best done on a playing field. The activity also incorporates mathematics, as students work with conversions of large distances to manageable sizes appropriate for the classroom or playing field.

MATERIALS

- large balloon (2–3 metres in diameter) or beach ball
- one marble
- two tennis balls
- one ping-pong ball
- basketball
- soccer ball
- two baseballs
- trundle wheel
- labelled stick markers (optional)

1. Choose nine pairs of students who will place the planets and the Sun.
2. Go through each of the planets and the Sun, comparing and contrasting their relative sizes. For example,
   - Sun: Large balloon or beach ball (should be much larger than a basketball)
   - Mercury: marble
   - Venus: tennis ball
   - Earth: tennis ball
   - Mars: tennis ball
   - Jupiter: basketball
   - Saturn: soccer ball
   - Uranus: baseball
   - Neptune: baseball
3. Place the Sun at one end of the field.
4. Have partners pace out each of the planets from the Sun: Mercury (4 paces), Venus (7 paces), Earth (10 paces), Mars (15 paces), Jupiter (52 paces), Saturn (95 paces), Uranus (191 paces), and Neptune (301 paces).

continued on next page

5. Have planets hold their positions while another pair of students uses a trundle wheel to measure and record distances from the Sun. You might take a photograph of the model solar system. Use place markers for each planet if you wish to revisit the solar system in another class.

6. Back in the classroom, discuss the creation of the solar system model. What was surprising? What do the relative distances from the Sun tell you about the conditions on the planets and the length of a year (one rotation around the Sun)? Ask students to complete a short journal entry about the size of the solar system.

7. *Assessment*: You might use a rubric to assess students' participation in the model construction and discussion. Anecdotal comments can be made in student journals.

TEACHING WITH ANALOGIES AND MODELS

Many of the concepts taught in science are not observable to the naked eye, or sometimes are too abstract in nature to fully grasp. Analogies and models can be powerful tools for helping students make sense of complex concepts or theories. *Analogies* relate two domains whose elements are semantically different but whose structural relations are similar (Yanowitz, 2001). Take, for example, the analogy of a cell as a factory, the mitochondria of a cell as a power plant, Earth's layers like those of a soft-boiled egg, and the eye operating like a camera. These analogies can help students understand, for example, that the cell has different parts and that each of those parts has a specific form and function. These are but a few of the analogies teachers can use to support learning in life science, physical science, and Earth and space science. Similar to analogies, models can also help students visualize or clarify abstract concepts by using three-dimensional illustrations. So, for example, teachers might use 3-D models of the solar system or plant and animal cells, or actively model the phases of the moon using a flashlight and a basketball or beach ball.

Analogies and models are used to help teachers creatively explain difficult concepts; they can be both engaging and fun for students (Harrison & Coll, 2008; Nashon, 2004). They can make abstract concepts familiar by comparing them to everyday objects and experiences. Most analogy researchers agree that their use can promote learning through constructivist pathways (Harrison & Coll, 2008). Students draw from familiar experiences, interests, knowledge, and ideas of how the world works (Harrison & Coll, 2008) to construct ideas, modify existing schemata, and challenge previously held ones.

Strategies for Using Analogies and Models

Analogies and models are thinking tools; they are not meant to be actual representations of concepts. When using analogies, we recommend the following (based on Harrison & Coll, 2008):

- Be sure that the analogy (sometimes called the *analogue*) or model is familiar to the students in your class.

- Discuss with your students how the analogy is *like* the science concept (sometimes referred to as the *target*).

- Discuss with your students how the analogy is *unlike* the science concept—in other words, where does the analogy fall apart?

- Ask yourself if the analogy is useful and clear, what could be confusing, how it can be improved, or is there a better one.

- Provide opportunities for your students to develop their own analogies. Be sure that they can explain why their analogy is useful and effective, and how it is like and unlike the science concept.

ACTIVITY 13.4

21st C

Connecting Practice and Theory: Using Analogies and Models

In small groups, create an analogy or model for teaching one of the following topics:

- daily and seasonal changes
- properties of liquids and solids
- electrical current
- blood vessels and blood flow
- rocks and minerals and erosion
- layers of the Earth

Watch

Water Wheels Part 2

Provide some context, describe the analogy or the model, and explain how you might use it. Answer the discussion questions below and be prepared to share your responses with your class.

DISCUSSION QUESTIONS

1. Describe how the analogy you created is similar to and different from the science concept.
2. Discuss how the model you created illustrates the science concept. What materials are needed to create the model?
3. Are the analogies you chose inclusive and familiar to your student population? Explain.
4. Is the model one that students will be actively involved in creating or using? If not, how might it be modified to involve students?

TEACHING WITH GAMES

For many, games are an important part of childhood. Played individually or collaboratively, games can entertain, challenge, teach, and sometimes inspire. They often generate curiosity (both sensory and cognitive) when students are confronted, for example, by paradoxes, incompleteness, or challenges. In this section, we briefly examine how games can be included in science instruction to actively engage students in learning.

Games are a useful strategy to motivate students to learn science. They are meant to be fun and challenging. Research suggests that games encourage problem-solving, learning about how we learn (meta-cognition), collaboration, learning new material, and reviewing concepts already studied (Moursand, 2007). Used appropriately, they can also facilitate peer instruction. Receiving and providing feedback from fellow players can improve one's level of expertise and enhance communication skills. Games often facilitate an environment that supports student discourse and social interaction—keys to meaningful learning.

There are a plethora of games to choose from (both digital and non-digital). No doubt you are familiar with the many commercially produced games available to educators, as well as traditional ones that can be easily modified for classroom use—for example, Taboo and Jeopardy. Puzzles and memory games are also useful teaching tools. Crossword puzzles, for example, can be used to help students recall or review content knowledge and vocabulary. Teachers can generate their own crossword puzzles at www.discoveryeducation.com.

More sophisticated games create immersive environments in which players engage in inquiry online (e.g., Martian Boneyards, Blue Mars). Such gaming activities can reflect the habits of practising scientists in professional communities who share data and observations, challenge, and confirm each others' claims, and work together to build theories (Asbell-Clark, 2011; Dunbar, 2000). Gaming can provide opportunities for students to explore science in more immersive environments.

Strategies for Using Games

Information about digital and non-digital games can be found online and through teacher resource catalogues. We encourage you to explore the different kinds of games available, and, as always, to develop a critical lens for determining their usefulness. Be sure to learn your school board policy regarding internet use and the consent needed for students to access it. Below we offer some questions for planning with games:

- Is the game inclusive?
- How does the game support the learning of CK?
- Is the game appropriate for your students and context?
- What will the students learn?
- How is it connected to the curriculum?
- Are there language issues that may cause barriers to learning for some students?

ACTIVITY 13.5　　　　　　　　　　　　　　　　　*21st C*

Analyzing Games

In pairs, locate one digital game and one non-digital game that could be used to teach or review science concepts. Describe and critique the game. Provide some context; for example, identify the grade, topic, connections to the curriculum, citation for the game, and how you would use it with your students. Post your findings on a class wiki or other sharing platform.

DISCUSSION QUESTIONS

1. What knowledge or scientific concepts are learned in this game?
2. What other learning goals are being met (for example, cooperation and numeracy)?
3. What are the strengths of the game?
4. What are the weaknesses of the game?

USING QUESTIONS TO PROMOTE LEARNING

Why do teachers ask questions? Knowing when and how to ask good questions is an important skill for teachers to develop. In this section we revisit the art of questioning from Chapter 6. There are many sound pedagogical reasons for asking good questions. The question-and-answer format can foster a classroom environment that is interactive and engaging. It can also help with classroom management issues. Asking questions provides opportunities to:

- probe students' prior knowledge on the topic
- probe any student misconceptions related to the topic
- check for understanding and consolidate recent teaching and learning
- confirm that goals have been met
- review material
- encourage critical and creative thinking
- help establish relationships and integrate groups that involve students and draw on students' experiences
- generate discussion and share insights
- motivate students

Watch
Curiosity and Interest

Types of Questions

The types of questions asked depend on purpose and context; for example, teachers use questions to probe students, to focus attention, and to check for understanding. Different questions elicit different responses and levels of engagement. In Activity 13.6 below, you will explore a particular category of questions.

ACTIVITY 13.6

21st C ❷ ❸ ❹

Identifying Questions

In groups of four, consider the questions in Group A and Group B. How are these questions similar? How are they different?

Group A:

1. Describe what happens to an apple after it is eaten and moves through the digestive system, from the perspective of the apple.
2. How could you reduce energy use in your home?
3. Why is soil important to all living things?
4. How might you determine the ideal conditions for plant growth?

👁 Watch

Invitation

Group B:

1. What happens when ice is heated?
2. Which planet from the sun is Jupiter (first, second, etc.)?
3. Name the three different types of rock.
4. What makes a mammal different from a bird?

DISCUSSION QUESTIONS

1. What are the strengths and weaknesses of using questions like those in Group A?
2. What are the strengths and weaknesses of using questions like those in Group B?
3. Which types of questions would you prefer to answer and why? Which types would you prefer to ask and why?
4. What are the implications for the classroom if you were to use only questions from Group A or from Group B?

No doubt you noticed that all of these questions have to do with content knowledge related to science. However, the Group A questions allow for multiple responses and for a range of possible answers. These are *open* or *divergent* questions. The Group B questions have a very limited number of acceptable responses, and are referred to as *closed* or *convergent* questions. There are several reasons you could cite for either preference. At times, it will be appropriate to ask more closed-ended questions; at other times, it might be best to ask open-ended questions. Your choice will depend on your goals for the lesson, the content, and the context. What is problematic, however, is an overemphasis or reliance on one type of question. The next section examines questions in more detail, with some suggestions for constructing different kinds of questions.

Bloom's Taxonomy

👁 Watch

Science—Response
Card Activities

Recall Bloom's taxonomy (from Chapter 6), which describes a range of cognitive thinking skills, from lower-order thinking skills (LOTS) to higher-order thinking skills (HOTS).

The taxonomy includes: Remembering, understanding, applying, analyzing, evaluating, and creating. Refer to Table 6.3 to help you with the following activity.

ACTIVITY 13.7

21st C ❷ ❸ ❹

Developing Questions to Teach a Concept

1. Choose a topic of interest from the list below.
   - Compare differences and similarities of series and parallel circuits.
   - Describe how heat is related to changes of state.
   - Describe the life cycle of a plant.
   - Name and describe six types of simple machines.
   - Describe the components of the universe.
   - Compare features of birds, mammals, amphibians, fish, and reptiles.
2. Use a textbook or the internet to locate resources that can be used to familiarize yourself with key ideas.
3. Review types of questions and Bloom's taxonomy.
4. Prepare a 10-minute mini-lesson, consisting of 10 to 12 questions in a logical sequence, in order to teach the material to one of your peers. You may want to use visuals, diagrams, or graphs to support your mini-lesson. Include a brief answer that you would expect for each question. The answers may be in point form. As you organize your questions, begin with a few that assess prior knowledge, and possibly define your terms. Ensure that you have a variety of cognitive levels, and identify the level of each question using the language of Bloom's taxonomy: remembering; understanding; applying; analyzing; evaluating; creating.
5. You may choose to begin with a flow chart if it will help you plan the sequence of questions.
6. Organize your questions in a chart like the one below.
7. Be prepared to teach your mini-lesson to a peer who will act as your student.
8. After teaching your mini-lesson, critique your questions with your classmate.
9. Switch roles with your peer and repeat.

Question	Anticipated answer	Cognitive level

DISCUSSION QUESTIONS

1. Critique the quality of your questions and their cognitive levels.
2. Comment on the variety of questions you created.
3. Comment on the sequence of the questions.
4. What went well? What did not go well?
5. How you might improve the questions with respect to type, order, and level?

TEACHING CONTENT KNOWLEDGE WITH AND THROUGH TECHNOLOGY

Hewitt (2005) outlines three compelling reasons for using technology: (1) concretizing abstract concepts; (2) providing students with tools for analyzing scientific processes; and (3) supporting connections among people as they learn. (See Chapter 1 for more details.) Many technologies can make an abstract theoretical concept more concrete. For example, simulations (such as Gizmos) allow a student to manipulate variables so that students can see relationships (e.g., what happens when water is heated). In addition, simulations help concretize *hypothetical* concepts. For example, processes such as succession or glaciation happen slowly over time. Simulations can allow a student to see these processes unfolding through a time lapse or other representations available through technology.

Technology can also be a powerful tool for analyzing natural phenomena and scientific processes. Consider, for example, probeware and sensors that allow students to collect data such as temperature, pH, and distance travelled over time (see Metcalf & Tinker, 2004). Other technologies, like a simple video camera, can be used to slow time so that students can study the wing movement of a bird in flight, or conversely to speed up time to observe a flower as it comes into bloom (Hewitt, 2005). Technology can be used to support understanding of scientific processes and conceptual development.

The third use of technology described by Hewitt (2005) relates to supporting connections between people as they learn, such as through social media technologies like blogs, Facebook, and Twitter. These technologies can be used in creative ways to help students collaborate with each other and with experts beyond the school. They have the potential to expand the classroom to include subject-specific experts and mentors (such as scientists working in labs and at universities). Technologies also remove the limitations of time and location and allow for communication in different ways. Students in different classrooms, schools, and countries can connect, for example, by sharing large-scale data. Technologies also permit students in the same classroom to create a shared dataset over a period of several weeks and to engage in knowledge building activities. (See Cober, McCann, Slotta, & Moher, 2012.) Other examples include the use of interactive whiteboards, wikis, clickers, and the web. There are many open-source platforms available to educators that encourage and support knowledge-building communities. (See, for example, Slotta & Linn, 2009.) These applications can be used to teach new content, assess prior knowledge, build knowledge collaboratively, and review material learned.

ACTIVITY 13.8   *21st C* ② ③ ④

Using Technology to Support Teaching Content

In groups of four, choose a topic from the Kindergarten to Grade 8 science curriculum and consider the CK learning outcomes or expectations for that topic. Create a student activity that incorporates technology in a meaningful way. For example, you might have students work together to measure and discuss weather patterns or events, or track and document animal growth and change. Prepare the activity in ready-to-use format so that your classmates can use it in the future. Provide context with respect to grade, topic, and how and when the activity might be used.

DISCUSSION QUESTIONS

1. What underlying prior knowledge are you assuming your students have in order to complete this activity?

2. How does the technology support learning of the material?

3. What are students asked to *do* while engaged with the technology?

4. What are the strengths of using this particular technology?

5. What are the challenges of using this particular technology?

👁️ Watch

Pinhole Cameras (Part 1)

Pinhole Cameras (Part 2)

Pinhole Cameras (Part 3)

ACTIVITY 13.9

Read and Reflect: Using Technology in the Science Classroom

Locate and read Niess, M.L. (2005). Preparing teachers to teach science and mathematics with technology: Developing technology pedagogical content knowledge. *Journal of Teacher Education, 21*(5), 509–523, and answer the questions below.

DISCUSSION QUESTIONS

1. Explain what is meant by *technology pedagogical content knowledge* (TPCK)?
2. What are some of the reasons for success and failure when integrating technology?
3. How will you go about learning more so that you can develop your own TPCK?

Developing a Critical Lens When Using Technology

As you develop your PCK around the use of technology in science education (Wallace, 2002), keep in mind the following:

- Knowing how to use technologies such as computers, blogs, and wikis is not the same as knowing how to teach using technologies.
- Use of technology is context-specific—for example, grade, subject matter, goals of the lesson, and student access to technology affect what is desirable and what is possible in a classroom.
- Teaching effectively with technology is time-consuming and requires careful planning and scaffolding.
- Use opportunities to learn from and with your colleagues and students to build your knowledge about the range of technologies available.

As you consider incorporating technology into teaching science, ask yourself some key questions: Is there an authentic purpose to the use of technology? How does the technology enhance student understanding? Is there a better or more effective strategy that does not involve technology? How will I scaffold student learning when students are using technology?

We would be remiss in ending this section without considering the development of a critical lens when accessing science content knowledge through information and communication technologies. There is a wealth of information available online about science content areas, which is both a blessing and a curse. We invite you to think about what you do when you are confronted with conflicting views from different sources. How do you determine if a source is trustworthy, accurate, and reliable? A district curriculum leader in science or a school librarian can be helpful in directing you to reputable resources and websites. However, what are your own critical skills for assessing sources and making decisions that impact your curriculum planning and pedagogy? Consider, for example, the topic of vaccines and vaccinations. What do you know about them? How are they related to disease prevention? Are they safe? Why do some parents refuse to have their children vaccinated? How do you know what you know about vaccines? Activity 13.10 presents a chance to explore your critical literacy skills.

ACTIVITY 13.10

Developing Critical Literacy Skills: Vaccines: Friend or Foe?

Research the following aspects of vaccines and vaccination: their development, how a new vaccine is tested, their disease prevention qualities, and any controversy around their use. Be sure to research widely; don't just stop at the first source that you find. Gather information from the following types of sources:

- at least one textbook (e.g., a medical textbook)
- at least one magazine or newspaper (e.g., a popular magazine that focuses on science)
- at least one peer-reviewed medical journal (e.g., *Nature*, *The Lancet*)
- at least one website (other than a website from which you would access any of the above)
- at least one human source (e.g., a person you trust who has knowledge of vaccines—this might be a person you speak to or a person who is interviewed on television or radio)

Make a list of the sources you used, the key points you learned from each source, and, in your estimation, whether the claims made are warranted and why you think so. Form small groups to compare your findings. A chart such as the one below may be helpful.

Source	Key points or claims	Do you believe the claims? Why or why not?

DISCUSSION QUESTIONS

1. What do you now know about vaccines that you did not know before?
2. How did you determine whether a source was reputable and reliable? What criteria did you use?
3. How would you help your students learn critical literacy skills?

ACTIVITY 13.11   *21st C* ❷❸❹

Read and Reflect: Teaching Elementary Science

Read one of the articles below and write a one-page reflection that (a) summarizes your reaction to the paper and (b) describes what you anticipate being your strengths and areas for professional growth as you prepare for teaching elementary science. Choose three points from your reflection to discuss with a partner. Mulholland and Wallace (2005) describe a teacher's growth with respect to PCK over a 10-year period, while Smith (1997) examines how elementary preservice teachers acquire science CK.

Mulholland, J., & Wallace, J. (2005). Growing the tree of teacher knowledge: Ten years of learning to teach elementary science. *Journal of Research in Science Teaching, 42*(7), 767–790.

Smith, R. G. (1997). "Before teaching this, I'd do a lot of reading": Preparing primary student teachers to teach science. *Research in Science Education, 27*(1), 141–154.

TEACHERS' WORK AND PROFESSIONAL DEVELOPMENT

Concerns around learning CK are ever present. Teachers need to navigate curriculum documents; follow school, school board, and provincial educational initiatives; organize materials, equipment, and resources; select teaching and assessment strategies; examine and learn how to use new technologies related to science; and evaluate student progress.

A Case Study: Teaching About Light and Sound

Karl is a first-year teacher with a teaching schedule of core Grade 7 (language arts and mathematics) in the mornings, and Grade 4, 5, and 6 science in the afternoons. He has been busy but is happy in his first year. His background is in physical education and biology, so he feels comfortable with such science topics as the human body, living things, and basic biochemistry. Next, he is going to teach light and sound to the Grade 4 students. This is outside of his expertise. Karl knows he has lots to learn, and so begins reading and preparing. With so many new terms and unfamiliar processes, he begins to feel a bit overwhelmed.

He begins to wonder: Light and sound are complex enough, but light travels in a straight path, while waves travel in all directions—what's that about? And properties of light, such as bending and refracting, add to his confusion. Diagrams seem to be labelled for the expert, not the learner, and he wonders how his students will cope. Frustrated, he asks a colleague for advice. She proves to be very helpful, but in talking to her he sheepishly admits that he had misunderstood some of the material and had been adding to his misconceptions about light and waves. She suggests a couple of good references. In addition, he does some reading about misconceptions, as it is easy to find information online.

Karl starts to wish there were two of him to get all the work done. Venting one day at lunch, another colleague suggests a website with lesson plan ideas and a computer simulation for teaching light and sound. He also gives Karl some good advice: "You have to stop reading and learning new stuff at some point, and plan some lessons!" Just when Karl thinks he could not do another thing, his principal asks if he'd like to attend a board professional development session. The session will focus on the Grades 4–8 science curriculum for the purpose of starting a professional learning community to help all teachers in the school teach science. Karl realizes two things: He needs more professional development and this would be a great opportunity, and he needs more hours in the day. So, as beginning teachers do, he says yes to the invitation and goes home to plan his lessons.

ACTIVITY 13.12

21st C **2 3 4**

Teaching and Learning for Beginning Teachers

The scenario above raises many questions about learning new content, especially for those of you teaching outside your area of expertise. Recognizing, unravelling, and addressing misconceptions; using technology as a teaching tool; and accessing professional development are ongoing challenges for teachers. With the scenario in mind, answer the questions that follow.

DISCUSSION QUESTIONS

1. Name all the challenges that Karl is facing in his work.
2. What is his approach to learning the new content?
3. What might be other ways for non-specialists to learn content they need to know in order to teach science effectively?
4. How might a teacher stay current? What are the best ways to explore issues that are in the news—for example, the claim that coffee is good for you because of the antioxidants it contains?
5. In using the internet to research, how might Karl ensure that he is using his time wisely and visiting reputable sites?
6. How might you approach identifying and addressing your own misconceptions?
7. What would you envision as the most meaningful professional development for yourself in your first year of teaching?
8. What is a professional learning community?

Professional Learning Communities

One form of professional development commonly used today is professional learning communities (PLCs). PLCs are often formed in schools by groups of teachers who come together for a common purpose. Teachers may establish PLCs, for example, to discuss the best implementation plan for a new or revised curriculum released by a province or territory, or to explore how to integrate literacy and numeracy into their science program. A community of practice can be defined as a group of people who share tools, rules, beliefs, tacit knowledge, and areas of interest through their engagement in common practices and goals—often with clearly defined, goal-oriented activities over an extended period of time (Lave & Wenger 1991; Pedretti & Bellomo, in press; Wenger, 1998, 2000). In Stoll, Bolam, McMahon, Wallace, and Thomas's (2006) review of the literature on PLCs, they write:

> There is no universal definition of a professional learning communities [sic]. PLC may have shades of interpretation in different contexts, but there appears to be broad international consensus that it suggests a group of people sharing and critically interrogating their practice in an on-going, reflective, collaborative, inclusive, learning-oriented, growth, promoting way. . . . [T]he notion, therefore draws attention to the potential that a range of people based inside and outside a school can mutually enhance each others' and pupil's learning as well as school development. (pp. 222–223)

Characteristics of PLCs include support and shared leadership, collective creativity, shared values and vision, supportive conditions, collaboration, and shared personal practice. (DuFour Eaker, & DuFour, 2005) Additionally, PLCs help build teacher confidence and enhance practice (Le Bouthillier, Bourgoin, & Kristmanson, 2011). In schools, PLCs can form across grades or divisions, across disciplines, and for different purposes such as school policy renewal; parent community involvement; and curriculum development, implementation, and assessment.

CONTINUING THE JOURNEY

We are happy to have been part of your professional learning journey to becoming a teacher. We wish you the very best as you embark on this new and exciting profession. Teaching science can be rewarding and joyous as you provide opportunities for your students to explore the wonders and beauty of the natural world. Central to teaching and learning science, indeed to teaching and learning in general, are student interests, needs, learning strengths, and aspirations. We invite you to re-imagine a science education that is empowering, engaging, and authentic for all students.

We have created several appendices to support you as you begin your teaching career:

- Appendix A: Strategies and Graphic Organizers
- Appendix B: Preparing for Your Practicum
- Appendix C: Making a Successful Beginning to the School Year
- Appendix D: Favourite Assignments
- Appendix E: Suggested Children's Literature for Elementary Science
- Appendix F: Planning for Field Trips

CONCLUDING THOUGHTS

In this chapter, we focused on teachers developing PCK in relation to teaching scientific knowledge that is conceptual, theoretical, or hypothetical in nature. Although we examined building questioning skills and using analogies, models, technologies, and games to enhance conceptual understanding, keep in mind that the learner is central to pedagogy. Teachers should begin with what the learner already knows, and work toward actively engaging students, utilizing different learning styles, and designing experiences that encourage students to explore new ideas. In this way, students can construct meaningful understandings of scientific concepts and the workings of the natural world.

What follows is a summary of the key ideas related to the learning objectives provided at the beginning of the chapter.

Content knowledge and pedagogical content knowledge

Content knowledge is knowledge of subject matter, while pedagogical content knowledge refers to the interaction of subject matter and effective pedagogy. PCK is how teachers transform content into meaningful learning experiences for students.

Levels of scientific concepts

Descriptive concepts allow teachers to order and describe experiences, and include knowing, for example, that fish have gills or that Earth is the third planet from the sun. *Theoretical concepts* are those that are not directly visible, but are understood and accepted based on empirical evidence, other theories, or models—for example, the concept of gravity and the properties of sound. *Hypothetical concepts* are those that are difficult to observe because of the length of time in which they occur—for example, climate change or the rock cycle.

Questions that promote learning

Knowing how to ask good questions is an important skill for teachers. Question-and-answer formats can foster a classroom environment that is interactive and engaging, and they can probe students' prior knowledge, check for understanding, encourage critical thinking, motivate students, and consolidate teaching and learning.

Bloom's taxonomy and its relevance to pedagogy

Bloom's taxonomy captures an array of cognitive thinking skills, ranging from lower- to higher-order skills. Bloom's original taxonomy includes knowledge, comprehension, application, analysis, synthesis, and evaluation. More recently, this taxonomy was modified slightly; synthesis was replaced with creating, and knowledge with recall or remembering.

Using analogies, models, and games

Analogies can be powerful tools for helping students visualize and understand concepts that are too abstract or conceptually complex. Similarly, models also help students understand abstract concepts or concepts that are too *small* or *large* in scale. Games can stimulate curiosity, challenge, motivate, and inspire students in learning science content.

The role of technology

Three compelling reasons for using technology to teach science content include (1) concretizing abstract concepts, (2) providing students with tools for analyzing scientific processes, and (3) supporting connections between people as they learn.

Education research related to content and pedagogy

Research focusing on CK in science and the development of PCK is vast. We have drawn upon several researchers in the field, including Benjamin Bloom, Richard Coll, Allan Harrison, Jim Hewitt, Anton Lawson, Marsha Linn, Samson Nashon, Margaret Niess, and James Slotta. We encourage you to read the work of these researchers as well as the many others who have contributed to this field over the past few decades.

BRINGING IT ALL TOGETHER: FINAL QUESTIONS

1. What content areas are you concerned about teaching?
2. Discuss the relationship between CK and PCK.

MyEducationLab®   Visit MyEducationLab® to access an electronic version of the text, as well as a variety of topics that enhance the text material. The topics include the following to support your learning in the course:

- Assessments, including interactive case studies, activities, and video assignments
- Discussion board questions
- Videos, simulations, a lesson plan builder, and other useful course resources

MyEducationLab®

Appendix A
Strategies and Graphic Organizers

Teaching science makes use of a number of strategies, some of which are particular to the discipline, such as conducting science investigations. In this appendix, we describe instructional strategies and graphic organizers that can be powerful tools in science curriculum and instruction. This is not meant to be an exhaustive list, but rather reflects some of our favourite strategies and organizers—some that we have referenced in earlier chapters. Many strategies and graphic organizers need to be explicitly taught to students to ensure success. The more practice students have using a strategy or graphic organizer, the richer the experience and the product. For convenience, we present these ideas in alphabetical order and, at the end of the appendix, provide a bibliography of additional readings.

Strategies and Graphic Organizers:

- Carousel
- Concept Map
- Consequence Mapping
- Debate
- Flow Chart
- Jigsaw
- Learning Centres
- Literature Circles
- Know, Want to Know, Learned (KWL)
- Mind Map
- Role Play and Drama
- Science Notebook
- Six Thinking Hats
- Think-Pair-Share (and Share Again)
- Town Hall Meeting
- Values Continuum
- Venn Diagram
- Word Wall

CAROUSEL

Carousel is a cooperative brainstorming strategy that can be used to help students access prior knowledge, review what they have learned, or explore a new topic. This is accomplished by having students work in small groups to think about and record their ideas about subtopics within a broader topic. Initial ideas are shared, critiqued, and expanded through interactions with other groups.

Process

1. Choose a topic for the activity and divide it into subtopics (e.g., *animals* can be broken down into *mammals*, *amphibians*, *reptiles*, *birds*, and *fish*).

2. Put the title of each subtopic on a separate piece of chart paper. Alternatively, you might use interactive whiteboards or tablets for recording ideas. If doing so, please substitute that technology throughout the process that follows.

3. Divide students into small groups. The number of groups should equal the number of subtopics.

4. Provide each group with one piece of labelled chart paper and a different colour marker. Let students know that they will have five to ten minutes (less time for younger students, more for older students) to record all of their ideas related to the topic on their sheet. Encourage students to use key words or short phrases. Students can also include pictures and diagrams (sometimes called *graffiti*).

5. Have students display their chart papers in designated spaces on walls around the classroom, creating a circle of charts. Create a circle of tablets if you are using them.

6. Groups rotate from one chart to the next in a carousel, circling to read the charts of other groups and add their own ideas. Begin this step by having each group stand in front of their own chart. Specify the direction of movement; have each group move to the chart next to them in the specified direction. Give groups three to five minutes to read each chart and add ideas or queries to it in a different colour. By having each group use a different colour marker, you will be able to assess each group's thinking and contribution to the activity. Continue until each group has contributed to each chart.

7. By the end of step 6, groups should be in front of their original work. Have them read the additions and respond to any queries.

8. Finally, collect all the charts and post them at the front of the classroom. If using tablets, display all of the ideas on an interactive whiteboard. Use the sheets to stimulate a broader discussion of the big ideas of the topic or to facilitate the review.

Benefits

- Carousel allows for movement around the classroom and social interaction.
- The strategy provides a climate in which students can take ownership of their learning by constructing meanings with each other rather than relying solely on the teacher's authority.
- It provides opportunities for all students to participate in the discussion, especially students who find it difficult to share ideas in large groups.
- As with all cooperative learning strategies, carousel helps foster friendships and social development.

Additional Tips or Variations

- The ideal group size for this activity is four members. Depending on class size, the chosen topic should be divided into enough subtopics to facilitate groups of four.
- To facilitate group work you can assign specific roles for students within groups (e.g., recorder, leader, time keeper, and checker).

- During the carousel (step 6), by the third or fourth move you may need to give students a little more time to interact with the charts or prompts since the more obvious ideas would have already been recorded.

- With younger students, or during students' first few times doing carousel activities, you might have adult or older elementary volunteers help guide discussions and scribe for each subtopic.

CONCEPT MAP

A concept map is a graphical tool for organizing and representing knowledge. Concept mapping is a strategy to help students deepen their understanding of the relationships between concepts. Concepts, usually denoted by boxes or circles, are connected with arrows in a branching structure. The relationship between concepts are articulated by linking phrases or words such as *produces*, *helps*, *needs*, and *is a part of*. Concept maps are similar to mind maps in that they both are graphical tools that use images, words, and symbols to represent thinking. However, where a mind map reflects what you think about a single concept, a concept map is a systematic view of a related set of concepts. It can have multiple branching hubs and clusters. Concept mapping can be done by individual students, small groups, or a whole class; these maps are helpful in determining students' prior knowledge at the start of a unit and what they have learned at the end of a unit. Figure A.1 depicts a concept map for green plants.

Process

1. Introduce a concept that is familiar to all students (e.g., weather, energy).

2. Ask students to list 10 other concepts that they associate with this main idea. If your students are new to concept mapping, you might get them started by providing three or four concepts. Ask them to think about how the concepts are related.

3. Have students connect the concepts two at a time, with directional links—that is, arrows with linking labels on them. Linking labels are short explanatory phrases of how concepts are related (e.g., *sun* can be linked to *energy* with the linking label *is a renewable source of*.

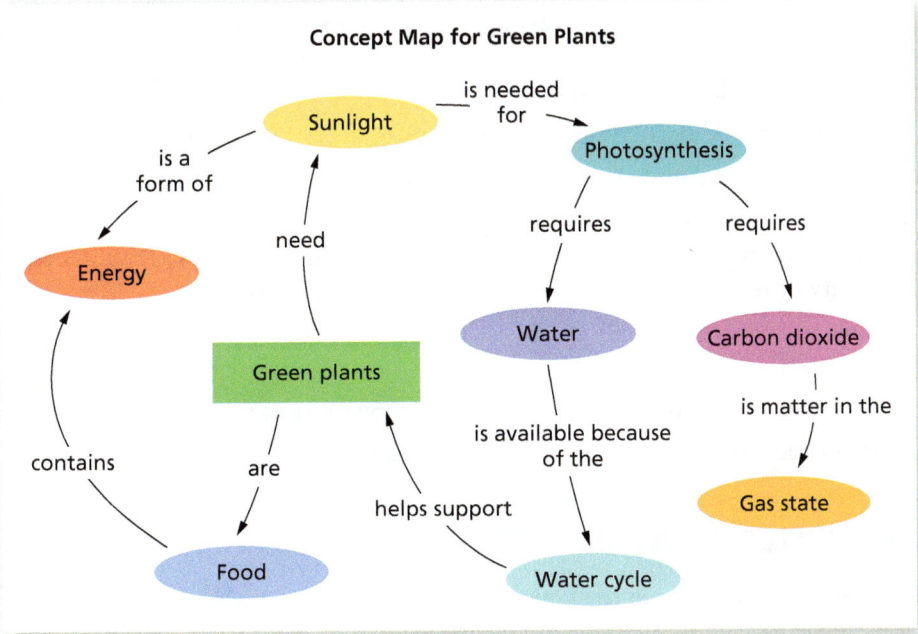

Figure A.1 Concept map

4. The students should continue this process until all the concepts appear on the map. Encourage them to include a lot of branching and many levels of hierarchy. Place special emphasis on cross-linking concepts in one area of the map to other areas. Suggest that they add as many additional concepts as they wish to make the maps personally meaningful.

5. At the end of the exercise, discuss the process of creating a concept map. Which concepts were easy to connect? Which were challenging to relate to each other? Select several students to share their maps with the class to demonstrate the diversity of thinking in the class.

Benefits

- Concept maps facilitate thinking about related concepts. Students can use them to consolidate key concepts, and teachers can use them to assess student understanding.

- Concept maps can also be used as advanced organizers to introduce a new topic in class.

- The strategy encourages higher-order thinking by revealing connections and helping students see how individual ideas relate to form a larger whole.

- Concept maps can be effective for visual learners or English language learners.

Additional Tips or Variations

- Students need to be taught how to create complex concept maps. For example, you might give students a list of concepts to work with instead of having them create a list on their own. You might also provide a partially completed concept map with blank concept boxes or linking labels. Another variation is to provide a focus question for students to work from. For example, instead of asking students to create a concept map for food, you might provide the focus question, How is food digested in the human body?

- Provide students with plenty of time (20 to 30 minutes) to create their maps.

- Have students create a concept map with a partner. Or, create a class concept map. This is particularly useful for students new to concept mapping or to introduce a topic.

- Ask students to revisit their concept maps throughout a unit and make additions based on their learning. Additions can be made in different colours, allowing you to easily follow their developing understandings.

- Include pictures or diagrams in the concept map.

- Use science vocabulary from your word wall as the concepts to be connected. This can provide a good unit review.

- Circulate the room to support students as they create their maps. Try to encourage creativity by reminding students there is no one correct answer.

- Encourage students to use short, precise linking phrases and only one or two words in concept boxes.

- Students can modify or redraw their maps as many times as they like.

- Students can also use software programs to complete their concept maps.

CONSEQUENCE MAPPING

In this strategy, students have the opportunity to illustrate in a visual diagram the range of effects related to a real or imaginary event, issue, trend, or technology. It encourages students to imagine future possibilities. Consequence mapping involves creating a flow diagram stemming from a central *what if* question and can be particularly useful when teaching science, technology, society, and environment (STSE) topics. Depending on the question posed, consequence mapping can be used across the elementary grades.

Process

1. The teacher provides a central *what if* question. Examples include: What if there were no trees in the neighbourhood? What if we did not have access to clean water? What if we had no electricity? What if a chemical dump was planned for your community? What if there were more robots in society? The *what if* questions are repeatedly posed and consequences considered.

2. Students can be provided with a template that includes the *what if* question, or they can draw their own on chart paper or a tablet.

3. Students complete the diagram, considering scientific, social, ethical, legal, economic, environmental, and personal consequences. Consider your students' level and the depth of the consequences that you would like them to explore.

Figure A.2 shows a consequence map that corresponds to the question: What if the oil ran out?

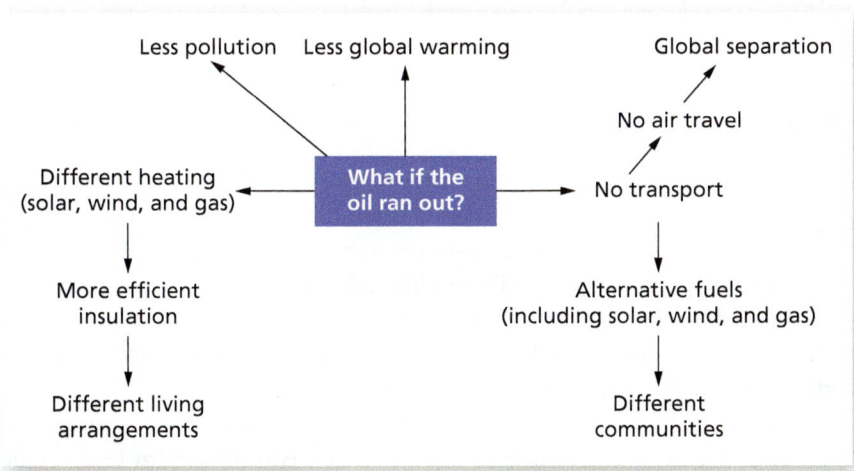

Figure A.2 Consequence map: What if the oil ran out?

Adapted from Alsop & Pedretti (2001).

Benefits

- Consequence mapping can provide an opportunity for students to consider science in relation to larger social, cultural, political, environmental, and economic forces.

- Consequence mapping encourages discussion, collaborative learning, and creative thinking.

Additional Tips or Variations

- Approach consequence mapping in steps. Begin by having your students consider just one or two consequences (e.g., environmental and social). Consequence mapping can be overwhelming, so it is best to start off small, gain confidence and comfort with the process, and build from there.

- Have students work with a partner or in small groups to encourage discussion and collaborative meaning making.

- It is helpful to provide students with prompts to guide their thinking, particularly if consequence mapping is new to them. The following questions can help students extend their mapping. The questions will need to be modified to meet your curricular outcomes and your students' level.

A.   Scientific consequences: What science is this based on? What scientific information, if any, might change your view on this issue?

B.   Social consequences: Who does this affect? How are different groups of people affected? Who does it bring together, and who does it exclude? What effects will it have on how we live?

C.   Ethical and legal consequences: What individual rights might be violated? Does the issue harm people or environments? Do the positive effects outweigh the negative impacts? What are the related ethical issues?

D.   Economic consequences: Is it desirable or undesirable in global, national, regional, or local contexts? What is the impact on employment or economic stability?

E.   Environmental consequences: How does it affect our environment in the short term? In the long term?

F.   Personal consequences: How does it affect you, your family, and your friends in the short term? In the long term?

DEBATE

In this strategy, students have the opportunity to debate an issue. Debating is structured argumentation in which two opposing teams defend and challenge a given proposition. The intent of the strategy is to engage learners in a combination of activities and skills, such as research, active listening, public speaking, decision making, and critical thinking, and to enable them to actively interact with controversial topics arising from the curriculum. Formal debate is bound by rules that vary by location and participants. The process can be adjudicated and a winner is declared based on the quality of their arguments, their defense, and their rebuttal of opponent's arguments. A formal debate strategy follows a Lincoln-Douglas debate, a one-to-one strategy in which two sides of an issue are debated. This format has long been used to stage classroom debates. Depending on the age and level of your students, you will need to adapt the format accordingly by modifying and omitting steps as you see fit. Do not shy away from having primary students participate in modified debates—they often have very strong opinions! The formal process is summarized below.

Process

1. Make a statement or provide a question to the class; for example, Should we have only meatless school lunches?

2. Divide students into two sides based on their agreement (Affirmative side) or disagreement (Negative side) with the topic. Each side should have at least six students. A third group of students can be assigned to act as judges.

3. Allow students several days to research the topic and prepare their arguments.

4. While all students should assist in preparing for the debate, each team should choose a speaker. Other students on the team can take on other roles—for example, acting as time keepers or note takers.

5. On the day of the debate, the Affirmative side begins the process, which is structured as follows:

    a. Affirmative debater presents constructive debate points (6 minutes).
    b. Negative debater cross-examines affirmative points (3 minutes).
    c. Negative debater presents constructive debate points (6 minutes).
    d. Affirmative debater cross-examines the negative points (3 minutes).
    e. Affirmative debater offers first rebuttal (4 minutes).
    f. Negative debater offers first rebuttal (6 minutes).
    g. Affirmative debater offers second rebuttal (3 minutes).

6. During the debate, the teacher acts as a moderator and ensures the format is followed.

7. Students judging the debate should be asked to keep a running tally of points as they are introduced by each team.

8. (optional) After the debate, the judges should be allowed time to decide which side won. In giving their decision, they should present a summary of all points for and against the issue and justify how they chose the winner.

Benefits

- Debates can help students formulate arguments based on evidence.
- Debates can foster open-mindedness and respect as different views are considered.

Additional Tips or Variations

- Students need to be taught how to debate. Discuss with them the ideas of arguing differences of opinion in a calm, rational manner. Suggest that debating is simply a structured way of arguing one's position.
- Introduce vocabulary associated with debating, such as proposition, rebuttal, evidence, and hypothesis. Introduce some of the devices of argument and ways to spot faulty arguments.
- Choose a controversial topic for debate. It should not have a simple yes/no answer, but should be one with many dimensions, which students can explore in a meaningful way.
- Encourage the formation of equally strong teams.
- Provide students with a clear format for the debate.
- Provide students with a rubric that lists the criteria on which they will be judged.
- Although competition is part of the debate process, for classroom use, emphasize that it is not the success at winning but rather the evidence of preparation and quality of delivery that are important.
- On the day of the debate, prepare the room layout to facilitate the activity.

FLOW CHART

A flow chart is a graphic organizer that visually links a series of steps (for example, steps in an investigation of magnets). Flow charts are a useful tool for communicating how processes work or for clearly documenting how a particular task is done.

Process

1. Choose a process or task for which students will make a flow chart.
2. Students may work individually or in small groups.
3. Ask students to list the decisions that need to be made to accomplish the process or task.
4. Write the steps in the order they should be completed.
5. Next, ask students to map the steps in flow chart format, using appropriate symbols for the start and end, for actions to be taken, and for decisions to be made.
6. Finally, ask them to review the flow chart to ensure that it is an accurate representation of the process or task.

Benefits

- Flow charts highlight and reinforce the importance of temporal order in particular tasks.
- Creating flow charts from oral, visual, or written text can help clarify students' understanding of a process by fostering thinking skills, especially reflective thinking about the process.
- Flow charts can encourage clarity and can prevent cognitive overload. They clearly connect steps to lab work and classroom tasks. Students can concentrate on each individual step without feeling overwhelmed by the bigger picture.

Additional Tips or Variations

- Students can be taught a few basic symbols in order to create uniform flow charts that everyone can understand (e.g., elongated circles signify the start and end of processes; rectangles show instructions or actions; and diamonds show decisions that must be made).
- There are several ways the teacher can introduce a subject using flow charts. One way is to provide students with text describing the process or task, which students can use to create the flow chart. Another is to name the process or task and have students brainstorm steps and put them in order.

JIGSAW

The jigsaw activity is an effective way for students to become experts in one area, and then to share that knowledge with peers. Jigsaw involves making groups and regrouping. Clear instructions on movement into and between groups are important for a jigsaw to be successful.

Process

1. Divide the class into small Home Groups. The size of each Home Group is dependent on the number of tasks or questions; for example, if there are four questions to be researched, each Home Group should have four members.
2. Within each Home Group, students negotiate who will be responsible for each question or task. Alternately, you can assign roles by drawing numbers.
3. The students from each Home Group who have selected the same question or task come together to form Expert Groups.

4. Expert Group members work together on what is now a common question or task. Through discussion, research, and collaboration, the group members learn with the understanding that they will return to their Home Groups (as the experts) to teach the material to their peers.

5. Experts go back to their Home Groups. Each expert teaches her or his Home Group members the newly acquired expertise.

Benefits

- A jigsaw strategy can be useful when there are different perspectives to be considered or several topics to be covered.
- Working through a jigsaw activity fosters collaborative learning.

Additional Tips or Variations

- The teacher needs to decide if she or he will provide resource material to be used in class or if students are expected to research using the internet or school library. Consider the time you have for the activity and other learning goals (e.g., internet research skills) for your students.
- Handouts can provide guidance as students begin addressing the questions or tasks.
- Consider the length of time that students will need. Be flexible; productive and collaborative jigsaws often take longer than anticipated.
- Jigsaw activities can be complicated. To help you and your students stay organized, especially when moving from Home to Expert Groups and back, you may wish to make use of labels, colours, or team names.

KNOW, WANT TO KNOW, LEARNED (KWL)

Know, Want to Know, Learned (KWL) can help students recall prior knowledge about a topic, identify what they would like to know or what they wonder about, and share what they have learned. KWL is revisited throughout a unit; the K and W are completed at the start of the unit, and the L is added to over the course of the unit and at its conclusion. It can be completed by students individually, in small groups, or as a whole class and will help you to determine your students' existing understandings. A sample KWL chart follows.

Process

1. Identify the topic for which the KWL chart will be made. Typically this is the topic of a unit of study (e.g., flight, simple machines).

2. Have students work individually, in small groups, or together as a class. With younger students, it is advantageous to work together on a class KWL, particularly when first working with the strategy.

3. Ask students to draw three columns—labelled K, W, and L—on a piece of chart paper or tablet. If working as a class, consider using an interactive whiteboard and ask a student to act as a scribe.

4. In the K column, ask students to list everything they know about the topic. This can include words, pictures, and diagrams.

5. In the W column, ask students to list everything they would like to know about the topic. Here, students can pose questions or list things they want to know more about.

6. Revisit the K column and move any points that students would like to know more about to the W column.

7. If students are working independently or in small groups, have them regroup with the rest of the class and share what they know and what they would like to know. With your students, brainstorm ways that the class can learn about topics and answer questions. You might choose to leave this out of the KWL chart and make your own notes of student ideas.

8. At the end of the unit, as well as at various points throughout, students can revisit the table and summarize what they have learned (L).

K What I know	W What I want to know	Plan for learning	L What I learned
Students record what they already know about the topic.	Students record what they would like to know about the topic.	Brainstorm ideas for how questions can be answered.	After the lesson or unit is complete, students record what they learned.

Benefits

- The KWL organizer is an effective way to access students' prior knowledge. In doing so, KWL charts can help teachers determine students' existing understandings and thus guide planning.
- The strategy can be used individually and can support students' reflections on the unit.
- Students are able to add their voice to curriculum planning.
- KWLs can be particularly effective for young learners, visual learners, and English language learners. As noted, pictures can and should be used in place of words when appropriate.
- Teachers can share what they had planned and negotiate with students what will be included in the unit.

Additional Tips or Variations

- You can provide students with a worksheet of the graphic organizer or can project a KWL chart using an LCD projector so that it is done as a whole class activity.
- At the end of the unit, you can include another column for additional questions or for questions that remain unanswered.

LEARNING CENTRES

Learning centres (often called *activity centres* or *centres*) are spaces in your classroom that are created to allow students easy access to learning materials. Learning centres are designed to encourage active learning, and can be used by individual students or small groups, and with or without direct adult guidance. They might relate directly to a curricular topic (e.g., properties of water), connect to broader skills and understandings (e.g., science process skills), and typically feature materials that can be manipulated or media that can be explored. Often centres are cross-curricular and thematic in nature and integrate science with, for example, social studies, visual arts, literacy, and numeracy. As students are able to interact with the learning materials in their own way, learning and understanding become personalized. Learning centres take time to plan and create. Creating centres with another teacher or including students in planning your centres can be helpful. The benefits to your students' learning make the preparation well worth it!

While learning centres vary widely depending on student interests, abilities, and learning styles and teacher goals and comfort, there are generally three types: enrichment centres, skill centres, and exploration centres. Enrichment centres offer students the opportunity to freely explore ideas and phenomena related to a unit being taught in class. Usually these centres are used following a class lesson on a topic (e.g., characteristics of solids and liquids). Skill centres, like enrichment centres, are used following a class lesson but are more structured and focus on reinforcing ideas taught in class. Exploration centres build upon the interests of students and do not necessarily align with the curricular sequence. Here, students might explore simple machines through play with a range of toys, even though the topic being covered in science class is habitats and communities. Centres can be permanent (such as a reading centre) or created for specific topics (such as exploring levers and pulleys).

There is no set process for using learning centres in your instruction. Practically, though, there are some questions and considerations to keep in mind.

- How many centres will you have in your classroom? You might have a science lesson that consists of four different centres for groups of students to explore different aspects of a concept. Alternatively, you might have one centre that individual students rotate through. The number of centres will influence how and when they are included in the day.

- When will your students use the centres? It is often a good idea for students to work at centres early in the day when they are alert and focused, allowing for rich and meaningful learning; this is also typically a convenient time for classroom volunteers. Determine what time of day will work best for your students.

- For what period of time will students work at the centres? Again, this depends on the number of centres as well as the activity at each. If you are using centres for a class period, you might have students work at a centre for 20 minutes and then switch to another. In general, younger students will be able to work for shorter periods of time while older students will be able to work for longer.

Benefits

- Learning centres can bring together all areas of the curriculum.
- Learning centres allow students to actively participate in hands-on learning experiences.
- Groups working together at learning centres learn collaboratively as they interact with the materials; this also supports social skill development.
- Learning centres can allow students to choose what they explore and how they explore it, making learning personalized.
- Learning centres can allow students to participate in a range of science investigations that might not be possible in whole-class lessons.

Additional Tips and Variations

- Vary the use of centres. Use several in a lesson where groups of students rotate through them, and also use centres that students visit individually outside of a lesson.
- Vary the types of learning centres you create (enrichment, skills, and exploration).

LITERATURE CIRCLES

Literature circles (or reading circles) are much like book clubs. Students meet regularly to discuss readings in depth. The group's discussion is directed by student responses to the reading (fiction or non-fiction); these include conversations about themes, characters, and plot; concepts; and the students' personal connections to the reading. Each group member takes on a role to guide the discussion, dependent on what your goals are as well as their age, ability, and experience. Possible roles include director (creates questions for the group to consider), passage selector (chooses excerpts from the reading that are important or particularly interesting), vocabulary finder (chooses new, unfamiliar, or challenging vocabulary from the reading), connector (makes connections between the reading and prior knowledge and other readings), and summarizer (summarizes the main points of the reading and the discussion). As students work collaboratively and engage in critical thinking and reflection, they are able to enrich their understandings and construct new meanings with peers. Used in science teaching, literature circles can be used for science-related children's literature or non-fiction books. Schlick Noe and Johnson's (1999) *Getting Started with Literature Circles* and Daniel's (2002) *Literature Circles: Voice and Choice in Book Clubs and Reading Groups* are valuable resources that can help you incorporate literature circles into your teaching. Please see Appendix E for a list of children's literature that can be included in science literature circles.

Process

1. Create literature circle groups of four or five members. Students can choose their own groups or be assigned.
2. Have group members select their roles. If you wish, you can assign roles.
3. Assign the reading to be completed and decide on a meeting date.
4. Prior to the meeting, students read the book and prepare for their meeting, keeping their role in mind.
5. On the meeting date, have students move into their groups and begin their discussions.
6. Circulate between groups, helping to facilitate discussions where needed and posing questions to extend thinking.

Benefits

- A deeper, richer meaning can be made of text through collaboration with peers.
- Students are able to enhance their social skills as they work together.
- Literature circle discussions, while guided by teacher input, are directed by students' responses and connections to the text, and as such they can encourage student ownership of learning.
- Literature circles can bring literacy seamlessly into all subject areas, including science.

Additional Tips and Variations

- Literature circles can be more or less teacher-directed depending on your students' needs and experience. Initially, it can be helpful to provide a list of questions or prompts to guide students' reading and participation. As your students gain experience and confidence with the process and with their role in it, allow them to take the lead and reduce the amount of scaffolding you provide.

- Combine literature circles with jigsaw. Have each circle discuss in depth a particular aspect of the reading (e.g., plot, characters, setting) and then use a jigsaw to rearrange groups to share their discussions.

- Have each group read a different, but thematically related, book. For example, groups might read different books related to Earth, the sun, and moon.

MIND MAP

Mind mapping can help students structure and visually organize their thinking by physically mapping words, phrases, pictures, and symbols in relation to a central idea or concept. Mind maps are similar to concept maps; however, where a concept map may have several concepts and connecting relationships, a mind map focuses on a single, central concept. Depending on your own and your students' preferences, you may or may not choose to use rectangles and ovals to frame central concepts and related ideas, respectively. It can be useful to create mind maps with Post-it notes; this will allow you to easily group related ideas together. Similarly, using a computer program to create the map will allow for ease of rearranging ideas and clustering thoughts. Once completed, you may wish to extend students' work by having them identify and label relationships between ideas along the connecting lines (similar to a concept map). Figure A.3 provides an example of a mind map.

Process

1. Draw a rectangle in the centre of a page with several radiating lines or branches and ovals as a starting point.

2. Inside the rectangle identify a topic in words or in an image that you want to mind map.

3. Brainstorm and record related idea in the connected ovals.

4. Check each idea to see whether it is an extension of an existing idea. If it is, then continue on that branch. If it is a variation of an existing idea then draw another side-branch. If the idea is something new, then draw a new branch from the rectangle in the centre.

5. After the mind map has taken shape and you have finished generating ideas, look for linkages or clusters between pieces of information. Highlight linkages and groupings with symbols, arrows, or colours.

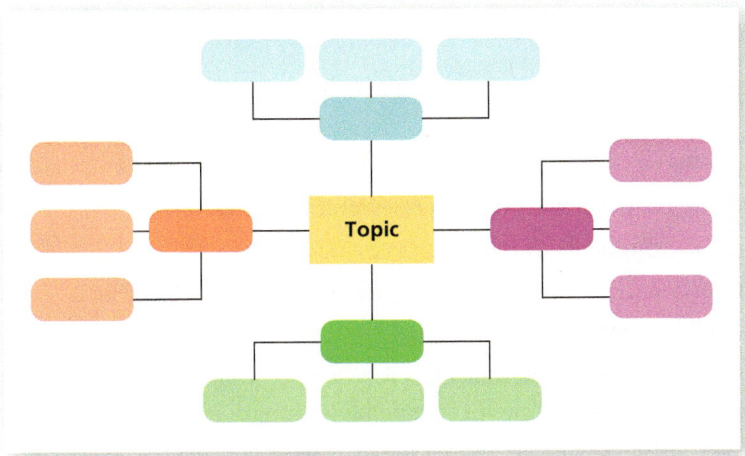

Figure A.3 Creating a mind map

Benefits

- Mind maps are visual, easy to use, can be made in little time, and can help to start a conversation around a given topic.

- There are many ways to use mind maps. They can be developed into strategies for brainstorming, note taking, studying, and report writing.

- Mind maps are visual, and can be easier for some students to remember than linear notes.

- Mind mapping can stimulate creative thinking and assist during problem-solving activities because they work the way the brain works—in an associative rather than a linear way.

- The strategy encourages students to take ownership of their learning and to develop connections to new ideas rather than relying solely on the teacher's direction.

Additional Tips or Variations

- There is no correct starting point once the central image or word is established, and it is not necessary to work in a sequential order. Add branches and ideas as they come to mind.

- With young students, or if mind mapping is a new strategy for your students, work as a class.

- Vary the size of words to denote importance.

- In addition to words, key symbols and images can convey ideas. This is especially helpful for younger students.

- Use different colours to highlight or separate different ideas.

- Try not to get stuck in one area; if you get stuck, work in another part of the map.

ROLE PLAY AND DRAMA

In this strategy, students take on a role in order to personalize or dramatize an event or perspective. Role play incorporates research, reflection, planning, rehearsal, and performance. This strategy encourages students to use their artistic talents and imagination.

Process

1. The teacher identifies a context (e.g., topic, story, historical event, socio-scientific issue).
2. Students choose or are assigned roles.
3. Students are provided with time to research their roles.
4. Allow time for students to rehearse in character.
5. Students enact their roles in small groups or before the class. Some examples of possible formats include the following:

    - Create a TV panel show: The class is split into groups, each representing interested parties. Each group assesses or researches information around a given topic. A panel member introduces his or her group's position, and questions are invited from the audience.

- Assume the role of a scientist: In this format, students assume the role of a scientist (i.e., Eugenie Clark, Rachel Carson, Jane Goodall, Stephen Hawking, David Suzuki). Through reading biographies and conducting research, students begin to learn about the socio-cultural context in which the scientist lived and worked. Students then prepare to assume that role in a dramatic presentation and question-and-answer period.
- Re-enact a significant historical event, such as Neil Armstrong's and Buzz Aldrin's walks on the moon.
- Conduct a town hall meeting on an issue such as the possibility of wind turbines being built in your community. Students are asked to role play various stakeholders (e.g., farmers, environmentalists, citizens, industry) and to develop and present an argument based on a particular position.

Benefits

- This strategy encourages integration of dramatic arts and science.
- Role play can foster appreciation, empathy, reflection, and understanding of different perspectives.
- Role play contextualizes topics and brings issues to the fore in creative and engaging ways.

Additional Tips or Variations

- Be sure to review class expectations with your students (e.g., respectful listening, positive feedback for actors).
- Encourage your students to use props, costumes, and so on to bring their roles to life.
- Start small (e.g., still images or freeze frames) and, as students develop their role-playing skills, move on to more elaborate formats.

SCIENCE NOTEBOOKS

Science notebooks help students develop and strengthen their science understanding while integrating reading, writing, and mathematics. They allow students to record and communicate their science learning from activities such as inquiry-based investigations, class discussions, research, or design technology projects. Students can use them as scientists would—before, during, and after the investigation. Consider reading Michael Klentschy's (2005) *Science Notebook Essentials* as you plan to include science notebooks in your curriculum and instruction.

While components of science notebooks depend on the students' needs and the teacher's curricular intentions, several elements are common. The following process outlines what is typically included in a science notebook; please make adaptations to best fit your students' learning and your teaching. Scaffold the use of the science notebook as your students begin to use them. As they gain more experience, students will take more ownership over their organization and use.

Process

1. First, the question or purpose is stated. These often take the form of *how* or *what* questions.

2. Next, students might note predictions for an investigation, which often take the form of *if…then* and *I think…because* statements. The predictions should relate directly to the question posed or the stated purpose of the investigation.

3. Students might next outline the steps to be taken and any other planning prior to conducting the investigation. This component might include the procedural sequence, materials, and a graphic organizer (e.g., tables, charts, Venn diagrams).

4. During the investigation, students make observations using writing, drawing, or both. It is important to remind students to record what they actually see and do, rather than what they think you are looking for. They should also formulate claims or conclusions based on their findings.

5. Next, students consider what they have learned, both explaining their results and reflecting on their understandings. It can be very useful to have a class discussion as students make meaning of their findings.

6. Finally, students look back on the investigation and outline next steps or further questions. These should be extensions to the investigation's original stated question or purpose.

Benefits

- Science notebooks can help students develop and enhance their science understanding.
- Reading, writing, and mathematics skills can be strengthened through the use of science notebooks.
- Students can easily refer back to their notes regarding planning, conducting, and analyzing results from investigations.
- Science notebooks allow teachers to easily assess student achievements and provide feedback to support further growth.
- Students have a record at the end of the year of all the science investigations they have done.

Additional Tips and Variations

- Add, remove, or adapt science notebook components from the above list. For young students, you might include a question: *What do I think will happen? What did I observe? Why do I think this happened?* For older students, you might have them decide on five components to include for a particular investigation.
- Provide students with structured handouts. This can be particularly helpful for young students, those with unique learning needs, and those who are new to using science notebooks.
- Have students create electronic science notebooks.

SIX THINKING HATS

This strategy (de Bono, 1985) is often used to help students in the decision-making process, particularly around tricky ethical questions. Each student adopts a certain "thinking approach," symbolized by a coloured hat (real or imaginary).

Process

1. Organize students into groups. The number of students per group will equal the number of hats or approaches you wish students to take on. For example, you may wish to have

students consider *emotions* and *questions* related to an issue. In this case, you would have groups of two students.

2. Each student in the group picks a coloured hat out of the "thinking hats envelope," and then assumes that role.

- White hat (information and questions): Students should focus on the data available. Have them review the information and see what they can learn from it, looking for gaps in knowledge and trying to fill them. The student with the white hat is the fact finder.

- Yellow hat (benefits): This hat symbolizes values and benefits about an idea or plan—for example, simplicity, effectiveness, efficiency, acceptability, opportunity, lower cost, lower risk, or increased value. The student wearing the yellow hat looks for strengths.

- Black hat (caution, judgement, and assessment): This hat requires the student to play the devil's advocate. He or she should check for evidence, logic, feasibility, impact, and weaknesses of the decision. This hat is used cautiously and defensively. The student wearing the black hat looks for weaknesses.

- Green hat (creativity, different ideas, suggestions): This hat helps students think positively and provides a perspective on the decision. It also calls for creativity, and makes use of phrases like *what if*, *possibly*, and *suppose* to develop creative alternative solutions to a problem. The student with the green hat thinks of new ideas and solutions.

- Red hat (emotions, feelings, and hunches): The student wearing the red hat looks at problems using intuition, gut reaction, and emotion. He or she has empathy, and tries to imagine how other people will react emotionally. The student wearing the red hat expresses emotions and feelings.

- Blue hat (thinking about thinking, process control): The student in the blue hat defines purpose, sets out the agenda, makes observations, facilitates the group's thinking, and decides on next steps. The blue hat controls the sequence of events in the process of decision making, and exercises a role similar to a meeting chairperson. The student with the blue hat acts as the group leader.

3. Have students record their ideas. They might use a table like the one below. Bring the groups together and, as a class, discuss the ideas from each of the hats.

4. Finally, as a class, consider how the input from each hat guides decision making about the issue.

White Hat:	Yellow Hat:	Black Hat:
Looking for Facts	Finding Strengths	Finding Weaknesses
Green Hat:	Red Hat:	Blue Hat:
Offering New Ideas	Expressing Feelings	Recording Processes

Benefits

- Six thinking hats can encourage critical and higher-order thinking skills as students consider different perspectives in the decision-making process.
- Students work collaboratively and can develop positive social interactions with peers.

Additional Tips and Variations

- With elementary school students, particularly K–3 students and those for whom this strategy is new, it is a good idea to start with only one or two thinking hats. For example, students might read a news article or view a news report and, wearing white hats, look for the facts shared in the story. Or, students might work in pairs, with one partner wearing a yellow hat and the other wearing black, to determine the strengths and weaknesses of an issue. As students become more skilled, they can explore multiple hats.

THINK-PAIR-SHARE (AND SHARE AGAIN)

This cooperative discussion strategy is often used during a teacher-centred lesson. It gets its name from the three stages of student action that occur during the activity. The teacher asks the students to think about a specific topic, pair with another student to discuss their thinking, and then share their ideas with the group.

Process

1. Present a question to the class.
2. *Think:* Ask students to quietly ponder their thoughts about the question for a minute or two. They may write down some of their ideas.
3. *Pair:* Ask students to pair up.
4. *Share:* In pairs, students share their thoughts about the question, allowing sufficient time for each partner to talk about his or her ideas.
5. *Share again:* This can be done in several ways. One is to ask each pair to choose one partner to share the group's thoughts with the class. Another way is to ask all students to stand. After each student responds, she or he sits down, along with any other student with a similar response. This continues until all students are seated. During "share" time, the teacher can record responses on the blackboard, whiteboard, or overhead projector.

Benefits

- Participation in a linguistically rich environment enhances learning, especially processing, organization, and retention of ideas.
- The think-pair-share (and share again) strategy fosters higher order thinking skills by actively engaging students in discussing ideas with others.
- The strategy provides the climate for students to take ownership of their learning.
- Students who find it difficult to volunteer an answer in a large group may develop confidence after having discussed their thoughts with a partner.
- Think-pair-share-share ensures that students have sufficient time to formulate responses (sometimes called *wait time*).
- It provides teachers with an opportunity to check for understanding and to determine if it is appropriate to move on.

Additional Tips or Variations

- Students should be given the opportunity to pair with a variety of partners.
- Allow adequate think time for students to formulate and talk through their ideas.

TOWN HALL MEETING

The town hall meeting is used to conduct research about and make personal topics in the science curriculum. Generally speaking, a town hall meeting gives members of a community an opportunity to come together to discuss issues or concerns. A typical town hall meeting includes citizens, representatives of stakeholder groups, and officials. Everyone is given a chance to state their position or raise questions from their own perspective. The culmination of a town hall meeting can vary. Sometimes people are asked to make a decision by voting after considering all the perspectives. At other times the meeting may end with a summary of the main points of discussion. These points may be used to draft policy or to guide further decision making on the issue. As with debating, town hall meetings are commonly used to resolve issues and make decisions in societies.

The town hall meeting strategy represents an authentic introduction to living in a democracy. The following is one format for conducting a classroom town hall meeting. It can be modified to suit teacher and student contexts.

Process

1. The teacher, acting as the moderator, introduces an issue to the class. (For example, the community is debating the potential building of a garbage incinerator near the outskirts of the town.)
2. The town hall date should be set well enough in advance to allow students time to research the issue and prepare supporting arguments.
3. The goals of the town hall meeting should be clearly established. For example, will your students be asked to write position pieces (supported by evidence) once the meeting has ended? Will they work in small groups to set policy?
4. The teacher establishes at least five different perspectives or stakeholder positions, and may choose to provide some information as a starting point.
5. Choose groups of students to role-play each perspective.
6. Allow time for all students to research the issue from the perspective of the stakeholder they represent. Be sure that students research the risks and benefits to society, the environment, and so on, and include information that will back up their positions. They can also generate questions for other stakeholders.
7. Allow time for stakeholder groups to construct supporting statements for their perspectives and choose a speaker to represent their group.
8. On the day of the town hall meeting, the moderator begins by restating the issue and explaining how the meeting will run. During the meeting, one representative speaker from each stakeholder group is allowed five minutes to present the group's arguments. Throughout these presentations, all students should be engaged in taking notes and formulating queries. Following the presentation of perspectives, the audience is given a chance (15 to 20 minutes) to ask questions about stakeholder positions. At the end of the question period, the moderator should present a summary of the main points.

Benefits

- Town hall meetings can foster listening and speaking skills.
- Town hall meetings contextualize topics and bring issues to the fore in creative and engaging ways.

- Students are exposed to a variety of perspectives and learn to appreciate the complexity of issues.

Additional Tips or Variations

- Choose an issue for the town hall meeting that is controversial and has several different, valid perspectives.
- Teach students how to build arguments using facts, claims, and evidence.
- Provide students with a clear format for the meeting.
- Encourage students to make the activity as authentic as possible by dressing appropriately for their roles and adopting appropriate language and manners.
- On the day of the activity, prepare the room to facilitate the meeting.
- Throughout the process, the teacher should ensure that all perspectives are equitably explored and particular views are not privileged.
- Consider asking students to write a reflection on their personal experience of the activity.

VALUES CONTINUUM

In this strategy, students or groups are asked to respond to a thought-provoking statement by saying to what degree they agree with it. It is a method that allows the teacher to quickly garner how students feel about an issue. Figure A.4 shows an example of a values continuum.

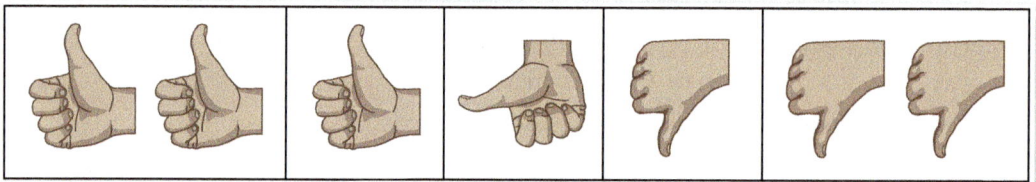

Figure A.4 Values continuum

Process

1. Inside the classroom create an imaginary or real line (using tape or string) or, if outside, paint or tape a line on the ground. The line represents a continuum with opposing views at each end.
2. Students are asked to stand at a point on the line that represents their opinion or position.
3. If you are using the values continuum more than once, be sure to keep the extremes the same way around to avoid confusion.
4. To simplify the activity the two extremes can be labelled *Yes* and *No*, with *Maybe* in the middle.

Benefits

- This strategy allows you to quickly determine students' views on particular issues.
- The values continuum gets students out of their seats, providing a physical break.

- It allows students to share their opinions without verbal communication. Sometimes this is preferable—particularly if the issue is sensitive.
- The results of the activity can lead to class- and small-group discussions.

Additional Tips or Variations

- Students can be asked to discuss a statement in groups, and then one of the group members steps on the line at the spot that represents the group's position. This can be particularly effective when comparing responses to different questions, challenging alternative positions, and finding contradictions in thinking.
- Teachers can create a continuum on the whiteboard or a wall by using smiling and frowning face cards that represent *really agree*, *agree*, *not sure*, *disagree*, and *really disagree*. Students stand near the face that represents their view.

VENN DIAGRAM

Venn diagrams are graphic organizers that can help students identify distinctive and shared features of two topics that are similar conceptually and share overlapping features. Figure A.5 depicts a Venn diagram comparing plants and animals.

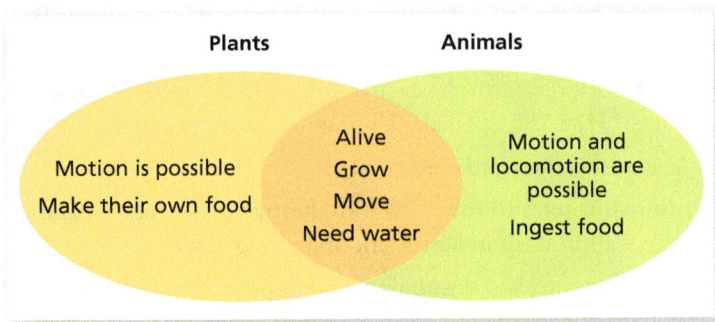

Figure A.5 Venn diagram: Comparing plants and animals

Process

1. The teacher identifies the topics and provides a template.
2. Individually or in small groups, students complete the table.
3. Students record traits, characteristics, or features that are distinctive to each category (i.e., each circle).
4. Students record shared traits, characteristics, or features that belong to both categories in the overlapping space.
5. As a class, groups share and compare answers.

Benefits

- Venn diagrams provide a visual for organizing ideas and comparing two topics.
- They are a useful technique for reviewing and consolidating knowledge.

Additional Tips or Variations

- Depending on the level of your students, you may use more complicated Venn diagrams (i.e., three circles with overlapping spaces).
- Students need to know a lot about a topic.

WORD WALL

A word wall is a common feature in most elementary classrooms, particularly primary classrooms. It is an organized and cumulative list of key terms and vocabulary used in a unit of study or from across subjects. Word walls offer a visual reference as the words are used in a range of activities. Word walls offer visual cues for topic-specific or challenging vocabulary—for example, words such as *there*, *their*, and *they're; condensation*, *evaporation*, and *melting*; or *force*, *power*, and *work*. Word walls can be helpful to incorporate into your science teaching, particularly in units that include specific or new vocabulary. Tailor their usage to fit best with your students' learning needs and your own teaching style.

Process

1. Prior to the start of a unit, brainstorm a list of vocabulary and key terms that your students will be learning and applying. Create word wall cards on thick card stock.
2. In the first lessons of a new unit, introduce your students to the new words. How is the word pronounced? How is it spelled? What do you think it might mean?
3. Add the new words to the word wall.
4. Throughout the unit, refer to the word wall during your teaching, and encourage students to use the wall in both independent and group work.
5. Also throughout the unit, add vocabulary and key terms that arise.

Benefits

- Word walls support the teaching and learning of key terms and unit-specific vocabulary as well as general words in context.
- Word walls can foster student independence as they provide a visual support for reading and writing.
- Visual cues provided by word walls support English language learners.
- Word walls can be used to review key terms at the end of a unit.

Additional Tips or Variations

- Use different colours of card stock for each subject or unit of study.
- Add pictures or icons to further support beginning readers and visual or English language learners.
- Students can illustrate word meanings using a diagram or photograph.
- Include definitions with words.

BIBLIOGRAPHY

Buzan, T., & Buzan, B. (1993). *The mind map book: How to use radiant thinking to maximize your mind's untapped potential.* London: BBC Books.

Canadian Student Debating Federation (2012). *Resources.* Retrieved from http://csdf-fcde.ca/debate-in-canada/resources.

Daniel, H. (2002). *Literature circles: Voice and choice in book clubs and reading groups* (2nd ed.). Portland, ME: Stenhouse Publishers.

Dunbar, R.E. (1994). *How to debate.* New York: F. Watts.

Franck, R. H. (2000). Why is cost-benefit analysis controversial? *Journal of Legal Studies, 29*(2), 913–930.

Gelb, M. (1996). *Thinking for change: Discovering the power to create, communicate and lead.* London: Aurum Press.

King, A. (1993). From sage on the stage to guide on the side. *College Teaching, 41*(1), 30–35.

Klentschy, M. (2005). Science notebook essentials. *Science and Children, 43*(3), 24–27.

Larrick, R. P., Morgan, J. N., & Nisbett, R. E. (1990). Teaching the use of cost-benefit analysis in everyday life. *Psychological Science, 1*(6), 362–370.

Lipton, L., & Wellman, B. (1998). *Patterns and practices in the learning-focused classroom.* Guilford, VT: Pathways Publishing.

Lyman, F. T. (1981). The responsive classroom discussion: The inclusion of all students. In A. Anderson (Ed.), *Mainstreaming Digest* (pp. 109–113). College Park, MD: University of Maryland Press.

Margulies, N., & Maal, N. (2002). *Mapping inner space: Learning and teaching visual mapping.* Tucson, AZ: Zephyr Press.

McAleese, R. (1998). The knowledge arena as an extension to the concept map: Reflection in action. *Interactive Learning Environments, 6*(3), 251–272.

Mintzes, J. J., Wandersee, J. H., & Novak, J. D. (2005). *Teaching science for understanding: A human constructivist view.* Burlington, MA: Elsevier Academic Press.

Mishan, E. J., & Euston, Q. (2007). *Cost-benefit analysis.* New York: Routledge.

Novak, J. D. (1991). Clarify with concept maps: A tool for students and teachers alike. *The Science Teacher, 58*, 45–49.

Novak, J. D. (1998). *Learning, creating and using knowledge: Concept maps as facilitative tools in schools and corporations.* Mahwah, NJ: Lawrence Erlbaum Associates.

Rutherford, P. (2002). Think-pair-share. In P. Rutherford (Ed.), *Instruction for all students* (pp. 104). Alexandria, VA: Just ASK Publications.

Schlick Noe, K. L., & Johnson, N. L. (1999). *Getting started with literature circles.* Norwood, MA: Christopher-Gordon Publishers.

Slavin, R. (1994). *Using student team learning* (4th ed.). Baltimore, MD: Johns Hopkins University.

Tate, M. L., & Phillips, W. G. (2011). *Science worksheets don't grow dendrites: 20 instructional strategies that engage the brain.* Thousand Oaks, CA: Corwin.

TeacherVision. (2012). *Think, pair, share.* Retrieved from http://www.teachervision.fen.com/group-work/cooperative-learning/48547.html.

West, C. K., Farmer, J. A., & Wolf, P. M. (1991). *Instructional design: Implications from cognitive science.* Englewood Cliffs, NJ: Prentice Hall.

Appendix B
Preparing for Your Practicum

This appendix is meant to help you prepare for your practicum. During your practicum, you will have the opportunity to observe, prepare, teach, and assess lessons and reflect upon your teaching. Teaching in an open and welcoming environment with a supportive associate teacher can be a powerful learning experience on your journey to becoming a teacher.

PREPARING FOR THE PRACTICUM

As you prepare for your practicum, you will have many questions. The following list outlines some considerations to keep in mind.

1. Discuss the following with your associate or host teacher:

   - The students: It can be helpful to go through a class list with your associate teacher to help you get to know the students and their particular needs (e.g., allergies, IEPs). Also, check pronunciation of students' names. Make a copy of the class list.
   - A safe place to store your belongings (e.g., in the classroom, staff room)
   - What to do if you need to be absent (e.g., call school office, associate teacher)
   - Staff meeting dates (if you are invited to attend)
   - Routines for fire alarms and emergency drills (e.g., earthquake, stranger)
   - Supervision duties, times, and locations
   - Weekly and daily timetables (make copies for yourself and your faculty advisor)
   - Times that are convenient to meet for planning and discussion
   - How students should address you

2. Introduce yourself to school staff:

   - Principal and vice-principal (if applicable)
   - Teachers
   - Administrative assistants (be sure they have a contact number for you)
   - Librarians, counsellors, and education assistants
   - Custodians

3. Find the location of the following:

   - Stationery supplies: Sometimes these will be in a central location; other times teachers will have their own
   - Staff computers and printers: Find out your login name and password
   - Photocopiers: Find out what code you should use
   - Computer labs
   - Library: Check with the librarian about your borrowing privileges
   - Audio-visual equipment: Ensure it is in good working order before a lesson
   - Medical room

- Counselling office (if applicable)
- Custodial office (if applicable)
- Lunch room (if applicable)
- Staff room
- Staff washrooms
- Prep room (if applicable)

4. Familiarize yourself with the science supplies and equipment in the classroom and at the school. Consider the following:

- Safety (e.g., first-aid kit, fire extinguisher, goggles)
- Location and storage of science equipment (e.g., pulleys, magnets). Each school will vary depending on space and resources available; some schools might have a science storage room, others might have a storage cupboard, and some teachers keep equipment in their classrooms.
- Location and storage of chemicals
- Location of broken glass container or procedure for disposing of broken glass
- Procedure for disposal of chemicals or biohazardous material
- District or board central stores for lending science supplies, equipment, curriculum boxes, or science kits

ON THE FIRST DAY OF YOUR PRACTICUM

- Arrive early! Give yourself at least 45 minutes before the day begins. Check with your associate teacher about when he or she would like you to arrive.
- Ask your associate teacher if you may circulate in the classroom during your observation sessions or if she or he would prefer you to be seated.
- Plan a fun and engaging way to introduce yourself to your students. This might be with a favourite story, personal anecdote, or game.
- Learn students' names as quickly as you can. It can be fun to play a game or sing a song to get to know names. Do not rely solely on names on desks!
- Observe students in the classroom, hallways, school yard, and cafeteria.
- Participate in small ways in the beginning (for example, look at student work or help students individually). Negotiate how you can best participate with your associate teacher.
- Walk around the school or in the school yard during breaks and noon hour.
- Talk to students: Ask them questions about their hobbies and interests and be open to sharing stories with them.
- Circulate in the classroom while students are working. You should not be sitting idle at any point during your practicum!

FAMILIARIZING YOURSELF WITH CLASSROOM AND SCHOOL CULTURE

Classroom

- Do any students have allergies? If a reaction occurs, what measures should be taken and how (e.g., EpiPen)?

- What are the expectations regarding entrance to and exit from the classroom?
- How is attendance taken? What are the school and classroom procedures?
- What are the opening and closing routines for the class?
- How are materials distributed and collected (e.g., by teacher, by student volunteers, placed at a specific location for pick up, or handed in)?
- How is student work displayed?
- What are the classroom expectations for creating a safe and respectful environment?
- What is the procedure regarding going to the washroom? For going to the water fountain?
- How are group activities organized (e.g., numbering, student-chosen groups)?
- Is there a schedule for parent or guardian volunteers who help the class? How do they participate (e.g., lead small groups, read with individual students)?

School

- When and how are announcements made?
- Is the national anthem played each morning?
- Are inspirational readings or prayers part of the daily routine?
- What are the expectations for conduct in the school?
- What is the process for accessing and reserving audio-visual resources or technology?
- How are other spaces at the school booked (e.g., gym, computer lab, school garden)?
- What other resources are available in the school or from the district board office?
- Is there a blanket consent form for local community field trips?

Classroom Observations

How does your associate or host teacher:

- begin the class or focus student attention
- use routines
- make transitions between activities
- ensure that all students are included
- encourage active student participation
- provide direction
- validate student ideas
- deal with incomplete or missing work (including homework)
- respond verbally and nonverbally to students who are not on task
- reinforce appropriate behaviour
- respond to disruptive behaviour
- encourage critical thinking
- recognize and celebrate student diversity
- keep a record of classroom observations
- keep a record of student achievement

ABCS: TIPS AND TOOLS

Below is an ABC of what we hope are helpful hints as you begin to establish your own norms and practices. Many of these could be addressed as part of your orientation. Keep in mind that schools vary in terms of resources, science investigation set up and materials, and expectations.

A Attendance—What are the school rules and your associate teacher's expectations regarding recording and reporting student attendance and tardiness?

B Boards (chalk, white, and interactive white)—What is available? How do you use the interactive whiteboards?

C Curriculum documents and resources—Ask your associate teacher to show you relevant curriculum documents and support materials for units and lessons that you will be teaching.

D Directory of important phone numbers—Create a list of important contact phone numbers and email addresses (e.g., school office, associate teacher).

E Evaluation and assessment—How does the associate teacher evaluate and assess student learning? How is achievement recorded?

F Flexibility—This is an asset in teaching, and as your confidence and comfort grow, so will your flexibility and ability to change plans at a moment's notice.

G Goals—Always be clear about what you expect from your students.

H Homework—What is the class and school board homework policy?

I Illness—Who do you contact if you are ill, and by what time? Are you expected to submit lessons for the day that you will be absent?

J Justice and fair practices—Think about how you will create a safe and respectful environment, being particularly mindful of issues related to bullying and equity.

K Keep copies of your unit and lesson plans (electronically or on paper)—Make notes about what went well and what could be improved the next time you teach the unit or lesson.

L Library and librarian—Where is the library and who is the librarian? What are your borrowing privileges for library books and resources?

M Mentor—Try to develop this relationship with your teacher—listen, ask questions, and be willing to try her or his suggestions.

N Names—Learn your students' names as quickly as possible. Use a game or other fun way of doing so.

O Openness—Be open to new ideas and constructive feedback.

P Punctuality, preparedness, and planning—Arrive at school well before school begins so that you are prepared, and do not rush out at the end of the day. Try to keep at least a day ahead with your planning; this will allow you time to discuss any difficulties with your associate teacher.

Q Questions—Ask questions. Remember, you are there to learn. However, be mindful of when you ask. Do not expect your associate teacher to answer your questions while she or he is teaching. Write them down and ask later.

R Routines—What are the routines in the classroom? Your associate teacher will have established some, and you should, wherever possible, follow them.

S Sense of humour, sleep, and sustenance—Get enough of all of these so that you remain healthy and happy.

T Technology—What technologies are available to you and your students, and how can you access them?

U Unwritten rules—Find out what teachers do about such things as food in the classroom, iPods, hats, etc.

V Visual and audio equipment—What equipment does your classroom or school have? Where are they stored, and do you need to book them?

W Willingness to participate—Be prepared and eager to participate in staff meetings, parents' night, and extracurricular activities; these are all learning opportunities for you. Check with your associate teacher about how you can participate.

X Xerox—Where are the photocopiers and printers located? How can you access them? Is there a code?

Y Yesterday—Think about what you did the day prior with your students and let that inform your planning.

Z Zeal—Enthusiasm is contagious.

Appendix C
Making a Successful Beginning to the School Year

Your first interactions with a new group of students are important for creating a safe and productive classroom environment. Some of your students may be new to the community or new to Canada, and may be facing related challenges. This appendix provides some suggestions for making a successful start to your school year, not only in your teaching of science but across the curriculum. It is organized by what you might do before the school year begins, on the first day, during the first week of school, during the first month, and throughout the school year. You will be able to adapt many of these strategies should you take over a class from another teacher at some point during the year; this can happen in the case of, for example, a maternity leave or other teacher leave of absence. We wish you all the best of luck as you begin your teaching career!

Before the School Year Begins

- *Become familiar with the school community.* This includes the physical aspects of the community: the school building, the playground and school grounds, and the local neighbourhood. Get to know the social and cultural communities—introduce yourself to other teachers, school staff, and also community members. This will allow you to richly and meaningfully embed your curriculum and your students' learning within the local environment. A diverse student population brings a variety of strengths and cultural landscapes to the classroom.

- *Organize your classroom.* For elementary school teachers, this can be a massive undertaking! Take stock of what is already in the classroom and find out what is available at the school (e.g., additional tables and chairs, flip-chart easels). Check the number of desks and chairs against your class list. Think about how you will arrange your classroom furniture. Will desks be in small groupings? Rows? Will you have a central meeting space? A quiet reading corner? Permanent learning centres? Consider your storage. Do you have ample storage? Is everything clearly labelled? Be sure that materials are easily accessible to students. Look at your own workspace. Identify what school supplies you might need to order (e.g., scissors, glue sticks, chart paper, markers) or that might be in some central location at the school. Determine what audio-visual equipment and technological resources are available. Find out how to reserve shared resources. Create welcoming and visually appealing displays in your classroom and on the bulletin board outside. Throughout the year, student work can be displayed. Decorate your room in a way that is fun, inviting, and engaging for your students.

- *Set a school supply list for your students.* Many elementary schools have a supply list that goes out to parents and guardians in the summer. Some lists are set at the school level; others can be modified to meet your curricular needs. Determine whether you will use DuoTangs, binders, folders, or portfolios for science. School supplies can be very expensive; be sensitive to families' abilities to purchase supplies, and encourage reusing supplies from previous years.

- *Plan ahead.* Make general long-term plans for the subjects you will be teaching and also year-at-a-glance plans that make connections across the curriculum. Think about field trips, and make bookings well in advance. (See Appendix F for details about planning field trips.) Look at your prep, gym, music, and French schedules (if applicable); if changes need to be made, speak with teachers and administrators early, but remember to be flexible.

On the First Day

- *Save handouts and newsletters for later in the week.* Often the school office has many forms to go home on the first day of school. The first day is very exciting and busy and it can be better to send class letters home at the end of the first week.

- *Ask students to introduce themselves to each other and to you.* This helps you learn your students' names and allows you to learn about their interests, which can inform your curriculum. Your students will also get to know each other, and together, you can start building a strong and supportive learning community.

- *Do an activity.* On the first day we suggest that you ask students to work on an activity together. Circulate as the students work and have some fun. A student-centred activity gives students an opportunity to get to know each other. It also allows you to observe how they work with others and to negotiate and practise class expectations for cooperative work, following instructions, and cleanup. The following activity can be used with your students on the first day of school.

Build the Tallest Free-Standing Tower

Materials for each group:
Toothpicks
20 mini marshmallows

Challenge:
In assigned groups, students will build a free-standing tower that is as tall as possible using only the materials provided. The tower must be free-standing for at least five seconds and cannot be taped to the surface it rests upon. As a group, have students brainstorm how they might construct the tower. Then, working together, students can build the tower. They will only have 20 marshmallows, which must not be torn into smaller pieces. Students can build with as many toothpicks as they wish.

During the First Week of School

- *Expectations and routines.* Negotiate with your students the expectations and routines for the year. You may have some ideas about what you would prefer and about what is appropriate, but the expectations are more likely to be adhered to if you negotiate them with students. Try to keep your class list of expectations to five or so clear and concise statements (too many can become complicated), and post them in a conspicuous place in the classroom for easy referral. By the end of the first week, routines and expectations should be clear to all. The time required to firmly establish routines will depend on the class, but whatever time you do invest will be wise!

- *Seating plans.* For the first days of school, you may wish to allow students to choose where they would like to sit and create a plan from this. However, after a few days, you may recognize that some students would do well to sit apart or that some students are not feeling included in the class; as such, you might create your own seating plan. Regardless of whether you or your students create the seating plan, keep an updated copy on hand for prep and supply teachers. During the first week, have students create name tags (laminate them if possible) that can be attached to their desktops.

- *Notebooks.* Organize notebooks, binders, DuoTangs, folders, and portfolios. It can be a good idea to have students use the same coloured notebooks for subjects (e.g., red for mathematics, green for science, and so on). This will help your students find their notebooks quickly and easily. Specific to science, you might have your students begin to set up a science notebook, (see Appendix A), with the tower activity from above as the first entry.

- *Textbooks (if applicable).* Textbooks are available in some elementary schools and school boards. If textbooks are in your class, determine how they will be used. We suggest that they supplement your science curriculum rather than form the foundation of it. Consider as well whether the books will stay at school or if students will be able to take them home. Textbooks are very expensive and it is often easier to have a class set for use at school only.

- *Homework (if applicable).* Depending on the grade of your students and your school and board policies, the amount of homework assigned (if any) varies. Younger students might read with a parent or guardian for 15 minutes each day. Upper elementary students may have up to 45 minutes or an hour of homework. You will need to determine what types of homework you will give, and share this with your students and parents.

- *Safety and science investigations.* Explain what expectations are in place for science investigations and why these expectations are important. If your students understand the reasons for rules in science investigation classes, they will be more likely to follow them. See Chapter 9 for suggestions on planning science investigations with safety in mind.

- *Learning centres.* If you choose to use learning centres in your teaching, create some at the start of the school year. Establish with your students the expectations for their use in content learning and skill development and also for student behaviour when attending them. See Appendix A for more information on learning centres.

- *Use of technology.* Learn your school and school board policies regarding the use of devices (e.g., smartphones, iPods) in class. Devices can distract students, and lack of access to such devices is a social justice issue. Consider what is best for all of your students.

During the First Month

Sometimes after a few weeks, teachers have a vague feeling that things are not going as well as they could be, and yet they are unable to name the problem. On the following page, organized by theme, are some statements you might reflect upon in order to analyze your teaching and to achieve some insight.

Lesson Organization	My lesson planning is clear and logical.
	My lesson, as presented, has no relationship to my written plan.
Interactions with and Inclusion of Students	I know all of my students' names and their interests.
	I understand and am sensitive to diverse student needs.
	I am careful to include all students in every lesson.
	I address specific needs, such as those of English language learners and students with unique learning needs.
	I provide enrichment and choice for students.
Content Knowledge	I have a solid understanding of the content.
	I am sometimes asked questions that I cannot answer.
	I am often asked questions that I cannot answer.
Timing and Pacing	I start the class on time.
	I never start on time because I'm always looking for my notes, book, equipment, or attendance sheets.
	The overall pace is too fast for most of the class.
	The overall pace is too slow for most of the class.
	I bring closure to each class.
	I never bring closure to my lessons; we often scramble to finish before the bell.
Classroom Organization	My printing (or handwriting) on chart paper, whiteboards, and chalkboards is clear, easy to read, and organized.
	I manage classroom disruptions with patience and fairness.
	I manage classroom disruptions idiosyncratically—sometimes I ignore issues, sometimes I address them, and sometimes I raise my voice.
	The students talk to each other throughout class and often ignore me.
Communication	I use my voice effectively in the classroom—not too loud and not too soft.
	I use precise language.
	I find I'm always raising my voice, sometimes yelling.
	I always check and provide feedback in student planners or agendas, and they are always signed by parents and guardians.
	I do not regularly check and provide feedback in student planners or agendas; they are inconsistently signed by parents and guardians.

Throughout the Year

- Establish a balance between work and the rest of your life.
- Be sure to include activities that help you grow professionally and personally (e.g., go to a conference, attend a time-management workshop, volunteer for a committee).
- Get involved in an aspect of school life to which you feel you can contribute (e.g., coach a team, supervise a club, join a curriculum committee).
- Ask for help and advice when you need it. Many of your colleagues will be glad to help, but might respectfully wait to be asked.
- Take time for yourself.

TAKE TIME[1]

1. Take time to work…it is the price of success.
2. Take time to think…it is the source of power.
3. Take time to play…it is the secret of eternal youth.
4. Take time to read…it is the foundation of knowledge.
5. Take time to worship/to be reflective/to nourish your spirit…it is the highway of reverence and washes the dust from your eyes.
6. Take time to help and enjoy friends…it is the source of happiness.
7. Take time to love…it is a gift that we give and receive.
8. Take time to dream…it hitches the soul to the stars.
9. Take time to laugh…it is laughter that helps with life's burdens.
10. Take time to plan…it is the secret of being able to have the time for the first nine things!

Final Suggestion

Read! There are many books for beginning teachers, and your school may have new teacher mentor programs. Check your school library or staff room for professional resources that might also be useful in your first year of teaching. Below are a few books that might be helpful.

Kronowitz, E. L. (1999). *Your first year of teaching and beyond.* New York: Addison Wesley Longman Inc.

MacDonald, R. E., & Healy, S. D. (1994). *A handbook for beginning teachers.* New York: Addison Wesley Longman Inc.

Wong, H. K., Wong, R. T., & Seroyer, C. (2005). *The first days of school: How to be an effective teacher.* Mountain View, CA: Harry K. Wong Publications.

---

[1]Thank you to our former colleague Don Galbraith, who always shared this *old Irish poem* with his students and colleagues.

Appendix D
Favourite Assignments

This appendix contains five popular assignments. They have evolved over the years to the form presented here and represent a blending of practice and theory. Micro-teaching and conducting a demonstration involves presentation and analysis, while creating an integrated unit plan is part of curriculum development. There are two reading assignments: One entails reading a popular science book and writing an annotation; the other focuses on science education research literature and gives teacher candidates the opportunity to read, summarize, and reflect upon a peer-reviewed journal article in an area of personal interest. Some of the assignments include a specific assessment tool, while others can be evaluated more holistically. Assessment tools can be adapted as needed.

List of assignments:

1. micro-teaching
2. creating an integrated unit plan
3. reading and summarizing a popular science book
4. reading a research article and writing a précis
5. doing a demonstration for the class

1. MICRO-TEACHING

Introduction

Teacher candidates will prepare a 10- to 12-minute micro-lesson to teach to a small group of their peers. The teaching episode will be video-recorded for later review. This assignment will provide opportunities to generate some useful data about strengths and areas for growth.

Rationale

We rarely have an opportunity to watch ourselves teach, and this assignment gives teacher candidates that experience. The assignment is a scaled-down version of a teaching situation that allows you to plan, teach, and reflect on a short teaching episode, or micro-lesson. Additionally it provides opportunities to hear feedback from peers in preparation for feedback from the practicum experience. Teacher candidates will teach the micro-lesson and later analyze the video in order to examine their ability to demonstrate key concepts using concrete materials, to ask questions at various cognitive levels, and to answer questions. A suggested reading to accompany this assignment is Wilkinson, G. (1996). Enhancing microteaching through additional feedback from preservice administrators. *Teaching & Teacher Education, 12*(2), 211–221.

Details of the Assignment

In planning, consider an appropriate activity, demonstration, or short exploration. Though much shorter in duration than a regular lesson, the micro-lesson should include a clear beginning, middle, and end. During the micro-lesson we suggest that you avoid lecturing and rather aim for student involvement by using student answers to guide the lesson and using concrete materials where appropriate. Please refer to Chapter 6 to review lesson planning, and Chapters 8 and 9 to review science explorations.

Part One: Choosing a Topic in Home Group (Jigsaw Style)

The class will be divided into home groups of six individuals. Within each home group, each member will choose a different topic on which to plan a 10- to 12-minute micro-lesson. Later, on a specified recording date, teacher candidates will present their micro-lessons to the home group.

Choose from these topics (or from those provided by the instructor):

1. Demonstrate and describe the effects of magnets on different materials.
2. Demonstrate and describe the purpose and basic operation of a pulley system.
3. Identify properties of air that make flight possible.
4. Demonstrate and describe properties of sound.
5. Describe the basic structure and function of the human muscular and nervous systems.
6. Explain obstacles unique to exploration of a specific extreme environment.

Part Two: Making a Plan in the Expert Group

Once teacher candidates have chosen a topic they will meet with peers from other groups who have chosen the same topic—this is the expert group. Within the expert group, brainstorm and discuss ideas for the micro-lesson. Teacher candidates may want to refer to resource materials provided by the instructor in order to generate some ideas. Each member of the expert group may use the same lesson idea, since the micro-lessons will later be presented to home groups. However, in part three, teacher candidates are expected to personalize the plan.

Part Three: Planning Individually

Each teacher candidate will prepare their own micro-lesson plan. They can use the ideas generated from the expert group meeting or plan for something different. The micro-lesson plan should be brief, be used during the actual teaching episode, and include the following:

- the topic, grade level, and curriculum outcomes or expectations supported by your lesson
- a flow chart or concept map for the lesson (optional but recommended)
- list of materials, props, or visuals needed
- time sequence for the lesson
- clear introduction
- questioning sequence and possible answers (margin notes or hints)
- concluding idea or summary of concepts covered

Teacher candidates can refer to Appendix 6.B for sample lesson plan templates or create their own.

Part Four: Implementing the Micro-Lesson

Each home group will be assigned to a classroom or space in which they will teach the micro-lesson. In home groups, each teacher candidate will present her or his micro-lesson. During lessons, those teacher candidates not teaching will take on the role of elementary school students in terms of participation and asking questions. All video recording should take place during the regular class period. Students may choose to record their micro-lesson using their laptops, camcorders, phones, or digital recorders provided by the teacher. Be sure to submit the recordings to your instructor.

Part Five: Reviewing and Critiquing the Taped Lessons in Home Groups

After the taping, the home groups will view their micro-lessons and provide feedback in the form of a group discussion. Have one group member act as a scribe, taking notes of the feedback and suggestions. Feedback might include constructive criticism regarding communication skills, timing, use of interactive materials, questioning, and level of peer engagement. Each participant will use the feedback from peers to inform her or his reflection.

Part Six: Writing a Personal Reflection

Each teacher candidate will write a reflection using her or his own notes and the group discussion notes to analyze their micro-teaching. The reflection should include a self-analysis of the micro-lesson implementation and some discussion of strengths and areas for growth.

Submission

- micro-lesson plan
- video recording of micro-lesson
- group discussion notes
- personal reflection

Assessment Tool for Micro-Teaching: Rating Scale

Criteria		Points
Planning		
The Micro-Lesson Plan	The complete lesson containing expectations, materials, timing, introduction, question sequence, and conclusion.	2 4 6 8
Teaching		
Topic	The topic was appropriately presented with evidence of subject mastery.	1 2 3 4 5
Timing	The lesson flowed well at a consistent and appropriate pace with a timely finish.	1 2 3 4
Verbal Communication	Communication skills were good. Language use was appropriate; voice was dynamic, well modulated, clear, and adequately loud.	1 2 3 4
Questioning	The questions were concise, sequenced, well-distributed with a variety of cognitive levels; appropriate wait time was used; good use was made of answers. Lecturing was kept to a minimum.	2 4 6 8
Non-verbal Communication	Eye contact, posture, comfort level, and movements were appropriate. No distracting mannerisms.	1 2 3 4
Materials	Materials were appropriate and helped further the lesson.	1 2 3 4
Student Involvement	Students were involved, attentive, actively participated in all activities.	1 2 3 4 5
Reflecting		
Personal Reflection	After consideration of the group discussion notes and self-analysis, the reflection shows insight into personal strengths and areas for growth. The reflection makes use of specific examples from the micro-lesson to support the analysis. Group discussion notes were included.	3 6 9 12 15 18
	TOTAL	/ 60

2. CREATING AN INTEGRATED UNIT PLAN

Introduction

In this assignment, teacher candidates will choose a K–8 science topic and create an integrated unit plan of six to eight lessons. Along with covering a science topic, the unit will also integrate two other subject areas (e.g., mathematics and social studies, fine arts and language arts). The unit plan itself should include the outcomes or expectations to be covered (for science and other subject areas), assessment strategies directly related to each learning outcome or expectation, and a description of the teaching and learning strategies for each lesson.

Rationale

Unit planning is an important component of successful teaching. Because every elementary school teacher has her or his own planning style, a common unit plan will not be used for this assignment. Instead, you are encouraged to work with and adapt a template or style of unit planning that works for you.

Details of the Assignment

Unit planning will be discussed at length during class time; please refer to Chapter 6 for details. Build upon and adapt templates to develop a style of your own. In the early stages of unit planning, begin with the end in mind. Determine what you want your students to know by the end of the unit. Using a web for brainstorming teaching and learning ideas can be helpful. This can be a good way to make connections between science concepts and skills, learning goals, lesson ideas, and activities across disciplines. From this initial planning, you might create a unit plan chart that outlines learning outcomes and expectations, assessment strategies, and learning experiences for each lesson. These do not need to be as detailed as your lesson plans; your unit plan helps you to organize large blocks of teaching, not specific details.

Whichever format you decide to use, your unit plans for this assignment must clearly provide the following information: 1) learning outcomes or expectations from the science curriculum as well as from two other disciplines; 2) assessment strategies related to each learning outcome or expectation; and 3) a description of the teaching and learning strategies to be incorporated into each lesson. Plan for a unit of six to eight lessons: one lesson should be used to introduce the unit, four to six lessons to teach the big ideas of the unit, and a final lesson to bring the unit to a close. Teacher candidates will share their integrated unit plans and their preplanning methods with a small group of peers who will use Two Stars and a Wish to provide feedback. The teacher candidate will also complete a self-assessment using Two Stars and a Wish. (See Chapter 11.)

Submission

Teacher candidates will submit their integrated unit plans, their preplanning work, and their peer and self-assessments.

Assessment Tool for Integrated Unit Plan: Rubric

Criteria	Level 1	Level 2	Level 3	Level 4	Notes
Preplanning	Little or no evidence of preplanning and connecting between ideas	Adequate evidence of preplanning and connecting between ideas	Good evidence of preplanning and connecting between ideas	Exemplary evidence of preplanning and connecting between ideas	
Learning Outcomes or Expectations	Learning outcomes or expectations from science and other curricular areas are minimally or not appropriate to the topic	Learning outcomes or expectations from science and other curricular areas are somewhat appropriate to the topic	Learning outcomes or expectations from science and other curricular areas are appropriate to the topic	Learning outcomes or expectations from science and other curricular areas are very appropriate to the topic	
Assessment Strategies	Assessment strategies are minimally or not aligned with learning outcomes or expectations	Assessment strategies are somewhat aligned with learning outcomes or expectations	Assessment strategies are well aligned with learning outcomes or expectations	Assessment strategies are very well aligned with learning outcomes or expectations	
Teaching and Learning Strategies	Teaching and learning strategies are minimally or not suited to outcomes and are unlikely to engage students	Teaching and learning strategies are somewhat suited to outcomes and will likely be somewhat engaging for students	Teaching and learning strategies are well suited to outcomes and will likely be engaging for students	Teaching and learning strategies are very well suited to outcomes and will likely be very engaging for students	
Cross-Curricular Integration	Inadequate or no integration of topics through activities, concepts, or skills	Adequate integration of topics through activities, concepts, or skills	Good integration of topics through activities, concepts, or skills	Exemplary integration of topics through activities, concepts, or skills	
Unit Plan (overall)	Lessons are not cohesive and do not build upon each other; unit is not feasible, well planned, or engaging	Lessons are somewhat cohesive and build upon each other; unit is somewhat feasible, well planned, and engaging	Lessons are cohesive and build upon each other; unit is feasible, well planned, and engaging	Lessons are very cohesive and build upon each other; unit is very feasible, well planned, and engaging	

3. READING AND SUMMARIZING A POPULAR SCIENCE BOOK

Introduction

As is clear from the title, this assignment involves reading a science-related book (not a textbook) and creating a one-page summary that gives a brief summary of the book and suggests ways that it might be used in teaching science.

Rationale

The intent of this assignment is to encourage a lifelong commitment to reading books that are intended for a wide audience and are useful for teachers as they develop breadth of knowledge in science. It can be helpful for teachers of science to include in their repertoire, knowledge of significant works and accomplishments in the field. For example, Wade Davis, Stephen Hawking, Stephen Jay Gould, and Barbara McClintock are significant figures in the science narrative. This assignment will give you a range of popular science resource materials from which to draw.

Details of the Assignment

Select and read a popular science book. Be prepared to write a brief summary of the book (one to two paragraphs) and suggest ways that it might be used in teaching science (one to two paragraphs). The summaries will be shared among the class in either electronic or print form and graded holistically by the instructor.

Below is a suggested list of books. This list is not exhaustive and other books might also be appropriate—for example, biographies of scientists, books by important scientists, or a book of historical significance such as *On the Origin of Species* by Charles Darwin.

Suggested Titles

Capra, F. (1996). *The web of life*. New York: Anchor Books.

Davis, W. (1997). *The serpent and the rainbow*. New York: Touchstone.

Dawkins, R. (1976). *The selfish gene*. London: Paladin-Granada Publishing.

Diamond, J. (1999). *Guns, germs, and steel: The fates of human societies*. New York: W.W. Norton & Co.

Gould, S. J. (1981). *The mismeasure of man*. New York: W.W. Norton & Co.

Gould, S. J. (1989). *Wonderful life*. New York: W. W. Norton & Co.

Hawking, S. (1996). *A brief history of time: The updated and expanded tenth anniversary edition*. New York: Bantam Books.

Hubbard, R., & Wald, E. (1999). *Exploding the gene myth*. Boston: Beacon Press.

Kingsolver, B. (2010). *Animal, vegetable, miracle*. New York: HarperCollins.

Krauss, L. (2007). *The physics of Star Trek*. Philadelphia: Basic Books.

Kuhn, T. (1996). *The structure of scientific revolution* (3rd ed.). University of Chicago Press.

Lewontin, R. (2000). *The triple helix: Gene, organism, and environment*. Boston: Harvard University Press.

Rees, W. & Wackernagel, M. (1996). *Our ecological footprints*. Gabriola Island, BC: New Society Publishers.

Ridley, M. (1999). *Genome*. New York: HarperCollins.

Roach, M. (2003). *Stiff: The curious lives of human cadavers*. New York: W. W. Norton & Co.

Shermer, M. (1997). *Why people believe weird things*. New York: W.H. Freeman and Company.

Shiva, V. (1997). *Biopiracy: The plunder of nature and knowledge*. Toronto, ON: Between the Lines.

Smith, A., & MacKinnon, J. B. (2007). *The 100 mile diet: A year of local eating*. Toronto, ON: Random House.

Suzuki, D. (2002). *The sacred balance*. Vancouver, BC: The Douglas & McIntyre Publishing Company.

Wilson, E. O. (2013). *Letters to a young scientist*. New York: Liveright.

Submission

Please submit the summary electronically to the instructor. Include the reference for the book using an agreed upon citation format.

Holistic grading means that a grade will be assigned for the overall impression or value of a piece of writing. A simple rubric can be used to arrive at one grade rather than an average of several criteria.

Assessment Tool for Reading and Summarizing a Popular Science Book: Holistic Criteria

Excellent (Level 4)

Writing is on topic. Content is informative and well developed.

Writing is clear. Information presented will be valuable for helping others decide if they want to read the book.

Good (Level 3)

Writing is on topic. Content is helpful and well developed but could have more detail.

Writing is clear.

Fair (Level 2)

Writing is generally on topic but could be more detailed and more informative.

Writing is mostly clear but needs some editing.

Unsatisfactory (re-submit)

Writing needs improvement and editing, and content does not have enough detail to be helpful.

4. READING A RESEARCH ARTICLE AND WRITING A PRÉCIS

Introduction

Teacher candidates will prepare a summary in the form of a précis, of an article from a peer-reviewed science education research journal. They will choose an article of personal interest and submit both the précis and a copy of the article. Be sure to include the article's citation in an agreed upon citation format.

Rationale

Teachers seldom have the opportunity to explore the theory that underpins practice. This assignment is meant to introduce teacher candidates to the vast field of science education research literature and allows for careful consideration of a piece of research. Teacher candidates may want to extend their reading in a particular area of science education research—for example, nature of science (NOS); inquiry; science, technology, society, and the environment (STSE); environmental education; equity, diversity, and social justice issues in science; Aboriginal science; curriculum development; or scientific literacy.

Details of the Assignment

A précis is a cogent reduction of a text, or a summary of a reading. It is not about personal opinion or arguing a position. Teacher candidates might choose an article they agree with, disagree with, or find compelling. They might also choose a particular researcher's work to read. (The names of Canadian and other researchers in science education are provided throughout the text.) The précis will be graded holistically, based on the clarity and quality of the writing or presentation and the demonstrated understanding of the article. A list of peer-reviewed education journals follows:

- *Canadian Journal of Environmental Education* (CJEE)
- *Canadian Journal of Science, Mathematics and Technology Education* (CJSMTE)

- *Cultural Studies in Science Education* (CSSE)
- *Environmental Education Research* (EER)
- *International Journal of Environmental and Science Education* (IJESE)
- *International Journal of Science Education* (IJSE)
- *International Journal of Science Education, Part B: Communication and Public Engagement* (IJSE [B])
- *Journal of Environmental Education* (JEE)
- *Journal of Research in Science Teaching* (JRST)
- *Journal of Science Teacher Education* (JSTE)
- *Journal of Science Education & Technology* (JSET)
- *Public Understanding of Science* (PUS)
- *Research in Science Education* (RISE)
- *Research in Science and Technology Education* (RSTE)
- *Science Education* (SciEd)

Submission

Two possible forms for a précis are outlined below. The first is a précis written in prose, while the second takes a more free form.

Précis written in prose

A précis should include all of the important ideas in the original text, using your own words. Only ideas of primary importance are included. A précis does not involve commentary on, or analysis of, the text, and the writer of a précis should not express an opinion about the content. The ability to understand and to state clearly another person's ideas in one's own words is what counts. Do not present merely the conclusions or the general idea. An excellent précis paraphrases the argument and conclusions of an original text.

The précis should clearly state the topic or main thesis, the purpose of the research, the methods used, the results (or insights) gained, and conclusions. It should convey the author's emphasis and argument.

Source: Adapted from www.architecture.uwaterloo.ca/faculty_projects/.../precis2.html and Constance DeVereaux, www.cgu.edu/pages/905.asp.

Précis in free form

This form of précis can be represented as a mind map, a web diagram, or another visual form. Feel free to represent the reading in a way that is reflective of the content and context of the text itself, of your interpretation of it, and of you as a reader. In the example below we have summarized key ideas and created a patchwork of broad themes found in a research publication. The squares are connected by the foundational characteristics—for example, place, care, complexity, and interdependence—described in the reading.

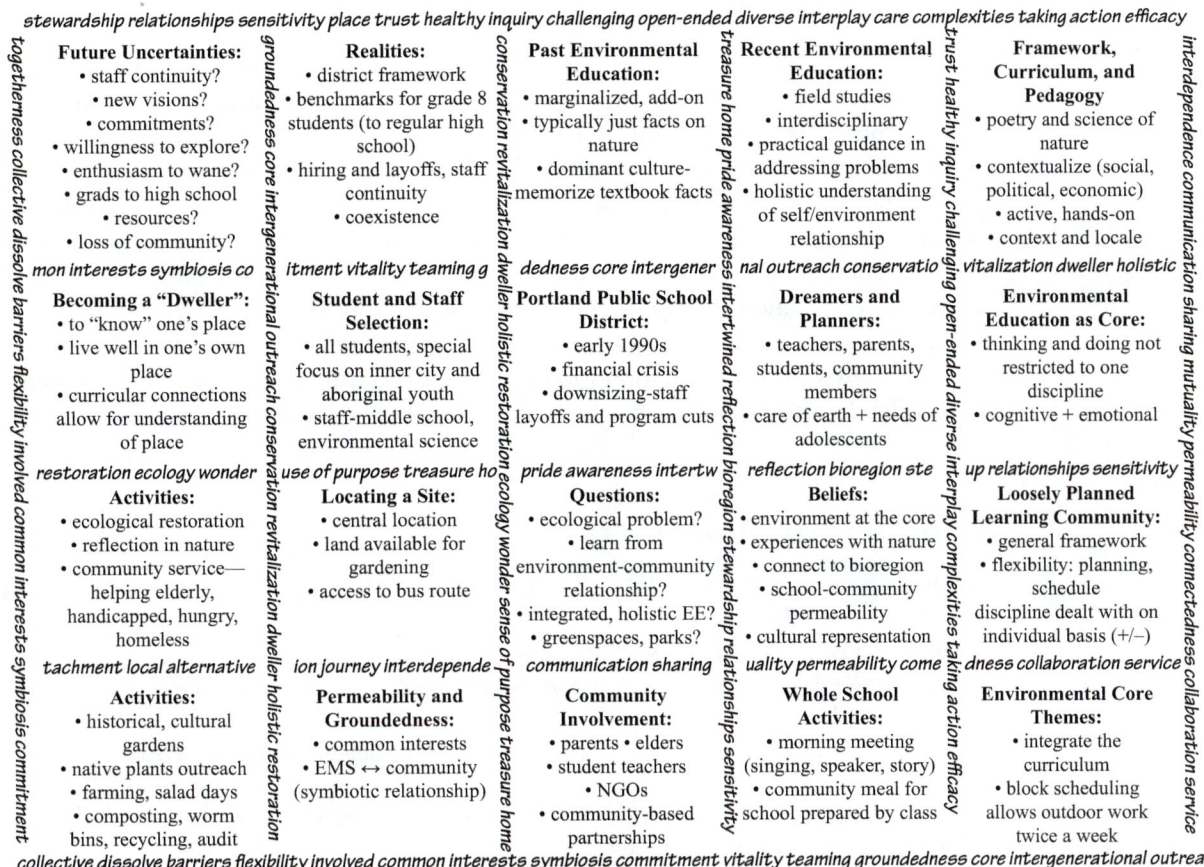

Figure D.1 Sample of a free-form précis. This example was created as a summary of the key ideas presented in Williams, D. R., & Taylor, S. (1999).

5. DOING A DEMONSTRATION FOR THE CLASS

Introduction

Demonstrations are an important and fun part of science teaching. This assignment provides teacher candidates with an opportunity to plan and perform a demonstration for their peers.

Rationale

There are many important aspects of science that are best viewed by students rather than conducted as an investigation. For example, dropping potassium into water creates the explosive interaction of an alkali metal and water. However, due to safety issues, it is an inappropriate activity for students. This assignment will provide opportunities for each teacher candidate to explore demonstration resources (both in print and online), to practise a demonstration, and to present it to the class. In this way teacher candidates can build a repertoire of demonstrations for use in the future. Research suggests that most teachers are more comfortable doing demonstrations they have seen or tried.

Details of the Assignment

Individually or in pairs, choose, practise, and present a demonstration to the class. The demonstration might be an attention grabber to start a unit, an activity that addresses a misconception, or something fun and interesting that is worth sharing. The demonstration should take about 10 minutes to perform and should include some questions that promote critical thinking and peer participations. (Please refer to Chapter 6 for a discussion of questioning.) Two weeks prior to the presentation date, submit to the instructor the demonstration choice and equipment or materials needed. Try to use supplies and equipment you would find readily available at an elementary school; often elementary science demonstrations and experiments are done with supplies from a supermarket or drugstore. It is expected that the demonstration will be practised in advance of the class. Upon completion of the demonstration, the teacher candidate will submit a summary to be shared with peers.

Sources for Demonstration Ideas[*]

Bilash, B., & Shields, M. (2001). *A demo a day: A year of biological demonstrations.* FLINN Scientific Ltd.

Bosak, S. V. (1991). *Science is...* Markham, ON: Scholastic.

Gross, G.R., Koob, J., & Bilash, B. (1995). *A demo a day: A year of chemical demonstrations.* FLINN Scientific Ltd.

Liem, T. L. (1987). *Invitations to science inquiry* (2nd ed.). Lexington, MA: Ginn Press.

[*]Online resources can also provide ideas; however, they *must* be carefully vetted for safety, accuracy, and appropriateness.

Submission

Teacher candidates will submit a summary of the demonstration; these will be shared with peers to help build each teacher candidates' repertoire of classroom-ready demonstrations. The summary should include the following:

- A brief lesson plan or notes for teachers (approximately one page) that include safety considerations, materials needed, a description or diagram of the set up, a description of what to do, questions to ask during the demo, and an explanation of the theory or science underpinning the demonstration

- Student handouts. These might include, for example, a student worksheet or data table for recording, questions for students, or a predict-observe-explore chart. (See Chapter 9.)

Assessment Tool for Doing a Demonstration: Rubric

Criteria	Level 1	Level 2	Level 3	Level 4
Planning				
Evidence of preparation and practice; demonstration occurs in a 10-minute time frame.	Little evidence of preparation and practice	Some evidence of preparation and practice	Good evidence of preparation and practice	Exemplary evidence of preparation and practice
Presentation				
Presentation to the class is smooth, clear, and engaging.	Inadequate presentation to the class	Adequate presentation to the class	Good presentation to the class	Excellent presentation to the class
Teacher Notes				
Notes are complete and clear with respect to safety materials, a description of what to do, questions, and an explanation of the science.	Inadequate teacher notes; plan is not easy to follow	Adequate teacher notes; plan is somewhat easy to follow	Good teacher notes; plan is easy to follow	Excellent teacher notes; plan is very easy to follow
Student Handouts				
Student handout is complete, clear, and ready to use.	Inadequate student handout	Adequate student handout	Good student handout	Excellent student handout

Appendix E
Suggested Children's Literature for Elementary Science

As an elementary school teacher, bringing children's literature into your curriculum and instruction is beneficial for many reasons. Stories can engage and capture the attention of your students. Most children love to be read to; do not underestimate the power of reading aloud to your upper elementary students! Literacy is inherent in all areas of the curriculum, and by incorporating children's literature into your teaching, you will open up opportunities for all components of literacy—reading, writing, speaking, and listening—to be developed in your students.

Children's literature can enhance your science teaching. The following are examples of children's literature that can be incorporated into your science curriculum. We have provided an annotated bibliography as well as the strands (life science, physical science, Earth and space science) that the books connect with. The list is by no means exhaustive but will help you to bring stories into your science teaching and build your library of science-related titles.

Life Science Titles

Atkins, J. (2000). *Girls who looked under rocks: The lives of six pioneering naturalists.* Nevada City, CA: Dawn Publications.
The stories of six female scientists are shared: Maria Merian, Anna Comstock, Frances Hamerstrom, Rachel Carson, Miriam Rothschild, and Jane Goodall.

Base, G. (2001). *The water hole.* New York: Puffin Books.
Base's beautifully illustrated book depicts the story of animals from around the world coming to drink at a water hole. As more animals come to drink, the water hole gets smaller and smaller. Will the animals have enough water?

Bouchard, D., & Vickers, R. H. (2004). *The elders are watching.* Vancouver, BC: Raincoast Books.
Bouchard's poetry and Vickers's art come together in a poignant plea to respect and honour the gifts of the natural world as the voices of past Aboriginal leaders call out to the people of today. *The Elders are Watching* beautifully presents the rugged nature of Canada's West Coast and the knowledge and wisdom of the First Peoples.

Brett, J. (2004). *The umbrella.* Toronto: Putnam.
Brett's colourful, richly illustrated tale tells us the story of Carlos, who climbs a tree in a Costa Rican rainforest to get a good view of the animals there. In doing so, he drops his banana leaf umbrella. All of the animals of the forest, from the tree frog to the jaguar, pile into the umbrella as it floats by, and poor Carlos wonders why he is unable to see them.

Brett, J. (2005). *Honey, honey…lion!* Toronto: Putnam.
In the plains of Africa, the honey badger and honeyguide bird work together to find and eat honey. However, one day Badger keeps all of the honey to himself! Honeyguide bird hatches a plan to teach Badger a lesson.

Bunting, E. (1996). *Sunflower house.* Markham, ON: Houghton Mifflin Harcourt.
A boy creates a circular summer playhouse of sunflowers and, over the summer, watches the flowers grow and change. He saves the seeds to build a house again the following spring.

Bunting, E. (1999). *Butterfly house*. Markham, ON: Scholastic.
With her grandfather's help, a girl builds a house for a larva and watches it grow, letting it go when it matures. As the girl grows older, the butterflies return to spend time with her.

Butterworth, C. (2011). *How did that get in my lunchbox?* Somerville, MA: Candlewick Press.
Butterworth traces the story of food production from the ground to the lunchbox. The stories of several common foods are followed, and information on food groups is provided.

Cannon, J. (1993). *Stellaluna*. Markham, ON: Houghton Mifflin Harcourt.
When little Stellaluna—a bat—is knocked from her mother's arms by an attacking owl, she lands in a birds' nest. The story follows her adaptations to what she perceives as an upside-down world as she is adopted by the birds.

Cannon, J. (1997). *Verdi*. Markham, ON: Houghton Mifflin Harcourt.
Verdi is a young snake who doesn't want to grow up; he likes his bright yellow stripes and thinks all adult snakes are lazy and boring. As he begins to turn green, Verdi tries everything he can think of to stop the change and realizes that his change of colour does not mean he is changing himself.

Carle, E. (1996). *The grouchy ladybug*. Toronto: HarperCollins.
The grouchy ladybug refuses to share aphids with another ladybug, and takes on a succession of fights with progressively bigger animals. Carle brings together the concepts of time and size with manners in this classic book.

Carle, E. (2002). *Slowly slowly slowly said the sloth*. Toronto: Philomel.
The sloth hangs quietly in the tree, moving very slowly, as all the other animals rush about around him in the rainforest. Why is the sloth so slow? Carle's timeless classic reminds us of the value of slowing down and enjoying the world.

Cherry, L. (1990). *The great kapok tree*. Markham, ON: Houghton Mifflin Harcourt.
A man exhausts himself in his efforts to fell a great kapok tree. During the night, as he sleeps, residents of the rainforest whisper in his ear of the importance of the trees and how all living things in the forest rely on each other for life. The book is a vibrant celebration of the biodiversity of the rainforest and its critical importance.

Cherry, L. (1997). *Flute's journey: The life of a wood thrush*. Markham, ON: Houghton Mifflin Harcourt.
This story follows Flute, a young wood thrush, through his first year and migration across thousands of miles to Costa Rica. Flute encounters countless challenges en route, including natural predators and habitat loss.

Cherry, L. (2003). *How Groundhog's garden grew*. Markham, ON: Scholastic.
After Groundhog tries to take some vegetables from Squirrel's garden, Squirrel teaches Groundhog how to plant and grow his own food. It is a gentle story of the interrelations of all living things and the value of working together.

Cole, J. (1996). *The magic school bus gets eaten: A book about food chains*. Markham, ON: Scholastic.
Arnold and Keesha have forgotten their report on two beach things that go together; they have only a tuna fish sandwich and some green pond scum. Ms. Frizzle jumps behind the wheel and the class takes the magic school bus into the ocean to learn about food chains.

Dendy, L., & Boring, M. (2005). *Guinea pig scientists: Bold self-experimenters in science and medicine*. New York: Henry Holt.
Guinea pig scientists are those who use their own bodies in scientific experiments and testing; this book shares the stories of some of these remarkable scientists.

Ehlert, L. (2001). *Waiting for wings*. Markham, ON: Houghton Mifflin Harcourt.
Through rhyming text and vibrant collage, Ehlert follows the life cycles of four butterflies from eggs to caterpillars to beautiful butterflies. This lovely book by the author of *Chicka Chicka Boom Boom*, *Waiting for Wings* also includes instructions for planting a butterfly garden and identifying butterflies and flowers.

Ehrlich, A. (2003). *Rachel: The story of Rachel Carson*. Markham, ON: Harcourt.
Ehrlich tells the story of Rachel Carson's life, from her childhood days of curiosity and her sense of wonder in the natural to her pivotal *Silent Spring*, which motivated the current environmental movement.

Fogliano, J. (2012). *And then it's spring.* New York: Roaring Brook Press.
    And then It's Spring is the gentle tale of a boy and his dog, who plant a garden and wait, and wait, and wait patiently for the brown earth to spring into green.

Jenkins, M. (2011). *Can we save the tiger?* Somerville, MA: Candlewick Press.
    Jenkins explores how humans and their actions can threaten or conserve the species of Earth. Beautifully illustrated, with examples from history, *Can We Save the Tiger?* presents reasons to save endangered species.

Knudsen, S. (2011). *Eggs, legs, wings: A butterfly life cycle.* North Mankato, MN: Capstone Press.
    In graphic novel format, this book tells the story of the butterfly life cycle through brilliant illustrations and text.

Larson, G. (1998). *There's a hair in my dirt!* Toronto: HarperCollins.
    A fun story of invertebrates, Larson's tale begins with a young worm who is fed up with his wormy life. In response, Father Worm shares the story of a maiden and her adventurous stroll through the forest. Larson's humorous prose and hilarious illustrations make this a fun trip through ecology.

Lionni, L. (1973). *Swimmy.* New York: Random House.
    A happy school of fish live deep in the ocean but are afraid of the dangers around them. When Swimmy comes along, the fish learn that, by working together, they can overcome their fears.

McFarlane, S. (1991). *Waiting for the whales.* Victoria, BC: Orca Books.
    A young girl and her mother go to live with her grandfather at the seaside and join him in watching the whales return to the bay each year. Over the years, the girl grows up and her relationship with her grandfather deepens as he shares his knowledge and wisdom. Set on the beautiful West Coast, *Waiting For the Whales* gently alludes to the cyclical nature of life and death.

McFarlane, S. (1992). *Jessie's island.* Victoria, BC: Orca Books.
    When Jessie's cousin Thomas writes her a letter about all the wonderful things he can do in his city, Jessie decides to write a letter back sharing with him the magic of her home. A simple yet poignant tale, *Jessie's Island* shares the richness of place and the joy of nature in its vivid descriptions of the natural world on the west coast of Canada.

McGinty, A. B. (2009). *Darwin.* Markham, ON: Houghton Mifflin Harcourt.
    This picture book biography shares the story of Charles Darwin through a series of handwritten entries.

Munsch, R. (1992). *Moira's birthday.* Toronto: Annick Press.
    Moira invites her whole school to her birthday party, but her parents don't find out until the last minute.

Okimoto, J. (2007). *Winston of Churchill, One bear's battle against global warming.* Seattle, WA: Sasquatch Books.
    Winston is a polar bear living in Churchill, Manitoba. He has big dreams: He wants to stop global warming but finds that he first needs to look at his own actions. The book includes information about global warming and the bear's namesake, Winston Churchill.

Parr, T. (2004). *The peace book.* New York: Little, Brown, and Company.
    Parr's beautiful and accessible book for young readers shares simple but powerful messages about the importance of peace, tolerance, and celebration of difference.

Pratt, K. (1991). *A walk in the rainforest.* Nevada City, CA: Dawn Publications.
    Kristen Pratt presents the exotic animals and plants of the rainforest in a colourful, alphabet style. This is Pratt's first book, written and illustrated when she was only 15.

Pratt, K. (1994). *A swim through the sea.* Nevada City, CA: Dawn Publications.
    Led by Seamore the Seahorse, *A Swim through the Sea* takes readers on an alliterative tour of animals living in the ocean.

Rockwell, A. (2002). *One bean.* Toronto: Bloomsbury.
    One Bean takes the reader through the plant growth cycle, from a planted bean in a cup to a grown plant. Its three-dimensional paper sculptures and simple narration make this an ideal first look at plant growth.

Ryder, J. (1996). *Earthdance*. New York: Henry Holt.
Through brilliant pictures and powerful prose, Ryder's story encourages readers to become not only part of Earth, but Earth itself.

Ryder, J. (1996). *Where butterflies grow*. New York: Puffin Books.
Beautifully written by Joanne Ryder and vividly illustrated by Lynne Cherry, *Where Butterflies Grow* follows the life cycle of a black swallowtail butterfly from caterpillar to green creeper to brilliant butterfly. The book includes suggestions on how children can grow butterflies in their gardens.

Seuss, Dr. (1971). *The lorax*. New York: Random House.
Dr. Seuss's classic tale tells of the Lorax's efforts to stop the Once-ler from destroying the forests of Truffula trees. While the Lorax says he speaks for the trees, this book speaks volumes for Earth.

Van Allsburg, C. (1990). *Just a dream*. Markham, ON: Houghton Mifflin Harcourt.
Walter does not appreciate the gifts of the environment or understand his role in the natural world—that is, until a fantastic journey that shows him what might happen if he and other humans are not more careful. This is a classic book, richly illustrated in Van Allsburg's unique style.

Williams, V. B. (1981). *Three days on a river in a red canoe*. New York: Mulberry Books.
This is the story of a girl, her cousin, and their mothers' canoe trip, in which they learn to pitch a tent, build a fire, and lower their canoe over waterfalls.

Winter, J. (2008). *Wangari's trees of peace*. New York: Harcourt.
When Wangari returns to her home in Kenya, she sees that most of the trees have been cut down. She responds by planting nine seedlings in her backyard, and her plans bloom and grow from there.

Physical Science Titles

Allen, P. (1996). *Who sank the boat?* New York: The Putnam & Grossett Group.
A cow, a donkey, a sheep, a pig, and a mouse decide to go for a boat ride one day. You wouldn't believe who sinks the boat!

Burton, V. L. (1977). *Mike Mulligan and his steam shovel*. Markham, ON: Houghton Mifflin Harcourt.
First published in 1939, this is the story of Mike and his steam shovel, Mary Anne. Mike and Mary Anne have worked together to dig canals for ships, mountain passes for trains, and hollows for skyscrapers, but new machines are being created and the pair are soon out of work. Mike must prove how hard Mary Anne can work to save her from the scrap heap.

Busby, P. (2003). *First to fly: How the Wright brothers invented the airplane*. New York: Crown Publishers.
With riveting text, paintings, photographs, and diagrams, *First to Fly* retells the history of Orville and Wilbur Wright, from their childhood spent building things, to adulthood and mechanical work, to their trial-and-error invention of the airplane.

Drummond, A. (2011). *Energy island*. New York: Farrar, Straus, & Giroux.
The people of the Danish island of Samso reduced their carbon emissions by 140 percent in just 10 years. *Energy Island* shares the inspiring story of how this was accomplished.

Kamkwamba, W., & Mealer, B. (2012). *The boy who harnessed the wind*. Toronto: Penguin.
Drought and crop failure in his Malawi village motivate 14-year-old William to figure out how to bring electricity to his people. William successfully builds a windmill out of junkyard scraps and harnesses energy from the wind. The story is beautifully told and illustrated with vivid pictures.

Marrin, W. (2013). *Black gold: The story of oil in our lives*. New York: Random House.
While oil is much disputed, it has played a pivotal role in all aspects of our lives and shaped the history, politics, society, and economy of all nations on Earth. Marrin's books explores oil and its influence.

Seuss, Dr. (1949). *Bartholomew and the oobleck*. Toronto: Random House.
This is the story of a boy, Bartholomew, who must contend with a sticky substance, Oobleck, that has fallen from the sky. In the end, Bartholomew helps his king rid the kingdom of this strange, sticky stuff.

Strauss, R. (2007). *One well: The story of water on Earth*. Toronto: Kids Can Press.
Water connects all beings on Earth, and how we treat water impacts all living things. This book illuminates our power to conserve water and protect our shared well.

Wells, R. E. (1995). *How do you lift a lion?* Park Ridge, IL: Albert Whitman and Company.
Wells's delightful book looks at levers, wheels, and pulleys as simple machines lift a lion, pull a panda, and get a basket of bananas to a baboon's birthday party.

Young, C. (2011). *Ten birds*. Toronto: Kids Can Press.
Young's incredible chiaroscuro pen-and-ink drawings illustrate this story of 10 birds given the task of crossing a river. The book uniquely explores the inadequacy of labels in identifying abilities and characteristics.

Earth and Space Science Titles

Baylor, B. (1985). *Everybody needs a rock*. Toronto: Aladdin.
Baylor's story tells the tale of a rockhound with very particular rules for finding the right rock.

Carle, E. (2002). *Little cloud*. New York: Puffin Books.
While other clouds drift across the sky, Little Cloud is lagging behind. This is because he is busy changing shapes—from a sheep to an airplane to a clown. Carle's story will inspire you to look up and see what shapes Little Cloud is making.

Cassino, M., & Nelson, J. (2009). *The story of snow: The science of winter's wonderland*. San Francisco: Chronicle Books.
The Story of Snow investigates the science of snow and answers commonly asked questions. The book features pictures of snow crystals and instructions for snow catching.

DePaola, T. (1974). *The cloud book*. New York: Holiday House Inc.
This book describes the 10 most common cloud shapes and explores cloud and weather-related myths and sayings.

Hesse, K. (1999). *Come on, rain!* Markham, ON: Scholastic.
A lyrical delight, *Come On, Rain!* shares the sensory experience of a refreshing and renewing summer rainstorm following an urban heatwave. Hesse's simple yet beautiful prose is complemented by light watercolour illustrations.

Hiscock, B. (1999). *The big rock*. Toronto: Aladdin.
Hiscock's story is one of a very old rock, formed millions of years ago. The history of the granite boulder is traced through the ages, from mountain formation and wearing down, to flooding, to the age of dinosaurs. *The Big Rock* will make you appreciate the silent witness that is a rock.

Hooper, M. (1997). *The pebble in my pocket*. London, UK: Pan Macmillan.
The Pebble in my Pocket follows the path of a pebble from formation in a volcano 480 million years ago through rock formation and erosion to the present.

Hurst, C. O. (2001). *Rocks in his head*. Toronto: HarperCollins.
Hurst's father was a collector of rocks, and through difficult times, he continued to collect, trade, label, and display his rocks. No one thought his obsession would amount to anything until a museum found that his eccentricity was just what they needed.

Locker, T. (2003). *Cloud dance*. Markham, ON: Houghton Mifflin Harcourt.
Through poetic prose and lovely illustrations, Locker introduces the science of clouds in a journey through cumulus, cirrus, and stratus clouds.

London, J. (1998). *Hurricane!* Toronto: HarperCollins.
The sun is shining on the mountains of El Yunque rainforest in Puerto Rico until suddenly the sky turns deep purple and a hurricane bears down on the island.

Martin, J. B. (2009). *Snowflake Bentley*. Markham, ON: Houghton Mifflin Harcourt.
Bentley loved to photograph snowflakes and his enthusiasm paid off as he revealed that no two snowflakes were alike. With beautiful woodcut illustrations, readers see the passion and vision of a scientist.

Martin, Jr., B., & Archambault, J. (1988). *Listen to the rain*. New York: Henry Holt and Co.
The authors beautifully and gently present the magic rhythm of rain's sounds and silences through poetic prose and abstract paintings.

McNulty, F. (1990). *How to dig a hole to the other side of the world*. Toronto: HarperCollins.
Follow an exciting 8000-mile journey through the centre of Earth and discover what is inside our planet! This book presents information about Earth's composition in a fun and engaging way.

Polacco, P. (2002). *Thunder cake*. New York: Puffin Books.
A grandmother and her granddaughter hurry to collect ingredients from the farm and get the Thunder Cake in the oven before an approaching thunderstorm arrives. Polacco's touching story retells how her own grandmother helped her to overcome her fear of thunderstorms.

Rey, H. A. (2008). *Find the constellations*. Markham, ON: Houghton Mifflin Harcourt.
Rey's passion for astronomy and star gazing is clear in this classic book. It contains star charts, constellation guides, and information about seasons and celestial movements. The second edition features additional information, including the reclassification of Pluto as a dwarf planet.

Shaw, C. G. (1993). *It looked like spilt milk*. Toronto: HarperCollins.
Children will be motivated by this book to create their own cloud identification games. On a blue background, the white cloud changes shape on each page. What shape will be next?

Simon, S. (1994). *Comets, meteors, and asteroids*. Toronto: HarperCollins.
Throughout history, these celestial bodies have mesmerized and puzzled scientists and star gazers. Simon's book explores the characteristics of comets, meteors, and asteroids and shares what they can tell us about our universe.

Steig, W. (1999). *Sylvester and the magic pebble*. Toronto: Aladdin.
Sylvester finds a magic pebble that makes wishes come true. On his way home, he is frightened by a lion and makes a wish that brings unexpected results. Through magical storytelling and beautiful illustrations, the reader joins Sylvester as he is reunited with his family and his true self is restored.

Stolz, M. (1989). *Storm in the night*. Toronto: HarperCollins.
It is a dark night, lit only by flashes of lightning. Thomas and his grandfather rediscover the magic of the world and each other.

Sweeney, J. (1999). *Me and my place in space*. New York: Random House.
Sweeney's book is a lovely introduction to space. Its clear language, diagrams, and images bring fun and detail to the young astronaut's tour of the planets and stars.

Tresselt, A. (1988). *Hide and seek fog*. Toronto: HarperCollins.
Children play in the fog that envelops a seaside community, but the fog has strange and mysterious effects.

Waldman, N. (2005). *The snowflake: A water cycle story*. Minneapolis, MN: Lerner Publishing.
From precipitation to evaporation to condensation, the path of a water droplet is traced through the water cycle.

Appendix F
Planning for Field Trips

When planning for a unit of study, you may want to include a field trip that will be both educational and fun. Field trips can enhance learning and help develop social and interpersonal skills. For some students, your field trip might be the first time they have experienced a farm, science centre, zoo, laboratory, or other setting. While valuable, field trips require a great deal of preparation and planning. Planning often begins with a sense that a particular part of a unit is best supported by learning beyond the classroom. For example, a unit on ecology might warrant a trip to a local wetland, or an astronomy unit might include a trip to an observatory. Regardless of the destination, be sure that the substance of the field trip supports your curriculum outcomes or expectations. A well thought-out rationale for taking students out of school may be required by your principal and by parents. Be sure to carefully review related rules and regulations set out by your jurisdiction. What follows is a guide to help you plan effective field trips.

At the Start of the School Year (or Earlier)

- As you make your year plans (or long-term plans), think about places you would like to visit with your students to complement your curriculum.
- Book visits to special exhibitions and programs. Some destinations and programs are in high demand. Best to book early rather than be disappointed. Also check about cancellation policies. If you are planning a field trip during a busy time (e.g., in June), book even earlier.
- Make connections with other teachers at your school or in your district who are also interested in attending the exhibition or program. Sharing a bus can reduce the cost of transportation.
- Ask students about places they have visited in the past and places they would like to explore. This will help you to tailor your curriculum to meet student interests. Also ask parents about previous field trips.
- Determine whether you have funding for field trips. Plan for fundraising if needed.
- Visit the site ahead of time. This will help your trip planning, especially if you have not yet attended the venue with a student group. Many venues have a special teacher's evening or a reduced rate for teachers.
- Find out what the legal supervision ratios (adult: student) are for your board. While these are the legal requirements, err on the side of having more adults. This will allow you to have smaller groups—always a good thing!

Two Months Before the Field Trip

- Find out if your school board or local jurisdiction requires particular permission forms. Sometimes requests for field trips need to be approved at the board level.
- If needed, book transportation for your field trip. Look into taking public transit; this can be much less expensive than paying for a bus. Some cities and municipalities offer

reduced fares for school groups. Also, taking public transit can be a learning experience for many students.

- Send a letter home to parents and guardians that describes the field trip (date, place, purpose, etc.) and invites parents to volunteer as supervisors. By giving ample time for parents and guardians to make adjustments to their schedules, you will be more likely to have enough adult support on your trip.

One Month Before the Field Trip

- Determine the cost of the field trip and how it will be paid for. Consider whether you will ask parents or guardians to contribute to the cost. Be sensitive to the situations of your students' families and what is feasible to ask. Confirm contributions from your school budget and any fundraising you may have done.

- Start to bring the field trip into your teaching. For example, you might relate a concept from a science exploration to a simulation that students will get to experience at the science centre. Or, you might begin a project that cumulates with the field trip.

Two Weeks Before the Field Trip

- Create an itinerary for the day. If appropriate, leave free exploration time; it can be a good idea to have more structured activity at the start of your visit so that students become familiar with the venue and can note exhibits or sights they would like to revisit later in small groups.

- Plan activities for the field trip and create any materials (e.g., exhibition inquiry worksheets, booklets) for your students. Look at specific resources that are available from the venue and adapt as needed to fit your curriculum needs.

- Talk about the field trip with your students. This is particularly important for younger students. Discuss the activities that students will be taking part in and your expectations for the trip. You might wish to practise some of the expectations and signals beforehand (e.g., walking hand in hand with a partner in the hallways).

- Prepare and send home permission forms to be signed by parents and guardians and returned. Some school boards have generic permission forms. Include a space for volunteers to indicate that they will be attending. While your school will have records of student medical information, include this on your permission form as well. Be sure to have your students write reminders in their agendas or planners to bring back their forms. Have additional copies on hand; some will undoubtedly get lost.

One Week Before the Field Trip

- Contact parent and guardian volunteers by phone or email to confirm their attendance and to let them know when to meet at the school on the day of the trip.

- If you have a school lunch program, arrange for packed lunches for your students for the day of the trip.

- Make arrangements for those students who will not be taking part in the field trip. This might be with another class at the same grade level or as a special helper with another class.

- Make a handout for volunteers, briefly outlining the itinerary for the day, expectations for students, volunteers' responsibilities, and emergency contact numbers.

During the Week Before the Field Trip

- Prepare your field trip backpack or bag. Include a class list with emergency contact details, pencils and clipboards (if needed), a first-aid kit, and any medications your students might need. Depending on your destination, pack trip-specific supplies (e.g., spare dry socks and a compass for a hike). Also consider bringing a camera (or cameras for each group) if allowed at the venue; these allow for quick and easy data collection and the pictures taken can be used in many learning activities back at school.

- Double check that you have permission forms signed for each student. Contact parents and guardians for those students whose forms have not been returned, to gently remind them.

- Think about how you will group your students. Which students work well together? Which students work better separately? How many groups, and students per group, are needed for any programs in which students will participate? Try to form small groups (three or four students per parent) if possible. Also, consider *not* having a group for yourself; this will allow you to circulate among groups to check on learning and behaviour.

- Talk to your students about what to bring in terms of clothing and food.

- Remind students of what to expect on the field trip and what they will be doing.

- Prepare work for any students staying at the school with another class during the field trip.

- Watch the weather forecast and ask your students to bring weather-appropriate gear and supplies.

- On the day before the field trip, make all final preparations—less to worry about on a busy field trip morning!

The Day of the Field Trip

- Double check your trip backpack for supplies.

- Let the office know which students will not be attending and those who will be spending the day with another class at the school.

- If your students get school lunches, pick up packed lunches.

- Ask students and volunteers to arrive at school 15 to 20 minutes before departure time. This will leave some wiggle room for students and volunteers who might be running late.

- Organize students into partners and groups while still at the school if possible. You might have students create group names for themselves. Be sure that volunteers know which groups and individual students they are responsible for.

- Remind students of expectations for the field trip before you leave the school and also at various points through the day as needed.

- Regularly take a head count and have a volunteer do so with you.

- Set a central place for students to go if they get separated from the group (e.g., information desk, atrium).

- Have fun!

After the Field Trip

- Debrief the field trip. This might be done informally on the journey back to school and more formally the following day. This is the time to have a class discussion about the trip and make connections to what is being learned at school. Let students share their stories of exciting things that happened on the field trip, as well as the science content they learned.

- Make explicit connections to your teaching, both in science and any other curricular areas that your visit supported. Make sure that the trip is not an isolated event, with no connection to your curriculum and instruction.

- Send thank-you notes or emails to parent and guardian volunteers, program guides, bus drivers, and others who helped. Knowing that you and your students appreciate their efforts will increase the likelihood of their support in the future.

In summary, there are many considerations to keep in mind when planning field trips. Carefully planned trips are more effective and enjoyable for everyone. Benefits to students include learning new material, experiencing new environments or locations, developing social and interpersonal skills, and experiencing science beyond the classroom. Have a wonderful field trip!

References

Abd-El-Khalick, F., & Lederman, N. G. (2000). Improving science teachers' conceptions of the nature of science: A critical review of the literature. *International Journal of Science Education, 22*(7), 665–701.

Aikenhead, G. (2001). Students' ease in crossing cultural borders into school science. *Science Education, 85*(2), 180–188.

Aikenhead, G., & Michell, H. (2011). *Bridging cultures: Indigenous and scientific ways of knowing nature.* Toronto: Pearson Canada, Inc.

Aikenhead, G. S. (1994). What is STS teaching? In J. Solomon & G. Aikenhead (Eds.), *STS education: International perspectives on reform* (pp. 47–59). New York: Teachers College Press.

Aikenhead, G. S. (1996). Science education: Border crossing into the subculture of science. *Studies in Science Education, 27*(1), 1–52.

Aikenhead, G. S. (2006). *Science education for everyday life: Evidence-based practice.* New York: Teachers College Press.

Aikenhead, G. S., Allen, N., Jegede, O. J. (1999, March). *Culture studies in science education: Current issues.* Workshop presented at National Association for Research in Science Teaching Annual Conference, Boston, MA.

Alberta, Manitoba, Saskatchewan, Northwest Territories, Nunavut, and the Yukon. (2011). *The Western and Northern Canadian Protocol.*

Allen, M. (2010). *Misconceptions in primary science.* Maidenhead, UK: Open University.

Allen, P. (1996). *Who sank the boat?* New York: The Putnam & Grossett Group.

Alsop, S., & Bencze, L. (2012). In search of activist pedagogies in SMTE. *Canadian Journal of Science, Mathematics & Technology Education, 12*(4), 394–408.

Alsop, S., & Fawcett, L. (2010). After this nothing happened. *Cultural Studies of Science Education, 5*(4), 1027–1045.

Alsop, S., & Pedretti, E. (2001). Science, technology and society. In S. Alsop & K. Hicks (Eds.), *Teaching science* (pp. 193–208). London, UK: Kogan Page.

Alsop, S., & Watts, M. (2003). Science education and affect. *International Journal of Science Education, 25*(9), 1043–1047.

American Association for the Advancement of Science. (1989). *Project 2061: Science for All Americans.* Washington, DC: Author.

Amirshokoohi, A., & Kazempour, M. (2010). The biodiversity community action project: An STS investigation. *The American Biology Teacher, 72*(5), 288–293.

Anderson, L., & Krathwohl, D. A. (2001) *Taxonomy for learning, teaching and assessing: A revision of Bloom's taxonomy of educational objectives.* New York: Longman.

Aoki, T. T. (1993). Legitimating lived curriculum: Towards a curricular landscape of multiplicity. *Journal of Curriculum and Supervision, 8*(3), 255–268.

Apple, M. W. (2004). *Ideology and curriculum* (3rd ed.). New York: RoutledgeFalmer.

Appleton, K. (2006). Science pedagogical content knowledge and elementary school teachers. In K. Appleton (Ed.), *Elementary science teacher education: International perspectives on contemporary issues and practice* (pp. 31–54). Mahwah, NJ: Lawrence Erlbaun.

Asbell-Clark, J. (2011). *Martian boneyards: Sustained scientific inquiry in a social digital game.* Unpublished dissertation. Toronto: University of Toronto.

Aspen-Baxter, L., Brockman, A., Molnar, C., & Shields, K. (2013). *Saskatchewan science 3.* Toronto: Pearson Canada Inc.

Aspin, D. (2002). An ontology of values and the humanisation of eduction. In S. Pascoe (Ed.), *Values in education.* Deakin, ACT: The Australian College of Educators.

Assessment Reform Group. (2002). *Assessment for learning: 10 principles.* Retrieved from www.assessment-reform-group.org

Atlantic Canada Science Curriculum. (no date). *Foundation for the Atlantic Canada Science Curriculum.* Retrieved from http://www.ednet.ns.ca/files/curriculum/camet/foundations-science.pdf

Ausubel, D. P. (1968). *Educational psychology: A cognitive view.* New York: Holt, Rinehart & Winston.

Baker, J. (2002). *Window.* London, UK: Walker Books Ltd.

Banchi, H., & Bell, R. (2008). The many levels of inquiry. *Science and Children, 46*(2), 26–29.

Banks, J. A. (1996). The canon debate, knowledge construction and multicultural education. In F. Schultz (Ed.), *Education 96/97* (pp. 163–173). Guilford, CN: Dushkin Publishing Group.

Barman, C. (1997). Students' views of scientists and science: Results from a national study. *Science and Children, 35*(1), 18–24.

Barnett, J., & Hodson, D. (2001). Pedagogical context knowledge: Toward a fuller understanding of what good science teachers know. *Science Education, 85*(4), 426–453.

Base, G. (2001). *The waterhole.* New York: Puffin Books.

Bash, L., & Zezlina-Phillips, E. (2006). Identity, boundary and schooling: Perspectives on the experiences and perceptions of refugee children 1. *Intercultural Education, 17*(1), 113–128.

Bateson, G. (2000). *Steps to an ecology of mind.* Chicago: University of Chicago Press.

Baylor, B. *(1985). Everybody needs a rock.* New York: Macmillan.

Bazzul, J., & Sykes, H. (2011). The secret identity of a biology textbook: Straight and naturally sexed. *Cultural Studies in Science Education, 6*(2), 265–286.

Bell, R., Smetana, L., & Binns, I. (2005). Simplifying inquiry instruction. *The Science Teacher, 72*(7), 30–33.

Bellomo, K. (2003). Towards the development of an inclusive science curriculum. In D. Hodson (Ed.), *OISE Papers in Science Education, 4* (pp. 59–78). Toronto: OISE.

Bellwood, C., Denyes, K., Friar, L., Windsor, C., & Mahoney, K. (2007). *The three cueing systems. Hastings and Prince Edward District School Board C.O.D.E Project.* Retrieved from http://www.hpedsb.on.ca/ec/services/cst/elementary/literacy/documents/ThreeCueingSystems-detail.pdf

Bencze, J. L. (2001). "Technoscience" education: Empowering citizens against the tyranny of school science. *International Journal of Technology and Design Education, 11*(3), 273–298.

Bencze, J. L., & Bowen, G. M. (2009). A National Science Fair: Exhibiting support for the knowledge economy. *International Journal of Science Education, 31*(18), 2459–2483.

Bencze, J. L., & Carter, L. (2011). Globalizing students acting for the common good. *Journal of Research in Science Teaching, 48*(6), 648–669.

Bencze, J. L., & Sperling, E. R. (2012). Student-teachers as advocates for student-led research-informed socioscientific activism. *Canadian Journal of Science, Mathematics and Technology Education, 12*(1), 62–85.

Bencze, L., Bowen, M., & Alsop, S. (2006). Teachers' tendencies to promote student-led science projects: Associations with their views about science. *Science Education, 90*(3), 400–419.

Bencze, L., DiGiuseppe, M., Hodson, D., Pedretti, E., Serebin, L., & Decoito, I. (2003). Paradigmatic road blocks in elementary school science "reform": Reconsidering nature-of-science teaching within a rational-realist milieu. *Systematic Practice and Action Research, 16*(5), 285–308.

Bennett, B. B., & Rolheiser, N. C. (2008). *Beyond Monet.* Toronto: Bookation.

Bennett, J., Lubben, F., & Hogarth, S. (2007). Bringing science to life: A synthesis of the research evidence on the effects of context-based and STS approaches to science teaching. *Science Education, 91*(3), 347–370.

Bilash, B., & Shields, M. (2001). *A demo a day: A year of biological demonstrations.* Batavia, IL: FLINN Scientific Ltd.

Blades, D. W. (1997). *Procedures of power and curriculum change.* New York: Peter Lang.

Blades, D. W. (2006). Levinas and an ethics for science education. *Educational Philosophy and Theory, 38*(5), 647–664.

Bloom, B. (1956). *Taxonomy of educational objectives: The classification of educational goals; Handbook I: Cognitive domain.* New York: Longmans Green.

Bobbitt, F. (1918/2004). Scientific method in curriculum-making. In D. J. Flinders & S. J. Thornton (Eds.), *The curriculum studies reader* (2nd ed., pp. 9–16). New York: RoutledgeFalmer.

Bosak, S. V. (1991). *Science is…* Markham, ON: Scholastic.

Bouchard, D., & Vickers, R. H. (2004). *The elders are watching.* Vancouver, BC: Raincoast Books.

Boulton, J., Brockman, A., Johanson, T., Wallace, M., & View, T. (2000). *Saskatchewan science 8.* Toronto: Pearson Canada, Inc.

Bowen, G. M., & Bencze, J. L. (2009). Print media representations of science fairs. *Canadian Journal of Science, Mathematics, and Technology Education, 9*(2), 100–116.

Bowen, G. M., & Roth, W. M. (2005). Data and graph interpretation practices among pre-service teachers. *Journal of Research in Science Teaching, 42*(10), 1063–1088.

Bowers, C. A. (2002). Toward an eco-justice pedagogy. *Environmental Education Research, 8*(1), 21–34.

Braund, M., & Reiss, M. (2006). Towards a more authentic science curriculum: The contribution of out-of-school learning. *International Journal of Science Education, 28*(12), 1373–1388.

Brickhouse, N. W. (1990). Teachers' beliefs about the nature of science and their relationship to classroom practice. *Journal of Teacher Education, 41*(3), 53–62

Brickhouse, N. W., & Potter, J. T. (2001). Young women's scientific identity formation in an urban context. *Journal of Research in Science Teaching, 38*(8), 965–980.

British Columbia Ministry of Education. (1995). *Environmental concepts in the classroom: A guide for teachers.* Victoria, BC: Author.

British Columbia Ministry of Education. (2005). *Science K–7 integrated resource package.* Victoria, BC: Author.

British Columbia Ministry of Education. (2007). *Environmental learning and experience: An interdisciplinary guide for teachers.* Victoria, BC: Author.

Buxton, C. A. (2010). Social problem solving through science: An approach to critical, place-based, science teaching and learning. *Equity & Excellence in Education, 43*(1), 120–135.

Caduto, M. J., & Bruchac, J. (1997). *Keepers of the animals: Native American stories and wildlife activities for children.* Golden, CO: Fulcrum Publishing.

Cakir, M. (2008). Constructivist approaches to learning in science and their implications for science education: A review of the literature. *International Journal of Environmental and Science Education, 3*(4), 193–206.

Calabrese Barton, A. (1998). Teaching science with homeless children: Pedagogy, representation, and identity. *Journal of Research in Science Teaching, 34*(4), 379–394.

Calabrese Barton, A. (2001). Science education in urban settings: Seeking new ways of praxis through critical ethnography. *Journal of Research in Science Teaching, 38*(8), 899–917.

Calabrese Barton, A. (2003). *Teaching science for social justice.* New York: Teachers College Press.

Calabrese Barton, A., & Upadhyay, B. (2010). Teaching and learning science for social justice: Introduction to the special issue. *Equity & Excellence in Education, 43*(1), 1–5.

Canadian Council of Learning. (2007). *Lessons in learning, the cultural divide in science education for Aboriginal learners.* Retrieved from http://www.ccl-cca.ca/ccl/Reports/LessonsInLearning.html

Carlone, H. B., & Johnson, A. (2007). Understanding the science experiences of successful women of color: Science identity as an analytic lens. *Journal of Research in Science Teaching, 44*(8), 1187–1218.

Carson, R. (1956/1998). *The sense of wonder.* New York: Harper Collins.

Carson, R. (1962). *Silent spring.* New York: Houghton Mifflin.

Carter, Majora. *Greening the Ghetto.* Retrieved from http://www.ted.com/index.php/talks/majora_carter_s_tale_of_urban_renewal.html

Cavallo, A. (2007). Draw-a-scientist/mystery box redux. *Science and Children, 45*(3), 37–41.

Chambers, C. (1999). A topography for Canadian curriculum theory. *Canadian Journal of Education, 24*(2), 137–150.

Chambers, D. W. (1983). Stereotypic images of the scientist: The draw-a-scientist test. *Science Education, 67*(2), 255–265.

Cherryholmes, C. H. (1988). *Power and criticism: Poststructural investigations in education.* New York: Teachers College Press.

Clough, M. P. (2000). The nature of science: Understanding how the game of science is played. *The Clearing House, 74*(1), 13–17.

Cober, R., McCann, C., Slotta, J., & Moher, T. (2012). Materials that scaffold collective inquiry: The role of aggregate representations. *Proceedings of the Tenth International Conference of the Learning Sciences—Volume 2* (64–71). Sydney, Australia: International Society of the Learning Sciences, Inc.

Cobern, W., & Loving, C. (1998). The card exchange: Introducing the philosophy of science. In W. F. McComas (Ed.), *The nature of science in science education: Rationales and strategies* (pp. 73–82). London, UK: Kluwer Academic Publishers.

Cobern, W.W. (1996). Worldview theory and conceptual change in science education. *Science Education, 80,* 579–610.

Cochran-Smith, M. (2003). Learning and unlearning: The education of teacher educators. *Teaching and Teacher Education, 19*(1), 5–28.

Cochran-Smith, M. (2004). *Walking the road: Race, diversity, and social justice in teacher education.* New York: Teachers College Press.

Colburn, A. (2000). Constructivism: Science education's "grand unifying theory." *The Clearing House, 7*(41), 9–12.

Connelly, F. M., & Clandinin, D. J. (1988). *Teachers as curriculum planners: Narratives of experience.* New York: Teachers College Press.

Cook, J. L., & Cook, G. (2005). *Child development: Principles & perspectives.* Boston, MA: Allyn & Bacon, Pearson Inc.

Cooper, S., Motley, T., & Thomas, J. (2011). No duck left behind: Fourth grade students' data analysis supports scientists' theory of declining duck populations. *Science and Children, 48*(5), 45–49.

Corson, D. (1998). *Changing education for diversity.* Buckingham, UK: Open University Press.

Costa, V. B. (1995). When science is "another world": Relationships between worlds of family, friends, school, and science. *Science Education, 79*(3), 313–333.

Council of Ministers of Education, Canada. (1997). *Common framework of science learning outcomes, K–12: Pan-Canadian protocol for collaboration on school curriculum.* Toronto: Queens' Printer for Ontario.

Council of Ministers of Education, Canada. (2010). *Pan-Canadian education for sustainable development framework for collaboration and action.* Toronto: Author.

Crouch, C., Fagen, A. P., Callan, J. P., & Mazur, E. (2004). Classroom demonstrations: Learning tools or entertainment? *American Journal of Physics, 72*(6), 835–838.

Crowther, D. T., Lederman, N. G., & Lederman, J. S. (2005). Understanding the true meaning of the nature of science. *Science and Children, 43*(2), 50–52.

Cuban, L. (1995). The hidden variable: How organizations influence teacher responses to secondary science curriculum reform. *Theory into Practice, 34*(1), 4–11.

Cummins, J. (1981). Age on arrival and immigrant second language learning in Canada: A reassessment. *Applied Linguistics, 2*(2), 132–149.

Cummins, J. (1996). *Negotiating identities: Education for empowerment in a diverse society.* Ontario, CA: California Association for Bilingual Education.

Cummins, J. (2011). *Teaching English language learners.* Retrieved from http://www.etfo.ca/resources/researchforteachers/pages/default.aspx

Cummins, J., & Early, M. (Eds). (2011). *Identity texts: The collaborative creation of power in multilingual schools.* Stoke-on-Trent, UK: Trentham Books.

Dagher, Z. R., & Ford, D. J. (2005). How are scientists portrayed in children's science biographies? *Science & Education, 14*(3–5), 377–393.

Davidson, S., Passmore, C., & Anderson, D. (2010). Learning on zoo field trips: The interaction of agendas and practices of students, teachers, and zoo educators. *Science Education, 94*(1), 122–141.

Davis, B., & Sumara, D. J. (1997). Cognition, complexity, and teacher education. *Harvard Educational Review, 67*(1), 105–125.

Davis, B., Sumara, D., & Luce-Kapler, R. (2008). *Engaging minds: Changing teaching in complex times* (2nd ed.). New York: Routledge.

Dawson, V. M. (2001). Addressing controversial issues in secondary school science. *Australian Science Teachers' Journal, 47*(4), 38–44.

de Bono, E. (1985). *Six thinking hats: An essential approach to business management.* London: Little, Brown, & Company.

de Jong, T., & Ferguson-Hessler, M. G. M. (1996). Types and qualities of knowledge. *Educational Psychologist, 31*(2), 105–113.

DeCoito, I. (2009). *Improving teachers' and students' nature of science conceptions using reading and writing activities to reflect on the nature of science.* Germany: Lambert Academic Publishers.

Delpit, L. (1995). *Other people's children: Cultural conflict in the classroom.* New York: The New Press.

Dewey, J. (1925/1997). *Experience and nature.* Chicago: Open Court.

Dewey, J. (1938/1997). *Experience and education.* New York: Touchstone.

Dolan, T. J., & Zeidler, D. L. (2009). Speed kills! (Or does it?) *Science and Children, 47*(3), 20–23.

Doll Jr., W. E. (1993/2004). The four R's—An alternative to the Tyler rationale. In D. J. Flinders & S. J. Thornton (Eds.), *The curriculum studies reader* (2nd ed., pp. 253–260). New York: RoutledgeFalmer.

Driver, R. (1989). Students' conceptions and the learning of science. *International Journal of Science Education, 11*(5), 481–490.

Driver, R., Guesne, E., & Tiberghien, A. (1985). *Children's ideas in science.* Milton Keynes, UK: Open University Press.

Driver, R., Leach, J., Millar, R., & Scott, P. (1997).*Young people's images of science.* Philadelphia: Open University Press.

DuFour, R., Eaker, R., & DuFour, R. (2005). Recurring themes of professional learning communities and assumptions they challenge. In R. DuFour, R. Eaker, and R. DuFour (Eds.), *On common ground: The power of professional learning communities.* (pp. 7–29). Bloomington, IN: National Education Service.

Dunbar, K. (2000). How scientists think in the world: Implications for science education. *Journal of Applied Developmental Psychology, 21*(1), 49–58.

Egan, K. (1978). What is curriculum? *Curriculum Inquiry, 8*(1), 9–16.

Eisner, E.W. (1979). *The educational imagination: On the design and evaluation of school programs.* New York: Macmillan.

Eisner. E.W., & Vallance, E. (Eds.). (1974). *Conflicting conceptions of curriculum*. Berkeley, CA: McCutchan.

Ellis, L., Hounjet, C., Johanson, T., Walter, C., O'Soup, D., Racette, C., & View, T. (2012). *Saskatchewan science 5*. Toronto: Pearson.

Emdin, C. (2010). Affiliation and alienation: Hip-hop, rap, and urban science education. *Journal of Curriculum Studies, 42*(1), 1–25.

Emdin, C. (2011). Droppin' science and dropping science: African American males and urban science education. *Journal of African American Males in Education, 2*(1), 66–80.

Eslinger, J. C. (2012). Navigating between a rock and a hard place: Lessons from an urban school teacher. *Education and Urban Society*. doi: 10.1177/0013124512446221.

Falk, J., & Dierking, L. (2001). *Free-choice science education: How we learn science outside of school*. New York: Teachers College Press.

Fensham, P. (2002). Time to change drivers for scientific literacy. *Canadian Journal of Science, Mathematics and Technology Education, 2*(1), 9–24.

Fleer, M. (1996). Fusing the boundaries between home and pre-school to support children's scientific learning. *Research in Science Education, 26*(2), 143–154.

Fleer, M. (2009). Understanding the dialectical relations between everyday concepts and scientific concepts within play-based programs. *Research in Science Education, 39*(2), 281–306.

Fogliano, J. (2012). *And then it's spring...* New York: Roaring Brook Press.

Foster, A., & Linney, G. (2007). *Reconnecting children through outdoor education. A research summary*. Toronto: The Council of Outdoor Educators.

Franklin, U. (1999). *CBC Massey Lectures. The real world of technology*. Toronto: HarperCollins Canada Ltd.

Freire, P. (1970). *Pedagogy of the oppressed*. New York: Continuum.

Frykholm, J. A., & Glasson, G. E. (2005). Connecting science and mathematics instruction: Pedagogical context knowledge for teachers. *School Science and Mathematics, 105*(3), 127–141.

Furman, G. C., & Gruenewald, D. A. (2004). Expanding the landscape of social justice: A critical ecological analysis. *Educational Administration Quarterly, 40*(1), 47–76.

Gallagher, J. J. (1971). A broader base for science teaching. *Science Education, 55*(3), 329–338.

Gardner, H. (1985). *Frames of mind: The theory of multiple intelligences*. New York: Basic Books.

Gardner, H. (2006). *Multiple intelligences: New horizons*. New York: Basic Books.

Gaylie, V. (2008). The poetry garden: Ecoliteracy in an urban school. *Language and Literacy, 10*(2). Retrieved from http://ejournals.library.ualberta.ca/index.php/langandlit/article/view/9778/7692

Gaylie, V. (2009). *The learning garden: Ecology, teaching, and transformation*. New York: Peter Lang.

Gaylie, V. (2011). *Roots and research in urban school gardens*. New York: Peter Lang.

Gess-Newsome, J. (2002). Pedagogical content knowledge: An introduction and orientation. In J. Gess-Newsome & N. Lederman, (Eds.), *Examining pedagogical content knowledge* (pp. 3–17). Rotterdam, The Netherlands: Kluwer Academic Publishers.

Gill, D., & Levidow, L. (1987). (Eds.). *Anti-racist science teaching*. London, UK: Free Association Books.

Giroux, H. A. (2005). *Border crossings: Cultural workers and the politics of education*. New York: Routledge.

Gitari, W. (2003). Science literacy: Schooled science in the service of equity and social justice. In K.S. Brathwaite (Ed.), *Access and equity in the university* (pp. 349–374). Toronto: Canadian Scholars Press.

Gitari, W. (2008). Some issues of science education in Africa. In N. Damlini (Ed.), *New directions in African education, challenges and possibilities* (pp. 41–72). University of Calgary Press.

Government of Canada. (2007). *The framework for environmental learning and sustainability in Canada*. Ottawa: Author. Government of Canada.

Government of Nunavut. (2004). *Pinasuaqtavut 2004–2009: Our commitment to building Nunavut's future*. Retrieved from http://www.gov.nu.ca/pinasuaqtavut/engcover.pdf

Government of Nunavut. (2007). *Inuit Qaujimajatuqangit education framework for Nunavut curriculum*. Iqaluit, NU: Department of Education, C&SS.

Grant, C.A. & Zeichner, K.M. (1995). On becoming a reflective teacher. In G. Taylor & R. Runte (Eds.), *Thinking about teaching: An introduction* (pp. 54–68). Toronto: Harcourt, Brace & Company.

Gross, G.R., Koob, J., & Bilash, B. (1995). *A demo a day: A year of chemical demonstrations*. Batavia, IL: FLINN Scientific Ltd.

Gruenewald, D. (2008). The best of both worlds: A critical pedagogy of place. *Environmental Education Research, 14*(3), 308–324.

Grundy, S. (1987). *Curriculum—Product or praxis?* Lewes, UK: Falmer Press.

Hand, B. (1996). Diagnosis of teachers' knowledge bases and teaching roles when implementing constructivist teaching/learning approaches. In D. F. Treagust, R. Duit, & B. J. Fraser (Eds.), *Improving teaching and learning in science and mathematics* (pp. 212–221). New York: Teachers College Press.

Harding, S. (1991). *Whose science? Whose knowledge? Thinking from women's lives*. New York: Cornell University Press.

Harding, S. (1998). *Is science multicultural?* Bloomington, IN: Indiana University Press.

Harlen, W., & Holroyd, C. (1997). Primary teachers' understanding of concepts of science: Impact on confidence and teaching. *International Journal of Science Education, 19*(1), 93–105.

Harrison, A., & Coll, R. (2008). *Using analogies in middle and secondary science classrooms, the FAR guide, an interesting way to teach with analogies*. Thousand Oaks, CA: Corwin Press.

Hart, P. (2002). Environment in the science curriculum: The politics of change in the Pan-Canadian science curriculum development process. *International Journal of Science Education, 24*(11), 1239–1254.

Hart, P., & Nolan, K. (1999). A critical analysis of research in evnrionmental education. *Studies in Science Education, 34*(1), 1–69.

Hein, G. (1998). *Learning in the museum*. New York: Routledge.

Hewitt, J. (2005). Instructional technologies, technocentrism, and science education. In S. Alsop, L. Bencze, & E. Pedretti (Eds.), *Analysing exemplary science teaching: Theoretical lenses* and a spectrum of possibilities for practice (pp. 160–170). Buckingham, UK: Open University Press.

Hodson, D. (1993). In search of a rationale for multicultural science education. *Science Education, 77*(6), 685–711.

Hodson, D. (1998). *Teaching and learning science: Towards a personalized approach.* Philadelphia: Open University Press.

Hodson, D. (1998). In pursuit of literacy. In D. Hodson (Ed.), *Teaching and learning science: Towards a personalized approach* (pp. 1–8). Philadelphia: Open University Press.

Hodson, D. (2003). Time for action: Science education for an alternative future. *International Journal of Science Education, 25*(6), 645–670.

Hodson, D. (2008). *Towards scientific literacy: A teachers' guide to the history, philosophy, and sociology of science.* Rotterdam: Sense Publishers.

Hodson, D. (2011). *Looking into the future: Building a curriculum for social activism.* Rotterdam: Sense Publishers.

Hofstein, A., & Lunetta, V. (2003). The laboratory in science education: Foundations for the twenty-first century. *Science Education, 88,* 28–54.

Hollins, E. R. (1993). Assessing teacher competence for diverse populations. *Theory into Practice, 32*(2), 93–99.

Hollins, E. R. (1996). *Culture in school learning: Revealing the deep meaning.* Mahwah, NJ: Lawrence Erlbaum Associates.

Hood, G. H. (1998). Democracy and the Curriculum. In L. E. Beyer & M. W. Apple (Eds.), *The curriculum: Problems, politics, and possibilities* (pp. 177–198). Albany: SUNY Press.

Huber, R. A., & Burton, G. M. (1995). What do students think scientists look like? *School Science and Mathematics, 95*(7), 371–376.

Hume, K. (2008). *Supporting and sustaining differentiated instruction. An administrators' guide.* Toronto: Pearson.

Hurd, P. D. (1986). Perspectives for the reform of science education. *Phi Delta Kappan, 67,* 353–358.

Infoxchange Australia: Technology for social justice. *Social Justice in the Digital Age.* Retrieved from http://www.infoxchange. net.au/news/social-justice-digital-age

Islandwood. (2013). *Compute your ecological footprint.* Retrieved from http://www.islandwood.org/forkids/footprint

Jackson, P. W. (1968). *Life in classrooms.* New York: Holt, Rinehart, and Winston.

Jagger, S. (2009). *The influence of participation in a community mapping project on grade four students' environmental worldviews* (Master's thesis). Retrieved from http://hdl.handle. net/1828/2816

Jagger, S. L. (2013, in press). "This is more like home": Knowing nature through community mapping. *Canadian Journal of Environmental Education, 18.*

Jagger, S. L., Dubek, M. M., & Pedretti, E. (2012). "It's a personal thing": Visitors' responses to *Body Worlds. Museum Management and Curatorship, 27*(4), 357–374.

James, C. E. (2010). *Seeing ourselves: Exploring race, ethnicity, and culture.* Toronto: Thompson Educational Publishing, Inc.

James, C. E. (2012a). *Life at the intersection: Community, class, and schooling.* Halifax, NS: Fernwood Publishing.

James, C. E. (2012b). Students "at risk": Stereotypes and the schooling of black boys. *Urban Education, 47*(2), 464–494.

Jao, L. (2012). The multicultural mathematics classroom: Culturally aware teaching through cooperative learning and multiple representations. *Multicultural Education, 19*(3), 2–10.

Jenkins, E. (1990). Scientific literacy and school science education. *School Science Review, 7*(256), 43–51.

Jenkins, E. W. (2000). Constructivism in school science education: Powerful model or the most dangerous intellectual tendency. *Science and Education, 9*(6), 599–610.

Jickling, B. (1992). Why I don't want my children educated for sustainable development. *Journal of Environmental Education, 23*(4), 5–8.

Jickling, B., & Wals, A. (2008). Globalization and environmental education: Looking beyond sustainable development. *Journal of Curriculum Studies, 40*(1), 1–21.

Johnstone, A.H., & Al-Shuaili, A. (2001). Learning in the laboratory: Some thoughts from the literature. *University Chemistry Education, 5*(2), 42–51.

Jordan, A., Schwartz, E., & McGhie-Richmond, D. (2009). Preparing teachers for inclusive classrooms. *Teaching and Teacher Education, 25*(4), 535–542.

Jordan, B. (1992). Improving a playcentre science programme through action research. *Research in Science Education, 22,* 240–247.

Kallery, M., & Psillos, D. (2001). Pre-school teachers' content knowledge in science: Their understanding of elementary science concepts and of issues raised by children's questions. *International Journal of Early Years Education, 9*(3), 165–179.

Kennedy, M. M. (2008). Sorting out teacher quality. *Phi Delta Kappan, 90*(1), 59–63.

Kestner, B. (2012). Ben Kestner: Personalizing education. [Video file]. Retrieved from http://www.youtube.com/watch?v=3ifi_ fd4n9E

Khishfe, R., & Lederman, N. G. (2006). Teaching nature of science within a controversial topic: Integrated versus nonintegrated. *Journal of Research in Science Teaching, 43*(4), 395–418.

Klentschy, M. (2005). Science notebook essentials. *Science and Children, 43*(3), 24–27.

Knudsen, S. (2011). *Eggs, legs, wings: A butterfly life cycle.* North Mankato, MN: Capstone Press.

Kugler, C. (2002). Darwin's theory, Mendel's laws: Labels & the teaching of science. *The American Biology Teacher, 64*(5), 341–351.

Kuhn, T. S. (1996). *The structure of scientific revolutions* (3rd ed.). University of Chicago Press.

Laboratory School at the Dr. Eric Jackman Institute of Child Study, The. (2011). *Natural curiosity: Building children's understanding of the world through environmental inquiry.* Oshawa, ON: Maracle Press.

Ladson-Billings, G. (1994). *The dreamkeepers.* San Francisco, CA: Jossey-Bass Publishing.

Ladson-Billings, G. (1995a). But that's just good teaching! The case for culturally relevant pedagogy. *Theory into Practice, 34*(3), 159–165.

Ladson-Billings, G. (1995b). Toward a theory of culturally relevant pedagogy. *American Educational Research Journal, 32*(3), 465–491.

Lave, J., & Wenger, E. (1991). *Situated learning: Legitimate peripheral participation*. Cambridge, UK: Cambridge University Press.

Lawson, A. E., Alkhoury, S., Benford, R., Clark, B.R., & Falconcer, K.A. (2000). What kinds of scientific concepts exist? Concept construction and intellectual development in college biology. *Journal of Research in Science Teaching, 37*(9), 996–1018.

Le Bouthillier, J., Bourgoin, R., & Kristmanson, P. (2011). *Collaborating for success: Classroom teachers and researchers coming together through professional learning communities*. Conference proceedings for the International Conference of School Improvement. Limassol, Cypress.

Lederman, J. S., & Lederman, N. G. (2005). Nature of science is… *Science and Children, 43*(2), 53.

Lederman, N. G. (1999). Teachers' understanding of the nature of science and classroom practice: Factors that facilitate or impede the relationship. *Journal of Research in Science Teaching, 36*(8), 916–929.

Lederman, N.G., Gess-Newsome, J., & Latz, M.S. (1994). The nature and development of preservice science teachers' conceptions of subject matter and pedagogy, *Journal of Research in Science Teaching, 31*(2), 129–146.

Lee, E. (1985). *Letters to Marcia: A teacher's guide to anti-racist education*. Toronto: Cross Cultural Communication Centre.

Lemke, J. L. (1990). *Talking science: Language, learning, and values*. Norwood, NJ: Ablex.

Lemke, J. L. (2001). Articulating communities: Sociocultural perspectives on science education. *Journal of Research in Science Teaching, 38*(3), 296–316.

Lickers, F. H. (1999). The Creator. In Haudenosaunee Environmental Task Force (Eds.), *Words that come before all else: Environmental philosophies of the Haudenosaunee* (pp. 154–160). Hogansburg, NY: Native North American Travelling College.

Liem, T. L. (1987). *Invitations to science inquiry* (2nd ed.). Lexington, MA: Ginn Press.

Linn, M., & Slotta, J. (2000). WISE Science. *Educational Leadership, 58*(2), 29–32.

Liu, C., & Matthews, M. (2005). Vygotsky's philosophy: Constructivism and its criticisms examined. *International Education Journal, 6*(3), 386–399.

Llewellyn, D. (2005). *Teaching high school science through inquiry*. Thousand Oaks, CA: Corwin Press.

Lott, K. (2011). Fire up the inquiry. *Science and Children, 48*(7), 29–33.

Louv, R. (2008). *Last child in the woods*. New York: Workman Publishing Company Inc.

Lucas, A. M. (1979). *Environment and environmental education: Conceptual issues and curriculum implications*. Melbourne, Victoria: Australian International Press and Publications.

Lynch, S. J. (2000). *Equity and science education reform*. London: Lawrence Erlbaum Associates.

Manitoba Education and Training. (2000). *Education for a sustainable future: A resource for curriculum developers, teachers, and administrators*. Winnipeg: Author.

Manitoba Education and Training. (1999). *Manitoba curriculum framework of outcomes, Kindergarten to Grade 4 Science*.

Manitoba Education and Youth. (2003). *Integrating Aboriginal perspectives into curricula*. Winnipeg, MB: Author. Retrieved from http://www.edu.gov.mb.ca/k12/docs/policy/abpersp/ab_persp.pdf

Martins, I. P., & Veiga, L. (2001). Early science education: Exploring familiar contexts to improve the understanding of some basic concepts. *European Early Childhood Education Research Journal, 9*(2), 69–82.

Mawson, B. (2003). Beyond the design process: An alternative pedagogy for technology education. *International Journal of Technology and Design Education, 13*(2), 117–128.

Mayer-Smith, J., Bartosh, O., & Peterat, L. (2007). Teaming children and Elders to grow food and environmental consciousness. *Applied Environmental Education and Communication, 6*(1), 77–85.

Maynes, N. (2010). *Focus on learning: The art and science of planning, delivering, and assessing effective lessons*. Boston, MA: Pearson Learning Solutions.

McComas, W. F. (1996). Ten myths of science: Reexamining what we think we know about the nature of science. *School Science and Mathematics, 96*(1), 10–16.

McComas, W. F. (2004). Keys to teaching the nature of science. *The Science Teacher, 71*(9), 24–27.

McComas, W. F., Clough, M. P., Almazroa, H. (1998).The role and character of the nature of science in science education. In W. F. McComas (Ed.), *The nature of science in science education: Rationales and strategies* (pp. 3–39). Boston: Kluwer Academic Publishers.

McFarlane, S. (1991). *Waiting for the whales*. Victoria, BC: Orca Books.

McFarlane, S. (1992). *Jessie's island*. Victoria, BC: Orca Books.

McLaren, P. (1998). *Life in schools*. New York: Longman.

McTighe, J., & Thomas, R. S. (2005). Backward design. *Educational Leadership, 62*(5), 52–55.

Metcalf, S. J., & Tinker, R. F. (2004). Probeware and handhelds in elementary and middle school science. *Journal of Science Education and Technology, 13*(1), 43–49.

Milford, T. M., Jagger, S., Yore, L. D., & Anderson, J. O. (2010). National influences on science education reform in Canada. *Canadian Journal of Science, Mathematics, and Technology Education, 10*(4), 370–381.

Miller, J. P. (2007). *The holistic curriculum* (2nd ed.). Toronto: University of Toronto Press.

Moje, E. B. (2007). Developing socially just subject-matter instruction: A review of the literature on disciplinary literacy teaching. *Review of Research in Education, 31*(1), 1–44.

Morrison, (2006). *Complexity theory and education*. Proceedings of the 2006 Asia-Pacific Educational Research Association Annual Conference, Hong Kong.

Moscovici, H., & Holmlund Nelson, T. (1998). Shifting from activitymania to inquiry. *Science and Children, 35*(4), 14–17, 40.

Moursand, D. (2007). *Introduction to using games in education. A guide for teachers and parents*. Retrieved from http://pages.uoregon.edu/moursund/Books/Games/Games.pdf

Mulholland, J., & Wallace, J. (2008). Computer, craft, complexity and change: Explorations into science teacher knowledge. *Studies in Science Education, 44*(1), 41–62.

Mulholland, J., & Wallace, J. (2001). Teacher induction and elementary science teaching: Enhancing self-efficacy. *Teaching and Teacher Education, 17*(2), 243–261.

Mulholland, J., & Wallace, J. (2005). Growing the tree of teacher knowledge: Ten years of learning to teach elementary science. *Journal of Research in Science Teaching, 42*(7), 767–790.

Munsch, R. (1992). *Moira's birthday*. Toronto: Annick Press.

Murphy, C., Neil, P., & Beggs, J. (2007). Primary science teacher confidence revisited: Ten years on. *Educational Research, 49*(4), 415–430.

Nashon, S. (2004). The nature of analogical explanations: High school physics teachers use in Kenya. *Research in Science Education, 34*, 475–502.

National Research Council. (1996). *The national science education standards*. Washington, DC: National Academy Press.

National Research Council. (2000). *Inquiry and the national science education standard: A guide for teaching and learning*. Washington, DC: National Academy Press.

Nelson, C., & Ponder, J. (2010). Turtle girls: A visit to a sea turtle hospital inspires civic involvement. *Science and Children, 47*(6), 27–31.

New Brunswick Department of Education (2002). *Atlantic Canada Science curriculum—Science, Grade 5*. Retrieved from http://www.gnb.ca/0000/publications/curric/grade5science.pdf

Niess, M.L. (2005). Preparing teachers to teach science and mathematics with technology: Developing technology pedagogical content knowledge. *Journal of Teacher Education, 21*(5), 509–523.

Nieto, S. (1996). *Affirming diversity: The sociopolitical context of multicultural education* (2nd ed.). White Plains, NY: Longman.

Norris, S. P., & Phillips, L. M. (2002). How literacy in its fundamental sense is central to scientific literacy. *Science Education, 87*(2), 224–240.

North American Association for Environmental Education (2010). *Developing a framework for assessing environmental literacy: Executive summary*. Retrieved from http://www.naaee.net/sites/default/files/framework/EnvLiteracyExeSummary.pdf

Northwest Territories Education, Culture, and Employment (2004). *K-6 Science and technology curriculum*. Retrieved from http://www.ece.gov.nt.ca/files/Early-Childhood/K-20Science%20%26%20Technology%20CurriculumFINAL%20.pdf

Nova Scotia Department of Education (2005). *Atlantic Canada Science curriculum—Science, Grade 1*. Retrieved from http://www.ednet.ns.ca/files/curriculum/science_1_sec-web.pdf

Nova Scotia Department of Education (2006). *Atlantic Canada Science curriculum—Science, Grade 4*. Retrieved from http://www.ednet.ns.ca/pdfdocs/curriculum/Science4_web.pdf

Nunavut Department of Education. (2012). *2012–2013 Nunavut approved curriculum and teaching resources*. Retrieved from http://www.edu.gov.nu.ca/apps/UPLOADS/fck/file/NU%20CUR%20GUIDE%202012-2013.pdf

Ogawa, M. (1995). Science education in a multi-science perspective. *Science Education, 79*(5), 583–593.

Okimoto, J. (2007). *Winston of Churchill, One bear's battle against global warming*. Seattle, WA: Sasquatch Books.

Olson, J. K. (2003). Light students' interest in the nature of science. *Science Scope, 27*(1), 18–22.

O'Neill, T. B. (2010). Fostering spaces of student ownership in middle school science. *Equity and Excellence in Education, 43*(1), 6–20.

Ontario College of Teachers. (2010). Sketch of a three-part lesson. *Professionally Speaking*. Retrieved from http://professionallyspeaking.oct.ca/march_2010/features/lesson_study/three-part.aspx

Ontario Ministry of Education. (2003). *Targeted implementation & planning supports (TIPS): Grade 7, 8, and 9 applied mathematics*. Toronto: Queen's Printer for Ontario. Retrieved from http://www.edu.gov.on.ca/eng/studentsuccess/lms/tips4rm.html

Ontario Ministry of Education (2007a). *Ontario First Nations, Métis, and Inuit education policy framework*. Toronto: Aboriginal Education Office.

Ontario Ministry of Education. (2007b). *The Ontario curriculum, Grades 1-8, science and technology*. Toronto: Queen's Printer.

Ontario Ministry of Education. (2008). *Standards for environmental education in the curriculum*. Toronto: Queen's Printer.

Ontario Ministry of Education. (2009). *Equity and inclusive education in Ontario schools. Guidelines for policy development and implementation*. Toronto: Queen's Printer for Ontario.

Ontario Ministry of Education. (2010a). *Differentiated instruction educator's package: The differentiated instruction scrapbook*. Toronto: Queen's Printer.

Ontario Ministry of Education. (2010b). *Growing success—Assessment, evaluation, and reporting in Ontario schools, first edition, covering Grades 1 to 12*, Ministry of Education website, http://www.edu.gov.on.ca

Ontario Ministry of Education. (2011). Ontario Schools, K–12, Policy and program requirements. Toronto: Queen's Printer for Ontario.

Ornstein, A. C., & Hunkins, F. P. (1993). *Curriculum: Foundations, principles, and issues* (2nd ed.). Boston: Allyn and Bacon.

Orpwood, G., & Souque, J-P. (1984). *Science education in Canadian schools, Volume 1, Introduction and curriculum analysis*. Ottawa, ON: Science Council of Canada.

Orr, D. (1991). What is education for? *The Learning Revolution, 27*, 52–59.

Orr, D. W. (1992). *Ecological literacy: Education and the transition to a postmodern world*. Albany, NY: SUNY Press.

Orr, D. W. (2004). *Earth in mind: On education, environment, and the human prospect* (10th anniversary ed.). Washington, DC: Island Press.

Osborne, J. F. (1996). Beyond constructivism. *Science Education, 80*(1), 53–82.

Osborne, J., Simon, S., & Collins, S. (2003). Attitudes towards science: A review of the literature and its implications. *International Journal of Science Education, 25*(9), 1049–1079.

Padilla, M. J. (1990). The science process skills. *Research matters—To the science teacher, 9004*. Retrieved from http://www.narst.org/publications/research/skill.cfm

Palmer, J. (1998). *Environmental education in the 21st century: Theory, practice, progress, and promise*. New York: Routledge.

Pedretti, E. (1996). Learning about science, technology and society (STS) through an action research project: Co-constructing an issues-based model for STS education. *School Science and Mathematics, 96*(8), 232–240.

Pedretti, E. (2003). Teaching science, technology, society, and environment (STSE) education: Preservice teachers' philosophical and pedagogical landscapes. In D. Zeidler (Ed.), *The role of *moral reasoning on socio-scientificissues and discourse in science education* (pp. 219–240). Dordrecht, The Netherlands: Kluwer.

Pedretti, E. (2004). Perspectives on learning through research on critical issues-based science centre exhibitions. *Science Education, 88*(1), S34–S47.

Pedretti, E. (2005). STSE education: Principles and practices. In S. Alsop, L. Bencze & E. Pedretti (Eds.), *Analyzing exemplary science teaching: Theoretical lenses and a spectrum of possibilities for practice* (pp. 116–126). London: Open University Press.

Pedretti, E. (2012). The medium is the message: Unraveling visitors' experiences of *Body Worlds and the Story of the Heart*. In E. Davidsson and A. Davidsson (Eds.), *Understanding interactions at science centers and museums—A sociocultural perspective* (pp. 45–62). Rotterdam, the Netherlands: Sense Publishers.

Pedretti, E., & Bellomo, K. (in press). A time for change: Advocating for STSE education through professional learning communities. *Canadian Journal of Science, Mathematics and Technology Education.*

Pedretti, E., Bencze, L., Hewitt, J., Romkey, L, & Jivraj, A. (2008). Promoting issues-based STSE perspectives in science teacher education: Problems of identity and ideology. *Science & Education, 17*, 941–960.

Pedretti, E., & Little, C. (2008). *From engagement to empowerment: Reflections in science education.* Toronto: Pearson Education.

Pedretti, E., & Nazir, J. (2011). Currents in STSE education: Mapping a complex field, 40 years on. *Science Education, 95*(4), 601–626.

Pedretti, E., Nazir, J., Tan, M., Bellomo, K., & Ayyavoo, G. (2012). A baseline study of Ontario teachers' views of environmental and outdoor education. *Pathways: The Ontario Journal of Outdoor Education, 24*(2), 4–12.

Percy, J. (2002). Personal communication.

Peters, E. E., & Kitsantas, A. (2010). The effect of the nature of science metacognitive prompts on science students' content and the nature of science knowledge, metacognition, and self-regulatory efficiency. *School Science and Mathematics, 110*(8), 382–396.

Petrina, S. (1993). Under the corporate thumb: Troubles with our MATE (Modular Approach to Technology Education). *Journal of Technology Education, 5*(1), 81–89.

Petrina, S. (1998). Multidisciplinary technology education. *International Journal of Technology and Design Education, 8*(2), 105–138.

Petrina, S. (2004). The politics of curriculum and instructional design/theory/form: Critical problems, projects, units, and modules. *Interchange, 35*(1), 81–126.

Piaget, J. (1926). *The language and thought of the child.* London: Routledge & Kegan.

Piaget, J. (1929). *The child's conception of the world.* London: Routledge & Kegan.

Pinar, W. F., Reynolds, W. M., Slattery, P., & Taubman, P. M. (1995). *Understanding curriculum: An introduction to the study of historical and contemporary curriculum discourses.* New York: Peter Lang.

Pocovi, M. C. (2007). The effects of history based instructional material on students' understanding of fieldlines. *Journal of Research in Science Teaching, 44*(1), 107–132.

Polya, G. (1957). *How to solve it* (2nd ed.). Princeton, New Jersey: Princeton University Press.

Posner, G. J., Strike, K. A., Hewson, P. W., & Gertzog, W. A. (1982). Accommodation of a scientific conception: Towards a theory of conceptual change. *Science Education, 66*(2), 211–227.

Prime, G. M., & Miranda, R. J. (2006). Urban public high school teachers' beliefs about science learner characteristics—Implications for curriculum. *Urban Education, 41*(5), 506–532.

Quay, J. (2003). Experience and participation: Relating theories of learning. *Journal of Experiential Education, 26*(2), 105–116.

Quebec Education Program, Preschool and Elementary Education. (2001). *Chapter 6: Mathematics, science and technology.* Gouvernement du Québec Ministère de l'Éducation. Retrieved from http://www.learnquebec.ca/toolkit/documents/new/qepelem.pdf

Quebec Ministry of Education (Gouvernement du Québec). (1998). *A school for the future—Policy statement on educational integration and intercultural education.* Bibliothèquenationale du Québec.

Radakovic, N., & McDougall, D. (2012). From static to dynamic representations of probability concepts. In D. Martinovic, D. McDougall, & Z. Karadag (Eds.), *Technology in mathematics education: Contemporary issues* (pp. 221–241). Santa Rosa, CA: Informing Science Press.

Ramsey, J. (1994). The science education reform movement: Implications for social responsibility. *Science Education, 77*(2), 235–58.

Ratcliffe, M., & Grace, M. (2003). *Science education for citizenship.* Maidenhead, UK: Open University.

Read, J. R. (2004). Children's misconceptions and conceptual change in science education. Retrieved from http://acell.chem.usyd.edu.au/Conceptual-Change.cfm

Reid, N., & Shah, I. (2007). The role of laboratory work in university chemistry. *Chemistry Education Research and Practice, 8*(2), 172–185.

Reis, G., & Ng-A-Fook, N. (2010). TEK talk: So what? Language and the decolonization of narrative gatekeepers of science education curriculum. *Cultural Studies of Science Education, 5*(4), 1009–1026.

Reiss M. J. (2005). The importance of affect in science education. In S. Alsop (Ed.), *The affective dimension of cognition: studies from education in the sciences* (pp. 17–25). Dordrecht: Kluwer.

Reiss, M. (2008). The use of ethical frameworks by students following a new science course for 16-18 year olds. *Science & Education, 17*(8-9), 889–902.

Reiss, M. J. (2003). Science education for social justice. In C. Vincent (Ed.), *Social justice, education and identity* (pp. 153–165). London, UK: RoutledgeFalmer.

Rennie, L., Venville, G., & Wallace, J. (2012). *Integrating science, technology, engineering and mathematics: Issues, reflections and ways forward.* Philadelphia, PA: Routledge. Retrieved from http://www.carla.umn.edu/assessment/vac/evaluation/p_7.html

Rezba, R. J., Auldridge, T., & Rhea, L. (1999). *Teaching and learning the basic science skills.* Retrieved from http://www.pen.k12.va.us/VDOE/instruction/TLBSSGuide.doc

Richards, J. (2011) C.D. *Howe Institute Commentary—The education papers, Aboriginal education in Quebec*. Toronto: C.D. Howe Institute. Downloaded from http://www.cdhowe.org/pdf/Commentary_328.pdf

Roberts, D. (1982) Developing the concept of "curriculum emphases" in science education. *Science Education, 66*(2), 243–260.

Roberts, D. A., & Ostman, L. (1998). *Problems of meaning in science curriculum. Ways of knowing in science series*. New York: Teachers College Press.

Roth, W.-M., & Bowen, G. M. (2001a). Mathematization of experience in a grade 8 open-inquiry environment: An introduction to the representational practices of science. *Journal of Research in Science Teaching, 31*(3), 293–318.

Roth, W.-M., & Bowen, G. M. (2001b). Professionals read graphs: A semiotic analysis. *Journal for Research in Mathematics Education, 32*(2), 159–194.

Roth, W.-M., & Calabrese Barton, A. (2004). Science as collective praxis, literacy power, and the struggle for a better world. In W.-M. Roth & A. C. Barton (Eds.), *Rethinking scientific literacy* (pp. 1–19). New York: Routledge Falmer.

Roth, W.-M., & Désautels, J. (Eds.). (2002). *Science education as/for sociopolitical action*. New York: Peter Lang.

Rousseau, J.-J. (1911/1966). *Émile: Or, on education*. London, UK: J. M. Dent and Sons.

Russell, C., Bell, A.C., & Fawcett, L. (2000). Navigating the waters of Canadian environmental education. In T. Goldstein & D. Selby (Eds.), *Weaving connections: Educating for peace, social, and environmental justice* (pp. 196–217). Toronto: Sumach Press.

Sadler, T., Barab, S., & Scott, B. (2007). What do students gain by engaging in socioscientific inquiry? *Research in Science Education, 37*(4), 371–391.

Sandner, L., Ellis, C., Lacy, D., Little, C., & Mace, H. (2009). *Investigating science 9*. Toronto: Pearson Canada, Inc.

Saskatchewan Ministry of Education. (2011). *Saskatchewan curriculum science 5*. Retrieved from https://www.edonline.sk.ca/bbcswebdav/library/curricula/English/Science/Science_5_2011.pdf

Saskatchewan Ministry of Education. (2011). *Science 5*. Regina, SK: Author.

Sauvé, L. (2005). Currents in environmental education: Mapping a complex and evolving pedagogical field. *Canadian Journal of Environmental Education, 10*(1), 11–37.

Schon, D. (1987). *The reflective practitioner: How professionals think in action*. London, UK: Temple Smith.

Schubert, W. H. (1996). Perspectives on four curriculum traditions. *Educational Horizons, 74*(4), 169–176.

Schwab, J. J. (1969/2004). The practical: A language for curriculum. In D. J. Flinders & S. J. Thornton (Eds.), *The curriculum studies reader* (2nd ed., pp. 103–117). New York: RoutledgeFalmer.

Schwab, J. J. (1973). The practical 3: Translation into curriculum. *The School Review,81*(4), 501–522.

Schwartz, S., & Pollishuke, M. (2013).*Creating the dynamic classroom: A handbook for teachers* (2nd ed.). Toronto: Pearson.

Sen, A. (2009). *The idea of justice*. Cambridge, MA: Harvard University Press.

Seuss, Dr. (1971). *The lorax*. New York: Random House.

Shanahan, M.-C. (2010). Changing the meaning of peer-to-peer? Exploring online comment spaces as sites of negotiated expertise. *Journal of Science Communication, 9*(1), 1–13.

Shanahan, M.-C. (2011). Science blogs as boundary layers: Creating and understanding new interactions through science blogging. *Journalism: Theory, Practice and Criticism, 12*, 903–919.

Shapiro, B. L. (1994). *What children bring to light: A constructivist perspective on children's learning in science*. New York: Teachers College Press.

Shulman, L. (1986). Those who understand: Knowledge growth in teaching. *Educational Researcher, 15*(2), 4–14.

Shulman, L. (1987). Knowledge and teaching: Foundations of the new reform. *Harvard Educational Review, 57*(1), 1–23.

Silverstein, S. (1964). *The giving tree*. Toronto: HarperCollins.

Skinner, B. F. (1953). *Science and human behavior*. New York: Free Press.

Sleeter, C. E. (2000). Creating an empowering multicultural curriculum. *Race, Gender & Class, 7*(3), 178–196.

Sleeter, C. E. (2009).Teacher education, neoliberalism, and social justice. In W. Ayers, T. Quinn, & D. Stovall (Eds.), *Handbook of social justice in education* (pp. 611–624). New York: Routledge.

Slotta, J. D., & Linn, M. C. (2009). *WISE science: Web-based inquiry in the classroom. Technology, Education—Connections*. New York: Teachers College Press.

Smith, A., & MacKinnon, J. B. (2007). *The 100-mile diet: A year of local eating*. Toronto: Random House.

Smith, G. A. (2007). Place-based education: Breaking through the constraining regularities of public school. *Environmental Education Research, 13*(2), 189–207.

Smith, R. G. (1997). "Before teaching this, I'd do a lot of reading": Preparing primary student teachers to teach science. *Research in Science Education, 27*(1), 141–154

Snively, G., & Corsiglia, J. (2001). Discovering indigenous science: Implications for science education. *Science Education, 85*(1), 6–34.

Sobel, D. (1996). *Beyond ecophobia: Reclaiming the heart in nature education*. Great Barrington, MA: The Orion Society.

Sobel, D. (1998). *Mapmaking with children: Sense of place education for the elementary years*. Portsmouth, NH: Heinemann.

Solomon, J. (1993). *Teaching science, technology and society*. Buckingham, UK: Open University Press.

Solomon, J., & Aikenhead, G. (Eds.) (1994). *STS education: International perspectives on reform*. New York: Teachers College Press.

Sperling, E., & Bencze, J. L. (2010). "More than particle theory": Citizenship through school science. *Canadian Journal of Science, Mathematics, and Technology Education, 10*(3), 255–266.

Stenhouse, L. (1970). *Curriculum research and development in action*. London, UK: Heinemann Educational Books.

Stenhouse, L. (1975). *An introduction to curriculum research and development*. Oxford, UK: Heinemann Educational Books Ltd.

Stocklmayer, S., Rennie, L., & Gilbert, J. (2010). The roles of the formal and informal sectors in the provision of effective science education. *Studies in Science Education, 46*(1), 1–44.

Stoll, L., Bolam, R., McMahon, A., Wallace, M. & Thomas, S. (2006). Professional learning communities: A review of the literature. *Journal of Educational Change, 7*, 221–258.

Stone, M. K., & Barlow, Z. (Eds.). (2005). *Ecological literacy: Educating our children for a sustainable world.* San Francisco: Sierra Club Books.

Strauss, R. (2007). *One well: The story of water on Earth.* Toronto: Kidscan Press.

Sutherland, D. (2005). Resiliency and collateral learning in science in some students of Cree ancestry. *Science Education 89*(4), 595–613.

Suzuki, D. (2009). *The big picture: Reflections on science, humanity, and a quickly changing planet.* Vancouver, BC: Greystone Books.

Suzuki, D. (2010). *The legacy.* Vancouver, BC: Greystone Books.

Suzuki, D., & Hanington, I. (2012). *Everything under the sun: Toward a brighter future on a small blue planet.* Vancouver: Greystone Books.

Suzuki, D., & McConnell, A. (2002). *The sacred balance: Rediscovering our place in nature.* Vancouver, BC: Greystone Books.

Taber, K. (2005). Analysis 4: Conceptual development. In S. Alsop, L. Bencze, & E. Pedretti (Eds.), *Analysing exemplary science teaching:* Theoretical lenses and a spectrum of possibilities for practice, (127–135). New York: Open University Press.

Thadani, V., Cook, M. S., Griffis, K., Wise, J. A., & Blakey, A. (2010). The possibilities and limitations of curriculum-based science inquiry interventions for challenging the "Pedagogy of Poverty." *Equity & Excellence in Education, 43*(1), 21–37.

Thompson, F., & Logue, S. (2006). An exploration of common student misconceptions in science. *International Education Journal, 7*(4), 553–559.

Tomlinson, C. A. (1999). *The differentiated classroom: Responding to the needs of all learners.* Columbus, OH: Pearson Canada Inc.

Tomlinson, C. A., & McTighe, J. (2006). *Integrating differentiated instruction and understanding by design, connecting content and kids.* Alexandria, VA: Association for Curriculum Development and Supervision.

Turner, N. J. (2005). *The Earth's blanket: Traditional teachings for sustainable living.* Vancouver, BC: Douglas & McIntyre.

Turner, N. J., Ignace, M. B., & Ignace, R. (2000). Traditional ecological knowledge and wisdom of Aboriginal peoples in British Columbia. *Ecological Applications, 10*(5), 1275–1287.

Tyler, R. W. (1949). *Basic principles of curriculum and instruction.* University of Chicago Press.

Tyler, R. W. (1949/2004). Basic principles of curriculum and instruction. In D. J. Flinders & S. J. Thornton (Eds.), *The curriculum studies reader* (2nd ed., pp. 51–59). New York: RoutledgeFalmer.

UNESCO. (1975). *The international workshop on environmental education final report, Belgrade, Yugoslavia.* Paris, France: UNESCO/UNEP.

UNESCO. (2005). *United Nations decade of education for sustainable development (2005–14): International implementation scheme.* Paris, France: UNESCO.

UNESCO-UNEP. (1978). *The Tbilisi Declaration: Final report of the intergovernmental conference on environmental education.* Paris, France: UNESCO ED/MD/49.

United Nations. (n.d.). *World day of social justice.* Retrieved from http://www.un.org/en/events/socialjusticeday

Usak, M., Ozden, M., & Eilks, I. (2011). A case study of beginning science teachers' subject matter (SMK) and pedagogical content knowledge (PCK) of teaching chemical reaction in Turkey. *European Journal of Teacher Education, 34*(4), 407–429.

van de Walle, J. A., & Lovin, L. H. (2006). *Teaching student-centered mathematics: Grades 5-8.* Boston: Pearson.

van Eijck, M., & Roth, W.-M. (2007). Keeping the local local: Recalibrating the status of science and traditional ecological knowledge (TEK) in education. *Science Education, 91*(6), 926–947.

van Rooy, W. (2012). Bringing controversial issues into science teaching. In G. Venville and V. Dawson (Eds.), *The art of teaching science for middle and secondary school* (2nd ed., pp. 194–209). Sydney, Australia: Allen and Unwin.

Venville, G., & Dawson, V. (Eds.). (2012). *The art of teaching science for middle and secondary school* (2nd ed.). Sydney, Australia: Allen and Unwin.

von Glaserfeld, E. (1989). *Constructivism in education.* Oxford, UK: Pergamon Press.

Vygotsky, L. S. (1962). *Thought and language.* Cambridge, MA: MIT Press.

Vygotsky, L. S. (1987). Thinking and speech. In R. W. Rieber & A. S. Carton (Eds.), *The collected works of L. S. Vygotsky, Vol. 1: Problems of general psychology.* (pp. 39–285). N. Minick (Trans.). New York: Plenum Press.

Vygotsky, L.S. (1978). *Mind in society: The development of higher mental processes.* Cambridge, MA: Harvard University Press.

Wackernagel, M., & Rees, W. (1998). *Our ecological footprint: Reducing human impact on the earth.* Gabriola Island, BC: New Society Publishers.

Wallace, J., & Louden, W. (2000). *Teachers' learning: Stories of science education.* Dordrecht, The Netherlands: Kluwer.

Wallace, J., & Louden, W. (2002). *Dilemmas of science teaching: Perspectives on problems of practice.* London & New York: RoutledgeFalmer.

Wallace, J., & Loughran, J. (Eds.). (2003). *Leadership and professional development: New possibilities for enhancing teacher learning.* London & New York: RoutledgeFalmer.

Wallace, J., Venville, G., & Rennie, L. (2010). Integrated curriculum. In D. Pendergast & N. Bahr (Eds.), *Teaching middle years* (pp. 188–204). Brisbane: Allan & Unwin.

Wallace, R. (2002). *Technology and science teaching: A new kind of knowledge.* Retrieved from https://www.msu.edu/course/cep/953/readings/WallaceTimeFinal.pdf

Weaver, A. (2008). *Keeping our cool: Canada in a warming world.* Toronto: Penguin Books.

Wellington, J. (1998). Practical work in science: Time for a re-appraisal. In J. Wellington (Ed.), *Practical work in school science. Which way now?* (pp. 3–15). New York: Routledge.

Wellington, J. (2001). What is science education for? *Canadian Journal of Science, Mathematics, and Technology Education, 1*(1), 23–38.

Wellington, J., & Osborne, J. (2001). *Language and literacy in science education.* Philadelphia: Open University Press.

Wenger, E. (1998). *Communities of practice: Learning, meaning and identity*. New York: Cambridge University Press.

Wenger, E. (2000). Communities of practice and social learning systems. *Organization, 2*, 225–246.

Wertsch, J. V. (1985). *Vygotsky and the social formation of mind*. Cambridge, MA: Harvard University Press.

Western and Northern Canadian Protocol for Collaboration in Education. (2006). *Rethinking classroom assessment with purpose in mind*. Winnipeg: Manitoba Education, Citizenship and Youth. Retrieved from http://www.wncp.ca/media/40539/rethink.pdf

White, L. O. (1996). Medicine wheel teachings in native language education. In S. O'Meara & D. West (Eds.), *From our eyes: Learning from Indigenous peoples* (pp. 107–122). Toronto, ON: Garamond Press.

White, R., & Gunstone, R. (1992). *Probing understanding*. New York: The Falmer Press.

Wiggins, G., & McTighe, J. (1998). *Understanding by design*. Alexandria, VA: Association for Supervision and Curriculum Development.

Williams, D. R., & Brown, J. D. (2012). *Learning gardens and sustainability education: Bringing life to schools and schools to life*. New York: Routledge.

Williams, D. R., & Taylor, S. (1999). From margin to center: Initiation and development of an environmental school from the ground up. In G. A. Smith & D. R. Williams (Eds.), *Ecological education in action* (pp. 79–102). Albany, NY: SUNY Press.

Willinsky, J. (1998). *Learning to divide the world: Education at empire's end*. Minneapolis, MN: University of Minnesota Press.

Windschitl, M. (2002). Inquiry projects in science teacher education: What can investigative experiences reveal about teacher thinking and eventual classroom practice? *Science Education, 87*(1), 112–143.

Wong, H. K., Wong, R. T., & Seroyer, C. (2005). *The first days of school: How to be an effective teacher*. Mountain View, CA: Harry K. Wong Publications.

Working Group on Environmental Education, Ontario. (2007). *Shaping our schools, shaping our future: Environmental education in Ontario schools*. Toronto: Queens Printer.

World Commission on Environment and Development (WCED). (1987). *Our common future*. Oxford University Press.

Wright, H. K. (2000). Nailing Jell-O to the wall: Pinpointing aspects of state-of-the-art curriculum theorizing. *Educational Researcher, 29*(5), 4–13.

Yager, R. E. (1996). History of science/technology/society as reform in the United States. In R. E. Yager (Ed.), *Science/technology/society as reform in science education* (pp. 3–15). Albany, NY: SUNY Press.

Yanowitz, K. L. (2001). Using analogies to improve elementary school students' inferential reasoning about scientific concepts. *School Science and Mathematics, 101*(3), 133–142.

Yore, L. D., Bisanz, G. L., & Hand, B. M. (2003). Examining the literacy component of science literacy: 25 years of language arts and science research. *International Journal of Science Education, 25*, 689–725.

Yore, L. D., Hand, B., Goldman, S. R., Hildebrand, G. M., Osborne, J. F., Treagust, D. F., & Wallace, C. S. (2004). New directions in language and science education research. *Reading Research Quarterly, 39*(3), 347–352.

Young, M. (2008). From constructivism to realism in the sociology of the curriculum. *Review of Research in Education, 32*(1), 1–28.

Young, M.F. D. (1998). *The curriculum of the future*. Philadelphia, PA: Falmer Press.

Young, R. M. (1987). Racist society, racist science. In D. Gill & L. Levidow (Eds.), *Anti-racist science teaching* (pp. 16–42). London, UK: Free Association Books.

Zeidler, D. L., & Keefer, M. (2003). The role of moral reasoning and the status of socioscientific issues in science education: Philosophical, psychological and pedagogical considerations. In D. L. Zeidler (Ed.), *The role of moral reasoning on socioscientific issues and discourse in science education*. Dordrecht: Kluwer Academic Publishers.

Zeidler, D. L., Sadler, T. D., Simmons, M., & Howe, E. (2005). Beyond STS: A research-based framework for socioscientific issues education. *Science Education, 89*(3), 357–377.

Ziman, J. (1980). *Teaching and learning about science and society*. Cambridge, UK: Cambridge University Press.

Ziman, J. (1994). The rationale for STS is in the approach. In J. Solomon & G. Aikenhead (Eds.), *STS education: International perspectives on reform* (pp. 21–31). New York: Teachers College Press.

Name Index

A

Abd-El-Khalick, F., 27, 194
Aboriginal Education Office, 250
Aikenhead, G., 9, 12, 24, 45, 46, 47, 63, 65, 66, 68, 69, 70, 200, 202, 249
Aikenhead, G. S., 250
Alberta, Manitoba, Saskatchewan, Northwest Territories, Nunavut, and the Yukon, 45
Alberta Teachers Association Science Council, 177
Alkhoury, S., 268
Allen, M., 259
Allen, N., 250
Allen, P., 168, 336
Almazroa, H., 24, 27
Al-Shuaili, A., 151
Alsop, S., 47, 83, 134, 226, 228, 233
American Association for the Advancement of Science, 12
American Biology Teacher, 18
Amirshokoohi, A., 204
Anderson, D., 17
Anderson, J. O., 13
Anderson, L., 116, 251, 276
Aoki, T. T., 128, 131, 139
Apple, M. W., 129
Appleton, K., 140
Archambault, J., 338
Asbell-Clark, J., 273
Aspen-Baxter, L., 252
Aspin, D., 209
Assessment Reform Group, 94
Atkins, J., 32, 333
Atlantic Canada Science Curriculum, 152, 158, 207
Auldridge, T., 152
Ausubel, D. P., 109, 133
Ayyavoo, G., 52

B

B, Moje, E., 70
Baker, J., 49
Banchi, H., 154
Banks, J. A., 61
Banting, F., 229
Barab, S., 226
Barlow, Z., 58
Barman, C., 30
Barnett, J., 8, 109
Bartosh, O., 17
Base, G., 333
Bash, L., 68
Bateson, G., 205
Baylor, B., 220, 337

Bazzul, J., 68
BBC, 58
Beggs, J., 140
Bell, A. C., 44
Bell, A. G., 33
Bell, R., 152, 153, 154
Bellomo, K., 30, 52, 70, 237, 281
Bencze, J. L., 12, 15, 210, 211
Bencze, L., 27, 217, 218, 233
Benford, R., 268
Bennett, B. B., 118
Bennett, J., 202
Best, C., 229
Bilash, B., 161, 330
Binns, I., 152
Bisanz, G. L., 14
Blades, D. W., 132, 194
Blakey, A., 74
Bloom, B., 116, 275, 276
Bobbitt, F., 132
Bolam, R., 281
Bondar, R., 33
Boring, M., 33, 334
Bosak, S., 171, 177
Bosak, S. V., 161, 263, 330
Bouchard, D., 58, 333
Boulton, J., 47
Bourgoin, R., 282
Bowen, G. M., 14, 27, 89, 170
Bowers, C. A., 50
Boykin, O., 75
Braund, M., 17
Brett, J., 333
Brickhouse, N. W., 27, 33, 34, 63, 65
British Columbia Ministry of Education, 45, 54, 67, 78, 94, 123, 141, 152, 158
British Columbia's Scientist in Residence, 177
Brockman, A., 47, 252
Brown, J. D., 58
Bruchac, J., 58
Bunting, E., 115, 333, 334
Burton, G. M., 30
Burton, V. L., 336
Busby, P., 336
Butterworth, C., 334
Buzan, B., 307
Buzan, T., 307

C

Caduto, M. J., 58
Cakir, M., 261
Calabrese Barton, A., 9, 12, 18, 68, 70, 74, 211
Callan, J. P., 161

Canadian Council of Learning, 66, 67, 77
Canadian International Development Agency (CIDA), 77
Canadian Journal of Science, Mathematics, and Technology Education, 18
Canadian Network for Environmental Education and Communication (EECOM), 58
Canadian Student Debating Federation, 307
Cannon, J., 334
Capra, F., 326
Carle, E., 334, 337
Carlone, H. B., 63
Carson, R., 42, 58
Carter, L., 12, 210, 211
Carter, M., 50
Cassino, M., 337
Cavallo, A., 23
Chambers, D. W., 30
Cherry, L., 334
Cherryholmes, C. H., 131
Clandinin, D. J., 128, 130
Clark, B.R., 268
Clough, M. P., 24, 27
Cober, R., 278
Cobern, W., 22
Cobern, W. W., 249
Cochran-Smith, M., 63
Colburn, A., 258
Cole, J., 334
Coll, R., 272
Collins, S., 83
Connelly, F. M., 128, 130
Cook, G., 255
Cook, J. L., 255
Cook, M. S., 74
Cooper, S., 228
Corsiglia, J., 47
Corson, D., 80
Costa, V. B., 63
Council of Ministers of Education, 12, 13, 27, 44
Council of Ministers of Education Canada (CMEC), 40, 158, 191, 201
Crouch, C., 161
Crowther, D. T., 24, 27
Cuban, L., 128, 130
Cultural Studies in Science Education, 18
Cummins, J., 70, 85, 120
Curie, M., 33
Curriculum Services Canada (CSC), 77

D

Daniels, H., 296, 307
Darwin, C., 326

Davidson, S., 17
Davis, B., 254, 255, 257
Davis, W., 326
Dawkins, R., 326
Dawson, V., 209, 226
de Bono, E., 230, 300
de Jong, T., 251
DeCoito, I., 82, 134
Delpit, L., 2
Dendy, L., 33, 334
DePaola, T., 337
Derrida, J., 131
Désautels, J., 11, 210, 225
DeVereaux, C., 328
Dewey, J., 42, 51, 253, 255, 257
Diamond, J., 326
Dierking, L., 17
Dolan, T. J., 231
Doll Jr., W. E., 132, 139
Driver, R., 28, 29, 255, 259
Drummond, A., 336
Dubek, M, 241
Dubek, M. M., 17
DuFour, R., 282
Dunbar, K., 273
Dunbar, R.E., 307

E

Eaker, R., 282
Ehlert, L., 334
Ehrlich, A., 32
Eilks, I., 140
Einstein, A., 33, 229
Eisner, E.W., 128, 129, 132, 139
Emdin, C., 62
Environment Canada, 58
Environmental Educators Provincial
    Specialists Association (British
    Columbia), 58
Eslinger, J. C., 81
Euston, Q., 307
Evergreen, 58

F

Fagen, A. P., 161
Falconcer, K. A., 268
Falk, J., 17
Farmer, J. A., 307
Fawcett, L., 44, 47
Fensham, P., 11
Ferguson-Hessler, M. G. M., 251
Fleer, M., 158
Fleming, S., 229
Fogliano, J., 115, 262, 335
Foster, A., 51, 52
Foucault, M., 131
Franck, R. H., 307
Franklin, U., 15, 33
Freire, P., 7, 257
Frykholm, J. A., 14, 89, 134
Furman, G. C., 50

G

Galilei, G., 33
Gallagher, J. J., 200
Gardner, H., 84, 268
Gaylie, V., 42, 45, 53, 58
Gelb, M., 307
Gertzog, W. A., 260
Gess-Newsome, J., 109, 140
Gilbert, J., 17
Gill, D., 60
Gitari, W., 60, 249
Glasson, G. E., 14, 89, 134
Goethe, 79
Goldman, S. R., 14
Goodall, J., 33, 229
Gore, A., 58
Gould, S.J., 326
Government of Canada, 44
Government of Nunavut, 250
Grace, M., 226
Grant, C.A., 64
Green Leaf, 58
Green Thumbs Growing Kids, 58
Greenwood, D., 45
Greenwood, D. A., 50
Griffis, K., 75
Gross, G.R., 161, 330
Gruenewald, D., 51
Gruenewald, D. A., 50
Guesne, E., 255
Gunstone, R., 161

H

Hand, B., 120
Hand, B. M., 14
Hanington, I., 205
Harding, S., 69, 249
Harlen, W., 140
Harrison, A., 272
Hart, P., 45, 205
Hastings and Prince Edward District
    School Board, 87
Hawking, S., 326
Hayes, R., 171
Healy, S. D., 319
Hein, G., 253, 257
Hesse, K., 337
Hewitt, J., 16, 162, 163, 194, 217, 218,
    277
Hewson, P. W., 260
Hildebrand, G. M., 14
Hiscock, B., 337
Hodson, D., 8, 9, 11, 12, 17, 18, 23, 24,
    27, 28, 60, 70, 109, 150, 151, 153, 194,
    201, 210, 211, 226, 227, 241, 249, 260
Hofstein, A., 194
Hollins, E. R., 80, 81
Holmlund Nelson, T., 153
Holroyd, C., 140
Hooper, M., 337
Howe, E., 225
Hubbard, R., 326

Huber, R. A., 30
Hunkins, F. P., 253
Hurd, P. D., 18, 200
Hurst, C. O., 337

I

Ignace, M. B., 47
Ignace, R., 47
International Journal of Science Education,
    18

J

Jackson, P. W., 129
Jagger, S., 13, 206
Jagger, S. L., 17, 52, 241
James, C. E., 62, 65, 70, 81, 131, 233
James, W., 253
Jegede, O. J., 250
Jenkins, E., 11
Jenkins, M., 335
Jickling, B., 45
Jivraj, A., 217, 218
Johanson, T., 47
Johnson, A., 63
Johnson, N. J., 296
Johnson, N. L., 307
Johnstone, A, 151
Jordan, A., 85
Jordan, B., 158
Journal of Research in Science Teaching, 18

K

Kallery, M., 140
Kamkwamba, W., 336
Kazempour, M, 204
Keefer, M., 194
Kennedy, M. M., 3
Kestner, B., 116
Khishfe, R., 27
King, A., 307
Kingsolver, B., 326
Kitsantas, A., 28
Klentschy, M., 299, 307
Knudsen, S., 195, 335
Koob, J., 161, 330
Kool, R., 45
Krathwohl, D. A., 116, 251, 276
Krauss, L., 326
Kristmanson, P., 282
Kronowitz, E. L., 319
Kugler, C., 27
Kuhn, T., 326
Kuhn, T. S., 69

L

Ladson-Billings, G., 71, 80, 81, 131
Larrick, R. P., 307
Larson, G., 335
Latz, M.S., 140
Lawson, A. E., 268
Leach, J., 28

Lederman, J. S., 24, 27
Lederman, N. G., 24, 27, 140, 194
Lee, E., 65
Lemke, J. L., 14, 18, 83, 86
Levidow, L., 60
Lewontin, R., 326
Lickers, F. H., 46
Liem, T. L., 161, 330
Linn, M., 162
Linn, M. C., 16, 162, 194, 277
Linney, G., 51, 52
Lionni, L., 335
Lipton, L., 307
Little, C., 9, 11, 75, 201, 204, 227
Liu, C., 256
Llewellyn, D., 152
Locker, T., 337
Logue, S., 259, 260
London, J., 337
Lott, K., 154
Louden, W., 8
Louv, R., 41, 52, 58
Lovin, L. H., 89
Loving, C., 22
Lubben, F. Hogarth, S., 202
Lucas, A., 48
Luce-Kapler, R., 254, 255, 257
Lunetta, V., 194
Lyman, F. T., 307
Lynch, S. J., 80

M

Maal, N., 307
MacDonald, R. E., 319
MacFarlane, S., 115
MacKinnon, J. B., 206, 326
Manitoba Education and Training, 73, 205
Manitoba Education and Youth, 250
Margulies, N., 307
Marrin, W., 336
Martin, J. B., 337
Martin, Jr., B., 338
Martins, I. P., 158
Matthews, M., 256
Matzeliger, J. E., 76
Mawson, B., 167
Mayer-Smith, J., 17, 45
Maynes, N., 112
Mazur, E., 161
McAleese, R., 307
McCann, C., 278
McClintock, B., 326
McComas, W. F., 24, 27, 28
McCoy, E., 229
McDougall, D., 207
McFarlane, S., 58, 335
McGhie-Richmond, D., 85
McGinty, A. B., 33, 335
McLaren, P., 45, 63
McMahon, A., 281

McNulty, F., 338
McTighe, J., 106, 268
Mealer, B., 336
Mendel, G., 33
Metcalf, S. J., 277
Michell, H., 46, 47, 65, 66, 249
Milford, T. M., 13
Millar, R., 28
Miller, J. P., 7, 132, 211
Mintzes, J. J., 307
Miranda, R. J., 62
Mishan, E. J., 307
Moher, T, 278
Molnar, C., 252
Morgan, J. N., 307
Morrison, K., 257
Moscovici, H., 153
Motley, T., 228
Moursand, D., 273
Mulholland, J., 5, 65, 140
Munsch, R., 141, 335
Murphy, C., 140

N

Nashon, S., 272
National Research Council, 150, 152, 207
National Science Fair, 169, 170
Nazir, J., 52, 228
Neil, P., 140
Nelson, C., 228
Nelson, J., 337
New Brunswick Department of Education, 78
Ng-A-Fook, N., 47
Niess, M. L., 278
Nieto, S., 80, 81
Nisbett, R. E., 307
Nolan, K., 205
Norris, S. P., 12, 14
North American Association for Environmental Education, 40
Northwest Territories, Education, Culture and Employment, 73, 78
Nova Scotia Department of Education, 72, 73, 78
Novak, J. D., 307
Nunavut Department of Education, 47

O

Ogawa, M., 249
Okimoto, J., 58, 335
Olson, J. K., 27
Ontario College of Teachers, 112
Ontario Ministry of Education, 17, 45, 66, 73, 78, 82, 84, 85, 87, 92, 93, 94, 113, 126, 152
Ontario Society for Environmental Education (OSEE), 58
Ornstein, A. C., 253
Orr, D. W., 58
Osborne, J., 88

Osborne, J. F., 83, 253
Ostman, L., 137
Ozden, M., 140

P

Padilla, M. J., 158
Palmer, J., 48, 49, 50, 205
Parr, T., 335
Passmore, C., 17
Pedretti, E., 9, 11, 17, 52, 75, 200, 201, 210, 217, 218, 221, 225, 226, 227, 228, 237, 241, 244, 281
Percy, J., 33, 270
Peterat, L., 17
Peters, E. E., 28
Petrina, S., 132, 139
Phillips, L. M., 12, 14
Phillips, W. G., 307
Piaget, J., 255, 257
Pierce, W., 253
Pinar, W. F., 128, 139
Plato, 248
Pocovi, M. C., 28
Polacco, P., 338
Pollishuke, M., 80, 112
Polya, G., 92
Ponder, J., 228
Posner, G. J., 260
Potter, J. T., 63
Pratt, K., 335
Prime, G. M., 62
Psillos, D., 140

Q

Quay, J., 258
Quebec Education Program, Preschool and Elementary education, 78
Quebec Ministry of Education, 17

R

Radakovic, N., 207
Ramsey, J., 226
Ratcliffe, M., 226
Read, J. R., 259, 260
Rees, W., 42, 326
Reid, N., 151
Reis, G., 47
Reiss, M., 17, 194
Reiss, M. J., 60, 83, 134
Rennie, L., 17, 225, 251
Rey, H. A., 338
Reynolds, W. M., 128
Rezba, R. J., 152, 153
Rhea, L., 152
Richards, J., 67
Ridley, M., 327
Roach, M., 327
Roberts, D., 137
Roberts, D. A., 137
Rockwell, A., 335, 336
Rolheiser, N. C., 118

Romkey, L., 217, 218
Roth, W.-M., 9, 11, 12, 14, 47, 89, 131, 210, 221, 225, 244
Rousseau, J.-J., 42
Russell, C., 44, 45
Rutherford, P., 307

S

Sadler, T., 226
Sadler, T. D., 225
Sandhu, G., 75
Saskatchewan Ministry of Education, 66, 207
Sauvé, L., 45, 48, 49, 50
Schlick Noe, K.L., 296, 307
Schon, D., 2
School Science and Mathematics, 18
School Science Review, 18
Schubert, W. H., 128, 130
Schwab, J. J., 128, 129
Schwartz, E., 85
Schwartz, S., 80, 112
Science and Children, 18
Science and Education, 18
Science Council of Canada, 201
Science Education, 18
Science Scope, 18
Science Teacher, 18
Science Teachers' Association of Ontario, 177
Scott, A., 47
Scott, B., 226
Scott, P., 28
Sen, A., 60
Seroyer, C., 118, 319
Seuss, Dr., 58, 88, 336
Shah, I., 151
Shanahan, M.-C., 16
Shapiro, B. L., 256
Shaw, C. G., 338
Shermer, M., 327
Shields, K., 252
Shields, M., 161, 330
Shiva, V., 229, 327
Shulman, L., 8, 268
Shulman, L. S., 109
Silverstein, S., 49
Simmons, M., 225
Simon, S., 83, 338
Sina, I., 75
Skinner, B.F., 254
Slattery, P., 128
Slavin, R., 307
Sleeter, C. E., 69
Slotta, J., 162, 278
Slotta, J. D., 16, 162, 194, 278
Smarter Science, 177, 197
Smetana, L., 152
Smith, A., 206, 327

Smith, G. A., 51
Snively, G., 45, 47
Sobel, D., 52, 58, 206
Solomon, J., 200, 201, 203
Sperling, E., 210, 211
Statistics Canada, 58
Steele, Astrid, 45
Steig, W., 338
Stenhouse, L., 239
Stocklmayer, S., 17
Stoll, L., 281
Stolz, M., 338
Stone, M. K., 58
Strauss, R., 241, 337
Strike, K. A., 260
Sumara, D., 254, 255, 257
Sumara, D. J., 258
Sutherland, D., 249
Suzuki, D., 41, 58, 205, 327
Sweeney, J., 338
Sykes, H., 68

T

Taber, K., 268
Tan, M., 52
Tate, M. L., 307
TeacherVision, 307
Thadani, V., 74
The Laboratory School, 58
Thomas, J., 228
Thomas, R. S., 106
Thomas, S., 281
Thompson, F., 259
Tiberghien, A., 255
Tinker, R. F., 277
Tomlinson, C. A., 82, 268
Treagust, D. F., 14
Tresselt, A., 338
Turner, N. J., 46, 47, 58
Tyler, R. W., 80, 132, 139

U

UNESCO, 40, 41
UNESCO-UNEP, 41, 42
United Nations, 62
Urquhart, F., 195
Usak, M., 140

V

Vallance, E., 132
Van Allsburg, C., 336
Van de Walle, J. A., 92
van Eijck, M., 47
Van Rooy, W., 216, 226, 240
Veiga, L., 158
Venville, G., 209, 225, 226, 251
Vickers, R. H., 58, 333
View, T., 47

von Glaserfeld, E., 253, 255, 257
Vygotsky, L. S., 158, 256, 257

W

Wackernagel, M., 42, 326
Wald, E., 326
Waldman, N., 338
Wallace, C. S., 14
Wallace, J., 5, 8, 65, 140, 225, 251
Wallace, M., 47, 281
Wallace, R., 278, 281
Wandersee, J. H., 307
Watts, M., 83, 134
Weaver, A., 58
Wellington, J., 9, 88, 151
Wellman, B., 307
Wells, R. E., 337
Wenger, E., 281
Wertsch, J. V., 256
West, C. K., 307
Western and Northern Canadian Protocol for Collaboration in Education, 94
White, R., 161
Wiggins, G., 106
Wildlife Federation, 58
Wilkinson, G., 321
Williams, D. R., 58
Williams, V. B., 336
Willinsky, J., 63
Wilson, E. O., 327
Windschitl, M., 152
Winter, J., 336
Wise, J. A., 74
Wolf, P. M., 307
Wong, H. K., 118, 319
Wong, R. T., 118, 319
Working Group on Environmental Education, Ontario, 45, 48
World Commission on Environment and Development (WCED), 42
World Health Organization, 58
Wright, H. K., 129, 131

Y

Yager, R. E., 200
Yanowitz, K. L., 272
Yore, L. D., 13, 14, 86, 134
Young, C., 337
Young, M. F. D., 130
Young, R. M., 69
Youth Science Canada, 169

Z

Zandvliet, David, 45
Zeichner, K.M., 64
Zeidler, D. L., 194, 225, 231
Zezlina-Phillips, E., 68
Ziman, J., 200, 203, 228

Subject Index

Note: Pages followed by *f* and *t* denote figures and tables, respectively.

A

Aboriginal peoples. *See also* Indigenous
   peoples
      and beaver, 67
      Cree, 67
      and environmental education,
        46–48
      and place, 51
      provincial policies, 66–67
      and social justice in science
        education, 65–68
      and stewardship, 205
      and water, 47–48
about-in-for the environment, 48–49
academic language proficiency, 85
access, 69–70, 97
action, 204t, 210–211, 214, 233–234
Activities
      Aboriginal science education, 66–67
      about-in-for, 49
      action, 211–213
      action-based community project,
        234
      affect, multiple intelligences, unique
        learning needs, 86
      analogies and models, 272, 273
      animal life cycles, 194–195
      assessment, 192
      assessment strategies, 95, 191–192
      assignment design, 137
      balanced approach, 103
      biographies, 32–33
      blast off, 184–186
      border crossings, 68
      classroom management, 119,
        120–121
      commercially produced curriculum,
        138
      community building, 4
      conceptions of teaching and
        learning, 5–6
      conceptual change theory, 261
      content knowledge, 269, 281
      critical literacy skills, 279–280
      cueing systems, 88
      curriculum, 129
      curriculum, analyzing, 252
      curriculum documents, 13–14, 101,
        134
      curriculum examples, 135
      curriculum quotation, 131–132
      curriculum theory and development,
        139
      data management, 164–166
      debates, 231–232

      demonstrations, 162
      design technology, 168–169
      differentiated instruction, 82
      disruptive behaviours, 118–119
      doing science, 25–26
      ecological footprint, 42–44
      elementary science, 280
      environmental education, 40–41,
        45–46, 49–50
      equity, diversity, and social justice,
        61
      field trips, 35–36
      First Nations, 47–48
      games, 274
      graphing, 90–91
      human body systems, 140–141
      identity and ideology, 218
      identity wheel, 64
      inclusive approach, 81
      Indigenous and neo-Indigenous
        content, 250
      instructional strategies, 111–112
      issues-based approach, 228
      Kitchen Detective, 182–184
      knowledge, 249, 252
      laws and theories, 27
      length and distance, 270–272
      lesson plans, 110
      literacy and numeracy in children's
        literature, 14
      locavore movement, 206
      magnets, 170–171
      media literacy and NOS, 213
      misconceptions, 260, 261
      nature of science, 22–23
      not in my backyard, 209–210
      paper helicopters, 155–158
      planning for NOS, 34–35
      planning for STSE, 238–239
      plastic shopping bags, 208–209
      power, place, and the environment,
        51
      questions, 275, 276–277
      resources for planning, 54
      rock cycle, 219
      rubrics, 192
      safety, 188–189, 189–190
      scale, 270
      science and society, 201
      science curriculum, 9–10
      science education research, 18
      science in the media, 29
      scientific inquiry, 152
      scientific investigations, 150–151,
        155, 176, 180–181, 182–186

      scientific literacy, 10–11
      scientists, concepts of, 30–32
      seasons, 262–264
      simulations, 166–167
      skill development, 158–159
      social justice teaching, 73–74
      STSE, 202–203, 204, 204t,
        214–215, 224, 232–233, 238–239
      student identity, 63
      teacher beliefs and practices, 34
      teacher characteristics, 2
      teacher roles, 217
      technology, 17
      textbooks, 89
      theories of learning, 258
      unit planning, 102, 107–109,
        114–115
      using technology, 278
      water cycle, 242–243
      work habits, 136
      working with resources, 27–28
activity centres, 294–295, 317
advocacy and eco-justice, 50t
affect, 83, 86t, 134
affective argument, 151
Agenda 21, 42
alternative frameworks, 259
analogies, 272–273
analogue, 272
analyzing, 192
animal life cycles, 194–195
annotating, 321
application software, 16, 163
assessment
      defined, 93
      for demonstrations, 331
      for, as, and of learning, 94t
      formative, 94t
      and lesson planning, 113
      for micro-teaching, 324
      peer assessment, 96, 236f
      planning, 191–192
      purpose of, 92–93, 94
      for reading and annotating, 327
      and scientific investigations,
        191–192
      self-assessment, 96, 236f
      strategies and tools for, 93, 95t, 107,
        191, 234–236
      and STSE education, 234–237
      summative, 94t
      types of, 93
      and unit planning, 104, 107
      for unit plans, 325
assignment design, 137

assignments
demonstrations, 329–331
integrated unit plan, 324–326, 325t
micro-teaching, 321–323, 324
précis, 327–329, 329f
reading and summarizing, 326–327
attitudes, 13

B

baking soda, 182–184, 184–186
balance, 217
balanced approach, 102–103
banking model, 7
Bartholomew and the Oobleck, 88
basic process skills, 158
beaver, 67
behaviourism, 254
Belgrade Charter, 42
bias, 25, 61
big ideas, 104
biographies, 32–33
blast off, 184–186
Bloom's taxonomy, 116, 116t, 275
bodily-kinesthetic intelligence, 84t
border crossings, 68, 69t, 250
Brundtland Report, 42
buoyance and density, 259t
butterflies, 195

C

Canadian Journal of Environmental Education, 58
card exchange, 37
carousel, 285–287
cars, idling, 233t
centres, 294–295, 317
children's literature, 115, 333–338
citizenship science, 9
classifying, 158, 160
classroom management, 117–121
classroom organization, 315
Clearing, 58
closed questions, 275
clothes-sorting activity, 114
coercive control, 120
cognition, 256
cognitive argument, 151
coherence theories, 255–257, 258, 261
collaborative control, 120
commitment, 216–217
commonplaces, 129, 130f
community, 74
community-informed pedagogy, 71
complexity theory, 257
computer technologies, 114, 162–166, 163
concept map, 34, 287–288, 287f
conceptual change theory, 260–261
conceptual knowledge, 251t
concrete operational development, 255t
confirmation, 153
consequence mapping, 230, 288–290, 289f
conservation education and stewardship, 50t

constructionism, 256–257
constructivism, 255–256
constructivist-informed pedagogy, 255
content, 82
content knowledge, 8, 258, 277–279, 282–283
context knowledge, 8, 109, 129f
controversy, 239–241
convergent questions, 275
conversational language, 85
correspondence theories, 254–255
creativity in science, 140, 170, 194, 218, 242, 262
Cree, 67, 249
critical knowledge, 251t
critical reconstructionist, 131
critical scientific literacy, 12
cueing systems, 87–88, 87t
cultural and critical theories, 257
cultural and social contexts, 257
The Cultural Divide in Science Education for Aboriginal Learners, 67
culturally relevant pedagogy, 71
culture
and curriculum, 80–81
inclusion, 24
and knowledge, 250
and nature of science, 25, 28
and pedagogy, 71
and social justice issues, 65
and student identity, 68
curriculum
analyzing, 252
assessment and evaluation, 92–96
assignment samples, 135
commercially produced, 138
commonplaces, 129, 130f
and culture, 80–81
curriculum-as-plan, 131
defined, 128
development of, 132–134, 139
differentiated instruction (DI), 82
explicit curriculum, 129
hidden curriculum, 129
implicit curriculum, 129
inclusive approach, 80–82
issues and influences, 138–139
learned curriculum, 130
lesson plans. *See* lesson plans
lived curriculum, 131
ministry documents, 134
null curriculum, 129
official curriculum, 130
planning and implementation, 100
politicization of, 217
practical considerations, 134–136
quotations on, 131–132
for social justice, diversity, and equity, 61, 70, 72–74
and student needs, 80, 133–134
summary, 96–97, 142
taught curriculum, 130

and technology, 16–17
terminology, 101
tested curriculum, 130
textbooks, 88
theories, 128–129, 128t, 139
theorists, 128t, 129–131
types of, 129–131
unit plans. *See* unit plans
validations, 137, 138t
what, why, and how, 133, 133t
curriculum-as-plan, 131
curriculum knowledge, 8

D

data collection sheet, 245
data management, 162, 163
debates, 230, 231–232, 290–291
decision making, 204t, 207–208, 214
defining operationally, 159
demonstrations, 161–162, 329–331
descriptive concepts, 268
design technology, 167–169
development, stages of, 255t
development education, 50t
differentiated instruction, 82, 83, 100, 109, 124, 268
discovery learning, 256
divergent questions, 275
diversity, 60–62, 61f, 63
drama, 229–230, 298–299
drawing, 115

E

Earth Summit, 42
eco-justice, 50, 50t
ecological footprint, 42–44, 57
ecological theories, 257
ecology, 55
economy, 55
effectiveness, 3
emancipatory knowledge, 251t
empowerer, 120
enduring understandings, 104, 107
energy, 259t
English language learners, 85
environment, 40
Environmental Concepts in the Classroom: A Guide for Teachers, 45
environmental education (EE)
and Aboriginal perspectives, 46–47
about-in-for, 48–49
in Canada, 44–45
challenges in, 55–56
conceptualizing, 48–50
critical approach to, 50–51
and curriculum, 139
curriculum and policy, 45–46
history, 41–42, 48
introduced, 40
orientations, 49–50, 50t
reasons for, 41
resources for, 53–54, 55t, 58
summary, 56

Environmental Education Research, 58
Environmental Learning and Experience: An Interdisciplinary Guide for Teachers, 45, 54
epistemology, 248
equipment, 106, 113, 178, 179–180
equity, 60–62, 61*f*
Eurocentric science, 249–250
evaluation, 92–93, 108
existentialism, 253, 253*t*
expectations, 101, 113, 316
experientialist, 131
experimenting, 158
experiments, 153–154
explicit curriculum, 129

F

facilitator, 120
factual knowledge, 251*t*, 268
field trips, 35–36, 121, 193, 339–342. *See also* science beyond the classroom
first day of school, 316
First Nations. *See also* Aboriginal peoples
first year of teaching, 315–319
flow charts, 291–292
formal operational development, 255*t*
The Framework for Environmental Learning, 44
frameworks, alternative, 259
free-standing tower, 316
fundamental concepts, 104

G

games, 273–274
geologic time scale, 270
graffiti, 286
graphing, 89, 90–91, 114
grapho-phonic cues, 87, 87*t*
gravity, 259*t*
The Green Teacher, 58
groups, 178
guided inquiry, 153

H

heart-rate monitoring, 164–166
helicopters, 155–157, 174
hidden curriculum, 129
higher-order thinking skills (HOTS), 116, 116*t*
historical approach, 228–229
history of science, 25
holistic grading, 327
homework, 317
human body systems, 140–141
The 100 Mile Diet, 206
hypotheses, formulating, 158
hypothetical concepts, 268, 277

I

idealism, 253, 253*t*
identify-design-make-appraise, 167–169
identity
    identity wheel, 64*f*
    and ideology, 218
    and marginalized students, 62–63, 63*t*
    teacher identity, 63–64
ideology, 218
implicit curriculum, 129
inclusion, 69–70, 110, 178
Inclusive Education for Ontario Schools, 92
independent study, 111*t*
Indigenous peoples, 67–68, 249–250. *See also* Aboriginal peoples
inferring, 158
informal learning, 17–18
information and communications technology (ICT), 16
initiating, 191
inquiry, 74. *See also* scientific investigations
instructional strategies, 105, 111–112, 111*t*, 113
integrated process skills, 158
intellectual traditionalist, 130
intelligences, multiple, 84, 84*t*, 86*t*
intelligible, 260
interactive technologies, 16
interest, 138*t*
interpersonal intelligence, 84*t*
interpreting, 192
interpreting data, 158
intrapersonal intelligence, 84*t*
intrinsic value, 9
inventors, 75
investigations. *See* scientific investigations
issues-based approach, 48, 225–228, 227*f*

J

jigsaw, 292–293, 322
Journal of Environmental Education, 58
journals on science education, 328

K

Kitchen Detective, 182–184
know, want to know, learned (KWL), 293–294
knowledge
    categories of, 251–252, 251*t*
    factors related to, 248*f*
    Indigenous and neo-Indigenous, 249–250
    introduced, 248
    pedagogical content knowledge (PCK), 8, 139–140
    philosophies of, 253*t*
    scientific, 24, 105
    subject matter content knowledge, 105, 139–140
    summary, 264–265
    theories of, 252–254
    ways of knowing, 248–251
knowledge base, 8, 13
knowledge construction, 29
knowledge scaffolding, 178
Kyoto Protocol, 218

L

language, 85, 87–88
launching the unit, 104
laws of science, 24, 26
learned curriculum, 130
learning
    coherence theories, 255–257, 258
    constructivism 255–256
    correspondence theories, 254–255
    situated learning, 257
    summary, 264–265
    theories of, 83, 254–258, 258*f*
    unique needs, 85
learning centres, 294–295, 317
learning goals, 113
length and distance, 270–272
lesson design, 112–114
lesson plans
    closure, 114
    components of, 113–114
    defined, 100, 110–111
    instructional strategies, 111–112, 111*t*, 113
    lesson design, 112–114
    materials, equipment, and safety, 113
    misconceptions, 109
    motivating students, 110
    overview, 109
    post-lesson reflections, 114
    prior knowledge, 109
    sequence, 113
    student needs, 109–110
    summary, 121
    templates, 123–126
    three-part lesson, 112
    timing, 113
    versus unit plans, 100
light and sound, 280–281
Lincoln-Douglas debate, 290
liquids, 88
literacy
    and butterfly study, 195
    and curriculum, 133–134
    importance of, 87
    and the rock cycle, 220
    scientific. *See* scientific literacy
    and scientific investigations, 171
    and seasonal change, 262
    understandings of, 14
    and water cycle, 243
literature circles, 296–297
literature for science, 115, 333–338
lived curriculum, 131
locavore movement, 206
logical-mathematical intelligence, 84*t*
lower-order thinking skills (LOTS), 116, 116*t*

M

magnets, 154*t*, 170–171, 171–172
major projects, 104–105

manager, 120
Maori, 67–68
matching memory game, 115
materials, 113, 180
mathematics
    graphing, 89, 90–91
    importance of, 89
    problem solving, 89, 92, 92*t*
matter, properties of, 259*t*
measuring, 158
media, 29
media literacy, 213
memory game, 115
mentalism, 255
meta-cognitive knowledge, 251*t*
metaphors, 5–6
micro-teaching, 321–323, 324
mind maps, 297–298, 297*f*
misconceptions, 109, 259–260, 259*t*
models, 158, 272–273
modest realist position, 253
modified card exchange, 37
modules, 101
motivation, 110
mousetrap, 143
multiple intelligences, 84, 84*t*, 86*t*
musical-rhythmic intelligence, 84*t*
mystery powder identification, 182–184

N

naturalist intelligence, 84*t*
nature of science
    arguments for inclusion of, 28–29
    in the classroom, 32
    and curriculum, 139
    described, 22–24
    and inquiry, 74
    and media literacy, 213
    planning for, 34–35
    and power, 69–70
    in STSE education, 204*t*, 213, 214
    summary, 36
    teacher beliefs about, 33
    teaching through, with, and for, 27–30
    tenets of, 24–25
    tensions and challenges, 30
nature study, 50*t*
neutrality, 216
New Zealand, 67–68
non-western traditions, 75
not in my backyard, 209–210
notebooks, 146–148, 299–300, 316
null curriculum, 129
numeracy
    and butterfly study, 195
    in curriculum, 133–134
    importance of, 14
    and the rock cycle, 220
    and scientific investigations, 171
    and seasonal change, 262
    and water cycle, 243

Nunavut Approved Curriculum and Teaching Resources, 47

O

objectives, 101
observing, 158
official curriculum, 130
oikos, 55
one-minute reflection, 83
open inquiry, 153–154
open questions, 275
outcomes, 101, 113
outdoor education, 50*t*, 52–53

P

Pan Canadian Framework, 12–13, 158, 191–192, 201
paper helicopters, 155–157, 174
parent and guardian involvement, 106
pedagogical content knowledge (PCK), 8, 139–140
pedagogy
    content knowledge, 268–272
    meaningful understanding, 268–272
    professional development, 280–282
    strategies for STSE, 229–233
    and STSE education, 224
    summary, 282–283
    teaching with analogies and models, 272–273
    teaching with games, 273–274
peer assessment, 96
performance, 3
performing, 191
personal knowledge, 251*t*
personal resources, 3
philosophies
    of knowledge, 253*t*
    of teaching and learning, 5–9
Piaget's stages of development, 255*t*
Pinasuaqtavut 2004–2009, 47
place-based education, 51–52
planets, 143–146, 259*t*, 270–272
planning
    and assessment, 191–192
    historical approach, 228–229
    issues-based approach, 225–228
    lesson planning. *See* lesson plans
    long-term, 315
    and nature of science, 34–35
    pre-investigation planning, 176–181
    resources for, 54
    for scientific investigations, 176–186
    for STSE education, 225–229, 237–239
    as student skill, 191
    unit planning. *See* unit plans
plastic shopping bags, 208–209
plausible, 260
post-discourses, 131
post-implementation reflections, 109

power, access, and inclusion, 69–70
practice and theory, 34, 54, 214, 232, 238, 252, 273
practicum, 309–314
pragmatism, 253, 253*t*
pre-investigation planning, 176–181
pre-operational development, 255*t*
pre-planning, 103–106
précis, 327–329, 329*f*
Predict, Observe, Explain (POE), 161
predicting, 158
prior knowledge, 109
probeware, 163
problem solving
    with design technology, 167–169
    four-phase model, 92, 92*t*
    importance of, 89
    and social justice, 75
    structured inquiry, 153
professional development, 280–282
professional learning communities (PLCs), 237, 281–282
program planning, 118
properties of matter, 259*t*
propositional knowledge, 251*t*, 268

Q

Qaujimajatuqangit, 47
question and answer activities, 114
questions
    the art of, 115–117
    to promote learning, 274–277
    types of, 275
    what if questions, 289

R

reading and annotating, 326–327
reading circles, 296–297
realism, 253, 253*t*
recording, 191
recording devices, 95
recursion, 132
reflection statements, 318
reflective practitioner, 2
relations, 132
research, 18, 217–218
research project, 143–146
resources
    on Aboriginal science education, 67
    for environmental education, 53–54, 55*t*, 58
    personal resources, 3
    for social justice education, 77
    and unit planning, 105
    working with, 27–28
richness, 132
rigour, 132
rock cycle, 219–220, 269
role-play, 229–230, 298–299
routines, 316
rubrics, 97, 192, 235*t*

S

safety
      in classroom, 188–189
      contract for, 190
      and planning, 113, 317
      and scientific investigations,
           187–191
      symbols and procedures, 189–190,
           198
scaffolding, 178, 187, 256
scale, 269–270
science
      as culture, 250
      exploring creatively, 140, 170, 194,
           218, 242, 262
      history in non-western traditions, 75
      humanizing, 28
      and language, 87–88
      and mathematics, 89–92
      as a way of knowing, 248–251
science, technology, society, and the
      environment (STSE)
      and action, 210–213
      action-based community project,
           233–234
      and assessment, 234–237
      benefits of, 201–202
      challenges and tensions, 215–218
      characteristics of, 203–215, 204t,
           214–215, 224
      and controversy, 239–241
      and creativity, 218
      criticisms of, 202
      and decision making, 207–208
      described, 13
      historical approach, 228–229
      history of science, 200–201
      introduced, 200
      issues-based approach, 225–228,
           227f
      and NOS, 213–214
      pedagogy, 224, 229–233
      planning, 225–229, 237–239
      and politicization of curriculum, 217
      provincial positions, 202
      research perspective, 217–218
      and social justice education, 70, 75
      and stewardship, 205
      student identity, 215–216
      summary, 220–221, 243–244
      teacher positioning, 216–217
      and values, 209
science beyond the classroom
      field trips, 193
      informal learning, 17–18
      and nature of science, 35–36
      outdoor education, 52–53
      place-based education, 51–52
      science fairs, 169–170
      STSE education, 241
science education
      conflicting visions of, 19

enhancing, 28
issues in, 18–19
purpose of, 9–10
research into, 18
science education journals, 328
science expertise, 138t
science fairs, 169–170
science for all approach, 12
science notebooks, 146–148, 299–300
science specialists, 19
scientific inquiry
      defined, 150
      demonstrations, 161–162
      and scientific investigations,
           152–154
scientific investigations
      assessment, 191–192
      classroom considerations, 179–180
      communication of findings, 163
      computer technologies in, 162–166
      connections, 177
      data management, 163, 164–166
      with design technology, 167–169
      doing the investigation, 181
      for elementary students, 171–172
      experimental, 153
      independent study, 111t
      introduced, 150
      issues and debates in, 194
      and literacy, 171
      with magnets, 154t
      and numeracy, 171
      planning, 176–186
      post-investigation planning,
           181–182
      problem solving, 153, 167–169
      purpose of, 150–152
      and safety, 187–191
      and scaffolding, 187
      and science notebooks, 146
      simulations, 166–167
      skills development, 158–161
      student considerations, 178–179
      summary, 172–173, 196
      teacher considerations, 177
      testing, 177
      types of, 152–154, 154t, 158
      verification, 153
scientific literacy
      comprehensive vision of, 11–12
      in curriculum documents and
           policies, 12–13
      described, 10–11, 12
      importance of, 14
scientific method, 22, 25–26
seasons, 259t, 262–264
seating plans, 316
self-assessment, 96
semantic cues, 87, 87t
sensorimotor development, 255t
Shaping Our Schools, Shaping our Future,
      44–45

simulations, 16, 166–167
situated learning, 257
six thinking hats, 230, 300–302
skateboarding, 231–232, 245
skills, 13, 158, 191–192
skills argument, 151
skills development, 158–160
small-group activities, 111t
Smarter Science, 197
social behaviourist, 131
social constructivism, 255, 256
social cultural theory, 131
social justice
      and Aboriginal science education,
           65–68
      classroom teaching, 70, 72f
      and curriculum, 70, 72–74, 139
      in digital ages, 62
      foundations for, 69–74
      framework for, 60–62, 61f
      introduced, 60
      pedagogy of, 70, 71
      and power, access, and inclusion,
           69–70
      provincial guidelines, 77–78
      resources, 77
      and student identity, 62–63, 63t
      summary, 76
      world day of, 62
social media technologies, 16
social milieu, 25
social responsibility, 138t
socio-scientific issues (SSI), 225
software, 163
solar system, 270–272
solids, 88
special needs, 85, 86t
stability, 82
standardized testing, 18–19
standards, 101
*Standards for Environmental Education in the
      Curriculum*, 44
STEPWISE, 211
stewardship, 204t, 205, 214
strands, 101
strategic knowledge, 251t
strategies
      analogies and models, 272
      for assessment, 93, 95, 95t, 107
      carousel, 285–287
      for classroom management, 118
      concept map, 287–288, 287f
      consequence mapping, 288–290,
           289f
      debates, 290–291
      drama, 298–299
      to extend student thinking,
           116–117
      flow charts, 291–292
      games, 274
      instructional, 105, 111–112, 111t,
           113

strategies (*Cont.*)
    jigsaw, 292–293
    know, want to know, learned, 293–294
    learning centres, 294–295
    literature circles, 296–297
    mind maps, 297–298, 297f
    role-play, 298–299
    science notebooks, 299–300
    six thinking hats, 300–302
    for STSE education, 229–233
    think-pair-share, 302
    town hall meetings, 303–304
    values continuum, 304–305, 304f
    Venn diagrams, 305–306, 305f
    word walls, 306
structured inquiry, 153, 153–154
student-centred activities, 111t
student identity, 62–63, 63t, 68, 69t, 215–216
student needs
    and classroom management, 118
    in controversial issues, 241
    and curriculum, 133–134
    and lesson planning, 109–110
student tasks, 178, 179, 179f
    134-135, 134
students
    and content knowledge, 268
    knowing, 3–4, 83–86, 110
subject matter content knowledge, 105, 139–140
Sun's position, 114
supplies, 106, 315
sustainable development, 50t, 55, 205
syntactic cues, 87, 87t

T

"Take Time," 317–319
target, 272
Targeted Implementation and Planning Supports (TIPS), 113
taught curriculum, 130
Tbilisi Declaration, 42
teacher-directed activities, 111t
teacher knowledge, 8. *See also* pedagocial content knowledge
teacher positioning, 215–216
teachers
    characteristics of, 2–3
    role of in controversy, 240–241
    teacher identity, 63–64
teaching
    effective, 3
    enhancing, 28
    first year of, 315–319
    philosophy of, 5–9
    and social justice, 70, 71f, 72f

teamwork, 192
technological challenge, 143
technology
    computer technologies in investigations, 162–166
    and content knowledge, 277–279
    and critical lens, 278–279
    and curriculum, 16–17
    definition of, 15
    design technology, 167–169
    impact on science, 25
    information and communications technology (ICT), 16
    policies for, 317
    reasons for using, 277
    relationship with science, 15
    role of, 15–17
    for special circumstances, 85
TED conferences, 51
tested curriculum, 130
textbooks, 88–89, 317
themes, 104
theoretical concepts, 268
theories
    coherence theories, 255–257, 261
    complexity theory, 257
    conceptual change theory, 260–261
    correspondence theories, 254–255
    cultural and critical theories, 257
    described, 24
    ecological theories, 257
    of know, 252–254
    of learning, 83, 254–258, 258f
    terminology, 26
think-pair-share, 117, 302
ticket out the door, 83
titi chicks, 67–68
tower building, 316
town hall meetings, 230, 303–304
tracing shadows, 115
Traditional Ecological Knowledge and Wisdom (TEKW), 46–47
transaction orientation, 7
transformation orientation, 7, 7f, 8f, 12
transmission orientation, 7, 7f
truth, 253
Two Stars and a Wish, 236, 237f, 325
Tyler Rationale, 132

U

unit of study, 101
unit plans
    assessment, 104, 107
    assessment tool for, 325
    balanced approach, 102–103
    closing the unit, 104
    defined, 100
    drafting, 106

    equipment and supplies, 106
    equity, 102
    evaluation, 108
    fundamental concepts, big ideas, enduring understandings, 104
    instructional strategies and activities, 105
    integrated unit plan, 323–326
    launching the unit, 104
    versus lesson plans, 100t
    lesson sequence, 108
    major projects, 104–105
    overview, 101–102
    overview example, 122–123
    parent and guardian involvement, 106
    post-implementation reflections, 109
    pre-planning, 103–106
    resources, 105
    student needs, 106
    subject matter content knowledge, 105
    summary, 121
    themes, 104
usefulness, 138t
utilitarianism, 9

V

validations, 137, 138t
values
    in STSE education, 204t, 209, 214
    and student identity, 215–216
values continuum, 230, 304–305, 304f
Venn diagrams, 305–306, 305f
verbal-linguistic intelligence, 84t
virtual learning environments, 16
virtual manipulatives, 16
visual-spatial intelligence, 84t

W

wait time, 116–117
water cycle, 242–243, 269
weather chart, 114
The Western and Northern Canadian Protocol, 45
what if questions, 289
whole-class activities, 111t
whole-class focus, 111t
word walls, 306
work habits, 136
World Day of Social Justice, 62
world views, 249

Z

zone of proximal development, 256